Human Zoos
Science and Spectacle in the Age of Colonial Empires

Human Zoos
Science and Spectacle
in the Age of Colonial Empires

Edited by

PASCAL BLANCHARD, NICOLAS BANCEL,
GILLES BOËTSCH, ÉRIC DEROO,
SANDRINE LEMAIRE
AND CHARLES FORSDICK

Translations by
TERESA BRIDGEMAN

LIVERPOOL UNIVERSITY PRESS

First published 2008 by
Liverpool University Press
4 Cambridge Street
Liverpool L69 7ZU

British Library Cataloguing-in-Publication data
A British Library CIP record is available

ISBN 978-1-84631-123-9 cased
978-1-84631-174-1 limp

Typeset by Koinonia, Bury
Printed and bound by CPI Group (UK) Ltd, Croydon, CR0 4YY

Contents

Part II
Models of the Human Zoo: Populations On Display

Part III
National Identities: The Human Zoo in Context

Contributors

Nicolas Bancel Professor, University of Strasbourg II and University of Lausanne

Pascal Blanchard Affiliated Researcher, CNRS, GDR 2322, Marseille

Gilles Boëtsch, Director of Research, CNRS

Éric Deroo film-maker and Affiliated Researcher, CNRS, GDR 2322, Marseille

Sandrine Lemaire teacher, PhD, European Institute, Florence

Rosemarie Garland-Thomson Professor of Women's Studies, Emory University

Benjamin Reiss Associate Professor, Emory University

Nadja Durbach Associate Professor, University of Utah, Salt Lake City

Robert Bogdan Distinguished Professor Emeritus of Social Science, Syracuse University

Raymond Corbey Associate Professor, Tilburg University

Yann Ardagna teacher and Assistant Researcher, CNRS, UMR 6578, University of Marseille

Sam Maddra Lecturer, University of Glasgow

William H. Schneider Professor of History, Baker-Ort Chair of International Healthcare Philanthropy, Indiana University

Peter Mason Consultant, America Foundation, Santiago, Chile

Suzanne Preston Blier Allen Whitehill Clowes Professor of Fine Art and African and African American Studies, Harvard University

Hilke Thode-Arora Honorary Research Fellow, University of Auckland

Shane Peacock author, journalist and essayist, Canada

Catherine Servan-Schreiber Associate Researcher, CNRS, UMR 8564, EHESS; INALCO, Paris

Eric Ames Assistant Professor, University of Washington, Seattle

Roslyn Poignant Honorary Research Fellow, University College London

Bernth Lindfors Professor Emeritus, University of Texas, Austin

Elizabeth Edwards Professor and Senior Research Fellow, University of the Arts London

Arnaud Nanta Associate Researcher, CNRS, UMR 8173, EHESS

John M. MacKenzie Professor Emeritus, Lancaster University

Jean-Pierre Jacquemin journalist, Brussels

Tanfer Emin Tunc Assistant Professor, Hacettepe University, Ankara

Robert W. Rydell Professor of History, Montana State University

Fabrice Delsahut Lecturer, IUFM-Paris IV Sorbonne

Mary Jo Arnoldi Curator, Smithsonian National Museum of Natural History, Washington DC

Patrick Minder Lecturer, University of Fribourg

Nicola Labanca Professor, University of Siena

Guido Abbattista Professor, University of Trieste

Neus Moyano Miranda Art Historian, Center of Contemporary Culture, Barcelona

Herman Lebovics State University of New York Trustees Distinguished Professor, Stony Brook University

Charles Forsdick James Barrow Professor of French, University of Liverpool

Human Zoos:
the Greatest Exotic Shows in the West

PASCAL BLANCHARD, NICOLAS BANCEL,
GILLES BOËTSCH, ÉRIC DEROO
AND SANDRINE LEMAIRE

To see is to know.[1]

The 'human zoo' is exceptional in combining the functions of exhibition, performance, education and domination. Its study crosses disciplinary boundaries, drawing on the fields of history, anthropology and sociology, and it is as much a factor in the sociology of mass cultures as it is part of colonial history.[2] In embarking on the study of this phenomenon it is important to consider from the outset how it fits into a wider history of such practices. Linked, as it appears to be, to different types of display and areas of knowledge, the exhibition of 'exotic' humans can be said to number among the practices which contribute to the production of knowledge.[3]

This type of exhibition made its first real appearance as the result of a conjunction of political, social and economic factors in the nineteenth century, a period well known for its interest in distant lands, the discovery of the unknown, and the strange. This taste for far-off places, for exoticism, for the Other is, therefore, essential to our understanding of the links which can be established between 'human zoos' and earlier phenomena, such as the chambers of marvels which appeared in the great courts of Europe at the end of the sixteenth century,[4] the cabinets of curiosities which succeeded them and multiplied throughout the seventeenth and eighteenth centuries, bringing together entirely random groups of rare and strange objects drawn from the animal, vegetable, mineral and human worlds, or, again, menageries, zoological gardens and circuses.

In this long line of predecessors, the cabinets of curiosities are particularly important. First, such attractions, which were as diverse in their form as in the objects they contained, flourished throughout Europe from the end of the Renaissance. Second, it was these eclectic collections (containing juxtapositions of the most unlikely objects brought together by an all-consuming curiosity) that first motivated their owners to seek to understand their contents and to create systems of classification and hierarchies, making them the precursors of the museum.[5] Last, their compulsive attraction to the marvellous and their fascination with the curious provide us with part of the explanation for the emergence of human zoos, and for their success.

Early menageries – those collections of a variety of animals which were initially reserved for the enjoyment of Western aristocrats – also contribute to our understanding of those exhibitions of humans which were staged in zoological gardens. With the French Revolution, an upheaval occurred in the history of these menageries, which spread throughout Europe. In France itself, the animals from the Royal Menagerie at Versailles were transferred to the Jardin des Plantes in Paris, with the intention of furthering popular education and breaking with princely privilege. In the course of the nineteenth and twentieth centuries, London and other major cities in Europe gradually followed suit, opening zoos to the public. Such zoos were free, or charged a small entrance fee.

Another contributing factor to the growth of zoological gardens in cities was the urban development resulting from the first Industrial Revolution. These urban zoos became sites for combinations of collections that would not occur in the natural world; instead, they ordered Nature in accordance with the conceptions of eighteenth-century natural science. This recourse to a reconstructed nature corresponded to a deep social need brought about by the uprooting of millions of country people who came to work in the cities. Zoological gardens thus responded to a nostalgia (for nature), but also to the need to create an 'elsewhere' that could serve as the unlikely image of a lost paradise, a Noah's ark revisited by the Enlightenment, in which increasingly varied species of animal were to be found side by side, displayed in exotic settings. These were more the result of a desire to express the prodigality of nature than of any concern to recreate the natural environments of the animals on show. The animal zoo was thus a space both of curiosity and of fantasy, allowing the imagination free rein. It provided a divided and labelled space to which the public could come to contemplate advances in the knowledge of nature and the domestication of various species. And it was precisely at this juncture between exoticism and knowledge, between fantasy and rationality, that the human zoo appeared.

While the different zoological spaces were made available to scientists so that they could study or familiarize themselves with strange and wild beasts (and also confirm or disprove existing theories of the organization of life), they were soon opened to the public for purposes of entertainment and education (Blunt 1976; Baratay and Hardouin-Fugier 1998; Baratay 1999; 2002).[6] Now that the vegetable and animal worlds were becoming better known to scientists and the public, there was an increasing interest in the diversity of human morphology, stimulated by discoveries of new countries and colonial conquests. But human morphology needed to fit into current explanatory models of the world, and nineteenth-century physical anthropologists attempted to explain this diversity in scientific terms. Humans became a central topic of study, at first using skeletons or cultural artefacts; later moving on to reconstructed, desiccated or mummified bodies; and, finally through the use of 'live specimens'. These 'specimens' were first studied in their 'natural' environment, before being 'transported' and exhibited in the West.

In North America (where there were two local types of 'exotic' population: the African-American descendants of slaves and the Native Americans) the pattern was not the same. Here, towards the middle of the nineteenth century, the spectacle of 'elsewhere' was to be encountered in travelling circuses. These followed the European tradition of showing animals at fairs, but they did not retain the scientific and educational purposes of such shows. It was in these circuses that 'ethnic shows' and 'freak shows' would meet and cross-fertilize, producing the first popular manifestation of a systematic representation of human difference (if we exclude European cabinets of curiosities and a small number of shows for the benefit of the nobility). The similarity between ethnic shows and 'freak' shows demonstrates, moreover, the underlying connection between visual pleasure in exoticism and/or strangeness, and the (at least superficial) aim of acquiring knowledge through exhibition.

The reference point for such practices remains Phineas Taylor Barnum (who gave the anthropozoological model its name) and his enterprises, but we should also remember Buffalo Bill's Wild West show, which extended its influence across the world (Brown 1976). Of North American extraction, these 'professionals of the strange' were to organize worldwide tours and would travel to the greatest European cities, developing a new concept in mass culture. Their method was to exhibit the most 'savage' or 'outlandish' beings, hybrids of the human and the animal, who fascinated a still relatively naive public. The Wild West show transformed this model by integrating it into the technological progress of the industrial world and the concept of American nationhood, setting up an opposition between 'modern' America and 'Indian savagery'.

On both sides of the Atlantic, almost simultaneously, but in surroundings which were distinct and specific to each culture, there emerged the basic principles of a modern type of ethnographic exhibition that carried an identical message concerning exotic peoples.

The Genesis of Human Zoos

Of course, the Other has always been exhibited, shown and staged. Already, in Ancient Egypt, black 'dwarves' from the Sudanese territories were exhibited, just as, during the Roman Empire, conquered 'Barbarians' and 'Savages' were paraded through the streets of Rome in order to reinforce the message of Roman superiority and hegemony over the rest of the world. Later, during centuries of discovery and conquest, travellers and explorers brought living or dead human 'specimens' to the courts of the European monarchs. The strange, the different and the monstrous have thus long been objects of a lively curiosity.

The first 'exotic specimens' to be presented in the great courts of Europe were treated in quite different ways, repeating the varied pattern of the cabinets of curiosities which were so fashionable at that time. (These had begun with the Tradescants' collection, known as the Ark, which had been created in the early seventeenth century and would later form the core of the Ashmolean Museum collection in Oxford.) Among those on show were the Tupi Indians brought to Europe by Hernán Cortés and presented to the King of France in 1550; the 'savages' collected by Duke Wilhelm V of Bavaria in about 1580, who were displayed alongside an astonishing range of 'dwarves' and 'cripples'; the Tahitian brought back to France by Bougainville in 1769 (see Boëtsch and Ardagna in this volume; see also Bambridge 2002: 151–53);[7] and a 'troupe of Africans' who were established near Frankfurt in 1784 by Frederick II of Hesse-Cassel, in order to observe both their habits and their morphology (the bodies of some of their number were studied by Samuel Thomas Sömmering, see Blanckaert 2002: 229).[8] These cases illustrate a pattern that was slowly but inexorably being established in the West, along with the development of a passion for difference and exoticism.

The arts and the sciences were fully engaged in the study of humanity. Indeed, artists (such as Charles Le Brun) complained at the difficulty of gaining access to samples of all the full range of human forms which populated the earth and, in particular, to different 'racial' types. Their aim was to understand the relationship between the body and the soul. In the eyes of scholars and artists of the time, Europeans had the 'highest' type of facial structure, providing proof of their own genius compared with the abilities of other peoples (Baridon and Guédron 1999). But such hypotheses required confirmation through comparative study, creating a need for reference collections. The naturalist Johann Friedrich Blumenbach was the most conscious of the importance of forming an anthropological collection containing a large number of 'specimens'. His collection contained portraits of individuals from 'various races' and, in pride of place, 82 skulls. In France, museum professors rushed to form their own anthropological collections. Georges Cuvier, Etienne-Antoine Serres and, later, Jean Louis Armand de Quatrefages built one of the most famous such collections in the world (Quatrefages 1867).[9] The discovery of the Other by means of these collections of human skeletons became standard practice in the scientific world at a time when scholars were seeking to establish and understand human hierarchies.

To achieve this end, scientists needed anthropological and ethnographic collections, but they also needed to be able to see, touch, measure and study living humans. There were only two possible solutions to this problem: either it was necessary to 'go into the field' – which meant long, arduous and costly expeditions, available only to those with substantial means; or the objects of study had to be brought to the scientists. The desire at the beginning of the nineteenth century to 'collect' and 'display' the various 'races' was strengthened by this situation, as is demonstrated by an early project for an ethnographic park, recorded by the French architect Edme Verniquet in 1802, 'where each man would be dressed according to the traditions of his country, and placed in a setting appropriate to his way of life' (Verniquet 1802: 23; see also Baratay 2002: 36–37).[10] Elsewhere, an ethnological museum of the 'Scandinavian peoples' was created in Sweden in a similar vein, and various projects to form 'human collections' (whether living or not) were set in motion in Europe and the United States in the first half of the century. Although none of these enjoyed the success of the American Museum founded by P. T. Barnum in 1841 in New York, the process had nevertheless begun.

The North American model was central to this development. In New York, the American Museum, founded by Barnum in 1841 in the heart of Manhattan, became the most popular show in the country (Harris 1973; Lindfors 1983a). 'Freaks' were the lynchpin of the show (Garland-Thomson 1996). Barnum's invention was to stage his 'monsters' in an entertainment area, while simultaneously showing a programme of 'scientific' lectures, magical tricks, dancing and theatrical reconstructions. It was a new type of urban spectacle[11] and it would be taken up very quickly by the travelling circuses which were beginning to tour the whole of the United States and Europe. In 1884, Barnum created the Grand Congress of Nations, a sort of ideological culmination of these early commercial exhibitions, presenting 'strange and savage tribes' on a national scale. In it, he presented the American showman R.A. Cunningham's Australian Aborigines,[12] 'ferocious Zulus', Sioux Indians, a 'savage Muslim' 'Nubian', and several other 'exotic specimens'.

In Europe, a similar process had begun in the early years of the nineteenth century with the exhibition in London and Paris of the Hottentot Venus (1810–15), whose body would become an object of scientific study.[13] London rapidly became the capital of these 'exotic shows' (see Durbach in this volume; see also Altick 1978), with exhibitions of 'Indians' (Native Americans) (1817),[14] Lapps (Sami) (1822), Eskimos (Inuit) (1824), Fuegians (1829), Guyanese (1839), Bushmen (1847), and also several groups of Zulus, including in the major exhibition of 1859, which inaugurated a 'grand tour' through Europe (Lindfors 1999a: 205).[15] This tour fascinated Charles Dickens to such a degree that he later produced a pamphlet in which he argued against the myth of the 'good savage'.

It was during the nineteenth century that the paradigms for a normalization of the natural world developed in both the Old and New Worlds. In these, the world's visible phenomena were transformed into a combination of popular spectacle, science lesson (with the emergence of learned societies),[16] and explicit demonstration of the well-foundedness of existing colonial hierarchies and racial distinctions. Although society was progressively moving away from the age of slavery, through abolition, it was entering the age of empire, and the world order was divided into exhibited peoples on the one hand and spectators at the exhibition on the other. At the 1851 Great Exhibition in London (the first of its kind) the pavilions devoted to the Middle and Far East surprised the visitors by the quality of their artistic production. By contrast, the Egyptian pavilion was set apart from the technological progress of European industry. In addition to the antiquities on show, which were already familiar to Europeans, this pavilion caused a sensation with its imitation of a Cairo street, filled with traders, and with its own mosque, shops, dancers and cafés. This formula would be repeated at every subsequent universal exhibition. In Paris, Chicago, San Francisco, Berlin and Milan, the conventional exoticism of this Cairo street would draw hundreds of thousands of visitors (Aimone and Olmo 1993), and would stimulate a taste for exotic reconstructions which would persist throughout the period of great Western exhibitions.

A Changing Pattern

By the middle of the nineteenth century the pattern of shows was still a piecemeal affair (even though the Zulu tour of 1859 hinted at a new model to come) and had not yet developed into a fully fledged 'industry', with its own codes and professionals, playing an integral role in major colonial displays. The shows still staged essentially ludic displays of strength, strangeness, curiosity or cruelty. However, in the second half of the century a pattern emerged which led to the full development of the model of the human zoos as human exhibitions of 'exotics' with a certain racial element (from 'ethnic shows' to 'negro villages'), which were either independent or formed part of larger performances, such as the universal and colonial exhibitions.

The first troupe of this type was shown by Carl Hagenbeck in Hamburg in 1874, the year of Barnum's arrival in Europe. This date therefore acted as a watershed in the development of human exhibitions. Hagenbeck's troupe was composed of a family of six Lapps (Sami), accompanied by about thirty reindeer. As a result of the success of this exhibition, Hagenbeck exported his shows from Germany (not least to the Jardin d'Acclimatation in Paris, in 1877),[7] professionalizing them under the title of 'anthropozoological exhibitions'.[8] Almost simultaneously, in Philadelphia in 1876, Charles Rau of the Smithsonian Institution proposed a number of exhibitions of the same kind for the Philadelphia Centennial Exhibition, in order to demonstrate the 'extremely low level of our distant ancestors' and to facilitate the measurement of the degree of evolution of Western societies compared with 'primitive societies' (see Rydell 1984).

Alongside the German 'king of the zoos' and American Barnums, many impresarios would gradually establish themselves and develop their own companies (including those who were themselves from colonial backgrounds, such as John Tevi or J. C. Nayo Bruce).[19] From this time, the formula of the human zoo spread rapidly, becoming an historically significant pattern in just over a decade. The great novelty of these moments of scientific excitement, when compared with the eighteenth century and the first half of the nineteenth, was that travellers' tales and engravings were no longer enough to satisfy the public. Instead, a form of display was created which combined science with theatre and was staged in both private and public spaces, where men who were *different* were put on show.

This brought about a decisive transformation in the status of alterity, of *Otherness*, which became rationalized and *rationalizable* by means of a racial typology established (or in the process of being established) through science. The yardstick of this typology remained Western man and, in particular, Caucasian man, in whom the French naturalist Georges-Louis Leclerc, Comte de Buffon, perceived and admired a physical harmony. But the 'science of the races' would be overtaken in turn by Progress and the interests of international strategy. Accordingly, Japan, as an emerging modern power, would be included in the dominant model from the World's Columbian Exposition of 1893 in Chicago onwards.[20] To exhibit the Other became a visible and simple sign of modernity and greatness. Conversely, Russia refused to allow its citizens to feature in the shows, believing that this would diminish their status. The scientific rationalization of alterity produced a racial hierarchy at that time, which was then transposed and vulgarized in ethnic shows, bringing together a combination of features drawn from imaginary constructs of exoticism and the 'savage' (Courcelles 1997; Bensa 2006).[21]

The display of exotic peoples also suggested that they were inferior in status to the Europeans and therefore colonizable, even though there were doubts among some scholars concerning the state of 'backwardness' of some of them. One French anthropologist, Abel Hovelacque, explored the question of those peoples who represented 'the last (or the first) stages on the human ladder' (Hovelacque 1882: ii). In his work, he made reference to Australians, Veddas, Bushmen and the Botocudo of Brazil, whose material culture was, in his view, close to that of beasts: 'Is it not clear, is it not obvious that the most sophisticated dwellings of the Australian, the Bushman, or the Andamanite, are hardly superior in architectural form and comfort to the nests of anthropoids?' (1882: 266).

The appearance and the very rapid spread of human zoos has close links with other contemporary phenomena, for example, the quest for identity associated with the construction of nation-states, which affected the societies of the Old World; the affirmation of 'American specificity' following the end of the War of Independence; and the concept of Meiji modernity in Japan from 1878. These ethnocentric visions were constructed on the many fears that resulted from the combination of staggering advances in science and sudden social shifts. The new paradigm overturned all reference points: concepts of space were changed by the break between town and country and the development of transport networks; concepts of time were altered by the unprecedented speed of travel, the conquest of colonial spaces, and the acceleration of the rhythm of labour in the cities; concepts of society were changed by the emergence of the industrial working classes and the decay of communal and, sometimes, family ties; while concepts of culture shifted as local country traditions were replaced by a newly created political transcendence which lay at the heart of the creation of nation-states. These transformations, which occurred in the course of just two generations, were of a hitherto unexperienced brutality. Scientific positivism and faith in progress can be understood only against the backdrop of the profound anthropological concerns which permeated the social fabric, undoing the collective psyche and obscuring the future from view. Human zoos were part of a larger attempt to provide reassurance concerning identity.

In the case of the United States, which was both imperial and colonial in character, with a significant Afro-American minority and its own 'savages' in the form of Native Americans, it was necessary to define the essential form of the identity of the nation and its peoples, while confirming a racial model based in many respects on eugenics. In Japan we find a dual approach. First, it was important to establish a Japanese racial model (in which the Japanese were essentially superior), in contrast to the 'backward peoples' of the surrounding countries. Second, those peoples who were 'potentially' colonizable by the new elite groups in power were put on display, in particular, those whose countries were geographically close to Japan (Koreans, Taiwanese, Okinawans and Chinese).

The First National Industrial Exposition in Japan was held in Tokyo in 1877, but it was after the war with China of 1894-95 that exhibitions became more frequent, and 'colonial' exhibits appeared. Accordingly, the Okazaki (Kyoto) exhibition of 1895 included a pavilion of 'foreign colonial specimens' and also, for the first time, a pavilion representing Taiwan. This was only a year after the Chicago exhibition, where the Japanese pavilion had had such an impact on its visitors, influencing international opinion. This pattern was confirmed in 1903 at the Fifth National Industrial Exposition in Osaka, where the Japanese public first encountered an exhibition of colonial 'natives' and 'exotic' peoples in the Anthropological pavilion. The pavilion was supervised by the Tokyo Anthropological Society and linked to the Taiwan Pavilion and the Specimens Pavilion.[22] In it, the public could encounter Chinese, Ainus, Taiwanese, Okinawans, Koreans, Malays, Indians, a Javanese, a Turk and even a man from Zanzibar.

In Europe, the great powers supported their colonial choices through their exhibitions. Britain showed its links with India; France did the same with Algeria, Indochina and sub-Saharan Africa; Holland with the Dutch Indies; and, later, Belgium with the Congo; Germany with Togo and Cameroon; Italy with north-east Africa; and Portugal with east Africa. Meanwhile, Europe sought to reinforce its world hegemony by declaring its mastery over other 'races', whose destiny involved a simple choice: to be brought under colonial rule or to disappear. Each of the great centres of Western imperialism exploited this chance to 'exhibit difference' in order to reinforce its self-justificatory arguments concerning its policies overseas.

A Strange Strangeness ...

As the nineteenth century progressed, displays of difference were ratio- nalized and commercialized. Circuses, fairs, exhibitions and carnivals prospered throughout the Western world, particularly in America, bringing greater pleasure to the crowds and greater profits to their organizers. This popular craze for *monstrosity* cannot be separated from the distancing of various forms of alterity, and of this Guillermo Farini was without doubt a master (Peacock 1995; and the same author in this volume). First known as a tightrope walker and as the inventor of the 'human cannon', he later reinvented himself as an exhibitor of the monstrous and the exotic. In 1879 in London, for example, he exhibited a troupe of Zulu warriors, before going on to specialize in the exhibition of Bushmen whom he had himself sought out in the Kalahari Desert. Changing course again, he directed a touring troupe of blackface minstrels (white performers in black make-up), who travelled throughout the English-speaking world, including South Africa. His personal evolution (from the circus to ethnic shows and then to the minstrel shows) encapsulates the development of the genre at the turn of the century.

The concept of the 'monster' changed with the appearance of the ethnic shows (Twitchell 1990). The exhibition of the monstrous had, of course, been a form of popular culture since the sixteenth century at least, but it developed renewed vigour in the first half of the nineteenth century, as we have emphasized.[23] The arrival of the ethnic shows thus extended the characteristics of radical Otherness, which shifted from 'physical monsters' (Hevey 1992: 53) to 'exotics'.

In a dialectic process, the distancing of the 'abnormal' at the end of the eighteenth century was accompanied by its greater visibility in the form of the 'monster' (Truzzi 1979; McNamara 1974). Siamese twins,[24] the Last of the Aztecs,[25] the two 'savages of Borneo',[26] the 'cannibal warrior of Dahomey',[27] and troupes of 'Albino Africans' acted as links between the world of 'Freaks' and that of 'Ethnics'. These attractions were staged by Barnum[28] and by other impresarios in decors which were usually inspired by 'savage societies', with appropriate costumes and scenery (Barnum 1872; Saxon 1980; Reiss 2001),[29] opening up new spaces for the ordering of the world.

Although the formalized Otherness of the ethnic shows could be seen as an anthropological necessity, it also gave rise to stereotypes. This extension and redefinition of radical Otherness was cumulative in nature. We should note that ethnic shows, as new spaces for the display of difference, were the most recent products of a lengthy process, which began in the eighteenth century, in which madmen and those with disabilities were subjected to exclusion and incarceration (Foucault 1961). This segregation profoundly changed the face of rural and urban societies, where such figures had previously occupied a minority, but nevertheless legitimate, position as intermediaries for the supernatural. The disappearance of the 'abnormal' from the heart of social structures made it all the more imperative that a new form of Otherness should be displayed. Otherness was not simply a state, it was the alien element which resisted assimilation and made it possible to construct social, cultural and physical identities.

Thus, towards the middle of the nineteenth century, the exhibition of a 'cannibal from Oceania' in London or the 'monkey-woman' at Luna Park in Paris produced as many, if not more, thrills as (or than) the 'trunk-man', the 'Lilliputian' or the 'pig-woman', for it suggested that a whole people shared these physical, cultural and mental characteristics. The ethnic shows moved away from the display of exceptions or mistakes of nature; instead, they showed the extraordinary norms of the worlds surrounding the West, worlds which it would soon be necessary to dominate, colonize and change.

The colonial project was part of this urge towards uniformity, setting out to remodel the world in the West's *own image*, to make the 'savage' disappear, as the 'cripple' or the 'degenerate' had already done. This was a project based on Western reason and fed by the utopia of scientific transparency, which denied the need for the presence of the Other as testimony to what we are through what we are not.

Today it is hard to imagine the pull exerted by the theatricalization of fairground attractions in the visual culture of the second half of the nineteenth century. Despite the fact that, as Gilles Boëtsch suggests in this volume, it is hard to know the response of the vast majority of visitors to these exhibitions since they left no record of their reactions, only that of their presence there, three indicators are nevertheless available: the impressive (and profitable) sales of postcards of the exhibited peoples at the sites of the shows; the invariably large number of articles in the national and local press about such displays; and the consistently high number of visitors to all types of venue, be it a makeshift stage for a travelling troupe, a theatre or an official exhibition site.

A Contribution to Mass Culture

Such quantifiable information underlines the popularity of these shows,[30] including those in small towns,[31] and the financial benefits they brought to their many promoters are obvious. It tells us that profits rose steadily until the beginning of the First World War, and that the growing number of troupes and universal or international exhibitions from the 1880s generated a tenfold increase in the opportunities for the public to see the 'exotics'.

There remains, however, the complex issue of what this same public thought of the shows, given the lack of documentary evidence on the subject. It would appear that very few visitors or writers were critical of these exhibitions at the time. There were, nevertheless, a few exceptions in France (intellectuals and colonials), the United States (some religious groups), and Britain (anti-slavery groups). For example, Louis-Joseph Barot, a prolific French writer on sub-Saharan Africa and French colonial activities, who would later become Mayor of Angers, denounced 'ethnographic exhibitions' for treating the presentation of Africans as a masquerade. In his view, such exhibitions were nothing but 'gross caricatures', where 'specimens of the human race were presented alongside performing dogs and anatomical museums' (Bergougniou, Clignet and David 2001). And he concluded, in 1902, that 'Blacks should not be judged by the specimens which can be seen in the Dahomean and Senegalese villages that are touted from one town to the next in Europe'.

With regard to the opinions held by the general public, we can glean a range of reactions from newspaper articles (while recognizing the limitations of the use of such sources) that appear to form the background to public perceptions of these shows (as several contributions to this volume demonstrate). First, opposition to this sort of exhibition appears to have been the exception and, when it did occur, it was in special circumstances, such as the exhibition of men or women who were clearly sick, or their deaths as the result of the harsh conditions in which they were displayed. Most writers accepted the exhibitions and they show a nuanced range of responses, from open disdain to sincere admiration, in the vast majority of visitors.[32]

Although these exhibitions may appear shocking today in their conception and in their execution, they largely embodied the ideas of the day. Any analysis of the negative aspects of the attitudes they express towards the Other should take account of this. On a practical level, there are many suggestions that exhibited peoples were on occasion treated with cruelty. We thus encounter the use of cages (extremely rare); the use of wire fences (these were more common, and were intended to separate and protect visitors and those on show); the death of performers; the dramatic conditions in which some troupes lived; suicides while on tour, or on the performers' return to their native lands, along with significant trauma;[33] accommodation on the site of the exhibition itself, or in stockyards;[34] groups captured by force[35] and transported against their will (these were isolated cases, which ceased with the new century);[36] recruitment through a single agent under a one-sided group contract; studies carried out on living or dead bodies at the exhibitions;[37] the presence of children or publicly reported births in the ethnographic shows; and women deliberately stripped of their clothing in the travelling villages. Although the deaths in Tervuren in 1897, in Paris in 1892 (among the Kaliña), and in Barcelona in 1896, are proven facts, along with the smallpox outbreak in Chicago in 1893 and the dramatic tales of the Hottentot Venus (Coleman 1964; Strother 1999), Ota Benga,[38] and the pygmies presented at the Italian court in 1883 (Puccini 1999), these examples should not lead us to attribute the deaths involved only to the rigours they describe.

Very soon, though, two factors intervened to change the conditions under which 'performers' were engaged. First, the organizers recognized that, even more than deaths, sick people were bad for the financial health of their businesses. They led to damaging publicity surrounding the show and created distrust (and sometimes rebellion) among those on show, not to mention public concern (over infection) and compassionate impulses. A system of self-regulation developed to protect the major capital asset of these shows: the exhibited peoples. We can see this in Hagenbeck's response to the death of a whole troupe of Eskimos (Inuit) and many Fuegians. He was subsequently careful to vaccinate his 'performers' and to publicize the vaccination of the participants in the 'negro villages' he sent on tour in France, immediately on their arrival in each town. This public vaccination was intended to demonstrate the good conditions in which the participants were kept, but also to reassure the spectators concerning their health and, in particular, that they were not carrying any infectious diseases.

The second factor which improved conditions was the growing practice among the organizers, when faced with discontented performers, of recruiting whole families with children for their troupes (the presence of family members was believed to inhibit rebellion and desertion). A secondary effect of this was to make the shows more attractive to the spectators. Last, there was an increase in legislation by some colonial authorities against the recruitment of 'savages' (in the Belgian Congo in 1897, the German colonies in 1910, and the French Empire in 1931) and specific bodies were set up elsewhere to oversee the organization of such exhibitions (in the United States in 1893 and in France in 1906).

The troupes rapidly became professional and, from the 1880s, contracts were entered into with the recruiters, the performers often being represented by a third party. The use of contracts suggests a new perception of shared interests and of the relationships between the organizers and participants. While such relationships remained unequal and exploitative, we nevertheless see some troupes demanding, in addition to their contractual wages, special 'exhibition conditions' (refusing to perform in bad weather; striking in order to obtain a pay rise in Switzerland; calling for supervisory care of the animals on rest days; and demanding the payment of bonuses for all additional performances). Legal differences could lead to the formal prosecution of an impresario.

Economic interests were thus shared, albeit unequally. From now on, the troupes would, with good grace, travel from place to place playing the various roles assigned to them (cannibals here, native warriors there, or burlesque savages on a music-hall stage), illustrating the fantasies and projections constructed around the concept of the 'savage' by the Western imagination of the day. Some troupes remained on tour for a number of years and 'village chieftains' (Mamdou Seck, for example) directed dozens of villages in turn, crossing the Atlantic and travelling from one country to the next, communicating the skills they acquired to their descendants. The title of 'native performer' was, at the turn of the nineteenth and twentieth centuries, applied to a profession which employed 2,000–3,000 individuals a year on average in the dozen or so countries concerned.

It can be seen that a real economic system developed, involving recruiters in Africa, Asia, Oceania and South America, transporters, negotiating agents who entered into discussions with officials in towns and cities, and exhibition organizers, over the provision of troupes, each with its 'native' village headman and its 'performers' (with their families), and local businesses, which constructed the villages. 'Placed alongside all kinds of objects and products, colonial natives quickly became a standard part of world fairs, for the education and entertainment of Western citizens', writes Raymond Corbey in this volume. In the end, 20,000–25,000 performers from every part of the world were exhibited in the West in this way, over a period spanning just over half a century.

The similarity between exhibition models and schemata for the perception of the 'exotic' in operation throughout the northern hemisphere demonstrates a process of cultural transference and homogenization in the West. The contributions to this volume show that the creation of an imaginary construct of the Other based on difference not only accompanied but sometimes preceded the great movement of colonization by the European powers, as well as Japanese and American imperialism. We can propose that exhibitions of the exotic were not, therefore, a consequence of imperialism, but, rather, one of the cultural conditions which made it possible by demonstrating the inferiority of many human groups and thereby legitimizing their future submission.

Indeed, on reading the chapters which follow, it will be noticed that from the nineteenth century onwards, the wild animals with some claim to exoticism[39] and the small number of inhabitants of distant lands offered for the entertainment of Western elites were replaced by 'specimens' – representatives of a race (or a people), in a group or family, mostly displayed in an original frame or setting. This practice was widespread in nearly a dozen countries in Asia, Europe and the United States, and involved another twenty or so countries in a more marginal way, as the pioneering research of Bernth Lindfors[40] and Raymond Corbey[41] has shown, and the studies in this volume amply confirm. There is nothing anecdotal about this practice, then. It is part of the development of mass culture constructed around the expansion of different modes of communication, including periodicals, expositions and specifically human exhibitions. At the turn of the century, ethnological exhibitions constituted a key stage in the construction of an imaginary Other based on a vision which brought exoticism and racism together and, from the outset, was confirmed almost universally by scholars and anthropologists (Brace 1982), allowing it unprecedented exemplary value.

From the middle of the nineteenth century, the vast majority of Europeans, Japanese and Americans had their first visual contact with exotic peoples (who would soon mostly be of colonial origin) through the wire fences and other measures which kept them apart from the 'savages'. The 'savage', who had been a mythical figure until that time, appeared in the flesh before the fascinated or fearful eyes of Westerners, reaching the height of his glory, in various guises, throughout the entire northern hemisphere, from Tokyo to Hamburg, from Zürich to Paris, and from London to Chicago.

Between Science and Spectacle

The status of the Other within these exhibitions also gradually changed. At first reified as a 'savage', the 'exotic' figure was gradually 'tamed' during the period of colonial conquest and then 'civilized', in order to demonstrate the achievements of the colonial 'civilizing mission'. By contrast, those races who, in the contemporary view, were embarked on an irrevocable decline continued to be portrayed as 'savages', in anticipation of their disappearance when confronted with a civilization destined to act as guide to the whole of humanity. In the nineteenth century, the West was attempting to make sense of the world, while in the twentieth century it more obviously constructed it according to its own models, beliefs and interests. Against this backdrop, human zoos adapted themselves to the views of the time, the political context and the expectations of their visitors.

Scientists were, at first, essential to the legitimization of ethnic shows. Following the visits of certain French scientists to the Jardin d'Acclimatation in Paris, the Paris Exposition Universelle of 1878 gave them greater international exposure and provided them with a voice in the press: 'It will be an honour for our country to demonstrate that France is the chief home of the "science of mankind"' (Martin 1878: 8). Objects from the Stone Age, the Neolithic period and the Bronze Age were displayed. Alongside these relics of man's past and evidence of his evolution (Bordier 1878c), visitors could also encounter 'Foreigners of distinction, a native Prince from Java, Spahis, Turks, etc. These included living examples of distant races' (Mortillet 1878: 221). The exhibition was constructed along the same lines as those in the zoological gardens, where 'exotic races' were, by definition, interesting to see.

Indeed, since the innovative work of Linnaeus and Buffon in the eighteenth century, human beings had become proper objects of scientific investigation and anthropologists had begun to examine both objects and bodies (Blanckaert, Ducros and Hublin 1989). In the second half of the nineteenth century, the principle problem for scientists who were no longer content with travellers' narratives, ethnographic objects or skulls was how to gain access to living subjects. Human zoos thus arrived at a moment in the history of science when anthropology was in need of proofs, and were transformed from commercial fairground phenomena to objects of scientific study. A shift occurred from display to investigation, and from entertainment to education, which was facilitated by the interest of some anthropologists, and this situation lasted until the early years of the twentieth century.

These anthropologists did not remain idle when presented with the fertile grounds for study provided by such exhibitions, and turned them (in Paris at least) into extensions of their own laboratories. This practice became common in Paris from 1877[42] and in 1883, Ernest Chantre took it elsewhere, taking advantage of the arrival in Lyon of five Zulus to undertake anthropometric measurements of his subjects (Chantre 1884). In 1895, the director of the Sudanese exhibition on the Champ de Mars invited the members of the Société d'Anthropologie de Paris to come and view the several hundred 'negroes' it contained (SAP 1895: 479). Paradoxically, the majority of 'races' presented and studied in the Paris Jardin d'Acclimatation were not from the French Empire. At that time, rarity was valued, especially in the search for the missing link, which was the essential element in evolutionist thinking of the period.

Quite quickly, however, most anthropologists stepped back from their association with such displays, especially with regard to their commercial aspects (Copans and Jamin 1978).[43] This occurred between 1885 and 1890 in Western Europe[44] and some time later in Japan[45] and the United States.[46] Anthropologists also complained that the 'specimens' on show were lacking in 'authenticity'[47] a criticism made, in particular, by Paul Nicole about the Fuegians (*Bulletin de la Société d'Anthropologie*, 1880) and by the French anthropologist Léonce Manouvrier in 1882. Concerns were thus focused on the 'quality' of the 'specimens' shown. Gilles Boëtsch comments, accordingly, on the debates which raged among the members of the Société d'Anthropologie de Paris on the ethnographic exhibitions held from 1882–83. Its members refused in 1886 to visit the Ceylon (Sri Lanka) exhibition, not for any moral reasons, but because they considered it to more closely resemble a circus than an ethnographic exhibition. He concludes that 'in less than twenty years (from 1880 to 1900), anthropologists constructed a view of the world and a way of thinking about mankind which drove the chief mechanisms underlying colonial culture' (2003). It is for this reason that the Anthropology pavilion in the 1889 Paris Exposition Universelle took on a new significance in the minds of scholars.

In 1889, the vision the anthropologists wanted to promote was no longer one which demonstrated men's achievements in the field of technology, as had been the case in 1878. Instead, as Georges Berger cites in his account of the exhibition's themes: 'The retrospective exhibition

of labour [...] should re-trace [...] the different stages of the genius of
Man' (Girard de Rialle 1890: 289). We can infer from this that anthropologists wanted to situate their work within the field of modernity,
even if some, such as Deniker and Laloy, continued to take measurements of '145 individuals from a wide range of races' (1891: 257), despite
the fact that they had no clearly defined scientific goals.

These 'scholarly' preoccupations met with those of nation-states
which needed to justify their conquests. Racial difference was a key
argument frequently used in official colonial discourse. In the years
between 1880 and 1910, an active link developed between the aims of
the old colonial powers and the United States (in continuing the War
of Independence and in completing the pacification of the West) on the
one hand, and the requirements of the human sciences and the interests of private promoters on the other.

As Henry de Valigny emphasized in *La Nature*, writing on a visiting
troupe at the 1889 exhibition: 'never in their lives had natural men been
more squeezed, manipulated and examined, and I shall long remember
the intense curiosity with which one of the most eminent scientists
in Vienna helped himself to each native who came within his reach,
manipulating their skulls as though he wanted to crush them' (1889).
The anthropologists involved (we should remember that they were not
in any way the shows' organizers)[48] supported and validated such shows
until 1885–90 in France (Osborne 1994) and Britain, and for some time
after in Japan, Italy, Portugal, the United States and Germany, despite
the disapproval of some of their number for the policy of colonial expansion.[49] The twentieth century was beginning, and although the criticisms
of scholars were increasingly loud, it was too late for them to have the
least effect on the growth of such exhibitions. Moreover, as we have seen,
Paul Topinard was still expressing satisfaction at the interest taken by the
general public in 'savages' who, he anticipated, would soon disappear.

Although differentialist models cannot be laid at the door of the
physical anthropologists of the late-nineteenth century alone (Affergan
1987; 1991) (they had been circulating since the beginning of the century
through travel narratives, descriptions by geographical societies, and
popular literature, and were already well entrenched in the popular
psyche), there can be no doubt that physical anthropology would establish the differentialist concept in the field of science. Hierarchies,
both biological and cultural, were at this time combined with a range
of anthropometric experimental techniques which provided racial
discourse with a new regime of truth, just at the time when anthropological exhibitions were becoming common.

For the physical anthropologists, cultural phenomena were the direct consequences of biology. Accordingly, in a sociological work by Charles Letourneau, we find that the opening pages contain a list of the human 'races' and observations on their geographical distribution (1880b). In his explanatory model of the difference between the human races, intellectual and artistic capabilities, political organization and technical progress are linked to the particular physiology and morphology of each race. He thus suggests that 'only the white races have completely abandoned primitive savagery, at least at the level of society as a whole. Race is thus more influential than environment in sociological development' (1880b: 25).

In this context, the exhibition of the Other served to establish him or her as part of a logical order (that of reason and rationality), and objectivized him or her within a hierarchy (first as a deviant, degenerate or madman, and later as a representative of the 'inferior races', a 'primitive' or 'savage'), while setting him or her against the subjective world of popular representations of the Other, and elsewhere, creating a theoretical system of connections between learned discourse and the most recurrent stereotypes. Here was the reason why it was essential to exhibit the Other. To do so was to acknowledge that she or he had individual status and interest, but at the same time it legitimized, proved and stabilized supposed facts, effectively demonstrating an immeasurable difference.[50] In the first part of the nineteenth century, physical deformities, non-normative bodily or mental states, unusual or 'exotic' physical characteristics, signs of flexibility, strength or skill, and, in addition, social practices considered strange, such as cannibalism, formed the essential elements for display. Difference (because it crystallized both attraction and repulsion) was now an object of curiosity.

Human zoos are thus situated between popular representations of alterity and such scientific discourse (Blanckaert 2002). They provided a vulgarization of the hierarchical pattern, which, in the early years, was actively supported by anthropologists (in particular in Paris, London, Rome, Berlin, Vienna and the United States), while playing on the established tropes of exoticism and savagery. As a result, human zoos pandered to curiosity and aesthetic sensibilities, inducing surprise in the visitor while illustrating the hierarchy of races.[51]

The founding narrative structure of the human zoo, before forms of display became more complex, did not really need to be spelled out; the staging spoke for itself and communicated the underlying principle of difference more efficiently than words. Scientific interest, the contemporary colonial situation and political will were not alone sufficient to bring in the public, as was demonstrated by the failure (in terms of visitor numbers) of the Bella Coola exhibition in Germany, the Kalmyks in France, the Eskimos (Inuit) in Great Britain and the Egyptian caravans in the United States, none of which were considered by the general public to be sufficiently exotic, sensational or original.

From the 1890s, human zoos entered into a period of intensive spectacularization. Exhibitions had to be renewed constantly, new troupes had to be found, scenery had to be transformed, narratives had to be created (for example, the widespread staging of religious ceremonies, or the birth of children to members of the troupes). Ethnic shows, and 'negro villages' were increasingly billed as attractions, on a par with those of the fairground, at international exhibitions and world fairs, ceasing to be presented as strictly zoological exhibits. Although we can outline these underlying characteristics, we should not confine our interest to the ancestry of the human zoos alone. As the contributions to this volume demonstrate, the exhibition of the Other cannot be reduced to a simple demonstration of the hierarchy of races. It is part of a far more complex process.

It is a fact that some exhibitions led to fascination, even reverence and admiration. Many shows at the end of the nineteenth century laid great emphasis on the beauty of the bodies on display and their eroticism (see Bancel and Sirost 2002), on the admirable nature of the cultural artefacts on show, or on the physical skills of those exhibited (Bal 1996). There was thus a shift in the status of the Other, who changed little by little from an exotic object of curiosity into an exotic body which allowed the projection of Western fantasies (demonstrated by the immediate attraction of early cinema to such subjects).[52] The Other provoked desire (Gidley 1992). In this attraction towards the body of the Other, the 'savage' body was staged in such a way that it was eroticized, displayed naked or semi-naked, and made to move in 'ritual dances' in a way which escaped all the canons of Western movement. In order to understand why audiences were drawn towards bodies which were first exoticized and then eroticized (a major factor in bringing in the crowds) we need to remember that a physical norm had developed in nineteenth-century Western societies.

Although the Other was described as unreceptive to progress, lacking the necessary mental ability, he or she was possessed of a body which could be seductive in its strength, resistance, and sensitivity to musical rhythms. The armed forces would consider the exotic body to be a type that was well adapted to physical activity and, therefore, to combat. 'Exotic' women already had an established reputation for being beautiful and sensuous (Yee 2000). As a result, the body of the 'savage' appeared to have greater freedom than those of its audiences, thereby provoking desire in the visitor. Likewise, sexual transgressions attributed to 'savages' (such as polygamy, excessive sexual appetites, and incest), while reinforcing the divide between them and us, also implied a less constrained sexuality, acting as a source for fantasies throughout the century (Le Breton 2001; McClintock 1994). We should therefore distinguish between overtly stigmatizing shows with strong racial connotations and those that were part of a logic of civilizing colonialism, not to mention other, more ambivalent approaches, which mixed the objectification of 'race' with forms of 'recognition' of difference that had no pejorative force.

The Nature of 'Human Zoos'

We should remember that those human zoos which played on the trope of the exotic, and 'negro villages', in particular, appeared in Western Europe alongside faux Breton, Alpine, Flemish, Sicilian, Japanese (Hotta-Lister 1999), Irish, Alsatian, Swiss (Minder 2002), Scottish and Corsican villages. This pattern was born of a complex set of attitudes, in which we find the combination of an interest in ethnographic conservation (Clifford 1986) and a promotion of 'the land' and 'regional heritage', which also stemmed from a devaluation of regional cultures (when compared with the advances of urban modernity promoted by the dominant mid-century Positivist ideology) in favour of national identities.

Despite this context, there are, in our view, several essential differences between such exhibitions and the type of exhibition which grew up around 'exotic' villages. First, the human zoo was characterized by the explicit exploitation of racial difference. For the first decade of such shows, the exotic individual on display was seen as him- or herself, to a certain extent, without resort to a guiding narrative or staging (other than the scenery, which was supposed to recreate his or her environment). Here, the central focus was the representation of physical difference (Hartog 2001). Second, the initial scientific endorsement of the human zoos (founded on a biological racial hierarchy) was absent from the presentation of the 'regional villages'. This suggests that 'human zoos' were a new way of performing Otherness, with their own specific type of radical alterity.

The staging of 'minority cultures' in Europe demonstrates the sense of security of the unifying nation-states, sufficiently confident in their hegemonic power to be able to display their marginal populations as testimonies of the past, the last symbols of the ancient world. In a way, the 'exotic village' (in addition to its increasing conformity to colonial ideology) clearly demonstrates that the quality of strangeness was, in these final years of the nineteenth century, slipping away from provincial and European spaces and moving beyond Europe to more distant colonial spaces. This move anticipated a process of normalization which had yet to occur, projecting a colonizing and unificatory ideal into the future.

While it is thus necessary to make a distinction between anthropo-zoological exhibitions (De l'Estoile 2007), colonial pavilions at world fairs, travelling fairground and circus shows, and 'exotic villages', in terms of form and content, these different phenomena are nevertheless linked by their ultimate effect, whether explicit or implicit, which was to demonstrate the superiority of the white race and/or of Western civilization. We should therefore think of the broad range of such exhibitions within the context of such ends (along with admiration for some civilizations and reverence for the aesthetic beauty of some peoples), while remembering their function as creators of myths and fantasies based on archetypes of Western culture, going beyond their hegemonic role (De l'Estoile 2007). In this last case, the 'savage' was not just a menacing, limited, childlike, or animal figure, he or she also functioned as the irrepressible element in a desire to go beyond the rigidity and bodily constraints generated by the emergence of modernity (see Bancel and Sirost 2002), the metaphor for lost innocence, or for an Elsewhere which was the counterpart to the invasive rationality of the last years of the nineteenth century.

It is also important, faced with the diversity of forms taken by our definition of 'human zoos', to emphasize the chronological limits of the phenomenon. In the first edition of this book, we wrote with regard to this topic that human zoos, in their historical and etymological sense, occurred only in a precise period, from the early nineteenth century to the 1930s, if we accept a broad definition of their nature, thereby opening the debate on the concept of human zoos itself. It must be said that the problem of the categorization of human zoos was not fully resolved in that first edition and, moreover, the opening up of deliberately broad historical perspectives on the topic, which linked human zoos to the present day, may have led to confusion, despite our precautionary remarks in the Introduction. It is therefore necessary to continue here our attempt to provide a definition of the concept.

The issues of chronological limits and of the categorization itself led to debates and objections from the June 2001 French conference. Scholars criticized the breadth of the category (Merle and Sibeud 2003; in this particular case with an unfortunate lack of epistemological awareness), but also the link with the 'fact of colonialism' (Liauzu 2004). Others proposed that the official colonial exhibitions of the interwar years should be excluded from the category, as they were more 'humanist' in character (De L'Estoile 2007; Blanckaert 2002; Bergougniou et al. 2001). But Robert Rydell had already largely dealt with these points at the conference, as had many other participants, criticizing the 'recent tendencies in scholarship to treat world's fairs as theatre settings with performers who entertained crowds' (see Rydell in this volume), with no further attempt to discover their meanings and ideological implications (it should be made clear that this tendency is confined to a few researchers in France and Germany). The form of the human exhibition of 'exotics', which included ethnographic shows, 'negro villages' and theatrical performances within the specified time frame, seems to us to constitute a genuine historical pattern. But it is, of course, hard to establish the limits of the phenomenon with absolute certainty, given that the human exhibition of 'exotics' is effectively more a pattern and a process than it is a category in the strict sense.

Even the term 'human zoo', inspired by Hagenbeck's formula of the 'anthropozoological exhibition', seemed to some to be too 'strong' (even though it is really only rewriting a term of the period) or applicable only in a narrow sense to purely 'zoological' exhibitions. On the contrary, as we wrote in 2002, 'to place a man, with the intention that he should be seen, in a specific reconstructed space, not because of what he "does" (an artisan, for example), but because of what he "is" (seen through the prism of a real or imagined difference) is in our view the most precise definition of the human zoos' (Blanchard 2002: 419). We understand this concept to express a separation, 'a relationship of induced distance and exteriority, materialized through a physical spatial device (bars, fence, barrier, screen)' (2002: 419), which leads us to 'construct an invisible but tangible boundary between "them" and "us"' (2002: 420). In the context of this broad definition, the specification of the 'exoticism' of the exhibited peoples and the precise time frame seem to us to be powerful enough tools to delineate the pattern of human zoos.[53]

In a recent study Benoît De l'Estoile (2007) sets out a reasoned argument which questions whether a single concept (that of human zoos) should include the different forms of exhibition, describing a process which extended from the most racist of exhibitions to those which manifested respect in their reconstructions of other cultures (exemplified by the French Colonial Exposition of 1931 in Paris).[54] His

critique is indicative of an ongoing debate among a small number of
scholars, which, because it is still in progress, we feel it is appropriate
to address. Without denying that exhibitions took different forms (as we
have remarked here already), we believe that the concept of human zoos
does not imply any sense of particular degrees of racism (or humanism),
which varied from one exhibition to the next. Instead, it represents a
common process and similar devices. This is why, indeed, in the mosaic
of human zoos, we encounter the juxtaposition of strongly racialized
displays, and of exhibitions which were more ethnographic in character,
sometimes allowing a degree of admiration for the civilization of those
on show.

   This process is in any case well documented in this volume by
Boëtsch and Ardagna, who show that the move towards a 'more official
image of the colonies' which euphemized 'types', or more specifically
'races', was in evidence in France from the 1906 Marseille Exposition
Coloniale onwards, and would emerge fully at the 1931 exhibition, as
Lebovics demonstrates here in this volume (see also Lemaire 2002a).
This does not alter the fact that in all their complex manifestations,
human zoos led to the redefinition of the status of the Other, instituting
a boundary between two different humanities (Blanchard, Blanchoin,
Bancel et al. 1996).

Amusement, Information, Education

The spectacle of 'racial' diversity in the form of ethnographic scenes was
constructed around three distinct functions: to amuse, to inform and
to educate, appearing in different configurations in the various types
of exhibition. The same troupe could pass from the zoological gardens
to the music hall (Chalaye 1998; 2002), from the scientist's laboratory
to a 'native village' at a world fair, or from a colonial reconstruction to a
circus act. Boundaries were unclear, genres were mixed, and interests
varied. For the purposes of analysis, though, we need to separate the
tangled threads of this narrative. For, at the beginning of the twentieth
century, a visit to the zoological gardens, to the circus or to a 'negro
village', was not just a chance to witness the diversity of humanity, it
was an opportunity for the visitor to understand not only the Other's
place in the world, but also his own (Barthe and Coutancier 1995).

   Visitors to the exhibitions had little sophistication. They shared a
general idea of a European physiological norm and were influenced
by the new industrial and colonial culture. They were encouraged to
interpret what they saw as a demonstration of the progress of humanity

from savagery to civilization. The integration of savagery into the entertainment world had opened up new horizons.[55] Exhibitions were no longer passive, as they had been in the zoological gardens, but became active (Bogdan 1988). The entertainment value of the 'savage' was increased by activities considered to be primitive in nature, such as dance, music, games and traditional physical pursuits, in which the body of the 'savage' was the key element. This body was presented as the reflection of a universe far removed from the technical progress of the West and close to nature, where man's survival depended on his physical prowess.

Although Otherness is itself an ancient concept, that of exoticism is more recent. The latter belongs to a European conceptual framework, which was expressed through waves of public interest in particular countries or peoples. Persia, China and the Ottoman Empire were in vogue in the seventeenth century, and were considered to be mysterious and fascinating. Well before the bodies of foreign peoples were put on show, their metalwork, clothing, fabrics and drugs[56] were at first objects of curiosity, then became sought-after luxury goods and were appropriated by the arts. The colonial period gradually constructed a different kind of Other, which was less strange and more everyday in nature, since it had to form part of a colonial and racial hierarchy dominated by the white peoples. This construct became fully integrated into Western thought, permeating the popular imagery of the period and being perceived as a legitimate object of scientific study.

The anatomical criteria for the definition of different human categories were the same in physical anthropology and the figurative arts, both of which were based on appearances. Morphological analysis allowed the appearance of the human body to be broken down into a certain number of visible characteristics. In order to succeed in this observational undertaking, intended to determine the biological characteristics of each human type, physical anthropologists created a scientific classification system in which chromatic scales were utilized to categorize the colours of the skin and eyes, and measuring apparatus, tape measures and slide callipers were employed for the measurement of the body.

A major change in the gaze occurred with the emergence and establishment of the photographic medium, which was soon transferred to the cinematograph. The photographic image satisfied a need to capture, inventory, reproduce, study and distribute the 'true' forms of people and objects that haunted the minds of the curious, which were already filled with the nineteenth-century concepts of universalism and rationalism. Half scientist and half artist (the status of the former was still not fully established), the enlightened amateur would, through photography, photogravure and, later, the cinematograph, provide the dominant Western discourse with an extraordinary tool. Practitioners addressed an unsophisticated public, employing an iconographic style which could be immediately understood. Purporting to be expressions of the truth, available for rapid distribution in a variety of forms, photographs and, later, films, would provide a definitive validation of a particular representation of the world, complete with its human hierarchy, its scenographic devices, and its moral dramaturgy. These mechanisms, which were successfully tried out at world fairs (in particular by the Lumière brothers in France in 1896), thereafter became an important source for all modes of discourse, communication and identity.

Gradually, comparative anatomy and research in the natural sciences reduced the role played by fantasy in the Western understanding of the world and the bodies of others. But in order to be aware of the diversity of mankind and to portray it, a line still had to be drawn between the human and the animal worlds. Here, those who were considered to be at the limits of humanity would continue to cause problems in classification for scientists whose understanding of anthropology was founded on the European body.

In the field of artistic representation, this led to problems in the construction of normative human figures which were supposed to illustrate the typical morphology of each 'race', given that human groups could be expected to be as susceptible as individuals to changes in their environment or in social practice. For artists, the representation of the human body was expected to correspond to established canons, leading to a problem in portraying Otherness of whatever type, be it deformed, monstrous or savage. Indeed, within the context of an aesthetic where the body illustrated the work of the gods or of God, art could only be derived from perfection, and the canons were consequently composed of representations of perfection, leaving no place for alternative forms.

The common interest of the artist and the natural scientist in the human body had led them to follow parallel paths, at least until the beginning of the nineteenth century, which saw a rationalization of knowledge and a shift from qualitative approaches to quantitative methodologies in the field of science. From this time on, anthropology held itself apart, adopting a classificatory approach founded on a typological paradigm. Measurement did not, as it does today, allow the analysis of the spectrum of human biological diversity, but instead demonstrated the processes of degeneration (of hybridization) compared with 'pure types'.

In this environment, colonized peoples became worthy of a second look, for they could not remain for too long in the category of the 'savage' or the 'barbarous', given that this would have been a denial of the core principles of the colonial mission (August 1979). They gradually became the subjects of colonial empires, turning into 'the natives'. But, by focusing too closely on the colonial act in its strictest sense, some researchers (in France in particular) have neglected the fact that a *colonial culture* grew up in the home countries that fixed the status of 'races' and 'natives' and popularized this discourse through the visual image.[57] As Lebovics remarks in this volume: 'Living as we do in the postcolonial period, we tend to underestimate the sometimes Herculean efforts of the imperial propagandists to gain the support of the people for the conquest and administration of an empire and to make them accept their destiny as an imperial race.'

Understanding a Process

One of the major goals of our approach, it will have been understood, is to be able to question the representation of the Other through time and to understand the different forms which illustrate the concept of human zoos through their close relationship with racializing and/or eugenicist discourses, with arguments for colonization, and the creation of national identities. This approach also opens up a fresh spectrum of analysis through the study of new materials, enabling us better to redefine and understand the colonial space.

To allow the reader a cumulative understanding of this process, we have organized this volume on chronological–thematic lines into three major sections. We start the first part with an introduction of the particular characteristics of our core concept, which are to be looked for in a wide range of cultural forms (see Garland-Thomson), particularly in shows containing 'freaks' in circuses and fairs (see Bogdan and Corbey),[58] but also in the history of the importation to the royal courts of Europe of 'exotics', which merged with the frame of the animal zoo to become human zoos. Three events (two in Europe and one in the United States) appear to have served as turning points in this process: the exhibition of the Hottentot Venus between 1810 and 1815 in Britain and France (see Boëtsch and Blanchard);[59] the encounter between Barnum and Joice Heth in 1837, with the model that was subsequently established in the United States (see Reiss); and the professionalization of the phenomenon by Carl Hagenbeck in the early 1870s in Hamburg (see Thode-Arora).

The models for the exhibitions were not constructed on identical lines, nor did they precisely coincide chronologically. They were affected by local expectations, by the type of peoples who were displayed (although black Africans made up more than half the troupes or individuals on show), and by the spaces in which they were presented to the public (reconstructed villages, travelling troupes, exhibition pavilions, circuses). This is demonstrated by the contributions collected in the second part of this volume. In this vast panorama, we encounter formal adaptations of the model of the human zoo, which responded to local requirements and contexts. These include Buffalo Bill's Indians in his Wild West show (see Maddra in this volume; see also Moses 1996); the shows held in Germany in the last part of the nineteenth century (see Ames in this volume); exhibitions which were regularly held in particular locations, such as the Paris Jardin d'Acclimatation, which organized more than thirty exhibitions from 1877–78 onwards (see Schneider in this volume);[60] those which took place in Zürich and Basel;[61] the ethnic shows at White City in London (see MacKenzie in this volume);[62] and, of course, the dozens of troupes and villages which Hagenbeck sent out throughout Europe and the United States from 1874 until midway between the two world wars (see Thode-Arora in this volume).

There were also performances in a different style. The exhibitions of Aborigines, Kanaks or Dahomeans throughout Europe; the exhibitions of Onas in the Netherlands (see Mason in this volume) and Kaliñas in France (Collomb 1992; 1995); anthropological inventions such as Dr Kahn's Niam-Niams (see Lindfors in this volume); or the position occupied by Indian (or Sinhalese) troupes and populations in the West (Assayag 1999), all responded to the expectations of particular audiences.[63] Beyond these different models, the specific characteristics of each nation-state also affected the evolution of the process. The spread of different models was accompanied by variations in the staging of the Other and of the exotic in all fields of popular culture. From photography to cinema (see Edwards and Deroo in this volume),[64] from postcards to museums, the range of media in which they appeared goes far beyond the simple exhibition, affecting all cultural spaces at the turn of the nineteenth and twentieth centuries.

In the third and final part of this volume, we have looked more closely at national identities and their relationships with local identities and exhibition models. Faced with a wide range of forms, it is not possible to infer a progression of types from the end of the nineteenth century to the current day, but some more recent hybrid forms suggest the persistence of the racial model, each adapted to its particular context. Most of the European exhibitions (more than three-quarters of the shows took place on the continent of Europe) were based in four countries: Switzerland; Britain (see MacKenzie and Servan-Schrieber in this volume);[65] France (see Lebovics, Boëtsch and Blanchard, Blanchard, Bancel and Lemaire, and Schneider);[66] and Germany (see Thode-Arora and Ames).[67] Outside Europe, Japan (see Nanta) and the United States[68] (see Maddra, Emin, Rydell, Delsahut and Arnoldi) experienced comparable shows but for shorter periods (until the First World War in the United States, and until the Second World War in Imperial Japan).

Finally, a last group of countries which were more peripherally concerned with human zoos are presented, in particular Belgium (see Jacquemin), Spain (see Moyano), and Italy (see Abbattista and Labanca).[69] Elsewhere, only the occasional touring troupe would visit (perhaps while on a grand tour of Europe), and there were just a few local world fairs. Examples here are the Austro-Hungarian Empire, Poland, Portugal, Russia, countries of northern Europe, Australia, New Zealand, Argentina, Canada, India, Algeria (in 1930), South Africa (in 1936) and even what used to be French Indochina (Hanoi in 1901) and Upper Volta (now Burkina Faso) in 1934.

National Developments and Variants

With the fashion for colonial exhibitions and travelling 'negro villages' (including those in the United States, see Rydell 1999) the 'savage' was gradually transformed into a 'native', under the spectators' gaze. In Europe, these exhibitions were dreamed up in order to glorify the achievements and projects of the colonial powers, particularly those of France (Bancel, Blanchard and Lemaire 2000), Italy (see Abbattista and Labanca in this volume; see also Labanca 1992; Palma 1999); Britain (MacKenzie 1984); and Belgium (Jacquemin 1985; 1991). In the case of the Koreans exhibited in Japan and the Filipinos exhibited in the United States, the same process was in evidence. Although the lifestyle, clothes, dances and artisanal techniques were ambivalent in their function (both recognizing certain cultural aspects of the colonized nations, and still associating them with the burden of their archaic nature in comparison with Western modernity), skin colour (or racial differences) remained the emblematic sign of difference. In the nuanced palette of colours which determined the races, the graduation ran from the darkest to the lightest of skins. The blacker the individual, (or the blacker he or she was perceived to be), the more limited or non-existent his or her capacity for development was judged to be.

The spectacularization of the Other was far from homogeneous,

varying according to period and place. In France, there was a notice-
able shift in the presentation of colonized peoples at the 1922 Exposition Nationale Coloniale in Marseille, where racial stigmatization was
largely glossed over in favour of a paean to the 'civilizing mission'.
This continued in 1925 at the Paris Exposition Internationale des
Arts Décoratifs, and at the 1931 Exposition Coloniale Internationale in
Vincennes, outside Paris, becoming even more pronounced at the Salon
de la France d'Outre-mer in Paris in 1935, and reaching its height at the
1937 Paris Exposition Internationale des Arts et Techniques dans la Vie
Moderne. By 1940, 'native exhibitions' would completely disappear, to
be replaced by a purely economic focus.

In addition to France, which specialized in universal or international
exhibitions (1855, 1867, 1878, 1900, 1925 and 1937) and vast colonial
exhibitions and salons (1894, 1895, 1901–2, 1906 (2), 1907, 1909, 1911,
1914, 1922, 1923, 1924, 1927, 1930, 1931, 1935 and 1940), not to mention
its travelling 'negro villages', Germany and Switzerland also became
specialists in ethnic events, while Britain developed a hybrid genre
between the universal and the ethnic. As John MacKenzie suggests in this
volume, the British 'great exhibitions' gradually became dominated by
the theme of Empire, building on their combination of 'entertainment,
education, and trade fair on a spectacular scale'. As well as the exhibitions organized in Britain itself (for example those of 1886, 1888, 1901,
1907 and 1938 in Glasgow,[70] and, in London, the 1899 Greater Britain
Exhibition, the 1908 Franco-British Exhibition,[71] the 1909 Imperial
International Exhibition, the 1911 Coronation Exhibition, the 1914 Anglo-
American Exhibition, and the 1924–25 British Empire Exhibitions at
Wembley, which had 25 million visitors), this type of event was staged
throughout the British Empire: in New Zealand (on three occasions); in
Jamaica (1891); in Australia and Tasmania (1879, 1888, 1891, 1894, 1897);
South Africa (1877, 1936); and India (1883, 1910).

For the British Empire, the most important development occurred
between the Colonial and Indian Exhibition of 1886 and the Greater
Britain Exhibition of 1899 in London. At the latter, the central feature
(created by the master of the genre, Imre Kiralfy) was the Kafir Kraal,
which portrayed 'savage' South Africa tamed by the white man. It was so
successful that it was repeated in Paris in the following year at the Porte
Maillot under the title of 'Savage Africa'. In 1911, visitors to the Festival
of Empire Exhibition at the Crystal Palace in London experienced
another significant innovation: being conducted on a complete tour of
the Dominions and having the chance to view the riches, landscape and
peoples of each colony. After the First World War, the British Empire

Exhibitions of 1924–25 at Wembley marked a change in the character of colonial exhibitions. As in France, the following decade saw ethnic villages gradually relegated to the background, disappearing in the face of an imperial pageant which highlighted the economic progress and power of the British Empire.

In the United States, the process was more complex, although we can locate the change in the exhibition of the 'exotic' (albeit with many caveats) at the Panama-Pacific International Exhibition, San Francisco, of 1915 (Benedict 1983). The staging of minorities, like that of 'exotic' peoples, gained a new quality after this time, before gradually fading away as modernity became the central theme of the great American exhibitions. It was, above all, in the world of theatre, the circus and also the cinema that the invisible boundary between 'them' and 'us' continued to exist. 'Egyptian pavilions' and 'Red-Skin shows' were still to be encountered, but the dreams and spectacle of the Hollywood invitation to travel to foreign lands now dominated the minds of audiences.

Where Japan was concerned, colonial and ethnographic pavilions became common in exhibitions from 1914 until the Second World War (see Nanta in this volume). At the Tokyo-Taisho exhibition in 1914 there were pavilions from Taiwan, Karafuto (Sakhalin Island), Manchuria and Korea (as well as an 'enhancement' pavilion). These were the regions which were shortly to become part of the Japanese Empire. At the 1922 exhibition, the new Nanyo (South Sea) and Siberian pavilions also contained ethnographic features.

In these different geographical areas, the 'ethnic village' was the chief vehicle for the display of 'exotics', being the easiest form to include in both official exhibitions and local shows. From the Paris Exposition Universelle of 1878 onwards, there were calls for indigenous peoples to be included as part of the entertainment in colonial pavilions, and we can note that there were also plans to create ethnographic reconstructions on this occasion.[72] But at this time the link between private operators such as Hagenbeck and the public organizers of such exhibitions had not yet been forged.

It was in 1883, when East Indian peoples were presented at the Amsterdam International Coloniale en Uitvoerhandel Tentoonstelling, and again in 1886, at the Indian and Colonial Exhibition in Britain (with over five million visitors), that the first villages began to appear in official imperial displays. In France, the first formal villages appeared at the 1889 Paris Exposition Universelle on the Champ de Mars, in particular the Kanak village (Bullard and Dauphiné 2002) and the Javanese village with its troupe of dancers (Labrousse 2002: 171–72).[73] Four years later in the United States at the 1893 Chicago World's Fair, the same type of village was to be found (Bergouniou, Clignet and David 2001; Gilbert 1993; Rydell 1993; Scott 1991).[74] Last, in Lyon the following year (1894) an organized and structured Indochinese village was placed opposite an apparently archaic and savage 'negro village' with its 'one hundred and ten natives' (Bancel, Bencharif and Blanchard 2007).

In a single decade, the village model was not only rolled out to official exhibitions across the world but also appeared in most of the major cities of Europe (not to mention the United States) under the aegis of thirty or so private impresarios, most of whom were German, French and Swiss. The pattern was thus established and ethnic villages were to be found everywhere in the universal, national, and colonial exhibitions which followed, a fact which suggests that their surroundings were interchangeable. Why? No doubt because at this time these shows were already an international product, shared by the American and European publics. No doubt, too, because this formula was an effective one and responded to codes which had already been tried and tested in the private sector. Such villages offered a developed form of a world in miniature, which could now be visited without having to leave one's home town. These exhibitions had drawn closer to home, visiting small provincial towns on the heels of the circuses and small travelling troupes which, in the preceding decade, had prepared the ground for them, feeding the popular hunger for the exotic.

All of Europe and North America was affected by this pattern. The first to witness it were the cities of Basel, Berlin,[75] Hamburg, Zürich, Anvers, Paris, Brussels, Lyon, Dresden, Frankfurt, Marseille, Strasbourg, London, and Turin, which alone saw several hundred 'negro villages' or 'exotic' troupes presented as 'villages' (both individually and at exhibitions). We can also cite European and American towns and cities which hosted major shows, such as Barcelona, Budapest, Dublin, Düsseldorf, Ghent, St Petersburg,[76] Lyon, Freiburg, Geneva, Glasgow, Gothenburg, Vienna, Hanover, Cologne, Lausanne, Leipzig, Liège, Milan, Brest, Munich, Oslo, Moscow, Warsaw, Naples, Copenhagen, Palermo, Prague, Rotterdam, Stockholm, Chicago, Brussels, Bordeaux, Rouen, St Louis,[77] San Francisco, and Buffalo (Leary and Shones 1998). We should add to this number the Japanese world fairs, and those organized in the British Empire such as the Empire Exhibition of 1936 in Johannesburg,[78] where ethnic villages were constructed.

Visitors came to these villages not only to learn but also to gaze at and to 'encounter' the Other. For, as the *New York Times* wrote on a Senegalese village which appeared at the Pan-American Exposition in Buffalo in 1901, nothing had previously been seen which gave off such an impression of brutal savagery. In the villages, a touch of exoticism, the odd example of native crafts for the tourist, and a few rags to support the message of an ongoing civilizing mission were the essential elements of the programme, along with, of course, regular attractions and entertainments. They functioned along roughly similar lines: dances and processions with a musical accompaniment; picturesque costumes and interchangeable names for the troupes; reconstructed battles; close association with animals in an exotic setting; cultural or cult attractions; crafts designed as souvenirs, or reproductions of schools, in which children attempted to learn the alphabet. The attractions ranged from children diving into a pool to retrieve coins and the preparation of meals by the women, to 'village births'. They adapted equally to different places, cultures, current events and popular demand. Thus, following a practice which had been common among the travelling exhibitions, the same troupe could, for example, be 'from Dahomea' in France and 'from Togo' in Germany.

This was a euphemized form of the anthropozoological exhibition, which followed new codes. But essentially, despite the claims of some scholars (De L'Estoile 2007), there was no break with the earlier period, and the ethnic villages (especially those at exhibitions) continued to have an undeniably ideological function, namely to demonstrate who was already *civilized* and who still needed to become so. Of course, visitors could sometimes talk with those on show, craftsmen could explain their work, 'natives' could leave with their medals, or visit the local town (the visit being itself an attraction advertised by the press), but this did not serve to break down barriers, it only reduced the degree of distance between observers and exhibits. We also see an attenuation of the racializing elements, with interest being extended to cultural artefacts (objects, architecture, clothing and so on) and to productions which increasingly created a narrative. This accounts for the fact that, in most of the souvenir books and other official guides for exhibitions, these villages were classed among the attractions, sending a clear signal as to how they should be received (and perceived) by visitors.[79] The First World War seems to have acted as a turning point in the evolution of ethnic shows, as much in the United States and Japan as in Europe, although we should remember that ethnic exhibitions continued beyond this time in the context of circus performance, with little change in the forms they took.[80] With the increase in prominence of soldiers from the colonies (in France, Britain), minority groups from the United States, and contract workers from countries such as China, the discourse of the

Other took on new forms and exploited new media. Everywhere, exhibitions were adapting to national contexts (Benedict 1991).

The Demise of Human Zoos

In the event, exhibitions of all types, whether international, colonial or national, were used as a vehicle by every state to show off its social (and sometimes 'racial' or eugenicist) projects (Çelik and Kinney 1990), to impose its own view of the world, and to legitimize its overseas projects or the practice of racial segregation. In the United States, analysis of the practice reveals significant differences from elsewhere (Sears 1997), linked to the presence of 'ethnic minorities' within the home country. It is indisputable that the American nation was constructed on successive forms of exhibition, from 'freak shows' to eugenics,[81] and from ethnic shows to racial segregation, in a series of stages which together make up the American model of the exhibition of the Other and which were based on the status of minorities in American society. In Japan, as in France, Britain, Belgium and Italy, the link between the potential for colonization and the designation of peoples as 'appropriate for colonization', or already colonized, is clear. In the case of France and Britain, it is possible to follow the colonial situation (the phases of colonial conquests and events between 1880 and 1910) through the exhibited peoples.[82] Thus, in different but concomitant ways, human zoos were created in particular contexts, feeding the construction of national identities.

In order to reach the widest possible audience, human zoos were now organized everywhere and relied on a wide range of publicity devices, including posters, photographs, postcards, films, advertising leaflets, reports in the national press, and articles and reports in scientific journals. The tens of thousands of postcards produced demonstrate the degree to which these shows were promoted through the media, but they also anticipated their decline, while cinema sealed the fate of the live shows. As the shows developed national characteristics, they were thus also undergoing a profound shift in medium. From 'living spectacles' (exhibitions) they were transformed into 'living images' (the cinema), passing through the intermediate forms of the diorama and ethnographic sculpture. From the imported Other (the exhibited person) they moved to the duplicated Other (fixed images). This represented both a change in scale and the emergence of a new dimension of Otherness (Baudrillard 1987).

From the early 1930s we see a gradual and steady decline in human zoos, with some variation from country to country. For example, in 1934 (Exposição Colonial Portuguesa) and 1940 (Exposição do Mundo Português; see Léonard 1999), Portugal somewhat belatedly organized the visit of several 'native' troupes intended to support its colonial operations and to raise public awareness. Likewise, Italy, engaged in a wave of conquests in Ethiopia, maintained the presence of 'African villages' at its great exhibitions, the last of these being the East African village at the Naples exhibition of 1940. In Germany, (with the Deutsche Africa-Schau; see Forgey 1994) and in Switzerland (see Minder in this volume), where there was still a public for traditional ethnographical exhibitions, human zoos continued, but with reduced frequency.

But the time of great colonial exhibitions had passed and in Britain and France the display of 'native populations' was relegated to the background. In France, for example, a decision was made (imposed by Lyautey)[83] to exclude all exhibitions of an 'ethnic' character from the Paris 1931 Exposition Coloniale Internationale. These included the 'negresses with lip plates', Indochinese rickshaw boys (in response to a direct request from the League for Human Rights) and 'Kanak Cannibals'[84] (Hodeir and Pierre 1991; Blanchard and Lemaire, 2003). Their exclusion was intended to act as a gesture which would emphasize 'colonial humanity'. However, for the 2,000 'natives' at the Paris exhibition, of whom a large number were soldiers, while it can be said that the 'conditions of presentation had changed' as De L'Estoile underlines (2007: 61), it was nevertheless the case that they were still actors in a staged display, performing in a colonial show created by 'white' producers. Effectively, as Lebovics writes in this volume, this exhibition was like all other colonial exhibitions in that it remained a human zoo, in which the strange beasts of the colonies (and France) were on display.

Although the presentation changed, replacing racial inferiority with the quaint habits of 'native' cultures, the general aim of the demonstration was still to glorify the 'civilizing mission'.[85] It is indisputable, though, that Lyautey also wished to pay homage to indigenous cultures,[86] without, of course, questioning in any way the legitimacy of colonial rule. The Vincennes international exhibition thus presented many facets: it was propagandist; it presented other cultures as quaint; it was educational (thousands of photographs, hundreds of films, and a multitude of ethnographic objects were on display in the various pavilions); but it was also admiring of certain other cultures.

Some scientists (such as Henri Vallois), not placated by the presence of pirogues on the lakes, were still nostalgic for the old-style 'negro villages', regretting their absence and bemoaning the fact that the organizing committee would not allow scientists to study the 'natives', thereby preventing the continuation of the 'fine studies by Deniker and Laloy relating to those displayed in the 1889 exhibition' (Vallois 1932).[87] A report on the plans for the pavilions of Togo and Cameroon by André Bonamy in 1929 had already warned that 'exhibitions' would be forbidden at the 1931 Exposition, so as to provide a more 'modern' message concerning the French colonial endeavour and to emphasize France's civilizing influence. The concept of modernity was set in opposition to the vulgarity which was now considered to accompany the culture of the gaze generated by such shows.

It is clear to us, here, that we have a mixture of genres, blending scientific activity with the independent private tour (along the lines of a travelling circus) and official reconstruction. The days of the old ethnic shows were over. De L'Estoile comments in this respect that from 1931 'the negro village was seen as outmoded', suggesting that this exhibition 'marked a shift in the presentation of the colonized'. He argues that the performer had now been transformed into an 'artist' who had a particular role to play in the exhibition. The 'static display' of natives had disappeared (if it really ever existed), and performers 'were presented in active roles which emphasized their artistic abilities'. He concludes that this evolution demonstrates the fact that the ethos here was no longer that 'of the zoo', but rather that 'of the music and folk festival' (2007).

It is nevertheless necessary, in our view, to introduce a degree of nuance to the analysis of these changes. We cannot simply describe the 1931 exhibition as a 'music festival', interpreting it as an epistemological break with the human zoos. Instead, we must ask what it shared with these, and recognize that every era adopted different forms of such exhibitions. Indeed, as Lebovics remarks in this volume, we should probably view this exhibition as 'an imperialist ceremony of self-validation and the initiation of French visitors into the new society of spectacle'. It was therefore necessary to bring new life to the genre, and to emphasize, above all, that 'native peoples' were, thanks to France, on the road to 'colonial progress'. As Lebovics concludes, the organizers 'wished to see the reproductions of the Bois de Vincennes become a reality for the peoples of the Empire, and one which was centred on France.'

The homage to other cultures thus needs to be understood not only within the context of an unspoken intention to achieve political domination (legitimated by the intrinsic superiority of Western civilization), sealed by an inevitable 'common future' with France (see Lebovics in this volume). The change from the naturalizing archaism of the first human zoos to a more modern presentation was, in the final analysis, a way of demonstrating 'the benefits of colonial modernization' to the visitor in visible form, transforming the passive 'savage' into an 'artisan' at work (in the exhibition and, by extension, in the colony). This tendency was already present in the Marseille exhibition of 1922, and reached its height in France at the 1931 Exposition. The 'savage' could no longer be displayed; he needed to have disappeared under the influence of Western civilization, for the primitive peoples of earlier times had become both 'good Christians', under the influence of the missionaries, and 'good soldiers', who would demonstrate their valour in war, as they had during the colonial conquests (Deroo and Champeaux 2006). Women who had once been displayed in 'primitive' nakedness were now clothed and imbued with the moral values of Western society (Boëtsch and Savarese 1999). The two powerful lobbies involved in this process (the Church and the Army) expected colonized peoples to be treated with dignity, thereby becoming valuable economic assets. The presentation proposed by the organizers was influenced by these factors.

As a result, although we should rid ourselves of the idea of a radical shift in the perception of the 'native', we can note a change in the objectives of colonial propaganda which now set out to demonstrate that that the 'native' was on the road to civilization (see Lemaire 2002b), proof of which was provided by the military and religious organizations associated with colonial policy. The new mode of presentation in 1931 was now in line with these objectives and the desired image of a 'Pax Colonica'. The new 'humanism' which can be detected in this transformation cannot be dissociated from the process of colonial domination which, in this particular case, perpetuated the exhibition of the Other in accordance with the new pattern constructed by the colonizers for their relationship with colonized peoples.

In effect, six years later, in 1937, the presence of 'exotics' in Paris at the international exhibition made it resemble a 'village of craftsmen'[88] accompanied by a theatrical troupe more closely than an ethnic show (Lusenbrink 2002: 260–61), but this process is more properly part of a shift in the colonial relationship than it is the affirmation of a form of 'colonial humanism' supported by the French colonial authorities. Between the two exhibitions, the sidelining of human zoos by French exhibitions seems to have been completed. As Lemaire suggests: 'natives, who had previously symbolized the trophies of colonization in the period of conquest, had now become the trophies of civilization, displayed as visual proof of the rightness of activities in the colonies. It is true that they remained "inferior", but they were tamed, domesticated and moving towards progress' (Lemaire 2002b: 278).

To reinforce the message that these were 'new times', there were displays on colonial projects and the development of indigenous peoples under the colonial mission (demonstrating progress in conversions to Christianity and in education), but the role of these peoples in the accomplishment of the mission was also shown. This role was, of course, modest (represented by crafts, dances, and enrolment in the army), but was also a moving one, testifying to their enthusiastic participation in the establishment of their own domination.

The Legacy of the Gaze

The final manifestation of this process was Expo 58, the great Belgian Universal and International Exposition of 1958. Here, on the eve of the end of empire, 'native' performers were called on for the last time to participate in the general presentation of a colonial power. As we have seen, it was from the 1930s that the general public became tired of human zoos and that the latter found themselves increasingly out of step with social needs. In particular, the failure of Hagenbeck's two final shows in Germany (a troupe of Kanaks who came from France in 1931, and a troupe of Tcherkess riders in 1932) marked the sad ending of a story which had included more than seventy ethnic shows (see Thode-Arora in this volume).[89] The last ethnographic tours in Europe appear to have failed to attract the large numbers of visitors of the previous generation, whether in Basel (Switzerland), Stockholm (Sweden), Cologne (Germany – with a troupe of 'Sara Kaba negresses with lip-plates') or Milan (Italy).

In the United States, the same situation prevailed. The model established at the World's Columbian Exposition, Chicago, in 1893 (see Rydell in this volume) had changed and was no longer effective. In the 1893 Great White City of Chicago, everyone had been allocated his or her place in the world. The villages and exotic pavilions had occupied the centre of the exhibition space in a layout that underlined the metaphor of civilizing progress on the march. Thus, alongside a variety of attractions from Hagenbeck's menagerie, and sixty or so Dahomeans (both male and female) who had symbolized the defeat of Darkest Africa by the colonizing West, had been found the Sioux chieftains who had been defeated in 1890 at Wounded Knee (see Preston Blier in this volume; see also Rydell 1993).

That world of display had disappeared. Now, domination was presented in a more subtle fashion. The Other was no longer a 'still-savage' defeated figure, but a 'pacified native', enthusiastically rushing forward under the leadership of his or her benefactor to follow the path traced out for him towards 'progress'. This was the figure who appeared, as we have emphasized, at the Paris Exposition Internationale in 1937, at the Johannesburg Empire Exhibition of 1936, at the Naples exhibition of 1940, at the Glasgow Empire Exhibition of 1938,[90] and at the Deutsche Kolonial Ausstellung in 1939, now that the brutal tone of ethnic exhibitions was no longer appropriate for the demonstration of activities overseas. Ethnic shows had now become part of the heritage of both Western societies and ex-colonies: their day was past.[91]

A history of human zoos cannot, however, ignore how aspects of this phenomenon have continued in our culture, even to the present day (Blanchard and Bancel 1998b; Bancel 2007). It would certainly be simplistic to propose a continuous line from ethnic shows to modern forms of the display and perception of the Other (Moussa 2002). It is, nevertheless, still possible to propose that there are thematic threads in the representation of the Other which extend across the century (Alloula 1986; Blanchard 2002). As a consequence, all contemporary representations of the Other (in the cinema, live performances, advertising, the tourism industry,[92] sport, media images, ethnographic exhibitions[93] and museums of world culture) should be subjected to a long-term empirical analysis (Gosden and Knowles 2001) which, alone, can allow us to understand their ancestry and their transformations (Mason 1998).

The lack of interest (in colonial history, in the history of mass cultures, and the history of stereotypes) accorded not only to the mass phenomenon of human zoos (nevertheless one of the cultural conditions necessary for the growth of empire) but also to their influence, is still surprising. It would appear that the relationships between communities in Western societies need to be (re)considered as a diachronic process, and any such study should include these exhibitions, which constituted a fundamental stage of the process at the turn of the nineteenth and twentieth centuries (Boëtsch and Villain-Gandossi 2001). The stereotypes which created images of the Other until the time of decolonization made a significant contribution to the construction of the collective imagination and legitimized colonial practice in the eyes of the public.

Human zoos raise questions concerning spectacle and the creation of popular culture, but they also raise questions about a form of racist thought which spread across the globe (from Tokyo to Hamburg, from London to Chicago) in just three generations. This fact calls for the analysis of the building blocks of the construction of societies themselves or, put another way, the archetypes that contribute to a collective imagination that defines us, thereby allowing us to recognize and position ourselves in the world. Human zoos are, in the final analysis, the crystallization of a shifting barrier between the 'civilized' and the 'savage', between the 'modern' and the 'archaic', and these distinctions are still very much in force.

Notes

1 Motto of the Anthropology pavilion, World's Columbian Exposition, Chicago, 1893.
2 This research has followed a programme which began in 2000 and involves a number of academic research groups in Europe and America. It led to a first international conference at the University of Marseille 2 in June 2001 under the aegis of Research Group 2322 (Anthropology of the Representation of the Body) of the CNRS (Centre National de la Recherche Scientifique) and the research team at ACHAC (Association Connaissance de l'Histoire de l'Afrique Contemporaine).
3 This volume represents a shift in focus compared with the original French edition, the revised French paperback edition and the Italian edition (Bancel, Blanchard, Boëtsch et al. 2002, 2004 and 2003 respectively). In it, we have set out to refocus the analysis on the historical development of human zoos and as a consequence, we present here only half of the original contributions (21 articles out of 47). Equally, in order to take account of our own continuing thoughts on the topic and recent work in the field, we have included 11 new contributions, which provide a broader view of the different geographical spaces and types of exhibition and of their implications for the host nations. Ultimately, the 31 contributions published here, organized into three clear sections, allow a better understanding of the phenomenon of human zoos in all its complexity and specificity, providing a new perspective for readers.
4 See Falguières (2003) on this subject.
5 See Impey and MacGregor (2001 [1985]), and Martin and Moncond'Huy (2004).
6 As the director of the Marseille Jardin d'Acclimatation remarked in 1861, such zoos were 'made for the spectators, not the animals' (Siépi 1937: 7; Baratay 2002: 32).
7 A similar story occurred in Britain in 1774. Another Tahitian called Omai remained there for two years and was presented to King George III and to the University of Cambridge.
8 Some of this group died of cold, others of tuberculosis, while others committed suicide.
9 In 1854, the Muséum national d'histoire naturelle collection contained 865 skulls. The largest known collection of the time was that of the American polygenist Samuel Morton, which contained over 1,000 items (Meigs 1857). By 1867, though, the French collection contained more than 1,500 skulls.
10 At about this time, the Chinaman, Tchong-A-Sam, was brought to Europe and was studied by many learned societies.
11 See Bogdan in this volume.
12 See by Poignant in this volume.

13 See Fauvelle-Aymar 2002b, and Boëtsch and Blanchard in this volume.

14 It is claimed that members of the Cherokee tribe were exhibited in London as early as 1762 (Fox 1989).

15 See also Lindfors in this volume. The 2005 film by the French film director Régis Warnier, *Man to Man*, is a semi-fictionalization of this 1859 visit.

16 In 1800, the first learned anthropological 'society' was created in France. It was called the Société des Observateurs de l'Homme [Society of the Observers of Mankind]. However, it disappeared in 1803 as a result of lack of activity. In 1829, Dr W. F. Edwards published *The Physiological Characters of the Races of Mankind*, which viewed its subject matter from a historical perspective and was very influential in scientific circles. This work led to the creation of the Société d'Ethnographie in 1839, which was also the result of contacts with English scientists (a Society for the Protection of Aborigines had been founded in London in the previous year). The French society disappeared in 1848 after having contributed to the abolition of slavery in France.

17 See Coutancier and Barthe 2002, and Schneider in this volume.

18 See Thode-Arora in this volume.

19 There was, at that time, an autobiography by John Tevi. Tevi was one of the most noteworthy troupe directors, becoming a specialist in this area after having himself been exhibited and having participated in the major international exhibitions, Buffalo Bill's Wild West show, and Pawnee Bill's Wild West and Great Far East show. His book was published as *A Tour Around the World and the Adventures of Dahomey Village*. On this publication, see Rydell in this volume. Nayo Bruce, who was originally from Togo, directed a travelling troupe for more than twenty years, changing its name and its acts from country to country and according to fashion. He died in 1919.

20 At the Chicago Exposition, Japan was considered to be on a par with the Western powers and its pavilion was allocated the same exhibition area as those of France, England, Belgium, Austria and the United States. The pavilion contained, moreover, an anthropology section and an Ainu village.

21 In 1995, an initial investigation of the display of the Other and the creation of racial and colonial imaginary constructs was proposed within the framework of an international conference entitled 'Scenes and Types', organized in Marseille by the ACHAC research group. The papers given there are to be found in ACHAC (1996).

22 More than four million visitors attended the Osaka exhibition.

23 David Lynch's film *Elephant Man* provides a relatively realistic illustration of this.

24 The mythology of Siamese twins was one of the major attractions in 'freak shows', from the Chinese twins exhibited by Barnum in New York, onwards (Monestier 2007). Later, the fate of Chang and Heng, brothers from Thailand, who arrived in Boston in 1829, symbolizes the encounter between the worlds of spectacle and science. Indeed, Professor John Warren of the Harvard Medical School provided funding for this show and the tour of Europe which followed it in 1830. In 1835 the brothers joined Barnum and then, becoming their own managers, remained on show in the United States until 1869.

25 These were not, in fact, 'Aztecs', but were mentally handicapped.

26 These two brothers actually hailed from Ohio. They appeared in various shows

from 1852 to 1905.

27 This was an Afro-American called Henry Moss. He was on show in Philadelphia and noted for his dappled skin.

28 Barnum showed an Afro-American known as Vitiligo, who was an albino and was also microcephalic. He presented him as the 'missing link' between men and apes.

29 See also Reiss in this volume.

30 Hagenbeck himself, in his autobiography, was surprised at the high visitor numbers and wrote of their 'enormous impact', remembering that in Berlin, in one day, close to 93,000 people attended one of these exhibitions, necessitating 'mounted police and foot patrols' (1951: 78; see Deroo in this volume). Likewise, just under one million paying and free visitors were recorded in the annual report of the Paris Jardin d'Acclimatation in 1883. Later, the 1900 Paris Exposition Universelle would be attended by a little under 50 million visitors; the 1931 Paris Exposition coloniale internationale would sell more than 30 million tickets; and the British Empire Exhibition of 1924–1925 at Wembley in London would receive nearly 25 million visitors.

31 For example, the French towns of Nancy in 1909 (2.5 million paying visitors), Roubaix in 1911 (1.7 million visitors), and Reims in 1903 (300,000 paying visitors and an estimated 100,000 'guests'). These towns achieved greater visitor numbers for these 'negro villages' than on any previous public occasion.

32 A major limitation in this research concerns the reaction of the exhibited peoples themselves. Sources are patchy and, most important, produced at second-hand. We cannot assume, as some researchers hope to (see Bergougniou, Clignet and David 2001) that purported interviews of the time with the participants are reliable evidence. Orally transmitted memories, by contrast, are an important source in estimating the effects of these exhibitions. The Kanak remarks of 1931, collected by Joël Dauphiné and Didier Daeninckx (for his novel), demonstrate this clearly. The oral memories collected by Gérard Collomb on the display of the Kaliña are equally interesting, in that they show the handing down of memories across several generations: 'They were shut up so that the Whites could see them. Nobody had the right to leave. Each day, the Whites would gather to watch them' (Maliana's statement, cited in Collomb 1992: 129). But these few statements are insufficient to allow a systematic cataloguing of the reactions of either the public or the exhibited peoples.

33 An opposing view was adopted by some anthropologists (themselves revealing the attitudes of the day), who claimed that exhibited peoples became 'civilized' during the exhibitions. In 1881, Paul Nicole wrote on this topic in the *Bulletin de la Société d'Anthropologie*, commenting that initially 'savage' Zulus returned 'crafty and cunning' to their own countries (*Bulletin de la Société d'Anthropologie* 1881: 775).

34 Robert Rydell reminds us that this occurred at the Pan-American Exposition, Buffalo, New York in 1901, where 'natives' were housed in an animal stockyard until the construction of their villages could be completed and they could be moved in. See Rydell in this volume.

35 Aboriginal Australians, pygmies and Hottentots in particular.

36 For example, the Fuegians and Galibi Indians presented at the Paris Jardin d'Acclimatation.

37 Parisian and London anthropologists complained at the difficulties in dissecting those participants who died 'during their perfomance', while in St Louis in 1904, the American anthropologist Ales Hrdlicka removed the brains of a number of Filipinos (Rydell 1984: 164).

38 Ota Benga was a Congolese pygmy who was displayed at the 1904 Louisiana Purchase Exposition in St Louis, Missouri, and was persuaded to remain in the United States by various Protestant groups and missions. He was 'lodged' for a time at the Bronx zoo in the orang-utang cage and later committed suicide in 1916 (Blume 1999: 197–201).

39 The failure of the Basel zoo (before it specialized in the exhibition of humans and, more particularly, 'exotic' peoples), whose collection in the final years of the nineteenth century focused on European animals, reminds us that the visitors of the time were interested in 'exotic' species, and the public wanted 'strange savage wild beasts, very different from European species, so that they could escape their everyday environment and dream of distant lands' (Baratay 2002: 33).

40 In his innovative work, Lindfors, a specialist in African literature, brought together numerous writings on the exhibition of Africans in the West, most of which were published under the aegis of the African Studies Association (Lindfors 1999a). An article by Lindfors on Dr Kahn's famous Niam-Niams is reproduced in this volume.

41 Corbey's original article, 'Ethnographic Showcases, 1870–1930', which appeared in *Cultural Anthropology* in 1993, has been revised for this volume. This article was, for the editors of this book, the real starting-point for research on human zoos, beginning in Marseille with the ACHAC research group and continuing in collaboration with the CNRS research group GDR 2322 from 1999 (see above, n. 2).

42 A glance at the scientific journals of the day, such as *La Nature, Revue d'anthropologie, Le Journal illustré, La Science illustrée*, and the *Bulletin de la Société d'Anthropologie*, is sufficient to identify the major contemporary names in the field of anthropology, associated with reports on various troupes who were on show in the capital (more than eighty articles appeared in the period to 1909 in French scientific reviews on the Jardin d'Acclimatation exhibitions alone). See Boëtsch and Ardagna in this volume.

43 The members of the Société d'Anthropologie de Paris very quickly made the distinction between 'good anthropological attractions' and the others, as Bordier writes in the society's bulletin of 1877: 'The superiority of these scientific exhibitions compared with those which are just Barnum shows [is] what is sought here, neither a standard staging, nor the false local colour of armchair travellers, but the pure and naked truth' (Bordier 1877a).

44 In Germany, for example, the combination of spectacle and science reached its height in 1889. In that year, the Munich Ethnographic Exhibition was held. This was a sort of human gallery on a world scale, where the mummified body of the 'gorilla woman', Juliana Pastana, was displayed among other 'exotic peoples'. She was born in Mexico in 1832 and was thought by some to represent the missing link.

45 In Japan, the Tokyo Anthropological Society was not formed until 1884, but it played a major part in the ethnographic exhibitions subsequently staged in the archipelago (Nanta 2001).

46 The initiating moment in the United States remains, explicitly, the World's Columbian Exposition, Chicago, of 1893.

47 'While the anthropologists of the time often went to great lengths to collect their specimens, less attention was devoted to the documenting of the source and previous location of the specimens, whether through negligence or because the clandestine nature of some of their collecting methods prevented such information from being available' (Langaney 2002: 376).

48 In a review of the original French version of this book, entitled 'Spectacles ethniques et culture de masse au temps des colonies', in *Revue d'histoire et des sciences humaines*, 7, (2002), pp. 223–32, the French historian of science, Claude Blanckaert, suggests that the book is no more than a series of articles which are 'tedious simple repetitions, page after page on the "staging" of the "Other"'. He suggests that the book 'claims to set out the logic of exclusion which was carefully orchestrated by the anthropologists of the end of the nineteenth century'. Beyond the reductive nature of this criticism concerning the richness of the contents of the volume, it misunderstands something which is explained in almost all the contributions. In fact, anthropologists did not 'orchestrate' such exhibitions, they validated them, initially in a spirit of opportunism, chiefly out of interest in the 'specimens' displayed, and in the anticipation that such shows would make the general public, as political decision-makers, more aware of scientific research.

49 Here, again, Blanckaert's review, which suggests that many anthropologists were not in favour of colonization (believing that each 'race' should live in its own healthy environment), does not seem justified to us, as the author purports not to understand that the opinion of these scientists and the nuances of their individual judgement actually have little importance. What was essential for the world of entertainment was that they should support the principle of racial hierarchy which governed these shows, a principle that was endlessly repeated by the theorists and practitioners of colonial expansion.

50 The Other and his or her body, by escaping from Western norms, became a cultural construct. As Singleton comments: 'the pig, which we think we can objectively classify as an animal, is, in the ontology of some Papuans, grouped with humanity; whereas some Papuans, whom we think we can objectively classify as humans, are, in the ontology of the Asmats (other Papuans), grouped with edible foodstuffs' (Singleton 2004: 9).

51 Hilke Thode-Arora provides an excellent explanation of the initial pattern of these exhibitions, recalling the three main criteria for the selection of a group, namely strangeness, particular characteristics, and picturesque customs. See Thode-Arora in this volume.

52 See Blanchard and Deroo's 52-minute television documentary *Zoos humains*, broadcast by ARTE in December 2002, which contains archive film footage. The film received an award at the Festival du Film Ethnographique de Paris, organized by the Musée de l'Homme in 2003.

53 This is demonstrated by the behaviour of the Cossacks in Paris and of the Japanese in London in 1908, who insisted on being presented in a different way, not as 'savages' who were part of another sort of humanity.

54 See also De l'Estoile (2003), where he is far less critical of this pattern of ethnographic and colonial exhibitions.

55 It was, in its own way, the grand European tour of the Egyptian Pasha's three giraffes in 1827–28 which began this process, firmly embedding the 'exotic' in Western performance.

56 See Pierre de Taillac's recent work on this subject (2007).

57 An example of this attitude is to be found in an unpublished paper by Isabelle Merle and Emmanuelle Sibeud (2003). According to these scholars, this research topic ultimately boils down to a 'predilection for questions of presentation', which distracts from real research on colonization and is mere 'guilt-ridden soul-searching'! Human zoos are, in their view, a 'deliciously fascinating ghost story', which has hardly any impact on the history of the colonial fact, a sort of 'epistemological chauvinism [sic]' whose sole aim is to focus the analysis of our colonial past on relationships of 'domination'. These are somewhat surprising arguments if their authors wish to say that the historical topic 'human zoos' is simply not worth studying, because it ascribes guilt and distracts from the real history of colonization. Is this position not itself purely and simply chauvinistic? It appears to us that the cultural productions linked to imperialism (images, exhibitions, literature, the general press, and so on) are worthy of analysis. The West legitimated the 'right to colonize' through these cultural productions, and the creation of colonial culture which occurred in the cities demands a thorough analysis if we are to understand the 'colonial fact'. The violence of the attacks on the Human Zoos research programme in this text is a fair representation of the conservatism of some scholars of the 'colonial fact' on these matters.

58 See also Bogdan (1988) and Corbey (1993), which is an earlier version of Part 1, Chapter 6, in this volume.

59 See also Fauvelle-Aymar (2002b); Badou (2000a); and Lindfors (1983a).

60 See also Gala (1980). Some scholars have assumed, somewhat hastily, and on the basis of a single study (Osborne 1994), that the exhibitions at the Paris Jardin d'Acclimatation were commercial failures, and have drawn rapid conclusions concerning their lack of impact in France. Although there were no significant financial returns for the Jardin in the first two years, this was only because this new activity was in its infancy and required considerable capital expenditure (in bringing the foreign troupes over from Germany). After this, for nearly 60 years, troupes appeared regularly at the Jardin and this supplementary activity allowed it to balance its (annual) budgets, to renew its facilities, to repay its debts, and to rebuild following the collapse brought about by the 1870 Franco-Prussian war (Gala 1980). With regard to the year 1883, with four or so troupes on the annual programme and a more than positive review, the director, Geoffroy Sainte-Hilaire, was able to report to his administrative board that 'the operations were profitable from a purely financial standpoint as well as a scientific one'. This reference is easy to consult, as it is to be found in the chapter by Schneider in this volume. For the original source, see Saint-Hilaire (1871).

61 Although Switzerland had no colonies, it nevertheless acted as a major centre for ethnographic exhibitions, both at various regular sites where dozens of troupes appeared, and in the context of official national exhibitions (Debrunner 1979; Brändle 1992; 1995; 2002; Staehelin 1993). Work in Switzerland on the whole process of display is still patchy. See Minder in this volume. See also Brändle (2002); Arlettaz and Barilier (1991); and El-Wakil and Vaisse (2000).

62 See also Shyllon (1977).

63 The success of the Dahomeans was phenomenal, as is underlined by Preston
    Blier in this volume. In particular, their exhibition in Paris in 1893 received
    more than two and a half million visitors. See Preston Blier and Poignant in this
    volume. See also Bullard and Dauphiné (2002) and Bullard (1997; 2000).

64 See also Banta and Hinsley (1986).

65 The permanent exhibition 'Empire and Us' at the British Empire and Common-
    wealth Museum in Bristol covers the colonial period, international exhibitions
    and colonialist propaganda, ending with postcolonialism and immigration. A
    mural sums up this progression, emphasizing that our imperial heritage lives
    on in our multicultural society (in addition to the chapters in this volume, see
    also Walthew 1981; Woodham 1989; and Hoffenberg 2001).

66 See also, among the many works on this subject: Lusebrinck 1995; Leprun 1987;
    Lemaire 2002b; and Ruscio 2002. See the General Bibliography for further
    works.

67 See also Eissenberger 1996 and earlier works in the General Bibliography.

68 See also Bigham 2000. We should make it clear that many of the 'exotic' exhibi-
    tions in the United States were organized for profit by the International Anthro-
    pological Exhibit Company.

69 See also Delgado, Lozano and Chiarelli 2002 on Spain and Italy. Human zoos
    took a specific form in Italy (combining with missionary discourse) and there-
    fore continued for longer than elsewhere in Europe, being linked to Mussolini's
    conquests in Ethiopia and their associated propaganda (1934–40). Nevertheless,
    as Chiarelli (in Delgado, Lozano and Chiarelli 2002) emphasizes, almost all the
    colonial international exhibitions in Italy included ethnic villages, in particular
    those held in Turin in 1884, where Nubians and Ethiopians were on show, and
    in Palermo in 1894 and Turin in 1928, where Abyssinians were displayed. In
    Naples in 1940 it was the turn of a Somali village (as it had been in 1934 and
    1935), while 'African villages' were on show in Genoa in 1892 and 1913, and
    in Rome in 1931. Last, at the Turin exhibition of 1898, the whole of humanity
    was on display, with Indians, Chinese, Libyans, Nubians, Brazilians, Eritreans,
    Ethiopians and Bolivians (see Castelli 1998; and Labanca 1992).

70 The 1938 Empire Exhibition in Glasgow, despite the decline in interest in
    colonial exhibitions, nevertheless attracted 12 million visitors.

71 On the Franco-British Exhibition of 1908 in London, see Greenhalgh 1985.

72 Blanckaert (2005) writes that from the 1867 Exposition Universelle in Paris
    many French scientists, including Armand de Quatrefages, were keen for
    there to be a presentation of specimens from 'living races on earth'. The plan
    was apparently blocked by the French Empress, who found the idea morally
    unacceptable (Chinese participants were nevertheless on show at the Chinese
    pavilion). In 1878, the explorer Joseph Bonnat proposed the exhibition of a
    troupe of Africans, but this proposal was not retained by the organizers of
    the exhibition, a fact lamented by the reporters of the Petit journal, the first
    French newspaper, on 30 July 1878. By contrast, at the same exhibition, Algerian
    soldiers greeted the public in the Algerian pavilion.

73 The *Pall Mall Gazette* described this exhibition as 'colonies of savages' which the
    'French' were trying to 'civilize'. At this time, the 'Hairy Man of Burma' was the
    major attraction in the Paris café-théâtres.

74 Beyond the significant impact of the 1893 Chicago World's Fair, it should be

noted that the ethnographic collections presented there formed the basis of the Field Museum, which would go on to develop ethnographic studies and would, in 1937, create a permanent gallery of the 'races of humanity' (Arnoldi 1997).

75 The height of German colonialism was without doubt to be found at the Berlin Gewerbe-Aussetellung of 1896, where 'specimens' from throughout the German Empire were on show in their 'natural surroundings'.

76 In Chapter 13, Preston Blier reminds us of the familiarities which occurred between the audiences and the Amazons in St Petersburg and Hamburg.

77 See Delsahut and Corbey in this volume. The 1904 Louisiana Purchase Exposition was organized in St Louis, Missouri, to coincide with the Olympic Games. During the exhibition, which was among those with the greatest number of native exhibits, visitors could watch Igorots from the Philippines eating dog meat and African pygmies simulating beheadings (see Corbey's chapter in this volume).

78 At the 1936 Johannesburg Empire Exhibition there was a village encampment of Bushmen, which 600,000 people visited. Its primary aim was to justify the plan to create a reserve for the 'prehistoric' populations of the Kalahari.

79 For various studies of cases specific to France, we recommend a series of works containing a significant corpus of images, in particular *Le Paris Noir* (2001), *Le Paris arabe* (2003), *Le Paris Asie* (2004), *Marseille porte Sud* (2005), *Sud-Ouest porte des outre-mers* (2006), *Lyon capitale des outre-mers* (2007) and *Frontière d'Empire* (2008).

80 We can cite the example of Klikko, a young Khoisan, who was on show in Europe and Cuba. He was the star of the Wild Dancing Bushman show in 1913, before joining Barnum and Bailey's company. He died, a half-crazy alcoholic, in New York in 1940 (Parsons 1988). Another example is provided by Joseph Lee, the Afro-American who played the 'African Savage' from Dahomea and became a genuine star in the United States.

81 Between 1910 and 1935, the link between eugenics and the exhibition of 'monsters' or 'exotics' was an enduring feature of the activities carried out in the United States by the Eugenics Record Office (ERO). The activities of this body were intended to contribute to the definition of the 'necessary homogeneity' of the American nation (see Emin in this volume; see also Wiebe 1967, and Haller 1984). After a period of research between 1910 and 1920, national campaigns in favour of eugenics gave value to white identity, denouncing the dangers of miscegenation and the black presence (with, for example, the film *The Black Stork* of 1917), along with the risks of degeneracy linked to the transmission of mental illnesses. Conference series, exhibitions, films, databases and studies on migrant populations or 'healthy families' followed. Countless photographs were displayed from the ERO's photographic collections of 'exotics' in circuses or shows, not least those at Coney Island, just a few minutes away from the ERO. From 1935, the influence of the American eugenicists declined for a number of reasons: lack of income; few concrete results which could be brought before the public and federal authorities; an ambiguity in their relationship with the politics of migration, which had been established on a national level; and an increasingly clear link between their discourse and Nazi eugenicist theories which dominated the international stage.

82 For example, the Dahomeans were exhibited in many exhibitions and shows between 1891 and 1894, following Behanzin's defeat (a troupe was sent to the

Chicago World's Fair in 1893 after appearing at the Casino de Paris). A group of Madagascans were exhibited after the conquest of their island, and Tuaregs toured Paris and elsewhere following the fall of Timbuctoo in 1894.

83   Marshall Lyautey, who had been Resident-General in Morocco, was appointed by the French government in 1928 as general commissioner for the Paris Colonial Exposition planned for 1931.

84   De l'Estoile (2007) suggests that the Kanaks were brought to Paris privately in 1931, with the original intention of participating in the exhibition. In fact, as Dauphiné (1998) has amply demonstrated, the manner of their arrival was quite complex. They were recruited by a society of ex-colonials, with the agreement of the colonial authorities in Nouvelle-Calédonie. It was later, following the dramatic circumstances of their exhibition in Germany (where part of the troupe had been sent), that the authorities acted to forbid the recruitment of the natives of Nouvelle-Calédonie (circular of 27 July 1931). This decision followed the statement made by the Minister in charge of colonial affairs, Paul Reynaud, who denounced exhibitions of 'inferior human types', and called on the administration to refuse to respond favourably to what he described as the promoters of 'unhealthy curiosity' (Hale 2002: 317). In Paris, the Kanaks were presented at a show (with an explanatory brochure) in the Bois de Boulogne, which had the unequivocal title: 'Cannibalism'. Nevertheless, from September 1931, they would attend the exhibition in Vincennes every afternoon, on special occasions and for evening shows, in order to represent their island in various performances (Bullard and Dauphiné 2002: 125). These performers had, in short, interchangeable roles: in the morning they were 'cannibalistic savages' in the Bois de Boulogne; in the afternoon they were the 'picturesque representatives' of Nouvelle-Calédonie in the Bois de Vincennes.

85   See, on this topic, the retrospective exhibition which was held in Paris from December 2006 to February 2007 in the Bois de Vincennes, by the City of Paris in collaboration with the ACHAC research group. Information on this project, including the 30 two-faced totems created for it, is to be found on www.achac. com

86   Lyautey was a singular figure in the colonial army world. He had always been in favour of the preservation of the cultures of colonized nations (at a time when many foretold their disappearance) and set up a very modern form of indirect rule in Morocco which, in many ways, anticipated the changes in colonial strategy which would be introduced during the 1950s (except in Algeria and Indochina). See Rivet 1988.

87   Vallois was also extremely critical of the presentation of the Kanak dances, lamenting their lack of authenticity, and of the general tendency to make indigenous cultures appear quaint in the publicity material for the exhibition.

88   The small number of artesans from Senegal was even criticized by *Le Périscope Africain*, which expressed its regret that this display bore no relationship with the economic realities of the country, nor with the real work of local jewellers and shoemakers. The *Paris-Dakar* newspaper compared this new style (in August 1937) to that of the past: 'No obscene dances, no English missionaries in the pot. No cannibals behind bars, no death dances, no negro king seated on his throne of skulls' (quoted in Lusenbrink 2002: 265).

89   As Thode-Arora remarks in this volume, Hagenbeck's shows had tentatively

started up again in the 1920s, but had never regained their earlier complexity and success.

90 The Highland village, Indian temple and Zulu village on show there represented a more 'artisanal' form of display than the Wembley villages, which, only 15 years earlier, had continued to present the savagery and authenticity of imperial populations. But the most significant difference between the two exhibitions was one of scale. At Wembley, ethnic shows and villages were the central features of the presentation, while in Glasgow they had become merely peripheral attractions (see MacKenzie in this volume).

91 We note that a recent special number of the French publication *Sciences humaines* (November 2002) has as its title: 'L'abécédaire des sciences humaines: d'Aborigène à Zoos humains' [The ABC of the Human Sciences: from Aborigine to (Human) Zoo].

92 See Deroo and Lemaire 2006, and Bancel 2006.

93 See Barlet and Blanchard 2005.

PART I

The Specificity of the Human Zoo: Histories and Definitions

I

From Wonder to Error: Monsters from Antiquity to Modernity

ROSEMARIE GARLAND-THOMSON

Like exotic animals, people who are visually different have always aroused the imagination of their fellow human beings. Those of us who have since antiquity been known as 'monsters' and more recently as 'freaks' defy the ordinary and mock the predictable, exciting anxiety and speculation among our more banal brethren. The extraordinary body is fundamental to the narratives by which we make sense of ourselves and our world. The unexpected body provokes narratives and practices that probe the very contours and boundaries of what we take to be human. Stone-age cave drawings, for example, record monstrous births, while prehistoric grave sites evince elaborate ritual sacrifices of such bodies. Clay tablets at Nineveh, the Assyrian capital, describe in detail 62 of what we would now call congenital abnormalities, along with their prophetic meanings. Aristotle, Cicero, Pliny, Augustine, Bacon and Montaigne attempt to account for such disruptions of the seemingly natural order in their interpretative schemata. For these fathers of Western thought, the differently formed body is most often evidence of God's design, divine wrath, or nature's abundance, but it is always an interpretive occasion.

Perpetually significant, the singular body has been alternately coveted, revered and dreaded. Their rarity made exceptional bodies instrumental and lucrative to those who appropriated them, even in pre-capitalist societies. Egyptian kings, Roman aristocrats, and European nobles until the eighteenth century kept dwarves and fools as amusing pets. Cheap, popular 'monster ballads' in Renaissance England detailed the corporeal particulars of anomalous bodies and uncovered their hidden lessons: a cleft palate cautioned against lewd talk; missing fingers warned against idleness. In 1534, an anxious England made bestiality a capital offence, lest the occasional, unsettling birth anomalies which suggested hybridity might burgeon uncontrolled as testimonies to some threatening cousinship between man and beast (Thomas 1983: 135).

Tributes to Matthew Buchinger record that he dazzled eighteenth-century Europe with his conjuring, musical performances, calligraphic skills and marksmanship with the pistol (Jay 1986: 57).[1] Learned gentlemen of the early Enlightenment collected relics of the increasingly secularized monstrous body in their eclectic cabinets of curiosities, along with an array of oddities such as sharks' teeth, fossils, and intricately carved cherry stones (Impey and McGregor 1985: 4).

As scientific inquiry began to eclipse religious justification, the internal anatomy of exceptional bodies was exposed in the dissection theatres and represented in early medical treatises. The cabinet of curiosity became commercialized through the creation of popular museums such as P. T. Barnum's famous American Museum, all filled with 'monsters' (Harris 1973; Saxon 1980). The ancient practice of exhibiting anomalous bodies in taverns and on street corners consolidated in the nineteenth century into institutions such as American circus sideshows or London's Bartholomew Fair, where showmen and 'monster-mongers' proliferated in response to a seemingly insatiable desire to gawk contemplatively at these marvellous phenomena (Altick 1978). In a definitive split from the popular, nineteenth-century science officially assigned the name 'teratology' to the study, classification and manipulation of monstrous bodies. As scientific explanation took the place of religious mystery, becoming the authoritative cultural narrative of modernity, the exceptional body began increasingly to be represented in clinical terms as pathology. The 'monstrous' body now moved from the 'freak show' stage into the medical theatre. Thus, even though the discourses of the anomalous body comprise a series of successive re-framings within a variety of registers over time, the uneasy human impulse to textualize, to contain, to explain our most unexpected corporeal manifestations, has remained constant.

Exceptional Bodies in Modernity

Singular bodies become politicized when culture maps its concerns upon them as meditations on individual as well as national values, identity, and direction. Under the extreme pressures of modernity, the significances imposed on them have shifted from a narrative of the marvellous to an objectification of the deviant. As modernity develops in Western culture, discourse on the monstrous changes with it: the prodigious 'monster' is transformed into the pathological terata. What was once sought-after as revelation becomes pursued as entertainment; what aroused awe now inspires horror; what was taken as a portent becomes the object of research. In brief, wonder becomes error.

Saturated with meaning, the extraordinary body is never simply itself. Rather, its exceptionality betokens something else, becomes revelatory, sustains narrative and exists socially in a realm of hyper-representation. The word 'monster' – perhaps the earliest and most enduring name for the singular body – derives from the Latin verb *mostrare*, meaning to warn, show or sign, and which has given us the modern verb 'demonstrate'. 'Monsters' were taken to be a demonstration of divine will from antiquity until the hand of god seemingly loosed its grip on the world. When the gods lapsed into silence, 'monsters' became an index of nature's fancy or – as they now appear in genetics and embryology – as the Rosetta Stone which reveals the mechanics of life. As portents, 'monsters' were the most important manifestation of a varied group of astonishing natural phenomena known as prodigies, marvels or wonders. Under the sign of the miraculous, comets, earthquakes, six-legged calves, cyclopic pigs, and human 'monsters' confirmed, repudiated or revised what humanity imagined as the order of things. By challenging the boundaries of the human and the coherence of what seems to be the natural world, 'monstrous' bodies appear as sublime, merging the terrible with the wonderful, exciting attraction as much as repulsion. Whether generating awe, delight, or terror, the monstrous emerges from culture-bound expectations even as it violates them.

In a similar manner, the French surgeon Ambroise Paré brought together in 1573 what we would today see as the normal, the deviant, and the fanciful in an illustrated treatise on monsters. In it, he catalogues together marvels such as conjoined twins, giraffes, hermaphrodites, sea devils, elephants, unicorns, comets, incubi and Egyptian mermaids. Paré's *Des monstres et prodiges [On Monsters and Marvels]* (1982) straddles the seam between wonder and error, between marvellous and medicalized narratives of the anomalous body. Along with the traditional, divinely driven explanations, Paré initiates a secular, clinical approach to monsters, which runs parallel to and competes with religious interpretations, finally eclipsing them around the beginning of the twentieth century. This incipient scientific view, which depends on the fantasies of objectivity and sees regularity rather than exceptionality as its founding epistemology, imposes empiricism upon the narrative of wonder that had ranged relatively freely across earlier representations of monsters. By the seventeenth century, this alternative humanistic scientific discourse, which endorses the predictable, entwines itself with the idea of religious prodigies, casting extraordinary bodies as nature's benevolent whimsies, bestowed upon the world to delight man's curiosity and inspire his awe. This is not, however, the awe of divine warning, but rather an implication that, increasingly, the world exists not to glorify god but to please man, who is destined to be its master.

The notion of the 'monster' as prodigy disappears at this juncture, transfiguring singular bodies into lusus naturae – nature's sport or the freak of nature. What was once an ominous marvel now becomes a gratuitous oddity, as 'monsters' shift into the category of *curiosities*.[2] Curiosity fuses inquisitiveness, acquisitiveness, and novelty to the ancient pursuit of the extraordinary body, shifting the ownership of such bodies from god to the scientist, whose Wunderkammern, or cabinets of curiosities, antedated modern museums. Simultaneous with the secularism that finds delight in nature's corporeal jokes arises the contrasting empiricism which creates the knowledge used to drive fancy from the world.

'Monsters' in Science and Entertainment

Consequently, at the same historical moment as the foreboding 'monster' turns into a whimsical freak of nature, the logic of the Enlightenment produces teratology, the science of monstrosity, which sets out to tame and rationalize the marvellous. Formally articulated in 1832 by the French doctor Isidore Geoffroy Sainte-Hilaire, teratology recasts the 'freak' from astonishing corporeal extravagance into the pathological specimen of the terata. The marvellously singular body, whose terrible presence in the world gave rise to such cultural narratives as Genesis and *The Odyssey* is thus mastered and demythologized by modernity. Domesticated within the laboratory and the textbook, what was once the prodigious 'monster', the fanciful 'freak', the strange and subtle curiosity of nature, has become today the abnormal, the intolerable.

In response to the tensions of modernity, the ancient practice of interpreting extraordinary bodies not only shifted towards the secular and the rational but also flourished as never before within the expanding marketplace, where it became institutionalized under the banner of the 'freak show'. Especially in Victorian America, the exhibition of 'monsters' exploded into a public ritual that bonded a sundered polity together in the collective act of looking. In a turbulent era of social and material change, the spectacle of the extraordinary body stimulated curiosity, ignited speculation, provoked titillation, furnished novelty, filled coffers, confirmed commonality and certified national identity.

From the time of the democratic movement initiated by President Andrew Jackson in the 1830s, to the Progressive Eras, which worked their reforms in the first decades of the twentieth century, Americans flocked to 'freak shows'. As the older narrative of wonder still remained culturally tenable, and the newer narrative of error revealed itself to be increasingly compelling, the mid-nineteenth to early twentieth centuries comprised a heightened transitional moment for such ceremonial displays. The early exhibitions of human oddities in taverns put on by itinerant showmen, and the slightly more respectable performances in halls rented by managers, evolved in the mid-nineteenth century into institutionalized permanent exhibitions of 'freaks' in dime museums and later in circus sideshows, fairs, and amusement park midways.

The apotheosis of museums, which both inaugurated and informed the myriad dime museums that followed, was P. T. Barnum's American Museum, which he purchased and revitalized in 1841. Until the turn of the century, dime museums proliferated, offering spectacles of amusement parading as edification to all classes of Americans.[3] Human 'freaks' were the central magnets of Barnum's showplace and all successive dime museums. In the museums' curio halls and lecture rooms, as well as on the sideshows' stages and platforms, there gathered an astonishing array of corporeal wonders, from Wild Men of Borneo to Fat Ladies, Living Skeletons, Fiji Princes, Albinos, Bearded Women, Siamese Twins, Tattooed Circassians, Armless and Legless Wonders, Chinese Giants, Cannibals, Midget Triplets, Hermaphrodites, Spotted Boys and much more.

From the Prince of Wales and Henry James to workers' families and the humblest immigrants, Americans gathered together (as did their British counterparts) in this most democratizing institution to gaze raptly at the ineffable Other, who was both the focus and the creation of the 'freak' show's hyperbolic conventions of display (McNamara 1974; Truzzi 1979; Twitchell 1990: 57–65). The exaggerated, sensationalized discourse that is the essence of the 'freak show' ranges over the seemingly singular bodies that we would now call either 'physically disabled' or 'exotic', framing them and heightening their differences from viewers who are rendered comfortably common and safely standard by the exchange. 'Freak' discourse structures a cultural ritual that seizes upon any deviation from the typical, embellishing and intensifying it to produce a human spectacle whose every somatic feature becomes laden with significance for the gaping spectator. An animal skin, a spear and some grunting noises, for example, make a slightly 'simple' black man into the Missing Link. Irregular pigmentation enhanced by a loincloth and some palm fronds produces a Leopard Boy. Feathers, blankets, and a 3-kilogram (7-pound) hammer turn an 'ordinary nigger' into the

Iron-Skulled Prince (Fitzgerald 1897: 409). Shaved heads, topknots, and gaudy tunics render two microcephalics into the Aztec Children. Congenital anomalies and progressive or hereditary conditions yield imaginative hybrids of the human and animal, reminiscent of classical satyrs, centaurs or minotaurs.[4] At once dangerous and alluring, this cultural space of seemingly infinite licence is what the shows both amplified and contained with their conventions of display.

Commercial hyperbole drove all these narrative modes, even while the linguistic genres themselves varied. The fabulous was shot through with the scientific; truth claims abutted the credulous; the mundane flanked the peculiar. Tattooed white men were ostensibly captured and tortured by cannibals. Missing links were discovered in the jungles of Darkest Africa. The armless and legless used their alternative limbs to perform ordinary tasks on stage – such as violin-playing, calligraphy, needlework or taking tea – which were then detailed in inflated language that made them remarkable even as it laced them with pity and admiration. Autographed souvenir cabinet photographs or the extremely popular cartes de visite literally framed 'freaks' by surrounding them with enhancing props such as jungle backdrops, or by juxtaposing, for instance, giants with midgets or fat men with human skeletons, to intensify through contrast their bodily differences (Mitchell 2002). Costumes enhanced the extraordinary quality of the 'monster's' body, and staging established distance as well as literal hierarchies between the group of spectators and the lone spectacle on the elevated platform or in the sunken pit. Living Skeletons wore leotards; Fat or Bearded Ladies sported frills and jewels; Hermaphrodites dressed in half-male and half-female outfits; Zulu Warriors became alien by way of animal skins, spears, whoops and jungle scenes. Taken together, these mediating devices, as well as the cultural premise of irreducible corporeal difference upon which the 'freak show' is founded, comprise the process David Hevey calls 'enfreakment' (1992: 53).

By constituting the 'freak' as an icon of generalized embodied deviance, the exhibitions also simultaneously re-inscribe gender, race, sexual aberrance, ethnicity and disability as inextricable yet particular discriminatory systems legitimated by bodily variation – all represented by the single multivalent figure of the 'freak'. Thus, what we assume to be a freak of nature is instead a freak of culture (Stewart 1984: 109).

'Freaks' and the American Self

The 'freak show' makes more than 'freaks', though: it also fashions the self-governed, iterable subject of democracy – the American (or Western) self. Parading at once as entertainment and education, the institutionalized social process of enfreakment unites and validates the disparate throng positioned as viewers. The cultural work of the 'freak show' is to make the physical particularity of the 'freak' into a hyper-visible text against which the viewer's indistinguishable body fades into a seemingly neutral, tractable and invulnerable instrument of the autonomous will, suitable to the uniform citizenry democracy institutes. Yet the popularity of the 'freaks' – the strange blend of reverence and condescension audiences registered – suggests ambivalence toward such forfeiture of the bodily distinction that marked eminence in traditional societies.

This cultural work occurred specifically within the productive context of nineteenth-century America's swift and chaotic modernization. That rich cultural matrix provided a conducive environment for the archaic custom of exhibiting and interpreting extraordinary bodies and alien cultures to thrive in the invigorating form of the 'freak show'. But this dovetailing of cultural conditions pressured these shows to flourish and to fade at the same time. Ironically, the period of their most intense elaboration and popularity was simultaneously the period of their evisceration and decline. In the escalating upheaval of modernization from about 1840 to 1940, what we now think of as the 'freak show' flared like a comet and then vanished from view, re-emerging in almost unrecognizable forms in the late twentieth century (Brown 1976; Bogdan 1988: 2). The socioeconomic conditions that animated anew this ancient, almost anachronistic, practice composed the very context that at the same time rendered it obsolete, making the 'freak show' today virtually synonymous with bad taste, a practice that has gone the way of public executions.

Modernization reconstituted the human body. 'Freak shows' became ritual sites where the uncertain polity could anxiously contemplate the new parameters of embodiment wrought by cultural transformations. The changes in production, labour, technology, and market relations that we loosely call industrialization redeployed and often literally reconfigured the body, perhaps turning America's collective eyes more attentively on the extraordinary body for explanation, validation, or simply comfort. Machine culture created new somatic geographies. For example, the decline of the apprentice system and the rise of the machine and the factory, as well as paid labour, put bodies on arbitrary schedules instead of allowing natural rhythms to govern activity.

Rather than machines acting as prosthetics for the human body, as they had in traditional cultures, the body under industrialization began to seem more like an extension of the machine, which threatened to replace the working body or at the least restructure its relation to labour. Efficiency, a concept rooted in the mechanical, ascended to prominence as a measurement of bodily value. Mechanized practices such as standardization, mass production and interchangeable parts promoted sameness of form as a cultural value and made singularity in both products and bodies seem deviant.

The professionalization of authority, paid labour, the logic of slavery and the women's rights movement challenged the common citizen's sense of autonomy and mastery over his own body and others' bodies. Moreover, industrial accidents, as well as the technologies and scale of the American Civil War, literally changed the shapes of human bodies on a dramatic new scale. Both sentimentalism and realism, the major representational modes of the 'freak-show' period, register in differing ways the concern with the place and meaning of the body. If this new body felt alien to the ordinary citizen, the 'freak's' bizarre embodiment could assuage the viewer's uneasiness either by functioning as a touchstone of anxious identification or as an assurance of regularized normalcy (Laqueur 1990; Stone 1984; Seltzer 1992; Landes 1983; Sennet 1974).

Not only did modernization re-imagine and reshape the body, it relocated it as well. The new geography of labour changed the physical relationships between bodies, literally separating workers from owners, the skilled from the unskilled, men from women and children. Mental and manual work migrated apart. Transport systems and new work patterns moved people from farms and familial contexts into cities, as well as into anonymous social and labour hierarchies. Paid labour and urbanization created unstructured leisure time and forged situational, transient relationships, while change stimulated a taste for the novel. In addition to restless physical migrations, a surging marketplace both promised and threatened social mobility founded upon unstable incomes.

All these dislocations created anonymity, forcing people to rely on physical appearance rather than kinship or local memberships as indices of identity and social position (Halttunen 1982). Furthermore, secularization de-emphasized the condition of one's soul, while an intensifying market system spawned the anxious display of status, and technologies such as the democratization of portraiture photography located identity in one's exterior image. Social upheavals such as immigration, emancipation, and feminism – along with discriminatory responses like nativism, segregation and eugenics – depended upon the logic of visual corporeal differences for their coherence and enactment. Consequently, the way the body looked and functioned became one's sole resource as local contexts receded, support networks unravelled and mobility dominated social life.

In this way, modernity effected a standardization of everyday life that saturated the entire social fabric, producing and reinforcing the concept of an unmarked, normative, levelled body as the dominant subject of democracy. Clocks, department stores, ready-made clothing, catalogues, advertising and factory items sculpted the prosaic towards sameness, while increased literacy and the iterable nature of a burgeoning print culture fortified the impulse toward conformity. With its dependence on predictability, scientific discourse also re-imagined the body, depreciating particularity while valorizing uniformity. Statistics quantified the body; evolution provided a new heritage; eugenics and teratology policed its boundaries; prosthetics normalized it; and asylums cordoned off deviance. Additionally, allopathic, professionalized medicine consolidated its dominance, casting as pathological all departures from the standard body. Finally, the notion of progress and the ideology of improvement – always a fraught consolation against the vagaries of contingency – implemented the ascendance of this new image of a malleable, regularized body whose attainment was both an individual and a national obligation (Starr 1982; Rothman 1971).

As life and body standardized under modernity, a tendency towards compartmentalization and stratification accompanied that change. As, with modernization, culture became more dynamic, complex and literate, broad discourses tended to cleave into multiple discrete discursive systems inflected by an elaborate system of social markers. Such differentiation created, for example, myriad branches of specialized knowledge and work, each located somewhere on the ladder of social status. In democratized nineteenth-century America, class distinctions solidified, bifurcating cultural discourses into high and low (Levine, 1988; Blumin, 1989). Swept along on this wave, 'freak-show' discourse, which from pre-modern times had been primarily iconographic – that is, of the show, whether religious or secular – began, as we saw earlier, to be intersected by literate scientific discourse and to fragment into an array of specialized discourses, some popular and some elite. With this dispersion of discourses, Victorian middle-class decorum's project of self-definition increasingly repudiated the popular 'freak show', while sentimentality recast awe into pity, and other forms of visual entertainment like theatre – and, later, cinema – proliferated. Thus the 'freak show' itself – which although perpetually democratic, had always vexed respectability – came to rest irrevocably at the bottom of low culture (McConachie 1993). Yet before the 'freak show' broke off from respectable society around the turn of the century, it was a central element in our collective cultural project of representing the body. Indeed, 'freak' discourse did not vanish with the shows, rather, it proliferated into a variety of contemporary discourses that still allude to its premises. In 1830, however, the exhibition of 'freaks' was inextricably entwined with an array of now-discrete discourses that were then only beginning to differentiate from one another. Genetics, embryology, anatomy, teratology and reconstructive surgery – the discrete high-scientific discourses that now pathologize the extraordinary body – were once closely linked with the showmen's display of the 'freak' body. The equally elite discourses of anthropology and ethnology, as well as museum culture and taxidermy, were inseparable from the display of 'freaks' in the early nineteenth century.

The entertainment discourses of vaudeville, circuses, beauty pageants, zoos, horror films, rock celebrity culture, and Epcot Center[5] have descended from the 'freak show,' to which displays of these kinds were once fused. Although earlier 'freak-show' discourses – the somewhat contradictory hybrid of old wonder narratives, commercialized show narratives and clinical scientific narratives – seem today to have dissipated, to have become inappropriate for the public eye and ear, they have instead dispersed and transformed.

Notes

1 Buchinger was virtually armless and legless but nevertheless powdered his face and wore a wig.

2 All definitions are from the second edition of the *Oxford English Dictionary* (Oxford, Clarendon Press, 1991).

3 The words *muse* and *amusement* both descend from the related Old French and Old English words for staring, gaping or being idle. *Museum* comes directly into English from the Latin.

4 For example, Turtle Boy, the Mule-Faced Woman, Serpentina, the Camel Girl, the Dog-Faced boy, the Bear Woman, the Lobster Boy, the Lion Woman, the Alligator Man and Sealo.

5 Walt Disney's theme park, showcasing futuristic projects and innovations.

2

The Hottentot Venus:
Birth of a 'Freak' (1815)

GILLES BOËTSCH AND PASCAL BLANCHARD

The arrival in Europe of the Hottentot Venus at the beginning of the nineteenth century initiated a new way of exhibiting the Other. Although she was not the first to be exhibited in Europe (many 'savages' and 'exotics' had been put on show previously, the most famous of whom were the Arawaks brought back from the Americas to Ferdinand and Isabella of Spain's court by Christopher Columbus in 1492), this young woman has had the dubious honour of being an original, having served, in turn, as an object of entertainment, an object of media attention, a 'sexualized' object, a monstrous object, and a scientific object.

The 'Hottentot' myth was not new at the beginning of the nineteenth century. The Hottentots already symbolized the concept of an 'intermediate race' between men and animals, and this view had extensively penetrated the newly developed world of Western science, appearing in many travellers' narratives (Fauvelle-Aymar 2002a). Her arrival in Europe was not surprising, as she lived and moved in an historical and sociological context where the world was expecting some such appearance. The 'Hottentots' were fascinating to the West and they were fully equipped to act as the Missing Link and to demonstrate the possibility of degeneracy at the heart of the human species. They were seen as a sort of left-over from prehistoric times, which must be made available to the eyes of the public.

From the outset the Hottentot Venus had a double identity founded both on *femininity* and *savagery*. She set out from South Africa on 24 May 1810, having been put on board a British ship by a Royal Navy surgeon under contract.[1] She arrived in London on around 5 September 1810, after a sea voyage of several months. The 'Hottentot Venus' was a stage name given to her by her owners.[2] A domestic servant, her real name was Sawtche, and she was under contract to Hendrik Caezar (her owner's brother) and a seafarer called Alexander Dunlop. She was baptized Saartjie Baartman with the agreement of the Bishop of Chester. As the

Hottentot Venus, she travelled with fairs and circuses (Altick 1978) and appeared at a number of London cabarets and popular drinking holes after her owners had failed to sell her to the Liverpool Museum. She was about 20 years old when she arrived in Europe and her tour would last for nearly 2,000 days before ending in a dramatic way in Paris.

Her tour was the first of a certain type of exhibition of 'exotic peoples', anticipating the operations of P. T. Barnum in the United States in the middle of the century and of Carl Hagenbeck in Europe from 1894. It foreshadowed the 'era of exhibitions' of 'exotics', 'savages', and 'natives', which would appear in Europe from 1874 to 1940 and would entertain and, above all, educate vast crowds. In 1810, the Hottentot Venus established a particular pattern in the process of coming to know the Other. Put on show for her 'exoticism', she would attract both scientists and the general public. While the former studied her, the latter came to 'view' her. They observed her with different attitudes (enjoyment, curiosity, knowledge), but she was always seen as a 'curious animal', representing a continent and a race.

The Different Stages of 'Her' Story

In London, Saartjie Baartman went on show in the elegant Piccadilly area on 24 September 1810, where she provoked curiosity, fascination (inspiring popular songs and many newspaper articles) and fantasies in most of the many spectators. Such was her success that the police had to be called on to preserve order and direct the public. But a section of the audience were indignant at the show, and members of the African Institution, a humanitarian and anti-slave organization, succeeded in bringing a temporary halt to her 'shameful exploitation', by bringing a court case against her owners for her ill-treatment. Saartjie Baartman then had a choice: she could go home, with the certainty of resuming her life as a slave, or she could stay in Europe. She 'chose' the second option (although it is impossible to judge the reasons for her choice or estimate the pressure placed on her by her 'owners'), in the hope of gaining a little freedom and of earning some money (Holmes 2007).

From 1811 to 1814, little is known of Saartjie Baartman's activities on British soil. No articles or reports speak of her during this period of her life. After London, she may have toured in English ports or in Holland. All we know is that at the end of her travels she journeyed with Hendrick Caezar to Paris during the summer of 1814. Transferring her contract to a certain Henry Taylor, she was presented to the public in the rue Neuve-des-petits-champs from 18 September 1814 from 'eleven in the morning until nine in the evening', according to an advertisement in *Le Journal de Paris* on 18 September 1814. Her new impresario, Taylor, appears to have disappeared in turn, leaving Saartjie Baartman with a new contract, this time with a man called Réaux, who was an exhibitor of animals. She was then exhibited in strange and squalid surroundings in the rue Saint-Honoré, in the midst of other 'fairground creatures'. Following the fall of the monarchy in France, this area around the Palais-Royal had become a neighbourhood of prostitutes, gamblers, swindlers and publishers of licentious literature, attracting citizens and those new to the capital in search of excitement. Everything here was varied, mixed, colourful, marginal, and disturbing, and the bodies on show could have come from textbooks on anatomical aberrations (Baridon and Guédron 1999). It was hardly surprising, therefore, that Saartjie Baartman's 'new owner' should decide to exhibit her in this district.

The term 'Hottentot Venus' appears to have begun at this time to be associated with such exhibitions in the public mind. A luxury haberdasher's called 'La Vénus Hottentote' opened in Saint-Germain. On 24 October 1814 there was even the performance of a rather ridiculous vaudeville entitled *La Vénus Hottentote*, written by Théaulon de Lambert, Dartois and Brasier, which demonstrated the growing popularity of Saartjie Baartman in Paris. She was a successful draw for some time here, attracting many visitors. These were of all classes, including the Paris workers, the middle classes from Saint-Germain, and the prostitutes from the Tuileries (Badou 2000a). She was even put on show in middle-class salons, as the *Journal des dames et des modes* of 12 February 1815 reported.

Her physical appearance was rendered 'spectacular' by her steatopygia (an accumulation of fat around the hips and buttocks) and her macronymphia (unusually large labia). These features, judged to be extraordinary, led her to be considered an object of interest and study by the scientific community during her lifetime and after her death. Indeed, shortly before her death in March 1815, Étienne Geoffroy Saint-Hilaire, Director of the Natural History Museum in Paris and Professor of Zoology, requested official authorization to study her. She was taken to the museum to be examined. Geoffroy Saint-Hilaire knew Buffon's famous description of the Hottentot people in his *Histoire naturelle*: 'These Hottentots are very different from the other savage species. The women, in particular, have a sort of growth or broad area of hard skin over their pubis which hangs down to the middle of their thighs like an apron' (Buffon 1792: 139–40).[3] He wished, by means of this study, to define the characteristics of this very singular 'race', and to identify its place in the history of species.

An Object of Fascination

Saartjie Baartman would, after this, be regularly put on display for scientists to study (beginning with Georges Cuvier, followed by Blainville and Geoffroy Saint-Hilaire), but also for artists to observe (Nicolas Huet and Léon de Wailly) so that her anatomical characteristics could be recorded in the most minute detail. On 1 April 1815 Geoffroy Saint-Hilaire wrote a report in which he compared her face to that of an orang-utang and her rear end to those of female mandrill monkeys. For his part, Blainville presented her as 'the last race of the human species', situated between humanity and the simian world. Georges Cuvier confirmed this description, declaring that he had never 'seen a human head more similar to that of monkeys than this'. Thus, the official scientific discourse of the period irrevocably situated Saartjie Baartman in the world of beasts and bestiality, well before her tragic demise.[4] An object of spectacle, she also became an object of science, occupying the extreme margins of humanity.

What was more, her 'strange' body left her in an ambivalent position. Her anatomy made her an object suited to a 'cabinet of curiosity', but her behind, which was rumoured to have mysterious powers, and which would impress scientists at the beginning of this new century, turned her into a sexually fascinating object (Hobson 2005). The study of Saartjie Baartman would lead to the definitive classification of the Khoisan as a special human type. To describe a 'race' on the basis of one individual demonstrates the fallacious contribution which human zoos made to science, in particular in understanding the Other. In addition, in the case of Saartjie Baartman, this relationship can only be fully understood in the context of the pressing demands from the world of the stage for the anthropologists to provide the most 'amazing' explanations possible concerning her anatomy. As Fauvelle-Aymar writes: 'The Hottentot Venus had now become a member of the pantheon of anthropology [and became] the naturalists' muse' just as she was 'one of the mascots of a public greedy for displays in which savage children, knife-swallowers, Siamese twins, "Lilliputians", ventriloquists and other monsters and exotic curiosities performed side-by-side in no particular order' (2002b: 328). And, he concludes: 'she was the lynchpin on which the classificatory models of human kind turned: a half-way piece (between man and sign, simple-minded woman and four-year-old child, Black and yellow) which aroused bitter debates among specialists' (2002b: 359).

A Reference Model

Twenty-four hours after the death of Saartjie Baartman,[5] Georges Cuvier had already undertaken her dissection, but it would be many months before he reported on his work to the French Academy of Medicine in 1817.[6] In his report, he confirmed Geoffroy Saint-Hilaire's earlier impressions on studying this unusual specimen, claiming that 'races with depressed and compressed skulls are condemned to a perpetual state of inferiority' (Cuvier 1817). The anatomy of the Venus, in particular her *tablier*, or apron, was proof to Cuvier of what he considered to be the primitive sexual appetite of African women (Gilman 1986), as many works have emphasized (Kirby 1953; Altick 1978; Lindfors 1983b). Cuvier would later remove the sexual organs and the anus for preservation, along with other organs such as the brain, placing them in jars which would end up on the museum's shelves. Her brain would be studied thirty years later by Pierre Gratiolet, who published his conclusions in 1854.[7] The scientific community thus transformed her role once again: to that of *reference specimen*.

In later years, the Venus would continue to feed scientific debate on the relationship between the number of cerebral folds, or sulci, and intelligence: 'The rarity, the simplicity of the cerebral folds of the Hottentot Venus should not be seen as signs of idiocy, as some anatomists have claimed. In fact, this woman was not an idiot at all. If the comparison could be made under rigorous conditions, it might be found that the area covered by her brain's convolutions is equal, proportionately, if not to the exceptional surface of Cuvier's own brain, at least to that of the average White brain' (Quatrefages 1867).

While these scientific debates were going on, showmen were eager to find fresh Khoisan to satisfy the public in Europe and the United States following the popular success of Saartjie Baartman's exhibitions. Interest spread across the world, with scientific interest following in its wake. In 1829, another Venus (whether real or an impostor) was shown in Paris. Subsequently, a female Boschiman from Port Natal was displayed in London in 1852,[8] who would, after her death, be dissected at the Royal College of Surgeons in London.[9] From 1847 to 1853, a troupe of Bushmen (San) was on show in London and in France.[10] On the other side of the Atlantic, similar events were taking place. In Philadelphia in 1848 and then in Boston in 1862, 'specimens' were exhibited and studied. In the German city of Ulm, a young woman was dissected in 1866 after her sudden death and became the subject of numerous studies. According to Fauvelle-Aymar, there was:

a connivance between the circus world and the laboratory, as in many other spheres: in order to combat the practice of unscrupulous impresarios who exhibited false savages, recruiting them from among the local black population, a number of honest showmen requested authentication certificates from the scientists. In exchange, the scientists felt entitled to make their own observations. This joint interest is an essential element in the history of the Western view of the Other, because it suggests that the individuals who formed the basis of a century of scientific interest were those same individuals who were considered to be of greatest interest by the entertainment industry. In this context, scientific judgements could only serve to ratify and reinforce the criteria for authenticity which were in force in the entertainment world. (Fauvelle-Aymar, 2002a: 112).

There was certainly a double crossover here, where the world of the stage 'supplied' 'specimens' to the scientific community and, in return, the latter 'validated' the so-called 'learned' exhibitions, enabling them to deceive the public more effectively. But it is also possible that nobody was taken in by this game. Each participant was reassured, or saw what he wanted to see. The 'savage' was a best-seller, not only in shows but also when it came under the aegis of 'scientific work', fascinating public opinion and also the authorities, who were eager to find a scientific justification for their declarations of desire for colonial conquest.

Thus, everybody appeared to gain from the process, and each participant was dependent on the others. The public was amused by increasingly *amazing* scenarios, the exhibition organizers made money, the scientists were easily able to recruit scientific objects of study and expected to extend knowledge through their learned publications (while not failing to benefit from the publicity such exhibits brought to their own work). Exhibitions of extraordinary humans and ethnic shows would flourish in Europe in the second quarter of the nineteenth century, in a period which saw the development of policies of colonial expansion. In this context, the Hottentots would return to centre stage. In 1886, and again in 1888, Paul Topinard would be fascinated by the Hottentots[11] on show at the Paris Jardin d'Acclimatation, who comprised six men, five women and two children (Topinard 1888a and 1889). Other scientists (for example, Raphaël Blanchard, François Péron and Charles Le Sueur) were just as interested in the steatopygia of the Hottentot women exhibited in Paris. Some years later, in 1916, the Venus was still present in the public memory, and an article commemorating the centenary of her death appeared in *L'Anthropologie* (Verneau 1916).[12]

'Year after year', writes Fauvelle-Aymar, 'the scientific world literally grafted itself onto the structures of the world of entertainment' and backed, both directly and indirectly, the launching of the vogue for the exhibition of exotics: 'Working with incomplete information from the Cape, and resorting to much tinkering in the laboratory in an attempt to make it fit into a pattern which would conform with current scientific ideology, anthropologists created a racial universe which was totally out of touch with Khoisan reality. In the nineteenth century, neither the definition of anatomical groups nor the Hottentot–Bushman dichotomy was familiar in South Africa. They would only become so gradually, in a sort of re-appropriation of anthropological conclusions by the racist ideology which underlined apartheid' (Fauvelle-Aymar 2002a: 117). The history of the Hottentot Venus might have ended there. But the plaster cast of Saartjie Baartman was put on show in the Paris Natural History Museum, before being transferred, in 1937, to the newly-created Musée de l'Homme, Place du Trocadéro, where it was displayed until the mid-1970s.[13] As a result, the cast of her body became a symbol, from one century to the next, of the fascination produced by these human 'races', so different from our own.[14] She was then tidied away into the drawers of the Musée de l'Homme with the realization that she did not serve the greater glory of the human sciences. A generation later, she would again become the object of media focus, this time on an international scale.

A Far from Common Destiny... Across the Centuries

The history of the Hottentot Venus is certainly a key point in the birth of the practice of human zoos and this is no doubt why she is omnipresent in the Western *socius*. She teaches us about our way of *doing* science and the way in which we *construct* the identity of the Other. The fact that she was a woman already facilitated (in her own times) a quite radical distancing; that she was, moreover, a 'Hottentot' located her in an irreducibly distant space; and that she was considered to be misshapen linked her with the world of 'freaks'. Savagery was expressed in this body, which was catalogued under the heading of the monstrous, or at least the extraordinary, but it was above all a black, female and naked body on display; 'deformed' and born of savagery, set in opposition to the clothed white bodies of European women. It was also for this reason that the scientists classified her as beyond the anatomical norms associated with the Western canon. Such bodies would later be used by P. T. Barnum in his 'freak shows' (bodies which combined the 'exotic' and the 'monstrous'), but also by many European impresarios, situating side by side, and then face-to-face, 'ethnic' and 'freak' shows in a world which existed in parallel with the 'normatized' world.

Her story could not end on the shelves of the Musée de l'Homme. It would be taken up again at the beginning of the twenty-first century.[15] In April 2002, after long months of negotiations, the South African Embassy in France was the scene for the return of the 'remains' of Saartjie Baartman to the South African Ambassador to France, Thuthukile E. Skweyiya, in the presence of South African officials and the French Minister for Research, Roger-Gérard Schartzenberg.[16] The joint communiqué explained: 'In accordance with the Law of 6 March 2002, France has decided to return to the Republic of South Africa the mortal remains of Saartjie Baartman, who died in Paris in December 1815, and whose remains were preserved until now in the National Museum of Natural History. [...]. This return bears witness to the desire of France and the Republic of South Africa to restore her dignity to Saartjie Baartman and to enable her remains to rest in peace in South Africa.' On 9 August 2002 she was buried in the presence of the South African president, Thabo Mbeki, in a national ceremony.[17]

In the life of this young woman we can trace an individual story of our society, situated at the interface between science and showmanship, which had its heyday at the turn of the twentieth century. This story was accompanied by a scientific attempt, in physical anthropology, to construct a racial hierarchy built on anatomical characteristics. The construct was a very dynamic one at the time, feeding colonial discourse through its attempt to explain the aptitude of different 'races' (in particular, colonized races) for civilization and progress (Bordier 1884). These anatomical characteristics were very few in number but easily accessible. They included, essentially, height, shape of the skull, skin colour and hair type.

In truth, it was the strangeness of the bodies of others in relation to the *norm* constituted by European bodies which would always discredit her and would lead to a tendency to categorize her at the limits of the animal. The Hottentots were among the 'races' who were condemned to serve as the living proof of these limits. Even the plaster cast of the Venus became a scientific object: 'Hottentots, Boschimen are clearly, with the Australians, the lowest form of men in existence [...]. The women of the Boschimen display a remarkable feature rarely seen in the Hottentots: their buttocks show extraordinary development. To be convinced of this it is sufficient to visit the Natural History Museum and view the cast of the so-called 'Hottentot' Venus to be found in the anthropology gallery' (Brongniart n.d.: 247).[18]

Stephen Jay Gould, in his book *The Mismeasure of Man* (1996 [1981]) wrote of the sinister fascination exercised by Saartjie, not as a missing link, but as a result of her position half-way between man and beast. The morbid interest in her supposedly deformed body, her supposed bestiality, the belief in her unusual sexual appetite, fed fascination with her among men. Simultaneously, the strangeness of this female body reassured them of their superiority and made a significant contribution to a racist gaze. To be a woman and black at this time in France and to be subjected in this manner and this position to the gaze of men certainly constituted a major stage in the history of the construction of the Other in the West. This staging of a woman who was at once 'exotic' and 'monstrous' set three important boundaries which would construct the space of the Other in the West: between the 'normal' and the 'monstrous', between man and woman, and between the 'superior human races' and the 'inferior human races' (who were therefore susceptible to colonization or likely to disappear). At the time, Hottenots, Bushmen, Pygmies, Caribbeans, and Australian Aborigines occupied the lowest echelons in the hierarchy of 'races' proposed by anthropological discourse. They were barely above chimpanzees and orang-utangs (Gould 1985). And this vision of the world would influence the century which followed.

Out of this unchanging relationship between things would be born, too, a fixed structure of relationships between North and South. Between the exhibition of the Hottentot Venus in 1810 and the final great 'exotic' exhibitions in the West (Cologne and Hamburg in 1933, Brussels in 1935, Paris in 1937, and Porto in 1940), there would stretch a period of 125 years. This time was sufficient for the definitive creation of an invisible line between 'us' and 'them', but was also sufficient to see the colonial empires begin to crumble, before embarking on the road to independence after the Second World War. In the end, the history of colonial empire would dictate the pattern of the history of human zoos, and the decline of the latter would follow that of the empires themselves.

Notes

1 Marie-Claude Barbier (2003) reminds us that she was born 'on the banks of the river Gamtoos, in what is today the Eastern Cape, at a time when the indigenous populations of Khoikhoi and San were under the control of the Dutch settlers. The first were herdsmen who would soon be called Hottentots by the colonists. The San were hunter-gatherers who would later be called Boschimans, then Bushmen.'

2 François-Xavier Fauvelle-Aymar writes of the 'popular craze which probably had as one of its causes the association between the image of the venal woman and the savage which was encapsulated in the name Hottentot Venus'. Equally, he continues, 'what was important about this expression, which could provoke a smile or a shiver, was that it allowed it to be understood that there was something

unspeakably "Hottentot" in an area of the body which usually produced well-endowed Venuses, or even ordinary Venuses; the area below the waist' (2002a: 111).

3 After her death, other scholars would conclude on the basis of the analysis of her body that: 'The Hottentots are to be distinguished by their small stature, their dirty yellow skin, and their repulsive physiognomy' (Brehm, n.d.: 113).

4 Fifty years later, the German W. F. A. Zimmerman wrote: 'the Hottentots, also black, but lacking in the characteristics of the negro type. In the past, when man was believed to be descended from apes, it was thought that they represented the first stage in this strange succession' (Zimmerman 1864: 231).

5 She died on 29 December 1815 as the result of an illness which Cuvier described on 1 January 1816 as 'inflammatory and eruptive'.

6 The report was entitled 'Observations sur le cadavre d'une femme connue à Paris sous le nom de Vénus hottentotte' [Observations on the corpse of a woman known in Paris as the Hottentot Venus]. He announced on this occasion that he had 'the honour of presenting to the Academy the genital organs of this woman, prepared in such a way as to leave no doubt whatsoever on the nature of the Hottentot apron'.

7 These were unequivocal: the size of her brain explained the inferiority of 'her' race.

8 Like the Venus, she sang and danced on the London cabaret stage.

9 On this occasion, the conclusions of the scientists were more nuanced: she was certainly the product of an 'inferior race' but there was nothing to suggest that she was close to the world of apes.

10 Most of those displayed died in Europe, never returning to their homeland.

11 After being shown in Germany by the famous Farini, they were presented in Paris under the generic term 'African Pygmies', not least at the Folies Bergère. They were in fact Bushmen from South Africa.

12 Verneau was the source of, among other fantasies, the legend that Baartman was a prostitute in London and Paris.

13 The following commentary can be read on the subject from the proceedings of the Senate of 29 January 2002 relating to the return of her body to South Africa: 'So why was it only in 1976 that the skeleton and plaster cast of Saartjie Baartman were removed from the public galleries [of the Musée de L'Homme]? I prefer to see in this the result of carelessness rather than the indication of any degree of tolerance for scientific theories which, very fortunately, are no longer current, and have not been so for a long time. Finally, what has become of the jars containing the anatomical parts from Saartjie Baartman, removed by Cuvier during his dissection of her body? It would appear that they have purely and simply disappeared: they are not mentioned on any inventory. In response to my questions when I visited the site, the Museum responded with somewhat vague explanations: they were said to have been destroyed when the shelf on which they stood collapsed. When? We don't know; in 1983 or 1984. This reply is at least worrying, given that these are elements contained in national collections and, moreover, are human remains.' This type of reply is indeed 'worrying'.

14 In South Africa, she had not been forgotten, as Kirby (1954) illustrates.

15 The last public 'appearance' of Saartjie Baartman's skeleton was in 1994, in an exhibition at the Musée d'Orsay. 'Today, the remains of this woman are rotting

in a storeroom in the Musée de l'Homme,' wrote Nicolas About, Senator for the Yvelines area and the instigator of the legal proceedings to return her body to its homeland (in truth, little remained of her body). In the same year, Zola Maseko made a film for the South African television Channel 4, and shown on France 3 (released in 1998 as *The Life and Times of Sara Baartman, the Hottentot Venus*), which was largely responsible for the rediscovery of her story in Britain, France and South Africa.

16 Marie-Claude Barbier (2003) describes the return of the remains in detail: 'With the end of apartheid, the transformations in South Africa were at first of a political and economic nature. But the new government also wanted to take account of and promote the rich ethnic and cultural diversity of the country symbolized by the term "Rainbow Nation". Until then, history had been presented through White and mostly Afrikaner eyes, mainly those of the descendants of the Dutch settlers. This old history rested on a certain number of founding myths from which the indigenous peoples were absent. [...] The new South Africa, born of the ballot boxes in 1994, needed new founding myths which reclaimed the past and could act as a key to the "brighter future" promised by the ANC in its electoral campaign. [...] In 1994 [the year in which Maseko's film was shown on television], the descendants of the Griqua peoples, who belonged to the Khoisan group of tribes, demanded the return of Saartjie Baartman's remains to her native country. This demand was communicated to French President François Mitterrand on his official visit to South Africa in the same year, and was reiterated two years later by Mr Ngubene, South African Minister for the Arts, Culture, Science and Technology. There was communication between the South African Professor Tobias and Professor de Lumley, director of the Paris museum, but it failed to bear fruit. In October 2000, Mrs Skweyiya, the new South African Republic Ambassador in Paris, sent a written request to the Secretary General at the Quai d'Orsay, which the French government agreed to follow up, considering it to be legitimate, but this was followed by months of debate. The French Senator Nicolas About became the spokesman for this return, which he described as the "symbol of the rediscovered dignity of a people". However, he came up against the constraints imposed by Michel Duffour, Secretary of State for National Heritage and Cultural Decentralization, which were on three grounds: legal, moral and scientific. These obstacles were finally removed and the law of 6 March 2002 [six months after the publication of the French version of *Human* Zoos] authorized the return of the young woman's remains.'

17 Mr Mbeki declared that 'the story of Sarah Bartmann is the story of the African people of our country in all their echelons. It is a story of the loss of our ancient freedom. It is a story of our dispossession of the land and the means that gave us an independent livelihood. It is a story of our reduction to the status of objects that could be owned, used, and disposed of by others [...]'. ('Speech at the Funeral of Sarah Bartmann', 9 August 2002, www.anc.org.za/ancdocs/history/mbeki/2002/tm0809.html). This event can be seen in the film *Zoos humains* shown by ARTE at the end of 2002.

18 In 1880, the German anthropologist, Hartmann, would discredit this claim, explaining that this 'stéatopygia was also to be found in the Bantus, the Bongos, and even the Berbers. The Hottentot apron is not unique to South Africa, it is to be found everywhere on the continent and is even often found in Europe' (Hartmann 1880: 83).

3

Barnum and Joice Heth: The Birth of Ethnic Shows in the United States (1836)

BENJAMIN REISS

On 25 February 1836, P. T. Barnum orchestrated an event that would launch his career in show business and provide the nascent mass media with one of its first great spectacles.[1] This was the first of a series of exhibitions which would last for nearly a century in the United States and in Europe. At the centre of the story was Joice Heth. This African American woman had been exhibited by Barnum across the Northeast United States, for her great age (161 years) and her previous employment as George Washington's nurse. Her journey now ended as she lay dead on an operating table in New York's City Saloon under the scalpel of Dr David L. Rogers, who cut into her corpse before a vast and fascinated public. Dr Rogers concluded that Joice Heth was a fraud, touching off an intense journalistic debate, mainly in the penny press. Through this debate, a surprising number of improvisations on the themes of identity, authenticity and essence were seemingly wrung from Heth's corpse. Alternately she was still alive, dead but a fraud, or dead and the real thing. For others she remained an eternal mystery, was a waste of time, or was about to embark on a tour of Europe as an urn of ashes.

Reconstructing the Heth exhibit – in particular, its grisly aftermath – through its coverage in the media provides a microscopic view of some of the unsettling transformations that would shape culture throughout the nineteenth century. Underlying this show and those that followed, and often profoundly affecting the lives of those who saw Heth, were issues of modernization such as the new prestige of science, social atomization, the emergence of a commercial mass culture, rapid urbanization, and a felt loss of familial or class-based traditions. Many of these transformations produced anxieties about status, authenticity, and identity. In several of its aspects, the autopsy of Joice Heth appears as a moment in which science – mediated by popular journalism and other mass media – faced some of the crises of legibility, authenticity and recognition brought on by the process of modernization.

Before the Civil War, changing concepts of 'race' in the Northern states provided the context for these exhibits. In early nineteenth-century America, racial distinction was a relatively loose set of discourses, practices and ideas that separated and elevated one group from others, drawing on law, religion and science with little internal consistency. Heth's itinerant exhibit reflects some of this loose structure, in that it was an improvised racialist display, an open text that was given a wide range of readings in local media. These readings revealed her various publics' notions of race, which were inevitably filtered through their differences of region, class and ideology. But after her death, the question of what she meant to her viewers and to readers was displaced by the more imperious question of who she was, or rather, who was behind her. Her autopsy – like other spectacular displays of race created by the media – dramatized some of the new meanings of racial identity and allowed whites to debate them as they gazed upon her corpse. The episode thus offers the opportunity to construct an ethnographic miniature of white antebellum North Americans as they struggled to make sense of the issues of racial identification and modernization, and looked for symbolic resolution to those struggles in popular culture and the emerging mass media.

Freak Show, History Lesson or Disgrace: Heth on Tour

The small-scale itinerancy of Heth's tour with Barnum is located at a transitional moment for entertainment, between the wandering performers, orators and curiosities who had flourished since the late eighteenth century and the urban spectacles of the second half of the nineteenth century (Burke 1978; Wright 1927). Her first exhibitor was actually not Barnum but R. W. Lindsay, a hapless showman from Kentucky, who had exhibited her in towns and villages across Ohio and the South. Little is known about this early tour, but Lindsay, having failed to turn a profit, sold her to Barnum, who was at the time working in a dry goods store in New York.

Barnum thus became Heth's virtual owner and, with the assistance of a young lawyer named Levi Lyman, displayed her in taverns, inns, museums, railway houses and concert halls across the American Northeast for a period of seven months, until her death. Beginning with an extended stay in New York, Heth, Barnum and Lyman moved on to Providence, Boston, Hingham, Lowell, Worcester, Springfield, Hartford, New Haven, Bridgeport, Newark, Patterson, Albany and many towns in between, stopping back in New York several times. Wherever they went, newspapers avidly reported Heth's comings and goings, and crowds flocked to hear her tell how she had witnessed the birth of 'dear little George' and had been the first to clothe him, to breastfeed him, to hear him sing hymns she had supposedly taught him. Some asked her questions on the upbringing of the future father of the nation. Others came to judge for themselves the authenticity of her claims, which were supported by an impressive array of documents such as her birth certificate and bill of sale, as well as by the bodily signs of her old age, and to ponder the causes and implications of her extraordinary longevity. Her debility was a draw, too, for many came to gaze on – even to touch – her marvellously decrepit body. Joice Heth was advertised as weighing only forty-six pounds (about 21 kilograms); she was blind and toothless and had deeply wrinkled skin; she was paralysed in one arm and both legs; and her nails were said to curl out like talons. Visitors regularly shook hands with her, scrutinized her, and sometimes even took her pulse. 'Indeed', wrote one observer, 'she is a mere skeleton covered with skin, and her whole appearance very much resembles a mummy of the days of the Pharaohs, taken entire from the catacombs of Egypt' (*New York Baptist*, 1835). Doctors and naturalists were fascinated. Well before she died – in fact while some were predicting that she would *never* die – her autopsy was a greatly anticipated event.

Throughout her travels with Barnum and Lyman, a curiously multivalent power of attraction marked the exhibitions of Joice Heth. Did her decrepitude make her a human oddity, to be marketed like the Chinese woman with 'disgustingly deformed' bound feet, the Virginia dwarves, and the Siamese twins whose paths she had often crossed on the touring circuit? Was it her scientific value as an embodiment of the different aging processes of the various races that merited her display? Was she an attraction because of her patriotic value as a living repository of memories of a glorious past? Because she was a storehouse of ancient religious practices? Or simply because she was a good performer? The publicity surrounding her exhibit played on these different levels of interest, and her audience's different interpretations of the display are of fundamental cultural significance.

Many newspapers across the North read Heth's exhibit primarily as a 'freak show'. Displays of human curiosities – lusus naturae, or freaks of nature, were among the most popular travelling entertainments of the late eighteenth and early nineteenth centuries. By the 1830s, though, while the display of grotesquely embodied human forms was for some a populist, carnivalesque entertainment, for others it was an offence to genteel sensibilities (Bogdan 1988: 10). The contested meanings of

Heth's extraordinary body reveal much about regional and class-based notions of race and cultural propriety, and point toward a larger struggle for cultural power in 1830s America.

In New York she was a favourite of the lively Jacksonian press, including the *Evening Star* and the first three-penny papers (the *Sun*, the *Transcript* and the *Herald*). These periodicals, the first entirely commercial serial publications in America, were perhaps the most compelling voices of Jacksonian individualism. Their brash displays of hostility for the culture of the upper classes, their sympathies for the urban working and upwardly mobile classes, their freedom from political patronage, and their fierce egalitarianism for whites, mixed with overt anti-black racism all marked their distinctiveness from the more genteel six-penny papers (Saxton 1990: 95–108; Schudson 1978; Tucher 1994). For the most part, the Jacksonian press peddled images of Heth's debility, her great appetite and fondness for tobacco, and her grotesque appearance. But although some articles continued the kind of coverage Heth had received in New York, Barnum and Lyman had to respond to a number of opprobrious reports.

In Boston, many journals attacked the publicity created around Heth. In particular, the protest of the *Courier* expressed fear that viewers' morals would be corrupted by the display, while appealing to readers' sympathy for Heth herself:

> Those who imagine they can contemplate with delight a breathing skeleton, subjected to the same sort of discipline that is sometimes exercised in a menagerie to induce the inferior animals to play unnatural pranks for the amusement of barren spectators, will find food to their taste by visiting Joice Heth. But Humanity sickens at the exhibition. (*Boston Courier*, 1835)

In response to these attacks, Barnum and Lyman wisely advertised Heth's cleanliness and her religiosity, rather than her freakishness, on the rest of her New England tour. According to a puff piece planted in the *Hartford Times*, 'There is nothing about her appearance which can possibly be unpleasant to the minds of the most fastidious' (*Hartford Times*, 1835). Apparently to pre-empt further criticism, they even printed a pamphlet biography of Heth which stressed, in addition to her propriety, the roughness of her treatment in slavery and the humane qualities of her current exhibitors (Barnum 1855: 5).

Behind the differing representations of Joice Heth lay a radical disagreement about the role of the human body in public display, the stakes of which were connected to a wider argument about who controlled culture (Stallybrass and White 1986). Editors of the 'penny-a-liners' typically saw themselves as cultural populists, providing what the readership wanted for the cheapest price possible. In their protests against the Heth exhibit, the more genteel editors viewed its solicitation of voyeuristic interest as a kind of naked public aggression that threatened their moral guardianship of culture.

'Freak shows', perhaps more than any other popular antebellum practice, helped disseminate the lessons of racial solidarity because they acted as a hinge between scientific inquiries into racial essence and the popular desire for images of white domination. Exhibits typically highlighted the physical anomaly, grotesque features, extreme disability, or exotic racial or cultural difference of the displayed human object, and often more than one such quality at a time.

For example, towards the end of the eighteenth century, Henry Moss, a black man afflicted with a disease that gave him spotted skin, exhibited himself in Philadelphia and became the subject of great popular attention, including that of Benjamin Rush, who concluded that Moss was undergoing a spontaneous 'cure' of his blackness. This popular scientific interest was institutionalized in the next century by Barnum, who exhibited in his American Museum African Americans with vitiligo, albinism and microcephaly, claiming that they were the missing links in an evolutionary chain extending from black to white and from monkey to man. The difference between the earlier and later exhibits is telling. The control exerted by Moss over his own exhibit in a major urban centre would have been unthinkable in the following decades, as racial attitudes hardened in the North and as cultural entrepreneurs like Barnum, circus managers, and proprietors of dime museums began to corner the market in human curiosities (Mitchell 2002). This increasing control of the 'freak's' body was accompanied by the incorporation of freakishness into developing notions of racial science.

Whereas Rush found that Moss blurred the distinctions between white and black, the later displays tended to refine and enforce those distinctions: the 'missing links' demonstrated the racialist implications of the new Darwinian theories (Cook 1996). Finally, Rush's interest in Moss was simply one voice among many about the nature of 'human curiosities', who were still often viewed in terms of religious wonder or the rituals of carnival that extended back to medieval Europe.

By Barnum's time, starting with the Heth autopsy, science became the dominant discourse for interpreting the 'freak's' body (Garland-Thomson 1996, 1997). Not surprisingly, then, the papers that emphasized Heth's freakishness also debated her scientific value (Bogdan

1988; Savitt 1978: 281–307), in particular, the 'fact' of her extraordinary old age. Also, amid the swirling possibilities and anxieties attending modernization and urban life that these papers so brilliantly chronicled, race stood as an island of fixity. From now on, the laws of nature decreed that each race should remain in its proper place, and those laws could be read on or through the body.

Death, Dissection and Cultural Commodification

Following Heth's death, her autopsy was an early instance of the imperious gaze of anatomists which made the racialized body a crossroads of science and popular culture. A precedent had been set in Europe in 1815 with the death of Saartjie Baartman (the Hottentot Venus). The popular press commented extensively on the 'findings' of scientists who undertook the scrutiny of racial 'types'. Popular exhibitors (led by Barnum) often called on these scientists to authenticate their exhibits, and the exhibits themselves often led to further scientific research. This emergent pattern would become the driving force for exhibitions towards the end of the nineteenth century.

As Barnum and the editors of the penny press saw, the cluster of social meanings adhering to Heth's corpse made it an object of considerable value. Its connection to Washington made it a curiosity in its own right and it was prized material for scientists because of its rarity and because of its significance in the loaded debates about race, biology, and region. In addition, Heth's blackness exempted those responsible for her autopsy from the clamour against human dissection and turned them into actors in a scene of white domination. Finally, popular interest in racial science translated her scientific value into commercial value. Soon after Heth died, Barnum contacted Dr David L. Rogers to perform the autopsy in the City Saloon in New York, which he had rented for the occasion, converting its exhibition room into a makeshift operating theatre, and opening the doors to the public. Despite the steep 50-cent admission price, 1,500 spectators showed up, netting a large profit for Barnum. The spectacle (a precursor of anatomical museums) also provided a windfall for the commercial press.

Following the conclusions of Dr Rogers that Heth could not be more than 80 years old and that the entire exhibit had been a hoax, Barnum and Lyman decided to pay a visit to James Gordon Bennett, the notorious editor of the *New York Herald*. They convinced him that Heth was still alive and well and that the corpse on the operating table was that of another aged black woman called Aunt Nelly.

The Dark Subject: A Fantasy of White Domination

As the Joice Heth episode progressed from itinerant road show to urban spectacle, from wondrous display of human curiosity to medical specimen, from historical relic to fraudulent commodity, it traversed many of the geographical and conceptual spaces of the modernizing antebellum North. Her living display had been given a range of readings contingent on the regional and ideological interests of her visitors. Her autopsy, in contrast, shows mass media and science converging on the black body in search of a fixed text in a changing world. In this sense, the autopsy anticipates the work of racial anatomists, like one Dr Caldwell, whose 'personal examination of dissection of the entire negro anatomy' led him to conclude that it is easier to 'distinguish an African from a Circassian skeleton' than that of a dog from a hyena, a tiger from a panther (cited in 'On the unity of the human race' 1854: 299).

This type of work established racial difference as a zone of distinct legibility and fixed boundaries; this essential fixity when reported in the popular press was a dialectical counterweight to the popular fascination with hoaxes and conspiracy theories that grew out of modern anxieties. The autopsy can also help us perceive the links between nascent racial essentialism and the grotesque popular essentialism of the 'freak show' and minstrelsy, which were beginning to emerge as dominant mass cultural representations of blacks in the modernizing, urbanizing American North. Scientific ideas on the biological nature of racial difference provided a conceptual framework for popular images of degraded, deformed, and otherwise humiliated blacks on stage.

Throughout his career, Barnum himself often circled back in his writings to the Heth exhibit, which had launched the series of 'ethnic' and 'freak' shows that made him famous. In his 1855 autobiography, he finally gave away the secret that he had not dreamed up the Heth act but had seen Lindsay's exhibit of her in Philadelphia and had decided to purchase her and continue the tour himself. As to the identity of Heth and her origins, he pretended to be as ignorant as anyone else, predicting that the 'dark subject' of her authenticity would remain a mystery (Barnum 1872: 80). Soon after the triumph of the Heth exhibit in 1837, Barnum lost his entire fortune and set out on a series of tours of the United States and Canada with small circuses, before publishing his articles in *Atlas* and the series of autobiographical writings which brought him renewed success. The new attractions dreamed up by Barnum for his American Museum from 1841 began another history of American showmanship, and Barnum's travelling shows would eventually arrive in Europe in 1874.

The story of Joice Heth exposes how entrepreneurs of culture in the antebellum American North borrowed images from the slave-owning South to construct fantasies of northern white mastery, in which the slave's body was subjected to the modern disciplines of scientific and mass-cultural scrutiny. This process set in place some of the underlying conceptual structures of racism for the next two centuries.

Note

1 This is a revised version of an article which appeared in March 1999 in *American Quarterly*. For a more extensive discussion of the topic, see Reiss 2001.

4

London, Capital of Exotic Exhibitions from 1830 to 1860

NADJA DURBACH

In 1855, John Conolly, President of the Ethnological Society, remarked on the number of exotic performers, who increasingly passed through Britain's capital: 'There is scarcely a year in which, among the miscellaneous attractions of a London season, we do not find some exhibition illustrative of the varieties of mankind.' But, he cautioned his learned readership, 'some of these are unsatisfactory, some deceptive, and all nearly unprofitable, because not rendered instructive to the public' (Conolly 1855: 5). While these performances might have been unsatisfactory to Conolly and his colleagues, and many were indeed deceptive, they were clearly not unprofitable. In fact, displays of exotic peoples were so common in the period between 1830 and 1860 precisely because the public clamoured to see examples of the 'varieties of mankind', and treated these ethnographic exhibitions as little different from the countless displays of wild animals, ancient Egyptian mummies, and freaks of nature, which could also be seen for a penny or two in the show shops and exhibition halls that dotted the urban landscape in the early and mid-Victorian period.

During the years between 1830 and 1860, the display of 'exotic' peoples was an important feature of the cheap entertainment industry and was embedded in the larger category of the 'freak show', which in Britain dates at least as far back as the sixteenth century. In the first half of the nineteenth century, Londoners developed a seemingly insatiable appetite for 'monsters', 'human oddities', lusus naturae, 'prodigies', 'novelties' and 'freaks', interchangeable terms for those who displayed their unusual bodies to the curious for entertainment purposes. While scholars have often argued that the 'freak show' and the ethnographic exhibit represent two different traditions of human display, and thus have treated them separately, commercial displays of 'exotic peoples' were not, in fact, a wholly distinctive category of performance. Since the earliest years of the nineteenth century, human zoos had existed along-

81

side exotic animal displays and exhibitions of human novelties (Qureshi 2004; Altick 1978). At Bartholomew Fair in 1834, the 'Beautiful Spotted Boy', the original 'Siamese twins', an albino woman, and a 'Wild Indian' were all exhibited side by side. But were the conjoined twins Chang and Eng, who often performed in oriental costume, freaks of nature or 'ethnographic specimens'? Was the Spotted Boy – an African youth suffering from a skin pigmentation condition – an exotic act, or merely another *lusus naturae*? By positioning the non-white body alongside bodies that were congenitally anomalous, and by blurring the distinction between the 'racial exotic' and the 'human oddity', these exhibitions configured racial Otherness as freakish bodily difference, thus naturalizing and normalizing the white British body. Thus, while Conolly may have considered these shows uninstructive, preferring that audiences learn about 'the great history of man on the globe' (Conolly 1855: 44) from experts such as himself, these exhibitions of non-Western peoples were, in fact, highly educational in that they contained critical messages for British spectators about their own place within the hierarchy of races and civilizations.

Long before the rise of international exhibitions, which in 1883 began to feature 'native villages', exotic peoples could be seen on display in the capital cities of Europe. In November 1853, the *Illustrated Magazine of Art* declared that a 'man, now-a-days, need not encounter the perils of the sea and the dangers of the land to make himself acquainted with the varieties of the human race'. For, its reporter maintained, 'there are at the present moment exhibiting in London [...] various members of those families of men with whom we have hitherto cultivated but slight acquaintance'. Between 1830 and 1860, Londoners could have seen, among others, a variety of North American peoples (including Ojibbeways, Ioways, Hurons), three different groups of Khoisan, several troupes of Zulus, a party of Australian aborigines, a Rarotongan youth from the Cook Islands, a group of Inuit from the Cumberland Strait, some Fiji Islanders, an albino from Barbados, several indigenous inhabitants of the Torres Strait, and a 'Small-Footed Chinese Lady' whose bound 'lotus' feet were the main attraction. Since these commercial displays of exotic peoples were likely the only context in which most Londoners came into contact with non-white peoples, they served as the primary vehicle for instructing a mass public about the distinctions among 'the varieties of mankind'.

Conolly encouraged his colleagues to visit and report on these shows in order to be able to instruct the public and prevent them from 'imbibing erroneous information' about 'the races of mankind' (Conolly

1855: 11). Ethnologists, newly emerging as experts on racial difference, were thus concerned about the content of these shows precisely because they believed them to be instrumental in shaping popular understandings of race. They were especially anxious to distinguish authentic acts from the countless patently fake ethnographic 'specimens' that could also be seen in this period. The painter George Catlin often hired fake troupes of Native Americans for his 'Tableaux Vivants Indiens', which accompanied his exhibitions of American paintings in the early 1840s. These Western extravaganzas included 'traditional' native dances and wigwams pitched on the Lord's Cricket Ground, and attracted over 35,000 spectators in London alone. They clearly pre-date Buffalo Bill Cody's equally successful Wild West shows by over forty years.[1] In an attempt to capitalize on this interest in North Americans, in 1846 the dwarf actor Hervey Leech appeared in the role of the 'Wild Man of the Prairies' or 'What is it?' billed as both the missing link between man and monkey and as a Native American 'wild man' character. The act was short-lived, since Leech, a minor celebrity with a distinctive physique, was instantly recognizable to the public[2] and his masquerade backfired, proving commercially unpopular. Furthermore, it was common knowledge that most of the 'Red Indians' on display in the early nineteenth century were in reality only 'Paddy Murphy' Indians, that is, run-of-the-mill Irishmen (Riach 1973: 237). In 1835, a newspaper report on Greenwich Fair maintained that there were the 'usual number of Indian warriors (thick lipped Irishmen from St. Giles's [London's quintessential Irish slum] painted, with their ears and noses adorned with rings)'.[3]

If Conolly felt it necessary to distinguish between the real and the fake, most spectators were not necessarily deeply concerned with the authenticity of these entertainments. Indeed, fake Red Indians and Africans were sometimes as popular as the genuine variety, as the financial success of the contemporaneous blackface minstrel shows attests (Pickering 1991). While some audience members may have been angered at being duped, many people continued to pay to see what they may or may not have known was a fraud, primarily because they were entertained by the messages about racial and cultural difference that these acts literally embodied. It was not always the authenticity of the exhibition that was important, but rather the security of one's own relationship to the performance.

Whether bona fide or counterfeit, these shows drew in audiences by reinforcing the comfortable binary of savage/civilized that encouraged even working-class audiences to imagine themselves to be members of an imperial ruling race. In the 1840s and 1850s, the discourses of the 'primitive', who was savage but civilizable, tended to dominate exotic exhibitions. When 'Eleven Native Canadian North American Indians' appeared at the Egyptian Hall in Piccadilly in 1843, their handbill maintained that despite the fact that these were 'Children of the Forest', and thus truly primeval peoples, they were nevertheless good British subjects. Indeed, it declared that they had 'long intended to visit the country of their "Great Mother", the Queen, for the double purpose of seeing Her Majesty and her great country, as well as to collect some funds for the purpose of educating the Indian youth'. Similarly, when nine 'Ojibbeways' from the British territory of Upper Canada appeared at the same venue two years later, the fact that they were 'wild indians from the Forests of North America' was tempered by their apparent patriotism. These individuals, their promotional materials insisted, belong 'to one of the most numerous and powerful tribes, which has at all times been devotedly attached to the British Government' (*Programmes*, 1840–80).[4] 'Red Indians', however wild and savage, these acts seem to suggest, could nevertheless be educated and forged into respectful and educated subjects of the Crown.

The exhibition of Khoisan peoples from southern Africa in the 1840s and 1850s similarly reinforced these narratives of primitiveness, and at times proposed that these seemingly archaic peoples could in fact be rescued from extinction through the benevolence of British civilization. The appeal of these 'Bushmen' was that they were living examples of 'Stone Age' peoples, 'the lowest grade' of mankind, 'sunk in the scale of humanity to the level almost of the beasts of the forest', and thus destined to disappear (Tyler 1847: 2).[5] Lecturing on the troupe of Khoisan he was exhibiting across Britain in 1847, J. S. Tyler maintained that it was inevitable that the Bushmen would soon be 'exterminated'. 'Even now, London and Paris, in their museums, have stuffed skins of these people', he declared. 'A short time, alas! and such will be the only relics left of them' (1847: 6).

If the Bushmen were often seen as 'a race sentenced to speedy extinction', even before Darwin proposed the theory of natural selection, many believed that they had a duty 'to their nearly helpless and half-famished brethren' to bring them 'within the broad area of civilisation' ('Now Exhibiting at the Egyptian Hall' 1847[6] Erdermanne 1853). Two Khoisan children, exhibited in 1852 as Martinus (or sometimes Martini) and Flora, the 'Earthmen', served as perfect proof of the success of this civilizing mission. About 1 metre (3 feet) tall, with 'skins of a bright bronze hue', the children sang and danced for the spectators, reported the *Illustrated Magazine of Art* (1852), clothed in nothing but animal hides. Their repertoire featured the popular minstrel songs, 'Buffalo Gals' and 'I'm Going to Alabama'. Ironically, these African-born performers, often labelled 'white negroes' because of their pale skin, were mimicking the performance of other 'white negroes', the Englishmen who blacked up to impersonate African–Americans in minstrel shows. But the Earthmen also performed 'Rule Britannia' with its memorable last line, 'Britons Never Shall Be Slaves', underscoring on the one hand the difference between the free white Englishman and the only recently liberated black African, but on the other that South African 'natives' could also identify themselves as British subjects. As Bernth Lindfors has argued, the Earthmen were a great success precisely because they charmed their audiences, demonstrated that they were 'acquiring the rudiments of European civilization', and even provided, according to one contemporary account, 'a direct Contradiction to the Theory lately set forth, of the Impossibility of Rendering the Savage a Thinking, Feeling Being' (Lindfors 1996: 16).

In December 1854, the Earthmen were paired with the Aztecs, a new act that had first appeared on the London 'freak show' circuit the previous year, and continued to tour with them until 1860. Maximo and Bartola, 'The Last of the Aztecs', were fake. They were nothing more than two microcephalic dwarfs of mixed race, but these exotic Others were among the most popular of all mid-Victorian 'freak show' acts (Aguirre 2005; Goodall 2002). Conolly had argued that exhibiting these two groups together did nothing for either of them, for the Earthmen, whom he had also seen exhibited before the Ethnological Society, were 'perfect in their kind', lively, witty, and clearly intelligent, while the Aztecs, he declared, were 'arrested in their growth', both mentally and physically (Conolly 1855: 27). Indeed, once they had been exhibited with the Aztecs, Martinus and Flora's promotional material ceased to underscore their lively intelligent natures and, instead, emphasized the similarities between what their souvenir admission ticket proclaimed were 'Two New Races of People, the First of either Race ever discovered'.[7]

These newly discovered people, their publicity materials maintained, were extremely primitive. 'The Earthmen', the souvenir ticket stated, like 'The Aztecs', cannot speak. They 'burrow under the earth in South Africa', it recounted, 'subsisting upon insects and reptiles'. Indeed even before they were joined on stage, these two groups were seen as analogously primitive peoples equally incapable of advanced civilization. A contributor to *Blackwood's Magazine* in September 1853 declared that he was astonished to learn of the ability of underwater coral polyps to produce magnificent structures. This was much the same sort of surprise one would express, he maintained, upon discovering, say, 'that the pyramids and temples of antiquity had not been constructed by Egyptians or Romans, but by a race like the Earthmen of Africa, or by a set of pigmies like the Aztecs now exhibiting in London'.

The marketing of these acts together thus tempered the hopeful discourse of a benevolent civilizing mission that could rescue and uplift even the most primitive people. Instead, this exhibition firmly distinguished between those peoples who were destined to decline, and those more 'favoured' races, who would not only survive but would flourish and dominate the earth (Brantlinger 2003). Maximo and Bartola's exhibitors constructed them as degenerate members of the now defunct Aztec people. 'Forbidden, by inviolably sacred laws, from intermarrying with any persons but those of their own caste', their souvenir pamphlet explained, the Aztec people had 'dwindled down, in the course of many centuries, to a few insignificant individuals, diminutive in stature, and imbecile in intellect' (*Illustrated Memoir* 1853: 25). Further evidence of their degeneration, and thus of their civilization's decline, emerged in a debate over whether these 'Last of the Aztecs' could, in fact, speak, whether they had language, a key element of culture. Their publicity material declared that they had no language. The *Athenaeum* (9 July 1853) and the *Freeman's Journal* (4 October 1853) both asserted that Maximo and Bartola had 'no means of communicating with each other by language'. Indeed, The *Standard* (12 July 1853) declared that the 'only vocal noise they emit is a short indefinite grunt'. This suggested that these 'last Aztecs' were extremely primitive beings, whose civilization had deteriorated to such an extent that even its language had disappeared.

The 'Last of the Aztecs', particularly when paired with the Earthmen, whom *The Times* (7 May 1853) billed as 'the last link in the human chain', offered visible proof of the fate of primitive peoples who lived mired in the past, did not evolve, and therefore degenerated as a civilization and died off as a race. Maximo and Bartola thus served as an object lesson in the decline of civilizations and the extinction of inferior races. At the same time, however, they threw into stark relief the many reasons why Britain, which championed itself as the epitome of modern civilization, was destined to evolve, expand and ultimately endure. Far from being uninstructive, as Conolly had claimed, their exhibition helped Britons to articulate their own understanding of their position vis-à-vis other empires, peoples and civilizations.

This narrative of dying races that had framed both the various Bushmen acts and The Last of the Aztecs in fact served as a justification for the violence of colonialism and the extinction of indigenous peoples that rapidly followed the settlement of southern Africa and Australia. It was soon paired with a discourse of savagery that cast African peoples as cannibalistic, brutish and violent. Although the Bushmen were rarely exhibited as little more than a quaint archaic people, other Africans, and Zulus in particular, were regularly portrayed in these shows as brutes that needed to be subdued because their passions were animalistic and thus, unlike civilized Englishmen, lacked self-control. When the circus showman 'Lord' George Sanger's father attempted in the early nineteenth century to pass off two mulatto children as African 'pigmies', he played on the discourse of the bloodthirsty savage. These, 'savage cannibal pigmies', he insisted,

> were captured by Portuguese traders in the African wilds, and are incapable of ordinary human speech. Their food consists of raw meat, and if they can capture a small animal they tear it to pieces alive with their teeth, eagerly devouring its flesh and drinking its blood (Sanger 1908: 14).

As this spiel suggests, showmen often advertised Africans as wild, dangerous and depraved. While, as Michael Pickering has argued, '"[s]avagery" as spectacle was "savagery" domesticated and tamed', a demonstration of the disciplining of the 'wild man' was nevertheless central to the performance precisely because it underscored the need for subjugation (Pickering 2001: 60). Ropes and cages were used as containment devices, but more significantly the 'savage' was seen to be actively tamed: Sanger used to parade his own patently fake 'savages' around the fairground, buying them sweetmeats, and thus indicating their ability to be restrained and controlled by an essentially benevolent keeper. These narratives of savagery, cannibalism, and thus the need for violence to subdue 'the natives', became more pronounced in the second half of the nineteenth century when Zulu warriors, who had in fact defeated British soldiers in a series of colonial skirmishes, became the most popular exotic act. But these discourses were already deployed by promoters in the period between 1830 and 1860, thus setting the stage for the more overtly imperialistic exhibitions of the later nineteenth century.

That these acts were influential, and in fact helped to shape the British public's understanding of racial difference (and thus the nature of the imperial project), is evident in Charles Dickens's reaction to a series of ethnographic displays. A visit to a Bushmen exhibit, and later a display of 'Zulu Kaffirs' at Hyde Park corner, filled Dickens with disgust. He was only too pleased to learn of the impending and inevitable disappearance of what he ironically termed 'the Noble Savage'. In a caustic essay published in *Household Words* (11 June 1853), Dickens not only claimed to 'abhor, detest, abominate, and abjure' the 'howling, whistling, clucking, stamping, jumping tearing savage', but maintained that is was, in fact, 'highly desirable' for them to be 'civilised off the face of the earth' (Lindfors 1999b).

In the years between 1830 and 1860, then, these human zoos were a key feature of mass entertainment. While it might be tempting to dismiss them as merely voyeuristic and tawdry, not worthy of historical analysis, these shows played a critical role in the making of modern imperial identities. As one of few forms of entertainment whose appeal cut across lines of class, gender, age and region, exotic exhibitions instructed a diverse group of curious spectators how to position themselves in relation to the 'varieties of mankind'. They thus primed the metropolitan British public for the Age of Imperialism, which, as many historians have recently demonstrated, required the full co-operation of all members of British society.

Notes

1 See 'A Collection of Handbills, Newspaper Cuttings, and Other items, 182096', Guildhall Library, G.R.2.5.7.
2 See 'Egyptian Hall 1845–73' Folder, London Theatre Museum.
3 Newspaper Clipping, Greenwich Fair, 1835, Noble Collection, Guildhall Library, C 26.5.
4 See 'A Collection of Handbills, Newspaper Cuttings, and Other items, 1820-96', Guildhall Library, G.R.2.5.7.
5 See 'A Collection of Handbills, Newspaper Cuttings, and Other items, 1820–96', Guildhall Library, G.R.2.5.7.
6 'Now Exhibiting at the Egyptian Hall, Piccadilly. The Bosjesmans, or Bush People, From the Interior of South Africa', n.pub., 1847.
7 See Favour Ticket for 'Aztecs and the Earthmen', *St. Martin's Scrapbook, Leicester Square*, volume 1.2, City of Westminster Archives Centre.

5

When the Exotic Becomes a Show

ROBERT BOGDAN

Respectable Americans did not always despise 'freak shows', be they exhibitions of wonders or of monsters of modern times. For a long time, upstanding citizens were connoisseurs of the exhibition of people with physical, mental and behavioural anomalies (alleged and actual), as well as 'natives' from exotic lands. For close to one hundred years (from 1840 to about 1940), the shows thrived in circuses, fairs, carnivals, dime museums and amusement parks. In the mid-nineteenth century, celebrated 'freak' entrepreneur P. T. Barnum ran one in his American Museum in the heart of Manhattan, just across the street from City Hall. The rich and the famous of New York, as well as commoners, flocked to his establishment to feast their eyes on the likes of The Last of the Aztecs (a brother and sister with pointed heads, who had mental disabilities), The Swiss Bearded Lady, The Original Siamese Twins, an African–American mother with her two albino children, and domestic and foreign 'savages'. The opening of the Ringling Brothers' Barnum and Bailey Circus in Madison Square Garden, the event that heralded the coming of spring for Americans, sported a large 'freak show' until the early 1950s.

It was not until well into the twentieth century that more scrupulous showmen came to see such shows as indecent and cruel, shamelessly exploiting their exhibits. 'Exhibitions of curiosities' were still to be seen occasionally at country shows and fairs, but these were pale imitations of the prestigious attractions of earlier days. Although the grand tradition of 'freak shows' is now deplored and almost extinct, the exhibition of physical deformities, far from disappearing, has been adopted by other media in forms which are less identifiable to the unwary. Indeed, in cyberspace, in cinema, in chat shows, and in other television programmes, we still encounter the tradition of the ancient fairground attractions.

The 'freak show' community was extremely close-knit and shared a very individual philosophy. In their eyes there were two sorts of people: those in the business, who were 'in the know', and everybody else. This solidarity was expressed through a corporate style of life, a particular vocabulary, secrets of the trade, and an open distrust of those who were not part of their world. The 'suckers', 'gulls', 'mugs' and other credulous outsiders were the targets of systematic hoaxes, cons and swindles. Presented as healthy, instructive and scientific entertainments, 'freak shows' were, above all, about making money, and resolutely participated in a world of show business where anything went. Masquerades and deceptions were therefore common currency.

Exhibitions became carefully staged productions which were researched, choreographed, and presented with a perfectly constructed patter. From Mr Loyal's harangue – intended to draw in the punters – to the showstopper that, for a few extra pennies, held out the promise of an extraordinary surprise, these displays differed only in their minor details. Their fixed formula bound them in a ritual: their giants were always the tallest in the world and their dwarves the smallest. Refuting charges of frivolity and voyeurism, their owners and managers all prided themselves on the educational qualities of their shows, which rendered them highly commendable.

In order to promote their trade, managers, often in cooperation with the exhibits, embellished and lied about the identity and backgrounds of those who were on the stage. For example, the Davis brothers, who were small and mentally handicapped, had grown up on a farm in Ohio. But from 1852 to 1905 they were presented as the Wild Men of Borneo, captured after a bloody fight by the crew of a ship in the distant Pacific and subsequently tamed. By knowingly drawing on images and symbols which appealed to public sensibilities, organizers and showmen created public identities for their exhibits which were guaranteed to 'pull in the punters'. Each 'freak' was a lure in the strict sense of the term. Many were certainly gravely handicapped, or disabled (to use contemporary terminology), but almost all, with a few exceptions, were falsely presented.

Although there was more than one way to exhibit a 'freak', the exotic mode of presentation was a favourite. By 'mode of presentation' I mean a standardized set of techniques, strategies and styles that showmen used to construct the exhibit. The exotic mode provided a formula for advertising literature, the staged appearance, the banners and other aspects of the 'freak' promotion and display.

With the exotic mode, showmen presented the exhibit so as to appeal to people's interest in the culturally strange, the so-called primitive, and the bestial. As with the Wild Men of Borneo, promoters told the audience that the exhibit came from a mysterious part of the world – darkest Africa, the jungles of Borneo, a Turkish harem, or an ancient Aztec kingdom. Dressed in a style that was compatible with the story, the exhibit would behave consistently with the front. 'Wild men' or 'savages' might grunt or pace the stage, snarling, growling and letting off warrior screams. Dress might simply be a loincloth and a string of bones around the neck, and, in a few cases, the scene was embellished with chains, which were allegedly there to protect the public from the attacks of the 'beast' who paced the stage before them. In the case of people who were supposedly from the Middle East or Asia, the presentation and the performance would be characteristically more sedate, with the 'freaks' acting out in exaggerated, stereotypical ways the presumed mannerisms and customs of the countries they represented. Their dress consisted of flowing robes, turbans and silks.

The stories used in presenting exhibits were created to maximize interest. Because this period was one of intense world exploration and Western expansion, news events provided some of the scripts and descriptions for the presentation of 'freaks'. Thus, when Stanley and Livingstone were lost in the 'dark continent' and the imperialist British were fighting those they were colonizing, the 'savage African' was a popular motif. Late in the nineteenth century and early in the twentieth, when the United States took the Philippines from Spain and fought the indigenous people, the Philippine backdrop was prominent in shows.

Where Science and Theatre Meet

An important source of stories to package 'freaks' was provided by the scientific reports and travelogues of nineteenth- and early twentieth-century natural scientists. Pre- and post-Darwinian discussions about the place of human beings in the great order of things and the relationship of the various kinds of humans to each other and to baboons, chimps and gorillas were in the air. Scientific writing on teratology or on the classification of the 'races of man', and theories of 'missing links' provided the ideas for show decorations and for details of the plots to be presented in the exotic mode. While the different-species explanation was the most popular in presenting 'exotic' exhibits, scientists provided a broader range of theories for showmen to choose from.

Exotic-mode explanations of people who were blatantly different or who had obvious physical and mental disabilities were sometimes bolstered by the 'hybridity' theory, for example. The theory posited that certain malformations were the result of crossbreeding man with beast. The comparisons showmen made between an exhibit's malformations and certain animal structures ('the lion-faced boy', for example) also implied a biological link. Another popular explanation which fit nicely with certain exotic presentations was the 'atavistic' or 'throwback' theory. The basic premise here was that humans could give birth to children who were reversions to more 'primitive' forms of life, including less developed species of humans.[1]

In the most blatant distortion under the exotic mode, native-born Americans were misrepresented as foreigners – a very tall, black North Carolinian was presented as a 'fearsome warrior' from Dahomey. Many of the exhibited 'freaks' were, nevertheless, from the non-Western lands, and some were even born in the countries claimed as their mother-lands by the promoters. Here, the distortion and misrepresentation came in the exaggerated details of the culture and the person exhib-ited, highlighting the odd, the bizarre, the erotic and the savage. Favou-rite themes included cannibalism, human sacrifices, head-hunting, polygamy, unusual dress, and food preferences that were disgusting to Americans (such as eating dogs, rodents, insects and dirt).

Non-Western people with demonstrable physical differences – those who were very tall, very short, without arms and legs, Siamese twins, and so on – were exhibited within the exotic mode through emphasis on their physical anomalies as well as their 'strange ways'. But it was standard sideshow practice from the days before Barnum to the 1950s for people from the non-Western world who had nothing 'wrong' with them to climb on to the 'freak show' platform to be gawked at by Ameri-cans. They did not have disabilities, nor were they unusually tall or short. They did not even perform some novelty act like fire-eating or tumbling. Those whose only difference lay in the fact that they belonged to an unfamiliar race and culture had value as show pieces. Dexter Fellows, exalted press agent of the amusement world, explained: 'The Borneo aborigines, the head-hunters, the Ubangis, and the Somalis were classi-fied as freaks. From the standpoint of the showman the fact that they were different put them in the category of human oddities' (Fellows and Freeman 1936: 296). They were generally referred to as 'freaks' and often shared the 'freak show' platform with people we would describe as having a disability, but all that made them 'freaks' really was the promoters' racist presentations of them and their culture.

People from Oceania, Asia, Africa, Australia, South America and the Arctic – people from all over the non-Western world – were brought to the United States. In addition, American Indians played a part in the famous Wild West shows. All were presented in early museums and circuses and later filled the human exhibit ranks at fairs, amusement parks and carnivals. Large groups were brought to populate 'native villages' along midways. They also came alone and in small groups to take their place in the 'freak show' proper.

Bringing people from far away to show them was quite a complicated and expensive business, beyond the resources of the smaller showmen. To reduce the costs and simplify the process, during the period when these exhibits were at their most popular, African-Americans and other ethnic minorities of the United States were willingly recruited to perform as the populace of distant lands. Less commonly, white Americans were blacked up with wax and passed off as non-Westerners. These hoaxes are as revealing of the credulity of the public as of the showmen's lack of concern for authenticity.

'Native people' as exhibits fit well into the nineteenth-century framework in which 'freak shows' doubled as scientific presentations. Explorers took along natural scientists to collect all forms of animal and plant species; in this scheme, aborigines constituted the living specimens for the human kingdom. By 1850, a new science, ethnology, the early cousin of cultural anthropology, had begun to lay claim to non-Western people. The use of the word 'primitive' seems as appropriate for these early practitioners of the science as for their subjects. Not until the 1930s and Franz Boas did the idea of cultural relativism – that a culture should be evaluated by its own standards, not by those of another – gain currency in learned circles. Non-Westerners as exhibits fit the early twentieth-century mentality well. Indeed, belief in their inherent racial inferiority and the undisputed superiority of Western culture remained part of the American frame of mind well past the 1930s, and lingers today.

The Imported Native in the United States

The presentation of imported non-Western exhibits was big business. Major circuses and other amusement establishments had full-time agents who combed the globe for cultural curiosities. With the whole non-Western world as their hunting grounds and sensitivity to exploitation undeveloped, there was a ready supply of exhibits and no opposition to the use of oppressive tactics to capture 'specimens'. The legal status of many of the foreign exhibits in the United States is difficult to determine. Some came there under contracts arranged with the governments of origin. In some cases the period of service was specified in their contracts. In other cases, when no such arrangements were made, exhibits were referred to as being 'owned by' their exhibitors, and they remained indefinitely in the United States.

Adjustment to amusement-world life varied considerably. 'Freak show' exploitation caused suffering for many non-Westerners, but some of these exhibits nevertheless adjusted quickly and even became 'showmen'. Those who did not lived miserable lives. But these matters did not seem to concern pre-1940s American audiences or the exhibitors – after all, to them, the people being exhibited really were cannibals, savages and barbarians. Through costuming, staging and advertising pictures and booklets, showmen fabricated a conception of 'natives' that accurately captured (or, rather, reflected) what they were to US citizens. The presentation reinforced pictures already in the American mind.

Around 1925, Jack Earle, a beanpole of a man, who was a student at the University of Texas at the time, went to see the Ringling Brothers' circus. Clyde Ingalls, the famous director of the circus, immediately spotted him in the audience and after the performance suggested that Earle should play the giant in his show. This anecdote sheds light on a fact which was perfectly understood by those in the business, but ignored by others: to be very tall is a matter of physiology, but to be a giant is something else. Likewise, to be a 'freak' is neither a personal quality, an illness, nor a social position. The fairground 'freak' is 'freakish' only on stage. What makes a 'freak' is a state of mind, a set of practices, a way of seeing individuals and of presenting them, the staging of a tradition, the theatricalizing of a sophisticated display.

'Freak' shows therefore tell us less about 'freaks' than about ourselves. Our way of perceiving individuals who are different from us derives less from their physiological and ethnic identity than from our own cultural identity. As the example of Jack Earle demonstrates, the simple fact of physical disability or of being from an 'exotic' country is not sufficient in itself to turn an individual into a 'freak'. 'Freak shows' teach us not to confuse the performer with the role, whether it is acted freely or under duress.

Note

1 This was the theory which gave the now-unacceptable label of 'mongolism' to trisomy.

6

Ethnographic Showcases:
Account and Vision

RAYMOND CORBEY

'To see is to know': this motto was attached to the anthropological exhibits of the World's Columbian Exposition of 1893, one of the many world fairs during the era of imperialism and colonialism (Rydell 1984: 44). At these gigantic exhibitions, staged by the principle colonial powers, the world was collected and displayed. Natives from a wide range of colonized cultures quickly became a standard part of most manifestations of this kind. Together with their artefacts, houses and even complete villages, so-called 'savages' or 'primitives' were made available for visual inspection by millions of strolling and staring Western citizens. Comparable places of spectacle such as zoos, botanical gardens, circuses, temporary or permanent exhibitions staged by missionary societies and museums of natural history, all exhibited other races and/or other species.

In this chapter, I shall put these ethnographic exhibits in the wider context of the collecting, measuring, classifying, picturing, filing and narrating of colonial Others during the heyday of colonialism.[1] All these modes of dealing with the exotic, with colonial Otherness, functioned in a context of European hegemony, testifying to the successful imperialist expansion of nineteenth-century nation-states and to the intricate connections that developed between scientific and political practices. Of course, I cannot bypass the historical changes and national differences in exhibitionary practices in the period under study – the last decades of the nineteenth and the first decades of the twentieth century – but I will concentrate on the similarities which in my view are predominant, arguing that it is possible to have a wide range of seemingly divergent modes of dealing with the Other within one single analytic field.

World fairs or international expositions were very large-scale happenings that combined features of trade and industrial fairs, carnival, music festivals, political manifestations, museums and art galleries. But primarily they were 'pilgrimage sites of commodity fetishism' as

Walter Benjamin (1984: 441) put it rather pointedly. The idea was to show progress in all fields – not only in industry, trade, and transportation but also in the arts, the sciences and culture. Meanwhile, there was no mention of poverty, sickness and oppression, or of social and international conflicts.

'Savages' on Show

Placed alongside all kinds of objects and products, colonial natives quickly became a standard part of world fairs, for the education and entertainment of Western citizens. Not only the citizens themselves but also the natives figured as categories in Western representations of self, as characters in the story of the ascent to civilization, depicted as the inevitable triumph of higher races over lower ones and as progress through science and imperial conquest. Often ethnologists were ahead of their times concerning interpretations of other cultures, but Charles Rau, for one, who created the ethnological exhibits at the Philadelphia Centennial Exhibition in 1876 on behalf of the Smithsonian Institution, stated that 'the extreme lowness of our remote ancestors cannot be a source of humiliation; on the contrary, we should glory in our having advanced so far above them, and recognize the great truth that progress is the law that governs the development of mankind (see Rydell 1984: 24).

Two years later, the Paris world fair of 1878 was the first one in which many people from non-Western cultures were exhibited, in specially constructed pavilions and 'native villages'. The display of 400 natives from the French colonies met with huge success, as did the exhibits of indigenous peoples from Java, Samoa, Dahomey, Egypt and North America itself at the World's Columbian Exposition in 1893.

Native villages were a standard part of world fairs from 1878 onward. Equally popular were the 'foreign streets', such as the 'Rue du Caire'. Around the turn of the century, the International Anthropological Exhibit Company commercially exploited exhibitions of non-Western people in the United States in several settings, including world fairs. At the Dutch Internationale Koloniale en Uitvoerhandel Tentoonstelling in Amsterdam in 1883, natives from the Dutch East Indies and West Indies were shown. The Greater Britain Exhibition of 1899 included a Kaffir Kraal – A Vivid Representation of Life in the Wilds of the Dark Continent, an exhibit featuring African animals and 174 natives from several South African peoples brought under control only shortly before. They were divided into four native villages, showing their crafts, performing

'war dances', and riding ponies. Among them were San, who characteristically were exhibited as part of the natural history of Africa, together
with baboons (MacKenzie 1984: 104). Often the European impresarios
travelled from one world fair to another with the same group of people
– the Senegalese who constituted the well-known Senegalese Village,
for example – and had them perform at other venues and on other
occasions as well.

It was light against dark, order against violence, and a European nation
as the bringer of civilization. 'Amazons', depicted as both barbarous
and alluring, true personifications of the Dark Continent, performed
throughout Europe. When they appeared in the Moskauer Panoptikum
in Frankfurt in 1899, they were introduced as 'wild females' – *wilde
Weiber*. A group of women from Samoa, however, was described by the
press and in brochures as a breathtakingly beautiful, always cheery,
erotically permissive, and lazy people from the paradisiacal Pacific
Ocean (Schmidt-Linsenhoff 1986: 257). North American Indians were
similarly idealized and romanticized.

The 1909 world fair that featured the Amazons also included a native
village of nomadic Kalmyks from Central Asia, brought under the
control of the Russian Empire shortly before. At the Berliner Gewerbe-
Ausstellung of 1896, which led to the foundation of the Deutsches
Kolonialmuseum, over a hundred natives from the German colonies
were present, each group in its own carefully imitated cultural and
natural setting. They had to call 'hurrah' at set times in praise of emperor
and *Reich* (Schneider, G. 1982: 167). Governments were keenly aware of
the opportunity to publicize their colonial policies and to manipulate
public attitudes toward the newly acquired territories. German, Dutch
and Irish villages were also (re)presented at the world fairs as part of the
national exhibits, staged in this case, however, by the exhibited peoples
themselves, not their colonizers.

The *Völkerschau* and Other Exhibitions

Persons from non-Western cultures appeared not only at world and
colonial exhibitions but also at special ethnographic shows, called
Völkerschauen in German, where this type of manifestation had proliferated since 1874 when Hagenbeck staged his first show.[2] Fear was but
one of the mixed feelings German citizens experienced when visiting
ethnological exhibitions. Another reaction was sexual fascination
and curiosity, as is clear from contemporary press coverage and from
preserved posters. Admiration of the supposedly great sexual potency of

the scarcely clothed 'primitives' competed with deprecation because of their alleged bestial lust (Goldmann 1985: 263–64; Thode-Arora 1989: 115–19). Disgust alternated with exalted attention, wonder, and enchantment when Western citizens were confronted with picturesque scenes from 'savage' life.

In the Netherlands, too, ethnological exhibits took place. In the year 1900, for instance, the *Groote Achantees Karavanen* [large Ashanti caravans] attracted much attention in Amsterdam, Rotterdam, The Hague, Utrecht and Nijmegen. The Ashanti, usually shown at the Jardin d'Acclimatation in Paris, now toured the rest of Western Europe. In the Netherlands, they were described on a poster as 'old natives from the Gold Coasts of Africa ... Warriors, fetish, priests, snake-charmer, women, girls and children. The most uncommon human race that has ever been seen in Europe. Most interesting for everyone' (Municipal Archives, Rotterdam). A few years earlier, *De Boschmannen of wilden van Afrika* [The Bushmen or savages of Africa], as the title of the accompanying brochure reads, were on tour. Judging from their appearance, this brochure states, 'they show more similarity to Apes than to people ... Notwithstanding their ferocity these Bushmen are nearly harmless, and even the most fearful person can approach and feel all over them with the greatest confidence' (Municipal Archives, Rotterdam). The suggestion that they could be touched indicates how close the attitude toward these people was to the attitude toward animals. That the exhibited people were similar – metonymically, metaphorically, qua appearance and behaviour – to animals, especially apes, was indeed a common perception, fed by contemporary scientific theory. In recent decades, in contrast, Bushmen once again came to play a positive role in Western imagination, similar to the one they played in the eighteenth century – that of 'noble savages', spontaneously and innocently enjoying a pure, natural, paradisaical existence.

The natives performed in several roles. The American firm William Foote & Co. African American Characters exploited a show with African-Americans – as the letterhead of the firm stated – appearing as 'savages, slaves, soldiers and citizens' (Thode-Arora 1989: 41). Crafts, hunting techniques, rituals, dances and songs were among the activities staged, as well as stereotypical 'authentic' performances like warfare, cannibalistic acts and head-hunting. At the 1904 Louisiana Purchase Exposition in St. Louis, Igorots from the Philippines could be seen eating dog meat, a food taboo in the West, while African Pygmies illustrated decapitation. The above-mentioned Dahomey 'Amazons', heavily armed, simulated fights. On exhibit at the Frankfurt Zoo and elsewhere in May 1885, Aborigines from Queensland, Australia, presented as 'Austral Neger', were described on posters as cannibals and bloodthirsty monsters [*wirklich blutdürstige Ungeheuer*]. Another poster, printed for their appearance in England, continued a European iconographical tradition reaching back to De Bry's late sixteenth-century *Grands Voyages* and earlier, by depicting them engaged in a ferocious cannibal ritual, with the following text: 'Male and female Australian Cannibals/ R.A. Cunningham, Director/ The first and only obtained colony of these strange, savage, disfigured and most brutal race ever lured from the remote interior wilds, where they indulge in ceaseless bloody feuds and forays to feast upon each other's flesh/The very lowest order of mankind, and beyond conception most curious to look upon' (Schmidt-Linsenhoff 1986: 228).

Commerce and Science

Hagenbeck was certainly not the first to take such an initiative. Christopher Columbus and Hernán Cortés had already brought back American Indians and Aztecs from the New World. European princes such as the Medici in Florence had scores of aliens at their courts as curiosities and for purposes of prestige. During the age of European expansion, virtually every generation of Europeans could see Nubians, Inuit, Saarmi, North American Indians and Pygmies at fairs, in inns – like the Amsterdam Blaauw Jan, precursor to the Artis Zoo – in theatres or, together with exotic animals, in zoos and princely menageries. An analogous practice was that of exhibiting the insane, who were usually presented in cages, with an admission fee. In eighteenth-century France, insanity was seen as a decline to a state of wildness and unruly animality, associated traditionally with all that was wicked and unnatural (Foucault 1961); at the same time there existed a whole body of publications theorizing on similarities of physical appearance between particular types of insanity and particular animal species. 'What was presented here,' Dörner writes, 'was wild and indomitable nature, "beastliness", absolute and destructive unruliness, social danger, which, behind the bars installed by reason, could be staged the more dramatically for showing at the same time to the public reason as the necessity of controlling nature, as a constraint upon unlimited freedom and as securing the order of the state' (1984: 22).

The way exotic animals were – and still are – shown and handled in circus performances elucidates practices of discipline and the concomitant idiom of wildness and taming that were present more implicitly in many exhibits involving people. P. T. Barnum's shows and, somewhat later, the German Circus Sarrasini had for decades ethnological acts on their programme, often combined with acrobatics.

During the eighteenth and nineteenth centuries, exhibits of live 'specimens' were increasingly re-framed in terms of science, especially physical anthropology and natural history. Aside from their entertainment and curiosity value, their educational value came to be stressed more and more. Hagenbeck, for instance, advertised his manifestations as 'anthropological-zoological exhibitions' [Anthropologisch-Zoologische Ausstellung]. In many ways, exhibitions of human individuals were related to scientific practices and purposes anyhow. The lunatic asylums where the insane were put on show were in the process of being medicalized; what was 'monstrous' or 'exotic' was often as interesting from a scientific point of view as it was shocking or fascinating to the general public. Anthropologists used to be represented on the committees heading the anthropological sections of world fairs, often quarrelling with those who wished to cater more to commercial than to scientific or educational interests.

In anthropometric and psychometric laboratories at the world fairs, visitors could witness and even take part in scientific research on racial characteristics. Phrenology, craniology, physiognomy and anthropometry shared the assumption that in the outward shape and physical appearance of the body, the inner character – of different races, but also of criminals, prostitutes and deviants – was manifest. So science, commerce and imperialism went hand in hand.

It is not difficult to show the central role of narrative structures in nineteenth- and early twentieth-century world fairs, museums, or missionary exhibitions. Narrative plots are as pervasive in the civilizatory, imperialist, missionary and scientific discourses of the period as in the three-dimensional spectacles that, to a considerable degree, were governed by these discursive activities. As many contemporary book titles suggest, the history of mankind was narrated essentially as a heroic ascent toward the natural and ultimate goal of cosmic evolution: the industrial civilization of white, European, middle-class citizens of the nineteenth century. Other races followed the same path, it was postulated – especially in evolutionist ethnology, which was a scientific manifestation of the discourse on progress – but lagged behind culturally and physically. Imperialist expansion was represented in terms of a social Darwinist natural history, and European hegemony as a natural and therefore desirable development. There has been some controversy over the question of whether the master narrative of progress and civilization is essentially a secularized avatar of the Christian idea of world history as God's working, but in any case, it was not formulated in religious terms. The implied development was from lack of civilization to civilized state, from wildness to civility, achieved heroically by the white, Caucasian race under its own power, and by the other races with the help of the Caucasian one, insofar at least as their constitutions allowed them to progress. The stage-by-stage development from savagery through barbarism to civilization was suggested by organizing museum and world fair exhibits into evolutionary sequences.

Sekula's stress (1986: 58) on the spirit of optical empiricism and encyclopaedism of pictorial archives, with their purely iterative character, is heuristically useful and certainly justified to a certain degree; but in many contexts of collecting, filing and exhibiting, an order was imposed on the data that went beyond mere iteration and taxonomy. In many cases, all essential ingredients of the story, or at least of a certain type of story, are present: a beginning where some desirable good is lacking; an end that is somehow implied by that beginning teleologically; acting subjects; strife and struggle; and other plot elements. World fairs and museums not only categorized peoples, races, cultures, species and artefacts, by creating taxonomies, but also ordered them syntagmatically, creating the well-known plots of civilized/Christian whites bringing light to the savage/heathen in the name of some higher instance. The same goes for many photographs from colonial contexts, showing moments from the story they presuppose and illustrate (Corbey 1988; 1989; 1990). Those well-known plots – flexible and capable of incorporating disparate elements, of outdoing alternative readings – are as pervasive in nineteenth-century discourses regarding Otherness as they were in the spectacles and pictures that were governed by these discursive activities. This century saw the proliferation of historicized, evolutionary frameworks of representation – of artefacts and natural history specimens, of human, racial and national origin.

One aspect of these spectacles, pictures, and narratives was that they neutralized the cognitive dissonance and the threat to Western middle-class identity constituted by the baffling cultural difference of new peoples. Colonial Others were incorporated narratively. In a 'mise en intrigue', they were assigned their roles in the stories told by museum exhibitions, world fairs and colonial postcards. They were cast as contemporary ancestors, receivers of true civilization and true religion. The radical difference of the Other was made sense of and thus warded off by a narrative 'discordant concordance' between 'civilized' and 'savage'. Money, trade and exchange mediated between peoples, but on another level stories were created in order to mediate the basic contradiction between the two states of mankind. Here I concur with Lévi-Strauss's interpretation of myth as a struggle with contradictions or paradoxes, as a syntagmatic mediation of paradigmatic oppositions.[3] Carol Breckenridge points out the analogy between the building of private collections by colonial officials, creating an illusion of cognitive control over a colonial experience that might otherwise have been disturbingly chaotic, and the world fair as a reminder of the orderliness of empire, which consolidated the sense of imperial knowledge and control in the imagined Victorian ecumene (1989: 211).

To return now to the 1893 world fair motto we began with – 'To see is to know' – we do not, of course, know how things are by simply looking. The eye is not innocent. The motto succinctly expresses an underlying ideology that is at work in a range of seemingly disparate practices in colonial times: photography, colonialist discourse, missionary discourse, anthropometry, collecting and exhibiting, and so on. What people saw, rather than reality as it is, was, to a considerable extent, reality as perceived, as actively constructed by images, conceptions, native taxonomies, stories and motivational attitudes in the spectator's mind. The perceived order was an imposed one; the citizen's gaze on alien people was determined to a considerable degree by stories and stereotypes in his or her mind.

Persons from tribal cultures, on show in the West, were cast in the role of backward, allochronic contemporary ancestors, receivers of true civilization and true religion in the stories told by museums, world fairs, and imperialist ideologies, thus becoming narrative characters in the citizen's articulation of identity – of Self and Other. Their own voices and views – ironically often as ethnocentric and omniscient as Western ones – were neutralized. Fitting cultural Others into narrative plots, we suggested, was a way the citizen's panoptic eye/I dealt with their wondrous, disturbing difference without annihilating it completely.[4] These plots came with the illusion of the panoptic position of an omniscient spectator, functioning as another strategy of power – the illusion that 'to see is to know'.

Over the last centuries the 'we'-group, as an emic category of Western middle classes characterized by true humanity, has been expanding continuously to include many categories that were formerly excluded or considered ambiguous: women, slaves, peasants, the poor and non-Western peoples. In this chapter, occasional reference was made to analogies between how other races and species were thought of and treated in the late nineteenth and early twentieth centuries. By now the boundary of the human species has been reached and, in fact, is being questioned – not least as to its moral significance – and transgressed. The discussion is now shifting towards zoos, circuses, dolphin shows, bio-industry and animal experiments; towards 'simian Orientalism' (Haraway 1989), and other forms of anthropocentrism. It would seem that our observations on ethno-/euro-centric ethnographic exhibits during the heyday of colonialism are in many ways readily extendable to present-day forms, in theory and practice, of anthropocentrism and 'speciesism'.

Notes

1 An earlier version of this article was published as Corbey 1993.
2 See Thode-Arora on Hagenbeck in this volume.
3 At the same time, as may be clear to insiders, we take some inspiration from the structuralist narratology of A. J. Greimas and the Paris School – without necessarily subscribing to all its presuppositions. For an as powerful but more radical, poststructuralist, analytical approach to exhibitionary practices, see Bal 1996.
4 For a more extensive analysis of the relationship between the quasi-panoptic perspectives of the eye, the camera and the narrator, see Corbey 1997.

7

From Scientific Racism to Popular and Colonial Racism in France and the West

PASCAL BLANCHARD, NICOLAS BANCEL AND SANDRINE LEMAIRE

In two preliminary publications in 2000 and 2001 we examined the nature of 'human zoos' and the impact of these exhibitions in the West.[1] Key questions concerned their effects on our relationship with the Other; on inter-colonial relations; and on the schism which occurred in the course of the nineteenth century between the West and 'elsewhere'. We attempted, there, to demonstrate that, in barely half a century, a shift occurred in what we described as 'human zoos' (in a wide sense of the term), from a form of racism which was exclusively scientific in nature to a popular racism, which spread rapidly, taking root throughout Europe. This shift began with exhibits in the zoological gardens of the middle of the century and ended with the great universal and colonial exhibitions of the first third of the twentieth century, with the 'freak show' as its intermediate form.

Anthropozoological exhibitions were the first points of mass contact between so-called exotic worlds and large swathes of the population of Europe (from Paris to Moscow). As such, they established a relationship with the Other which would last for several decades and which was founded on the twin processes of objectification and domination. By staging a world in which the divide between civilized peoples and 'savages' was clear to see, they contributed to the legitimization of the colonial project and to interracial xenophobia. This text is reproduced here, with additional contextual information and materials from the lively debates at the Marseille conference of June 2001.[2]

Difference: collect it, examine it, measure it and promote it

The appearance, and increasing success, of the fashion for human zoos resulted from the conjunction of three concomitant processes: the construction of a social imagination of the Other (whether colonized or not); the scientific theorization of the 'hierarchy of races' in the wake of advances in physical anthropology; and the construction of a fast-growing colonial empire. Over a relatively short period of about fifty years, these three elements formed the basis of a model which has yet to be deconstructed, and whose repercussions are still to be felt.

The idea of promoting a zoological show of exotic peoples emerged in several European countries in the 1870s (although its origins went back to the beginning of the nineteenth century), as well as in the United States, in particular through the agency of the famous P. T. Barnum, who had been one of the first to set up 'living museums', to popular acclaim.[3] In Germany, from 1874, Carl Hagenbeck, a dealer in wild animals and the future promoter of the major European zoos, decided to create regular exhibits of Lapps (Sami) and Samoans, who were presented as 'entirely natural' peoples for the entertainment of visitors avid for new sensation. The success of these first exhibitions led him, in 1876, to send one of his colleagues to the Egyptian Sudan in order to bring back animals and Nubians to renew the display. The latter embarked on a tour which took in various capital cities such as Paris, London and Berlin and, like most of the peoples put on show by Hagenbeck, were immediately successful throughout Europe.

This success undoubtedly influenced Geoffroy Saint-Hilaire, director of the Paris Zoological Gardens (the Jardin zoologique d'acclimatation), who was looking for new attractions to improve his establishment's problematic finances. Noticing, moreover, that the 'native' camel drivers provoked greater curiosity in their audience than the animals they were accompanying at a Parisian display, he decided to organize two 'ethnological shows' at the Zoological Gardens in 1877, presenting groups of 'Nubians' and 'Eskimos' (Inuit). The shows were an immense success. Attendance at the Gardens doubled and in that year reached a million paying visitors. Parisians rushed to discover what the general press described as a 'band of exotic animals, accompanied by no less singular individuals'. From 1877 to 1912, about thirty 'ethnological exhibitions' of this type were put on at the Zoological Gardens (Blanchard 2001) with repeated success, making it the main site (in terms of numbers and number of shows) for human zoos in France.

Many other venues would soon promote similar shows, or would adapt them to more political ends, for example the Parisian Universal Exhibitions of 1878, 1889 (this exhibition presented a 'negro village' with 400 'native' performers as one of its chief attractions) and 1900, where 50 million visitors saw the famous living Diorama of Madagascar. The exhibits continued in the later colonial exhibitions in Marseille in 1906 and 1922, and in Paris in 1907 and 1931. Certain venues specialized in lighter entertainment, such as the Champ de Mars, the Folies Bergère and Magic City, while the Porte Saint-Martin theatre presented the reconstruction of the defeat of Behanzin's Dahomeans by the French army. In order to respond to a more commercial market and to the draw of the provinces, regional fairs and exhibitions soon became the major promotional sites for such shows. As part of this process, troupes were quickly put together. They moved between exhibitions and regional fairgrounds, and the famous 'black' or 'Senegalese villages' became popular, appearing, for example, at the Lyon exhibition of 1894. Henceforth, there was not a town or exhibition which did not have its 'exact' reconstruction of 'savage' lands, allowing all French citizens to view the exotic human and animal inhabitants of such lands between an agricultural competition, Sunday Mass and a walk beside the lake. It was in this context that millions of French men and women, between 1877 and the early 1930s, encountered the Other. This was a staged Other, whether it was a strange people from the far corners of the earth or a native of the empire, and for most of those in the home country it represented the first contact with difference. The social impact of these shows in the construction of the image of the Other appears considerable, all the more so because they were combined at that time with an omnipresent colonial propaganda (conveyed through word and image), which profoundly influenced the imagination of the French.

With the establishment of colonial empires, power of representation over the Other was asserted in a new political context and in a period of unprecedented territorial expansion. The key turning-point remained colonization, for it demanded that the Other be dominated, tamed and, consequently, represented. Superposed over earlier ambivalent images of the 'savage', which were marked by both a negative difference from and positive memories of Rousseau's myth of the 'noble savage', there now lay a new vision which clearly stigmatized 'exotic' peoples. In this new order, images were used to inferiorize the native, and human zoos unquestionably played a significant role in the construction of paradigms relating to colonized peoples.

It is an irony of history that these troupes who crossed Europe (and even the Atlantic) often stayed away from their home countries for ten to fifteen years and accepted their own staging in return for payment in hard cash. Behind the scenes of savagery in the zoo, the 'savage' demanded a salary from the organizers.[4]

The ethnological shows of the last third of the nineteenth century were the product of a specific scientific and media-related context. Indeed, a popular racism appeared in the general press and public opinion, constituting a backdrop to colonial conquest. All the major media, from the most popular illustrated papers (such as *Le Petit Parisien* and *Le Petit Journal*), to publications with claims to scientific content (such as *La Nature*, or *La Science amusante*), not forgetting papers devoted to voyages of exploration (such as *Le Tour du Monde*, and *Le Journal des Voyages*), portrayed exotic peoples as the relics of early states of human-kind. Their vocabulary stigmatized savagery ('bestiality', 'bloodthirsti-ness', 'mystic fetishism', 'atavistic stupidity') and was reinforced by an iconographic production of unprecedented violence, giving credit to the concept of a stagnant sub-humanity that was to be found at the further-most boundaries of empire, existing on the margin between the human and the animal (Bancel, Blanchard and Gervereau 1993).

At the same time, the inferiorization of 'exotic' peoples was reinforced by the trinity of positivism, evolutionism and racism, in a period where knowledge of the Other was in its infancy. Indeed, the members of the Société d'Anthropologie (founded in 1859, at the same time as the Zoological Gardens) often attended exhibitions for anthropological research purposes. Physical anthropologists obses-sively sought to establish a racial hierarchy, with the consequence that 'race' became a central paradigm in explanatory theories of human diversity. Human zoos provided a representation of this classification of the 'races of man', creating a metaphor of the evolutionary model. Such categorization was to be found in the planning of the Parisian human zoos and acted as the major influence on the ideology of such shows. When, for example, the Cossacks were invited to the Zoological Gardens, the Russian Embassy insisted that they should not be mixed up with 'negroes' from Africa. Likewise, when Buffalo Bill arrived with his troupe, his place in the Zoological Gardens was assured by the presence of Native Americans in his show. The system of racial differ-entiation became firmly entrenched in the collective conscious at this time. Highly significantly, exhibitions of so-called monsters (dwarves and Lilliputians in the Zoological Gardens in 1909; hunchbacks or giants in the many itinerant fairs; macrocephalics or 'negro' albinos in Paris in 1912) were extremely popular, accompanying and merging with the outstanding success of the human zoos. It is probable that a dialectic relationship developed between eugenics, social Darwinism and the belief in a racial hierarchy. It is likewise probable that their proponents experienced a common distress when faced with difference, a distress which found its outlet in a non-egalitarian rationalization of the 'races', stigmatizing both the 'degenerate' and the 'native'.

Scientific discourse, by legitimizing colonial domination through its theory of racial inequality, and by relentlessly rationalizing racism, created a truly horrifying vision of the world. These exhibitions provided a partial, but nevertheless crucial explanation which popularized evolutionist ideas on race. Through them, 'anthropological discoveries' attracted a large and captivated audience while conveying a clear hierarchical message promoting Western hegemony. They thus popularized the principle of the inequality of 'human races' and partly justified (by illustrating it) the domination associated with colonization in the context of the Third Republic's 'civilizing mission'.

Human zoos, quite obviously, combine scientific detachment and popular hierarchical racism, both of which are carried on the tide of colonial expansion. The 'ethnological exhibitions' in the Parisian Zoological Gardens provided a remarkable indicator of this combination. They were legitimized by the Société d'Anthropologie, whose members saw the different imported peoples as living specimens to be exploited in their own research. Even though, between 1890 and 1900, the Society clearly became more circumspect with regard to the 'scientific' nature of such shows, it could not help but appreciate the research potential of this stream of peoples from all the corners of the earth. The break would eventually result from the growing outlandishness of these entertainments and their increasingly popular and theatrical nature.

Taming the 'Savage'

The staging of these shows, along with the exhibitions at the Champ de Mars and the Folies Bergère, involved an increasingly complex portrayal of 'savagery'. Baroque props, frenetic dances, and simulations of 'bloody combats' or 'cannibal rites', were accompanied by advertising programmes which emphasized 'cruelty', 'barbarity' and 'inhuman customs' (human sacrifice and ritual scarring). During the period between 1890 and the First World War, a particularly bloody image of the savage dominated. Put together with no concern for ethnological authenticity, human zoos repeated, developed, updated and legitimized the most unhealthy racist stereotypes, which constituted the imaginary Other during the period of colonial conquest. Indeed, it is essential to emphasize that the 'supply' of these 'natives' closely followed the overseas conquests of the French Republic, was approved by the colonial administration, and supported the French colonial project. Thus, for example, the Tuareg were exhibited in Paris during the months which followed the French capture of Timbuktu in 1894; Madagascans appeared a year after the occupation of their island; and the success of the famous Abomey Amazons followed the much publicized defeat of Behanzin by the French army in Dahomey. The will to degrade the Other, to reduce him or her to the level of a beast, but also the need to glorify France abroad in the frenzy of ultra-nationalism which followed France's defeat by Prussia in 1870, was fully supported by the press, which depicted the colonists as faced by raging, cruel 'natives', who were blinded by fetishism and lusting for blood. Quite different 'exotic' peoples thus tended to be shown in the same unflattering light,[5] all the 'races' being presented in a uniform, caricatural way which made them almost indistinguishable from each other. Between 'them' and 'us', there was now a barrier which could not be crossed.

Without doubt, the 'savages' brought to the West were an attraction, but they nevertheless provoked a feeling of fear. Their actions and movements had to be strictly controlled. They were presented as completely alien and their European surroundings obliged them to act as such, since they were forbidden to show any signs of cultural integration for as long as the show lasted. Thus, at the turn of the century, in most instances, it was unthinkable that they should mingle spontaneously with the visitors, and usually few opportunities for such contact were provided. They were made up to conform to the most recent stereotypes and were equipped in the most outlandish manner possible. Furthermore, the exhibited peoples had to remain within a clearly circumscribed area of the exhibition space (they had to pay a fine, which was subtracted from their wages, for any infraction), marking the intangible frontier between their worlds and that of the citizens who came to see them. A frontier, both physical and mental, was established between the 'savage' and civilized worlds, between nature and culture.

The most striking element of this brutal animalization of the Other was the reaction of the public. During these years of daily exhibitions, very few journalists, politicians or scientists showed concern for the sanitary conditions of the 'natives', or for their confinement, both of which often had catastrophic results. Indeed, many deaths occurred among the visiting peoples, for example, among the Kaliña Indians on show in Paris in 1892 (Collomb 1995), who were unused to the European climate. A small number of writers did, nevertheless, emphasize the fear caused by these shows, noting that visitors would throw food or trinkets to those on show, comment on their physical appearance by comparing them with apes (adopting one of the mantras of the physical anthropologists, eager to flush out the 'simian characteristics' of the 'savages'), or laugh heartily at the sight of a sick and trembling African in his hut. These descriptions – albeit incomplete – are sufficient to demonstrate the success of the latent racialization of minds among contemporary visitors. In this context, the empire could start work with a clear conscience, creating internal structures which allowed judicial, political and economic inequalities between Europeans and 'natives', founded on an endemic racism.

Human zoos clearly tell us nothing about the 'exotic' populations exhibited. However, they are an extraordinary tool for analysing Western attitudes from the end of the nineteenth century to the 1930s, and for exposing declarations of popular racism in almost all the countries of the West. The aim of these zoos, exhibitions and parks was, essentially, to display the rare, the curious and the strange as expressions of the unusual and the different, set in opposition to a rational construction of the world that operated according to European standards (McClintock 1994). It is reasonable to ask what the meaning of these frenzied performances was. Were they not, in the end, the reverse image of the very real ferocity of colonial conquest itself? Can we not see in them the will, whether deliberate or subconscious, to legitimize the brutality of the conquerors by animalizing the conquered? It is probable that a central concept was that of the establishment of two distinct racial worlds: the world of the colonizers and that of the natives; that of a ruling civilization and that of a subjugated group. From this perspective, the use of language relating to the transgression of the sacred is a useful indicator, and the recurrence of the theme of cannibalism in these shows is revealing. While almost nothing was known at the end of the nineteenth century about this highly ritualized social practice, which was, in any case, extremely limited in sub-Saharan Africa, images of 'savage cannibals' pervaded every medium and were one of the greatest selling points for human zoos right up to the Paris Exposition Coloniale Internationale of 1931, where Kanaks were exhibited on the fringes (see Daeninckx 1998).

The Paris exhibition of 1878 marked the appearance of one of the first 'negro villages', legitimized by its appearance in this institutional setting. These villages would subsequently become an essential and inevitable feature of all exhibitions, whether colonial, international, universal or regional. Indeed, from the 1890s until the beginning of the Second World War, the number of exhibitions would increase, in particular colonial exhibitions. In almost every one, a 'negro', 'Indo-Chinese', 'Arab' or 'Kanak village' would be on offer to the curious eye of the visitor. Simultaneously, 'negro' then 'black' then 'Senegalese' villages (the interesting semantic shift took place following the First

World War) were turned into independent travelling attractions in the French regions, throughout Europe, and in the United States. Often, shows would succeed each other, year after year, as four or five distinct troupes worked their way between the major regional exhibitions, such as Amiens, Angers, Nantes, Reims, Le Mans, Nice, Clermont-Ferrand, Lyon, Lille, Nogent and Orléans, and the chief European cities, such as Hamburg, Anvers, Barcelona, London, Berlin and Milan, where as many as two to three hundred thousand visitors would attend each exhibition. Here, the decors were more 'ethnographic', and the 'villages' resembled card and paste sets worthy of contemporary Hollywood productions on Darkest Africa, anticipating an extremely rich crop of films on the theme in both Europe and the United States. Gradually, the fantastical reconstructions of 'native dances'[6] and famous historic episodes (the capture of Samory seems to have been a great morale booster) became less common.

Clearly, a new situation was emerging, where the 'savage' became peaceful (once again) and cooperative, mirroring the French Empire, which, on the eve of the First World War, was officially portrayed as completely and permanently under control. This was, in fact, the moment at which the limits of the Empire were finally set. Expansion was replaced by the 'civilizing mission', whose discourse was passionately defended by the colonial exhibitions. The soldier was succeeded by the administrator. Under the beneficent influence of the French Enlightenment, followed by a colonizing French Republic, 'natives' were put firmly back at the bottom of the scale of civilizations, while racist themes were cloaked in euphemism.

The 'negro' or 'black villages' were the sanitized successors to the human zoos of the preceding period, and the violently humiliating vision of the zoos was replaced by a less brutal objectification of the colonized peoples, as their image was re-orchestrated to respond to a new set of audience expectations. Certainly, the colonized native remained an inferior being, but he was tamed (as a step on the road to colonial redemption), and was now found to be possessed of a potential for evolutionary improvement, which justified the colonial act. This new perception of the 'native Other' would reach its peak at the 1931 Vincennes Exposition Coloniale Internationale, which, covering hundreds of hectares, was the most highly developed form of the human zoo, under the guise of colonial achievement and republican sainthood.

This exploration of some of the complex interdependences between the colonial endeavour, scientific movements and the visual appropriation of 'different' cultures in the context of ethnographic exhibitions and native villages allows us to understand to what extent those peoples put on show in the West were objectivized, decontextualized and racialized, stranded in an eternal backwater which justified the 'civilizing mission' of the colonizer. Human zoos were a new and essential cultural phenomenon, both in their vast scale, and in their contribution to our understanding of how the relationship with the Other was constructed in colonial France and across Europe. In fact, most archetypes generated by the human zoos can be said to represent the root of a collective unconscious (whose many faces change over time), which urgently needs to be understood today (Blanchard and Bancel 1998b). A century later, these types are still operative in different forms (cinema, television, the print media, stereotypes of the Other).

Human zoos can be seen as the crucial link between a nineteenth century that created the theory of the hierarchy of races and a twentieth century that put it into practice, from the heights of colonial empire to today's so-called 'war of civilizations'. This requires an examination of the manner in which racializing Western discourses were constructed and how and where they spread. This, in our view, is the most important aspect of human zoos: they reveal the basis on which we construct the Other.

Notes

1 The initial summary article on human zoos appeared in *Le Monde diplomatique* in Summer 2000 (Bancel, Blanchard and Lemaire 2000), while the study of their impact is to be found in a special issue of the same publication 'Polémiques sur l'histoire coloniale' (Blanchard, Bancel and Lemaire 2001).

2 This conference, 'Zoos Humains. Corps exotiques, corps enfermés, corps mesurés' [Human Zoos. Exotic Bodies, Incarcerated Bodies, Measured Bodies], brought together about fifty international specialists in the fields of colonial history and imagination, the representation of the Other, and the history of the social sciences.

3 Across Europe and in the United States, individuals, families and small troupes had formed exhibits from the beginning of the nineteenth century, appearing in fairs, circuses, other zoos, and also in touring shows such as those in Germany and Switzerland (Brändle 1995; see also the many contributions to the Marseille conference). They were not yet linked to the colonial project, or to the assertion of a structured racial discourse. They nevertheless foreshadowed later developments which would continue through the last third of the nineteenth century.

4 Not all the 'imported' groups had an exclusive and unique status. The Fuegians, for example, appear to have been 'transported' as genuine zoological specimens, whereas the 'Gauchos', who were closer to contracted artistes, were fully aware of the masquerade they were putting on for visitors.

5 See Blanchard, Blanchoin et al, 1996, in particular the articles by Beaugé on
   images and types; Coutancier and Barthe on the representation of the Other
   in the Paris Zoological Gardens; Collomb on photography; Dauphiné on the
   Kanaks, and Blanchard and Blanchoin on the idea of races in the French colonial
   imagination.
6 Some idea of these can be gleaned from the famous film, made by a Lumière
   operator in Lyon in 1897, of an Ashanti procession which had been reconstructed for the spectators and the camera.

8

Human Zoos: The 'Savage' and the Anthropologist

GILLES BOËTSCH AND YANN ARDAGNA

How were scientists involved in human zoos? Or, put another way, how, in that long process of the staging of the Other, did the world of science influence the various modes of display from the beginning of the nineteenth century onwards? In 1817, Cuvier published his famous article on the Hottentot Venus in the third volume of *Mémoires du Muséum* (Cuvier 1817). Saartjie (Sarah Baartman) was certainly not the first human to be put on show for her race, as the conquistadors had brought back American 'savages' and the French explorer Bougainville had returned with a Tahitian in 1769, but she was one of the first to be displayed from the dual perspectives of entertainment and scientific enquiry which led to the development of human zoos in their late nineteenth-century form. The presence of the Hottentot Venus allowed scientists to make direct observations of a living 'specimen', rather than have to depend solely on written texts of varying degrees of seriousness and on travellers' tales. Some years before Saartjie's arrival, a young Chinese man, Tchong-A-Sam, had been brought back from China and observed by the members of a learned society in 1800. This Society for the Observation of Mankind declared itself unable to ignore the 'public furore which greeted the presence in Paris of a Chinaman. It naturally felt the need, on such an occasion, to collect invaluable materials in order to further knowledge of a people that religiously held itself apart from the rest of the universe' (Jauffret and Leblond 1978 [1800]).

Although the West did not have a monopoly on the exhibition of other races (this also occurred in Egypt and Japan), the practice corresponded to a desire to create a shared body of knowledge, which at first focused on the natural world. This drive for knowledge developed during the Enlightenment (Thomson 1987). From the eighteenth century, following the work of Linnaeus on the classification of species, Western science threw itself into the meticulous study and identification of the different physical characteristics of the world's peoples. It was a major undertaking, and we can recall the difficulty experienced by European travellers in drawing the physical characteristics of native Americans which would distinguish them visually from their European counterparts. Lestringant (1995), studying the case of the Tupi, has demonstrated that the first physical and cultural representations by those such as André Thevet (1557) and Antoine Jacquard (Hamy 1907) followed a process of formalization based on the epistemological and aesthetic structures of the classical European model. In constructing bodies and poses according to classical norms, the travellers and artists of the time had wanted to reveal a primitive humanity which, nevertheless, already possessed the specific attributes of what Europeans of that period considered humanity to be. By contrast, the bodies of Africans were easily distinguished in Western art from ancient Egyptian and Greek civilizations onwards (Vercoutter et al 1976; Bucher 1977) through the combined use of black pigment and exaggerated physical characteristics.

It was Buffon, in his *Histoire naturelle* (1792 [1749]), who began a systematic description of the peoples of the earth drawn from travellers' narratives. Those who succeeded him abandoned such writings, as sources and built up increasingly complex and sophisticated systems of measurement which required direct contact with subjects. While Guérando was interested more in the 'customs' than the morphology of other races (Guérando 1978 [1800]), Cuvier suggested bringing back portraits and anatomical parts, mainly heads, from overseas. To this end, he recorded a technique to preserve the latter: 'boil the bones in a solution of soda or caustic potassium to strip them of their meat. This will take several hours. Sailors, to whom these operations appear barbarous, may not wish them to be carried out on board their vessels; but on an expedition whose goal is the advancement of science, the leaders should allow themselves to be governed by reason alone' (Cuvier 1978 [1800]). Dumoutier, who was on the scientific expedition of the *Astrolabe* and *La Zélée* which left Toulon for the southern seas under the leadership of Jules Dumont d'Urville on 7 September 1837, intended to put together a collection of 'phrenological' casts taken from the indigenous populations he encountered (Ackernecht 1956). The subject enthused the scientific world, which saw in it a means to continue and rationalize the earlier cabinets of curiosities.

The Naturalization of Man

This new scientific idea, which depended on the direct observation of cultural practices or of skeletons, was part of a process involving the naturalization of the human being. Previously, for theological reasons, man could not be studied using the scientific methods applied to other living beings (anatomical dissection, for example), but he now became an object of science. Beginning with the epistemological shift introduced by Linnaeus, who classified mankind with the animals, anthropology would little by little acquire the status of a scientific discipline, whose principle objects of study were the 'races' of the ancient and modern worlds.

At the beginning of the nineteenth century, J. F. Blumenbach, whose museum contained the most complete series of racially classified skulls in the world, marked a new development by integrating the practice of collecting into anthropology. In addition to the results obtained through the study of his specimens, Blumenbach collected written works on the 'races of man', which allowed him to note a great variety of observable 'types' in the human species. His classification of taxons began with the form of the skull, followed by the colour of the hair, the skin and the iris. Craniology became craniometry (study = measurement) and anthropology became human zoology. Blumenbach, in his treatise *De l'unité du genre humain et de ses variétés* [On the unity of the human type and on its varieties (1804 [1795]), advocated the vertical rule which, by viewing the head from above, allowed the measurement of the width of the skull and the angle of the profile.

From these beginnings, anthropology acquired a new position, becoming a discipline which divided humanity into classified subsections (taxons) which in turn allowed the development of sub-groups from which new disciplines emerged. The globalizing anthropology of Buffon, characterized as synthetic by Sonini in his introduction to the new edition of Buffon's works published in 1801, was replaced by an anthropology which was more analytical and more fragmented. The development of Camper and Blumenbach's approaches (craniometry and craniology) marked the appearance of a new era in the discipline. From now on, the human being would no longer be understood as a whole, but would be dissected into a series of morphological variables. Anthropology moved towards the questions and the methodologies of the emerging field of comparative anatomy (going back to Tyson [1699]), giving new life to an already existing racist ethnocentrism, replacing its cultural underpinning with biological explanation. The concept of difference, and hence inferiority, would no longer be a reflection of cultural developments, fast or slow, but would instead draw on biological distinctions that set out boundaries which could not be crossed. Gould (1996 [1981]) has already asked whether it was the introduction of deductive scientific methods which made it possible to construct a new racial classification system, or whether, on the contrary, it was the concept of classification which shaped scientific questions in such a way that they reinforced pre-established conclusions. Although Morton (1844) also made use of the concept of collection (which he applied in particular to the study of the peoples of ancient Egypt), his prejudices in favour of 'white supremacy' would nevertheless lead him to draw different conclusions from those of Blumenbach, and would feed the quarrel between the supporters of the theories of monogenesis and polygenesis.

It was in the context of the development of craniology that the French Imperial Museum of Natural History published, in 1860, the fifth edition of its *Instructions* for travellers and employees in the colonies on 'how to collect, preserve and expedite objects of natural history' (MIHN 1860). In the section on anthropology, it was proposed that, where possible, casts of living humans should be made. If this was not possible, then photographs should be taken. The role of the latter in anthropology had already been advocated by Ernest Conducré in an article which appeared in *La Lumière*, promoting the concept of the collection of anthropological photographs (1858). These 'Instructions for travellers' followed those of Guérando and Cuvier at the beginning of the nineteenth century, and would in turn be taken up by Broca in his *Instructions générales pour les recherches anthropologiques à faire sur le vivant* [General instructions for anthropological research on living subjects] (1879 [1865]).

The knowledge of the morphology of other races thus necessitated travel and periods spent in the field. But the arrival in Europe of the Chinese man Tchong-A-Sam and, above all, of the Hottentot Venus, had given access to unhoped-for sources of information and a new way to practise physical anthropology. These called for an opportunist approach founded on Comte's positivist perception of science. Such an approach would take advantage of the presence of such 'exotic' individuals to study them from an anthropological perspective, and was proposed by Bertillon in his book *Les Races sauvages* (1882), illustrated by an engraved frontispiece showing a 'group of Galibi in the Paris zoological gardens'.

Following Fitz-Roy's early attempt to show the 'individual-as-specimen' to the public in London between 1829 and 1831, using a group of four Fuegians (Corra 1882), ethnic shows in zoos, exhibitions, public parks and circuses grew in significant numbers from the mid-nineteenth century. Anthropologists turned them into a centre of study, a real laboratory, which gave rise to the most diverse anthropological observations. The first scientific research to be published by the Anthropological Society of Paris was that of Clémence Royer (1873), concerning a hirsute Russian and his son who were on show at Barnum's circus. Later research compared dwarves and pygmies (Bloch 1909) and discussed the Tuareg (Atgier 1909). Here, difference was constructed on a certain sort of strangeness: the Other – in order to be an object of public interest and curiosity – also needed to have the potential to be strange (Blanchard 1909; Forbin 1909). 'Primitive' peoples could, and must, either perform disturbing practices, such as cannibalism, or have suspicious physical characteristics which were exploited by romantic literature (Malchow 1993).

In 1877, Mazard wrote of the presence at the Paris Zoological Gardens[1] (the Jardin d'Acclimatation), of 'a group of Nubians who arrived accompanied by a group of animals. A committee was appointed to study these individuals, composed of Messrs Bordier, Dally, Girard de Rialle and Mazard' (SAP 1877a: 476). The committee began its work in mid-July and completed it in mid-October of the same year (SAP 1877b: 520). Again in 1877, a committee including Bordier, Broca, Dally, Girard de Rialle, Mazard and Topinard gave its attention to six Eskimos (Inuit) in the Zoological Gardens (Bordier 1877a; 1877b). In addition to an anthropometric description of the subjects and general reflections on their diet, a complementary study on breast milk was carried out (Coudereau 1877). In 1883, Ernest Chantre took the anthropometric measurements of five Zulus who had arrived in Lyon, and bought from them weapons and utensils, which he compared with similar objects from the Zambezi (Chantre 1884). In 1895, during the Sudanese exhibition on the Champ de Mars, Barbier, director of the exhibition, invited 350 'negroes' on show, and even offered three season tickets to those members of the society who wished to pursue their researches there (SAP 1895: 479).

These anthropological and ethnographic observations were published regularly in the scientific journals of the time (*La Nature, Bulletin de la Société d'anthropologie de Paris* and *Revue d'anthropologie*). In total, more than eighty articles were published, based on observations made almost exclusively in Paris during ethnographic exhibitions from 1873 to 1909. Paradoxically, only a minority of the 'races' who were put on show and studied in the Jardin d'Acclimatation were from the French Empire.[2] Beyond the spectacle which these exhibits offered the public, the anthropologists were careful, at least at first, to use them both as sources for the analysis of the 'races' and as a teaching tool for members of the public interested in anthropology. Topinard, Secretary General of the Société d'Anthropologie de Paris, noted in an article on the

'Races of Man' published in *La Nature* in 1888, that for 'about fifteen years, the public has developed a taste for exhibitions of savage races', in particular for those which displayed 'the last representatives of a dying age, on whom our grandchildren will no longer be able to gaze' (Topinard 1888b).

Topinard was discussing Australian Aboriginals, who followed Lapps (Sami), Fuegians, 'Nubians' and other 'exotic' peoples brought to the Paris Zoological Gardens by their director, Geoffroy Saint-Hilaire. Topinard viewed such exhibits as more than just the opportunity to study specimens directly. He saw them, above all, as a facility for the collection of precious facts on 'races' destined for extinction, thereby adopting a zoological perspective. He had already made similar comments on the Hottentots, explaining that their humanity differed from that of Europeans in that they were not capable of adapting to the 'new conditions posed by our civilization' (1888a). Last, in a climate of competition between different 'types' of society (archaic and civilized), he saw no possibility that the cultural structures of so-called less developed peoples might be transformed, instead predicting the radical disappearance of 'races' he identified as incapable of change.

Nadaillac would take this further by integrating the concepts of superiority and inferiority: 'The disappearance of the inferior races when confronted by the superior races is a fact recorded by history,' he wrote on the subject of 'Red Indians' (1891). As proof, anthropologists such as Hamy recreated prehistoric scenes at the Paris Universal Exhibition of 1889 which were intended to demonstrate the distance between the dawn of humanity and contemporary civilization following a linear developmental time-line. The exotic peoples of the late nineteenth century were, in the event, shown to share their humanity with European ancestors whose 'entire appearance [...] points to a still savage and barbarous race' (Nadaillac 1889).

The relationship between type, collection and exhibition was one which was developed beyond the limits of anthropology. It was a central feature of the Western classification of natural objects. To classify living beings was to seek to give a meaning to nature and to reveal its underlying organization. The concept of the zoological garden, developing from the cabinets of curiosities favoured by eighteenth-century scholars, allowed the display of a sample of the diverse inhabitants of the animal kingdom. From the anthropological point of view, the exhibition of 'exotic', 'savage', 'cannibalistic', dwarf and 'monstrous' humans was a demonstration of the curiosities, freaks and extreme limits of human nature, and one which reassured the majority of their own normality.

The exhibits of beings with strange bodies in reconstructed scenes of 'savage life' provide a good illustration of Western society's relationship with the world around it. Zoological gardens, like colonial exhibitions, set out to represent alien peoples and their living conditions as faithfully as possible. Colonial exhibitions soon became places of entertainment, where spectators would visit an archetypical zoo in which natives represented the species (the biocenose) and the pavilions represented the habitat (the biotope).

The Image of the Other

In the work of physical anthropologists, photography was not systematically employed in the same way as metric measurement, and it is still frowned on by many ethnologists, who consider it to be an invasion of personal space (Sontag 1973). However, anthropologists made use of photography in order to demonstrate the unquantifiable. This included not only expressions but also the unsayable and the unbelievable – those features of a culture which cannot be reduced to statistical tables. It was, moreover, this last step which met with the greatest success by transforming ethnological documents into images accessible to the general public. Photographs thus took over from engravings as the means to show primitive and savage humans, as yet unaffected by the 'virtues' of civilization, in the most unusual and strangest circumstances. Among these was, of course, the Hottentot Venus, but also those with self-inflicted bodily deformations (black African women with lip plates), decorations (scars and tattoos), bloody cultural practices (cannibalism, ritual crimes), and bodily deformations brought about by illness such as leprosy or amoebiasis. In this area, ethnologists aspired to become ethnographers as photography followed engraving in providing a visual inventory of objects. But even in this, the spectacular, the strange and the primitive triumphed over the banal and the local (Boëtsch and Ferrié 1997). We shall not expand here on the role of photography in the construction of categories, but the photographic collection can, through its arrangement, constitute an imaginary zoo. Apart from this, ethnographic and colonial exhibitions would in any case be fruitful hunting grounds for those seeking to photograph the 'primitive' (Dias 1994), as demonstrated by the work of Pierre Petit, Gustave Le Bon, and Prince Roland Bonaparte.

The image which Europeans, in particular the French, had of the inhabitants of their colonial empires would be changed by the events which took place between the height of colonial conquest and the

First World War. Indeed, Colonel Mangin's *Force noire* – in particular the participation of this force in the various operations suppressing the colonized countries of Africa, and the use of African troops on European territory in the First World War – would, for a time, change French perceptions of the inhabitants of their empire. The Senegal Rifles and Algerian Spahis would contribute to the construction of the colonial project, in which naturalist classification gave way to a far more pragmatic arrangement of peoples. Colonial exhibitions after the conflict would offer a new reading of the populations of the empire.

Thus, at the Marseille National Colonial Exposition of 1922, 'races' of the empire would disappear, to be replaced by soldiers of the empire. Beauregard in his work on the French Colonial Office (1922) reminds us that 'when the country was threatened, it was eight hundred thousand Frenchmen of colour who came, from their sunny lands, to bleed, suffer, and die with us in the mud of the Somme and Verdun'. At this exhibition, a fraternity born of bloodshed would offer a singular collection of ethnic military 'types' from the pencil of E. Burnand – for example, the Martiniquan gunner, the Algerian Spahi, the Moroccan rifleman, the Kabyle and Tunisian auxiliaries, and the Madagascan rifleman. Classification was still in operation, but it had become a double-entry system, responding to a logic of efficiency rather than of knowledge. Later, and even under the Vichy regime (Blanchard and Boëtsch 1994), the subjects of the empire would no longer be presented in the form of a human bestiary, but as military or economic agents who were gradually becoming indispensable to economic and social development and must be recognized as such (Dehon 1945).

Although Western cultures do not have a monopoly on the desire to know the Other, Western science made a speciality of it. The expansion of European colonial empires was one of the decisive factors in the creation of touring anthropological and ethnic exhibitions. Popular success led to their development (Schneider 1977), consolidating stereotypical views of the subjects. The thirst for knowledge, as much as a desire for entertainment, was fulfilled by the objectification of the Other in stereotyped form, first as a product of nature and later as the expression of a different culture. The study of the Other's body was achieved by its visualization, which needed to be standardized by reductionist methods, such as measurement, or the creation of images. But neither method could teach us about the Other, and such paths to knowledge set in place by Western science were incapable of explaining the complexity of difference. The description of the Other through a series of measurements, or the fixing of his or her image on a photograph, cannot help us to know him or her. It can, however, teach us much about ourselves, and it is this practice which defines our relationship with the world.

The consequences of these various ethnographic and colonial exhibitions are not, however, limited to questions of epistemology. Indeed, the construction of formal frameworks in which to display non-Europeans, which were more closely related to the field of zoology than to the world of entertainment (as occurred, for example, in the exhibitions of the Cossacks (Tissandier 1889a) and the inhabitants of the Far East (Laloy 1900)) inevitably had a negative effect on the public imagination. The exhibition of men, with animals or alone, in locations usually reserved for animals, such as zoological gardens, is hardly an anodyne act. And their presentation as specimens of un-evolved and uneducable 'races' played a major part in laying down the solid foundations of a popular racism which is almost as strong as ever in twenty-first century society.

Notes

1 On the beginning of the activities at the zoological gardens in Paris, see Blanchard, Bancel and Lemaire, and Schneider, in this volume.
2 Among these, we find articles on Galibi (Dally 1882; Capitan 1882; Girard de Rialle 1882; Manouvrier 1882), Kanaks (Moncelon 1885), Somalis (Bonaparte 1890), Dahomeans (Foa 1891; Zaborowski 1893; Regnault 1893; Binet 1900), Caribbeans (Coudereau 1892), Senegalese (Regnault 1895; Collignon 1896a), Madagascans (Deniker 1896; Collignon 1896b; Deniker and Collignon 1897), and finally, Tuareg (Deniker 1907; Atgier 1909). Only 18 articles out of the total of around 80 are on these racial groups.

9

The Cinema as Zoo-keeper

ÉRIC DEROO

As a fishmonger in Hamburg in 1840, Hagenbeck formed a personal collection of the rare animals – parrots, monkeys, seals – which the sailors and fishermen with whom he did business became accustomed to selling him. His passion expanded, and over time buildings were adapted to house the specimens he supplied to zoos, circuses, scientists and collectors. When his son, Carl, took over, the business moved on to a professional and industrial footing.[1] Carl guessed that the exhibition of humans would be more profitable than that of animals:

> it was the Laplanders who began it, one of my agents having succeeding in bringing a family of them to Hamburg. [...] They arrived towards the middle of September 1874 with about thirty reindeer. From the first I could tell that this would be a profitable venture. [...] The sight of the six members of the Lapp family drew thousands of curious spectators. This show was a triumph. [...] I willingly admit that the idea did not spring entirely from my own brain, but was suggested to me in a letter received in 1874 from my old friend the animal painter Heinrich Leuteman, who was replying to a letter of mine where I told him that I was thinking of importing a herd of reindeer. He wrote to me that it would be far more interesting if I invited a family of Laplanders to accompany them. (Hagenbeck 1951: 60–61)

The show was an immediate popular success and Hagenbeck soon employed representatives throughout the world to send dromedaries and Bedouins, elephants and Sinhalese, walruses and Eskimos (Inuit) back to Hamburg. 'The first trouble was in Copenhagen [...] where heads were shaken, and there was an outright refusal to participate in the trafficking of humans.' The intervention of well-known figures such as Professor Virchow from Berlin was necessary before 'Jacobsen could finally set out for Greenland. He managed to bring with him a group of pure-bred Eskimos, men, women and children, along with an ethnographical collection [...] sleigh dogs, household utensils, tents' (Hagenbeck 1951: 68–69).

A pragmatic showman, Carl Hagenbeck understood (like Barnum) that, in order to attract a public jaded by fairground monsters, it was necessary to reconstruct, whether in zoological enclosures or on the circus stage, scenes of 'exotic' life where, by means of a number of 'tableaux vivants', animals and humans would play their respective roles as 'naturals' before an audience 'avid for knowledge'. Local flora was symbolized by a few shrubs, palm trees, cactuses or rare plants; primitive life was represented by a pond and a few huts, among which a family with women and children would play. Pink flamingos suggested an Edenic harmony, while bears, tigers or lions paced their cages close by to suggest danger. 'In a set constructed rather like that of a theatre (but with plaster and wire mesh), and which measured over seven hundred metres in width, an authentic Somali village had been built, decorated with palm trees and various plants. Animals were fed here [...] You could watch here the assault of the slave dealers on this peaceful village' (1951: 80–81). The public rushed to see all the shows: 'In short, the Kalmyk exhibition had such a stunning success that it was necessary to repeat it in 1884. While the Parisian crowds were immense, those in Berlin surpassed anything I had seen until then. I still remember today the first telegram I received on the subject: So far we have received about eighty thousand visitors. Vast crowds. Order maintained by mounted police and foot patrols [...]. By the end of the evening, the number of visitors to the Berlin zoo reached ninety-three thousand' (1951: 78).

More Profit in Humans than Animals

From this time on, Hagenbeck dealt with the largest zoos and circuses in the world. From the United States to Great Britain, from Paris to Berlin, from Russia to Italy, he hired out troupes recruited at great expense from Asia, Africa and the North Pole who, on each appearance, drew hundreds of thousands of visitors. Banquets were held for artists, journalists and scientists, confirming his exceptional business sense and, more importantly, allowing his talents as a juggler to be legitimized through political and scientific discourse at a time when colonial conquests were growing rapidly: 'On some Sundays it [a Sinhalese troupe] received more than half a million visitors. The learned gentleman [Geoffroy Saint-Hilaire, director of the Paris Zoological Gardens] [...], with unparalleled honesty and modesty, replied that he merited only some of the compliments paid to him, and that they should mostly go to M. Carl Hagenbeck, who had prepared and staged this anthropozoological exhibition' (1951: 59–60).

The term 'anthropozoological', for the benefit of sceptics, was fully employed and authenticated at the banquet, and was adopted by the press, as well as by Hagenbeck in his memoirs. Convinced, like all Europeans, by a 'zoological view of human history in which cultural progress is the direct reflection of biological abilities' (Boëtsch and Savarèse 1999), Carl Hagenbeck and his customers created backdrops and scenarios for a staging of the Other which would shape most subsequent writings and performances, as well as the imaginary constructs which would be developed by photographers and film-makers with the growth of available techniques.

The 'reality show' was born. Strengthened by the Western hegemony, the commercial dealings of the end of the nineteenth century allowed the export of Lapps (Sami), 'Nubians', Eskimos (Inuit), Somalis, Kalmyks, Hindus, Sinhalese, Hottentots, Ashanti, Fuegians, Sudanese, Indians, elephants, tigers, dromedaries and zebras, while, simultaneously, the rationalist ideology of triumphant industry was developing. At the heart of this normative construct lay a formidable invention: that of photography. As both the subject and the object of a reality perceived as scientific, photography asserted itself as a tool for reproduction. Through postcards and, later, film, images became ideal vehicles for a process of popularization. The vast majority of Europeans and Americans, who were barely literate, would discover new worlds through the reproduction of the image. While these images allowed the discovery of the Other, they also allowed readers and viewers to become aware of their own status as observers.

Predetermined by a conquering ideology and restricted technical resources, the codes of reading in operation were so reduced and reductive that they were invalid from the outset. By putting a 'native' family and their animals in front of a few palm trees and rocks, Carl Hagenbeck and his imitators invented and imposed conditions on image-making which would be immediately adopted by film-makers. And it was quite natural after the First World War for Hagenbeck's business, which had begun in the zoos, to shift gradually towards cinema, at first making silent movies, soon followed by talkies. He acknowledged that the era of zoos was past, while that of cinema was beginning, with himself as one of its most active promoters. In this context, it is clear that the paths of human exhibitions and the cinema would cross, and the two genres would enter into dialogue and influence each other before fusing.

Cinema at the Zoo

The proof of this is to be found in the many early films in the history of world cinema which staged 'native' shows. For example, in 1894, at the Edison Studios (founded by the inventor of the Kinetoscope), W. K. L. Dickson made two 30-second films of Native Americans (Jordan 1992). *Indian War Council* and *Sioux Ghost Dance* were, in fact, performed by members of William F. Cody's Wild West show, then touring with his highly successful Wild West Rocky Mountain and Prairie Exhibition. Also in 1894, while in Paris, Antoine Lumière bought a Kinetoscope. In their Lyon studio, his sons Auguste and Louis would work to perfect the device while, for his part, Étienne-Jules Marey was improving his chronophotograph. The following year, Félix L. Régnault, who was a doctor and a member of the Société d'Anthropologie de Paris, created a series of 'ethnic chromophotographs' in his studio for the 1895 Champs de Mars Exhibition, entitled 'Wolof Potter' (two minutes), 'Oulof' and 'Peul'.

On 28 December 1895 the first public showing of the Lumière Cinematograph took place (Aubert and Séguin 1996). The commercial development of the machine rapidly led to an extraordinary craze. This enthusiasm, coupled with the repeated success of the exhibitions in the Paris Jardin d'Acclimatation, led the Lumière brothers to make some of their earliest films on ethnic subjects. In 1896, *Baignade de nègres* (Negroes swimming) was filmed there, and the Ashanti village at the Lyon exhibition of the following year was also filmed by them.

Of the 1,428 films produced by the Lumière brothers, 1,408 have been found and restored, among which 900 have been taken from the original nitrate negatives. About 30 are on European anthropozoo-logical topics. Nearly 100 others were filmed in the French colonies (Indochina, the French Antilles, and French North Africa, with the exception of Morocco) but not in sub-Saharan Africa. Their themes are varied (official visits, army, boats, docks, roads) and conform to stereo-types, providing such offerings as 'an Annamite village, fights, a burial, celebrations and various scenes and types'. The same is true of more than 50 'generic shots' (dances, rituals, acrobats, children) filmed in Japan, Egypt, and North and South America. A single film could be presented with more than one title and the films were constructed from various montages of the same elements (the average length was under 1 minute), so it is hard to establish a precise overview of these materials and, in particular, to gain a sense of what the catalogue's customers and their spectators thought of them. At first the brothers' own films were rented out, along with projection equipment, to franchise-holders, and appeared in catalogue form in several languages up to 1907. From this date, faced with competition from firms such as Pathé and Gaumont, from entrepreneurs such as Albert Kahn, and from individuals such as Eugène Pirou, the Lumière company decided to concentrate exclusively on the production of film stock and on the invention and improvement of technical procedures.

Classified alphabetically under 'General Scenes', 'Various Shots', *Baignade de nègres*, which is number 12 in the catalogue, is accompanied by a synopsis: 'Together, several negroes throw themselves into the water, dive, come back to the surface, etc.'. It appears between *Arrival of a Train in a Station* and *Swings*. A few lines later, after *Cat's Lunch*, comes *Javanese Jugglers*, followed by *Little Brother and Sister*. Number 441 has the general heading *Ashanti Negroes* and under this we find: *Sword Dances I and II, Young Girls' Dance, Women's Dance, Witch-Doctor's Dance, Tribal Procession, Piccaninnies' Meals I and II, A Piccaninny's Toilette I and II, Piccaninnies at Play, Piccaninnies at School, Men's Dance, Dance Lesson, Piccaninnies Swimming*. A note which follows the entry remarks: 'These shots were taken in an Ashanti village at the Lyon Exhibition. All these shots are very interesting, their titles are self-explanatory'.

Meanwhile, in August 1896 at the Crystal Palace in London, a group of 'Javanese' were filmed. This group were presented on the European mainland as Sinhalese, and the film appeared in the British distributors' catalogues under the title *Burmese Dance*, then, variously, as *Japanese Dancers, Japanese Jugglers*, and *Japanese Wrestlers*. The lack of precise identification and the territorial appropriations carried out by the various countries which saw the show, whether live or filmed, affected perceptions of the group. With colonial expansion and the progress made in techniques of filming, from the beginning of the twentieth century, the same operators moved out from the zoos to film 'on location'.

The Question of the Exotic

Linking the exploration and exploitation of the conquered areas, almost all films, whether they were described as documentaries, as novelized documentaries or, later, as fictions and major reportage (Leprohon 1945), followed the same constructs and presuppositions as the fairground and zoological exhibitions had.[2] Leprohon's work provides what amounts to a codification of this collection of rules, which had appeared in many earlier works of colonial propaganda. Cinema acted as an essential vehicle for the 'civilizing mission'. It allowed the colonizers to reflect on the results of their efforts, while allowing the colonized nations to recognize the extent of the power of their occupiers: 'A clear conclusion emerges from the above facts and ideas: the immediate creation of a new method of colonization and colonial propaganda through the use of colonizing cinema' (Madieu 1916: 26).

Although it was controlled, cinema production nevertheless aroused the public's interest. This was not simply vulgar curiosity: 'Cinematography is to be placed among the plastic arts [...] it follows the three great artistic principles of milieu, race and moment' (1916: 11).[3] With regard to the filming of foreign materials, Leprohon used two of these elements as a measure of the 'exotic': 'Once a film director requires that a distant country should provide not only the setting but also the actors for his film, we could say that his work falls into the category of exotic film' (Leprohon 1945: 268), and he was careful to emphasize that 'in France [...] the question of the exotic is a colonial question' (1945: 114).

He developed a line of argument which can be summed up in a series of aphorisms: if the exotic is founded on distance, then distant cultures which are considered to be strange (unknown and mysterious, non-evolving) are primitive. They are therefore unchangeable. And it is around this principle of immutability that filmic writing developed. Abdelkader Benali, in his book *Le Cinéma colonial au Maghreb* [Colonial Cinema in North Africa] provides a detailed analysis of the mechanics of this in relation to the film *Le Désir* (1928): 'The degree of exoticism is measured by the absence of spatial and temporal anchors. Corresponding to indefinite space we find the eternal nature of the practices of polygamy and the primitivism of those concerned' (Benali 1998: 137). From interchangeable troupes in the 'black' or 'Indian' shows to the absence of identification of the 'natives' in 1930s cinema, 'the image of the colonies transports the twentieth-century notion of the colonial (and its spectators with it) out of time' (Gilbert Meynier, quoted in Blanchard and Chatelier 1993: 25).

Photography and the cinema applied the Western concept that 'what is quantifiable is rational, and vice versa' to the field of the colonial exotic. Fixed in time, primitive man should, if he is to remain readable, provide only a minimum of information, constituting the 'essence of native life' (Leprohon 1945: 218).[4] A minimum of scenery (where emptiness expresses anticipation and danger); a minimum of costumes (reduced to loincloths and, even better, to nakedness[5] in Africa, Polynesia and Indochina); a minimum of action, which can be summarized as the survival relationships between man, fauna, and flora (the breastfeeding of children, meals, hunting); a minimum of religious material (magic, sorcery); a minimum, again, in the expression of joy (dance) or pain (brutal and violent death). For each of these stereotypes there was an appropriate frame and depth of field: wide, medium, close-up, forest, group, feet, paws, faces, muzzle.[6] The crowd (village or tribe) represented a spontaneity which was hard to control, and which was consequently menacing and savage. The individual only appeared as part of a larger ensemble: 'The Maghreban does not present himself, he merely represents' (Benali 1998: 183).

The Native as a Natural Actor

Any document which is successful in capturing the immutable thereby gains access to 'that great and useful truth: eternity'. The greater the immediacy of a scene, the more natural it is: 'the natural expresses beauty' (Leprohon 1945). To reinforce this belief, another commonly shared view is put forward, that the native is a natural actor. Marcel Griaule did not escape this assumption. In an interview about the film *Sous les masques noirs* [Under the black masks], he said: 'The shots were all taken direct from life, as in real newsreels. There is no need to ask the natives to re-enact anything, or even to rehearse. For them, everything is spontaneous, and if you load them down with details, they are lost' (1945: 185). In a move which converted lack of self-consciousness to lack of awareness, there emerged the cliché of the overgrown child and brave rifleman so dear to the colonial vision. In a self-reflexive loop, immutability led to the primitive, and the primitive to the child who, in turn, led to the natural, to beauty, to art (see Wastiau 2000) and, finally, to truth. For the expression of an intangible truth to spread, it must construct the primitive repeatedly.[7]

By intruding into 'uncivilized worlds', the movie camera, that tool of modernity, increased the rate at which they were disappearing. By fixing them on film, by archiving them, it allowed them, subsequently, to be tamed. 'It is important to capture what is about to disappear', proclaimed the colonial handbooks. 'Primitive peoples are very protective of their customs. The film-maker must, in most cases, steal the images which we see, employing cunning to calm their suspicions, not without risk' (Leprohon 1945: 103).

Without defence or protection, deprived of freedom of movement, the filmed object was already rendered inferior by the fact that he or she was condemned to disappear. In addition, the achievement of the cameraman who acted as an 'authentic witness' in filming a difficult or impenetrable subject provided further validation of its rarity. 'The image becomes a historical document' (1945: 97) because it bears witness to a lost situation. The guaranteed moral and financial success of the maker of the film led film-makers, scientists and their audiences to seek out new specimens from ever more distant lands to be captured on film, recorded, and historicized. The hunt for the scoop had begun.

This search thus opened up the physical and mental routes to the appropriation of the Other as effectively as empire-building expeditions.[8] By creating such an intermediate and experimental space (this was the space of French colonization, but also that of the American Far West, and of British India), cinematographic production carried within itself a fundamental contradiction. By 'taming' the subjects it filmed, the camera deflowered them, while lamenting their loss of virginity. This contradiction was itself soon scripted, creating nostalgia for a lost paradise by rearranging a journey across time, as Rousseau had done with the 'good Blacks' (Negroni 1992).

In Search of Paradise Lost, or Rousseau with the 'Good Blacks'

Western cinema acted out its own uncertainties by relying on the old drive to return to biblical sources. It projected the fear of its own disappearance, or self-destruction, on to the perpetually renewed image of the primitive. Confronted with the unexplainable, it pasted a realist world on to the 'exotic', which was built on theatrical codes inherited mainly from the eighteenth and nineteenth centuries: 'the most noble scenery is the least cluttered [...] a landscape is considered from an aesthetic point of view, it is the face which underlies the action, each country expressing its beauty, each race expressing its character' (Leprohon 1945: 296). Thus, humanity, in this case primitive humanity, was subjected to a dramatic fate. He polluted an innocent natural world and must either absent himself from it, or submit to it.[9]

This image of the intruder is, in fact, that of the white man. To escape from its ambiguities (their study would be left to so-called ethnographical and anthropological films) 1930s cinema, with the talkies now in full swing, created a new ad hoc character: that of the European misfit.[10] The native was relegated to supporting roles or to the status of enemy, enhancing the status of the new hero. Whether he was a Spanish legionary (Jean Gabin in Julien Duvivier's *La Bandera*, 1935) or a French crook (Jean Gabin, again, in Duvivier's *Pépé le Moko*, 1936), he personified both the urges of the 'primitive' and the culture of the *de-civilized* white man seeking salvation, caught between barbarity and redemption, between savagery and peace-bringing. Another even greater source of myth in France was Father Charles de Foucault, who inspired several films. Originally an aristocratic and debauched cavalry officer, he became an undercover explorer in Morocco, and then a wise man and religious hermit at Tamanrasset. He was assassinated in 1916 by rebel Tuaregs apparently in the employ of the 'murdering Boches'.

So, from the first scenarios put together by Barnum and Hagenbeck to Hollywood blockbusters (the Vietnam of *Apocalypse Now, Rambo,* the East of *Indiana Jones,* the Gulf Wars, Afghanistan, and future war zones), the same 'savage'-producing machine is at work. Westerners have superposed on much of the world, not least on Africa, 'a socio-historical preconception at the heart of which he [European man] has managed to create, through his imagination, a harmony between the constraints of his social environment and the requirements of his own drives, which is the expression of a true freedom to re-mythologize' (Boëtsch and Savarèse 1999).

This imaginary construct increasingly manifests itself through its worst possible scripts. Having failed to find personal paradise, hell is guaranteed for others, generating in all spectator-actors the same compulsion to create and then denounce images of the 'savage'. From the 'Splendour of the Great Satan', and 'Elusive Evil', to 'Savage and Evil Terrorism', the enemy is finally identified: he is, in all likelihood, the Devil. This offers a return to the immutable for many zoos to come. We can count on the cinema to lead us there.

Notes

1 See Hilke Thode-Arora in this volume, and her other work.

2 One exception was René Ginet who, in *Angola Pulmann,* made in the 1930s, attempted to show an Africa face-to-face with 'colonial modernity'. The film was a total failure and was withdrawn by the distributors.

3 These positivist principles were those followed by Zola and the Naturalist movement in art.

4 'The picturesque, primitivism, cruelty, tradition, all preserved in the shade of the virgin forest, which appears to constitute an almost impenetrable barrier between certain tribes and the outside world' (Leprohon, 1945: 218).

5 Hébert's cult of the sculptural body, developed at the beginning of the century, was adopted in fictional and documentary films, for example, Marc Allégret and André Gide's *Voyage au Congo* (1927), of which Leprohon wrote: 'A beauty of attitudes, the magnificent bodies of the Blacks, certain rhythmic dances with the violence inherent to this race' (1945: 216). This cult limited representations of the African body to the stereotypes of the athlete, the dancer, and the powerful lover, which all reappear in modern fashions for suntans, body-building, and the silicon enhancements of lips, chests and breasts.

6 The stereotypes began with the film titles: *In the Heart of Wildest Africa* (1922),

Unknown and Wild Australia (1923), *The Mysterious Continent* (1924), *Black Magic* (1926), *Exotic Passions* (1928), *At Home with the Man-eaters* (1928), *At Home with the Drinkers of Blood*, *Untamed Africa*, *A Race's Awakening*, *Exotic Symphony, Facing the Wild Animals*, *At Home with the Cannibals*, *Bring Back the Survivors, Eat them Alive*, *Trader Horn* (1930), *Village of Sin*, *Demon of the Steppes*, *Bare-Breasted Island* (1931), *Dance of the Virgins*, *Black Skins*, *Country of Sorcery and Death*, *Demon Island* (1933), *Hell and the Virgin Forest* (1935), *Exotic Spell* (1942). This is just a selection from a long list which extends without a break to the most recent international productions.

7   This process is still at work, especially in the media's treatment of news stories.
8   After the era of 'invented wildness' (Blanchard, Deroo and Manceron 2001) came that of geographical normalization, followed by that of tourism. *Across the Indies* (1922), *Across the Sahara*, *The Black Cruise* (1926), *The Conquered Desert* (1928), *A Bird's Eye View of Africa* (1929), *A Stroll in French Equatorial Africa, Symphony of the Virgin Forest*, *Sahara, Fertile Land*, (1933), *The Great Caravan Sentries of the Empire* (1940) and, finally, absorbing the entire colonial space, *France and her Empire* (1940).
9   Although they have been mythologized by the critics, Robert Flaherty's films, such as *Nanook of the North* (1922), *Moana* (1926), and *Tabu* (with F. W. Murnau, 1931), should perhaps be examined from this perspective.
10 This had, of course, been preceded in the 1920s by the *Tarzan* series and other 'Lords of the Jungle'.

PART I I

Models of the Human Zoo:
Populations on Display

American Indians in Buffalo Bill's
Wild West

SAM MADDRA

This chapter will explore how Buffalo Bill's Wild West show fits into the wider context of the human zoo, noting both the similarities and differences for the American Indian performers, before going on to explore the motivations of the Indian performers in greater detail. Buffalo Bill's Wild West show gave its inaugural performance in May 1884 in St Louis, Missouri. The show became an enormous success as it travelled around the United States of America, depicting the 'heyday of the West as a glorious period, based around the adventures of cowboys and Indians' (Pegler and Rimmer 1999: 12). The use of actual participants involved in the 'conquest' of the American West remained one of the exhibition's main sources of appeal. Next to the title attraction of 'Buffalo Bill' (William F. Cody), the most popular stars were the American Indians, who from 1885 until well into the twentieth century were all Lakota Sioux, hired at the Pine Ridge Reservation in South Dakota.[1]

In 1887 the show travelled to Britain for its first foreign outing and was an immediate success. It pitched up at Earl's Court in London, alongside the American Exhibition that was part of Queen Victoria's Golden Jubilee celebrations. The great success of this venture encouraged the management to tour Continental Europe and return to Britain a number of times. While the primary purpose of the show was certainly commercial, the managers asserted that one of their main objectives was education, and this claim appears to have been reinforced by contemporary commentators. 'It is not only entertaining because of its novelty, but is paramountly instructive, and no one who has read the history of the Western States for the past quarter of a century can fail to appreciate the object lessons of the Wild West Show' (*The Evening Citizen* [Glasgow], 17 November 1891).

Undoubtedly the Native American performers were one of the main attractions of Buffalo Bill's Wild West show. Furthermore, they were fundamental to the story of the show, as they played the role of the hostiles that the intrepid scout, Buffalo Bill, had to overcome. Richard White noted that 'in Cody's story Indians were vital. The scout, a man distinguished by his "knowledge of Indians' habits and language, familiar with the hunt, and trustworthy in the hour of extremest danger", took on meaning only because he overcame Indians' (1994: 9). Therefore, to legitimize Cody's role in the conquest of America he needed the Indian performers.

Much as in human zoos, the use of these natives worked on a number of levels. They were presented as the exotic Other, the 'savage' who needed to be tamed, legitimizing the conquest of the Other, and in so doing legitimizing American 'manifest destiny'. This, in turn, helped define American identity, with added resonance when the exhibition was performing in Europe. Buffalo Bill's Wild West show depicted a new, brash and confident America. The United States was celebrating its dominion over the West, and at the same time a number of Americans were even contemplating extending this 'manifest destiny' to an overseas empire.

The American Indians were commonly perceived to be a race in decline, and the Wild West show played on this idea by promoting the exhibition as being one of the last chances for the public to see a way of life that was vanishing. The *Manchester Weekly Times* (24 July 1891) clearly bought into this concept when they described the performer Lone Bull as being a 'fine specimen of the decaying red man'. There is plenty of evidence that illustrates the European view of the Indians as the Other. Numerous newspapers noted the difference in appearance; for example a journalist for the Leeds *Evening Express* (20 June 1891) remarked, 'Nearly all the men have long hair [...] and this, with their bare faces, makes them difficult to tell, at a glance, from the women.' A number also made fanciful assertions about the origins of the Lakota language, with a journalist in *Science Siftings* (30 July 1892) claiming: 'It is strange, but an actual fact, that the Manadad (Dakota) Indians use a Welsh dialect.' The Lakota's use of the sign language was also of great interest, and reporting about it reveals a sense of cultural and racial superiority, contrasting 'savages' conversing with their hands with 'civilized' people communicating with an advanced verbal and written language. None of the white performers were ever scrutinized in the same way as the Indians, and while the Lakota were undoubtedly novel and thus intrinsically interesting, the detailed descriptions of the Other and the concentration on their differences bolstered the idea of the white race as being more 'civilized' and, therefore, superior.

However, while there were clear similarities with the human zoos of the period, there were also distinct differences. The American Indians in Buffalo Bill's Wild West show were not just passive natives to be scrutinized by a European audience. This was clearly part of the appeal of the Wild West show. Audiences were encouraged to arrive early in order to view the so-called Indian Village pitched outside the arena, where members of the public could wander through the tepees and view the Indians going about their business. Nevertheless, the Indians did have the freedom to remove themselves from this gaze, by withdrawing inside their tepees.

The Indians were viewed as a spectacle both inside and outside the performance space, and even on trips into local towns; whether attending church, courting local women, or simply shopping, they were under constant scrutiny. Within the arena they had very little, if any, say about their roles in the performance, which, on the whole depicted them as the hostiles who needed to be eradicated in order to conquer the North American continent. The show did, however, include a short piece that claimed to depict the lifestyle and customs of the Indians pre-contact, thereby acknowledging the history of the Indians prior to the arrival of Columbus. Interestingly, one performer, Black Elk, noted 'I enjoyed the Indian part of the shows that we put on [...] but I did not care much about the white people's parts' (Demallie 1984: 246).

All of the American Indians who toured with the show entered into a contract of employment with Buffalo Bill's Wild West. Such work was viewed by the Lakota as a prized job for a number of reasons. As well as the obvious monetary reward, there was independence from government control, the ability to supplement family incomes that were solely reliant upon inadequate government annuities, and the chance to do a job that came from their own knowledge. The veteran performer Black Heart stated: 'We were raised on horseback; that is the way we had to work. These men furnished us the same work we were raised to; that is the reason we want to work for these kind of men' (Maddra 2006: 79). On top of this there were the added benefits of travel and excitement as opposed to the monotony of reservation life where traditional work patterns, especially for men, had been all but eradicated.

Finally, travelling with Buffalo Bill's Wild West show gave the Indians access to a much wider audience to air their grievances through interviews with the press. This is most obvious with Sitting Bull's brief engagement while the show toured Canada in 1885, and was reportedly one of his motivations for joining the show. Other Indian performers had audiences with heads of state, including royalty, the Pope, and political leaders (see Moses 1996, Reddin 1999, Rosa and May 1989, and Russell 1973 [1960]).

It should be noted that not all such exhibitions could be classified in the same way, and there are numerous instances of Indians being abused or abandoned many hundreds, even thousands, of miles from their homes when shows, for instance, fell into bankruptcy. There were also deaths on the tours as the Indians were bought into contact with European diseases, and from accidents inside the arena (see Moses 1996: 87–98). Indeed, the concern over the treatment of the Indians, coupled with what Indian Reformers felt were overtly liberal freedoms in wicked continental cities, led to a ban on all Indian employment in Wild West shows in the summer of 1890.[2]

To examine the Indian performers' motivations in greater detail, the 1891–92 tour of Britain provides an informative case study. During the summer of 1890, Buffalo Bill's Wild West had been touring in Continental Europe, putting on performances in all the major towns and cities. There had been a number of deaths during the tour, but when a returning showman died in New York City from an untreated injury, a campaign was initiated to put an end to all American Indians performing in such shows. This campaign was backed and, indeed, primarily driven by a group of individuals who saw themselves as 'the friends of the Indians'. Their aim in the latter part of the nineteenth century was the total assimilation of the American Indians into the mainstream of American society. They considered the Indians a 'vanishing race' and argued that the only way to save them was to change their identity completely (Maddra 2006: 4–5).

Lobbying groups, such as the Indian Rights Association, were supported in this campaign by the US government's Office of Indian Affairs, which had implemented policies such as off-reservation Boarding Schools and the Dawes Allotment Act of 1887, and banned traditional religious and cultural practices, in the hope that such measures would create financially independent individuals, no longer dependent upon the US government. The idea of the Indian Reformers was to replace the traditional Indian tribal identity with one they perceived as more progressive, which embraced the main tenets of Protestant Republicanism (see Adams 1995). These Indian Reformers viewed Wild West shows as an impediment to their aims, as the exhibitions celebrated the traditional lifestyles and customs of the American Indians. The Secretary of the Interior, John Noble, was persuaded to ban any more Indians from joining such shows when, in addition to the deaths, reports of Indians drinking, gambling and womanizing in the towns and cities of

Europe were published in the American press.

The Indian performers were integral to Buffalo Bill's Wild West show, so Cody put his show into winter quarters and returned his Indian performers to America, in order to counter the accusations reported in the American press. These Indians met with the Acting Secretary of the Interior, Robert Belt, on 15 November 1890, and they argued for the ban to be lifted in order that they could continue to work for Cody. Black Heart maintained that the Indians should be allowed to work wherever they chose, as whites did. 'If Indian wants to work at any place and earn money, he wants to do so; white man got privilege to do same – any kind of work he wants.... When this show is ready to go again, I want to go with it' (Maddra 2006: 79).

When the Indian performers were returned to their homes in South Dakota, the ban still stood. They were accompanied on the trains travelling towards South Dakota by troops arriving to suppress the Lakota Ghost Dance religion, and reporters from all over the US travelling to Pine Ridge to cover the so-called imminent 'Indian Rising'. The actions of these returning showmen speak volumes about how they regarded employment in Buffalo Bill's Wild West. Many worked for the government in the suppression of the Lakota Ghost Dance, in such roles as members of the Indian Police, scouts for the army or peace negotiators. A reporter for the Omaha *Morning World-Herald* (15 January 1891) noted:

> A good deal has been said about the Indians who were with Buffalo Bill and I took a good deal of pains to inquire about them, for many of them were the most prominent men among the Indians and they were all on the right side [...]. Their foreign travels have done them good and given them enlarged views. It would be a good thing if the government would employ Colonel Cody to take the whole Sioux nation on a European tour. Bill may not keep a Sunday school... but it is a better place than an Indian agency on half rations and nothing to do.

When the Ghost Dance crisis was concluded Cody was then able to demonstrate that 'his' Indians had all worked tirelessly in support of the government and often against friends and relatives who were adherents of the misunderstood religion (see Maddra 2006: 86–99). Thus, the actions of Cody's Indians rubbished the arguments of Indian Reformers that performing in Buffalo Bill's Wild West show was detrimental to the government's civilization programmes. Added to this was the argument that Cody was enabling the Indian performers to be financially independent by paying them a generous wage, much of which could be sent home to support families left behind on the reservations.

Not only was Cody able to overturn the ban imposed on Indian employment in Wild West shows, but he was also granted custody of the Lakota Ghost Dancers who had been removed to Fort Sheridan as prisoners at the end of the crisis. Twenty-three of these men and women, including the Lakota Ghost Dance leaders Short Bull and Kicking Bear, then travelled to Europe as part of Buffalo Bill's Wild West show for the 1891–92 tour.

So why would these Indian performers go to such extreme lengths to guarantee continued work with Buffalo Bill's Wild West? To understand this we must first understand the circumstances that these Lakota men and women faced at the end of the nineteenth century. Their ways of life had changed drastically since the coming of the whites and their military pacification in the aftermath of the Battle of the Little Big Horn. They were herded on to reservations; traditional roles for both men and women had been curtailed and altered. The warrior society of the Lakota was no more: even hunting had been drastically limited, and employment on the reservations was severely limited to a few select jobs. Families were now becoming more and more dependent upon rations doled out by US government officials, rations which, by all accounts, were inadequate and of poor quality.

The Dawes Allotment act was perceived by reformers to be one means of doing away with both the reservations and the deplored ration system. Each family would be given their own piece of land, thus breaking up the reservations and the communal tribal outlook. The Indians were encouraged to become self-sufficient farmers, and the excess land could then be opened up to white settlement. While the latter happened, the majority of Indians were unable to become self-sufficient on land inadequate for farming, and instead sank even further into dependence.

Families were torn apart as children were removed to far-off boarding schools, where their culture was under attack from all sides. These children were forbidden to speak their traditional languages, to wear their own clothes, or even return home during vacations. The white educationalists perceived the children to be the perfect target, more amenable to identity change, and thus the teachers set about their task of Total Assimilation.

The cultural attack was not restricted to the off-reservation boarding schools, but was also in full swing on the reservations. Religious and cultural practices deemed backward, unchristian, and contrary to American society, were banned. This ban was enforced by armed Indian Police and punished by quasi-legal Courts of Indian Offenses. The

Indians responded to these attacks in a variety of ways – some resisted outright, others accommodated or adapted, embracing those aspects of white culture that they perceived as being beneficial, but the majority in one way or another resisted the Total Assimilation being enforced by the Office of Indian Affairs.

The appeal of work in the Wild West exhibitions, is, then, perhaps quite understandable. The Indian performers were paid a good salary, much of which was sent home to families to help supplement the poor rations. There was escape from the reservations where being 'Indian' was frowned upon; in the shows they could celebrate their Indian identity. They were able to utilize traditional skills, especially their horsemanship, which was greatly admired by audiences. There was not only freedom from the US government's ever-pervasive attempts to control all aspects of the Indians' lives but also from the despair and monotony of reservation life. These Indian performers were enabled to travel the world, were given access to an expanded view of the world, and also to audiences, through interviews with, among others, journalists and statesmen. That is not to say that European audiences shed their perceptions of the Indians as the Other. On the whole they maintained their prejudices about the Indians, but these experiences educated the Indian performers about the white world in an unparalleled way. Furthermore, as Kasson has asserted 'newspaper stories continued to assert [that] the Indians were special favourites with audiences, and human-interest stories about Indians [...] complicated the racial stereotypes and hierarchies' (2000: 219).

In 1891–92 it could be argued that the employment of the Fort Sheridan Indian prisoners was a different case, but once again there was a certain amount of 'choice' involved, as not all of the prisoners decided to go. The freedom offered as an employee of Buffalo Bill's Wild West was much greater than that of a prisoner. Furthermore, these prisoners now also had a certain amount of economic control, which meant that they could aid their families suffering back home. Paradoxically, the closest the Fort Sheridan prisoners got to rebellion was playing the role of the hostiles within the exhibition arena. However, this in itself reinforced the audiences' perception of them as 'savages' and ultimately helped justify the US government's suppression of the Ghost Dance in South Dakota.

While there was definitely a certain amount of exploitation of the Indians by Buffalo Bill's Wild West, illustrated in part by the audiences' attraction to their exoticism, in reality it was much more complex than this. It also suited the needs of the Indian performers, and their participation, even for the prisoners, was their choice. The Lakota Indian performers used various forms of accommodation by seeking employment with Buffalo Bill's Wild West show, and as a result were presented with the chance to resist the dependence that the government's Indian policy had created, at the same time allowing them to maintain their Indian identity. Furthermore, the experiences of the Indian performers with Buffalo Bill's Wild West introduced them to the world of the whites from a position of relative security. As Vine Deloria (1981) noted:

> As a transitional educational device wherein Indians were able to observe [...] [white] society and draw their own conclusions, the Wild West was worth more than every school built by the government on any of the reservations. Unlike the government programs, the Wild West treated the Indians as mature adults capable of making intelligent decisions and of contributing to an important enterprise. Knowledge of white society gained in the tours with Cody stood many of the Indians in good stead in later years, and without this knowledge, the government's exploitation of the Sioux during the period before the First World War might have been even more harsh.

Notes

1 William Frederick Cody (Buffalo Bill) had risen to national fame as an Indian scout and buffalo hunter, but it was his role as a showman with Buffalo Bill's Wild West that brought him international renown. For further information see Kasson 2000, Moses 1996, Reddin 1999, Rosa and May 1989 and Russell 1973 [1960].

2 This ban demonstrates, however, not only the motivations of those Indians employed in such ventures but also the lengths they were willing to go to in order to ensure such employment. As will be discussed later, in the case of the Indian performers employed by Buffalo Bill's Wild West, this meant working for the government in the brutal suppression of the Ghost Dance religion in South Dakota, which culminated in the infamous Wounded Knee Massacre.

I I

The Ethnographic Exhibitions
of the Jardin Zoologique d'Acclimatation

WILLIAM H. SCHNEIDER

It was in the search for popular attractions to draw the public's interest that a new type of exhibition was presented by the Jardin Zoologique d'Acclimatation, the Parisian Zoological Gardens, in August 1877. It consisted of animals from Somalia and the Sudan in the Horn of Africa: camels, giraffes, exotic species of cattle, elephants, dwarf rhinoceros and ostriches. In addition, 14 Africans, 'Nubians' as they were called, accompanied these animals. The inclusion of the 'Nubians' was only an afterthought. As a member of the Société d'Anthropologie de Paris who visited the exhibition reported:

> The convoy belongs to a foreign merchant whose specialty is furnishing interesting specimens to the zoological gardens of Europe and who is supplied in the countries from which he draws his animals by paying local hunters. This time, instead of leaving them in Africa, he wanted to bring them to Europe and, if rumour is to be believed, he will not be poorly rewarded. (Girard de Rialle 1877c: 198)

The new attraction was an immediate success. 'Crowds turn out with little hesitation; every day visitors abound', noted *L'Illustration* (4 August 1877). The results were so encouraging that later in the year, in November, usually a slow month, the Jardin presented six Eskimos (Inuits) from Greenland as its second ethnographic exhibition. The increase in attendance at the Jardin for the year was dramatic: 830,711 visitors in 1877 compared to the previous high of 606,979 in 1875. In his report to the annual meeting of the stockholders, Albert Geoffroy Saint-Hilaire, the director of the Jardin, identified the reason for the increase: 'We recognize that we owe a very considerable portion of this augmentation to the "Nubians" and the Eskimos. Given the costs and receipts, they brought in a profit of 57,963 francs' (Saint-Hilaire 1871).

The following year a similar pattern of ethnographic exhibitions was presented: a winter exhibition of Lapps (Sami) and a summer exhibition of Argentine Gauchos, which lasted three months. With the Exposition Universelle drawing many people to Paris from the provinces and foreign countries, a record 985,000 visitors came to the Jardin. In 1879 the 'Nubians' were once again presented; and, with only a few exceptions, in the years that followed the ethnographic exhibitions became a regular feature of the Jardin d'Acclimatation. In the three years when no ethnographic exhibitions were held – 1880, 1884 and 1885 – yearly gate receipts were significantly lower than any year when exhibitions were held. Throughout the period, gate receipts consistently accounted for two- thirds of the total income from the Jardin. They averaged 69 per cent during years when exhibitions were presented and 61 per cent in other years.

The presentation of the ethnographic exhibitions did not immediately jeopardize the relationship between the Jardin d'Acclimatation and the French scientific community. On the contrary, the Société d'Anthropologie de Paris welcomed the exhibitions as enthusiastically as the mass public. The Société's reporter on the first Nubian exhibition noted:

> [This exhibition] evoked not only the simple curiosity of those in society. In addition, men of science, those who are especially concerned with anthropology, did not wish to allow such a good opportunity to study a group of humans from the great African continent to pass them by. As soon as it heard of the exhibition, the Société d'Anthropologie immediately designated a committee under the direction of its eminent general secretary, Dr Broca, charged with examining carefully the natives camped at the gates of Paris. (Girard de Rialle 1877a)

For his part, Geoffroy Saint-Hilaire offered every encouragement to the Société d'Anthropologie de Paris to visit the exhibitions by sending formal invitations, courtesy tickets, and even allowing special viewings for members prior to the opening of exhibitions. It is, perhaps, an indication of the state of the discipline of anthropology at the time that the Société's response to the exhibitions, at least initially, was favourable. The special committees named by the Society visited the exhibitions not once but several times during their stay at the Jardin; and the committees' findings were published in lengthy articles in the *Bulletin* of the Société . Often the ensuing discussions at meetings were as long as the reports themselves (e.g. Manouvrier 1882). This was the time when physical anthropology was dominant in France; physical differences were thought to be the key to classifying human races.

What interested members of the Société d'Anthropologie were not just skull measurements, but all aspects of human anatomy. One can well imagine the scene as the distinguished members of the Société arrived in the early morning at the Jardin d'Acclimatation armed with their tape measures, callipers and photographic equipment to measure the latest specimens to arrive at their new outdoor laboratory. Their thoroughness was meticulous, but sometimes it had its limits. Léonce Manouvrier, who visited the exhibition of inhabitants from the Tierra del Fuego five times in September 1881 to make measurements, reported to the Société: 'We were able to take fifty measurements of each, approximately all that are recommended in the *Instructions* [to travellers] of the Société d'Anthropologie. The only thing that we could not do was to examine and measure the genital organs. It was not possible to see any lower than the upper part of the pubis' (Manouvrier 1881: 767).

After the initial favourable response by the Société, other doubts began to be expressed by members as to the scientific value of the ethnographic exhibitions. One concern was with differences that might exist between people living in their home environment and the groups camped outside Paris. Questions were raised about how representative the individuals in the exhibitions were. Concern was also expressed about the effect that the ocean voyage and living away from home might have on the groups. One Société member, Paul Nicole, complained at a meeting in 1881 that the inhabitants on exhibit from Tierra del Fuego were not like those people described in accounts he had read by travellers who had been there. 'They have been recruited by an individual who wanted to promote them in Europe. They have not come directly to Paris, but have spent a month in Europe before coming to Paris' (*Bulletin de la Société d'Anthropologie* 1881: 782).

By this time, several cities in Europe were showing ethnographic exhibitions. Financial considerations made the promoters, who had spent their time and money to recruit a group, anxious to 'exhibit' them in as many cities as possible. This meant that for anthropologists, the longer a group toured in Europe the more likely it was to pick up 'contaminating' influences. One of the most widely travelled of these groups had been several Zulus brought to Europe by a promoter shortly after the Zulu War in 1879. Nicole noted that by the time of their performance at the Folies Bergère in Paris, they had learned quite a few things they had not known in Africa. 'They set foot on our continent as savages; when they left, they were crafty and cunning' (Nicole 1881: 775)

Another source of criticism about the exhibitions by the anthropologists and other circles of French society was the setting in which the exhibits were presented to the public. Reflecting the original nature of the Jardin d'Acclimatation, the animals of the exhibitions and the reproductions of the subjects' houses were enclosed by a fence, which separated them from spectators. The real, as well as the symbolic effect was to relegate the human subjects of the exhibitions to the level of the animal attractions at the Jardin. Letourneau described the 'Nubians' in 1879 as being 'set up at the Jardin d'Acclimatation a little like savage animals' (1880a). Despite these growing concerns on the part of the anthropologists, the mass public continued to flock to the ethnographic exhibitions. The Tierra del Fuego exhibition attracted over 400,000 visitors in August and September 1881, with one Sunday crowd of 54,000 people.

It is not surprising, therefore, that complaints from the French scientific community counted little compared to the financial benefits brought by the popularity of the ethnographic expositions. Virtually any promoter who showed up in Paris with a troupe from an 'exotic' land could expect a stay at the Jardin d'Acclimatation. In 1882, a group of Galibi Indians from French Guyana attracted almost 400,000 visitors, but the most unusual year for exhibitions was 1883, when four different groups were presented at the Jardin.

In June 1883 a troupe of 18 Sinhalese, accompanied by ten elephants, appeared at the Jardin, and in July a coincidence brought two families of Araucan Indians from the Andes for a short stay. For six weeks beginning in August, 22 Kalmyks from Siberian Russia appeared at the Jardin, and in October and November, 15 'Redskins' from Nebraska, 'already a little civilized' but appearing in their native costumes, camped on the exhibition grounds of the Jardin. The public response was impressive: 917,501 visitors for the year, the highest total since the 1878 Exposition Universelle. Geoffroy Saint-Hilaire was elated and boasted to the annual meeting of stockholders, 'the operations were profitable from a purely financial standpoint as well as a scientific one'.

Saint-Hilaire's observation about this latter point was based on his invitation to the Société d'Anthropologie de Paris to these exhibitions in 1883 and the visits by the special committees, which had been reported at the Société's meetings. But the reports and discussions at those meetings indicate that the exhibitions had become a major bone of contention between members. In 1886, the exhibition on what was then Ceylon was markedly different from all previous ones in that it had few of their scientific pretensions. Instead there was a direct attempt to draw crowds and provide them with entertainment. A programme was printed for sale at the Jardin, which described the exhibition as 'a trip around the world on the lawns of the Jardin, around the world in a few hours'. The caravan of 70 people, 13 elephants and 14 oxen strikingly resembled a circus. Every day at 2pm, a performance began with an elephant show. This was then followed by a 'devil dance' and a 'dance on stilts', then entertainment by snake charmers, dwarves, and clowns, and races between chariots pulled by the oxen. The finale at 6pm was the 'perra-herra' procession in which the whole troupe paraded around carrying two monks in a canopied chair. The total effect, the programme concluded, 'transports the imagination to the enchanted countries of the distant Orient' (Fulbert-Dumonteil 1886).

This new type of exhibition signalled the end of the Jardin d'Acclimatation's ties with the scientific community. The Ceylonese exhibition of 1886 was the first that was not visited by the Société d'Anthropologie de Paris and none was visited or reported on thereafter. The West African ethnographic exhibitions illustrate the consequences of this change.

West African Ethnographic Exhibitions

The Ashanti exhibition in 1887 was the first ethnographic exhibition from West Africa at the Jardin d'Acclimatation, and its timing was significant. West Africans were presented to Frenchmen only after ethnographic exhibitions had moved from the realm of science to that of sideshow. As a result, the medium of the ethnographic exhibition, much like the mass illustrated magazine, presented West Africans in a setting of spectacle and sensation. Bizarre customs, ferocity and savagery were emphasized in order to attract and entertain crowds.[1]

Promoters hurried to assemble troupes from far-distant corners of the globe that had only recently gained notoriety in the press, such as Dahomey and Madagascar. Exhibitions became so popular that other places, besides the Jardin d'Acclimatation, began to be used for their presentation. In Paris, the Champ de Mars was the scene of a Dahomean exhibition in 1893, an exhibition from Senegal and the Sudan in 1895, and Madagascar in 1896. The Casino de Paris sponsored a troupe of Dahomeans on their way to the Chicago World's Fair in 1893. Many of the promoters took their troupes on extensive tours of French provincial cities, as well as the major capitals of Europe. One Dahomean exhibition, which appeared at the Jardin d'Acclimatation in the spring of 1891, was reported in Prague in October 1892 (*Petit Parisien*, 1 October 1892).[2]

In general, these exhibitions followed the format which had evolved at the Jardin d'Acclimatation in the 1880s. They differed, however, in their timing and subject matter. Although exhibitions continued to be brought to Paris because they happened to be touring Europe, like the

Somali and Egyptian ones, most were more topical. Promoters sought to take advantage of the interest created by the increase in French colonial activity after 1890. The exhibitions of Dahomeans in 1891 and in 1893 followed closely each of the two Dahomean Wars.

One result of the timing and subject matter of these exhibitions was a recognition by the French government of the powerful role they played in publicizing the new colonial empire. The 1889 Exposition Universelle is the most obvious example, where the government itself recruited and presented an exhibition from Senegal. This was quite a change from the 1878 Exposition, when a proposal by the explorer Joseph Bonnat to bring a troupe of West Africans to Paris was declined in favour of a more traditional display of local products and artefacts in an exhibition hall (*Petit Journal*, 20 September 1877; 30 July 1878). In 1889, model villages, temples and markets were reconstructed not only for Senegal but also for Indochina, Gabon and Tahiti. Although the rest of the exhibitions presented in Paris in the years that followed were the work of private promoters, there was another way that the government could use them to publicize its colonial policy: visits by government officials. The president of the Republic, Sadi Carnot, visited the Dahomean exhibition in 1891, and the following year he attended the Carib exhibition from French Guyana along with Maurice Rouvrier, the Minister of Finance, and Jules Roche, the Minister of Commerce. These visits also bestowed an element of legitimacy on the exhibitions. That purpose had earlier been served by the visits of the special committees of the Société d'Anthropologie, but given the changes in the nature of the exhibitions, it was fitting that government officials should now fill that role.

The practice of giving a performance each day for visitors was continued in the West African exhibitions, but the nature of the performances reflected the new developments in colonial affairs. Most important was the beginning of full-scale, highly publicized colonial wars, in which the local inhabitants changed from being just another curiosity of the local countryside to formidable military opponents.

Even the military performances could become stale, and promoters often went to great lengths in order to present unusual attractions or performances that would draw crowds by their novelty. At the Sudanese exhibition there was a marriage, which was publicized in advance and drew large crowds. The most unusual attraction dreamed up by promoters, however, was the great baggage porters' race at the 1893 Dahomean exhibition at the Champ de Mars, which lasted three days. This second exhibition of Dahomeans in Paris was by far the largest undertaking of its kind since the beginning of the ethnographic exhibitions. France had just concluded a long and victorious war in Dahomey that had received a great deal of attention in the press.

Ethnographic Exhibitions and Popular Attitudes

What did the ethnographic exhibitions contribute to popular French conceptions of Africans? The preceding analysis has indicated that ethnographic exhibitions placed West Africans in a setting of spectacle and emphasized their warlike and savage nature. This was the result of changes in the nature of ethnographic exhibitions and of broader developments in colonial affairs in West Africa. Any attempt to gain a deeper insight into spectators' reactions presents a much more difficult problem.

The average visitors to the exhibitions did not leave any record of their reactions other than their attendance, and even that record is incomplete. The observations of the scientific community exist only for the early exhibitions and are too narrow to indicate subjective reactions. The only other descriptions that may be of value are the comments by reporters sent to the exhibitions by the *Petit Journal*, the *Petit Parisien*, and other newspapers. The fact that they expressed certain common reactions indicates that their responses may also have been shared by other visitors to the exhibitions. In addition, since their reading audience most likely overlapped a large part of the audiences that attended the exhibitions, their observations may also have influenced visitors' reactions. One of the most frequent reactions was to the physical appearance of the West Africans. Any lengthy article contained a perfunctory description of the customs and land from which the exhibition came, but the descriptions of physical appearance, based as they were on first-hand experience, were often very revealing.

It is true that many of these descriptions reflect the traditional European predisposition to find animal-like qualities in Africans, but some observers could bring themselves to an overall aesthetic judgement that was grudgingly complimentary. The women of the 1891 Dahomean exhibition were called 'for the most part young and pretty [...] in their own way'; a warrior in the 1893 Dahomean exhibition was described as 'not ugly at all, for a negro'; and it was noted 'the Pai-Pi-Bri woman is not lacking a certain grace'. These physical descriptions were by no means glowing portraits of noble savages, but they do indicate, if only indirectly, that Frenchmen began to appreciate that there was a difference between the simplified caricatures of Africans as described in the mass press and the live human beings in the ethnographic exhibitions.

Despite this positive effect of the ethnographic exhibitions, there was one unexpected feature that observers found very denigrating to the subjects. This was the practice of visitors throwing them money.[3] How it started is difficult to determine, but it appears to have been part of the earliest exhibitions. By the time of the 1893 Dahomean exhibition, a reporter from the *Petit Journal* concluded: 'Whether it is Buffalo Bill's redskins, the Ceylonese, or Hottentots, Galibis or Dahomeans, all seem to give the impression that passing round the hat is the basis of existence [...]. It is always, in its inferior form, the chasing after money which spurs us on in Europe ... and elsewhere' (22 May 1893).

The physical layout of the exhibitions did much to encourage the practice. The subjects were physically separated from the visitors by a fence or, later, when performances became more important, by a railing. It was only natural for spectators to respond to cries of *'donne-moi un sou'* from women and children leaning over the railing by tossing coins or notes. It was not very different from any spectator tossing peanuts or popcorn to other attractions at the zoo.

The money that was accumulated in this manner also served as a significant bonus to members of the exhibition who, from all accounts, had been recruited at a fixed amount while still at home. It was reported that in the three days following his victory in the baggage porters' race, the winner, Ahivi, received over 500 francs in 10- and 20-franc pieces: 'A tidy sum for a Dahomean warrior' (*Petit Journal*, 28 May 1893).

The ethnographic exhibitions were a product of the Age of Imperialism. By the end of the 1890s there was an effective administrative control in the colonies, and the Colonial Ministry in Paris had a stake in emphasizing the positive aspects of colonies. This change, already visible at the Paris Exposition Universelle in 1900, became even more marked at the first colonial exhibition in Marseille in 1906, where a more official image of the colonies was presented to the French public.

Notes

1 Visitors were entertained by snake fetishes, war dances, and a grand finale consisting of a full-scale mock battle, which was fitting for these enemies of the British in the 1873 Ashanti War. As an observer described it, the scene was a far cry from the outdoor ethnographic laboratory for scientific study that Manouvrier had hoped for: 'You are positively frozen by the sight of these black men in fantastic attire, crawling on the ground as in an ambush and then springing with a prodigious agility, shouting a war cry and swinging their sabres in a dizzying whirl' (*Petit Journal*, 18 September 1887).

2 References in the French press alone mention ethnographic exhibitions in London, Brussels, Berlin, Hamburg and Prague, as well as the major French provincial cities.

3 In the film made at the Jardin d'Acclimatation by the Lumière brothers, probably in 1896, spectators can be seen throwing coins into the water to encourage the young children of the troupe to dive for them.

12

The Onas Exhibited in the Musée du Nord, Brussels: Reconstruction of a Lost File

PETER MASON

Among the records of the aliens police in Brussels is a section dealing with *'Troupes d'étrangers exhibés en public, 1888–1904'* [Foreign troupes exhibited in public, 1888–1904]. One particularly tantalizing item is the file whose envelope bears the words *'Troupe des Onas exhibés en février 1890 au musée du Nord et qui ont été renvoyés en Angleterre'* [Troupe of Onas exhibited in February 1890 at the Musée du Nord who were sent back to England]. The envelope is empty (Vervaeck 1968: no. 834, 106C). Nevertheless, with the aid of textual and visual clues from Brussels, Paris, London, Argentina and Chile, it is possible to solve some of the questions posed by this laconic title. We can discover more about the 'Onas' and the Musée du Nord, what they were doing there in February 1890, where they came from, and where they – at least the survivors – went to afterwards. The advantage of such a micro-historical approach to human displays is that it enables us to examine more precisely the geographical and historical contextualization of a particular case, going beyond the familiar broad generalizations about the colonial period. In this respect, the present article shares with Felix Driver's *Geography Militant* (2001) the desire to investigate the cultures (in the plural to emphasize their diversity) of exploration and empire in the heartlands of the colonial empires themselves.[1]

Human Troupes and Groups

Among the files which have survived, we commonly find a heading: 'Profession', which is filled in by a term of nationality or place of origin: 'Senegalese', 'Samoans', and so on. The description is tellingly accurate, for it was the profession or job of these groups of non-Europeans to function as troupes, putting on a performance in which they literally re-presented the allegedly typical practices of everyday life as they knew it. Their job was to *be* Africans, Samoans, etc., to present a spectacle of exotic existence to a European audience for whom the indigestible mores of non-Europeans could only become a cultural object of consumption after they had been through a process of exoticization.

We can gain some insight into the modalities of the display of 'Onas' in Brussels from an entry in the *Journal de Bruxelles* on 6 February 1890:

> A troupe of cannibals imprisoned in the Petits-Carmes – On Tuesday, M. Le Jeune, Minister of Justice, ordered the arrest of the group of cannibals on show at the Castan museum. The unfortunate Onas are currently behind bars in the Petits-Carmes prison, as foreign nationals without means of support. The honourable Minister of Justice took this decision at the request of the English government. Apparently, these Indians were captured from the English territories of Tierra del Fuego and forced to board a French vessel. One of them was even killed attempting to defend himself. The Indians were first put on show in London. And the English police were about to investigate the events surrounding the capture of these poor people when they were sent to Brussels.

To start by locating the events in question, both the Musée du Nord and the Musée Castan were situated in the Passage du Nord, Brussels. The former, which opened in 1877, presented a wide variety of live attractions, including electrical and mechanical devices, together with a Théâtre Bébé, where children and dwarves put on farces and pantomimes, and a Salle des Fêtes, where variety shows were presented. The Musée Castan, which moved to the passage in May 1888, followed the same pattern. In addition to a permanent show of waxworks, its Salle des Fêtes presented string puppets, exotic dancers, illusionists, and other spectacles. In 1890, the year in which the 'Onas' were exhibited there, attractions included 'les Jewells Holden', Spanish dancers, 'Fatma and her Moorish troupe', Amazons from Dahomey, and Aztecs (Renieu 1928: 877–88). And from the *Journal de Bruxelles* of 22 February 1890, we know that ten male Samoans were on show in the Musée Castan, where they played billiards and performed song and dance acts.

The theatre or variety show was one of the three main types of venues at which non-Europeans were put on show for a European audience. The second was the setting of the world fair, inaugurated at the Crystal Palace in London in 1851, where the different nations of the world were presented on a single site, along with representative samples of the different manufactures and natural products of the various regions of the colonial world – what has been called 'The World as Marketplace' (Hinsley 1991: 344). The Exposition Universelle in Paris in 1889 was the first in which ethnographic villages were a key component. If the theatrical setting calls to mind the name of Phineas Barnum, the deployment of exotic human groups in world fairs seems to be associated with, or even to have been the initiative of, Carl Hagenbeck, who had been staging mixed anthropological-zoological exhibitions in the Hamburg Tierpark since 1874.[2] This brings us to the third setting, the zoo or menagerie, the most famous example being the Jardin d'Acclimatation in Paris. This secluded environment where animals could reproduce and be studied under competent supervision was the scene of a new kind of exhibition in August 1877, when for the first time 14 Africans ('Nubians') were put on show, in addition to African camels, giraffes, exotic species of cattle, elephants, rhinoceros and ostriches. The addition of humans to the animal display was such a financial success that it was repeated in November of the same year when six Eskimos (Inuit) from Greenland were put on show.[3]

Naturally, there was a good deal of exchange between these three types of setting. For example, the Mapuche (Araucanians) from southern Chile, who were on show in the Jardin d'Acclimatation in the Summer of 1883, were regularly visited there by the French pretender to the Araucanian throne, Achille Laviarde (Achille I of Araucania from 1878 to 1902), who took them to the Chat Noir, a favourite cabaret of the French intellectual elite, to introduce them to literary and political circles (as well as to bolster his political ambitions). As we shall see, the 'Onas' were to pass through all three types of setting.

Each of these settings involved a particular mode of presentation of the exotic. The vaudeville setting conferred on them a 'freak' quality to satisfy the popular demand for sensation. The setting of the world fair pointed out the economic advantages to be obtained from the colonies, as well as reinforcing a hierarchy of European/non-European through the juxtaposition of the two categories within the same spatial framework. In this respect, photographs of 'exotic' peoples kept in check by their European masters replicate the desired model of colonial relations. Finally, the zoo or menagerie setting sought to underscore the feeble division, if any, between certain non-European peoples and the animal world. In this respect, the native peoples of Tierra de Fuego played a special role. Charles Darwin, who became personally acquainted with four of them on board the *Beagle*, delivered the following verdict on them: 'These poor wretches were stunted in their growth, their hideous faces bedaubed with white paint, their skins filthy and greasy, their hair entangled, their voices discordant, and their gestures violent. Viewing such men, one can hardly make oneself believe that they are fellow-creatures, and inhabitants of the same world' (Darwin, 1839).

Natives of Tierra del Fuego, then, played an important part in the Darwinian scheme of things, and their presence in Europe in the late nineteenth century was inevitably overdetermined by that intellectual and emotional background.

'Native' Deaths

Who were these 'Onas' who were displayed in the Musée Castan in Brussels in 1890? The Onas, or Selk'nam, came from the southernmost part of South America, where they inhabited the interior of the main island of Tierra del Fuego and its northern and eastern coasts. The population of the Selk'nam and the neighbouring Haush has been estimated at between 3,500 and 4,000 in the period prior to the 1800s, but during the last two decades of the nineteenth century (the show in Brussels falls exactly in the middle of this period) their numbers decreased dramatically as white settlers and missionaries moved into their territory. Within the space of twenty years or so, their numbers had dropped to around 500 as the result of intentional genocide and unintentional infection by European diseases. The last of the Selk'nam to live in accordance with their traditional culture, Lola Kiepja, died in 1966 (Chapman 1986).

In 1888 a Belgian whaler kidnapped eleven Selk'nam on the Strait of Magellan. He took them to Europe in chains 'like Bengalese tigers'. They were displayed in Paris by the impresario Maurice Maître in a cage in one of the main buildings erected in the shadow of the Tour Eiffel during the Exposition Universelle of 1889. At this event held to celebrate 100 years of *Liberté, Égalité* and *Fraternité,* the Selk'nam were presented to the Parisian public as cannibals, and at feeding time pieces of raw horse meat were thrown to them. In a photograph of the impresario Maurice Maître with 'his' group of Selk'nam in front of a painted backcloth at the Exposition Universelle, the pose is that of a hunter with his trophy. This conforms to a type of photograph that recurs in similar settings, such as that of the Surinamese displayed not far from Brussels at the Amsterdam World Exposition in 1883.

Another, more sinister, recurrent pattern is betrayed by the photograph of Maître: though the sources refer to the kidnapping of eleven Selk'nam, only nine can be seen in the photograph. Presumably two of the original eleven had died by the time the photograph was taken. Mortality rates were constantly high for those non-Europeans who were brought to Europe to appear in such shows. During the earlier display of a different group of native peoples from Tierra del Fuego (eleven Alakaluf, a canoe people from the western parts of the archipelago) in Paris in 1883, the young daughter of one of them (Petite-Mère) died there. One of the women died when the group was on the way to Switzerland, and four more died in Zürich. At this point it was decided to send the five survivors back home. One of them, Antonio, died on the voyage. Only four of the original eleven Fuegians managed to return to the Punta Arenas (Brändle 1995: 7-21).

To return to Maurice Maître and 'his' Selk'nam, the nine surviving members of the group were taken from Paris to London, where they were exhibited at the Westminster Aquarium. Their diet remained unchanged: raw horse meat and raw fish. The *Pall Mall Gazette* (23 January 1890) reported that their 'savage customs were for a time the talk of the town'. After one of the women became ill, Maître abandoned her in London. She was sent to the Infirmary of the Saint George's Union, where she died at four o'clock on the morning of 21 January. The nurse who attended her described her case as follows: 'When she came into the infirmary she had on only an old rug tied on like a cloak, a rope tied round her waist, and a pair of slippers made of string. Not another stitch of clothing did she possess of any kind. She was filthy dirty; the filth was in layers and she objected by every sound and sign she could make to being washed. The stench from her body was horrible.'

The resident physician, Dr Webster, acquainted a representative of the South American Missionary Society with the facts of the case. He commented: 'I consider it a most shameful thing that these poor creatures should be permitted to be taken from their native land, and brought to this country, where they are almost sure to fall sick' (South American Missionary Society 1890: 29–30). Appeals by the South American Missionary Society to the directors of the Westminster Aquarium, to Maître, to the Aborigines' Protection Society, and to the Chilean authorities in England, were in vain. Maître defended his actions by stating that the Selk'nam were not English, that they were not under the protection of the South American Missionary Society, and that they had joined him voluntarily. The Foreign and Home Offices, though slow to act at first, did begin to take an interest in the matter. Feeling that the ground was getting too hot under his feet, Maître fled with his remaining captives to Brussels.

The presentation of them in the Musée Castan must have been short-lived, since it had already been closed down, and the Selk'nam had been sent to Petits-Carmes by 6 February. But the shows went on; as we have said, by 22 February the Musée Castan was host to the display of ten

Samoans. There were seven Selk'nam in Petits-Carmes, two fewer than the nine photographed in Paris, four fewer than the eleven who were originally captured in Tierra del Fuego. They were a man of about thirty, who had a slight beard, three women, and three children, the oldest of whom was estimated to be about four years old. They had no tools or implements with them, though they would certainly have known how to use a bow and a lance. They were dressed in rags, and walked barefoot in the snow (*Bulletin de la Société d'Anthropologie* 1890–91: 45).

Maître was arrested in Brussels, and the survivors, certainly no more than four by now, and perhaps less, were returned via Dover and Liverpool on board the *Oruba* to Tierra del Fuego. Reactions to the phenomenon of human shows in Brussels were mixed. On the academic side, the Société d'Anthropologie de Bruxelles took a lively interest in the activities of the *musées* in the Belgian capital. Its *Bulletin* for 1888–89 contained a report to the society by E. Houzé on the Hottentots (San) who had been presented in the Musée du Nord, though adding that 'it is a banal exhibition of no scientific value' (1888–89: 286). Nevertheless, despite the lack of scientific value of the shows presented in the Musée du Nord, the following issue of the *Bulletin* contained a report of a lecture given by the same E. Houzé on the group of Samoans who were being shown in the Musée Castan (1889–90: 241–55). The haste with which the exhibition of Selk'nam in the same museum was closed down meant that there was no time for the Société d'Anthropologie to visit them at the Musée before their incarceration pending return to England. However, they were visited in prison by a member of the society, V. Jacques. He had hoped to organize a special session for the society in the Musée du Nord before he learned about their incarceration. Prison conditions prevented him from carrying out the measurements which were so dear to physical anthropologists of his time; for instance, the so-called anthropologist Roland Bonaparte had taken advantage of the presence of natives from Surinam at the Amsterdam World Exposition in 1883 to carry out a systematic work of physical anthropology, published the following year (Bonaparte 1884). But not everybody was happy with the closing down of the show. The records of the Brussels aliens police include complaints that, if such events are to be barred from the Belgian capital, it will no longer be able to compete as a cultural metropolis with its European counterparts.

Not only ethical attitudes towards the human shows were mixed; opinions also varied on their informative value. As we have seen, non-Europeans on display in Europe were expected to perform as exotic Others. However, by the very fact of being taken to Europe, they had already lost some of that alterity. After the display of the 'wild' Fuegians in the Jardin d'Acclimatation in Paris in 1881, the exhibition of fourteen 'Araucanians' (Mapuche) from the south of Chile in the same venue in 1883 was considered to be less spectacular. Indeed, anthropologist Léonce Manouvrier declared that 'many of the men and women we saw could very well, their colour aside, be presented as natives of the Auvergne' (Manouvrier 1883a: 728). While Manouvrier was led to think of the Auvergne, Girard de Rialle, another visitor to the Jardin who saw the Mapuche, was transported in time by the spectacle:

> Deprived of their mounts, the Auracanians in the Jardin d'Acclimatation could not provide an idea of their daily occupations; nevertheless the construction of their straw hut, the many trivial tasks carried out each hour, even the strange chant which one of them produced from a long goat's horn three metres in length, all of these carried you off for a brief moment to the distant country of Araucania whose proud inhabitants, grandiose countryside, and touching scenes inspired Ercilla, in the sixteenth century, to produce an epic which is one of the glories of Spanish literature. (Girard de Rialle 1883b: 154)

Clearly, the non-Europeans on display served to trigger reactions in the minds of the spectators. Their function was to activate a set of emotions associated with exotic stereotypes, and if they failed to do so, or if anything was out of harmony with that romantic image, the visitor went away disappointed.

Postscript

An anonymous photograph now in the Archivo de la Nación in Buenos Aires carries the text: 'José L. M. Calafacte ten years after in the Salesian Mission of Rio Grande, in 1899, Tierra del Fuego.' This precious piece of evidence tells us that at least one of the Selk'nam displayed in Paris, London and Brussels in 1889–90 returned to his native country and was still alive ten years later. In fact, it was the missionary José María Beauvoir who met him in Montevideo and took him back to Tierra del Fuego. He became Beauvoir's main informant for the latter's dictionary of the Selk'nam language (Gusinde 1982: 152–53, 179; Beauvoir 1977 [1915]: 15).

Another anonymous photograph of two children now in the same photographic archive identifies them as 'The two Ona Fuegian children J. Luis M. Calafacte and José Fueguino when they were at the exposition in Paris in 1889.' The two boys can clearly be identified as two of the children in the photograph of Maître with his human trophy.[4] However, the European with his stick has been replaced by a tree to furnish a 'natural' setting for the Selk'nam boys. The European intrusion has been erased from the photographic record.

Notes

1 I would like to thank the following for their invaluable help: Christian Boeez Allende, Myriam de Alvarez, Marisol Palma, Anne Chapman, Florike Egmond and Christel Verhas.
2 See Reiss and Thode-Arora in this volume.
3 See Schneider in this volume.
4 The photographs of Calafacte and of Maître with his human 'trophies' in Paris are to be found in Mason (2002a).

13

Meeting the Amazons

SUZANNE PRESTON BLIER

The presence of a number of armed women among the warriors who attempted to safeguard their capital city, Abomey, against the onslaught of French colonial forces helped to create the myth of the Amazons of Dahomey. Months prior to the first French attack on 4 March 1890, a group of Dahomey Amazons were already on their way to Hamburg, in preparation for 'performances' which would begin in June. Soon, these and other troupes of African women warriors were travelling to other centres in Europe and the United States to perform in cities as diverse as Berlin, Frankfurt, Darmstadt, Zürich, Prague, St Petersburg, Paris, Lyon, London, Brussels, Chicago, San Francisco, Atlanta, Buffalo and St Louis.

Between the years 1890 and 1925 when these performances took place, the Amazons helped to shape the minds of millions of Western spectators with respect to ideas of race, gender and national identity. Many of the early Dahomey Amazon performances in Europe took place in settings which featured animals. Umlauff's Weltmuseum [World Museum] on Spielbundenplatz, in what was then the rough and bawdy Hamburg seaport suburb of St Pauli, was one such venue. The area was home to a panoply of trading-houses, bars and brothels, and today this tradition is still recalled through the St Pauli girl beer label. Founded by J. F. G. Umlauff, sister of the famed German animal purveyor Carl Hagenbeck, Umlauff's Weltmuseum was named for her late husband, a one-time sailor, who was renowned for having transformed a Hamburg bath house into a trade museum and sales depot featuring exotica and natural objects (from insects to elephants), acquired through earlier maritime contacts.[1] Opened in 1889 in the building of the former Hanseatic panopticons, Umlauff's Weltmuseum combined the characteristics of a curio cabinet and an exotic peep-show (Thinius 1975: 36).

Amazons à la Mode

A poster for one of Umlauff's Weltmuseum Amazon spectacles bears the date June–July 1890, suggesting not only that it was one of the first of the Weltmuseum's long tradition of ethnographic spectacles, but also that this was one of the earliest of the Dahomey Amazon performances in Europe. A news report describing one of the early Amazon shows gives a clear sense of the unique setting and the impact of the show:

> From the walls African landscapes greet us and the tops of palm trees sway above the heads of appropriate stuffed inhabitants of deserts, jungles, and swamps from the darkest corners of the world. But now none of the spectators is interested in these sights and rarities. Intense screams, the thud of feet, the clanking of shields and the monotone thud of a drum announce the beginning of the show in the hall. Closely packed masses of people stand before a decoratively painted massive podium, upon which stand the members of the Amazon corps, the bodyguard of the king of Dahomey (Thinius 1975: 36).

A year later, in August 1891, the Amazon troupes were appearing in the Berlin and Frankfurt zoos. As with Umlauff's Weltmuseum, the animal-park setting of the zoological gardens (still a popular choice today for family outings) served to reinforce local perceptions that the Amazons (and Africans more generally) were more comfortable with fauna and flora than with the world of humans. Eventually, other venues were secured in Germany, among them Castan's Panopticon in Berlin, which stood beside the city's zoological gardens. The sculptor Gustav Castan and his brother Louis had opened the Panopticon in Berlin's once-elite Kaiserpassage in 1873, modelling it on the then-popular Parisian wax museum prototype. Like the earlier zoo displays, the wax museum setting provided a far-from-neutral frame. In this bizarre world of wax, the Amazons on view evoked an equally potent emotional charge. Populated by darkly lit wax figures, the enclave of the Panopticon carried with it the widely accepted 'truth' that these women and, indeed, their entire continent were not only deviant and dangerous but real monstrosities of the world and mind. A wide variety of posters in glaring primary colours document these events, with key scenes often being recirculated in other forms.

Early Amazon performances in Paris (like those in Frankfurt and Berlin) took place in the city's zoological gardens (then part of the Bois de Boulogne). Ethnographic exhibitions had been introduced in the Jardin Zoologique d'Acclimatation in 1877 as a means of popularizing the newly emerging 'science' of ethnography (Schneider, W. H. 1982: 132, 135). Related exhibits dovetailed closely with colonial concerns. Among those in attendance at the 1891 Dahomey Amazon spectacle in Paris was the President, Sadi Carnot, who had overseen the 1890 French attack. It is perhaps not surprising, given the recent colonial campaign and the exotic setting of the zoological gardens, that the French public were fascinated by the Dahomean live performances. In 1891, the total number of visitors to the Jardin was 959,430, of whom around 800,000 had come to see either the fifty Dahomeans or another troupe from Egypt. Surrounded by a fence, which served both to enclose the native participants and to 'protect' the curious citizens of Paris, the women and men on display were living human complements to the flora and fauna on view nearby – fitting zoological taxonomical exemplars of the exotic, the rare, the frightening and the bizarre.

The Triumph of 1893

In 1893 a troupe of 150 Dahomey Amazons performed for a four-month season. This show was even more successful than the previous one, attracting over 2,700,000 visitors – the largest by far of any of the ethnographic exhibits (Schneider, W. H. 1982: 137, 142). The location of the exhibit on the Champ de Mars, named in honour of the Roman god of war, gave the spectacle special meaning. This site evoked the colonial military interest in Dahomey (including recent battles against the female troops) and the era's fascination with ancient myths. In 1889, President Carnot had welcomed a large group of representatives to the hugely popular Exposition Universelle, with its various displays (among them ethnographic shows) arrayed across the grounds of the Champ de Mars at the foot of the newly erected Eiffel Tower, itself constructed for the Exposition. Then, as now, the site was an important tourist Mecca. Running from the École Militaire to the Seine, the Champ de Mars had once served as the setting for Napoleon's triumphal march, with its display of African animals and other war booty from his recent European conquests. Still earlier, it had witnessed the bloody executions of 1791. By 1893, however, frenzied violence was attributed largely to the peoples and governments of Africa – particularly King Behanzin of Dahomey and his troupes of women warriors.

In France, as in Germany, large colour lithographs purporting to show the women on the field of battle served to convey a sense of the content of the performance. Perhaps not surprisingly in light of the recent French military campaign in Dahomey, the German posters featuring

'General' Gumma seem relatively tame when compared with French posters of the same troupe, which depict fierce, witch-like Amazons wielding bloody weapons and enemy heads.

In England, the Dahomey Amazons appeared in the Crystal Palace, transferred to its new location on the slopes of Sydenham Hill, 25 minutes by train from London's Victoria station. In what is now a residential suburb, one can still get a sense of the original performance surroundings – the broad sloping 81-hectare (200-acre) grassy park with magnificent views of distant London, a scaled-down version of the Eiffel Tower, flowerbeds, benches, fountains, shade trees and lakes for boating – all within a short walk of Gipsy Hill Station. Queen Victoria had described the original Crystal Palace at its opening as 'a noble monument of the genius, science, and enterprise' where 'treasures of art and knowledge may long continue to elevate and instruct, as well as to delight and amuse the minds of all classes'. By the summer of 1893, when the Dahomey Amazon performers appeared at the new Crystal Palace, 'entertainment' clearly preceded 'elevation and instruction' in the minds of most. Among those who appeared alongside the Amazons here was a troupe of circus elephants.

In this same summer of 1893, another 'Dahomey' troupe of 67 men and women crossed the Atlantic to perform on the newly opened Midway of Chicago's World's Columbian Exposition. Here, near the ostrich park, captive balloon, Hagenbeck's wild animal display and the newly erected Ferris Wheel (Chicago's engineering response to the Eiffel Tower), the Dahomey pavilion, and the Midway more generally, provided a striking contrast to the grounds and white-plastered halls designed by Frederick Olmstead, which came to be known (without irony) as the 'Great White City'.

Here, grand and elegant buildings – dedicated to industry, science, art and national pride – demonstrated America's new world stature. The Midway, a phallus-like appendage to this bright white utopia, privileged pleasure and the emotions over human advancement and the mind. Moreover, as Robert Rydell has noted (1984 [1974]: 66), the placement of ethnographic pavilions on the Midway (today part of the University of Chicago campus green) was intended to suggest the 'chain of human progress', from its so-called beginnings to the modern industrial era, an idea that closely dovetailed with social evolutionary theories of the time. Surrounding the Dahomey pavilion was a tall stockade fence reminiscent at once of the earlier French zoological park enclosures and of military forts used in the American West in the then recently concluded Native American 'pacification' programme. Indeed, also prominently displayed at the fair were leaders of the Sioux who had suffered defeat at Wounded Knee only three years previously.

A Reflection of Western Preoccupations

Whereas in Europe the Amazon spectacles were linked in vital ways to recent colonial moves, in the United States the Amazons were conceptualized in relation to quite different national issues: the aftermath of slavery, the persistence of racial discrimination, and the climate of violence which followed the reconstruction of the Union. Dahomeans as icons of 'savage' Africa were presented here as the anti-model to which African-Americans by their very ancestry were assumed to be bound. Sexual titillation was clearly a central part of the attraction of the Amazon spectacle and related visual appeal. As Thomas Theye explains for ethnographic shows of this era more generally, 'To see the naked body, mostly the female body, was one of the strongest impulses of the shows' (Theye 1989). The 16–23 July 1901 exhibit at the Zürich Panopticon was advertised accordingly as 'Wild Africa: 27 Black Vixens' (Brändle 1995). The responses of Pasternak and the early German reviewers to the Amazons in St Petersburg and Hamburg were typical of the voyeurism implicit in this genre. Indeed, an 1890 reviewer of the Umlauff Weltmuseum show noted of the Amazons specifically that 'they let themselves be touched and fondled by the openly aroused and pushy public, who give them cigars and sweets'.

Performance costumes added further to the sexual content. While photographs of German and other Western Amazon performance contexts indicate that on some occasions the women posed nude, the standard European costume consisted of a cowrie-decorated chest-harness, bloomers and a short cloth skirt-wrapper – far different from the Amazon attire in Dahomey. The dress of the men in the Amazon troupe was sexually provocative. Performance photographs show the men bare-chested with leopard-pelt pelvis-covers and tall, plumed head crests, the latter suggestive of both horse-trappings and chorus girl adornments. Cowrie armbands, leg-bands, belts, leather amulets and munition pouches completed the attire for both male and female performers. It is interesting that the costumes worn in Amazon spectacles in the United States were quite different from those of the European exhibits. For both men and women, the costumes here took the form of meagre shorts or grass skirts and open (very revealing) v-necked, sleeveless tunics of native cloth striped blue, yellow and white, somewhat reminiscent of Dahomey war dress.

In an era when ideas of civilization, respectability and class were closely associated with rules of dress (fashion), etiquette and sexual practice (the perceived demureness of women), the fact that the Dahomey women were obliged to perform naked or in skin-revealing, provocative attire suggested to Western visitors that these women were simultaneously 'uncivilized' and 'promiscuous', 'inaccessible' and 'available', features that complicated and heightened qualities of desire. Issues of sexual identity emerged in other ways as well, and among these was gender conflation. It was noted in the pamphlet for the English Crystal Palace Amazon troupe that: 'These extraordinary women have great muscular strength, and are extremely agile, as will be seen from their performances. They appear to possess as much vigour and national ferocity as the men, and intoxicate themselves, as it were, with their war exercises and dances.' In Europe and the United States, related issues of sexual challenge were played out against the era's growing women's rights movement. In Bachofen's well-known theory of social evolution, first published in the 1860s (1967: 153), the period known as 'Amazonianism' was purportedly accompanied by a marked degeneration of men. From the perspective of this theory, the powerful women of Dahomey lowered this culture on the social evolutionary ladder to a level well below that of even other Africans. In the context of the increasingly vocal movement towards women's suffrage of the early 1890s, the 'Amazons' represented to many a counter-exemplar, cautioning society against empowering women to vote, enter the job market, or hold community positions. At the same time, however, the Amazons clearly offered evidence that women could successfully engage in male activities, and in this way the model they presented was both potent and revolutionary.

Note

1　See Thode-Arora in this volume.

14

Hagenbeck's European Tours:
the Development of the Human Zoo

HILKE THODE-ARORA

The German port of Hamburg used to be a city of exchange for everything that ships – or sailors – could bring to it. In certain suburbs,
in particular that of St Pauli, all sorts of curiosity shops and places of
entertainment were to be found: theatres, panopticons, cabarets, fairs,
restaurants and public houses. It was in this lively area that, in 1848, the
fishmonger J. Hagenbeck charged the public for the privilege of viewing
a display of seals, which he then took on tour to Berlin. This enterprise gradually expanded into a veritable menagerie and animal trading
business, which Hagenbeck left to his son, Carl (1844–1913), when the
latter was 15 years old. The business prospered under his management,
but by 1874, the economic depression and the political situation in the
Sudan following the rise of the Mahdi led to a serious crisis. When
commercial relations with East Africa, which supplied most of the
animals, were broken off, it became necessary to find another source
of revenue. Hagenbeck must have already been familiar with ethnic
shows. It is known that there was an exhibit of 'Zulu-Kaffirs' on show in
St Pauli in 1854, which he may well have seen or of which he may have
been aware. Even more influential must have been his recent business
contacts with the American, P. T. Barnum, organizer of several ethnic
and 'freak' shows, who had been a regular customer of Hagenbeck's
animal trade since 1872. Beyond such local influences, Europe in any
case had a long tradition of putting 'exotic' peoples on display.[1]

Hagenbeck's first ethnic show of Lapps (Sami) opened in 1875. Its
immense success encouraged him to continue: in 1876 and in the
1877–78 season he organized shows of 'Nubians' from the Egyptian
Sudan. Here, his declared aim was to give the spectators an idea of
the ingenious methods employed by the African hunters in tracking,
stalking and catching the animals destined for the Hagenbeck menagerie. While the Sami were sent on tour to Berlin and Leipzig, the
so-called Nubians travelled as far as the Jardin d'Acclimatation in

Paris and Alexandra Palace in London, where they attracted visitors in their tens of thousands. Encouraged by this financial success, which helped to compensate for his losses in the animal trade, Hagenbeck engaged, or took over from other impresarios during the years that followed, troupes of Eskimos (Inuit), Indians and Sinhalese, Patagonians and Fuegians, Australian Aborigines, Kalmyks and Mongolians from the Russian empire, Bella Coola from America's north-west coast, Sioux, Samoans, Somalis, Maasai and Dualas, as well as more Lapps and Nubians. The animal trade recovered in the mid-eighties, and Hagenbeck, in a letter written in the nineties, complains that there was too much competition in ethnic shows to be able to make a decent profit from them any more. Other sources confirm this, showing an enormous increase in ethnic shows in Hamburg alone, not to mention other parts of Germany. Ethnic shows at Hagenbeck's were, nevertheless, to continue for some years, although they were no longer a central business activity, becoming merely a sideline.

In 1907 there came an important change, with the realization of Hagenbeck's dream of opening a permanent zoo in his Tierpark. This opened up new possibilities for the ethnic shows: the organizers were no longer forced to adapt the size of the troupe to the limitations of the stages and the requirements of each tour, but could keep the shows in the park for a whole season without restrictions on space. Accordingly, troupe sizes grew to several hundred members, tours became rarer, and 'native villages' were extravagant in their size and in the details of their staging. This new flowering of the ethnic show came to an abrupt end in 1914. In the 1920s, following the end of the First World War, Hagenbeck's ethnic shows staged a tentative come-back, but never again regained their former complexity and success. Cinema had appeared as a competitor which was far more capable of generating the illusion of the exotic dream than even the best-equipped ethnic show. In particular, the general public was attracted by the opulent silent movies of the twenties, with their exotic settings and locations, for example Joe May's *The Indian Tomb* (*Das indische Grabmal*; 1921). Such was the craze for the new medium that Carl Hagenbeck's heirs and their Umlauff cousins joined the film business, drawing on their expertise from the ethnic shows.

Hagenbeck staged his last ethnic show in 1932, with a troupe of Tcherkess riders, whose performance was more a circus number than an exhibit underlining ethnic difference. The New Caledonians (Kanaks), who had been under contract a year earlier, were already considered to have undergone too great a process of acculturation to present an exotic Other: they live on in the lore surrounding Hagenbeck as an unspectacular people who turned up in European dress rather than in the picturesque costumes likely to appeal to the public. As a consequence, South Sea garments had to be copied in a hurry from examples supplied by the Museum of Ethnology. To make matters worse, the boats which they were under contract to carve had capsized when they were launched, and the Hagenbeck employees found that the group had greater mastery of the foxtrot than of Pacific dances.

The Authentic and the Picturesque: Recruitment Criteria and Methods

As a businessman, Hagenbeck set out to maximize profit. The organization of ethnic shows entailed a considerable outlay, and in 1910, expenses were in the region of 60,000 Reichsmarks or more. In addition, for some time the shows had needed to compensate for the losses in the animal trade. As a consequence, the criteria applied in selecting ethnic groups and individuals for exhibition had to be carefully defined.

The list of about seventy ethnic shows organized by the Hagenbecks between 1874 and 1932 shows that only a very small percentage of the exhibits were recruited from German colonies. Rather, recruitment followed the pattern already established by the animal trade, where Hagenbeck had so many good contacts that he was able to bypass the colonial network. Quite a number of his recruitment agents were animal trappers or animal traders.

Before choosing an ethnic group for a show, a number of restrictions had to be taken into account. When, as was usual, the territory of another European state was involved, it was necessary to obtain the permission of its colonial administration and often a bond had to be deposited to cover fees and travel expenses. From 1901, it was forbidden to recruit for such shows from German colonies without a special permit. During the First World War and for some years after, recruitment from the territories of other states was impossible.

In addition to these external limitations, there were three essential criteria which had to be applied in selecting an ethnic group for exhibition: the group must be strange in some way; it must have particular physical characteristics; and it must have picturesque customs. The people in question must appear strange to the public, but it was impractical for them to be too strange. It was for this reason that the Hagenbecks experienced failure when they tried to contract the Wedda of Sri Lanka, the Andaman Islanders and the Kwakiutl Indians, who had neither the degree of contact with Europeans, nor the familiarity of at least some of their number with a European language, which were necessary for ease of recruitment and the smooth running of the show. Physical character- istics were an important aspect of selection. The group might display a special beauty and grace in the eyes of the European public – one of the reasons why there were so many Sinhalese and Somali shows at Hagenbeck's. The East Africans, in particular, with their Caucasian features and their tall and slender build, were a constant draw for the crowds, who returned again and again to see them. On the other hand, ugliness or 'freakiness', judged by European standards, also promised a good show. Although this did not occur frequently in Carl Hagenbeck's shows, as he favoured an ideal of 'ethnographic authenticity', individ- uals or groups with bodily or cultural deformations, such as the 'Sinha- lese dwarves', sometimes appeared in his shows. Hagenbeck refused, however, to stage such phenomena as 'negresses with lip-plates' or 'Burmese giraffe-neck women', considering them to be too extreme.

The concept of picturesque customs could encompass a variety of practices. John Hagenbeck, Carl's half-brother, who had settled permanently in Ceylon and provided many troupes and animals from that island, used the term 'picturesque' to include those members of Indian and Sinhalese society who were professional entertainers even in their own countries. He thus liked to recruit troupes consisting mainly of snake charmers, bear trainers, bamboo artistes, magicians, yogis and dancers, accompanied by artisans. Other recruiters sought out the picturesque in house forms, costumes or dances, when choosing an ethnic group. Selection could also be on the basis of customs which were unknown in Europe. Here, a female troupe would be presented as the 'Amazon Battalion' from Dahomey, or Kanaks would be presented as cannibals. These two 'hoax' troupes did not, however, meet with Carl Hagenbeck's standards: the 'Amazons' were under contract with his nephew, Umlauff, and the Kanaks were employed by his sons long after his death. A further factor in the choice of ethnic groups for display was the question of supply and demand: Indians, Sinhalese and Somalis were recruited many times because they were great crowd-pullers. By contrast, following the failure of the Bella Coola and Kalmyk shows, these groups were not employed again.

Once the ethnic group had been decided upon, the individuals who were to 'perform' had to be selected equally carefully. The most impor- tant factor was, once again, their physical appearance: those chosen should look like the ideal anthropological type for their region; in the words of the organizers, they should be 'genuine' types. After the death of a whole troupe of Eskimos (Inuit) and most of a troupe of Fuegians, Hagenbeck saw to it that every person had to be checked by a doctor and vaccinated before being recruited. To guarantee the smooth running of the show, he preferred most of his performers (with the exception of a few translators) to be unable to speak a European language, fearing that contact with the spectators might stir them up, inciting revolt or conflict. For the same reason, he once asked one of his recruiters to see to it that 'no drunkards or quarrellers' were among the contracted persons.

It was important when recruiting to produce a balanced group with regard to sex and age. The organizers felt that the presence of women and children made a show especially attractive and gave a better picture of 'the foreign peoples' family lives'. Some recruiters also tested the performing abilities of the potential recruits by paying them to compete in certain tasks. In the years before the opening of the zoo, the number of persons in the troupe was another essential factor, as they had to fit into different exhibition areas, or on to smaller stages when on tour. Touring was considered necessary to maximize profits. A time-consuming part of recruitment lay in the collection and/or purchase of ethnographic objects. Some of these were used to equip the show, while others were put on public display. After the end of the show, all were given away or sold, often to ethnological museums.

The extent of the Hagenbeck sources is such that it has enabled a detailed comparison of several recruitment tours to be made, revealing great disparities in the relative power of individuals and of the various ethnic groups. Some participants signed contracts to tour Europe for one or two years without having any idea of what it would be like. Others, such as the Sioux Indians, had long performed in such shows and were perfectly aware of what to expect. Some individuals came from a context of deprivation, signing up in order to escape poverty or debts, whereas groups such as the Sami had a wealthy background and dictated the terms of their contracts, even requiring that salaries be paid to replacement herdsmen for the period of their absence. All sources indicate that money was the most important motive for prospective participants in the ethnic shows. The main goal of the organizers and of the (voluntary) participants was thus basically the same.

Around the World for Fifty Pfennig: Organization and Exhibits

Unlike some other organizers, Hagenbeck's company always engaged in contracts with the participants of its ethnic shows. These documents set out all the arrangements for food and medical care, and specified what work was required, and salaries. The early shows were accompanied by a housekeeper, who cooked and washed for the participants, but it was later considered more practical for all concerned to allow the performers to cook for themselves. This enabled traditional and religious practices relating to the killing of animals, the preparation of food, and its consumption, to be respected. The organizers found that this brought with it an additional attraction, in that the spectators could watch the participants cook and eat their food.

The working day was from eight to ten hours in length, with as many performances, suggesting that performances lasted for about half an hour. On Sundays or bank holidays the hours could be greater because of the increased number of spectators. A comparative survey of about 50 shows staged by other companies has shown that this was the usual working pattern in Germany in this business. Two kinds of attraction were offered to visitors: planned performances and native villages. Almost all the performances comprised four main elements, whatever the origin, true or otherwise, of the performers. These were music, dance, fighting and a procession with animals. For Carl Hagenbeck, a central aim was to show the daily relationships with animals of the various groups from across the world. As a result, he did not speak of 'ethnic' shows, but of 'zoological-anthropological shows'. By 1895 at the latest, the performances were no longer a series of unconnected parts, but were turned into dramatic narratives with a peaceful opening scene, a dramatic incident and climax (for example, an abduction or an attack on the village), which allowed a fight to be staged, followed by a happy ending (for example, a peace treaty or a marriage ceremony) which provided the opportunity for singing, dancing and the animal procession.

From 1907 onwards, the native villages became the most important element. From the outset, Hagenbeck had tried to have the show participants live in, and act in front of, native dwellings. If these could not be transported, the raw materials for their construction were imported and they were built at the showground itself. The vast area of the permanent zoo allowed the construction of huge villages. Hagenbeck's nephew, Heinrich Umlauff, one of Germany's most important dealers in ethnographic objects, created enormous backdrops representing well-known scenes or buildings such as the Pyramids, or Indian temples. The publicity brochures offered a guided tour, pointing out all the highlights: the famous ruins of X, the variety of house types, the dwelling of the chieftain, or the warrior who had fought in the well-known battle of Y, the bazaar, and the artisans' stalls. The illusion of a trip to a distant land became increasingly complete. The visitor could watch the foreign peoples cook, eat, work with animals and produce crafts; he could taste exotic dishes, and ride a camel or in a rickshaw; or he could go to the barber's to have his beard shaved off. And this chance to tour the world for 50 pfennig could be even more marvellous when there were several ethnic shows from different regions present in the zoo at the same time. 'If you want to see Africa, don't set out on a long trip, but come to see the one hundred Somalis in Hagenbeck's zoo' read one advertisement, offering a risk-free journey with few expenses.

Impact on Scientists, Journalists, Spectators and Participants

Nearly all of the Hagenbeck ethnic shows went on tour within Germany, but also to France, the Austrian Empire, Switzerland, England, Belgium, Sweden, Norway, Italy, Holland and the Argentine. It is highly probable that they had a considerable impact on the crowds they drew and were more influential than any German colonial exhibition of more limited location and duration. The proliferation of these shows was in part due to the scientists of the time. Hagenbeck became a member of the Berlin Society for Anthropology, Ethnology and Prehistory, and saw to it that there was an extra performance of each new show for its members. Afterwards, anthropometric measurements could be taken and ethnographic interviews carried out. He would sometimes receive special requests that recruitment for future shows be carried out in particular areas. A number of scholars claimed to have confirmed their hypotheses through ethnic shows, or to have used materials collected there. University departments for non-European languages and musicologists used participants as informants. In the meantime, the general public could consult the 'race plates' in the successful German Brockhaus encyclopedia, displaying individuals from ethnic shows, until the 1950s. The Hagenbeck Bella Coola show of 1885–86 had a particular impact, inspiring the young ethnologist Franz Boas to such an extent that he spent the rest of his life carrying out research on the American northwest coast, using as his principal source the informant earlier employed by Hagenbeck's recruitment agent. Boas emigrated to the United States and became one of the most influential founding fathers of American anthropology.

Museums were great beneficiaries of the ethnic shows, acquiring large numbers of ethnographic objects, on whose use they interrogated the participants of the shows. In return, they provided information or teaching materials for the shows. Heinrich Umlauff was one of the main intermediaries between the shows and the museums. His father had founded a company dealing in stuffed animals, minerals, shells, and ethnographic objects. This meant that in a place like Hamburg practically everything a ship or sailor brought home could be bought and put to profitable use by the Hagenbeck-Umlauff family. Hagenbeck bought live animals, while Umlauff stuffed dead ones, collected shells, minerals, curiosities, and even people – who could sometimes be put to use in the shows. By the mid-1880s, the Hagenbeck-Umlauff family's business success was such that they owned almost every building in one St Pauli street. The family, who moved comfortably between the academic and show worlds, had considerable influence: they had contacts throughout the world with animal dealers, showmen, and collectors, including the aristocracy and the Dalai Lama of the time.

A systematic examination of thirty-five newspapers, each covering a period of approximately sixty years, has failed to find any negative commentaries on the exhibition of exotic peoples. The reaction of the German press to the exhibitions was friendly, commenting mainly on aspects of the performances or on the participants. However, many of the articles appear to be part of the publicity campaigns for the shows and cannot therefore be said to represent an unbiased view. Only a few church and missionary papers questioned the principle of putting people on display.

The reactions of the spectators manifest an overwhelming desire to make verbal and physical contact with the participants in the shows. Even though the organizers were careful to avoid the inclusion of too many participants who could speak a European language, the audience attempted to communicate with them as much as possible. Some sources report that the crowds were not willing to depart, even when the exhibition area was closing. According to other, mostly unpublished, sources, in particular impresarios, one aspect of this attraction was erotic in nature. Flirtations, sexual contacts, love affairs and marriages were not uncommon between participants and spectators. While these were tolerated between European men and non-European women, they caused a scandal when they were between European women and non-European men. Relationships between European girls and men from ethnic shows were reported as early as 1878.

The German public appears to have had a fixed set of expectations concerning most ethnic shows, albeit more so for some than others. For example, in the case of American Indians, the Plains Indians met the expectations of the audiences and were a success, while those from the north-west coast failed to draw the crowds. It would therefore appear that the Hagenbeck shows confirmed rather than created images of the 'ethnic Other', nevertheless having a considerable impact on a wide audience, as already discussed. As is demonstrated by the careers of the Hagenbeck show organizers, both the businesses and those who ran them had the capacity to transform themselves in a changing technical environment, moving from ethnic shows to silent movies (and, later, 'talkies'), influencing the way in which the exotic Other was constructed in this new popular medium.

Most of the sources on ethnic shows are by Europeans, providing very little insight into the views of participants. The latter were treated with more or less cruelty or humanity, depending on the character of the tour impresario. The most common attitude among the organizers appears to have been one of paternalism. One Inuit participant's diary records homesickness and boredom, the monotony of strange food, his panic in the face of large crowds, but also his astonishment and pleasure on a sightseeing trip, and his satisfaction at the perfect demonstration of his skills during performances (Taylor 1981; Thode-Arora 2002a). Occasional remarks by participants (American Indians and Kanaks) suggest a new impression that they were respected by Europeans outside the colonial territories. Correspondence shows, moreover, that some of the participants tried to take part in further Hagenbeck shows, once their contracts had ended, while others seem to have returned home to face a frosty reception and to have sunk into depression.

Note

1 The article draws on Thode-Arora 1989, 1992, 1997 and 2002a. For detailed references of sources, see these items.

15

Africa Meets the Great Farini

SHANE PEACOCK

The so-called Dark Continent drew its share of eccentric Europeans to its 'undiscovered' regions in the eighteenth and nineteenth centuries, but few, if any, matched Guillermo Antonio Farini. His life was a whirlwind of adventures, his attention shifting from one exploit to another, exploring each subject and then moving on. Africa and African people came into his rotating gaze in the late 1870s, and though he would exhaust this interest within a decade, his impact on the burgeoning business of African exhibitions was substantial.

He was afflicted to some degree by the racism of his time, but unlike some of his contemporaries did not emphasize the supposed inferiority of the people he exhibited. A consummate showman with a touch of genius and a preference for frightening his audiences, he had created many show-business sensations, and when Africans graced his performances he made them stars too; thus his shows were a disservice to people whom he had not set out to slander.

William Leonard Hunt, who would come to call himself Farini, probably saw very few people of African descent during his formative years. He was born on 10 June 1838 in Lockport, New York, but was actually the son of Canadian parents, and grew up in the little towns and countryside of southern Ontario. Here, slavery had long been outlawed and the population was relentlessly Anglo-Saxon Protestant.[1] Many, like Willie Hunt's mother, were United Empire Loyalists, Americans who had stayed loyal to the British crown at the time of the American Revolution and had fled north to find huge lots of land virtually handed to them by the king. They thus became pseudo-aristocrats by virtue of their holdings, and immediately considered themselves the upper class and the moral arbiters of the infant society they began to create; anyone non-English, non-Protestant and especially non-white fell distinctly below them on their social pecking order. Since the Scottish, the Irish and Roman Catholics were so lowly regarded, it was no surprise that

North American Indians, who had occupied this land before them, were accorded a place only slightly higher than the animals; people of African descent, though free in this new world, were so rarely seen and so obviously non-white that they were similarly disrespected.

Bill Hunt was a rebel in this society almost from the instant he was born into it. Blessed, or cursed (as his parents felt), with extraordinary energy, he was constantly in trouble: at school, at home and on the muddy roads of the villages. Brainy, muscular and imaginative, he found life in southern Ontario monotonous and restrictive. For him, only the travelling American circuses, which visited the area once or twice during the summers and were full of exotic feats and people, could momentarily explode the drudgery. But the unadulterated thrills it gave him were frowned upon by his parents and their friends, who considered circus people low and their shows immoral.

A Vocation

Bill secretly visited the circuses and then set out to learn the feats he witnessed. This he did extremely well and by the time he was 21 years old, despite having been diverted into medical studies by his father, was an accomplished amateur wire-walker, acrobat and strongman. When he debuted as Signor Farini (he took this name, of an Italian war hero and political leader, because using his own would have shamed his family) on a 'high rope' in the little town of Port Hope in 1859 he was an immediate sensation. But his father, who was conveniently out of town during the performance, essentially disowned him for his actions.

Farini then took to the road on a swashbuckling, careering life of adventure, disdaining the morality of his childhood in exchange for passionate adulthood. Convinced that his parents had lived false lives, he wanted to live truthfully. He loved excitement and thought that, deep down, so did everyone else; he vowed to give people what they really wanted, on stages throughout the world. Though he had only been a professional wire walker for ten months, in 1860 he challenged the legendary Blondin, who claimed that no other man could cross above the gorge at Niagara Falls. As huge crowds came to watch and newspapers around the world wrote of the treacherous duel, Farini matched Blondin feat for feat. When the Frenchman stood on his head on his 275-metre (900-foot) long rope above the whirlpool, Farini did the same on a cable more than twice that length, upriver, closer to the falls; when the veteran walked with a man on his back, the upstart carried a taller and heavier man; and when the great man brought out a stove and cooked an omelette at mid-wire, the rebel lugged a washing machine across and did his laundry 55 metres (180 feet) above the eddying river.

His versatility in the pursuit of excitement was astonishing. After several years of high-wire adventures, he expanded his repertoire to feature acrobatics, strongman displays and trapeze exhibitions, as well as lecturing to his audiences about physical fitness. Once he even stilt-walked along the edge of the American Falls at Niagara, just to see if it could be done. He also sought adventure with the Union Army in the American Civil War, travelled to Europe, Asia, Africa and Australasia, became the lead artiste in the famous Flying Farinis trapeze show, and created circus headliners in 'Mademoiselle Lulu' (who could jump 9 metres [30 feet] into the air from solid stage boards and was actually a man, Farini's adopted son, in drag), and 'Zazel the Human Cannon-ball' who performed Farini's classic invention. He also presented many famous 'freaks'. So extraordinary were the dangerous feats his protégés performed and so mesmeric was his presence that a rumour circulated that he was the model for George du Maurier's evil character Svengali.[2] But Farini was much more than a showman; he was an inventor with at least 100 patents to his credit (among them folding theatre seats), an explorer, an author, a respected horticulturalist, and a linguist who could speak seven languages; and in old age he was a painter, a financier and businessman.[3]

It was in mid-career, just after he turned 40, that he became interested in Africa. He had been retired from performing for nearly a decade, and was in full Svengali mode, sporting a long, black beard and scaring audiences who came to the dark, glass-roofed interior of the huge Royal Westminster Aquarium in Central London, where he presented his sensational shows. The Aquarium was not always a successful venture, but whenever Farini had it in his grip, it thrived.

Situated across Broad Sanctuary from Westminster Abbey, 'the Aq' had been created in 1876 as a kind of cultural institution, complete with libraries and educational exhibitions; and it hosted elegant concerts, as well as lectures by esteemed scientists. Exotic fish were also meant to inhabit its numerous tanks, their mere presence an enlightenment to the gentlemen and ladies who would gaze at them. But such a mandate had little general appeal and within six months the Aquarium's financial losses were mounting. Its well-heeled board of directors sought out the one man in all of the Empire who could create the sort of show-business sensations that could vastly improve their fortunes in an instant. Much to the disdain of 'respectable' people (many of whom surreptitiously enjoyed his shows), Farini then gave them what they wanted.

The acts he was creating for his many protégés in those days were mostly gymnastic, though many were of a decidedly sensational sort. Like his own performances of an earlier time, his athletes seemed to be testing the limits of human accomplishment; indeed, it sometimes appeared as though 'The Great Farini' was actually trying to make them fly. Restricted in his activities as a child and taught that life had limitations (both moral and physical), he was determined to push the envelope.

At the Aquarium he began things, literally, with a bang. The human cannonball act, never seen before by stunned London audiences, drew tens of thousands. Farini stood at the cannon, looking evil in his black beard, commanding the sweet, beautiful young Zazel to enter the mortar, and lighting the fuse to a great flourish, sending her across the Aq's great hall into a net of his own invention. Despite protests from moralists, Londoners (and the Prince of Wales, who was enthralled) wanted more. Farini, almost erotically charged by the thrill of such acts and by the challenge of digging further into his mind to invent even more spectacular ones, was happy to oblige.

Soon there was Pongo the Gorilla, a frightening animal from the 'dark continent', presented as the only gorilla in captivity; then there were white whales (belugas), never seen before indoors in England; and even a 'mermaid', one of those sirens of the sea who called sailors into watery graves (though Farini's was, as he admitted from the outset, actually a manatee). And he had more than animals: his human beings still flew through the air, causing his spectators the greatest of unease. Beside shooting performers out of cannons, he projected them horrifying distances from 'human catapults', taught them to dive ghastly heights from ceiling to floor, and even presented a woman (of African descent) named LaLa 'the Black Venus', who hung upside down from a trapeze bar with a cannon in her mouth as it was ignited and fired. The exhibition of unusual human beings, not for what they did, but for whom they were, was not far behind.

Human Curiosity

The 'freak show' had existed, in one form or another, for a long time before Farini presented his first 'human curiosity'. In fact, the activities of its practitioners are recorded as far back as medieval English fairs. It was experiencing a major growth spurt in the late 1870s: dime museums, some even luxuriously appointed, with classy clientele and wealthy owners, were sprouting up in the burgeoning urban centres, especially in the Bowery in New York City. So when Farini began his brief involvement with this sort of entertainment, he was riding a wave of public interest, not creating one. However, with his showman's verve, he certainly contributed to its popularity; and his reputation, his intelligence and his ability to deceive his audiences also helped to give it a sort of legitimacy. Immediately, he attracted some of the world's most sensational 'freaks' to his fold: Millie-Christine the Two-Headed Nightingale, who were a pair of African-American conjoined twins born to southern slaves; Herr Haag the Elastic-Skin Man, who could pull the skin from his chest up over his head; Captain Costentenus, who boasted that an oriental khan had ordered him stripped naked, tied to the ground and tortured by a beautiful woman with '7,000,000 punctures of the quivering flesh', rendering him 'the world's most tattooed man'; dwarfs with extraordinary names like Baron Littlefinger, Count Rosebud and the Countess of Lilliput; and the 'Leopard Boy', a piebald young man who, it was claimed, came from a white African tribe. And in the early 1880s Farini invented his own 'freak', 'Krao the Missing Link', a simian-like little girl, destined to become one of the greats of her profession.

Africa – exotic and freakish to much of the Western world – happened into the news just as Farini was hitting his stride as a 'freak' merchant. It had been of intense interest to people outside its borders for several centuries, and intrigue grew in the mid-Victorian period as the manly feats of men like Livingstone, Stanley and Burton were celebrated far and wide in the 'civilized' world. But early in 1879 Africa was news for less celebratory reasons: when the impis of the Zulu King Cetewayo fell upon a regiment of the British army at Isandhlwana in the south, and killed 800 of Her Majesty's soldiers, Africans shot to the Empire's front pages with the speed and impact of a Zulu-thrown assegai. The Anglo-Zulu War would be won by the British within a few months, but Isandhlwana was not the only shocking blow inflicted on the victors. On the first day of June, the son of the exiled Emperor of France, who had been trained in military schools in England so he might one day return triumphantly to his homeland as Napoleon IV, was in a small group of British soldiers who were attacked by Zulus. 'Loulou' fought bravely but fell under a hail of 18 assegais. On the home front, the citizens of the empire on which the sun never set reeled from the news. African people, whom the English had for the most part considered mentally and physically inferior, were outsmarting and butchering their brightest young men. Though Zulus were still not accorded much true respect, they began to rise in the British public's mind as larger-than-life warriors of nearly superhuman capabilities.

The wizard of the Westminster Aquarium, the Great Farini, saw an opportunity. There was almost a sense of glee in the speed and style with which he immediately brought Britain's deadly enemies into their midst and on to their respectable stages (to perform war dances), while English soldiers were still dying at the hands of such frightening foreigners.

Farini's shows, going all the way back to his Niagara crossings, were designed to give audiences jolts and put them in touch with the most intense of their emotions. He was convinced that most people, like his parents and the 'respectable' citizens who had criticized him as a child and often criticized his thrilling acts as an adult, were fakes, afraid to look certain truths in the face. He once proclaimed 'I courted peril because I loved it, because the very thought of it fired my soul with ardour, because it was what others were afraid to face.'[4] In early 1879 Farini showed the British public what they claimed they were afraid to face: those monstrous Zulus.

The build-up began in March when he presented the 'Zulu Kaffir Boy', the first in a series of increasingly spectacular living African exhibitions. Later in the month the Aq featured 'Umgame, the Baby Zulu', and in April Farini tempted citizens with the 'Maravian Wild Women', Pawchee and Flycheia Letiaway, who were advertised as the 'dusky daughters' of a Maravi chief, kidnapped from their central African home in their youth by the warlike Zulus. Though not the enemies themselves, these two women, aged 20 and 23, generated some interest, mostly because Farini presented them in a way that connected them to the war. The Aq's publicity machine told the public that: 'The manner in which they illustrate the method of killing their war victims is in itself enough to strike terror into the stoutest heart. The fiendish reality of their war dances and songs is marvellous in its true and horrible intensity.'[5]

But customers were not yet truly offended by what they saw, and it was Farini's experience that it was often only when the public claimed that they were genuinely outraged that they were really interested and a show could be a sensation. *The Times* of London spoke of the 'two savage African women' rather benignly,[6] and the *Daily Telegraph* wrote that the exhibition had 'at least the recommendation of being well timed and throwing some light on the manners and customs of barbarous nations'.[7]

Farini was an intelligent man with an endlessly enquiring mind and he often tried to educate his audiences as he thrilled them. There is no doubt that he was trying to enlighten them a little with these 'ethnological' exhibitions, and it is equally undeniable that he was occasionally racist and condescending in his characterizations of the Africans he employed. But as the above quotations from England's two most respected newspapers indicate, the press had nothing on him. It is instructive to look at these comments, since they are not meant to make any sort of point or to sensationalize: Africans are factually 'savages' from a 'barbarous' continent, no questions asked. This is the atmosphere in which Farini worked. The press certainly never took him to task for racism, mostly because they were incapable of detecting any in his style of presentation. When he offended them it was usually because he scared them, thrilling them just a little more than they wanted.

Later that year he was ready to really offend. In May, while the war still raged, he sent his associate and veteran circus man Nat Behrens to southern Africa to do the unthinkable: sign some genuine Zulu men, warriors even, to come to London to show to the British public. (A few years later a booklet entitled *The Zulu Spy* [1881], written by Hercules Robinson and published in New York, claimed that it was Farini himself who had gone to the war front that summer, and had ridden dangerously back and forth between the opposing armies seeking adventure, even challenging and defeating legendary white Zulu leader and traitor John Dunn, with his fists. It was also claimed that the Zulus whom Farini signed were the actual men who had killed the Prince Imperial. Though there is a very slight chance this is true, there does not appear to be any hard evidence that Farini was in Africa at that time and the fact that this booklet was used as promotional material for 'Farini's Zulus' on P. T. Barnum's Greatest Show on Earth renders the story even less credible.)

Behrens found six men willing to come to London with him and, on instructions from Farini, took the utmost care to prove to everyone that these Zulus were the real thing, and most importantly, that they had come willingly. A letter was even published in the London papers confirming as much, signed at the police station in Durban by George James Forrester, Sergeant of the Licensed Native Labourers. Forrester also admonished Behrens in print to 'Take good care of the boys and bring them back safe'.[8] Not satisfied with that, Farini made sure that Behrens had every crew member and passenger on the *Balmoral Castle* sign a statement confirming that the six men on board with them were genuine Zulus and had come from Africa. Some of these passengers were citizens of considerable reputation. Sir Theophilus Shepstone, the Secretary of Native Affairs in Natal, also put in writing, for public consumption, that one of these Zulus was the eldest son of Chief Somkali.

Such brilliant showman's tactics ensured that London was waiting to see the Zulus, and a good-sized crowd came to the Southampton docks in late June to watch them disembark (a crowd that the American showman W. C. Coup outrageously estimated at 100,000 in his autobiography). Farini, perhaps growing wary that government officials would not be as thrilled as the general public, let it be known that they were 'friendly Zulus', loyal to the British crown.

But the government, still shamed by the death of the young Napoleon, and not yet able to defeat the Zulus, viewed this prospective Farini show with contempt. Though they did not legally bar his exhibits from entering the country, the Secretary of State for the Home Department (R. A. Cross, who had also tried to censor the human cannonball act) made it known that Zulus, friendly or not, were not welcome. Officials also made this abundantly clear to the board of directors at the Royal Westminster Aquarium. And so, with the Zulus veritably en route to their debut, the show was cancelled.

Farini was enraged. A rebel from birth and an outsider wherever he lived, it was not his way to give in to authority. He considered his Zulu exhibition to be something that the British public needed to see: a palpable truth, Zulus in flesh and blood, who should be witnessed in person, and understood, not declared anathema. And, of course, it was a hell of a good show. By the first week of July he had negotiated a deal with a rival venue, St James's Hall at Piccadilly and Regent Street, to unveil 'Farini's Friendly Zulus' in London. Fittingly, this popular theatre was famous for its blackface minstrel shows.

They opened on 8 July and the crowds came in droves, thrilled by the mere presence of these exotic men but particularly excited by the spectacle of the terrific throws of their assegais, which they buried deep into targets. Whether any members of the big crowds or packs of reporters ever imagined the five-inch blades of these deadly spears tearing into the youthful bodies of their own soldiers or the hallowed flesh of the Prince Imperial is a question that is worthwhile considering, though it probably will never be answered.

The Success

From time to time the Zulus played tourists in London during that summer of 1879. They were always accompanied by their hosts and often, it seemed, journalists were invited to be part of the party. One outing involved a trip to the zoo. Farini knew that Victorians, some of whom still believed that Africans were only a few links superior to apes in the chain of being, would be fascinated to read what ensued; indeed the trip may have been arranged as a sort of promotion. Frank Buckland, a friend and eminent writer on zoological subjects (as well as 'freaks' and ethnological exhibitions) reported that the Zulus were intrigued by the sight of wild animals in cages and that the 'chief', entranced by a particularly beautiful young lady who served him at the refreshment department, made enquiries concerning how many cows her father would accept in exchange for her (Bompas 1885: 378).

When the war ended the following month, the Aquarium immediately set aside its high moral standards and brought 'the Only Genuine Zulus' to the Aq. Here they stayed to the end of the year and into 1880, a show-business sensation. Soon Farini added five more Zulu men to his show. They had apparently come to him via a Parisian showman who had treated them badly, and were wary of white men. When another London impresario, anxious to capitalize on Farini's success, offered them more money they tried to leave the Aquarium and were only thwarted when Farini confiscated their clothing (he also claimed that he did so in order to prevent them from wandering the streets of London alone, where mischief could befall them). The Zulus, apparently not without legal advice, proceeded to take their dynamic boss to court.

The case was given great play in the newspapers and something of the relationship between the Zulu men and Farini was revealed. Their complaints apparently had nothing to do with harsh treatment, nor did they seem in the least concerned about being displayed like animals before the public; they were merely dissatisfied with their salaries. Farini replied that he would not force the men to remain with him and would pay their way back to Africa if they wanted to leave, but that they had had full understanding of the details of their contracts when they signed them, and therefore, while he would let them work in non-show-business professions in England he would under no circumstances allow another English showman to exhibit his legally contracted performers. The Zulus, on the other hand, still concerned by their treatment at the hands of their French employer, were tentative about the rebuff Farini had given them when they enquired about bettering their situation. Understandably, they did not see why they were not free to take the best financial offer presented to them. A few sympathetic Englishmen, like Theophilus Shepstone and the son of the famously liberal Bishop of Natal (Colenso) appeared in court speaking to the Zulus in their native language and helping them understand the proceedings, but a more typical response to their dilemma came from the *Daily Telegraph*, which offered the racist opinion that the men were obviously just lazy, unprepared to work at anything. One cannot help but wonder how the *Telegraph*'s white English journalist would have fared had he been suddenly deposited in southern Africa and subjected to the subtleties of Zulu law and culture. But in those days all sides knew little of each other and it showed in their actions and their words. Calling the men 'wretched creatures' and 'savages' the reporter said they should be: 'Turned adrift into the streets for a day, and then taken up for the first misdemeanour they committed and punished like ordinary criminals. So far they have been enjoying life vastly, living on the police-court poor-boxes, and successfully defying their employers' efforts to make them fulfil their contract. Whether [...] [they] will eventually [...] [be persuaded] to be honest remains to be seen, but meanwhile London is threatened by an impi of outrageous Zulus, determined to live here, but equally determined not to work.'[9]

By contrast Farini, who soon settled amicably with his employees, seemed a relatively benign force. He even found some humour, and some publicity, in the court case, immediately advertising that his new show consisted of 'discontented Zulus, who are now becoming contented'.[10] But that wasn't the end of Farini's association with Zulu exhibitions, though the next phase was hastened by unwanted influences. By 1880 he was under extreme pressure from various government powers attempting to pass legislation that would ban his 'dangerous performances' (it should be noted that the exhibition of human beings was never considered unfit for the public and was therefore never part of this legislation). P. T. Barnum was simultaneously urging him to come to the United States. So in the spring of 1880 he left England and brought several of his famous acts to The Greatest Show on Earth; among them were four of the Zulus.

Americans, without any personal involvement in the war in southern Africa, had only a few preconceived notions about Zulu people and certainly did not regard them with horror. A satirical article in the 23 August 1879 *New York Clipper* (complete with a caricature depicting them as pitch-black, bug-eyed, thick-lipped and child-like) had even presented Farini's Zulus as harmless, as much in danger from the excesses of Western life as from their own 'savageness'.[11] Nevertheless, when Dingando, Possomon, Maguibi and Ousan ran into the circus ring in front of a big crowd in New York City that April dressed in full battle costume, they stirred and even frightened a great many spectators. Farini had their targets set up at one end of the ring, just in front of a portion of the audience, and when they hurled their assegais they struck terror into the hearts of many nearby spectators. The fascinated newspaper reporters called them 'copper-coloured men' and liked to write about their colourful ostrich feathers and the scantiness of their attire, referring to them as nearly naked. They also seemed incapable of not mentioning their well-developed and apparently not unattractive physiques.

Through that year, and the following two seasons in America with W. C. Coup's New United Monster Shows (of which Farini was part-owner) and the 1882 Barnum show, Farini's Genuine Zulus played on the biggest stages in the world. The circus was approaching its golden age and crowds of 10,000 for a single performance were not uncommon. Farini's intention was to give Americans a show unlike any they had ever seen before, to thrill them just as he had with the human cannon-ball act. But he (and each of his performers) was also creating a misconception: that all Zulus were savage warriors.

Those three years in America produced several intriguing incidents. In late May 1880 in Detroit one of the Zulus, a 'chief', dressed himself in American street clothes and left the show unannounced. That evening he was said to have been seen enjoying a drink at a local saloon, but it was not until a few days later that he was found by Barnum's men, across the Canadian border at 'a negro settlement' in Windsor.[12] Farini was an accomplished linguist and had apparently acquired a smattering of Zulu. One of his employees was dispatched to Windsor to speak to the chief, who shortly thereafter, apparently without coercion of any sort, agreed to return to the show when it played Chicago on 1 June. The reason for his hiatus in Detroit was never publicized, and he never again felt inclined to leave.

For Coup's shows Farini supplied the 'only Female Zulus ever brought to America', a foot-race between a Zulu and a North American Indian was sometimes run on the hippodrome track, and the circus's banners and advertisements often featured huge drawings of the Zulus in full war costume, making for curious sights on the front pages of frontier town newspapers. On Barnum's 1882 show the invidious concept of comparing African natives with animals was brought to a new low when Zulus were occasionally featured running in competition with horses. Later that season, on 21 August in Rome, New York, a stir was created when a Zulu child was born; the show's route book described the occasion: 'Arrival into the world of the first American Zulu born in captivity, to use a Jumbonian expression. Signor Farini was delighted, as there is a chance now of one of his many apprentices becoming President of this great republic.'[13]

Although Farini ended his direct association with the giant American circuses after 1882, he continued to manage several Zulu exhibits into the mid-1880s and booked some of them with US circuses, including Barnum's. In an interview in 1884 he remarked that he once had 33 Zulus working for him, divided into three troupes, and on the very day of the interview still had a dozen in his employ. Though he was not the first showman to exhibit Zulu people (they had been to England as early as 1853), he certainly did it in the most spectacular way. Who else but Farini would have graphically shown the English how you brutally murder an Englishman with a spear, at the very moment when fathers, sons and brothers were being similarly butchered? His Zulu shows were the best of their kind, if such a phrase can be used, and his performers (and they certainly were such) appear to have worked willingly and under at least tolerable conditions. It also seems apparent that his Zulus were actually who he claimed they were, a fact that is of note since it was not uncommon for Victorian promoters to exhibit 'exotic Africans' who were really from places like Hoboken or the Bronx. There are many stories of such hoaxes. W. C. Coup told a particularly interesting one, in which Farini himself was knowingly or unknowingly complicit:

About 1882 a very tall specimen of the African race walked into an Eastern museum looking for work. He was actually over seven feet in height, and had never been on exhibition. Knowing that his value as a negro giant would be but little, the proprietors resolved to introduce him as a monster wild African. After consulting Rev. J. G. Woods' *Illustrated History of the Uncivilized Races*, it was determined to make a Dahomey of the tall North Carolinian. A theatrical costumer was set to work to make him a picturesque garb. A spurious telegram was issued, purporting to be from Farini of London, stating that the Dahomey giant had sailed with his interpreter from London and would arrive in Boston on or about a certain date. The man, with his interpreter, was then taken by train to Boston, from which city they, in due time, wired the museum proprietor of their arrival. That telegram was answered by another telling them to take the first Fall River boat for New York City. The press was then notified, and the representatives of five New York papers were actually sent to the pier the following morning to interview the distinguished stranger from Dahomey. The man had been well schooled, and pretending not to know a word of English, could not, of course, converse with the reporters. But his interpreter managed to fill them up very comfortably. At all events, long and interesting accounts of the 'snuff-coloured giant from Dahomey' appeared in most of the dailies, and for several weeks this Dahomey was the stellar attraction at that particular dime museum. The advent of summer and its consequent circus season closing the city museums, the Dahomey 'joined out' with a side show in which, for successive seasons, he posed

as a Dahomey giant, a Maori from New Zealand, an Australian aborigine
and a Kaffir. This man's success was the initiative for a score of other
negroes, who posed as representatives of any foreign races the side-show
proprietor wished to exhibit. (Coup 1901: 47–49)

Return to London

Farini was back at the Royal Aquarium in London by 1883 and his interest
in Africa, stimulated by his contact with Zulus, was still growing. The
following year he sent W. A. Healey, his right-hand man at the Aq, to
the southern part of the continent to persuade a different sort of African
native to come to London. These people, six of whom returned with
Healey from the area of the southern Kalahari Desert, were presented at
the Aq as 'Earthmen', 'pygmies' or 'yellow dwarfs', but they were better
described as Bushmen and most accurately as San, the short-statured
indigenous people of the Kalahari who had lived in southern Africa for
15,000 years and had been pushed into residing in the desert by the
intrusion of Europeans. The six individuals who made their debut at the
Westminster Aquarium that year were described in the following way in
Farini's African Pygmies, an Aquarium publicity pamphlet: 'N'co N'Qui,
a kind of captain or chief, and a giant in his own country, aged thirty-
five years, height 4 feet 6 inches. N'Arbecy, the chief's wife, still taller,
height 4 feet 6¼ inches, aged forty years. N'Fim N'Fom, the chief's
favourite dancer, aged twenty-four years, height 4 feet 1 inch. N'Co, a
fine shot and good hunter, not afraid of tackling a lion single handed,
aged 19 years, height 4 feet 1½ inches. N'Icy, the daughter of two fine
specimens that ran away, aged twelve years. N'Arki, the son of the chief,
aged six years, and still nurses' (see Clement 1967: 178–82).

They were presented in 'Farini's Desert in the Aquarium', a show
that featured them stalking a lion and an ostrich, shooting poisoned
arrows, building their homes in ant hills and, of course, performing war
dances. Their shows were accompanied by a great deal of literature and
many lectures, detailing their appearance, customs, and history. This
was all part of Farini's 'aggrandized' style of ethnological exhibitions
and 'freak shows' in which he attempted to give some scientific integrity
to his presentations. For example, his 'Krao, the Missing Link', then a
sensation, was never exhibited as a leering, ugly 'freak', but instead as a
gentle young girl discovered in South-East Asia, whom scientists were
asked to examine, and whom Farini educated and adopted. At this point
in his life he was actually beginning to shed his former fascination with
terrifying his audiences, and his impending marriage to a German lady

of high breeding and social caste helped to push him towards a less sensational style of showmanship.

He did teach his Victorian spectators something about the San people, though he occasionally made errors, both intentional and unintentional, and was certainly motivated by show-business principles as well as by scientific ones. For example, he made the bizarre statement that the African 'dwarf's' yellowish skin colour was due to extended habitation underground and, as Robert Bogdan has pointed out, he showed his exhibits in leopard-skin shorts, so they would look 'primitive' and perhaps animal-like next to the Aquarium's elegantly attired white lecturers (1988: 189). However, while the San people were obviously not presented as equal to English citizens, the Farini show did not make their supposed inferiority its main focus. He gave audiences a sort of secondary-level, Anglocentric education about Africans while displaying them as human exhibits, a murky elucidation that one might argue was worse than no education at all.

The 'Earthmen' exhibition was not a typical Farini show. Unlike the Zulu presentation, it lacked danger and sensation; and though Farini was moving away from that to some degree, it was still unusual for him to give the public something without much adventure in it. San people were first brought to England more than thirty years earlier and though his show was an involved, exotic one that tried to give the British the sense of actually being in the Kalahari, it really made little 'progress', either scientifically or theatrically, over the 1850s. In fact in some ways it repeated the earliest shows. It did do well at the box office, like almost all of his shows, and that is its major legacy. Farini himself did not seem nearly as interested in this show as he had been in the Zulus, which perhaps accounts for some of its imitation of the tired and racist presentation methods of an earlier time.

Although it has been said that 'Farini's Dwarf Earthmen' were first exhibited at Coney Island, New York, and even that he actually discovered them there being presented by another showman, no evidence for that has been found, and it is almost certain that they debuted in September at the London Aq and then crossed the Atlantic for New York City appearances at Steinway Hall in December. There the *New York Clipper* reviewed them with typical nineteenth-century white man's chauvinism, displaying superficial knowledge of Darwin's theories and very little else: 'Their conversation is similar to the chatter of monkeys, yet it is said they are intelligent in their own way [...] their heads [are] narrow and unintellectual.'[14]

The 'Earthmen' toured the eastern United States that year and through 1885, appearing in the most prestigious dime museums, like the luxurious Austin and Stone's in Boston, and Kohl and Middleton's in Chicago. At the latter city the 'Queen' of the group gave birth, but the baby died. A great deal was written about the Sans' reaction: it was said they painted themselves, chanted and shrieked in grief. It was also reported that they were terribly distraught by the fact that their child was buried in the ground.

But Farini had no influence, either good or bad, on his employees' troubles in Chicago. By that time he was far away, in Africa, deep in the Kalahari Desert. Though this would be the pinnacle of his fascination with Africa, it was, curiously, also the beginning of the end. As with many of his interests, his African period had started slowly, then built to a climax, and would soon evaporate, as if he had experienced everything he wanted and needed a new challenge.

Unlike most show-business impresarios or 'freak show' promoters, Farini was capable of doing almost every feat he masterminded. For example, though some thought him cruel for asking a young woman to allow herself to be shot from a cannon, there is no question that he would have done it himself (and probably had in rehearsal) and had many times in his youth performed feats that were much more dangerous. Similarly, he was not just a merchant of exotic human exhibitions; he travelled to most of the places where his exhibits originated and sometimes even arrived in person, in jungles or deserts, to persuade people to come home with him.

The wonderful stories he had heard about the Kalahari from natives and friends, of seas of sand, undiscovered diamonds, ranch lands and unusual people, were irresistible. By January 1885 he was on board an ocean steamer with Lulu (his adopted son and protégé) and a Baster guide, and within another two months he was on a covered wagon in the midst of a perilous journey through parts of the Kalahari few people had ever visited. But he was undaunted: it was unparalleled adventure and that was what he lived for.

During the course of the seven-month trip he met a great variety of people: English, Boers, Germans, Malays, Basters, Khoikhoin, San, Zulus and others. Part way through he encountered several 'pygmies', whom he claimed were of unique appearance; he was fascinated by their peculiarities and convinced them to return with him to London. (He said he found them in the Lake N'Gami region and called them 'M'Kabba' dwarfs, though they may have been Koba.) He described them as averaging just slightly more than 1.2 metres (4 feet) in height, and recalled their strange customs of tattooing themselves with a blue dye and amputating the first joint of each little finger. He also commented, with typical Farini irreverence, that their projecting stomachs made them look like 'so many dwarf aldermen of the desert' (Farini 1973 [1886]: 253). It is difficult to ascertain who these people really were and whether Farini fabricated some of their unusual characteristics. But coming face to face with Africans in their homeland was just a very small part of his trip. So many other things caught his interest: he searched for diamonds, scouted ranch lands, explored rocky falls, hunted wild animals, ate everything the natives offered him, examined and carefully pressed flora and fauna, and nearly killed himself and his companions at least once or twice. And all the while he recorded what he saw in a diary and on his return wrote a book entitled *Through the Kalahari Desert* (1973 [1886]), which would be published in five countries in three languages.

Although this journey would give him his fill of Africa and he would start to wind down his African exhibitions upon returning to London, there were incidents during its course which give insights into Farini and his approach to the Dark Continent.

Discoveries

The first incident concerns one of the most intriguing stories in Farini's storied life. He claimed that when he was far into the unmapped depths of the desert he stumbled upon the ruins of an ancient civilization, in a place where history records no such African culture. It was as if he found Atlantis, peeking up through the sands.

Although his book was a success and it was reviewed in many major publications, leading him to be invited to speak at the Royal Geographical Society, London, and the Berlin Geographical Society (which he did, in German), little notice was taken of the book's brief account of his strange discovery. But in the twentieth century 'the Lost City of the Kalahari' has become one of the enduring legends of southern African lore. Two books have been entirely devoted to it (Clement 1967; Goldie 1963), while many others mention it, and dozens upon dozens of expeditions have been organized to find it, some government-sponsored, some including eminent professors, anthropologists, adventurers and even a famous author (Alan Paton). Searches have been conducted by jeep, car, truck and aeroplane; aerial photographs have been examined and re-examined. The bizarre stories of many individuals, native and white, have been recorded, many asserting that they have seen the mystical ruins and others even claiming that they house hidden treasures; Farini's biography has even been included in the *Encyclopaedia of Southern Africa*. But no one has ever found his city.

In a strange way the legend of the Lost City of the Kalahari is part of Farini's African entertainment legacy. Many believe he fictionalized parts of his book and that the lost city ruin was a particularly ingenious invention. Others, some of whom have searched for it and are well-informed, take the ruin very seriously and think it will be found some day. But whether it really exists or not sometimes appears to be beside the point: it is a marvellous story, a spectacular story, and Farini set it in Africa. He knew that Western civilization was deeply fascinated by the Dark Continent, and whether he was exhibiting its peoples or creating a legend situated in one of its most mysterious regions, he exploited the spectacle Africa provided. The Lost City of the Kalahari, among other things, is a show-business sensation.

But there is another, perhaps more important insight into Farini's attitude toward Africa and its peoples that can be gleaned from his account of his Kalahari exploration. This concerns the question of his racism. His book contains many observations and comments that we in the twentieth century (and even some in the nineteenth century) consider racist, and yet an even casual reading turns up contradictions. In fact, some are so striking that one might even build a case for Farini as an antiracist.

Early in the book he makes numerous comments about the laziness and uselessness of certain natives and is caustic in his criticism, but it soon becomes evident that the colour of one's skin does not excuse anyone from his wrath. The Boers, for example, are given a constant flogging and he undoubtedly despises them with a passion that supersedes anything he feels for natives. He is especially hard on them for the way they treat Africans, and becomes so disturbed about it that he occasionally can barely find the adjectives: for example, one dishonest Boer who tried to con him was characterized as one of many 'honourable, blackmailing, religious, sanctimonious, upright, thieving scoundrels' (1973: 82).

Another intriguing moment occurs when Farini and his party arrive in the dusty diamond town of Kimberley after an arduous trek and are told by the owner of their hotel that Gert Louw, their Baster guide, must sleep in the stables. Basters are actually the mixed descendants of Boers and Hottentots, but the owner is adamant that a 'black man' would never sleep inside the doors of his establishment. Farini then vociferously intercedes on Gert's behalf, a noble action that very few Victorian white men would have dared. Indeed, by the time Farini has finished putting his case to the owner, Gert is sleeping in his boss's hotel room, and in fact is bunked down in the coolest part of these decidedly hot accommodations. Within a few weeks Farini is bristling at Gert's laziness, but does so on the basis of his actions, not his skin colour. Farini thought just about everyone lazy, and relative to his own approach to life, he was probably correct.

When white officials at the Kimberley mines told him that thievery was rife and its practitioners were natives, he wrote in his diary that he felt they were being wrongly accused. And when he saw natives abused and disrespected in urban centres he wrote: 'The black man is not improved by a veneer of civilization. The real "savage", who has never been in contact with the whites, has a certain amount of honour and chivalry about him, and one cannot help admiring him; but the half-Christianized black is a lying, lazy scoundrel, without a spark of self-respect...' (Farini 1973 [1886]: 75).

Upon his return to England he wrote this surprisingly tender passage in his book: 'the poor Bushman is hardly dealt with. The big game is driven from the country by the Boers and their flocks; the small game he cannot hunt, as his poisoned arrow and bows are always taken from him; so he is obliged to steal some of the flocks to exist, for which he is punished by depriving him of his liberty which he loves so well. Is it a wonder he resists capture so desperately? But the march of civilization has no ears for the cries of those poor wretches whom it crushes if they stand in its way' (1973 [1886]: 442). These words come from the same man who exhibited Zulus and San people on 'freak-show' stages and in 1864 had supported George McClellan's presidential bid against Abraham Lincoln, in part because he was against the emancipation of the slaves (though it must be noted that his opposition probably had more to do with the speed and nature of the decision rather than any support for the institution of slavery); the same man who said of a grass-covered stretch of the Kalahari, 'In the hands of an energetic white race this country could surely be made one of the most productive grazing lands in the world' (1973 [1886]: 159). So a somewhat contradictory picture arises.

The answer to the problem seems to be that Farini possessed some of the prejudices of his time, but nothing that was truly deep-seated. In fact, if he had been questioned concerning the equality of races, he might even have turned out to be somewhat liberal, relative to his contemporaries. But he was obsessed by adventure, by anything or anyone who struck him as unusual, and by the excitement that a really powerful show-business sensation could generate. Those passions tended to override any other concerns.

He had also grown up in a secluded world where black people truly were exotic. It had been a society that believed fervently in human hierarchies and while he detested such beliefs, preferring to think that human beings should be judged by their actions and not their heritage, he still inherited these notions somewhat; he was never free from the assumption that the Anglo-Saxon way was usually the superior way. Nor was he above the Victorian habit of judging groups of people by characteristics found in a few of their number (an approach to others which our own era has not completely shaken off). This, combined with his inexorable pursuit of excitement, allowed him to present his Zulu and San shows without questioning whether or not they might be detrimental to the individuals thus exhibited. He was certainly not the worst of African exhibiters and it occupied only a brief period in his extraordinary life. But his showman's skills brought African people to the forefront in an explosive way, not necessarily to be looked down upon, but unfortunately, not to be considered equals either.

After a respite of nearly a decade Farini had a brief and final fling with another style of entertainment that, while it had not originated in Africa, it had taken a long and circuitous route from there, and certainly affected the public image of people of African descent. This was blackface or burnt-cork minstrelsy. In September 1894, the board of directors of the famous Moore and Burgess Minstrels asked Farini to take charge of their company. Believe it or not, this was considered a prestigious position. In fact, this style of entertainment was thought to be family-oriented, and the legendary Moore and Burgess troupe was renowned for the great numbers of ladies who attended their shows at a time when most musical hall fare was considered beneath such delicate observation.

Many of the most talented popular singers in the Victorian era performed in blackface, undaunted by tunes such as 'Happy Little Niggers', 'The Popping Coon' and 'The Darkey's Jubilee', and the Moore and Burgess Minstrels were one of the biggest things in London for nearly three decades. They performed downstairs at St James's Hall (where Farini's Friendly Zulus had made their debut), packing people into their 900-seat theatre every night, bringing their audiences to such a fevered pitch of enjoyment that the stomping of feet sometimes nearly drowned out the more elegant entertainments upstairs (such as, in their early years, lectures by Charles Dickens).

When Farini received the offer from the Moore and Burgess directors, he was in the midst of many other adventures. Just a few years earlier he had drawn 65,000 people to an outdoor London venue to see a parachute jump (he co-invented what was then the most effective version of the modern parachute) and would soon move on to other strange and diverse pursuits, like writing a book about growing begonias, becoming the vice-president of a gold mining company and experimenting with a tubular steel boat that spun like a huge rolling pin as it sailed. He would spend only six months as a blackface minstrel manager. He once said while exploring the Kalahari, 'I would put up with anything for the novelty of the thing' (1973 [1886]: 179). It seems that big-time minstrel music, like African exploration and daredevilry over the Niagara gorge, provided what he needed.

Farini spent the first three decades of the twentieth century, as he aged from 62 to 90, far from Africa and African entertainments but still in pursuit of novelty. He continued inventing, became an accomplished painter and sculptor, and played the stock market with abandon. During the First World War he lived with his wife in Germany, behind enemy lines. Perhaps because such an existence was not enough intrigue for his 80-year-old mind, he filled his days translating articles from German and other European newspapers and writing down his feelings about the war from Germany's perspective. When he was finished, he had written an astonishing 37 volumes.

Back in Port Hope by 1921, he approached his ninth decade at full speed, driving himself relentlessly, rising in the mornings to rotate his scalp, do his exercises, eat his yogurt and take 11-kilometre (7-mile) bicycle rides on unpaved roads to help harvest the crops on his farms. Many of his hours were spent at his easel, often recording in vivid colours some of the bizarre scenes he had witnessed during the whirlwind tour that had been his life. Whatever he was searching for, he never found, but when he finally died on 17 January 1929, a few weeks into his ninety-first year, he left behind one of the most extraordinary life stories the world has ever known.

It is important to view Farini's involvement with African exhibitions in the context of his many diverse adventures, the nature of other ethnological shows, and the time in which he lived. The day after Farini's fifteenth birthday, gained in the backwoods of a southern Ontario rural community, Charles Dickens, the great conscience of the most 'civilized' nation on earth, published his thoughts concerning an African exhibition he had just seen at Hyde Park, London. He said of the Zulu: 'I call him a savage, a something highly desirable to be civilised off the face of the earth... he is.... cruel, false, thievish, murderous; addicted more or less to grease, entrails, and beastly customs; a wild animal with the questionable gift of boasting; a conceited, tiresome, bloodthirsty, monotonous humbug... My position is, that if we have anything to learn from the Noble Savage, it is what to avoid' (see Lindfors 1999b).[15]

Every era has individuals as wonderful and terrible as Dickens and Farini. Life for such people is a race: the Englishman flying through marathon walks in the streets of London, staring at the poor he found everywhere in rags, his mind so overflowing with ideas and sympathies and emotions that it seemed his 58 years on earth were all he could stand; and the inimitable Farini, forever searching and exploring, hungry for any excitement, intrigue or danger he could find, and so inexhaustible at the end he seemed like that ancient character in one of Beckett's plays, the one who cries out 'MORE!' when she thinks she may die.

Farini was not an evil person, nor was he a saint. He was curious and passionate to a fault. He may have never even noticed, as he raced through life, that he sometimes knocked people down.[16]

Notes

1 Though slavery did exist for a short while in Canada, its practice was certainly never nearly as widespread as in the United States, and it was abolished in 1833.
2 Mrs Lucy Buck in the *Radio Times* (London), 1933. See notes on this in Clement 1967: 192.
3 For details about Farini's life see Peacock 1995; a thorough bibliography for this book is at the Ganaraska Region Archives in Port Hope, Ontario. For extensive primary sources see the Farini Papers in the Archives of Ontario, Toronto.
4 Quoted from Farini's handwritten autobiography in the Farini Papers at the Archives of Ontario, Toronto (pages not numbered).
5 *The Times* (London), 14 April 1879, 1.
6 *The Times* (London), 15 April 1879, 6.
7 The *Daily Telegraph* (London), 15 April 1879, 6.
8 The *Daily Telegraph* (London), 8 July 1879, 1.
9 The *Daily Telegraph* (London), 7 January 1880, 5.
10 The *Daily Telegraph* (London), 7 January 1880, 1.
11 *New York Clipper*, 23 August 1879, 180.
12 *Detroit Evening News*, 29 May 1880, 4.
13 *1882 Route Book, P. T. Barnum's Greatest Show on Earth*, entry for 21 August 1882, Rome, NY. This can be found in The Circus World Museum, Baraboo, Wisconsin.
14 *New York Clipper*, 13 December 1884, 613.
15 An important point regarding this quotation is noted by Lindfors (1999b): Dickens wanted to eradicate the 'savagery' of Zulus, not their very existence. In other words he was not advocating genocide.
16 This article is a revised version of Peacock 1999.

16

India and Ceylon in Colonial and World Fairs (1851–1931)

CATHERINE SERVAN-SCHREIBER

From 1838 onwards, troupes of Indian dancers had been brought to Europe to perform to enthusiasts of exotic art (Christout 1990; Assayag 1999: 128–33). The troupes were few, though, and lacking in organization, and it was not until London's Great Exhibition of 1851 that Europeans would see for themselves India's vast riches and the spectacular performances of its peoples. India, whose contribution to the success of the British Exhibition was striking, was called on to satisfy a public which had become accustomed to 'curiosities' over the past century. Entertained by a succession of exhibits such as Oronuto the 'Savage Ethiopian', 'albino negresses', a young woman who 'mistook her toes for hands', six Cherokee chiefs in war dress, and the famous Bengal tiger 'which looked like a human', Londoners were greedy for 'wild beasts' and 'monsters' (Picard 2000: 251–53).

The Beginnings: Crystal Palace

At the Crystal Palace in London's Hyde Park, the Indian section was one of the largest, exciting much attention. The products it displayed had mostly been lent by Nawab Nazim of Bengal. These included a throne set on a dais of blue silk supported by four silver pillars, the seat of which was covered in purple velvet and bordered with gold and silver.[1] Among the other exhibits were two palanquins, one of ivory and gold, carried by six bearers, an elephant howdah, a tent which was spectacularly furnished with carpets and cushions, rich silks and cottons, shawls, fans, minerals, medicines, dyes, rubber, luxurious furniture, precious stones, jewellery, ceramics, agricultural instruments, leatherwork, food and examples of traditional boats. A *Times* reporter, particularly impressed by this accumulation of riches, judged it to be a positive reflection of the way that England governed her Indian empire: 'We have ransacked that territory not after the fashion of ordinary conquerors but with a just appreciation of their hidden sources of labour and springs of commerce, which, in the end, are more remunerative than mines of silver and gold' (Leapman 2001: 106).

The celebration of the British imperial adventure was not confined to these stands, but extended to artistic works, such as the statue designed by Lord Ellenborough.[2] The central section of the statue was supported by three elephants lying down, and in front of its pedestal an Indian soldier in the service of the Raj stood over African and Chinese captives. Above them, Britannia embraced Asia, who, in return, crowned Britannia's helmet with a laurel wreath.

However, a voice penetrated this euphoric frenzy of colonial display, a voice that was humorous at first, but which became increasingly critical in tone. This was the voice of the poet Théophile Gautier, who was always quick to respond where India was concerned. Gautier had crossed the Channel to spend a day at the exhibition:

> Luckily for Frenchmen who can never make that magical journey, the English have packed up the whole of India in cases and have brought it to the Exhibition. And that gigantic empire, cradle of mankind, now an English province, has been set out artistically and methodically in display cases and catalogued with the same phlegm as Sheffield or Birmingham cutlery. As well as supplying plants and animals, the East India Company has exhibited an entire village so that visitors may form a complete idea of its eastern empire. It has also imported the population, by means of little models made out of coloured clay, created by the inhabitants themselves, and allowing us to experience the life of different castes at an intimate level. (Gautier 1852: 249).

But as he moved through the halls, having not deigned to cast a single glance at the 'copper and iron monsters', he was horrified by the terrible scenes he encountered. Moved by a vast system of poles which combined the characteristics of a circus trapeze and a swinging gibbet, Hindu penitents were suspended from forked prongs beneath their shoulder blades, revolving in circles over the heads of the spectators. This practice of expiatory self-mortification did indeed exist in the Indian tradition of pilgrimage and religious vows, but only among a minority of the faithful and, taken out of context, such acrobatics could only appear 'hideous' and 'monstrous' to the visitors.

Further on, but in a different vein, Indian members of the criminal sect of Thugs (or so it was claimed) had been released from prison and put on display, 'employing in industrious tasks the hands which had previously learned only to crush moaning throats'. Gautier was indignant at the inhumanity of this spectacle and shared in the humiliation of these men thus exposed to the curious eyes of the public as they laboured at 'Quaker or Moravian missionary tasks'.[3] He concluded that 'the Barbarians triumph over Civilization', and that 'the exhibition provides them with a complete victory in this matter'. But the voice of the poet remained a lone one, and the vogue for exotic and sensationalist tableaux only increased.

The Colonial and Indian Exhibition of 1886 occupied a site near to the South Kensington Museum (later the Science Museum), and was visited by 5,500,000 people. Indians living in London helped in its organization. Mancherjee Merwanjee Bhonaggree, for example, was rewarded by the Queen, becoming a Companion of the Indian Empire. Just over a decade later, Queen Victoria's Diamond Jubilee offered those at home the chance to become more familiar with the peoples of the Empire. On this occasion, rather than being consigned to zoos, or shown upon the stages of music halls, the troops accompanying the processions of exotic dignitaries were billeted in the London parks, setting up their quarters there.

From 1900, exhibitions and shows designed to entertain and instruct the populace on the benefits of empire would become common in the lives of Londoners. The year 1900 itself saw a particularly rich range of 'ethnic' attractions in London. Every evening in Portobello Gardens, 'savage' African Bushmen (San) could be seen killing a lion, while Bedouins galloped their horses at Sanger's Hippodrome and Circus. You could also visit the South African village at Earl's Court. This was, according to a contemporary observer, 'a real village inhabited by savages from the Dark Continent', where the aforementioned 'savages' could be seen making bracelets.

One of the most sought-after entertainments remained 'The Defeat by Prince Lobengula and his Troops of Two Hundred Savage Warriors', at the Empress Theatre (with 6,000 seats). The show at the Royal Agricultural Hall in Islington, where seventy Sinhalese and Tamils performed, including Nautch girls (dancers), fighters, magicians, snake charmers and monkey trainers, was also a great success. The public were fascinated by Ceylon and, in 1908, a subsequent show attracted more than five million spectators. In England, as in France, the educational aspect of these recreational sights was underlined by everyone concerned. But while the processions, parades and exotic shows of dignitaries and simple natives in England were part of an imperialist strategy, with the participants appearing as trophies, in France, Indian and Sinhalese troupes remained part of the world of the theatre, where they earned an unrivalled reputation.

Indian Exhibitions in France, 1878–1910

Indian art and handicraft exhibitions were prominent in the programmes of colonial and universal exhibitions in France, as were the picturesque performances of southern Indian and Sinhalese troupes. Which type of display dominated would depend on the year and on the availability of sponsors from the worlds of commerce and art, and the two would sometimes exist side by side. At the Paris Universal Exposition of 1878, a display from French India comprising 134 exhibits appeared in the Oriental Hall. This collection of carpets, weapons, vases, sandalwoods and ancient and modern Persian paintings reinforced preconceptions concerning the superiority of the West: 'The impression which this collection, however remarkable, left on art lovers was that oriental art had been greatly overrated by a public which did not know much about it, and that in reality it is inferior in every respect to the great Art of the West' (Ernest 1998).

More dazzling than the exhibit from French India was the British section, which included her Indian colonies. This occupied the largest space in the exhibition. According to the report published by Lacroix in 1878, 'the collection of products from India was made up largely of presents made to the Prince of Wales following the recent visit of His Royal Highness to India, but the stewards of the exhibition also purchased other objects, and the Maharajah of Kashmir made a number of generous gifts' (Exposition 1878). Jewel-encrusted works and ebonies from Bombay, ivories and sculpted horns, sandalwood, cut stones, artistic furnishings, jewellery, enamels, paintings on soapstone, lacquered objects, clay figures, embroideries, silks, cottons, harnesses and caparisons, potteries and carpets were on show, along with a collection of musical instruments. The author of the report had not only been struck by the tremendous refinement of the colours but also concluded from his discoveries that 'the Indian craftsman is a true artist' and that 'we would be greatly mistaken in believing that we have anything to teach to a people already in possession of traditions in the decorative arts founded on perfect principles' (1878).

At the Exposition Universelle of 1889 it was the turn of Indian architecture to be displayed to the Parisian crowds at the Champ de Mars, along the length of Avenue de Suffren. A palace was constructed there by the 'Tower Teas' company: 'A vast edifice designed by M. C. Purdon, Director of the Indian collections at London's South Kensington Museum, and which is a fair copy of the Panch Mahal, constructed in Agra in 1556... Natives in blindingly white national dress, which brings out their bronze complexions, sell goods in the shops and serve at the tea counters' (Champion 1991: 49).

Sinhalese rather than Indian troupes were the first representatives of the Indian subcontinent to participate in the series of ethnographic exhibitions at the Paris Zoological Gardens, preceding those from southern India. As the historian Hilke Thode-Arora shows, the fact that Carl Hagenbeck's nephew, John George, was of Sinhalese descent on his mother's side made the impresario extremely sensitive to the well-being of his troupes: 'He was known to have treated the participants in Indian and Sinhalese shows with special empathy, taking personal care of their food shopping and taboos, carrying opium for a yogi addicted to it, and attending the participants' ceremonies when invited' (Thode-Arora 2002a: 6).

The content of the shows was dictated by a desire to guarantee ethno-graphic 'authenticity' and therefore included various traditional activities which supposedly fulfilled this aim: singing, dancing, martial arts, parades of humans and animals, processions, and archaic and picturesque modes of transport and crafts. In 1883, the group of Sinhalese who were performing at the Paris Zoological Gardens was composed of twenty-one individuals: 'Thirteen men between sixteen and fifty-five years old, five women between twenty and forty, and three children from two months to seven years, accompanied by ten elephants and ten zebus. Half came from Kandy, once the capital of Ceylon, the other half from Colombo, which is now the capital' (Gala 1980: 26). On a 'racial palette' chosen for its impact, the Sinhalese show was ascribed a very precise position: 'Less "wild" than the Araucanians, the Fuegians, or the Redskins, certainly, but inferior to the Kalmuks, who where considered by anthropologists to be the most intelligent, the most eager to get to know others and, above all, the most curious of all the exhibited peoples' (1980: 26).

According to Girard de Rialle, 'it was a strange spectacle for us Parisians to see the Araucanians, those almost wild Americans with indomitable spirits, situated a few steps from the Sinhalese, who repre-sent one of the most ancient civilizations in the world. These gentle and frail inhabitants of Ceylon showed us how man in India had mastered the strength of the elephant to help him in his work. The Sinhalese attract spectators by working their elephants and racing their trotting zebus. You have to see, in the Zoological Gardens, these great animals as they move, transport, and manoeuvre enormous tree trunks with marvellous skill and precision. This spectacle and the zebu races are well worth a visit. In the recent days of great heat, under a beating sun, one might, with a little effort, have imagined oneself transported to

Ceylon' (Girard de Rialle 1883b: 131–34). The Sinhalese would return to the Gardens in 1886 to participate in zebu team races and to demonstrate elephant training by lifting and rolling beams. On this occasion, a Buddhist temple, decorated with sculptures and reflecting their Buddhist (as opposed to Hindu) faith, was erected on the plot assigned to them.

During the many visits of 'savages to the Gardens' (Gala 1980), the Parisian spectators were moved by a range of feelings: surprise, curiosity, mirth, compassion, scorn, fear, sympathy and generosity. But, as the brief messages sent on postcards of the time demonstrate, the surprise and admiration with which the senders responded to the skill of the Indian jugglers, acrobats, tightrope walkers and conjurors were without precedent. Three performances were given in Paris – in 1902, 1906 and 1907 – and these were followed by tours in the south of France, including the Parc Chambrun in Nice, in April 1908, and Marseille in September 1910.

It was certainly the case that the reputation of the skilled fakirs and magicians had preceded their arrival in France. Their mysterious talents had been described by writers such as Théophile Gautier (*Avatar*, 1856), Louis Rousselet (*L'Inde des Rajahs* [India of the Rajahs], 1871–74), Gobineau (*L'Illustre Magicien* [The Famous Magician], 1876), Jacolliot (*Le Spiritisme dans le monde* [Spiritualism around the World], 1880), *L'Illustration* ('L'Inde', 1894), and Paul d'Ivoi (*Le Docteur Mystère* [Doctor Mystery], 1900). The public knew, thanks to these writers, that 'they can accomplish astonishing feats which confound and humiliate our scientific pride, going so far as to reveal new laws, unknown to us in the West, that overturn all our acquired concepts and theories concerning movement, space, and time'. Powers such as levitation and the defiance of the laws of gravity were attributed to yogis, fakirs and other Indian magicians.[4]

While they did not quite achieve the level of magic vaunted by adventure narratives and believers in the occult in France, the balancing acts performed by 'Malabars'[5] from the Hindu caravan which visited the Zoological Gardens in 1902 were a tour de force. Some, with nothing to hold them up, were perched at dizzying heights on the tops of tall poles, standing on one leg, their arms crossed, and with three enormous earthenware pots on their heads. Others seemed to float over the crowd on their poles. Again making use of poles and held up by only a foot or leg, the members of the troupe would form enormous human pyramids. Snake charmers made women appear from their snakes' willow baskets. A new show appeared in 1906 and a caravan of a hundred or so people, including a dozen children, set up on the great lawn of the Zoological Gardens. There were snake charmers and performing bears. Richly dressed dancers of both sexes, and musicians, were surrounded by a group of actors in make-up and wild raffia headdresses, who represented the troop of monkeys in the epic Ramayana.

Fakirs on planks contorted their limbs in spectacular and dangerous poses, drawing on their yoga training. But the public could also view southern Indians going about other, more conventional artistic and domestic activities, such as cooking, engraving, embroidery and drawing.

In 1907, the main attraction of the Grand Colonial Exhibition at Nogent, outside Paris, was the troupe of wild elephants invited by the *Journal des Voyages*. At the edge of the Bois de Vincennes, in the section belonging to the Jardin Colonial (colonial gardens),[6] the Hindu village was on display, with its huts, mahouts and their elephants. And, as the correspondent for the *Journal* boasted in 1907:

> the moving scenes of capture and training and the reconstructions of elephant hunts in this charming setting are of the highest imaginable quality in both their picturesque effects and their realism. You will admire the skill of the elephant trainers and the intelligence of the tame elephants; the work and exercises of these enormous, strong and skilful pachyderms will captivate you; you will also learn – for this attractive show is also a most useful object lesson – the importance of the rearing of elephants to our colonies, where this admirable beast can be of the most distinguished service. (Terrier 1907: 3)

The services of many elephants, tigers and other great cats from India were also called on for the street and circus parades, for historical reconstructions, and for princely processions in which the Indian participants, usually displayed in skimpy loincloths on the lawns of the gardens, found themselves dressed up in luxurious borrowed finery in order to play their parts (Fox 1979). The advent of the First World War would bring these displays to an end, the final exhibition being that of bayadère dancers in September 1910 in Marseille. The 'exotic races' who had entertained Europe would now be employed by France to intimidate Germany and secure the defence of her citizens.

For the Indians, as for the African infantrymen, the First World War provided the opportunity for a change of perspective. More than a million Indian soldiers played a decisive role in the defence of the trenches, and they appeared indefatigable, impassive, or even joyful in the face of the enemy. The Indian Army had been formed and equipped to fight the marauding frontier tribes (and, on occasion, the Russians) in the Khyber Pass. With the 1914–18 war, their powers of self-sacrifice, one of the most lauded values of their civilization, were soon acknowledged: 'Neuve-Chapelle, 1914, the Hindus from the Lahore and Meerut divisions held the trenches between La Bassée and Estaires. Baluchis, Pathans, Sikhs, and Gurkhas died in the mud of Flanders for half a rupee a day and sacrificed themselves to war' (Debroka 1929: 1).

When French India came to Paris: 1931

Following the First World War, the French encounter with India, first established through Indian art, returned to this field. The trained racing zebus and the debonair pachyderms were gone, as were the dancers and magicians. Ethnographic shows were no longer in favour, and Asian art triumphed. This was the era of collections. At the 1931 International Colonial Exposition the dominant style was clean and unadorned. The French India pavilion – where Mr Jo Ginestou was commissioner – surrounded by palms and designed as a patio, was of the greatest sobriety, with the exception of the decorative columns and the two stone elephants sculpted by Jean Magrou which guarded the entrance. The organizing committee, which employed the architects Henri Girvès and René Sors, and the decorator Claude Salvy, did not contain a single Indian. An Indologist, Professor Jouveau-Dubreuil, acted as a consultant for the historical furnishings. Sets of garnets, copper and goldwork, laces, ivories, silver objects, agricultural and food products, paintings, carpets, walking sticks and waxes, fired clays, loincloths, shawls, fabrics, snakeskins, tortoiseshells, statues and carved furniture, all from Pondicherry, were on display, while the walls were decorated with paintings by Henri Montassier and friezes by Edouard Poisson and J. P. Poittevin. Twenty years after the disappearance of the 'ethnic shows', and thirteen years after the participation of the Indian regiments in the war, Indian life was once again represented in a sort of oriental blur that confused elements from many nations. In the frescos and murals, the scenery and people were more reminiscent of Egypt, Algeria, or even South-East Asia, than of India. In this pavilion representing French India, only the collection of statues belonging to the Chinese patron of the arts, Ching-Tsai Loo, provided an authentic representation of Indian art.[7]

The curiosity of those visiting the Villages and Caravans exhibit had, like Gautier's, been fuelled by their reading. Travel periodicals (such as *Le Tour du Monde*, *Le Journal des Voyages*, and *L'Illustration*), serialized novels (such as Eugène Sue's *Le Juif errant* [The Wandering Jew], 1844–45], and René de Pont-Jest's *Le Procès des Thugs* [The Trial of the

Thugs], 1878), as well as books for children,[8] had accustomed adventure-lovers to the image of a romantic, wild, and beautiful continent of tiger hunts in the jungle, idolatrous sects and princely splendours. The Hindu, who was associated with the wildness of the forest and its animals, was envied for 'the elasticity of his movements, his resistance to tiredness, his muscles of steel, and his free and wild life, running through the undergrowth, moving through the night with the supple speed of the great tawny beasts of the shadows' (Ivoi 1900: 29). We should remember here the role played by philology and comparative grammar in creating a scientific basis for racial anthropology. The linguists' terminological inventions and labels forged links between the Indo-Aryan (Indo-European) languages (and, very quickly, 'races') and the issue of European origins.[9] India had been considered, from the work of early Sanskrit scholars onwards, to be the first region in the world where humans passed from a state of 'savagery' to 'civilization', and it was viewed by those who pursued the new science of anthropology as a unique laboratory in which the inventory of the human races could be made.

Illustrations in the works of A. Urbain (1840), of Louis Enault (1861) and Louis Rousselet (1872–74) had emphasized the plasticity of the Aryan bodies, whose proportions were reminiscent of antique bronzes, and the spectacular practices of self-mortification to which they subjected themselves. Later, photography made it possible to view the 'panorama of Indian races', in British works such as E. T. Dalton's *Descriptive Ethnology of Bengal* (1872), and J. F. Watson and J. W. Kaye's *The People of India* (which appeared in eight volumes from 1868 and 1875).[10] Of all these 'races', the French only came to know the 'Malabars' and 'Singhalese' of Kandy and Colombo. Certainly, according to the organizers, the Vedas of Ceylon and the Indians of the Andaman Islands had supplied even more picturesque, or 'primitive' examples of their work but, as Hilke Thode-Arora points out, the organizers preferred to work with ethnic groups who had already had contact with Europeans, in order to make it easier to organize the exhibits.[11]

Dr Heinrich Hensold, a German scholar who had observed the tricks of Indian conjurers in the 1880s, promised them that 'if they would agree to come to Europe or America to show their marvellous skills, then a quick fortune awaited them' (Varigny 1987: 82). At best, some of the artists on show managed to sell their works to the public. The Indian women were not obliged to show themselves naked to the public, as the women of Tierra del Fuego, Dahomey and Guinea had done in 1881, 1891 and 1907. The postcards which popularized their shows always

respected the decencies.[12] None of the members of the troupes exhibited in France died, whereas in Germany eight of them lost their lives.
But in the history of colonial memory, there is still no evidence to tell
us what this 'prodigious people who made all of Paris rush to see them'
thought of the Europe which received them.

Notes

1　On the day of the opening ceremony Queen Victoria came to sit on this throne,
　　after which ladies visiting the exhibition sought to follow her example.
2　Ellenborough had just been removed from his post as Governor General of
　　India and recalled to England as a result of his repressive attitude towards the
　　Indian population.
3　In India itself, the idea of making these stranglers and their children weave
　　carpets was presented by the British colonizers as a redeeming act. It should be
　　remembered that the presence of the Thugs at the 1851 Exhibition was not by
　　chance, but was intended to serve the needs of contemporary phrenology. On
　　this use of the Thugs in the 1830s, see Woerkens 1995: 271.
4　We should remember that some of the tricks which were attributed to them in
　　colonial and travel writings became famous: sticks which turned into snakes;
　　mango and fig trees which grew to great heights; a gourd which became invis-
　　ible, then filled with water; a coconut which rose vertically into the air; and a
　　dead bird which came back to life. But the most extraordinary trick was a rope
　　with a knot on the end thrown into the air on which a man appeared to balance
　　in space.
5　Although this name designates the inhabitants of Malabar, the coastal region in
　　the south-west of the Deccan plateau, including Kerala, it was indiscriminately
　　applied during the colonial period to all southern Indians. In this particular
　　case, the performers were from Pondicherry, a French trading post in the south-
　　east of the Deccan plateau.
6　These gardens belonged to the Colonial Office, which was created in 1899 and
　　was responsible for the publicity for the Colonial Ministry (Lemaire 2000).
7　Ching-Tsai Loo had been a collector since 1902 and wanted the public to see
　　genuine Asian antiquities rather than the *chinoiseries* promoted by the Goncourt
　　brothers. A part of his Indian collection is on show in the Chinese pagoda
　　which he had built in the Parc Monceau.
8　For example, *Le Tour du monde en 80 jours* [Around the World in Eighty Days]
　　(1873), and *La Maison à vapeur* [The Steam House] (1880) by Jules Verne; *Le
　　Charmeur de serpents* [The Snake Charmer] (1910) by Louis Rousselet; *Le
　　Charmeur de serpents* (1919) by Léon Ambry; and *Le Tour du monde d'un boy-scout*
　　[A Boy Scout's World Tour] 1932) by Arnould Galopin.
9　On the philologists' dream in the nineteenth century, see Montaut, 1990.
10　On the role of these works in the relationship between 'inventory and surveil-
　　lance', see Corbey 1997: 549–52.
11　See Thode-Arora in this volume.
12　See Geary and Webb (1998) on the first Indian and Sinhalese postcards.

17

Seeing the Imaginary: On the Popular Reception of Wild West Shows in Germany, 1885–1910

ERIC AMES

When Indian troupes from North America came to Germany in the late nineteenth century, they initially appeared under the sign of ethnographic authenticity.[1] The 1893 edition of *Meyers Konversations-Lexikon* defined Buffalo Bill's Wild West show as the latest trend in 'anthropological exhibitions', or, 'Performances of representative foreign peoples for the satisfaction of visual pleasure and the dissemination of anthropological knowledge.' The Wild West offered an exciting (even thrilling) alternative to the more familiar tradition of anthropological spectacle. And the public evidently wanted an alternative. By 1890, so many troupes were touring Germany that there was speculation of 'a possible surfeit'. This scenario pertained to the number of troupes from Africa in particular, which had grown significantly in number over the previous decade. Indeed, there was a moment in colonial Germany when the physical presence of African performers, which was once enough to gather a crowd of gawkers, began to seem almost banal. 'Yes,' wrote one reporter in Berlin, 'black skin colour has become something so ordinary and familiar that even the most exotic, thick-lipped, heathen, uncivilized, ravenous Negro races can hardly arouse much interest with us anymore as display objects.' It was precisely at this moment, in 1890, that Buffalo Bill and his Wild West show arrived on the scene. To quote the same reporter, once again:

> There's something still different, however, about the Indian races and everything that has to do with Prairie life in North America. Today, despite the fact that steamships have already put 'North America' on the map of even the most casual tourists, despite the fact that things American no longer seem so 'distant', so exotic, so foreign to us, Indians and every-thing associated with them continue to exert a powerful, indescribable force of attraction. Today, as in our childhood, we remain under the magical spell of Cooper's *Leatherstocking Tales*, and for us the names of

chiefs and squaws such as 'Nimble Deer', 'White Dove', and the like have a sound transfigured by the actual poetry of the primeval forest.[2]

Native Americans continue to occupy a special place in the German imagination. However, the late nineteenth century – and particularly the arrival of the Wild West – marked an important phase in the historical development of this phenomenon and its expansion into the realm of visual culture. This essay focuses on the arrival of the Wild West and its historical reception in Germany.

Germany and the Wild West

Spectators saw the Wild West in many different and sometimes contradictory ways, but one aspect of the German reception stands out, namely, its ardent embrace of fantasy. Scientists and anthropological showmen might have treated Native Americans as bodies of data on the verge of extinction, but popular spectators saw them as living embodiments of figures from the novels of authors such as James Fenimore Cooper and Friedrich Gerstäcker. Thus, the German reception's governing logic was one of vivification. To be in the physical presence of actual cowboys and Indians but see in them fictional characters was not to commit a naive ontological error. Rather, to summon 'Cooper' or 'Gerstäcker' was a way for German spectators to take possession of the American entertainment and make it their own. They did so by means of the one thing that they alone, as spectators, brought to the Wild West – that is, their imagination. I should be clear: what follows is neither a literary analysis nor a pictorial history, nor a study of visual stereotypes. This essay documents a creative response on the part of spectators to the physical presence and live display of Indian troupes in Germany.

In a further step, brief consideration is given to the historical implications of the Wild West for the continued practice of anthropological exhibition in Germany. As I contend, the phenomenal success of the Wild West led established showmen such as Carl Hagenbeck of Hamburg to embrace the mythical aspect of 'Indians', while appealing to the spectator's powers of imagination and identification in ways that were formerly taboo for anthropological spectacles. Various troupes deserve to be mentioned, but the following discussion concentrates on four key examples of shows spanning a quarter of a century: namely Carl Hagenbeck's Bella Coola (1885), Buffalo Bill's Wild West (1890), Doc Carver's Wild America (1890) and Carl Hagenbeck's Oglala-Sioux (1910).

Carl Hagenbeck's very first Indian troupe, the Bella Coola of 1885, was supposed to attract mass spectators and appeal to an elite group of scientific experts at the same time. After all, Hagenbeck enjoyed a strong track record and an enviable public reputation as an anthropological showman. Since 1874, he had already assembled more than 20 troupes of peoples from around the world, developing his ethnographic enterprise largely in conjunction with the international trade in exotic animals, which was and remained the main branch of his company. Just as Hagenbeck brought the animal trade from the margins to the mainstream of colonial commerce, so he moved the practice of human display from the fairground to the zoological garden. In other words, he made it 'respectable' and therefore easily consumable by the widest possible audience, including (but not restricted to) the broad middle classes.

In assembling the Bella Coola troupe, Hagenbeck and his traveller, the Norwegian Johan Adrian Jacobsen, did all the necessary preparatory work – and more. Jacobsen had already been in British Columbia for some time, collecting objects for the Royal Museum of Ethnology in Berlin, when he landed upon the idea of importing a group of 'long-heads', or Kwakiutl, from Vancouver Island. While the spectacle of physical alterity augured well for the future success of exhibiting such Indians in Germany, or so he thought, it was particularly the kinetic scene of Kwakiutl mask dances which prompted Jacobsen to propose that Hagenbeck sponsor a troupe from this area. In a series of letters, Hagenbeck showed great enthusiasm for the idea. He also persuaded Jacobsen's employer, the museum's director Adolf Bastian, to release Jacobsen from his duties as collector for the museum. Bastian did more than that: he personally lobbied other members of the prestigious Berlin Society for Anthropology, Ethnology and Ancient History to support the project upon its completion (which they did). So, with the endorsement of Germany's leading ethnologist (Bastian), an experienced collector in the field (Jacobsen), the spectacle of physical as well as cultural difference ('long-heads' and mask dances) and ample resources to finance this endeavour, Hagenbeck had every reason to believe that he and Jacobsen would make 'a huge profit'.[3]

The ensuing troupe was made up of nine Bella Coola – all men – and a collection of more than 1,500 ethnographic artefacts. Jacobsen not only assembled the troupe but also served as the show's director on tour. From September 1885 to July 1886, they visited more than 20 cities, big and small, performing at a diversity of venues – including the zoological garden in Breslau, the Kaisersäle in Erfurt, the Stadthaus am Markt in Weimar and the Restaurant Bavaria in Aachen. The programme consisted almost entirely of music and ceremonial dance numbers, some of which were contextualized as the re-enactment of scenes from a traditional potlatch (i.e. a tribal feast and gift-giving ceremony). The dances were interspersed with sporting games and magic tricks, all framed by an ethnographic rhetoric of 'Indian ways and customs'. Over the course of the tour, the programme changed several times, substituting dances and adding a variety of more sensationalized and studiously grotesque numbers – such as the 'voluntary immolation of a shaman (magician)' – mainly for the purpose of accumulating customers, but also because the participants grew bored of the original routine.[4]

The Bella Coola created a sensation within the scientific community, as expected, but the show failed to find a broader public. Bastian's endorsement augured well for the troupe's success among professional scientists. In Halle, for instance, the troupe gave a special performance at the Institute for Geography, which was attended by a wide diversity of scholars, including the aspiring psychophysicist Carl Stumpf. The performance so inspired Stumpf that he arranged for a week-long series of private musical recitals with one of the troupe's performers. The results of his research, which he published in 1886 as 'Songs of the Bella Coola Indians', became a founding document of ethnomusicology.[5] Bastian's assistant, the young Franz Boas, also published a study of the Bella Coola language based on his experience of the troupe in Berlin. The well-known pathologist and long-time president of the Berlin Society for Anthropology, Rudolf Virchow, had this to say about the show: 'The Bella Coola Indians brought from British Columbia to Europe by Mr. Jacobsen are different from all American savages so far presented here. By virtue of the deformation of their heads, the peculiar formation of their faces, their quite singular language, their highly developed artisanship, they are immediately on first encounter rendered conspicuous among the multitude of American native peoples. For this reason they afford one of the most interesting objects for the observation of every thinking human being' (quoted in Haberland 1988b: 38).

Public Reactions

The public, however, saw it otherwise. The troupe's underlying assumption, that intellectual authority would help attract mass spectators, was evidently false. In his diary and private correspondence, Jacobsen complained of low attendance throughout the year-long tour. Part of the problem was competition from another Indian troupe, namely, The Sitting Bull Sioux Indians. Led by the American showman Frank Harvey, the troupe consisted of 30 men, women and children, a stable of sixteen horses, and a Texas sharpshooter named Happy Jack Sutton.[6] (Contrary to its name, the show did not include Sitting Bull, who was at that time touring the United States with Buffalo Bill.) When the Bella Coola came to Berlin, Harvey's troupe was already on exhibit at Castan's Panoptikum (a local wax museum). With their guns, horses and feathered headdresses, the cowboys and Indians created a loud, vibrant and visually potent spectacle. As spectators thrilled to the Wild West, and not to the Bella Coola, Jacobsen decided to leave Berlin ahead of schedule and take his troupe to Breslau. Several months later, in the hope that the memory of Harvey's troupe had by then faded, the Bella Coola returned to Berlin, this time appearing at Castan's Panoptikum – here, too, without success. One reporter had this advice for prospective viewers: 'If you are not to be disappointed, you must put away all preconceptions, formed perhaps by Cooper, of Indians' (quoted in Cole 1985: 71). Another lamented: 'Well, they are not those proud, red-skinned figures with cunningly bowed eagle-noses, dark-black, shimmering bushes of hair, and colourful feathers, which school boys reveling in Cooper and *Leatherstocking* like to dream about' (quoted in Thode-Arora 1993: 82). While Hagenbeck and his impresario claimed to deliver 'the real thing', spectators faulted the show for its lack of fictional reference points. This is not to say that Harvey's show was in some way more 'literary' than that of Hagenbeck (it certainly was not). Nor does it imply that the Sioux had anything more to do with Cooper and his *Leatherstocking Tales* than had the Bella Coola (they did not). The point here is one of reception: spectators forged a creative link between the idea of 'Cooper' and the physical presence of the Sioux, but not that of the Bella Coola. It was the act of imaginative identification on the one hand, and the lack of fictional reference points on the other that made the crucial difference.

The arrival of the Wild West in Germany captured the imagination of popular audiences. My signal figure here is, of course, William F. Cody ('Buffalo Bill') and his troupe of more than 200 cowboys and Indians. Buffalo Bill's Wild West show involved a colorful mix of national pageantry (a procession of cowboys, Indians and army scouts), historical re-enactment (scenes from the Indian wars, such as 'Custer's Last Stand'), military display (artillery exercises), sensational melodrama (dramatic narratives of frontier life), and sporting exhibition (with emphasis on trick shooting and horse racing). In Germany and throughout Europe this three-hour show followed the same basic pattern: the Pony Express; the attack on the emigrant train; a Virginia quadrille (a country dance) on horseback; 'cowboy fun' (horsemanship and lassoing); the attack on the Deadwood coach; Indian dances; and the buffalo hunt.[7] The show began its German tour on 19 April 1890, in Munich. Rows of portable bleachers held more than 5,000 spectators for daily performances on the Theresienwiese, which was also the traditional site of Oktoberfest. Over a scheduled ten-day visit, the troupe performed before 'sold-out' crowds (even the 'loges' at 4 Marks apiece were full). Prince Ludwig of Bavaria and his court were guests of honour on opening day. Hundreds of people camped out overnight in order to obtain tickets. Thousands of people from out of town placed orders via telegraph, in order to assure themselves of tickets. Each day, thousands more enjoyed 'free tickets', with some perched atop nearby buildings and others standing all around the arena's periphery. The Munich show was extended another eight days in response to continued demand. The tour then continued, with appearances in Vienna, Dresden, Leipzig, Magdeburg, Hanover, Braunschweig, Berlin, Hamburg, Bremen, Cologne, Düsseldorf, Frankfurt am Main, Stuttgart, Cannstatt and Strasbourg.[8]

Cody's was not the only Wild West show in Germany; Doc Carver's Wild America competed for the same entertainment-seeking public. William F. 'Doc' Carver was part of the original troupe, with Cody, when the Wild West show was first created in 1883. Now, however, they were bitter rivals. Unlike Cody, Carver had already toured Germany on two previous occasions. On 13 June 1880, the self-named Champion Sharp-Shooter of the World gave a 'shooting demonstration' for Kaiser Wilhelm I, his court, and 45,000 soldiers of the German army. Carver epitomized for German spectators the 'sharp-shooter' as a type of itinerant performer.[9] In the summer of 1889, while Cody was performing at the Exposition Universelle in Paris, Carver made his second tour of Germany, now with a Wild West show. Doc Carver's Wild America was made from the same mould as Buffalo Bill's Wild West, and it would exploit the latter's success by imitation. On his second tour of Germany, Carver 'got the greatest reception of his life', according to his biographer. On 4 July 1889, more than 35,000 people paid to see Carver's show in Berlin (Thorp 1957: 180). The following year he returned again, this time trailing Buffalo Bill across Germany, vying with him for spectators – sometimes directly. In Hamburg, for example, they set up camp on opposite sides of the street. Carver had arrived there a few days ahead of schedule, and thus claimed the prime location on the Heiligengeistfeld (the fairground). He also secured what was then the city's only available battery of lights, which allowed for evening performances in addition to the usual afternoon shows. In Hamburg, at least, Cody was left in the dark. When Buffalo Bill's Wild West show opened there, on 21 August 1890, the results were reportedly lopsided: 'Carver gave two performances and had 80,000 visitors, while Cody gave only one, which was attended by 7,000 persons."[10] While Carver might have solicited a larger audience on occasion, he did so almost inadvertently. Both showmen emphasized the 'reality' of the Wild West. Neither Cody nor Carver anticipated that 'fantasy' would be the key to their success in Germany.

Of the two American showmen, it was Cody who perhaps best represented 'real life' in the far West. As a US Army scout during the Indian Wars, an undaunted rider for the Pony Express and an equally intrepid buffalo hunter, he had years of first-hand experience. 'Buffalo Bill' was obviously a stage persona and a media personality created with the assistance of professional writers and publicists, but, unlike most other showmen, Cody had the experience, the evidence and the body to back it up. With his tall stature, flowing curls and ornate costumes, Cody's extraordinary corporeality fascinated spectators in Germany as well as in the United States. More important, Cody represented himself as a living embodiment of American history. Historical 'authenticity' was the stock-in-trade of Wild West shows, beginning with the exhibitions of George Catlin.[11] This idea had its ethnographic equivalent, as is evidenced by Hagenbeck's *Völkerschau*. In the age of scientific positivism, the process of verification and authentication was sometimes crucial to the success of an ethnographic troupe, with native performers being subjected to extensive physical examinations and prominent anthropologists acting as self-appointed cultural regulators. Not so in the Wild West. When Cody's troupe came to Berlin, one reporter asked: 'Who would dare question the authenticity of this enterprise?'[12] Indeed, Cody assembled a stunning cast of notable figures, including, over the years, Sitting Bull, Black Elk, Wild Bill Hickok and – most important – the celebrated showman himself. Historians of the Wild West usually emphasize that Buffalo Bill was probably the most famous living American at the time. A prototype of modern celebrity, Buffalo Bill became famous for being famous (Kasson 2000; McMurtry 2005). Of course, in Germany and throughout Europe the troupe could not rely on the same degree of familiarity and recognition that it had been able to assume in the United States. Yet the show was advertised here, as there, as 'a historical attraction', promising not only 'spectacular scenes and pictures from history' but also 'the people who actually experienced them'.

Acts of 'Vivification'

The rhetoric of historical authenticity that framed the Wild West makes the German reception all the more interesting. For it was the fantasy of the West, and not the show's claims to truth, that most inspired spectators. This required some adjustment on the part of American showmen. 'In Europe', historian Joy Kasson has shown, 'the Wild West had to accept – and to learn to trade upon – its own exoticism and its underlying fictionality' (Kasson 2000: 84). Add to this the historical reception in Germany (a context which Kasson does not examine), and a broad cultural trend comes into view. In a sense, the Wild West appeared as European audiences literally imagined it. These cowboys and Indians had to be literally freighted thousands of miles, via train and steamship, in order for the public to be able to see them here – in the flesh. And yet many spectators took their extraordinary presence as an occasion for reverie (not anthropology), while marvelling at the prospect of dreams becoming tangible.

In Germany, more specifically, the governing principle of reception can perhaps best be described in terms of 'vivification'. Other scholars have emphasized the tropes of loss, demise and preservation that link the shows to museums of the period – tropes that are by now very familiar, particularly in the context of ethnography. To be sure, American showmen invoked theories of imminent loss so as to confer a sense of urgency on their entertainments; critics in the German press pontificated on the romantic idea of 'vanishing Indians'; and museum directors such as Bastian openly lamented the loss of their material culture (which doubled as a self-serving argument for museum collections). I want to highlight a different but contemporaneous metaphor, one that gestures more towards life than death, according to the particular 'aliveness' of performance, even as it openly bypasses reality in favour of fantasy. The very idea of vivification in this context at once surprised and delighted viewers. 'That these our childhood dreams could one day assume tangible form – who would have ever guessed?'[13]

Here is a passage from a review of Carver's premiere in Hamburg – a passage that could just as well serve to summarize the German reception of Indian troupes in the late nineteenth century:

> This performance not only met the public's expectations but far exceeded them. Audiences familiar with the works of Cooper, Gerstäcker and others who write about Indian life, shall find here embodied everything that the active fantasy ever presented in the liveliest of images: boldness, skillfulness, primitive vitality and wildness appear before the eyes of the observer in such a colourful succession that one feels pleasantly excited from beginning to end.[14]

To many German spectators, the Wild West seemed to convert fictional characters into living tissue. The participants were seen not as 'preserving' the traces of peoples who were either presumably dead or on the verge of dying, as ethnographic museums would claim to do, but rather as giving life to figures that never existed (such as Cooper's Natty Bumppo). In Germany, the unintended effect of the Wild West, for all its claims to history and reality, was the vivification of a fictional universe. It was this fictional aspect of the American spectacle, its powerful grip on the German imagination – and not its obsession with the real and the authentic – that also had implications for the future success of Hagenbeck's Völkerschau and his own brand of Wild West show.[15]

Before returning to Hagenbeck, I want to emphasize that the fantasy world constructed through the reception was sometimes disrupted by the shared presence of performers and spectators. Indeed, the potential for disruption was also a special feature of live performance; unlike other forms of visual representation, itinerant troupes opened up the possibility for direct exchange and cross-cultural dialogue. Consider the group of seven Indians from Cody's troupe that attended a meeting of the Munich Anthropological Society, on 26 April 1890. The Lakota performer named Rocky Bear, leader of the Indian contingent in Cody's troupe since the 1880s, presented himself as a kind of keynote speaker. Also present was the troupe's interpreter, a cowboy named Broncho Bill (along with his Sioux wife and their two-year-old son). A member of the society named Dr Donebrink translated comments and questions from German into English, which Broncho Bill then translated into Lakota, and vice versa. Offering words of welcome and great anticipation, the society's president, Professor Johannes Ranke, convened the meeting, which was (in the words of one reporter) 'one of the most remarkable that the society ever convened'. It was an unusual gathering, indeed. 'The guests took their places at two reserved tables, and soon felt extremely relaxed and comfortable. With awe-inspiring tranquility, they helped themselves to the cigars and cigarettes that were offered to them, blew smoke rings into the air with pleased faces and a noble nonchalance, and enjoyed a beer or two. At the same time, however, they attentively followed the proceedings with their piercing, intelligent eyes.'[16]

Rocky Bear took the podium with the gravitas of an elder statesman. The performance that he gave on this occasion was different from that of the Wild West show: it was oratory, unrehearsed, non-diegetic, and overtly political in content. Augmenting his speech with hand movements that captured the audience's attention, Rocky Bear openly challenged the United States government, and he did so in terms that may have resonated with some of the older men sitting before him. 'My people and I have fought for our rights – for our freedom, our homeland,

and our fatherland.' In removing the Indians from their land, he argued, in denying their right to sovereignty and self-defence, 'the American people have done us great injustice'. Moreover, as Indians were categorically ineligible for US citizenship (nor would they be until 1924), 'The laws of the great American republic fail to protect us.' Joining the Wild West show also had political significance, he asserted. 'My position is that of a negotiator between the white men and the red men, and it is a difficult position to be in.' At the end of his speech, Rocky Bear gestured directly at the audience: 'Look at my hand! It is black, but the heart in my breast beats like your heart, in feelings of friendship; our skin colors are different, our hearts are one.'[17] In the words of one reporter, 'One saw from the speaker that his words came from the heart.' The room filled with applause. 'After the guests shook everybody's hand, they were put in carriages and driven to their homes on the Theresienwiese. The scheduled lectures were cancelled, for, as the president rightly said, the profound impression that this rare visit made upon us should not be diminished by academic discussions' ('Indianer Buffalo Bills', DPL).

On one level, this rousing speech and its transcription in the press are important because they document the voice of an Indian performer in Germany and show how it was also broadcast to mass audiences. On another level, Rocky Bear's speech inadvertently played into certain cultural fantasies that were also particular to the German discourse on Indians. First, in emphasizing the bond of friendship that he felt with this audience in particular (as opposed to the American people that he accused of widespread injustice), and soliciting their support, Rocky Bear seemingly confirmed the idea of a special affinity between Germans and Indians, based on mutual understanding and recognition. Second, the political argument reinforced the paternalistic notion that Germans were somehow morally superior to other colonizers. If Germans had settled the American frontier, so the logic went, they would have made better custodians of Indian culture than those Americans who shamelessly eradicated it. Both of these fantasies would be taken up again and given even greater circulation by Karl May.[18] Not surprisingly, they also informed and thereby helped transform Hagenbeck's future approach to the assembly and display of Indian troupes.

Revising Hagenbeck's *Völkerschau*

Carl Hagenbeck's Oglala-Sioux show of 1910 attracted more spectators than any troupe that the German showman ever assembled. If the choice of Sioux Indians seems obvious in retrospect, it is interesting to note

In the second half of the nineteenth century, the rapid increase of the number of images in circulation – due in large part to the development of new print technologies – offered an ideal means of providing the education for the masses implicit in the various universalist, positivist and scientist movements in Europe and the USA. Henceforth, media images and other forms of entertainment (most notably human exhibitions) would contribute to the production of collective imaginations and associated commonplaces shared by millions of people, from Tokyo to Hamburg, from Paris to Chicago...

1 'The Ashanti. Meal time.' Jardin d'Acclimatation [Zoological Garden], Paris. Stereoscopic image, Julien Damoy, 1895.

Populations put on display were depicted in a variety of forms, ranging from posters to illustrated programmes, from postcards (reproduced and translated into several languages to early films, from amateur photographs to the front pages of newspapers. Visitors, readers and spectators would be fascinated by these human subjects, while at the same time being convinced by them of the 'racial hierarchies' central to the contemporary context of colonial expansion.

Beyond the topicality of such 'ethnic shows', these millions of images, distributed to the four corners of the earth, greatly accentuated the impact of human zoos.

2 'Ethnographer and dancers.' Colonial Exhibition, Marseille. Postcard, Rosenthal and Cassan, 1906.

THÉÂTRE INTERNATIONAL
DE L'EXPOSITION UNIVERSELLE

TOUS LES SOIRS

EXHIBITION DE LA GRANDE SMALA
ou
TRIBU ARABE ALGÉRIENNE

Sous la direction de M. THÉLOU

PROGRAMME
PREMIÈRE PARTIE
CORPORATION DES DERDEBAS

Cette corporation reproduira la fête du Sebaa, dans laquelle les nègres exécuteront des danses variées, avec chant, tam-tams et castagnettes de fer. — Danse des Négresses agitant des *fontas*. — Danse des Nègres du Soudan ou danse des bâtons, avec chant. — Danse des Négresses avec des instruments tranchants.
Tous les Nègres réunis exécutent la grande danse de Tombouctou.

DEUXIÈME PARTIE
CORPORATION DES ZERNADJIA

Les Zernadjia exécutent la *Noûba*, qui est la musique du Sultan. Sur cette musique dansent et chantent les nomades du grand désert et les femmes de la tribu des *Ouled-Naïl*, dont le renom de beauté est célèbre dans tout l'Orient.

TROISIÈME PARTIE
CORPORATION DES LALIA

Les *Lalia* exécuteront tous les airs indigènes qui se jouent dans les *Serayas* ou soirées. Sur ces airs, les *Mauresques* et les *Juives* danseront et chanteront la DANSE DES ALMÉES.

QUATRIÈME PARTIE
CORPORATION DES AISSAOUA

Les exercices des *Aissaouas*, célèbres dans toute l'Afrique, sont les suivants :
1° Broyer des charbons ardents avec les dents;
2° Se mettre un fer rouge dans la bouche;
3° Manger des feuilles de figuier de Barbarie (ou cactus à longues épines) ;
4° Jouer avec des serpents et des scorpions en liberté;
5° Manger des scorpions, des lézards et une infinité d'autres animaux ;
6° Exécuter différents exercices avec des instruments tranchants, tels que yatagans, flissah, frida, etc.

Les Représentations auront lieu le soir, à partir de 7 h. 1/2 jusqu'à 11 h. au plus tard

PRIX DES PLACES

Fauteuils d'Orchestre, 1 fr. — Baignoires, Loges de Balcon et Stalles de Balcon, 2 fr. — Avant-Scènes, 3 fr. — Deuxième Balcon, 50 c.

Paris. — Typ. Morris et Comp., rue Amelot, 64.

3 Exhibition of the Grande Smala [Great Tribe], or Algerian Arab tribe. International Theatre of the Universal Exhibition, Paris. Programme, 1867.

5 'Zulus.' Folies-Bergère Theatre, Paris. Poster, 1878. © private collection.

4 'Tea sellers in the Chinese garden: Leao Ya Tchoe et Tcheou Ya Nai.' Universal Exhibition, Paris. Photograph, Bertail and Co. Photographers, 1867.

6 'Galibi.' Jardin zoologique d'Acclimatation, Paris. Photo-card (commercial), 1882.

7 'Chouli people.' Paris. Poster, Émile Levy, 1897.

8 Group of bushmen photographed on stage at the *Folies-Bergère*. Photograph from the anthropological collection of Prince Roland Bonaparte (Paris), 1886. © private collection/ all rights reserved.

9 'Savage – eats flaming hemp, live rabbits, cigar ends.' Paris. Trade vignette for the *Aux Buttes de Chaumont* store, 1890.

10 'Red Indians.' Jardin d'Acclimatation, Paris. Poster, Charles Tichot, 1883.

11 'Javanese kampong [native village].' Universal Exhibition, Paris. Photo-card (commercial), 1889.

Universal Exhibitions and Zoological Gardens

Designed from the outset to be profit-making shows, exhibitions of 'exotic' people aimed to operate in as many sites as possible. When legitimized by the scientific and rationalist discourses of universal and national exhibitions, human zoos were able to travel even more widely. Individuals exhibited in them played multiple roles – in *jardins d'acclimatation* (zoological gardens, such as the one in Paris) and theatres, in official exhibitions and circus troupes (such as Buffalo Bill's Wild West Show). In the major exhibitions, in the midst of colonial pavilions, they were a living justification of the colonial order.

At the end of the nineteenth century, images produced were dominated by posters, pictures in the press, and photographic cards. In the space of a few years, series of mass-produced postcards and then films (notably by the Lumière brothers) would permit contact with any increasingly large – and increasingly general – public.

12 'The Caribbean.' Jardin d'Acclimatation, Paris. Poster, Henry Sicard and Farrradeshe, 1882.

13 Colonial and Indian Exhibition, London. Daily Programme, 1886. © private collection.

14 Sinhalese in the Zoological Garden. Jardin zoologique d'acclimatation, Paris. Photo-card (commercial), 1886.

15 'Dahomeans in Paris. Training for war.' Jardin d'acclimatation, Paris. Cover of the *Petit Parisien*, March 1891.

16 'Mother and child, Dahomey.' Maritime Museum, Rotterdam. Postcard, 1896.

17 Geronimo. Pawnee Bill's Wild West Show, USA. Poster, Strobridge, 1904. © private collection/ all rights reserved.

18 Congolese village. Universal Exhibition, Anvers, Belgium. Chromolithographic postcard, 1894.

19 'Abyssinian village. Bride and groom, Kidica and Elmi.' Hagenbeck's show, Germany (the Abyssinian village visited Geneva in 1904). Postcard, 1899.

20 'The Black Continent.' Swiss National Exhibition, Geneva. Poster, Camis, undated. © coll. Kharbine-Tapabor/all rights reserved.

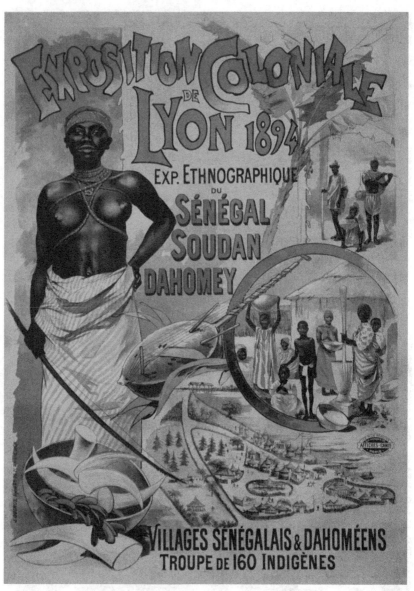

21 'Senegalese and Dahomean villages. Troupe of 160 natives.' Colonial Exhibition, Lyon, France. Poster, Francisco Tamagno, printed by Imprimerie Camis, 1894.

22 'Exhibition of Arabs of the Sahara Desert.' Olympia, Paris Hippodrome. Poster, Jules Chéret, 1897.

23 Cairo Street Waltz. World's Columbian Exposition, Chicago. Show programme, 1893.

24 'Greetings from Cairo.' Trade exhibition, Berlin. Chromolithographic postcard, 1896.

Travelling Villages

With technological progress – in particular in the areas of transport and information transfer – exhibition organizers were no longer reluctant to drum up custom by putting together real travelling villages and assembling troupes whose size depended on the revenue from the places in which they operated. The names of troupes and of populations on display were changed without compunction, like theatrical costumes or stage-managed customs. Although these exhibitions still illustrated some scientific theories or arguments directly linked to colonial expansion, they increasingly resembled the circus tours inaugurated by Barnum in the previous century.

25 Inuits in the Buen Retiro gardens. Madrid. Stereoscopic image, 1900. © Patrimonio Nacional, Madrid.

26 'Repas des négrillons [Piccaninny meal time],' Ashanti village. Photogram made from series of Lumière Brothers' films, Lyon, France, 1897. © Association des Frères Lumière/all rights reserved.

27 'Ashanti women.' Jardin d'Acclimatation, Paris. Stereoscopic image, Julien Damoy, 1895.

28 'Sudanese and Malagasies at the Champ de Mars. 400 natives, African villages.' Ethnographic Exhibition of East and West Africa, Paris. Brochure, 1896.

EXPOSITION ETHNOGRAPHIQUE
de l'Afrique Orientale et Occidentale
J. et L. BARBIER, Organisateurs

SOUDANAIS & MALGACHES
AU CHAMP-DE-MARS — 1896

400 INDIGÈNES

VILLAGES NOIRS

DIENA-BASSI Femme Toucouleur
Prix de l'Album : 0.15

Andenken an die Togo-Karawane.

29 'Souvenir of the Togolese caravan.' Berlin. Postcard, printed by Adolphe Friedländer (Hamburg, Saint-Paul), 1900.

Gruß aus Carl Hagenbeck's Indien 1898.
Ausstellung am Kurfürstendamm.

Kira-Ceylonese.

30 'Greetings from Carl Hagenbeck's Indians.' Hamburg. Postcard, 1898.

31 Tervuren. Palais des Colonies. Universal Exhibition, Brussels. Chromolithographic postcard, 1897.

32 Arab village. Prague. Postcard, 1899.

33 'Funfair. Museum.' Postcard, France, c. 1895.

34 Philippines Exhibition Album. Madrid. Photograph, Jean Laurent, 1897. © Patrimonio Nacional, Madrid.

35 Bangala canoers and the Congolese village. Universal Exhibition, Brussels, 1897.

36 'The Dahomeans.' Universal Exhibition, Paris. Postcard, 1900.

37 'Ponta Delgada Exhibition.' Porto, Portugal. Postcard, 1901.

38 'Buffalo Bill's Wild West.' Indians. Germany. Postcard, 1901.

39 'Africa in Song and Story. Two of Jas.H.Balmer's Kaffir boys.'
London. Postcard, 1904.

42 'Abyssinian camp.' Denmark. Postcard, 1904.

41 'Souvenir of the Sudanese
village.' Turin Exhibition. Postcard,
Gravier et Cie (Lyon), 1906.

40 'Interior view of the Virginia shoe shop.' Jamestown Exposition,
USA. Postcard, 1907.

43 'Igorrote Dog Feast.' St Louis Exhibition, USA. Postcard, 1904.

42 'Senegalese village. Porte Maillot. Main entrance.' Paris. Postcard, 1905.

44 Hagenbeck's Eritrean village. Milan Exhibition. Poster, 1906.

45 'Senegal village.' Franco-British Exhibition, London. Brochure, 1908. © private collection.

46 'Colonel Harrison and the Pigmies from the Congo forests.' London. Postcard, undated.

47 'Senegalese village: a birth in the village.' Amiens International Exhibition. Postcard, 1906.

Exotic and 'Traditional' Villages

In the major exhibitions, Scottish, Irish, Breton, Swiss and Flemish villages were often to be found alongside colonial and exotic populations. In addition to the pedagogical desire to put human evolution on display, there was a fascination with questions of origin as well as with 'endangered' worlds. Industrial civilization – rapidly in the ascendant during this period – ground down all distinctive identities. By comparing different worlds rebuilt together in a single place, spectators were better able to appreciate the 'progress' and 'veracity' of their own culture. In these ludic universes, the entry into 'modernity' seems to have been accompanied by a form of nostalgia for these gardens of Eden, exotic or European.

49 'Senegalese Village.' Franco-British Exhibition, London. Postcard, 1908.

50 'Souvenir from the Breton village.' Nantes. Postcard, 1910.

51 Samoans. Hagenbeck's show, Germany. Postcard, 1904.

52 'The Malabars.' Jardin d'acclimatation, Paris. Poster, G. Smith, 1902.

53 'The Tunisians.' Ethnic show,
Munich. Postcard, 1907.

54 'Laotians with hut.' Colonial
Exhibition, Paris. Postcard, 1907.

食人種サカイ

55 'Exhibition of savage cannibal from Formosa.' Taisho, Japan. Postcard, 1914.

AUSTRALSKÉ ČERNOŠKY.   Fotogr. Dr. Domin.

56 Aboriginal Australians Prague. Postcard, 1910.

57 A group of Senegalese. Barcelona. Photograph, 1913. © Centro Excursioniste de Catalunya, Barcelona.

58 'Bedouin ethnic show.' Carl Hagenbeck's Tierpark, Stellingen (Germany). Publicity leaflet, 1912.

59 African hunting village (Ethiopian). 1st International Hunting Exhibition, Vienna Postcard, 1910.

60 'A native duel. Somati Village.' Coronation Exhibition, London. Postcard, 1911.

61 'Völkerschau [ethnic show].' Colonial Exhibition, Stuttgart. Poster, Herdtle, 1928.

62 'Africa and the East.' Great Exhibition, London. Publicity brochure, undated. © private collection/all rights reserved.

63 'Giraffe-necked women.' Siebold's ethnic show, Germany. Postcard, c.1925.

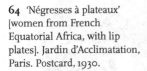

64 'Négresses à plateaux' [women from French Equatorial Africa, with lip plates]. Jardin d'Acclimatation, Paris. Postcard, 1930.

65 Gold Coast Africans in the native village at Wembley. London. Postcard, 1924.

人 ヌ イ ア 太 樺

66 Ainu people, Karafuto. Hokkaïdo Exhibition, Japan. Postcard, 1912.

The End of the Exhibitions

Moving images and the apathy of an increasingly blasé public explain in large part the decline of 'anthropozoological exhibitions'. A series of other factors made these spectacles appear more and more anachronistic: the widening of access to knowledge; the fact that the underlying message of human zoos had become normalized in the West; and the flood of images saturating everyday life. In the cinema, people could now witness entirely scripted worlds, set in natural scenery and presented in the light of a revitalized dramatic art. Representing a rupture with an imaginative world based on exoticism and fantasy, contemporary images aimed, from a colonial perspective, to be increasingly realistic: visitors were allowed fewer and fewer flights of fancy, and exhibitions were made to look more and more like shows presented by troupes of actors or like craftsmen's villages.

67 Abyssinian warrior.
Prague. Postcard, 1922.

MAUNG LAW PAW, BURMESE JUGGLER, AT WEMBLEY.

MARSEILLE - EXPOSITION COLONIALE 1922
Palais de l'Afrique Occidentale – Intérieur d'un Village Soudanais

68 'Maung Law Paw, Burmese Juggler.' Wembley. Postcard, 1924.

69 'Interior of a Sudanese village.' Colonial Exhibition, Marseilles. Postcard, 1922.

70 Galas. Hagenbeck's show, Hamburg, Germany. Photograph, 1924.

71 International Colonial Exhibition, Paris. Postcard, 1931.

72 'Prins Hessen Mohamed Troupe.' Indian Exhibition, The Hague
Postcard, 1932.

Aus der Völkerschau der **Kannibalen**
von den Südsee-Inseln

73 'From the ethnic show: cannibals from
the South Sea islands.' Germany. Postcard,
1931–32.

AU PAVILLON BELGE, A L'EXPOSITION COLONIALE

74 'In the Belgian pavilion at the Colonial
Exhibition.' *Le Petit Journal illustré* (Paris), 1931.

75 Maoris. Jardin d'acclimatation, Nice. Postcard, 1934.

EXPOSITION INTERNATIONALE - PARIS 1937

Le chef NYAMBI
dans la «Danse des Coupeurs de têtes»

76 'Chief Nyambi in the "headhunter dance"'
International Exhibition, Paris. Postcard, 1937.

THE EGYPTIAN PAVILION

77 The Egyptian Pavilion. Chicago World's Fair.
Postcard, 1933.

78 Guinean women. Porto, Portugal. Postcard, 1934.

78 Representation of the amount of Gold obtained in 1887, historical feature in the City's Jubilee procession. Johannesburg, South Africa. Photograph, 1936. © Museum Africa, Johannesburg.

Seminole Family Group at Tropical Hobbyland Indian Village, Miami, Fla.   604

79 'Seminole Family Group at Tropical Hobbyland Indian Village.' Miami, USA. Postcard, c.1940.

80 'Coming soon. The Robinson Circus and its savage peoples.' France. Poster, unattributed, 1900.

that Hagenbeck was initially averse to the idea, 'because he feared that the Indians would be too difficult to manage and, due to their knowledge of English, their contact with spectators would become too close' (Thode-Arora 1989: 76). He had to be persuaded by Jacobsen, who in 1909 invited Hagenbeck to a Wild West show in London. Impressed by what he saw, Hagenbeck dispatched Jacobsen to the Pine Ridge Reservation in South Dakota. The process of recruiting was competitive, not least of all because many Native Americans here relied on Wild West shows for their economic survival. To complicate matters, five other agents converged on Pine Ridge at the same time, and Buffalo Bill's representative was reportedly on his way.[19] Jacobsen managed to recruit 42 Indians and 10 cowboys. Several participants had previous experience in travelling shows, including Thomas American Horse, chief and leader of the Indian contingent of Hagenbeck's troupe, whose father had performed earlier with Buffalo Bill. With its exclusive engagement at Hagenbeck's new Tierpark (a zoo, containing an area of ethnographic villages) in Stellingen on the outskirts of Hamburg, the troupe attracted over a five-month period more than 1,100,000 visitors.

The Wild West changed Hagenbeck's image of Indians. Witness the 'Program' (or synopsis) for the Sioux show, as stated in the programme brochure:

> The presentations offer a picture of the dangerous life of farmers and trappers when the far West was first being settled. A real event frames the presentations – an event which took place in the Black Hills during the early 70s, as the settlers were pressing forward and the Sioux were on the warpath. A band of Indians appears at an isolated farm and, though warmly received, they take the opportunity to steal a horse. Responding to the sound of gunfire, cowboys track and capture the thief. The pony express passes by. At night, out of revenge for the capture of their friends, Indians ambush the stagecoach, attack the farm, and set fire to the lower log cabin. The farmhands are burned alive. Yet the farmer's family, having recaptured the stagecoach, races to the nearest fort, escorted by cowboys, and fighting the redskins all the way.[20]

The main elements of Hagenbeck's programme – cowboys and Indians with feathered headdresses, the conflict of horse-stealing, fight scenes on horseback, ambushes of settlers and the Pony Express, the revenge motif and last-minute rescues – were also the elements of Buffalo Bill's Wild West (Thode-Arora 1989: 110). Moreover, in contrast to the Bella Coola, the new show staked a claim to history, framing the scenes in terms of 'a real event' from the 1870s. The narrative programme description was augmented by an 11-page section entitled 'History', which includes brief entries on the Oglala, the Battle of the Little Bighorn in 1876, the so-called reservation system, Pine Ridge and the late Chief Red Cloud. Further details are provided about several of the troupe's oldest performers and their participation in the Indian wars, invoking their physical presence as further evidence of the show's historical authenticity.

The Wild West also changed the 'ethnographic' aspect of Hagenbeck's *Völkerschau*. By this I mean particularly the dances and ceremonies that interspersed the various action sequences of the Sioux programme. The Omaha Dance offers a good example. In contrast to the so-called Cannibal Dance of the Bella Coola, which traded on the fascination for the grotesque, the Omaha Dance exploited in particular the park's foreign-looking landscape and its link to the picturesque. The dance took place around and on top of the mesa-shaped artificial rockwork that was then located in the Tierpark's designated area for ethnographic villages. Artificial terrain and elaborate landscaping allowed the zookeeper to surpass itinerant American showmen and other rivals in at least one important respect: that of the show's setting. That was not all. Ironically, as one commentator pointed out, Germany as a country granted the Indian contingent fewer cultural restrictions and greater freedoms of religion and expression than it enjoyed at home: 'The Omaha Dance evokes the most passionate dancing of the Indians – so passionate, in fact, that the government of the United States of North America [sic] saw to it to fix specific days and times for this dance, because the sons of the prairie forgot all about work when it came to dancing. Here, where there is no authoritarian ban to hinder the redskins, one often hears even at midnight the faint sound of the drum and the peculiar type of song coming from the tents, as the dancers abandon themselves to the dance, often to the point of exhaustion.'[21]

At the same time, but in direct contrast to the Wild West shows of the 1890 season, Hagenbeck's Sioux troupe staked a claim not only to history but also to fantasy. What is more, going a step further than the Wild West troupes of 1890, Hagenbeck now provided the fictional reference points, urging the audience to draw the sorts of connections that earlier spectators made for themselves, without being prompted.

> When people speak of Indians, nobody thinks of the numerous tribes in Brazil or in the rest of South America, in Central America or Mexico. They always mean the famous Prairie Indians of legend and history. They are celebrated in countless novels, and they have given rise to a literature as vast as that of knighthood. These stories of knights and Indians, they will be told over and over again to the delight of our youth. The figures of Leatherstocking, Scout, Tecumseh, etc., with their sharp-cut faces, their

large hawk's noses, and their characteristic feathered headdresses, these figures are now brought to us and made tangible before our very eyes by this year's *Völkerschau*.[22]

Earlier, such references to imaginative fiction would have been anathema, as is evidenced by the Bella Coola. Rather than criticize this move, local reporters echoed and embellished the use of fictive referents. One journalist described the crowd in particularly vivid terms: 'The pale faces stride past the tents in a state of wonder. Their souls begin to soar when, like dreams from their childhood days, the famous chief of the Mohicans, Chingachgook, the Great Snake, his blood brother Leatherstocking, and the noble Uncas, who longed to take the scalp of the despicable Iroquois chief – all appear, living, before their very eyes. And none of this is imagined, for the copper-coloured warriors, Little Wolf and Yellow Thunder, Spotted Weasel and American Horse, and others have actually come from the land where Cooper's novels took place.'[23]

Learning from the Wild West, Hagenbeck sought to accumulate mass consumers by inspiring in them a set of strong memories and cultural associations, invoking explicitly the power of myth and legend and thereby encouraging spectators to take possession of the spectacle, as they had earlier, by means of the imagination. What makes this turn to fantasy all the more interesting is the idea that it fostered precisely the kind of imaginative role-play, passionate identification and ethnic impersonation that would shape the German fascination for Indians throughout the twentieth century.

Notes

1 This article is a revised version of Ames 2006. For a fuller account see Eric Ames, *Carl Hagenbeck's Empire of Entertainments* (Seattle and London: University of Washington Press, forthcoming).

2 'Wild-West in Berlin', *Lokal-Anzeiger* (Berlin), 24 July 1890, available in MS 6, William F. Cody Collection, Series IX: Scrapbooks, ledgers, etc. Germany, 1890, Microfilm Roll 2, Buffalo Bill Historical Center, Cody, Wyoming (hereafter cited as BBHC).

3 Carl Hagenbeck, letter to Johan Adrian Jacobsen, 5 January 1882, available at the Tierpark Hagenbeck Archive (hereafter cited as THA). It took Jacobsen years to actually bring a troupe to Germany from British Columbia, with several failed attempts along the way. For an account of this process, see Haberland 1988b. On Hagenbeck's ethnographic enterprise in general, see Thode-Arora 1989, and Dreesbach 2005.

4 Schedule and programme details appear in Haberland 1988b: 15, 17–35.

5 See Stumpf 1886. For an account of this encounter between science and entertainment, see Ames 2003.

6   See 'Die Sioux-Indianer', *Hamburger Fremdenblatt*, 20 November 1885. Harvey's was not the first Wild West show in Germany. For a list of other troupes, see Kocks 2004: 86–89.

7   The programme is detailed in Russell 1970: 33–35. For more on Buffalo Bill and on Wild West shows in general, see Russell 1973 [1960], Moses 1996, Reddin 1999, Kasson 2000, and Warren 2005.

8   In 1891, Buffalo Bill's troupe returned to Germany, with appearances in Karlsruhe, Mannheim, Mainz, Wiesbaden, Cologne, Dortmund, Duisburg, Krefeld and Aachen. Details on the Munich show come from 'Buffalo Bill', *Münchener Fremdenblatt*, 20 April 1890; 'Buffalo Bills Wild West', *Münchener Fremdenblatt*, 21 April 1890; 'Buffalo Bills "Wilder Westen"', *Münchener Neuste Nachrichten*, 21 April 1890; 'Die amerikanische Arena', *Münchener Fremdenblatt*, 22 April 1890; 'Indianer in der Stadt', *Münchener Nachrichten*, 25 April 1890; *Münchener Bote*, 26 April 1890. For a description of the programme in Munich, see 'Buffalo Bills Wild West', *Münchener Fremdenblatt*, 21 April 1890. All sources here come from the William Fredrick Cody/Buffalo Bill Papers, WH72, Western History Collection, of The Denver Public Library (hereafter cited as DPL).

9   On the 'shooting demonstration', see Thorp 1957: 116, 119–122. On 'sharp-shooting', see Saltarino 1895: 89–92.

10 'Cowboys Painting Hamburg', *San Francisco Examiner*, 28 August 1890, available in MS 6, William F. Cody Collection, Series VI: E, W. F. 'Doc' Carver scrapbook, microfilm roll 1 (BBHC).

11 On Catlin as forerunner to Buffalo Bill, see Reddin 1999: 1–52.

12 'Wild-West', *Freisinnige Zeitung*, 24 July 1890 (BBHC).

13 'Buffalo Bill's Wild West', *Münchener Tageblatt*, 21 April 1890 (DPL).

14 'Dr. Carver's Wild-Amerika', *Hamburger Nachrichten*, 22 August 1890, 2nd supplement. Similar statements can be found in 'Dr. Carver's Wild-Amerika', *Hamburger Nachrichten*, 7 September 1890, morn. edn; 'Dr. Carver's Wild-Amerika', *Hamburger Fremdenblatt*, 25 August 1890, 1st supplement; 'Buffalo Bills Wild West in Dresden', n. pub. (BBHC); 'Buffalo Bills Wild West-Truppe', *Presse* (Hanover), 3 July 1890 (BBHC); '"Wild-West" in Berlin', *Lokal-Anzeiger* (Berlin), 24 July 1890 (BBHC); an untitled report on the show's premiere in Dresden, *Anzeiger und Tageblatt* (Freiberg), 1 June 1890 (BBHC); 'Biographisches über Buffalo Bill', *Allgemeine Zeitung* (Munich), 15 April 1890 (DPL); 'Buffalo Bill und seine Karawane', *Münchener Tageblatt*, 17 April 1890 (DPL); and esp. the untitled report on the Munich show in the *Augsburger Abendzeitung*, 27 April 1890 (DPL).

15 Karl Markus Kreis (2002) has noted that Wild West shows in Germany made cowboys and Indians widely available for imaginative role-play. The metaphor of vivification would seem to enhance this hypothesis. For historical sources, see 'Indianer-Spielen', *Tageblatt* (Dresden), 4 June 1890 (DPL); and 'Die Wirkungen der Vorstellungen Buffalo Bill's', *Nachrichten* (Leipzig), 22 June 1890 (BBHC).

16 The quotations here come from 'Indianer Buffalo Bills in der anthropologischen Gesellschaft', *Münchener Nachrichten*, 27 April 1890 (DPL). The group is described in 'Die Indianer in der Münchener Anthropologischen Gesellschaft', *Münchener Fremdenblatt*, 28 April 1890 (DPL).

17 'Ansprache des Rocky Bear', *Münchener Nachrichten*, 3 May 1890 (DPL). Cody later echoed these criticisms of the US government when pressed by reporters

in Berlin (Reddin 1999: 114). Soon thereafter, Black Heart, Rocky Bear and other Lakota members of the troupe – all long-time employees of the Wild West show – allied themselves with Cody in defence of their work against attacks by so-called Indian reformers, US congressmen and bureaucrats in the US Indian Service. See Warren 2005: 358–89.

18 For a brief discussion of these fantasies in the context of May's *Winnetou*, see Zantop 2002. On their pre-history in German literature and culture, see Zantop 1997.

19 For an account of this troupe's recruitment, see Haberland 1988a: 11–15. See also Thode-Arora 2002c.

20 *Sioux-Indianer: Carl Hagenbeck's Tierpark, Stellingen, 1910*, souvenir guidebook and programme brochure with text by Johannes Flemming (Hamburg: Carly 1910), 5 (THA).

21 *Hamburger Nachrichten*, 2 June 1910. Historian Louis Warren has recently made a similar observation, adding that Wild West shows allowed some participants to resist native traditions, as well (2005: 363).

22 *Sioux-Indianer: Carl Hagenbeck's Tierpark*, 9.

23 *Hamburger Fremdenblatt*, 17 April 1910, quoted in Thode-Arora, 1993: 85. See also 'Sioux-Indianer bei Hagenbeck', *Hamburgischer Correspondent*, 16 April 1910; 'Wild-West bei Hagenbeck', *Hamburger Nachrichten*, 16 April 1910.

18

Billy the Australian in the Anthropological Laboratory

ROSLYN POIGNANT

On 19 November 1885, Billy, an indigenous Australian, met Paul Topinard, the French scientist. Picture the scene in the Paris Anthropological Laboratory at the École pratique des hautes études. Prompted by Topinard's questions about notions of time, Billy began to recite the names of all the places he and his companions had visited since their removal from their North Queensland home almost three years earlier by the showman, R. A. Cunningham, to be exhibited in the show places of America and Europe. Present at the seance with Billy was a woman called Jenny and her young son, Toby, and these three were the only survivors of the party of nine – six men, two women and the boy – who had set out. Jenny's husband and the boy's father, also called Toby, had died of tuberculosis in a Paris hospital about ten days earlier and, as Topinard explained, although he had done what he could for the body to be sent to the Broca laboratory for dissection, he had been unsuccessful.

Topinard's bare description (1885: 683–98) misses the significance of Billy's performance. He was retracing the song-line of the incredible journey they had made from Australia across the Pacific, through more than 100 towns and cities of America's north-west – at first with Barnum's circus, and later on the dime museum circuit[1] – and on, with Cunningham, to the bustling provincial towns and great metropolitan centres of Europe. Billy's litany of names transformed and extended an Aboriginal way of conceptualizing space – by memorizing the lie of the land and the stages of a journey – to encompass their world-journey. When interrupted – Topinard noted – Billy started again 'with the preceding town'. The order was important. Billy's great feat of memory was more than a mnemonic key to the route they had travelled, for each place-name had the potential for evoking a story, but the anthropologist wore his own cultural blinkers, and dismissed Billy's prodigious memory as of 'an automatic kind'.

For Billy, recollection through re-enactment was both a system for incorporating knowledge about his world and a way of *telling*; perhaps it was also for knowing – even willing – his way back home. Billy's predicament becomes our predicament: we want to hear what he has to tell. Instead, Topinard's culturally bound interpretation ensures that we have to settle for no more than a tantalizing intimation of Billy's side of the story. Aboriginal lives were made captive, not only in the sense of loss of personal control over their own actions but also within late nineteenth-century discourses that linked the colonial spaces of the frontiers to the metropolitan centres of America and Europe. Topinard failed to grasp the significance of Billy's performance because his concerns were not with Billy as an individual, but with his type – a racial type. In his report, he mainly discussed the physical characteristics of Billy, Jenny and her son, Toby, in relation to his earlier findings published in *Instructions sur les races indigènes d'Australie* (1872). This work drew not on direct observations of living people but on travellers' descriptions, as well as on the examination of skeletal material and 'onze bustes d'Australiens' [eleven Australian torsos] lodged in the Paris natural history museum. In this upside-down realm, Topinard, as the recognized authority, declared the three visitors to be 'authentic' Aborigines, and he provided a written testimonial to that effect for their impresario, Cunningham. At the same time, in a letter of 25 November 1885, he urged that 'these Curious examples of Man must be seen as their Race is fast dying away' (Cunningham 1887). Such a specific exchange between showman and scientist was not an isolated incident, it was indicative of the inter-layering of these two spheres of operation – popular and scientific. Cunningham also obtained 'certificates as to their [the Aborigines] being what they are represented' from other eminent professors throughout Europe. Most anthropologists regarded the showmen's initiative in touring these groups of indigenous 'performers' as advantageous for their special field of study, and instructive for the general public.

Topinard rejected the idea that Billy's reserve, even coldness of manner, and Jenny's indifference to the proceedings, were a response to the trauma of Toby's death – even though he wrote of an apparent sadness in her, which he considered might relate to that event. For the classificatory project in which Topinard played a leading part – what Stephen J. Gould (1996 [1981]) has described as the mismeasurement of man – meant that his attitudes reflected the misconceptions of the period, namely that the physical and mental characteristics attributed to Australian Aborigines consigned them to the lowest position in a hierarchy of races. Thus, like many others in his day, both scientists and laymen, Topinard attributed the rapid reduction in number of hunter-gatherers whose lands had been colonized, not so much to policies of dispossession, which led to dispersal and death, as to their innate nature, which 'doomed them to disappear' (Topinard 1878). Such ideas have a lineage.

An Antipodean World

In the century after Renaissance navigators brought the knowledge of the Americas to European consciousness, Terra Australis Incognita, the Unknown South Land, became a site for Europe's antipodean imaginings. The makers of a collection of maps known as the Dieppe maps, supposedly derived from one source, a lost Portuguese original (c.1530), laid down the first fragmentary outlines of its coasts, and sketched on its supposed landmass exotic representations of its animal and human occupants and their dwellings (Dauphin Map, 1536). By the early seventeenth century, however, when the Dutch began to make landfall on the coasts of Arnhem Land and Cape York Peninsula, Northern Australia, Aboriginal resistance to the white intruders gained for them a reputation of being 'bad' and 'barbarous' (Heeres 1899).

At the century's end, the Englishman William Dampier's account of the inhabitants of north-western Australia, widely disseminated the view of Aborigines as 'the miserablest People in the World' (Dampier 1697).[2] In 1770, however, Captain Cook decided that although the 'natives of New Holland' were among 'the most wretched people on earth', they were 'in reality [...] far happier than we Europeans' (Beaglehole 1955). In spite of the eighteenth-century traveller-ethnographers' preoccupation with the search for 'natural man', the Aborigine's reputation for 'miserableness' clung to him, and became the prevailing view after the establishment of the penal colony at Botany Bay in 1788.

The accounts of travellers, missionaries and colonizers, as well as the more systematic observations and collections made on the scientific voyages, were a source of the comparative data that contributed to notions relating to the origins and development of humans, which, from the eighteenth century, found expression in the concept of the Great Chain of Being. In the course of the nineteenth century, these developmental ideas were gradually transformed into the more structured socio-cultural evolutionary ideas about a hierarchy of races that became the paradigm for thinking about the physical, social and cultural diversity of humankind. These ideas – formulated by the 'Gentlemen of Science' – were seen as powering the engine of progress that was propelling the European nations towards the commanding heights of civilization, but they were by no means uniform. Some saw the developmental sequence as stemming from a single origin (monogenesis), while others explained the diversity of humankind as an outcome of separate developments (polygenesis), and even thought of the races as separate species.

Charles Darwin's own ethnographic observations of the inhabitants of Tierra del Fuego, made on his voyage round the world in HMS *Beagle*, were notable for their overwhelmingly negative tone. Viewing such 'abject and miserable creatures', he wrote, 'one can hardly make oneself feel they are fellow-creatures ...', and he relegated them to the lowest grade of savagery, along with 'the Australians', in spite of the latter's superiority in weapons (1839: 209). In 1864 Alfred Russell Wallace carried the argument further by maintaining that not only had the operations of natural selection (in which he included the effects of environmental influences) produced the diverse and distinct races of man that had led to 'the superiority of the Germanic races of the temperate zone', they would also lead to 'the inevitable extinction' of 'those lowly and mentally undeveloped populations' with whom Europeans were now coming into contact (see Stocking 1987: 148). My concern, however, is less with how the scientific expression of these ideas developed, and more with how, particularly in their popularized form, they both shaped and were shaped by the relationships of colonizers to the colonized.

By mid-century the growing contempt for the 'savage' was given popular currency by writers such as Charles Dickens, whose description, in an article entitled 'The Noble Savage' in *Household Words* (1853: 168), of the exhibition of 'Pygmy Earthmen' (the San of South Africa, also called Bushmen at that time) at the Westminster Aquarium in London, declared 'I call a savage a something highly desirable to be civilized off the face of the earth'. Similarly, the influential writer, Anthony Trollope, in his travel book *Australia* (1873: 474–75) criticized the missionaries' Christianizing and civilizing project as futile.

The occupation of the Australian continent by the British has been justified on the grounds that it was *terra nullius* (a land without owners) – a legal concept applied to European possession of non-European lands that was propounded by Grotius in the seventeenth century. In practice, however, the white land-takers more frequently rationalized the act of dispossession by the claim that the 'wandering Aborigines' had forfeited their rights to land because they had failed to make productive use of it. More than that, their failure to cultivate was seen as determining their lowly place in the social order. The idea that the industrious were the

natural inheritors of the land had deep roots in European Enlightenment thought – particularly in that of John Locke – and it had already
been used in the earlier British colonies in America to justify the appropriation of land on the grounds that the colonizers would make more
rational use of the it, for 'the public good'. By extension, it was argued
that the dependence of the 'savage' 'on the spontaneous hand of nature'
for sustenance meant that he lacked the capacity for rational thought. In
his *Two Treatises of Government* (1690), Locke proposed that those who
opposed men of reason exposed themselves to being treated as 'beasts
of prey'. As Peter Hulme has observed, here was 'the language in which
all colonial wars [...] have been justified' (1990: 18).

   The events that propelled Billy, Jenny, her son, Toby, and their companions on to a world stage had their epicentre in their North Queensland
homelands. When the full thrust of invasion, both overland and from
the sea, was felt in their area in the early 1860s, Toby, the oldest in the
group, was a young man of 20, while the youngest adult in the group,
Sussy, who was the wife of Tambo, was an infant. This couple, Toby's
family, and a young man called Jimmy were Manbarra from the Palm
Islands, and the other three men, Billy and his two Biyargirri companions, Bob and another whose name remains uncertain, were from nearby
Hinchinbrook Island (Dixon and Blake 1983). In the early 1870s, Billy
was a young man and his Biyargirri clansmen were still children when a
succession of punitive drives on Hinchinbrook Island and the mainland
opposite reduced their people to a handful of survivors. Happenings on
the North Queensland frontier were shaped by attitudes forged not only
on earlier Australian frontiers but also in other theatres of empire. As
one visitor, George Carrington, observed with regard to the decimation
of the Aborigines, on seeing 'the process in full work in the colony of
Queensland [...] we understand the mystery of Tasmania, New South
Wales, Victoria and Western Australia' (Carrington 1871: 144).

   The diaries, letters and settlers' accounts from this frontier (as from
earlier Australian frontiers) reveal the fear and anxiety engendered by
the 'invisibility of the natives', and their unpredictability, which was
attributed to their 'treacherous' nature. As one later reminisced: 'In
Melbourne we looked on North Queensland as a terra incognita inhabited by fierce tribes of cannibals and all sorts' (Rowe 1931). In actuality,
however, on this frontier, as on other frontiers, these well-established
'cultural representations of Aborigines [...] as treacherous beings [...]
in effect authorized and inspired greater acts of terror' (Morris 1992:
86; see also Lattas 1987; Taussig 1992). The space of terror became
the site for a series of retaliatory acts, where the supposed savagery

of the 'native' could only be extinguished by a greater savagery perpetrated in the name of civilization (Queenslander 1880: 28). There is a circularity here, for the cultural representations (in visual, textual and verbal forms) of Aborigines as treacherous, conceived on earlier frontiers, when transferred to North Queensland were re-enforced and re-inscribed in published frontier tales of that place and time, such as Eden's *My Wife and I in Queensland* (1872) and Finch-Hatton's *Advance Australia!* (1885). In turn, these texts framed the presentation of Billy and his companions, removed overseas by Cunningham, and contributed to their reception as 'savages'. These professional 'savages' were re-inscribed yet again in American and European texts, written and graphic, popular and anthropological, and in photographs that represented them as examples of the Australian type.

The Making of Professional 'Savages'

The circus touring season of Barnum Bailey and Hutchinson's 'Greatest Show on Earth' had already begun when Cunningham and his troupers joined up with it in May 1883. Billed as 'The last of the Cannibals', in the *Advance Courier* circulated ahead of the show, the public were urged: 'Now or never is the time to see them', as 'they are not only the first, but the last, of their race that we of America will ever behold'. Recruited to take part in Phineas T. Barnum's 'Ethnological Congress of Strange and Savage Tribes', Billy and his companions were exhibited alongside other indigenous performers – billed as 'Ferocious Zulu', 'Wild Moslem Nubian', 'Extraordinary Todars' and 'Sioux Warriors' – similarly dispossessed on other colonial frontiers.

From the 1870s Barnum had led the way in developing the travelling circus as an industrialized form of mass entertainment. He and his partner, W. C. Coup, made use of the expanding railway network to penetrate the largest and most profitable centres on the east coast and mid-west of North America. Dismountable carriages made the show highly mobile. Duplicate sets of canvases reduced the time lost between show places. The success of such an operation depended on capturing the attention of whole communities, a cast of hundreds, seen by tens of thousands, very often in the course of a single day. Illustrated newspaper ads and promotional publications – advance couriers, posters and billboards – summoned the crowds from the surrounding district, and excursion trains brought them in. Before the movies, the circus was probably the most influential instrument of mass culture in shaping public attitudes. The troupe was presented as a living picture

of savagery in a narrative of civilization's triumph over a savagery that
was 'destined for extinction' – and the processes of circus promotion,
presentation and performance served to fix the stereotype.

As the circus reached a peak of popularity in the 1880s, so the 'Dime
Museums of Curiosities' also entered their heyday throughout the cities
of North America (McNamara 1974), and at the end of the circus season,
in the winter of 1883–84, the Australian 'Boomerang-throwers' joined
the other 'attractions of wonder' on the dime museum circuit. There
they were exhibited on the so-called 'freak' platform, alongside the
Elastic-Skinned man, the Bearded Lady, Admiral Dot and others. Not
only were these geographically marginalized peoples exhibited with the
congenitally impaired, but Cunningham's 'savages' were also described
in the language of impairment – as 'deformed', with 'distorted' features,
and 'ranting' (i.e. lacking language). Thus the circus and dime museum
literature, and the shows themselves, were a popular reflection of a
range of scientific and fringe-scientific debates concerning humankind's origins and place in nature.

Towards the end of the Dime Museum tour, first Tambo, then
another young man died, and this traumatic event seems to have
caused Cunningham to change his plans (Poignant 1997). The troupe
was schedule to rejoin Barnum's 'Ethnological Congress' for 1884, but
instead, Cunningham moved the seven survivors to Europe, where they
continued to tour the European show places: The Crystal Palace in South
London, the Folies-Bergère in Paris, Castan's Panoptikum in Berlin,
Arkadia in St Petersburg and many zoos and music halls throughout
provincial Europe. They were also examined by anthropologists,
particularly E. Houzé and V. Jacques in Brussels and R. Virchow in
Berlin. One by one others of the group died, until, in Paris, only Billy,
Jenny and her young son Toby remained.

Cunningham continued to tour these three across northern Europe,
through Russia to Constantinople, and back to London in 1887, and
thence to America. In 1888 he returned them to North Queensland,
where what happened to them remains uncertain. While thinking about
their European travels and their ultimate fate, I turned to the Universal
Exposition of 1889 in Paris.

The Apotheosis of 'Billy – Australien'

In an elegant essay on the Eiffel Tower Barthes writes: 'The tower looks
at Paris' in such a way that it transforms it into a 'kind of nature' – 'a new
nature that is human space [...] a passive overview' which offers itself

for decipherment. He suggests that each onlooker imagines a history as he looks (Barthes 1983: 241). Among the histories Barthes considers, surprisingly, he neglects the world of spectacle that filled the show-space at the tower's base on the occasion of its inauguration in 1889. The mix of peoples and cultures to be found there, and their commodification, prefigured the new brew of the twentieth century. So multi-layered is the symbolism embedded in the constructed world of the Paris Exposition that there are several possible starting points to unravel its meaning. The relevant one for my purpose is the Palace of the Liberal Arts, which contained four pavilions devoted to anthropology and related subjects. Surrounding the palace were the streets containing the pavilions of various nations, and the reconstructed streets from the colonial towns of North Africa, and the Far East. Then – according to the publicity – 'in the back settlement behind all the gorgeous finery of the pagodas and palaces ... the ingenious French have established colonies of savages whom they are attempting to civilise. They are the genuine article and no mistake, living and working and amusing themselves as they and their kinsfolk do in their own country' (*Pall Mall Gazette*, 1889).

Anthropology, which was acclaimed as the modern French science, was a main focus of the exhibition, the layout of which is well documented by plans and photographs in the *Catalogue Général Officiel* (see Exposition 1889b; see also Alphand 1892). If one entered the pavilion at the end nearest the Seine, one came first to the Great Buddha of Nara, from Japan, which was the meeting point for anthropologists while the exposition was in progress. To the left were the casts of two Bushmen (San, who had been exhibited as living people in 1884 in London and elsewhere in Europe). Enclosed within the pavilion, in a central court, were tableaux depicting stone toolmakers, grain growers, builders, paper makers and metalworkers, arranged around central tableaux of 'Samoièdes'. This visualization lent authority to a conjectural history of progress and civilization.

The eight entrances to these diverse internal spaces were each framed by pairs of decorative panels depicting a selection of racial types, one pair of which represented Esther the Hottentot and Billy the Australian – the latter being based on Prince Roland Bonaparte's photograph taken in 1885. And, as a photograph of the entrance shows (Bibliothèque Nationale, Cartes et plans), just within the chamber, on either side of a figure of Western man with his musculature and nervous system exposed, stood skeletons of a gorilla and an orang-utan, the whole forming a visualization of contemporary evolutionary notions. It seems the panels themselves no longer exist, thus the faded photographic record survives as the end point of a series of representations, each more lifeless than the preceding one, and Billy's containment within them is analogous to his entrapment in western anthropological discourse. Billy is gone and only his fugitive image remains.

Notes

1 Succeeding the museums of curiosities at the end of the nineteenth century, dime museums drew their name from their low entry fees which also gained them a popular audience.
2 Apparently the phrase is attributable to Dampier's publisher rather than to Dampier himself.

19

Dr Kahn and the Niam-Niams

BERNTH LINDFORS

Long before Darwin, European scientists were wrestling with the question of humanity's relationship to other living creatures. In the Great Chain of Being that was presumed to link all forms of sentient life, humans were thought to stand midway between the apes and the angels, a favoured if somewhat ambiguous position that made him both animal and spirit. But just as there were different species in the animal world, so were there different varieties of people who could be classified as inferior and superior types and placed accordingly on a graded scale of innate ability. In the animal world, Homo sapiens obviously lorded it over the rest, and in this supreme category Europeans were considered – at least by Europeans themselves – to be at the very pinnacle of earthly creation. It may have been the scientists' preoccupation with taxonomic tidiness that led logically to the postulation of an absent transitional figure or missing link, which was believed to have served as a direct genetic connection between men and brutes.

Some scientists were, of course, of the opinion that the link was not missing. By calling attention to the close resemblance of the lowest humans to the highest apes, they sought to prove that the great chain was intact and unbroken. In their theories non-Western peoples, particularly Africans, were cited as examples of debased creatures sufficiently different in mind and body from European peoples to constitute a separate and unequal branch of the human family, if indeed they deserved to be called human at all. Charles White in *An Account of the Regular Gradations in Man* concluded that 'the African, more especially in those particulars in which he differs from the Europeans, approaches to the Ape [...] the characteristics which distinguish the African from the European are the same, differing only in degree, as those which distinguish the Ape from the European' (1799). Sir William Lawrence in his *Lectures on Physiology* (1819) stated that the Negro structure approximates unequivocally to that of the Monkey. It not only differs from the Caucasian model, but is distinguished from it in two respects: the intellectual characters are reduced, the animal features enlarged and exaggerated. This inferiority of organization is attended with corresponding inferiority of faculties; which may be proved, not so much by the unfortunate beings who are degraded by slavery, as by every fact in the past history and the present condition of Africa.

Even Baron Georges Cuvier, widely regarded as the greatest naturalist of his day, believed that it was 'not for nothing that the Caucasian race has gained domination over the world and made the most rapid progress in the sciences, while the Negroes are still sunken in slavery and the pleasures of the senses [...]. The shape of their head relates them somewhat more than us to the animals' (quoted in Coleman 1964: 166). Africans, whether manlike apes or apelike men, belonged at the bottom of the ladder, were the lowest anthropomorphic link in the great chain.

The End of Slavery and the Appearance of Public Exhibitions

These racist theories were founded less on direct observation than on an acceptance of reports from biased eyewitnesses. Travellers, missionaries, slavers and plantation-owners had told tales of their encounters with Africans, and these accounts, sometimes heavily embroidered with misconceptions, rumours and outright lies, were accepted as truth and cited in the scientific literature of the day. Cannibalism, for instance, was reported to be rampant throughout Africa, even though few European authorities on the subject went so far as to claim to have actually watched Africans eat human flesh. Hearsay and imaginative projection remained convenient substitutes for first-hand observation. One could theorize boldly, unencumbered by facts.

By 1833, when slavery was officially abolished in England, London had a small but very visible black population. Black servants, soldiers and entertainers could be seen in many parts of the city, but most of them hailed from the New World rather than directly from the Dark Continent. Autochthonous Africans were still hard to find, and when a few of them started to turn up on stage or at fairs exhibited as anthropological curiosities, they invariably created a sensation. A steatopygous San woman, suggestively billed as the Hottentot Venus, had made a small fortune for her managers between 1810 and 1815 before she died in Paris, whereupon her body had been handed over to the anatomists and had been dissected by the great Cuvier himself, who studied the peculiar aspects with great enthusiasm (1817).[1] In the 1840s, shortly after

Tom Thumb's conquest of Europe, a family of five diminutive 'Bosjesmans' (two men, two women and a child) were exhibited with enormous success all over the British Isles. They were followed in the early 1850s by a pair of young 'troglodytes' or 'Earthmen' (probably also San) who sang and danced their way across England, Scotland, Wales and Ireland, sometimes in the company of two 'Aztec Lilliputians' with whom they formed a popular short partnership. In 1853 a troupe of thirteen Zulus (eleven men, a woman and a child) were a smash hit for four months in London before going on tour in the major cities of France, Germany, and Prussia (see Lindfors 1999a).

All these shows excited the curiosity of Europeans, but the peoples exhibited could hardly be called typical Africans. Indeed, the reason they were chosen for public display was that they were abnormal in some spectacular way: the Hottentot Venus had a huge rump, the Bosjesmans and Earthmen were unusually small, the 'bloodthirsty' Zulu warriors were represented as culturally exotic. Yet it was 'savages' of this outlandish sort who were paraded as representative inhabitants of Africa. 'Freaks' and anomalies were palmed off as the norm.

The Logic of Races

Naturally, scientists flocked to these exhibitions and took careful measurements as well as eager mental notes. When a performer died, he or she was subjected to even closer scrutiny, the skeleton, skull and other durable remains being preserved for posterity. The nineteenth century saw the rise of comparative anatomy and ethnography as important interrelated sciences, and African subjects, alive or dead, furnished some of the data crucial for forming and testing theories about human variation. Debates raged about how to measure intelligence, how to account for cultural differences, how to classify the various peoples of the world. Many scientists of this period agreed with the famous anatomist Robert Knox, author of *The Races of Men*, that 'race or hereditary descent is everything' (1850). African 'specimens' were needed as objective proof in support of subjective notions of European racial superiority.

One of the most interesting European efforts to merge show business and ethnographic science took place at Dr Kahn's Celebrated Anatomical Museum near Piccadilly Circus in London in December of 1854. Joseph Kahn, allegedly a German doctor of medicine, had made a profitable business of exhibiting wax models of anatomical wonders at various centres of learning in Europe before moving to London to cater to Victorian curiosity about the human body. His museum contained

hundreds of natural and artificial preparations illustrating physiological phenomena such as the formation of the human embryo (seen as
through a microscope), the development of the foetus, the process of
deglutition, the anatomy of the skeleton, muscles, arteries, veins and
nerves, the development of the face and genital parts, the deformation of various bodily parts (including a special display on the 'dreadful
effects of tight lacing'), and the occurrence of monstrosities and other
extraordinary aberrations. For 'medical gentlemen' (i.e. anyone interested in exploring these mysteries further), there was also an obstetrical
room, where closer attention was given to sexual organs and childbirth,
and a pathological nook, where venereal disease was illustrated in all
its ulcerous varieties. Among the more memorable sights here were
preparations showing 'gangrene and mortification of the scrotum',
'elephantiasis of the female sexual parts [...] the result of onanism', and
the 'figure of a man who had his penis torn off by a horse, rendering
the constant wearing of a small silver tube necessary for the passage of
urine' (all from *Catalogue*, c.1855). Needless to say, this was sex education of a very engaging kind – lurid but illuminating, serious but slightly
kinky. Separate hours had to be established for ladies who wanted to see
these marvels. To top it all off, Dr Kahn made himself available in an
adjoining office to anyone who needed professional advice or treatment
for venereal disease. And as a sideline, he sold replicas of his most
popular wax models.

Dr Kahn's contribution to ethnological science took the form of a
'Gallery of all Nations', consisting of 'a series of figures representing
the different varieties of the human race and arranged with due regard
to geographical position and mental development [...]. Explanations
are given every hour, pointing out the peculiarities of each race, and
embellished with anecdotes of their manners and customs' (*Manchester
Courier*, 13 December 1851).[2]

The accompanying lectures were given by a 'Dr George Sexton,
F.R.G.S. and F.E.S.', who at other times had been employed by Dr
Kahn to speak authoritatively on topics such as food, air, tobacco, lactic
acid, eyesight, brain disease and the mutiny in India (see Altick 1978:
340–41).[3] Ethnological expertise must have come easy to so versatile an
expert. On 27 December 1854 an astonishing new anatomical attraction
was advertised in London's *Morning Herald*: 'Niam-Niams, or the Tailed
Family (Man, Woman and Child) from Central Africa, are Now, for the
first time in Europe, at Dr. Kahn's Museum' (27 December 1854). The
advertisement may have led some readers to expect that these curious
creatures could be seen in the flesh, but anyone entering the Museum

would have discovered that the Niam-Niams were only three more waxen figures in the Gallery of Nations. However, nobody could deny that these Africans were fundamentally different from all the other folks on display, for each of the three – mama, papa and baby Niam-Niam – sported what Dr Sexton sententiously described as 'a caudal appendage, called in common or vulgar language, a tail' (Sexton 1855: 6).

The belief in people with tails has had a rather long history, stretching back at least as far as Ptolemy, in the second century, who maintained that in his time they lived on certain islands. In the twelfth century, Marco Polo claimed that there were such people inhabiting the kingdom of Lambry (in the vicinity of Sumatra), and later travellers reported finding them in Egypt, Tripoli, Borneo, Formosa and the Philippine Islands.

Linnaeus had, in fact, placed some credence in the seventeenth-century account by a Swedish sailor telling of a race of cannibals 'with tails like those of cats' living on one of the Nicobar Islands in the Gulf of Bengal. In most of these stories the people endowed with caudal appendages were said to be black, but there was at least one example cited of a teacher of mathematics in eighteenth-century Scotland whose tail, 'about half a foot long, which he carefully concealed during his life [...] was discovered after his death' (1973 [1773–92]). An enthusiastic advocate of the theoretical possibility of 'an elongation of the rump-bone' was James Burnet, better known as Lord Monboddo, who wrote of tailed people in his six-volume study *Of the Origin and Progress of Language* (1973 [1773–92]),[4] but his views had been immediately dismissed as eccentric, irrational and sacrilegious; James Boswell had alluded to him as a 'grotesque philosopher' (Cloyd 1972: 105).

The debate about caudal appendages was revived in the middle of the nineteenth century by contemporary reports from French travellers who claimed to have seen tailed anthropophagi called Niam-Niams and to have heard corroborating accounts of them from many other African peoples as well as from slave dealers. These travellers were no ordinary tourists, but explorers sent out on official expeditions by the French government. Their reports were taken seriously by the Academy of Sciences in Paris, and other explorers who had collected anecdotal evidence of the existence of tailed people in the same general vicinity delivered supporting papers on the subject at meetings of the Oriental Society and Geographical Society in Paris. Within a few years, Niam-Niams had supposedly been sighted not only in their native land (said to be located somewhere in Central Africa between the Gulf of Benin and Abyssinia; a vast expanse of uncharted territory) but also in the slave quarters of Mecca and Constantinople.

By 1854 a book and a pamphlet on Niam-Niams had appeared (du Couret 1854; de Castelnau 1851), and the topic was extensively treated in French academic journals (see Penel 1982). The book, du Couret's *Voyage au Pays des Niam-Niams*, was reviewed in the London *Literary Gazette and Journal of Science and Art* on 28 October 1854. Just a week earlier a reputable French medical magazine had carried a circumstantial summary of new findings on the question of tailed men, prompting the British medical journal *The Lancet* to give some attention to this interesting tale in its November issue. While Dr Kahn may have been aware of the earlier controversy in France, he seems to have been inspired to take action only after the story had appeared in the British medical media. But then he moved very swiftly; within a month he had his three Niam-Niams moulded and mounted and had published a pamphlet entitled *Men with Tails* (1855).

This pamphlet, which was sold for sixpence at the exhibition, contained an introduction by Dr Kahn, an 'Essay on the Anatomical View of the Question' by Dr Sexton, reprints of the articles that had appeared in *The Lancet* and the *Literary Gazette*, and an 'engraving of a Group of these Extraordinary Beings'. In his introduction, Dr Kahn said that in addition to the testimony offered in the sources quoted, he himself had:

> received a few weeks since, a communication from a valued friend of mine who has spent many years in Africa, and who is now in Constantinople, wherein he informs me that he has on two or three occasions come in contact with the Niam-Niams, and had one with him which he intended to bring to this country, until a few days before he posted the letter to me, when, to his great regret, the tailed man died. The skeleton, however – which will probably be almost as interesting to the scientific as the living man – my friend still has with him. Having, therefore, received this intelligence, together with drawings of a group of these curious species of humanity, I have taken the earliest opportunity of adding models of them to my collection, trusting they may both interest and instruct those who derive pleasure from the study of the various branches of science relating to man.

Sexton then weighed in with his 'Anatomical View', which consisted of a preface applauding the continual progress of science, a long series of rhetorical questions concerning caudal appendages, and a corresponding string of pat answers bolstered by glib hypotheses about the proliferation of lower vertebral bones: 'Yet what, after all, is there remarkable in men with tails? What law of nature does it violate? What axiom in natural science is it in opposition to? What established principles of anatomy does it overthrow? We answer, none [...] A tail is simply an elongation of the vertebral column [...] What is the difference in these parts, between those animals with tails, and those destitute of that appendage? Simply this: that the coccygeal vertebrae are more numerous. And what is therefore to prevent the existence of an additional vertebra or two in some of the races of man? Nothing.'

The evidence Sexton supplied to support these assertions was entirely speculative, but included mathematical theorems and an impressive chart, taken from Agassiz and Gould's *Comparative Physiology* (1851), that gave vertebral bone counts for various mammals, birds, reptiles and fishes. The articles reprinted from *The Lancet* and the *Literary Gazette* were much more cautious about coming to a firm conclusion, but they reviewed the French explorers' accounts at some length, retailing all the pertinent anatomical details that had been published in Paris up to that time. *The Lancet* opened by asking a few rhetorical questions of its own: 'Are we truly promoted monkeys? What if Lord Monboddo, the much ridiculed, should have the laugh on his side?' But no attempt was made to answer such questions. Instead, *The Lancet* suggested that more hard evidence was needed to prove 'our affinity with the monkey tribe. [...] Whether the Niam-Niams will be a creation of Oriental fancy, like the Yahoos of Captain Gulliver, or a race actually existing, it is at any rate an object of interest to extend our ethnological inquiries in Central Africa. Should any enthusiastic traveller determine to solve the question, we counsel him to bring home the finest-tailed specimen that can be found.'

The *Literary Gazette* devoted more space to the matter, quoting copiously from passages in du Couret's narrative that emphasized the animalistic appearance and cannibalistic nature of the Niam-Niams. Here are some of the descriptive details singled out for translation: 'The Niam-Niams, or Ghilanes (their name signifies cannibals) form a race of men who have a great similitude to the monkey. Shorter than other negroes, they are rarely more than five feet high. They are generally ill-proportioned; their bodies are thin and appear weak; their arms are long and lank; their feet and hands larger and flatter than those of other races of man; their lower jaws are very strong and very long; their cheekbones are high; their forehead is narrow and falls backwards; their ears are long and deformed; their eyes small, brilliant, and remarkably restless; their nose large and flat, the mouth large, the lips thick, the teeth big and sharp, and remarkably white (they sharpen their teeth).'[5]

An example was given of a middle-aged Niam-Niam slave who had been captured as a young boy and carried off to Mecca, where he had been converted to the Islamic faith. Even though he was a devout Muslim and had lived so long abroad that he had forgotten his mother tongue, he still retained a 'frightful appetite' for human flesh, which his master sought to allay by tossing him large pieces of raw mutton from time to time. The slave himself was said to be self-conscious and genuinely worried about this strange dietary preference but claimed that it was an instinctual penchant that he could not control, no matter how hard he tried. In other words, once a Niam-Niam, always a Niam-Niam. Eating people just came naturally to anyone with a caudal appendage. It was a genetically acquired characteristic, custom-tailored to fit a backward African tribe at the very bottom of all humanity.

Dr Kahn's Gallery

Dr Kahn made the most he could out of such details. The figures he constructed to represent the Niam-Niams in his Gallery of all Nations were not only fitted with tails but also framed as cannibals. The description he wrote to accompany the engraving of these 'marvellous beings' was based entirely on du Couret and stressed the unsavoury symbolic significance of the male Niam-Niam's eye, ear, and nose: 'The man, in his rude and savage state – diminutive stature, black skin, large flat negro foot, long arms, repulsive figure, large jaws, enormous mouth, high cheek bones, narrow and receding forehead, long ears, thick lips, large white and sharp teeth, curly hair, vertebral column prolonged, so as to form a tail about three inches in length, and, in a word, a frame approximating toward the lower animals – is seen leaning upon one of his implements of warfare; his eye keenly piercing the distant view, and watching for prey (human, or otherwise); his ear intently listening to catch the first faint sound of approaching footsteps; his large broad flat nose, with the nostrils expanded, sniffing the air – even this sense appropriated to the uses of discovering prey, and detecting danger.' One could almost hear this Niam-Niam murmuring 'Yum-yum'!

The number of spectators Dr Kahn conned with this extraordinary exhibition is not known, but the British scientific community at large – with the possible exception of Dr Sexton – appears to have been sceptical of the whole enterprise from the outset. The *Literary Gazette* refused to take sides on the issue 'for if, on the one hand, it be hard to believe that M. du Couret, M. de Castelneau [sic] and other distinguished scientific men, are foolish victims of credulity, or dupes of impostors, on the other hand it is not a little singular that the precise whereabouts of the Niam-Niam country is not described, and more singular still, that none of the tailed race should have yet been sent to Europe, though, as we are told in the book before us, they are by no means rare at Mecca, in the towns on the coasts of the Red Sea, and in the Arab slave markets'.

John Conolly, President of the English Ethnological Society, was not at all impressed with the French explorers' accounts because so many of them were based on hearsay rather than on actual observation: 'These particular descriptions seem scarcely reconcilable with entire error, or defective observation, or downright falsehood; but are still very far from being satisfactory, or even credible. The evidence of tails remains, indeed, still as defective as that adduced long ago by Lord Monboddo. We never arrive at the actual person who has visited the tailed nations' (Conolly 1855: 37). In Conolly's view, Dr Kahn's exhibition, based on such flimsy evidence, was 'at least rather premature'. It was probably no more than a tall tale in wax.[6]

But most of the spectators drawn to Dr Kahn's Celebrated Anatomical Museum may not have been so incredulous. Indeed, they may have been predisposed to believe in any fabulous foreign tale put before them, especially if it came out of Africa. In the public mind the humanity of Africans was still in question, and Dr Kahn, by capitalizing on the curiosity aroused by reports of tailed cannibals in Central Africa, was only pursuing this question to its logical end. Niam-Niams may have been merely a half-baked figment of the European racial imagination, but in 1854–55 the British public ate them up.

Notes

1 See Boetsch and Blanchard in this volume.
2 The Catalogue of the museum (c. 1855) stated: 'Here will be found in one view the graceful Circassian, the angular Copt, the erect European, and the ungainly and ill-poised Ethiopian; the agile Arab contrasted with the languid and effeminate Hindoo; the gigantic Patagonian in juxtaposition with the squat and stolid Laplander; and the keen and warlike native of North America side by side with the immovable and pacific Chinese.'
3 Altick (1978) calls Kahn 'the most famous anatomical showman of his era'.
4 He deals with tailed people in Volume 1, Book 2, Chapter 3 (1973: 257–69).
5 The writer continues: 'Their hair is curly but not very woolly, short and not thick. What, however, peculiarly distinguishes this people, is the external prolongation of the vertebral column, which in every individual, male or female, forms a tail of from two to three inches long [...] They live in numerous bands, in a completely savage state, without any clothing, and feed on what they get by the chase or fishing, on roots, and on plants and fruits, which, without the least labour a bountiful Paradise puts within their reach, and causes to grow spontaneously. They are armed with small lances, bows and arrows, and they poison the latter skilfully; with clubs of very hard wood; with shields made from the

skins of the elephant, rhinoceros, hippopotamus, and crocodile; they often seek quarrels with neighbouring negro tribes with the sole object of carrying off their women, to whom they are very partial, their children, and other victims, whom they devour without pity. They are idolatrous. Formerly the Arabs bought great numbers of them from the slave-dealers (Djelabs), but at present they will not take any of them, because the children belonging to this race who were sold to them became, on growing up, dominated by the ferocious instincts natural to their species, and devoured the children of their masters.'

6 Such tales continue. Circus manager Al Barnes, in his autobiography (1938) tells the following story with a straight face: 'I had heard of a tribe of long-tailed men in a certain part of Africa. It seemed to me that a specimen would make a good side-show feature, and I sent a man to Africa to capture one of the men. After many trials and struggles he succeeded, and brought one to the United States. The captive was placed in quarantine at Alcatraz Island, in the Bay of San Francisco, where I went to inspect him. The long-tailed specimen proved to be a hideous-looking negro, with a tail something more than a foot long. He was too shocking in appearance, I considered, to exhibit in a side-show, and I gave orders that he should be sent back to his home in Africa. No doubt he would have proved a wonderful attraction, but his appearance was so repulsive that I didn't want to have him around, he would have been distasteful to some of the spectators, and I have made it a policy never to display anything in the show that would offend good taste.'

20

Photography and the Making
of the Other

ELIZABETH EDWARDS

The role of photography in making 'The Other', as well as its entangle-
ments with colonial culture, with anthropology, and with the definition of
the self, have been extensively discussed (see, for example, Pinney 1992;
Lalvani 1996). Much analysis has focused on the images themselves:
their iconography, semiotics and associational aesthetics. However, this
is only part of their stereotypical force. I shall suggest, rather, that it is the
whole visual economy in which images operated and the specific sites of
consumption which are fundamental in creating the Other, for photographs are objects made precisely to be reproduced and disseminated
across space and time. Further, images accrue value through the social
processes of accumulation, possession, and exchange. It was through
these processes that, for instance, images were absorbed into anthropology and thus became 'science'. Equally, the way in which science was
visualized through photography informed the popular production of
photographs of non-European peoples and legitimized their consumption within an encompassing visual economy (Poole 1997: 9–13).

This symbiotic relationship emerged from a common conceptual groundwork of systems of value and exchange. Within it, images
flowed between the sites of anthropological and colonial observation,
the studies, drawing-rooms and albums of upper- and middle-class
Europe and North America, the scholar's study, laboratory and museum
in mutually sustaining and overlapping relationships. The making
and movement of photographs had a massing effect, cohering around
certain kinds of imagery which assumed the force of truth.

The nineteenth- and early twentieth-century Other was defined
through two powerful and interrelated ideological contexts. The first
was constituted by theories of race and the moral values projected on
to racial difference, articulated through the emerging science of anthropology. The second was the expansion and maintenance of European
colonial power. In this, a belief in the biologically determined nature of

239

culture which informed a dominant evolutionary, or at least progressivist, model was fundamental. Non-European races were perceived as inferior and doomed to extinction. The Other was not merely racially other but, by implication, culturally and morally other. Through its scientific agendas, combined with its aspiration to realism, photography promoted a type of image which was saturated by general assumptions about racial and cultural hierarchies, the fear of contamination, political expediency, and which, paradoxically, marked the disappearance of the 'primitive' through which the self could be defined, thereby gaining a political dimension in its support of colonial practices.

While these processes were not unique to photographs, as other essays in this volume make clear, the nature of photography gave it a particularly persuasive power. Through mechanical means photography traces on to a chemical medium the physical presence of what was before the camera. While giving the appearance of an unmediated reality, those realities are culturally constituted; we photograph what we already 'know'. The imagined Other could thus be realized through the act of photographing. In addition, photographs make fragments held within the frame, focusing attention. They disrupt the relationship between the specific and the general as fragments come to stand for wholes, as an expression of an apparent essence, what it is 'to be something'. Thus, photographs acted as symbolic and reifying constructions, translating and transforming observed realities through an interpreting cultural grid. Indeed, a number of writers have characterized this as a fetishistic desire and reification of the qualities of difference and danger (be it moral, physical or sexual), focussed on the body of the Other, as photographs performed as both allegory and reality.

Significant in the making of the Other is the way photographs fracture time and space. Evolutionary thought was premised on ideas of time, 'primitive' peoples standing for times past, and 'civilization' for achievements over the passage of time. Yet photographs in many ways exist outside time, the 'there-then' becoming the 'here-now', present in the same space and time as the viewer yet always of the past (Fabian 1983). Likewise, one of the defining features of the exotic Other is that it is never at home, always elsewhere, a distant object (Mason 1998: 1–15). The temporal and spatial ambiguities of the photograph both confirm and deny the space of the Other. Photographs permitted a controlled domestication that allowed consumption and possession while maintaining the crucial distance between self and Other.

At the same time, the realities for which photographs stand shift according to the contexts in which they are read. While the content appears fixed, meanings are fluid, filtered through dynamic ideas which are complex and historically specific. Indeed, Tagg (1988: 63) has argued that photography has no identity of its own, but draws its meanings, chameleon-like, from the ideologies that employ it. The great interpretative dilemma of photographs is ultimately that they are never as complete a statement as they might appear.

Visual Economy

It was through the visual economy, however, that meanings were made as images moved through different photographic and interpretative spaces. Linking to earlier image forms, there was a technical and social production of photographs on a massive scale from the 1850s onwards, which extended the visual economy (Poole 1997: 9–13). From the 1860s, there was an enormous volume of images of the exotic Other circulating throughout the world, in which the scientific and popular existed in a symbiotic relationship. This increased markedly in the 1880s with the introduction of high-quality half-tone printing processes and of picture postcards, which allowed photographs a vast circulation. While, through overtly objectifying practices, anthropometry attempted to define racial and thus cultural difference through measured bodies in the laboratory, there was a systemic naturalizing of scientific ideas of race and culture at a popular level. Publications such as the fortnightly British magazine *The Living Races of Mankind* (1902–03), for example, reproduced ideas of the exotic and classified them through the realist rhetoric of the photographs which adorned nearly every page. The everyday assumptions about race, legitimated by scientific debate, informed the production and consumption of repetitive tropes of 'cultural' images which had been naturalized through photography's reality effect.

Before further considering the making of the Other within the visual economy, it is worth outlining the global scale on which images circulated. While images existed in local concentrations within the colonial world (for example, a photograph of Dufty Brothers' studio in Fiji shows Fijian portraits displayed for passers-by), colonial images could also be bought at the metropolitan centres. For example, by the 1870s, the Bonfils studio in Beirut carried a stock of over 10,000 photographs of Middle Eastern landscapes and local types, which could also be purchased through photographic dealers in Paris. Such photographs were also shown at the major expositions. For instance, those of German photographer A. Frisch, one of the first to photograph the indigenous peoples of the Amazon, were shown in Paris in 1867, while prints could be purchased through Leuzinger & Co. in Rio de Janeiro. C. Woolley's celebrated portraits of the so-called 'last-surviving' Tasmanian aboriginals were made specifically for the 1866 International Colonial Exhibition in Melbourne, Australia, yet they circulated widely for many years in many different but overlapping spaces, such as anthropological archives, museum collections and travellers' albums. In England, Bourne and Shepherd's photographs of India could be bought through London photographic suppliers Marion & Co., while Mansell's of London advertised scenes of the South Seas, 'native' types from 'The East' and Morocco, and claimed to be able to supply photographs from 'any photographic house in the world.'

Metropolitan photographic firms also employed photographers to take photographs for them throughout the world for sale in the cities of Europe and North America. Such images were displayed in shop windows and, therefore, seen by those who could not necessarily afford to buy them. Photographs of indigenous people were a relatively small proportion of the overall metropolitan market, which was dominated by views and celebrities, although at one level the Other existed as an extension of the natural landscape. For example, the New Zealand photographer Josiah Martin included portraits of Maori chiefs and scenes from Maori life in a catalogue entitled 'New Zealand Scenery'. The circulation of such photographs allowed them to permeate contemporary visual consciousness. Their exoticizing rhetorics played out in the live shows of 'savagery' in music halls, shows, and exhibitions across Europe and North America, and were related to the consciousness of empire, for the political Other was never far beneath the surface of the racial and cultural Other.

It is not, however, merely image content that constitutes the visual economy. The physical form of photographs was at least as powerful as the iconography itself. What things are made of, and how they are materially presented, relates directly to their social, economic and political discourses. Not only did different formats demand differences in composition, the way in which photographs were arranged, circulated, printed or viewed (as albums, lantern slides, carte de visite prints or mounted prints) was integral to people's experience of them, structuring visual knowledge (see Edwards and Hart 2004). Likewise, the actual act of viewing was determined by material form, for example, holding an album or looking at lantern slides in a darkened room. The material literally 'performs' images. For instance, the technical choices represented in printing a photograph on an albumen paper or a platinum paper, as Samoa-based photographer Thomas Andrew did for his Samoan 'types', results in a substantial difference in affective tone, and consequently in the reading of his photographs. Such choices of format and texture were conscious decisions to create certain effects. The visual economy and the meanings it generated were dependent on material forms, and it was material forms that made images of the Other available to an increasingly wide audience, thus disseminating colonial values.

However, despite my argument so far, meanings attributed to photographs of the Other should not be over-determined or over-homogenized. Indeed, one of the problems with much analysis of colonial imagery is the assumption that all members of a society 'thought the same' and responded to images in the same way. Foucauldian theories of discipline and surveillance have been extremely influential in the consideration of the photographic construction of the Other in the colonial context. However, applications of Foucault's theories, such as those of Tagg (1988) and Sekula (1986) have tended to suggest a unified absorption of images into a homogenized colonial desire for the Other, obscuring the sometimes contradictory meanings of photographs. There were, as I have suggested, different contexts of production and consumption, and a constant flow of images between categories, with differentiated truth values and ideas of evidence. One must distinguish, for example, between images which created a scientifically determined racial Other and those which simultaneously fed on and constructed a loosely defined, more generalized and pervasive, exotic alterity. The Other of the scientific laboratory is related to, but not necessarily the same as, the Other of the popular imagination in the exposition. If we are to understand how photographs constructed Others, it is important to allow space for both differences and similarities in the role of their images. The model of the visual economy is useful because it allows for differential values, complex relationships, and ambiguity. If response to photographs cannot necessarily be reduced to a direct causal link between ideology and a specific image, visual economy allows us to recognize the conceptual basis which made such images thinkable in the first place.

Likewise, the relationship between colonialism and photography, while grounded in systemically unequal power relations, was not a monolithic given, but rather something complex, nuanced, contradictory, anxious, and processual. Colonialism 'was made up of a mass of small processes with global effects' (Gosden and Knowles 2001: xix). Photographs are like this too. For it is not enough to ask what specific images 'mean', to decode specific semiotics, as one might an advertising image, but rather to show how images accrue value and meaning within specific historical performances. Layers and facets of imaging reveal the making not of the Other, but of many shifting Others within the complexity of the colonial imagination.

Iconographic Confusions

If the photographs in the visual economy are active in overlapping spaces, the iconography and the imagery also overlap. As has been well documented, photographic imagery of the Other drew its visual dialects from on one hand, the exotic, and on the other, the scientific. In both cases, they drew on iconographical and stylistic devices which go back centuries in Western culture (Edwards 1992). The iconographic forms of the grid and frontal and profile poses of anthropometric photography, such as those advocated by Broca, Topinard and Huxley, were directly derived from the conventions of anatomical drawing and description dating back to at least the seventeenth century. Such representations saturated the visual and textual language of systematic science, creating objectified 'type' specimens in a taxonomic array of 'Otherness'. The language of science is most clearly articulated in the popular through the idea of the 'type' which de-individualizes and generalizes the subject, reifying the Other as object. Its stylistic influences framed both the legitimation and consumption of other images. For example, the frontal pose, the pairing of full face and profile, and the use of the word 'type' in captions, both framed the objectifying reading of the images and legitimated the consumption of photographs produced far from the scientific laboratory (Edwards 2001: 141–44).

Other forms of imagery also go back to pre-photographic representations, reproducing an established way of seeing and knowing, reinforced by the realist nature of the photograph. The origins of such forms are to be found in literary and philosophical devices rather than observed reality. However, considered in conjunction with the realist nature of the photograph and the reifying tendencies of both scientific thought and popular consumption, discussed above, these conventions take on a powerful stereotypical force. For example, the nobility of the classical warrior can be traced through the paintings of artists such as David, through the illustrations of the great voyages of the late-eighteenth century, such as Parkinson's engravings from Cook's voyages, to the photographs of Im Thurn's Macusi wrestlers from Guyana, where it is translated into the 'noble savage'. The odalisk of orientalist imagination is photographically reproduced as a trope of Otherness on women from

Tahiti to Togo. In all cases, the iconography points to the intellectual space in which the photographs were intended to operate, contributing to their rhetorical and reifying force.

Yet such photographs became scientific ('ethnological' or 'anthropological') as they were collected and institutionalized by learned societies and universities. The assessment of their evidential value was based on the perception and categorization of their subject matter, rather than being premised on any specific scientific methodology and its photographic manifestations. The photographic frame was often saturated with cultural markers of the stereotype, and anchored through a distancing or generalizing text: 'African warrior' with spear; 'Aboriginal hunter' with a boomerang; the 'Village Maiden' carrying a water pot; or the 'Tahitian Belle' with flowers in her hair. This privileging of content over form constituted an ethnographic massing of representations of peoples, regardless of photographic discourse from which they emerged. Within the visual economy, commercially produced images from photographic studios all around the world, which had drawn on the culture of science, became reabsorbed as being of 'anthropological interest' in a mutually sustaining relationship. Indeed, much scientific effort in the nineteenth century was effectively an effort to counteract this – in other words, the representational and intellectual flaws were well-recognized, even if the political underpinnings were not.

Yet such images are not unambiguous. An interesting intersection of race, culture, photographic inscription and photographic style is found in the series of photographs taken by Prince Roland Bonaparte of the Omaha people at the Paris Jardin d'Acclimatation in 1883, where the subjects were 'performing' their culture for popular entertainment. Bonaparte trained with the founding physical anthropologist Paul Broca in the 1870s and his work draws heavily on the visualizing rhetorics of this tradition (Dias 1997). The images all contain strong scientific references, being arranged in pairs of full face and profile. Yet at the same time, their culture is displayed through careful rendering of the subjects' 'full dress' of buckskins, beads, feathers and abalone shell. Yet the qualities of 'vernacular' photography (the delicate garden chair, the wriggling child) insinuate themselves into the carefully controlled photographs, destabilizing the scientific and allowing the individuality of the sitters to emerge.

Another example of the ambiguity, which operates differently from that of Bonaparte, is a series of portraits of Native American chiefs taken in Washington by Charles Milton Bell for the Bureau of American Ethnology in the early 1880s. Individually, the photographs appear as fine portraits within the conventions of Western portrait photography – a concentrated focus and revelation of individual identity. However, viewed as a group, the individuality of each sitter becomes suppressed. Photographic style asserts itself through the hard frontal pose, the plain background, the shallow picture plane, and even light. It heightens the objectifying properties of the image as the individual is transformed into type, to function as a specimen for the laboratory, or as stereotype for mass consumption. What is important is the levelling effect, the repetitive photographic pose and iconographical device, which produced an equivalence of style, positioning the content within the specific value systems which create the Other. Here, contrary to the Bonaparte photographs, science, with its ethnographic massing, destabilizes the photographic aesthetic. Through visual dialects of scientific reference, working with the mutability of the image, the subject shifts to object.

The 'making' of my title therefore works on several axes: iconography; reproduction; circulation; consumption; and archiving. All are sites for making the Other within the visual economy. However, within this it is necessary to distinguish different levels of intention and different, but overlapping, theatres of consumption. For photographs have many meanings; those found in scientific archives are equally found in albums of tourists, travellers and colonial officers. I have tried to suggest the fluid and sometimes ambiguous ways in which photography makes the Other, the relationship between the general and the specific, the scientific and the popular, and ultimately the different truth values with which photographs perform within a unifying visual economy.

PART III

National Identities: The Human Zoo in Context

21

Colonial Expositions and Ethnic Hierarchies in Modern Japan

ARNAUD NANTA

During their Golden Age between 1851 and the Second World War, industrial and universal expositions gave nation-states a chance to compete with each other. Great powers demonstrated their national strength at these events, through exhibiting first their industrial capabilities, and later their colonies and influence in the non-European world. In the nineteenth century, nation-states and imperialism – all the powerful states were colonial empires – were phenomena that concerned Western Europe, Russia, the United States and Japan. Japan itself barely avoided falling under Western colonial domination, but succeeded in joining the group of world powers after crushing China in 1895, a victory consolidated by the 1902 Anglo-Japanese Alliance treaty and the defeat of Russia in 1905.

This raises the question of patterns of imperialist activity, especially as regards anthropology and expositions. Their role in Western Europe and the United States is well known, but little attention has been paid to the case of Japan. What was the nature of Japanese participation in international expositions, and to what extent did Japan exhibit indigenous people from its colonies? Here we examine the case of the colonial pavilions erected during the Japanese industrial expositions after 1895, especially in Osaka in 1903, the anthropologists who organized this exhibition, and the kind of resistance such exhibitions encountered. Finally, at the end of the chapter, we attempt to assess more general issues relating to this aspect of colonial history.

Modern Expositions in Meiji Japan

After the Meiji Restoration (1868), regional expositions, organized for educational or commercial purposes during the second half of the Edo period (1603–1868) and especially during the first part of the nineteenth century,[1] were merged with the model of industrial exhibitions adopted by the great powers after the Great Exhibition of 1851 in London (Aimone and Olmo 1993). The First National Industrial Exposition of Meiji Japan took place in Tokyo in 1877, in Ueno Park, where the Ueno Museum, which opened in the same year (although first established in 1871), was also located. The exposition lasted 120 days and received about 16,000 exhibitors and 450,000 visitors. From that point on, industrial expositions [*hakurankai*] would be held regularly, gradually producing a new view of Japan and the world, in keeping with a configuration typical of modern nation-states. The 1877 industrial exposition was organized despite the Second Japanese Civil War being under way at the time,[2] a fact that shows the importance it had for the state. The purpose of the exposition was mainly economic, intended to further the industrial development of the country through the exchange of technical know-how among exhibitors and through the general propagation of knowledge. This exposition and the two that followed (1881 and 1890, again in Tokyo) were strictly national events, closed to foreign participation; they aimed to support a robust, autonomous development of the Japanese economy at a time when the country was subjected to unequal treaties by the Western powers.[3]

This characteristic feature of expositions underwent an important modification after the fourth session in 1895,[4] held in spite of the First Sino-Japanese War (1894–95). This war confirmed the place of Japan among the powers and made Taiwan its colony – until then, the island had belonged to the frontiers of the Qing Empire and was inhabited by aboriginal tribes and some Chinese from southern China. The 1895 exposition in Okazaki in Kyoto included a pavilion of colonial specimens planned for foreign exhibitors, and, for the first time, a Taiwan Pavilion, i.e. a colonial pavilion introducing arts and objects assumed to be 'traditional' to the island's aboriginal population. It was through this general movement that Japanese industrial expositions, originally aimed at industrial and economic *development*, turned into sites of power devoted to the *demonstration* of national strength on the economic, industrial and colonial stage, as Japanese pretensions on the international scene increased. In other words, by becoming exhibitions of the colonial empire, these expositions could satisfy the conditions required to become 'universal expositions'.[5] This type of exhibition of living human beings resulted in their 'essentialization' in terms of an unchangeable, inferior Otherness, a genuine counterpoint to modern civilization (Matsuda 1996: 61).

The 1903 Osaka Exposition and the Anthropological Pavilion

This trend of the colonial empire to exhibit itself within industrial gatherings was reinforced during the Fifth National Industrial Exposition organized in Osaka from 1 March to 31 July 1903, at which visitors could see many indigenous or 'exotic' people for the first time in Japan. All these people were shown in an Anthropological Pavilion (*Gakujutsu jinrui kan*), which was added to the Taiwan Pavilion and the Pavilion of Specimens (where the Dutch colonial exhibition attracted considerable attention). The Osaka exposition, which lasted for 153 days and drew about 4,350,000 visitors, is a typical example because it reveals the underlying tendencies of all great imperial powers at the beginning of the century. It clearly shows that, beyond the concrete socio-historical differences between Western European countries and Japan, all the great modern powers were governed by the same type of logic and world view, which resulted in the adoption of similar sets of practices. Or was it perhaps designed, like the 'forced' Westernization of Japan, to show the West that the Japanese were not barbarians?

The coordinators of the Anthropological Pavilion were anthropologists from the Imperial University of Tokyo,[6] most notably Tsuboi Shôgorô (1863–1913),[7] a charter member and president of the Tokyo Anthropological Society. This academic society, the first of its kind in Japan, was founded at the university in 1884.[8] It had, since 1886, been the scene of a violent controversy between two groups, one led by Tsuboi and the other by the physical anthropologist Koganei Yoshikiyo (1858–1944). They discussed the racial nature of the inhabitants of the archipelago's prehistoric era. Koganei concluded that the Ainu, a northern indigenous people systematically subjected by Japan after the incorporation of Ezo Island [Hokkaido] in 1869, were the descendants of the 'anthropophagous barbarians of the Stone Age', judging they were an 'inferior race' and would die out in the near future (Nanta 2003; Nanta 2006). He also assumed the Ainu people could never be assimilated into the nation, in opposition to the pro-assimilation stance of Tsuboi, who defended the value of an open, racially mixed Japan based on a historical vision of the nation. This position would lead him, however, to support imperialism during the Russo–Japanese War (1904–05), combining a pro-assimilationist attitude with a condescending view of the Otherness he sought to protect. In any event, beyond vast differences between researchers, Japanese anthropology played a major role in shaping a reifying view of the populations of the colonial empire and national minorities, despite its criticism of the hierarchical categories of European anthropology.

The 1903 exposition served as an occasion to exhibit Otherness from an anthropological perspective. There were 'many different races gathered close to the city, in reconstructions showing their concrete practices, their daily tools and their customs', noted the newspaper *Ôsaka shinbun* at the time (Matsuda 1996: 47). The following people were exhibited: seven Ainu from Hokkaido, one 'raw barbarian', two 'cooked barbarians',[9] two 'indigenous' people from Taiwan, two Okinawans,[10] two Koreans, two Malaysians, three Chinese, seven Indians (from India), one Javanese, one Ottoman Turk, and one 'insular' from Zanzibar – in all, thirty-one people.[11] Photographs of all these 'races' were displayed along with scientific notes on the wall of the entrance to the pavilion. After receiving this initial information, visitors could observe real-life examples of each of them inside a fixed space that included a house 'reconstructed as their everyday habitation'. The whole pavilion was designed with education in mind, which satisfied the curiosity of visitors, for whom it was a unique occasion to see 'specimens' of all these populations – though in a version in keeping with the way the anthropologists imagined them.

To show their characteristic features, all these special actors had to perform fixed roles assigned by the scientists. For example, the aboriginals of the Taiwanese mountains, who were called 'raw barbarians' and had been subjected to horrible 'cleansing operations' by colonial troops (Ôe 1993), had to stand in the midst of a replica of the forest and mime a religious rite using human heads. One can imagine the astonishment of the public, but we must also remember that, at that time, the island of Taiwan was no more than a peripheral space, comparable, perhaps, to Black Africa. However, the performance reduced the picture of Taiwanese daily life to that image, the propagation of which was precisely the point of the exposition.

The distance and the effect of Otherness were reinforced between exhibitors and visitors on the one hand, and the exhibited people on the other – just as in Paris in 1889. (Tsuboi, who was in charge of the exposition and a professor of the Faculty of Sciences at the Imperial University of Tokyo, had visited the 1889 Exposition Universelle in Paris, where he was completing his academic training in Europe.) He assumed colonial pavilions to be 'of great value from the point of view of anthropological research', especially the reconstructions of 'villages where one could observe the life of barbarians and undeveloped races'.[12] Similarly, he assumed (Tsuboi 1903: 164) that the Osaka exposition 'enabled anthropologists to learn many things about physical and morphological differences' among the exhibited races. The exposition itself was legitimated by the intellectual framework offered by scientific anthropology, with racial hierarchies produced by researchers, or generated by the essentializing identification of culture and race. Anthropological knowledge itself was at the heart of the exposition, lending legitimacy to discourse about 'inferior people', while using the event to assert its usefulness as a form of colonial knowledge when modern imperialism had reached its peak (Matsuda 1996: 52). Finally, the exposition was supplemented by ethnological objects from the Laboratory of Anthropology, which were considered the 'daily tools' of the Ainu and of the 'raw barbarians' of Taiwan. They were exhibited along with a map, drawn by Tsuboi, showing the distribution of 'races' throughout the world,[13] with fifty pairs of figurines representing men and women of 'races' selected from the map (Matsumura 1903b). While most of the figurines were of non-European peoples, one can note among them representations of English, American and Japanese people (Tsuboi 1903: 165) – who would never have agreed to be exhibited live.

The exposition also provided the opportunity to conduct an anthropological study. Matsumura Akira (1875–1936),[14] who was then preparing his PhD at the Imperial University of Tokyo, wrote a report for the *Journal of the Anthropological Society of Tokyo*, in which he presented his observations (Matsumura 1903a). Prefiguring the attitude of Henri Vallois, who was to criticize the authenticity of the indigenous people during the Exposition coloniale in Paris in 1931 (De L'Estoile 2001), Matsumura expressed doubts about the quality of the reconstructions. He was convinced, nevertheless, that the exhibited people were, in fact, representative of their races. Through an 'essentialization' of the idea of race, typical of the early twentieth century, the anthropologist considered, above all, that a person was a representative of his race and only a representative of his race (Affergan 1991). For example, Matsumura described questioning a person from Zanzibar who defined himself as 'Arab':

> This person from the African island of Zanzibar appeared to me to be a rare type. When I asked him where he came from, he answered he was an Arab. However, his frizzy hair, his chocolate-coloured skin, his flat nose, his big lips and his flat, wide face, all these features were unquestionable evidence that he was of a type similar to the Negro. When I told him the names of a few tribes living near Zanzibar, he recognised the Swahili. Therefore, I assumed he must be a mixed-type of Arab and Swahili. Moreover, due to his morphology close to that of Negroes (in the broad sense), one can assume his ancestors must have been Arabs a few generations earlier. (Matsumura 1903a: 290)

Furthermore, convinced that the population of Zanzibar was composed of a mixed 'Negro-Arab race', the scientist confirmed his impression by 'measuring the widest and longest dimensions of the skull, then establishing a cephalic index of 76.5'. He finally concluded (1903a: 291) that the man was 'in fact not a pure-race Negro but, rather, a pseudo-Negro'. Here we can observe in action the discourse of modern anthropology, complacent in its self-congratulatory vision, while asserting that 'it is possible to know with precision' the origin of people through the shape of their skulls. As the historian Inoue explained: 'no one criticised the fate of these exhibited people. There is certainly no system that shows more extreme contempt for the humanity of nations than imperialism' (1968: 296).

Criticism of the 1903 Exposition

The exposition had unexpected effects, however, and came under external criticism. Alongside its purely scientific aims, it also possessed an aspect of entertainment that could, at any moment, divert attention from its primary objective. In addition to attempting to grasp Otherness through the 'specimens' arranged in well-defined, fixed spaces, within the scientific framework provided by anthropology, the Pavilion had also a 'stage' to enable each race to give performances of dancing and singing. This dimension of spectacle presented Otherness not as an object of knowledge, but rather as an entity belonging to funfairs, which had been greatly enjoyed by the Japanese public as far back as the Edo period (Ukigaya 2005).

No doubt the exhibitors did not foresee the risks of this dimension, not least that it had the further effect of enabling some of the exhibited people to talk with spectators. For example, from the stage, the headman of the Ainu village of Tokachi made 'a speech about the religion and education [of the Ainu people] in the language of the Metropolis', thereby arousing considerable interest among visitors. This problem raises two points. First, if the Ainu headman and other Ainu agreed to participate in the Osaka Industrial Exposition, it was in exchange for a subsidy promised by the Hokkaido authorities to invest in the creation of schools for 'former indigenous people of Hokkaido'.[15] Secondly, one can observe that public opinion in the 'Metropolis' judged the mental faculties of these indigenous people according to their ability to speak a 'civilized' language, in this case Japanese. During the 1903 Exposition, the case of the Ainu, rather than the Chinese or Koreans, is exemplary because they were the only group declared to be (former) 'indigenous people' [*dojin*] and also because they were the preferred objects of Japanese anthropological study at the end of the nineteenth century, before it turned its attention to Taiwan after 1895.

Furthermore, the exposition was far from conflict-free. Matsumura reported in April: 'aside from this list [of exhibited people], there were also two Korean women, but for some reason they left the exposition today' (Matsumura 1903a: 290). The fact is that these people, especially when they had a state capable of representing them, by no means accepted being exhibited as curiosities. An incident broke out a month before the exposition, when the Ambassador of the Qing in Tokyo learned that Chinese were to be exhibited and aired his grievance at the Japan Foreign Affairs Ministry; the Chinese were withdrawn from the exposition. The problem arose again after the exposition began, when Korean visitors discovered to their astonishment some of their countrymen on exhibit. They complained to the Osaka Police Department at the time; three weeks later, the Koreans were withdrawn.

Then, the inhabitants of Okinawa – annexed to Japan in 1879 – began levelling harsh criticism in the newspaper *Ryûkyû shinpô* in April, which was repeated on 7 May in the Japanese newspaper *Ôsaka Mainichi shinbun*. The exhibition of Okinawans was stopped the same day, putting an end to the criticism. Although it is difficult to assess Japanese public opinion at the time, there was clearly hostility to the exhibition of indigenous people in Japan from the very beginning of the practice. Nevertheless, can we conclude this was a 'victory for anti-colonialism'? The situation was not as straightforward, for those exhibited shared many of the racial prejudices of the exhibitors and it is impossible to analyse this affair in First-World/ Third-World terms. Moreover, those who succeeded in having their voice heard belonged to states capable of speaking on their behalf (China, Korea) or to politically organized groups (Okinawa), while all the others were exhibited until the end of the exposition without any such recourse.

In reality, the exhibited people were not all colonized people, but belonged rather to the populations that the modern nation-state looked upon with contempt. And the prejudice of race and civilization, far from being an exclusive monopoly of Europe or Japan, was in fact widely shared (Dikötter 1992; Liauzu 1992). Indeed the content of the complaints about the 1903 Exposition shows that the racism of those exhibited was even more virulent than that of the organizers, who often hid behind the objectifying scientific discourse of anthropology.

Chinese students – of whom there were many in Japan after the victory against China in 1895, with the country offering a model of development which fascinated the region – seized upon the exposition in two of their magazines.[16] They expressed hostile criticism of the exhibitors' desire 'deliberately to show old Chinese customs in order to [make the Chinese] look like barbarians'. However, neither the epistemological framework nor the explicit hierarchy underpinning the exposition were criticized. What posed a problem for them was the fact of being exhibited. Not only did they fail to question the system or its logic but they even legitimated the exhibition of the other people. Thus, the Chinese critics explained: 'India and Ryukyu [Okinawa] are two countries that have already disappeared, to become mere slaves of England and Japan; today, Korea is a protectorate of Russia and Japan and, incidentally, formerly subject to our Country [China]. The people from Java and Ezo [the Ainu of Hokkaido] and the raw barbarians from Taiwan, are among the lowest races of the world, barely different from pigs or deer. It is true we are in a inferior position today, but do we really have to be exhibited with these six races?' Lastly, the Chinese countrymen assumed that: 'from the standpoint of race or degree of civilisation, we are not different from the Japanese or the Aryans' (Sakamoto 1995: 78).

Similar contempt shows through in the complaints of the Koreans and the inhabitants of Okinawa. The editorial of the *Ryûkyû shinpô* asserted once again that the population of Okinawa was certainly 'of the Japanese race', while expressing their anger at being exhibited alongside 'savages' like the 'raw barbarians from Taiwan and Ainu from Hokkaido', or Koreans (Kaiho 1992: 158–59). Iha Fuyû (1876–1947), an Okinawan intellectual who supported the incorporation of the former kingdom of Ryukyu into Japan, would explain in 1907, using the European hierarchical and evolutionist categories, that the Okinawan archipelago had always been a 'nation', while the Ainu could not develop beyond the stage of a pre-political 'people', or be assimilated into the Japanese nation (Kaiho 1992: 160). In reality, the aboriginals of Taiwan and the Ainu from Hokkaido were the 'real indigenous people' and victims of the exposition, systematically isolated and veritable foils for modernity, an image used by everyone to reaffirm the superior degree of their 'race' or 'civilization'. Thus, it should be pointed out that, contrary to the case of Okinawans, the exhibition of the Ainu did not create an incident among the populations of Hokkaido, who, despite the 1899 'law of protection of former natives of Hokkaido', were forgotten in the modernization movement. The fact is, they were not in a position to refuse an opportunity to improve their living conditions or to complain.

In every case, therefore, the focus of criticism was not on the explicit hierarchy asserted by the exposition, but rather the rank assigned to each group by the exhibition. The fact that Chinese, Koreans and Okinawans visited the exposition is certainly the best proof that they fully agreed with its principle and with the imperialist *Weltanschauung* it presupposed – as long as they were not exhibited themselves.

Attitudes Towards Otherness and Modern Identity

Like the other great colonial powers, Japan was to stage multiple, supposedly edifying exhibitions of indigenous people. The 1893 World's Columbian Exposition confirmed that Japan was henceforth considered on a par with the other great powers;[17] the Japanese Pavilion during the 1904 Louisiana Purchase Exposition in St Louis contained an anthropological section showing an Ainu village, thus exhibiting the 'internal Otherness' of Japan once again. However, this movement worked both ways: at the very same time, news from the Russo–Japanese war also intensified Western racism against 'Asiatic' Japan. The 1910 Japanese-British Exhibition in London again presented reconstructions focused on the Ainu and the aboriginals of Taiwan.

It was not until after 1914, however, that colonial pavilions systematically appeared in Japanese expositions up to the Second World War (Yoshimi 1992: 213–14; Yoshimi 2005). During the 1914 Tokyo-Taisho Exposition, in addition to the Taiwan Pavilion there was a Karafuto Pavilion,[18] a Manchurian Pavilion, a 'Development' Pavilion and a Korean Pavilion, that is, exhibits from all the regions of the colonial empire – Korea had been annexed in 1910 – or semi-protectorates like Manchuria. All these pavilions were 'aimed at introducing the new territories to Metropolitans' (1992), in terms of culture, geography and travel facilities, as well as presenting the inhabitants of these areas. At the 1922 'Tokyo Exposition in commemoration of Peace', the new Nanyo [South Seas] and Siberian pavilions contained ethnographical presentations of the inhabitants of Micronesia, over which Japan would soon obtain a mandate from the League of Nations in 1924, and of Siberia. Thus, the content of expositions always reflected the advance of the armies and the expansion of the empire, with colonial and metropolitan minorities being systematically exhibited.

In the early twentieth century, expositions thus served – by emphasizing the modern dichotomy between 'civilization' and 'savagery' – as devices to confirm the position of Japan as a colonial empire of the first rank.[19] However, this cannot be seen as a 'project' specific to the organizers' ambitions, for this view of racial and civilizational hierarchies was widely attested at the time. The best proof of this is that this view was shared almost universally – by Europeans, Japanese, the organizers and those on show – and it is thus impossible to 'victimize' all the exhibited people in terms of a dichotomous writing of history, dividing the world into imperialists and colonized people. While Japan dominated after 1895, it should be remembered that the purpose of the 1894–95

Sino-Japanese war was to gain control of the Korean peninsula, which was contested by these two countries, and that China harboured ongoing imperialistic aims similar to those of Japan.

The reifying view of anthropology was clearly shown by Tsuboi, the organizer of the 1903 National Industrial Exposition in Osaka. His discourse continually emphasized the exoticism and Otherness of the recently incorporated minorities – the inhabitants of Okinawa and Ainu – as well as that of neighbouring populations. He saw Japan as ideally situated in the middle of a 'vast anthropological museum', ready to be studied. The Japanese anthropologist thus made use of his privileged position in East Asia: there would be no locking of people into zoos, but, instead, edifying reconstructions of ethnic categories for pedagogical purposes to accompany the scientific fieldwork. Furthermore, it might be advantageous for some of the people, such as the Ainu, to be exhibited, for it would introduce them to the public and, in any event, the exhibited Asians (including the Ainu) or Arabs were not viewed in the same ways as those from sub-Saharan Africa, because they were seen as too 'civilized' to be animalized. In the end, in both Europe and Japan, anthropological discourse constructed the 'modern' identity of the observer through an altero-referential process that constantly directed attention to the Other (Taguieff 2001). Ultimately, the problem lay not in the act of exhibiting people, but rather in the image thereby created of them – an image which was presupposed by expositions. According to the circular logic of anthropology, of which these expositions were a high point, modern nations asserted themselves as the producers of discourse on the 'barbarian', who was reduced in the process to a mere scientific object.

Notes

1 This does not mean there were no expositions or exhibitions of this kind before 1877. There is documentation, for instance, relating to those described by Ishii Kendô for 1872 and 1882 (Yoshimi 1992: 122).

2 The Seinan war (1877) was a conflict between the new government and part of its political staff led by Saigô Takamori (Takahashi 2005).

3 These treaties limited national sovereignty by restricting Japanese customs rights and fixing extraterritoriality for Westerners. They were gradually abolished between 1894 and 1911, when the Western Powers, slightly modifying their racial prejudice, accepted the presence of an 'occidentalized' Japan.

4 These expositions attracted growing numbers of visitors, with 1,137,000 people in 1895.

5 In Europe, too, after the first exhibition of indigenous people in the Jardin d'acclimatation in Paris in 1878, a similar shift was observed, with the 1889 Paris Universal Exposition presenting for the first time an exhibition of colonized

people in 'human tableaux' reconstructing their so-called natural daily life.

6 This university, established in 1877, is at the heart of the state university system, along with the Imperial University of Kyoto (established in 1897).

7 Following the custom in East Asia, the last name comes before the first name.

8 Its foundation occurred, therefore, only twenty-five years after that of its French equivalent in Paris by Paul Broca in 1859.

9 The Chinese terminology, which distinguished between 'raw barbarians' and 'cooked barbarians' according to the degree of assimilation to Chinese culture, was adopted by the Japanese to refer to populations formerly subject to China.

10 The kingdom of Ryukyu had been annexed by Japan in 1879, and the archipelago's name was changed to Okinawa.

11 There is a lack of precise information on the people who were exhibited, as the documents were not all based on the same 'categories'.

12 Tsuboi reported his impressions in a special column ('News from Paris') of the *Tôkyô jinrui gakkai hôkoku* (Bulletin of the Tôkyô Anthropological Society).

13 i.e. a map of the same kind as those drawn up by Joseph Deniker (1852–1918) at the very same time (Tsuboi 1903: 163).

14 Matsumura was to be in charge of the Laboratory of Anthropology in the 1920s and 1930s.

15 This 1899 law was similar to the 1887 Dawes Law in the United States of America concerning Native Americans. According to the law, the state could dispose of the 'yielded' lands at will (Nanta 2006).

16 One was a constitutionalist and the other was revolutionist, as Chinese modernists were divided about the way to alter China (Dikötter 1992; Sakamoto 1995).

17 At this exposition, Japan was given the same amount of floor space as France, Great Britain, Belgium, Austria and the United States.

18 Karafuto is the Japanese name for Sakhalin. It was inhabited by Japanese from 1905 to 1945.

19 Expositions would also become a means of legitimating aggression against China in the 1930s, when the Fifteen Years War (1931–45) began. After 1932, expositions focused on Japan and its army would be organized; they would offer occasions for huge demonstrations of military power.

22

The Imperial Exhibitions of Great Britain

JOHN MACKENZIE

The great exhibitions which, from the 1800s, came to be dominated by the imperial theme offer the most striking examples of both conscious and unconscious approaches to imperial propaganda.[1] The secret of their success was that they combined entertainment, education and trade fair on a spectacular scale. By the end of the century, they were enormous funfairs, coupled with, in effect, museums of science, industry and natural history, anthropological and folk displays, emigration bureaux, music festivals, and art galleries, together with examples of transport and media innovations, all on one large site. They were a wonder of their age, highlighted in the press and other contemporary literature. They seemed perfect exemplars of 'rational recreation', combining pleasure and instruction, and millions attended them. Even if most went for the fun, some at least of the imperial propaganda cannot have failed to rub off.

The exhibitions were, however, marvels that were ephemeral, constructed for a season, invariably dismantled and scattered at the end. That very transience heightened the sense of urgency to attend, and the need to capture them in leaflets, programmes and photographs. They provided the greatest opportunity to disseminate printed and visual ephemera of all kinds, for the high point of these exhibitions, the almost continuous sequence from late-Victorian times to the First World War, together with the great imperial and colonial examples between the wars, coincided with the peak of production of pamphlets, booklets, postcards and advertising matter.

Much has been written about the manner in which the Great Exhibition of 1851 marked the apex of Britain's industrial and commercial supremacy, and conveyed an impression of overweening pride and self-confidence. It is perhaps the later exhibitions, however, that provide the best insights into national obsessions, character and morale. Their theme was gradually transformed from the international industrial exposition, as in 1851 and 1862, to imperial and colonial display. They came to have a predominantly imperial flavour from the 1880s, precisely the decade of the new aggressive imperialism. This would disappear only after the Second World War. All the exhibitions from 1851 to 1951 effectively chart the rise and fall of imperial sentiment.

The exhibitions of the mid-nineteenth century largely followed the classification originated by Prince Albert and Lyon Playfair for the Great Exhibition at the Crystal Palace in 1851, in which exhibits were divided into raw materials, the manufactures created from them, and the arts that decorated the manufactures (see Gibbs-Smith 1950). Geographical origins were at first almost incidental. In 1851, only 520 out of 14,000 exhibitors were colonial. At the Great London Exposition of 1862, this imperial content had already grown considerably. Indian exhibits were prominent, occupying four times the total space taken up by the thirty other British colonies on show. From 1886 the exhibition became almost entirely concerned with empire, and as the Empire grew, the balance with India was correspondingly redressed. In this the exhibitions were charting the growth of, and contributing to the development of national perceptions about, the Empire.

At the British Empire Exhibition in Glasgow in 1938 there was a separate rubber pavilion, the only tropical product to be so honoured. Control over the natural world was exemplified in other ways. Stuffed animals first made their appearance in 1851 and aroused Queen Victoria's interest. Later, live animals representative of their region were to wander among the exhibits, as at the Greater Britain Exhibition of 1899 and the Coronation Exhibition of 1911. But it was living anthropological exhibits, villages of colonial peoples only recently 'pacified', that most reflected European man's control of his contemporary natural history.

In the Dominions, exhibitions seemed to be a necessary rite of passage for pubescent responsible government, and were invariably held in the wake of notable economic advance. They were mounted in New Zealand (1865, 1906–07, 1924–26), Cape Town (1877), Sydney (1879–80), Melbourne (1888), Kimberley (1893), Brisbane (1897), and Johannesburg (1936–37).[2] British India produced exhibitions at Calcutta (1883–84) and Bombay (1910); even smaller territories such as Sierra Leone (1865), Jamaica (1891), Zanzibar (1905)[3] and Tasmania (1891–82 and 1894–95) got in on the act.

Some indication of the popular impact of these exhibitions can be secured from the figures of attendance. In 1851 and again in 1862 the exhibitions topped 6 million visitors. The Colonial and Indian Exhibition of 1886 failed to match this figure, at 5.5 million, but it was a smaller affair, covering only half the area of 1851 and 1862. The Glasgow International Exhibition of 1888 actually surpassed it, with 5.7 million visitors. Later ones in that city in 1901 and 1911 were equally successful, the former drawing no fewer than 11.5 million people and the latter 9.4 million. It is of course true that these figures would include some multiple attendance by locals, a habit which must have become more pronounced as the funfair aspect developed. The peak was reached at the 1924–25 British Empire Exhibitions at Wembley, with more than 27 million visitors, whereas the 1938 Glasgow Empire Exhibition attracted only 12 million, although 15–20 million were expected. This may represent a decline of public interest in empire and exhibitions, or it may be indicative of the anxieties of the period, both financial and international.

None of the British exhibitions matched the great successes of the Paris Expositions Universelles – with the whole Continent to draw on – in 1889 (32 million) and 1900 (48 million), the 1931 Exposition Coloniale Internationale (33.5 million), the Exposition Internationale des Arts in 1937 (34 million) – or Chicago's World's Columbian Exposition of 1893 (27.5 million) and Century of Progress International Exposition of 1933–34 (48.7 million). Figures for the great series of commercial exhibitions at the Crystal Palace, White City and Olympia between the 1890s and the First World War are more difficult to come by, but as virtually annual events, open for months each year, they must have had considerable impact on the population of London.

The Peak Years: 1899–1911

The Greater Britain Exhibition of 1899 was a remarkable affair. It was perhaps the most ambitious effort of the exhibition entrepreneur Imre Kiralfy, as is well demonstrated by the *Official Guide and Libretto*, which was 150 pages long. The main buildings at the exhibition included the Imperial Court, the Queen's Court ('truly a regal spot'), with oriental façades, the Queen's Palace (which at one stage exhibited relics of the East India Company), the Central Hall, and the Empress Theatre, described as the largest in the world. There were also a Street of Nations, a Cairo Street (a common exhibition feature), a Grand Panorama, and a Royal Bioscope (presumably an early cinema).

Even more extraordinary was the Kaffir Kraal and the 'Savage South Africa' display, 'A Vivid Representation of Life in the Wilds of the Dark Continent'. At the Kaffir Kraal there were 174 Africans, Zulus, Basuto, Matabele and Swazi in four villages, infested apparently with strutting cranes and giant tortoises. A wide variety of activities could be seen here, for 'Unlike the Indian, the South African native is a restless native savage, and he will be seen to be very busy grinding corn, making the native drink, working beads, and most attractive of all, particularly to the fairer sex, the manufacture of kaffir bangles, which are said to be lucky amulets'.

There were five interpreters and headmen, and the public were reassured that the spiritual welfare of these exhibits was catered for by divine service each Sunday. Frank Fillis, a South African showman, contributed to this human natural history by a display in which 'baboons and bushmen take part', together with the Zulus, Basutos on ponies, ten picked Swazis 'magnificent of physique', some Transvaal Boers, two Malay families, some 'pretty little wildebeests', a 'battle of the elephants', and Miss Lillian Reiner, the champion lady shot of South Africa. As if that were not enough, there were re-enactments of the Matabele War of 1893, complete with a long programme 'libretto' describing 'Lobengula's Indaba', the 'Grand War Dance', 'Throwing the Assegai', 'Lobengula's Army on the March', 'the Matopos Hills', 'the Plunge over the Cliffs', 'British Troopers' and 'Major Wilson's Last Stand'. Breathlessly, the show rushed on to the Rhodesian revolt of 1896–97, featuring, in particular, 'Gwelo Stage Coach' in scenes entitled 'Infested with hostile Matabeles', 'The Last Cartridge', 'The Campbell Family', and 'Howling Matabeles'.

It may well be thought that such reminders of the dangers of white pioneer life might have counteracted the emigration propaganda elsewhere, but the impresarios seem to have assumed that any such fears would be allayed by the transformation of war, revolt and death into sentimental spectacle and entertainment. The displays in fact reflect a striking topicality, a powerful application of Social Darwinism to entertainment, and an extraordinary illustration of the imperial exhibition's capacity to chain and tame people who, a mere three years earlier had been enemies, now sadly acting out their former resistance. Representations like these contributed to the late-Victorian taste for theatrical spectacle, which in the exhibitions as in the theatres, set out to create living imperial icons. To Gordon's Death at Khartoum could now be added Major Wilson's Last Stand and the Gwelo Stage Coach. What critics have described as a 'visual living taxonomy' was, as we shall see, to be a feature of many exhibitions.

From 1908 Kiralfy moved his interests to the White City and, as he had previously, mounted annual exhibitions, all with imperial connotations: the Franco-British of 1908, the Imperial International of 1909, the Japan-British of 1910, the Coronation of 1911, the Latin-British of

1912, and the Anglo-American of 1914. In 1911 there were no fewer than two imperial coronation exhibitions in London, the one at the White City and a rather more official affair at the Crystal Palace, as well as a Glasgow exhibition the same year. Kiralfy's style was strongly orientalist. The late-nineteenth-century orientalist craze arrived in exhibition architecture from the 1860s and came to predominate by the 1890s.[4] Many exhibitions had 'sets' that rendered them forerunners of Cecil B. de Mille epics. The epic of the exhibition was the contemporary world and all its wonders brought on to a single site, and expressed invariably in temporary wood-and-plaster architecture. It was at the White City that the Hollywood film-set characteristic was taken to its highest point, with white stuccoed oriental-style buildings which were used, like many of the amusement park features, over and over again. As with orientalism generally, the exhibitions created a vision of what the East ought to look like, rather than the actuality. 'Moorish' kiosks and exhibits were to appear repeatedly, the Americans and British probably deriving the style from the French.

The Crystal Palace Exhibition of 1911 was intended 'to demonstrate to the somewhat casual, often times unobservant British public the real significance of our great self-governing Dominions, to make us familiar with their products, their ever-increasing resources, their illimitable possibilities' (Festival of Empire 1911: 7). The exhibits were displayed in three-quarter-size scale models of all the Dominions' parliament buildings, and they were connected by a train journey through the Empire in a series of extraordinary geographical juxtapositions. This trip was called, inevitably, 'The All-red Tour' and started in Newfoundland, passing a paper-making plant and Newfoundland scenery before reaching Canada, where wheat-growing and lumbering were featured. From Canada, the travellers passed through a Jamaican sugar plantation, a Malay village, Indian jungle ('with a variety of animals running wild'), an Indian palace (with 'wonderful inlaid gold and jewel work'), a 'typical Indian bazaar' and, *mirabile dictu*, the Himalayas. The train continued past Sydney harbour and the Blue Mountains, a sheep farm, orchards, vineyards and so on, to New Zealand, with its hot water geysers, a 'quaint Maori village', and much wool and mutton. The journey ended in South Africa, with gold and diamond mines and the traditional 'native kraal' featured.

The idea of the Empire Exhibition was first mooted by the British Empire League in 1902. The Liberal Party victory in 1906 killed the idea, but it was revived in 1913 by Lord Strathcona. He consulted Imre Kiralfy, thereby bringing the commercial and official streams of exhibition organization together. The Metropolitan Railway had reached

Wembley in the 1880s. But it was the Empire Exhibition which was to put Wembley on the map and lead to its rapid growth (Hewlett 1979; WHS [Wembley History Society] 1974; Walthew 1981). In 1920 an Act of Parliament empowered the government to become joint guarantor, and of the £2.2 million subscribed the government contributed half.

Thus, in 1924–25, Wembley became the greatest of all the imperial exhibitions – in area, cost, extent of participation, and, probably, popular impact. The official guide described its purpose as:

> To find, in the development and utilisation of the raw materials of the Empire, new sources of Imperial wealth. To foster inter-Imperial trade and open fresh world markets for Dominion and home products. To make the different races of the British Empire better known to each other, and to demonstrate to the people of Britain the almost illimitable possibilities of the Dominions, Colonies, and Dependencies overseas.[5]

Following the success at Wembley, the 1938 Empire Exhibition in Glasgow was conceived in 1931 at the depth of the Depression as a conscious effort to provide employment and to advertise home-based depressed industries. Yet the exhibition remained imperial – in appearance, in tone and in name. By the time the scheme reached fruition, at a cost of £10 million, a new world crisis was about to break. Classical architecture was abandoned for a much more contemporary 1930s style, although some pavilions, as in 1924–25, attempted to illustrate local styles, like the Dutch gables of the South African house or the carved teak of the Burma pavilion.

The official guide book of the exhibition stressed that it was 'the greatest held anywhere in the world since Wembley 1924–25' (which was something of an exaggeration, given the size and massive success of the Continental and American exhibitions) and emphasized its accessibility to the public:

> It has been built by Great Britain, the Dominions, and close on forty of the colonies. Within 175 acres of parkland and a huge stadium, the Empire is presenting itself to the World. Although the exhibition contains over 100 palaces and pavilions, the admission charge to the Park – 1/- for adults and 6d for children under 14 – admits visitors to all but a few of the buildings.

As always, the glories of the funfairs came in for particular treatment, including 'the latest and greatest devices that human ingenuity can devise', the Rocket Ride, the 'biggest dodg'em track in the world', the Brooklands Racer, and the Stratosphere Plane, the Trip to the Moon, the New Ride to Heaven, and the Flying Fleas, among many others.

The Zulu Village and the Indian Temple were mentioned in the same breath, although the main village feature was the clachan, or highland village. The year 1938 can, then, be placed in the classic exhibition tradition, combining fun with information, economic propaganda with ethnic display.

Ethnic Villages

From the 1870s, 'native villages' were in fact among the most enduring features of all the exhibitions. They repay closer attention because they were the prime way in which people in the metropolis were brought into contact with the conquered peoples of the Empire. Here were racial stereotypes illustrated, Social Darwinism established in the popular mind, and control of the world expressed in its most obvious human form. Moreover, the numbers of programmes and postcards of these exhibits that can still be found seem to indicate that they caught the public imagination. Yesterday's enemies, the perpetrators of yesterday's 'barbarism', became today's exhibits, showing off quaint music, dancing, sports, living crafts and food – but now well on the path to civilization. In the exhibitions, representatives of African and oriental peoples were brought cheek by jowl with all the trappings of the world-wide economy. It was a concentrated and speeded-up version of what was happening in their own countries.

Usually these living exhibits were set against the backdrop of the 'primitive village', but grander pieces of architecture, generally divorced from present-day inhabitants, were introduced in replica. One of the most popular French exhibits, which made its first appearance at Paris in 1889, and reappeared at the International Colonial Expositions in Marseille in 1922 and Vincennes, Paris, in 1931, was a full-size model of the temple of Angkor Vat. The king of Annam made his first visit to France in connection with the exhibit in 1922. A replica of the Taj Mahal was, rather surprisingly, constructed in Philadelphia in 1926, but generally the message was primitiveness rather than splendour.

The practice of bringing peoples from overseas seems to have begun in 1867, when Parisians were served exotic products by those who allegedly produced them. Thus 'a Mulatto offered cocoa and guava' and there were 'even Chinese women with their little tea shop' (Allwood 1977: 45). The French fascination with North Africa was reflected in Tunisian and Egyptian architecture. In Paris in 1889, there was a large colonial section with several native villages and a Cairo Street, complete with belly dancers and camel rides. The Cairo street was to reappear at

Chicago in 1893, Antwerp in 1894, and St Louis in 1904, indicating the new accessibility of Egypt after the opening of the Suez Canal. Imre Kiralfy seems to have caught it between Belgium and United States for his 1899 Greater Britain Exhibition, but that extraordinary impresario may well have had his own.

In the British exhibitions the native villages always performed one function: to show off the quaint, the savage, the exotic, to offer living proof of the onward march of imperial civilization. As we have seen, the 1899 Greater Britain Exhibition had its astonishing southern African displays, but they did not reappear. No doubt a fresh outbreak of Zulu resistance in 1906 made them a rather less attractive proposition. Imre Kiralfy went on to create a Pageant of Women, complete with an Amazon village, which must have helped satisfy an enduring fascination.

The two most common villages were, however, from the French Empire. These were the Senegalese and the Dahomean villages, which made frequent reappearances. The French had apparently perfected the organization of travelling troupes of 'native' entertainers, who entertained by being themselves and pursuing supposedly normal activities. The Senegalese were at the Scottish National Exhibition in Edinburgh in 1908, exhibiting music, crafts and wrestling; they (or presumably another team) were at the Franco-British Exhibition in the same year, and they made a surprising comeback at the North East Coast Industries Exhibition in Newcastle in 1929, together with 'members of the Fullah tribe'. The Senegalese also appeared as an attraction at seaside resorts in the years when they were not at exhibitions. The Dahomean village was a feature of the Imperial International Exhibition at White City in 1909. It was joined there, most surprisingly of all, by a nomad Kalmyk camp from Central Asia, only recently incorporated in the Russian empire. At the Scottish National Exhibition in Glasgow in 1911 there was an 'equatorial colony' with 'West African natives', whose precise origins were not identified.

Booklets and dozens of postcards were published to commemorate these displays. A guide to the Senegalese Village at the Franco-British Exhibition in 1908 was written by Aimé Bouvier and Fleury Tournier, who described themselves as 'explorers' who had brought out 150 people from Senegal by permission of the Governor, after what seems to have been a sort of human *Zoo Quest*. The booklet described the buildings and activities of the village, including the shop 'where goods of European merchants have penetrated to the remotest villages of Western Africa [...] tempting the native [...] by their brightness and cheapness'.

So far as African eating habits were concerned, 'though you may be amused you will not be shocked'. The strength of the wrestlers ('two colossal negroes, who look like statues of ebony as they prepare to grip') is contrasted with the weakness of African education. A hierarchy of peoples, even within West Africa, is established, the Wolofs being described as superior to the Mandigoes. All this was presented with the help of Mr Victor Bamberger, 'who presents pictures of the life of India and its natives in the British Colonial section'.

The villages are present in strength at the 1924–25 Empire Exhibitions in London at Wembley and, on a somewhat lesser scale, at the 1938 Empire Exhibition in Glasgow. But by the Second World War a new tradition was beginning to emerge. The last colonial exhibitions were to be small, mobile, and devoted to particular problems. Some of them were sent all over the country.

The great exhibitions provide a valuable study because with them we have the rare opportunity to gauge public reaction, through press reports, and through the figures of attendance. They left behind large numbers of cheap publications of all sorts, which seem to have had a wide distribution, and these publications illustrate the predominant imperial ideas and racial attitudes that were disseminated for public consumption. None of these ideas show any sign of dilution in the years between the wars. The exhibitions of the period emphasized the economic justification of Empire all the more strongly, and continued to convey Social Darwinian views on race. Only after the Second World War did the tone of propaganda change, although by then it was in a sense even more overtly and officially propagandist, government agencies consciously preparing the public for colonial developments. By then, however, many of the popular attitudes towards empire were deeply embedded and were to remain so into the era of decolonization itself.

Notes

1 This article is a revised version of the chapter 'The Imperial Exhibitions', in MacKenzie (1984).
2 The Official Catalogue, Empire Exhibition, Johannesburg, September 1936–January 1937, indicates that the UK, Canada, New Zealand, Australia, Northern and Southern Rhodesia, East Africa, the Bechuanaland Protectorate, Ceylon, and Nyasaland all had substantial exhibits there. The Dominions exhibitions were almost all 'imperial' rather than international. There seems to have been virtually no international representation at Johannesburg at all.
3 This was an exhibition of products from British East Africa, German East Africa, Portuguese East Africa, British Central Africa, Uganda, the Comoros Islands, Madagascar, Réunion, Mauritius, Italian Benadir (i.e. Somaliland), the Seychelles and Zanzibar. See official catalogue.

4 When the American architect Louis Sullivan castigated the 1893 Chicago Exposition for its architectural conservatism, he himself contributed a building of distinctly oriental flavour (Allwood 1977: 84, 89, 92).

5 In addition to the official programme, a free map and guide was issued with the admission price of 1/6d, with children admitted at half price. *The Times* (30 September 1924) reported that no fewer than 5.5 million copies of this map and guide had been issued. The paper extolled the role of the exhibition in issuing vast quantities of useful ephemera, including posters, handbills, leaflets and postcards. By that date 10 million exhibition postage stamps had been sold.

23

The Congolese in 'Imperial' Belgium

JEAN-PIERRE JACQUEMIN

If we try to find a single figure to symbolize the status of the Congolese people in the history of Belgian social thought and imagination, we need look no further than Coco, Tintin's 'boy' in *Tintin in the Congo*.[1] As a character, he is a minor presence, and his contribution to the plot is a strange disappearance. It should also be said that few commentators on Hergé's questionable best-seller have given Coco's fate its due. Indispensable factotum and useful comic fall-guy, this miniature Man Friday, having remained in the foreground for a brief period (he appears on the cover beside the great hero), suffers the fate of all puppets: he spins around three times and is gone. However, nothing in the narrative either anticipates or, above all, provides any logical justification, however slight, for such a sudden disappearance. We are obliged to conclude that he is no longer *useful* ...

This may, of course, simply be an iconographical manipulation, an exploitation of the essential ambiguity of metaphor to our own ends. But if we look at the images and texts published in Belgium on the Congolese we encounter the recurrent elements of absence, of undervaluation, and of misrepresentation through propaganda. There was Massala, the supposed 'king' who was Stanley's 'boy' or 'companion' in Lumumba. At first considered to be a likeable figure fit to visit the children of the motherland, he would later become a suitable target for assassination. In the 1920s, Stephano Kaoze, the 'first black man to be ordained a priest', was exhibited, along with his writings, as a justification for the missionary movement. And Panda Farnana, the agronomist, was revered for his academic gifts, but later reviled and demonized for having sunk into the 'darkness' of 'ancestral atavism'. The whole of this sparse corpus cries out for re-examination and, given its nature, inevitably begins to feel like evidence for the prosecution.

It is important to remember that, unlike France and England (who, as owners of vast colonial empires, received considerable numbers of their foreign subjects in the home country), Belgium, and most of her citizens, had practically no opportunity for extended physical (let alone intellectual) contact with representatives of Congolese humanity, whether for better or for worse. As a consequence, their encounter with the Congolese was almost entirely mediated by images and words, leaving their perception of them at the level of the imagination.

A Brief Appearance

In Belgium, as elsewhere in Europe, there were certainly fairground exhibitions which were deliberately anthropozoomorphic in nature. There were also major colonial exhibitions which temporarily imported human 'specimens' on a limited scale in order to attract the curiosity of the crowds. In 1885, the year in which Leopold II successfully negotiated in Berlin his personal right to found the 'independent' state of Congo, the first international exhibition was held in Antwerp. The focus of l'Exposition Universelle d'Anvers, was the pavilion which housed Massala, Stanley's companion, accompanied by several men, women and children of his entourage. The souvenir photograph of the event is disturbing in that it does not conform to the standard presentation of the human zoos: all of those depicted, in Western dress, are named individually. Only the Belgian posing authoritatively in the background remains anonymous (the better to preserve his distance?). But this was the time of the earliest exotic shows, and the visit was so exceptional that Massala could become a star, received on the royal estate of Laeken by Leopold II himself.

Nine years later, at another exhibition in Antwerp, the 1894 Exposition Internationale d'Anvers, the perspective had shifted. This time, the public were eager to view 114 'natives' in a Congolese village and to applaud twelve soldiers from the Force publique, the newly formed colonial army. But it was Tervuren (known today for its world-famous museum) which hosted in 1897 the most paradigmatic and spectacular exhibition, attracting 1,111,521 visitors, a substantial number for that time. Alongside the Congolese products which provided evidence of profits to come, 260 Congolese were on show to the Belgian public, including 90 soldiers, 34 wives and children, 123 villagers from Bas Congo and the Equator, 'plus two dwarves from the Upper Aruwimi, an Arab and his modest suite and a few boys of different origins', according to *Bruxelles-Exposition* (1897), which recorded the event. Installed in reconstructed villages, they mimed the typical actions of their daily lives (cooking, dances, discussions, fishing, water tournaments on the neighbouring lakes, etc.) for the benefit of the visitors. The enthusiasm of the public was such that they had to be restrained: signs were erected bearing the message 'Do not feed the Blacks, they have already been fed.' The newspaper *L'Étoile belge* wrote in a critical tone of 'the indulgences and familiarities of the Whites, especially the women!' towards the Congolese who had been thus installed and displayed (*L'Étoile belge* 1897).

However, scandal was to dampen these questionable enthusiasms. The climatic hardships of a poor summer led to seven deaths from pneumonia among the Congolese.[2] The inhabitants of the village nearest to the exhibition site refused to have the corpses of 'heathens' buried in their cemetery. The conservative press attempted to keep the matter quiet but other newspapers, hostile to the established church and the King's colonial activities, were vocal on the subject. Even before the major campaigns against Leopold at the beginning of the 1900s, resulting from the exposure of the violent exploitation involved in the production of red rubber, attitudes were cooled by the scandal of the first Congolese to die on Belgian soil. This no doubt explains why most subsequent official exhibitions avoided the practice, however attractive it had proved to be, of importing 'real natives'. From then on, they mostly limited themselves to pictures, posters, books, talks, artefacts and, as technology moved on, films, which provided risk-free interpretive access to the colonies.

It would not be until Expo '58, the Brussels World Fair of 1958, that inhabitants of the Congo would return in any significant numbers (several hundred) to demonstrate, by means of a range of symbolic displays, the benefits of colonial rule. Still carefully supervised, and once again housed at Tervuren, many of them nevertheless contrived to establish links with various Belgian groups and individuals. Until this time, a covert form of apartheid had deprived the Belgians themselves of any opportunity to encounter the Congolese and engage in a mutual cultural exploration. Without wishing to establish a causal link in a mechanistic way, it can nevertheless be noted that two months after the end of the fair, on 4 January 1959, riots in Leopoldville served as a rude awakening to the Belgians, and led in the following year to the independence of what they had long been led to believe was 'the most beautiful colony'.

It would be inappropriate, clearly, to accuse the colonial expositions of being the sole cause of the undervaluation and absence referred to above. Many other factors contributed to this. But we must recognize the facts. Throughout the colonial period, the Congolese were rarely present in Belgium and had little social impact. This is a far cry from

Claude McKay's *Banjo* (1930) and from the popularity of the *bals nègres* [negro balls] and Josephine Baker in Paris (see Blanchard, Deroo and Manceron 2001).

A Hidden Diaspora

From the end of the nineteenth century until the middle of the twentieth, and even up until independence, those Congolese who did appear in Belgium seem to have been exceptions: sailors who broke their contracts after having shuttled between Matadi and Anvers for a while; servants who accompanied their masters when the latter finally returned to Belgium (becoming the most discreet of shadows in the already shadowy society of ex-colonials); travelling salesmen who sold *karaboui͏̈a,* liquorice and other dark sweets at provincial markets (although many of these probably came from the French colonies); wandering ex-seminarians who had abandoned their studies, etc.

Very little is known of their stories and in documents they mostly appear as vague silhouettes.[3] Nevertheless, it is a frequently stated fact that the official system disapproved of such settlement. The main concern was that these individuals, having lived on the margins of white society, would return to the Congo and contaminate the minds of others with their tales, thereby threatening the myth of white superiority.

Those of mixed blood, with white fathers and black mothers (the opposite was unthinkable at that time), known as mulattos, were in a number of cases absorbed into their paternal families, required to become 'good Belgians' and to allow their 'tainted' origins to be forgotten.[4] But there is also a vast and troubling store of popular materials from both Flanders and Wallonia. Here, songs, jokes and anecdotes demonstrate how hard it was for Belgian society at that time to accept wholeheartedly a difference in skin colour associated with 'primitive' culture. We should remember that the whole of 1930s Europe was steeped in racist assumptions and theories.

It is important to remember how different the Belgian experience was from that of neighbouring France. Twice occupied, in 1914 and 1940, Belgium remained almost entirely unaffected by the major shift in opinion brought about by the presence (and sacrifice) of the Senegal Rifles. During the First World War, Belgian colonial troops fighting for the Allies did so largely in Africa, facing the German colonial forces in the Cameroon, Rhodesia and the Tanganyika area. Likewise, in 1941, the Abyssinian campaign ended with the victories won by three battalions of the Force Publique over the Italian garrisons of Asosa and Gambela, but the Force Publique did not have to fight in Europe. As a result, the media showed little or no positive recognition of heroes and martyrs from the colonies. Here, there was neither the outpouring of gratitude nor the mocking popularity which find their most famous expression in the dubious archetype of the jolly rifleman in the French Banania advertisement, as well as in a host of other contemporary and later images. The willing contributions to the war effort made by the population of the Congo were extensive but they were mostly economic in nature and, for this reason, they remained abstract, intangible and opaque in the eyes of a Belgian public, which had, since colonization began, remained unengaged and unenlightened.

Not all the reasons for such a comprehensive absence and collective blindness can be explained. Whole swathes of social history remain to be examined and more detailed research might contradict the hypothesis advanced above. But if we examine the front pages and covers (in the case of periodicals) of the Belgian national press from 1908 to 1960, we are forced to recognize that the Congolese presence there is entirely minor, allusive and almost non-existent. Only the Royal visits of Albert I and, later, Baudouin I appear on the front page. It is in the specialized and widespread missionary press that we find an obsessive litany which creates and perpetuates the myth of the Congolese as a 'big child', who must be cared for, educated and reformed. In parallel with this, equally specialized propaganda was emanating from colonial circles and the social divisions of the giant mining and agricultural companies, which would, until 1959, continue to publish the self-congratulatory news of their paternalist actions.

There are a few trips by 'notables' (the usual chiefs and major traders) and 'evolved natives' (the first members of middle management to open up communication channels within the system), who make special appearances sparsely scattered through the 1950s. But only a handful of individuals were permitted to study at university in Belgium during this period. And the colonial authorities have been reproached many times for having obstinately clung to the maxim 'no elites, no problem'. In 1960, less than fifty years ago, the idea of an independent Congolese intellectual who could engage reliably in debate was perceived as a fantasy, if not a dangerous utopian dream. For a long time, the dominant attitude towards the Congolese would continue to be distrust, for they were still considered to be tarnished, despite their cultural assimilation, by the dark and tenacious inheritance of the 'Bantu mind'.

Future Dialogue

It was in the academic world that the decolonization of minds would eventually occur. It was in this environment that the students of the two peoples would, in the most positive of cases, learn to know, respect and value each other. From the beginning of the 1960s, firm friendships were formed and many people managed to throw off the weight of their earlier ignorance. We must assume that the growth over time of a settled and established minority community of Congolese in Belgium (between 15,000 and 20,000 today) has served to normalize and improve this mutual knowledge. But this lengthy labour of human discovery has not prevented the continued existence of what can be called 'ordinary' racism, nor the revival of old prejudices in response to the violent crises which have overtaken the Democratic Republic of Congo in the last decade, any more than it has been able to prevent the various waves of xenophobia which still occur throughout Europe, encountering only desultory opposition. Although footballers and musicians benefit, as elsewhere, from popular support, their general situation is far from ideal and in their daily lives they remain exposed to administrative troubles and other types of abuse.

The final point which needs to be made about the Congolese presence in Belgium in the last few decades is that, contrary to what might be expected, the Congo, as an ex-colony, has not become an exporter of labour. Instead, at the beginning of the 1960s it was Morocco and Turkey which played this role.[5] As a consequence, it appears certain that Congolese immigration in Belgium has played no significant economic role and has, generally, remained minimal. Things happened elsewhere, in the inner sanctums of banks, administrative committees and religious groups. There was a parroting of propaganda, a cacophony of information, followed by weighty silences. But times are changing. When will they finally be ripe for genuine dialogue, without the parasitical interference of the lurking shadows of Tintin and Coco?

Notes

1 The extensive use and possible abuse of quotation marks in this chapter is deliberate.

2 A recent Belgian film, *Boma-Tervuren, le voyage* (Boma-Tervuren: The Journey) by Dujardin (52 minutes, 1999) narrates the event and its implications.

3 The doctoral thesis of the Congolese researcher Zana Aziza Étambala, who himself studied in Belgium, is devoted to this hidden diaspora (Étambala 1989). In the field of Belgian literature, the exception is 'Gim', a strange short story by the naturalist writer Camille Lemonier (1900). Gim, a Congolese adolescent

who has come to Belgium as an 'exotic' and lost 'boy', kills himself for love of his mistress, an inaccessible white goddess.

4 Most, however, remained in the Congo, in their mothers' families, or entered (willingly or unwillingly) religious orphanages called upon to manage the 'problem' they represented.

5 A theory exists, unverified as far as I am aware, which suggests that Mobutu himself turned down the offer of a special agreement with Belgium on the movement of labour. He is said to have feared the threat of too large a Congolese community outside his own country.

24

Freaks and Geeks: Coney Island Sideshow Performers and Long Island Eugenicists, 1910–1935

TANFER EMIN TUNC

The dancer known as Little Egypt was a sensation. Imitators soon gathered in Coney Island, hoping to attract the large crowds that surrounded the exotic belly dancer. They came in droves during the summer of 1910: pleasure-seekers from New York City, immigrants from the Bronx, and eugenicists from Cold Spring Harbor, Long Island,[1] drawn by the following advertisement: 'This way for the Streets of Cairo! One hundred Oriental beauties! The warmest spectacle on earth! Presenting Little Egypt! See her prance, wriggle, and dance the Hoochy-Koochy! Anywhere else but in the ocean breezes of Coney Island she would be consumed by her own fire! Don't crowd! Plenty of seats for all!' (McCullough 1957: 255).

American Progressivism and Eugenics at Cold Spring Harbor

Beginning in 1910 and continuing through 1935, scientists from Cold Spring Harbor's Eugenics Record Office (ERO) visited Coney Island to photograph and document the sideshow performers who were on exhibit. Their visits, however, were not out of mere curiosity. The ERO, with its interest in unusual, 'exotic' and 'abnormal' individuals, was a product of early twentieth-century American progressivism and its desire to categorize, homogenize and cleanse the nation. As Robert Wiebe illustrates in *The Search for Order* (1967), American progressive reform was a panacea to the nation's illnesses and a mixture of less positive initiatives. According to Wiebe, implicit in the progressive attempts of some middle-class intellectuals and activists was a racist, nativist agenda. Under the guise of science, a number of progressive reformers began to encourage eugenics programmes with the aim of eliminating the immigrant, working and 'degenerate' classes in the United States. Because they 'lived and worked comfortably' with

276

minorities and immigrants, the working class, which included Coney Island sideshow performers such as Little Egypt, also became a target of eugenic programmes. Even white sideshow performers were targeted, for, as historian Matthew Jacobson delineates, skin colour itself did not simply determine race – association often did (1998: 57). Using these social definitions, scientists, specifically eugenicists, began to label these Americans as genetically inassimilable menaces to the homogeneity of the American landscape.

In 1910, Charles Davenport, a committed eugenicist who maintained that plant and animal breeding theory could be applied to human beings to reduce the social threat of genetic 'undesirables', established the Eugenics Record Office at Cold Spring Harbor. The ERO served as the centre for all major eugenics research in North America until 1939 (Haller 1984: 65). In its early years, the ERO functioned as a testing ground for research and propaganda in eugenics, such as Davenport's *Heredity in Relation to Eugenics* (1911). Cited by one-third of the high-school and college biology textbooks used in the interwar years, *Heredity in Relation to Eugenics* tied fears of social chaos with fears of race, class, disease and immigration. Using the newly acquired scientific legitimacy of eugenics, these theories were quickly extrapolated to include 'exotic' figures such as Little Egypt, as well as mental and physical 'degenerates', many of whom could be found on display at Coney Island.

The academic fascination with eugenics entered popular culture during the 1920s, when the ERO began a national eugenics campaign. Through the use of cultural institutions, such as state fairs, eugenicists were able to establish a form of cultural hegemony which defined normality and abnormality, and reinforced the goals of positive and negative eugenics. As the ERO-sponsored *Fitter Family Contests* illustrated, the ultimate goal of this eugenics campaign was to produce the 'fittest' (i.e. whitest) families possible, who could then be promulgated as examples of Anglo-American genetic purity and racial superiority. Eugenic films, such as *The Black Stork* (1916), reinforced why degenerates should be eliminated by invoking in the American public a tangible fear of genetic monstrosities (1984: 80). This early film, as well as later ones, such as Tod Browning's *Freaks* (1932), stressed the thin line that existed between normal and abnormal, between 'us' and 'them'. By portraying strange individuals who, like immigrants, formed their own cliques and lived by their own social and moral codes, these films constructed in the collective mind of the nation the potential result of unchecked breeding: genetic 'freaks'.[2] They also reinforced the power of science, especially eugenics, to eliminate these human monstrosities:

'Never again will a story [such as *Freaks*] be filmed, as modern science and teratology [the study of birth defects] are rapidly eliminating such blunders of nature from the world.'[3]

Eugenicists such as Davenport believed that the study of human disabilities could provide them with evidence for their eugenics theories. As a result, in 1910 Davenport also established a summer school at the ERO which, over a span of fourteen years, trained a total of 258 men and women to be eugenics fieldworkers. The students were taught by Davenport himself and became experts in recording family histories and constructing pedigrees. To supervise the activities of the genetic fieldworkers, Davenport recruited a zealous eugenicist from Missouri, Harry H. Laughlin. Under Laughlin's direction, the ERO became the epicentre of the American eugenics movement, amassing thousands of family pedigrees, case studies, photographs and medical records. Their activities ranged the spectrum from trips to mental asylums to visits to Coney Island (1984: 65–66).

Although performers in 'freak shows' were originally intended as curious spectacles, eugenicists interpreted their disabilities as examples of 'degenerate heredity', and raided 'freak shows' for observations and 'specimens'. Aware of the research possibilities inherent in an isolated community such as Coney Island, Davenport began a project which objectified and placed scientific value on sideshow bodies. However, the eugenicists who visited Coney Island were not merely searching for scientific proof for their theories. Their reports, photographs and constant surveillance facilitated the medical identification, and elimination, of deviant, or 'pathological' bodies, all with the hope of *normalizing*, or homogenizing, the population of the United States. Normalization thus became a strategy, or a mechanism, of social inclusion or exclusion which, on Coney Island, targeted race, class, gender, sexuality and culture.

The Spectacle of the Exotic

Once 'commanding two miles of beach on the south-western end of Long Island, New York', Coney Island represented the culmination of turn-of-the-twentieth-century mass consumerism and low culture. Not only did its amusement parks and sideshows entertain the nouveau riche bourgeoisie but they also promoted conspicuous consumption. At Coney Island, middle-class Americans displayed their wealth and status through their clothing and jewels, while promoters profited from the presentation of human spectacles. Understandably, the glorification of abnormality, the rising number of immigrants at the parks, and the licentious, decadent and unchaperoned atmosphere of Coney Island troubled Long Island eugenicists. Moreover, Coney Island's 'Bowery', with its promenade of 'distorting mirrors, furnished the illusion that the [curious] spectators themselves had become freaks'. Thus, Coney Island seemed charged with a magical, and eugenically dangerous, 'power to transmute customary appearances into fluid new possibilities'. It represented an alternative world, a dream world, perhaps even a *nightmare* world (Kasson 1978: 1, 50–53, 66).

Coney Island's Manhattan and West Brighton beaches, with their replica minarets, exotic, elephant-shaped hotels, 'authentic' tribal warriors and vaudeville-influenced orientalism, served as the literal and figurative *stage* for performances of 'race', class and culture. There, eugenicists found Lionel, the lion-faced boy, who embodied the Tarzan-like, primitive *enfant sauvage*. Marketed as a product of the uncivilized Russian forest, where he had survived by picking berries, hunting like a wolf and roaring like a lion, Lionel became the quintessential missing link. In reality, he was raised on the fairgrounds of Europe, travelling from sideshow to sideshow with his equally hairy father, Homme-chien (or Dog Man; Fiedler 1978: 166). As Lionel entered adolescence, however, he could no longer be cast as *l'enfant sauvage*, for he could not play the part of the 'savage': his interest in reading had somehow been discovered by the media, transforming his barbaric image – and his class – virtually overnight. In later photographs, Lionel is often attired in upper-class, even aristocratic, clothing and is captured in erudite poses. In one studio photograph, for example, Lionel is wearing gold-embroidered leggings, and is reading a book as he reclines on an elaborate cushion (1978: 167).

Eugenicists were undoubtedly fascinated by Lionel's sudden makeover. His ability to transform himself from the missing link into an almost acceptable aristocrat challenged the limits of normality. Clearly, Lionel presented a eugenic threat: in their pedigrees, Cold Spring Harbor eugenicists noted that Lionel and his father both exhibited the same trait – hypertrichosis (excess face and body hair) – and that such a trait could be passed on from generation to generation by hereditary means. Eugenicists believed that if such a pattern continued, the number of Lionels in American society could eventually outbreed the eugenically fit population, resulting in social, and genetic, chaos.

The conflation of genetic degeneracy with race and primitive *animal-like* qualities is prevalent throughout the Coney Island records compiled by the ERO. Defying categorization, these abnormal specimens existed between the animal and human realms. Toney, the Alligator Skin Boy, and Susi, the Elephant Skin Girl, in reality suffered from the genetic disorder ichthyosis, or elephant-like skin, which covered their bodies with tough, dark, square scales. Prince Randian, an armless and legless native of New Guinea, who at the climax of the film *Freaks* is shown inching his way through the mud with a knife between his teeth (in real life he was married with five 'normal' children), was known not only as the Living Torso but also as the Snake Man and the Caterpillar Man (1978: 168). Phocomelics, such as the Prince, whose hands and feet extended directly from their torsos, were often called 'seal boys' or 'seal girls' (the medical term itself meaning 'seal limbs'). Coney Island performer Alice Bounds, known as the Bear Lady, was not only a phocomelic but was also a woman of colour. Born in Calcutta to a phocomelic mother, Alice could easily pass as an African-American, which the race-conscious eugenicists most likely noticed.

The nineteenth-century fascination with jungle-esque primitivism and stage personifications of the *dark* 'savage' through exotic costumes and dance movements were common spectacles at Coney Island. These exhibits, which sought to romanticize native culture through displays of quotidian indigenous activities, resulted in a zoo-like public gaze, which objectified and dehumanized the bodies of black subjects.

Eugenicists, many of whom were still interested in craniometry, reaped tremendous benefits, as these exhibitions provided them with a laboratory in which to measure not only skull shape and volume – that is, the brain size and therefore the supposed intelligence of their black subjects – but also various aspects of human anatomy. As Davenport noted, 'There are structural differences that are innate and racial and need to be measured and studied. It is known that the baby of two full-blooded Negro parents will develop black skin, wooly hair, a large nose, and large eyes' (1940: 14). This could explain the ERO's fascination with Chief Pantagal, a 'savage' jungle man, or *glomming geek*, who performed with live snakes and chickens, biting off, chewing and swallowing their heads as part of his racialized 'wild man' performance. Intrigued by the Chief, the ERO agents collected a sample of his hair, which they described as 'frizzy, dark and curled'. In their notes, they also drew a short pedigree, which included the Chief's sisters, his wife (a 'full blooded Negro woman'), and his daughter, all of whom, not surprisingly, exhibited the same kind of hair.

Another so-called *wild man* whom the ERO photographed, Chief Amok, 'A Bantu Head Hunter', further illustrates the social binaries that existed between the sideshow performers and their audiences.

Dressed in tribal regalia, with an almost serene look on his face, the Chief was the quintessential 'noble savage', willing to tell his story to sympathetic onlookers while denouncing his fellow tribe members. Moreover, his anachronistic, pseudo-title of 'Chief', like the titles of 'King', 'Queen', or 'Prince', blurred the boundaries between high and low culture, suggesting a sort of perverse aristocracy that would naturally be denigrated by *democratic* Americans (Garland-Thomson 1997: 61).

Clearly, 'freak shows' acted out a relationship in which exoticized and disabled peoples functioned as physical opposites of the ideal white American. However, it is interesting to note that these sideshow performers often became wild men only after applying burnt cork to their faces, frizzing their hair and affixing gold rings to their noses, thus *performing* exotic culture and the black race. Their popularity and, therefore, eugenic threat, stemmed from the fact that they fitted the mental image of the 'savage degenerate' that was embedded in the psyche of white, turn-of-the-twentieth-century, America. Believed to be mentally inferior, blackface characters such as these 'wild and primitive' Africans reinforced racism, thus guaranteeing racial domination even in the imaginary realm of the sideshow. This undoubtedly increased the cultural authority of eugenicists as they sought to eliminate the abnormal and 'uncivilized' individuals which American society shunned.[4]

Beauty and the Beast: The 'Freak' as Erotic Threat

According to Frantz Fanon, the black man in white society is not simply perceived as racially different. His darkness embodies the savagery of the jungle; he symbolizes the *uncontrollable beast* and the embodiment of lustful hyper-sexuality: 'One is no longer aware of the Negro, but only of a penis; the Negro is eclipsed. He is turned into a penis. He is a penis' (1952: 170). As illustrated by images of the nude torsos of Chief Pantagal and Chief Amok, eugenicists associated this portrayal of race and sexuality with the human exhibits. Davenport even expressed these sentiments in a 1913 ERO Bulletin when he characterized individuals of African ancestry as having 'a strong sex instinct without corresponding self-control' (1913: 34). Clearly, in spite of its appeal to objective reason, eugenics, and its fascination with the unusual, contained elements of fantasy, longing and desire. Moreover, Davenport's attitude towards the sideshow performers illustrates that the fin-de-siècle preoccupation with the dark, exotic body did not fail to invoke the phallic/colonialist gaze of these male scientists.

The search for scientific 'truth' became an endorsement to display the black body in a variety of 'primitive' and sexualized situations. Countless examples of bare-breasted or totally nude men and women of colour exist. In Coney Island, scantily clad and consumed by her own 'sexual fire', Little Egypt danced the 'Hoochy-Koochy' in front of crowds of American men, who were, no doubt, enthralled by her exotic body and the cultural spectacle she presented. Because these racialized characters were reduced to sexual creatures who were no different than the wild animals of the African jungle, standards of decency, to a certain extent, were overlooked. Photography and documentation by organizations such as the ERO merely reinforced this characterization of the black body.

These explicitly sexual sideshows stood in stark contrast to displays which, by exhibiting aesthetically unappealing women, hoped to deter thoughts of exotic sexual encounters with 'freaks'. Billed as the 'Ugliest Woman in the World', Mary Ann Bevan presented an 'inverted' beauty pageant (Garland-Thomson 1997: 71). In reality, her masculine and distorted appearance was brought on by acromegaly, or a pituitary tumour, which, at the age of 32, caused the abnormal bone growth of her face and limbs. Fat Ladies, who, because of their overabundance of flesh and maternal figures, were potentially the most erotically appealing 'freaks', were blatantly portrayed as eugenically unfit to produce their own children. Billed under cute names such as 'Dolly Dimples', 'Jolly Holly' or 'Baby Doll', these women, like Browning's female dancing pinheads, Zip and Pip, were constructed as perpetual children and, therefore, sexually, and eugenically, undesirable.

Similar to the Fat Ladies were the 'Midget Madames', such as Duchess Leona, Lady Little and Wee Jeanie. While, as noted by ERO eugenicists, these individuals suffered from inheritable hypopituitary disorders, they tended to be well proportioned and physically attractive. Spectators who visited Lilliputia, a Coney Island municipality of 300 midgets, were permitted to touch these 'cute' people. Consequently, in Lilliputia, the little person became a social, and potentially sexual, object, which disturbed eugenicists. To de-emphasize the compelling nature of this midget world and accentuate the eugenic danger of such 'freaks', ERO fieldworkers often photographed sideshow performers next to 'normal' individuals. Such images clarify the extent to which the coercive tactics of *negative eugenics* (race separation and the elimination of the abnormal) coexisted with the *positive eugenics* of selective breeding during the first few decades of the twentieth century.

Closely related to the sexual threat of the sideshow performer was the ability of the 'freak' to transcend social constructions of gender. Clearly, the full-breasted bearded lady challenged the bipolarity of the sexes. Bearded women with hair reaching to their ankles not only confronted gender distinctions but also crossed the borders which distinguished customary and uncustomary behaviour. Like masculine women such as Mary Ann Bevan, they presented forms of deviant gender expression which defied concrete categorization. Through their bodies, these women revealed the fluid nature of gender and the fallacies of anatomical construction. What was on the outside of their bodies – masculine faces – did not correspond to what was on the inside of their bodies – female sexual organs. These women were particularly problematic because they represented *gender-reversals*. In other words, their 'gender was at odds with their sex. Moreover, their apparent masculinity was at odds with their supposed femininity' (Halberstam 1998: 24).

The full-breasted bearded lady's ability, and inability, to transcend gender lines illustrated the extent to which these constructions were staged on, and derived meaning from, the female body. The spectacle of a masculine woman was problematic not only because it challenged the twentieth-century stress on female beauty but because it also implied impotent masculinity in a heavily patriarchal society. Because of its resemblance to the masculine form, the bearded face became a gendered object, which women such as Grace Gilbert used to negotiate power within the realm of the sideshow world. Not only did she, as a bearded woman, provide the abnormal state over which male eugenicists obsessed but she also presented a social and political challenge: she was a non-conformative woman in an age that stressed female docility and domesticity (Birke 1999: 46–47).

Because of their gender ambiguity, bearded ladies should have been socially, and eugenically, marked as unworthy of marriage and reproduction. What troubled eugenicists was most likely the fact that these bearded women, in spite of, or maybe because of, their deviant gender expression, had little trouble finding husbands. Rosine Muller, Annie Jones, Clementine Delait and Grace Gilbert were all married at least once. Lady Olga, who was billed as originating from an aristocratic plantation of the Old South, and was featured in the film *Freaks* as the mother of a gender-bending baby girl, whose father was a living skeleton, was married four times (Fiedler 1978: 147). The ability of these freakish women to marry and procreate, however, was not simply limited to bearded ladies. The famous conjoined twins, the Hilton sisters, were happily married to two separate men in *Freaks*. Mary Ann Bevan married and produced four 'normal' children. Midget men and women also found spouses and, in some cases, produced children who, ironically, if it were not for their unfit heritage, could have been poster children for the ERO's Fitter Family Contests.

By 1935, the year in which the last Coney Island photographs were taken, the heyday of eugenics research at Cold Spring Harbor had come and gone. As funding subsided and new benefactors refused to donate to an organization which, up to that point, had done little to improve the human condition, Davenport began to spend less and less time at the ERO, opting, instead, to explore the lecture circuit. Evidence of serious methodological flaws in their research, and Laughlin's exploitation of 'data' to illustrate the genetic threat of immigrants, did not help the ERO's reputation. The horrific Nazi abuse of eugenics theory proved to be the death-knell of the American movement: the ERO curtailed its research in 1939 and permanently closed its doors in 1944.

Nevertheless, Cold Spring Harbor Laboratory still struggles with its eugenics legacy. Initially, the institution's ambivalent attitude towards explaining its eugenics activities stemmed from the fact that the scientists involved with this movement genuinely believed they were fostering public good. While it is true that eugenicists such as Davenport and Laughlin were preaching the socially sanctioned, 'progressive' idea that science could solve many of the complex problems facing American society, they were undeniably scrutinizing, classifying and marginalizing the less fortunate with a sinister agenda in mind (e.g. compulsory sterilization, which they were able to implement on over 60,000 'degenerate' Americans during the first half of the twentieth century). In the end, however, they did not succeed in perpetuating the power and cultural hegemony of 'eugenically fit' WASP America. All that remains of their efforts are the texts, notes and enduring images of the Coney Island sideshow performers whom they unsuccessfully tried to eliminate.

Notes

1   My thanks go to Professors Gene Lebovics and Ruth Cowan for their help with this work. Cold Spring Harbor Laboratory maintains a website documenting its involvement in the eugenics movement: http://www.eugenicsarchive.org/eugenics/list_topics.pl Much of my research is derived from this website, especially its images of Coney Island 'Circus Performers'. I suggest pairing the reading of this article with a visit to the website, which also contains images of ERO fieldworkers, eugenicists, 'fit' families, and other historical documents, which will help illuminate and contextualize my research.

2   In turn-of-the-twentieth-century America, terms like 'freak' and 'monstrosity' were part of the national lexicon. While they were not as 'sensitive' as terms such as 'feebleminded', Americans used these words in everyday speech. Hence, my

use of these terms is not in any way pejorative; rather, I am using these terms in the same way in which lay people and scientists used them in the context of early twentieth-century discourse. Terms such as 'freak' and 'monstrosity' are currently being reclaimed by some members of the disability movement, just as the word 'queer' has been reclaimed by the gay and lesbian movement to denote difference and diversity. For more information on language, please consult Fiedler (1978).

3 This quotation comes from the introduction of the film *Freaks*.

4 It is unclear whether or not eugenicists were aware of this racial role-playing, or if they considered the possibility in their analyses. What is clear, however, is that the media's exposés of these impostors helped discredit the ERO's eugenics research, which ultimately contributed to the demise of the entire movement.

25

Africans in America: African Villages at America's World's Fairs (1893–1901)

ROBERT W. RYDELL

The history of African involvement in America's world's fairs is best understood in terms of efforts by people of colour generally to negotiate the terms of their representation at expositions that were intended to propagate ideologies of racism and imperialism. To be sure, world fairs were sites of exploitation, but they were also sites of contestation and collaboration – a range of responses consistent with the range of responses of indigenous people around the world who lived as subjects of Western imperial powers. If world fairs were human zoos, or 'iron cages of race', then it is imperative to remember that people put on display as anthropological 'specimens', or people who put themselves on display as performers, consistently looked back at world fair audiences and struggled to make meaning for themselves and for world fair visitors (Takaki 1979; Rydell 1984 [1974]).

That world fairs were agents of Western imperialism is well known. Beginning with the 1851 Great Exhibition at the Crystal Palace in London and continuing well into the twentieth century, the nation-states that hosted world fairs and participated in them regarded expositions as primary instruments for advancing colonialism abroad and for winning public support at home for specific imperial actions and policies. What is less well known is that world fairs, especially in the Victorian era, were primary venues for propagating a host of diseases associated with imperialism, in particular measles and smallpox. At most American fairs held between 1876 and 1909, indigenous 'performers' from around the world, especially people denoted 'Eskimos', were exhibited in horrifying conditions. In Chicago, they were forced to perform in the heat of the summer in sealskin suits. In Buffalo, they were forced to live in a stockyard while their village was under construction. In Seattle, they were forced to live in a cold-storage warehouse to help them acclimatize to Seattle's weather conditions. The result for the Inuit was disease, especially measles, that killed several performers at each of these fairs.

More devastating was the smallpox outbreak at the 1893 fair. In its wake, at least 3,000 people died.

Rethinking International Exhibitions

Thinking of world fairs, or other human zoos, as disease environments is important, given recent tendencies in scholarship to treat world fairs as theatre settings, with performers who entertained crowds. The point is simple: if fairs were like theatres, they were also unlike them in important ways.[1] Another facet of world fairs that makes them highly unusual performance sites is that at the fairs, individual performers, if that is the best way to regard them, especially if they were indigenous people, were the objects of horrific forms of medical intervention. For instance, following the example of French anthropologist Georges Cuvier, who removed Saartjie Baartman's genitals for study and preservation at the Musée de l'Homme in Paris, American physical anthropologist Ales Hrdlicka removed the brains from several Filipinos who died at the 1904 Louisiana Purchase Exposition in St Louis, and sent them to the Smithsonian Institution for examination and preservation. If this was theatre, this was theatre with a vengeance (see Rydell 1984 [1974]: 164–66).

These conditions of display and performance were important for Africans as well. As was the case with Filipinos and Chinese, who travelled great distances to and from world fair cities, Africans sometimes died en route. Once at world fairs they, too, had to combat the absence of proper sanitation facilities (the famous Midway Plaisance at the 1893 fair reportedly lacked any toilets for public use) and struggle for proper food. At the 1901 Pan-American Exposition in Buffalo, the Midway was layered with a coating that gave off a foul smell probably because it came from the slag produced by local smelters. Furthermore, there was a terrible incident concerning an infant who died at the Buffalo fair. The corpse was taken to the hospital, but, for some reason, was left in the vehicle. When cleaning crews found it, they threw the corpse in the trash. Ultimately, the coroner rescued it for examination, but not before extraordinary pain and suffering was endured by family members (Leary and Shones 1998: 104). To be sure, we know very little about the disease environments of these fairs, but it is certain that they posed public health risks to visitors and indigenous people alike.

There are other aspects of these performance sites that need to be considered. First, the people brought to perform and/or to be displayed at the fairs had little input into how their villages were located and built. Second, they had little, if any, input into how performances were scripted. Indeed, in the case of the Africans, contracts with the owner of the African concessions at the Chicago and Buffalo fairs made clear that the Africans were expected to 'present the racial peculiarities and customs [of their tribes]'. Third, for the performers, there was no going home after the day's performance concluded. Dwellings built within the village encampments for indigenous people were open to visitors who could examine, study and, on occasion, prod with sticks those who participated in village shows. Fourth, while most, if not all, of the performers were supposed to receive some kind of compensation, it is clear that show managers sometimes held money in 'trust'. For some performers, like the American Indians, an argument can be made that performing at fairs generated more income than working on reservations. But it remains to be proven, however, that payment promised by managers was actually received by the performers. Furthermore, it is clear from the entrepreneur Xavier Pene's payment ledgers that his performers were not exactly paid a fair wage. Pene's 1893 concession earned approximately $90,000 for the concessionaire. His performers received about 150 francs (or about $30) per month. Fifth, there is evidence to suggest that some village performers along the Midway were prohibited from leaving the fairgrounds. The performers, in other words, were not free agents, even when on their own time. Finally, one should never forget the occasional episodes of violence that could be directed at the indigenous people at the fairs – for instance, the Filipinos at the 1904 St Louis fair who dated white women and were assaulted by members of local police and US military units stationed at the exposition. Whether Africans suffered similar hate crimes is not, as yet, clear (Moses 1996).

What is clear is that evidence exists to support the contention that ethnological villages at America's world fairs can be regarded as human zoos that enclosed performers in an 'iron cage of race' and often deprived them of their full agency as human beings. But at the same time, it is important to realize that, if these sites were human zoos, they were *not* 'total institutions' that can be likened to the extermination camps set up by the Nazis during the Second World War. The African villages at the 1893 and 1901 fairs are cases in point.

The Dahomean village at the 1893 Chicago fair was inspired by the colonial villages that had been created for the 1889 Paris Universal Exposition and fuelled by accounts in the popular press of Stanley's search for Livingstone and of Richard Burton's tales of fierce Dahomean 'Amazon women'. After receiving two proposals for an African village concession, the exposition authorities settled on the one proposed by Xavier Pene, a shadowy imperial entrepreneur who owned several small plantations in Dahomey and who saw a pathway to fame, and possibly wealth, through the management of African shows, which had been gaining popularity across Europe. Pene proposed a concession that, according to the contract he received, would present a 'faithful' representation of a Dahomean village with at least 60 inhabitants, including a 'king or chief', who would perform religious ceremonies and military exercises on a daily basis. Pene succeeded in finding 67 Africans to journey to Chicago for his village. The exposition authorities located it at the extreme end of the Midway Plaisance, as part of the outdoor anthropological lessons presented at the fair, in order to reinforce the distance between the 'savagery' that was supposed to be represented in the concession and the 'civilization' that was supposed to be represented in the fair's main buildings, dubbed the 'White City' and located some distance away. Popular accounts in the press and in novels written about the fair made it clear that the African village succeeded in reinforcing dominant white supremacist attitudes about blacks. 'The habits of these people are repulsive', declared the author of one guidebook, 'they eat like animals and have all the characteristics of the very lowest order of the human family' (Rydell 1999). Pene apparently made the performers he managed dance while drinking from pint beer bottles.

The fundamental ideological structures of the Darkest Africa village at the 1901 Buffalo fair replicated the Chicago example, which is not surprising since, once again, Pene held the concession. This time Pene secured an endorsement from the Buffalo Museum of Natural History and boasted that he had a commission from the Smithsonian Institution, though no corroborating evidence of the last claim has been found. Shortly after the fair opened, Pene brought between 70 and 98 Africans to Buffalo, and they once again met with overwhelming hostility in the press. 'Nothing else I have ever seen conveys such an impression of wild savagery', declared one educator in the pages of the *New York Times*. Housed in a compound that was next to the 'Darkness and Dawn' concession and not far from a concession featuring a trained chimpanzee described as 'The Missing Link', Africans were once again demeaned and relegated to the shadows of the world's progress as projected by the fair (see Rydell 1984 [1974]: 126–53).

Beyond Human Zoos: Motivations of the Exhibited

If ever there existed human zoos, surely the African shows at these two fairs serve as prime examples. But, while the analogy may be apt, it is also incomplete. The reasons are several. First, there is no evidence that the Africans were brought to either fair against their will. Second, although they were relatively powerless, they were not completely so. For instance, at the 1893 fair, where the Africans had to parade up and down the Midway in a daily parade of 'ethnological types', the African women were heard to shout in their own language: 'We have come from a far country to a land where all men are white. If you will come to our country we will take pleasure in cutting your white throats.' Third, we need to know much more about the motives that propelled the Africans to travel to the United States. One of the performers, a man by the name of John Tevi, used his experiences at the fairs to propel him and his family into organizing their own African shows. Although many of the details of his life are not yet known, Tevi's career allows us to explore little-known areas of American society and to gain insights into the complexities African shows posed for Africans themselves (Scott 1991: 297–98).

Like Xavier Pene, John Tevi's life is shrouded in a great deal of mystery. We have no exact birth or death dates for him and it is unclear exactly where he was born. But, unlike Pene, who left behind only the faintest of traces, Tevi at least tried to make some sense of his life through a pamphlet entitled *A Tour Around the World and the Adventures of Dahomey Village* (1912).[2]

How should we understand Tevi's life and involvement with the exhibition culture of the late Victorian era? There are several, probably overlapping ways of understanding Tevi's quite extraordinary life. First, there are points of comparison between Tevi and the Sioux religious leader Black Elk, who travelled to Europe with Buffalo Bill's Wild West show. Black Elk makes clear that he was interested in finding out about the sources of power that underlay American – and by extension, English – society. The exhibition circuit provided an opportunity for doing just that. And, I think, there is good reason to believe that Tevi was deeply interested in learning about American society and about the world. Very few Americans, or Europeans for that matter, could boast of a life that took them across the West Coast of Africa, through the heart of Europe, and several times across the United States. Second, Tevi, in addition to learning about the West, may well have been inter-ested in educating white audiences about Africa. He may well have taken to heart the educational claims of world fair promoters and tried, through various artefacts, such as throwing knives, ritual masks, axes and magnificently carved ivory tusks, to give Americans some insights into African cultures. Third, Tevi, like Xavier Pene, was an entrepreneur interested in making money. While there are no precise figures about Tevi's earnings, he certainly earned more money in show business than he would have earned as an indigenous labourer along the West Coast of Africa. Fourth, given the levels of violence in French West Africa and the Congo, Tevi may have seen an opportunity for himself and for his family to escape the ravages of war and explore alternative possibilities for the future. Fifth, to the extent that travel enhanced his prestige and status at home, Tevi may well have seen through the bars of the human zoo to greater possibilities beyond. Whether any of these explanations are correct is speculative, at least for now.

There is, however, another possible explanation for Tevi's involvement in world fairs and Wild West shows that is more troubling. This explanation holds that Tevi, like other world fair operatives, was complicit in the imperial strategies that world fairs were intended to promote. This explanation validates his agency and capacity for acting and thinking in his own self-interest, but calls into question the rightness of the decisions he made. We know from the involvement of other indigenous groups at fairs, and from the history of imperialism generally, that collaboration with imperial officers was both a survival strategy and a means of gaining revenge against one's internal enemies. At America's Victorian-era fairs, anthropologists relied on the active collaboration of particular Native Americans, especially Antonio Apache, to help them secure participants in their anthropologically validated displays. At the 1904 St Louis fair, the exposition authorities relied on the deployment of members of the Philippine Constabulary – the police and paramilitary forces that assisted the United States to suppress the Philippine Insurrection – to help them control nearly 1,000 Filipinos sent for exhibition in the Philippine Reservation at that fair. Within the United States, there were also African-Americans, notably Booker T. Washington and his lieutenants, who collaborated with Federal and state government officials to promote acceptance of social segregation. Plausibly, therefore, a case could be made that Tevi was simply a broker, a go-between, funnelling resources in the form of Africans and their cultural artefacts to an exhibition world that rested on an ideological assumption that a display of something called 'civilization' required a display of something else called 'savagery' (Rydell 1984 [1974]).

So how should we think about John Tevi? The pamphlet, mentioned above, that either he, or someone close to him, assembled from notes

and newspaper articles, provides some important clues, beginning
with its title, *A Tour Around the World and the Adventures of Dahomey
Village*. From this, it seems clear that Tevi identified himself squarely
in a tradition of travel-writing that includes countless books generated
by tourists and explorers who had visited every corner of the globe in
the late nineteenth century. By Western standards, Tevi's pamphlet is
a poorly organized and disjointed presentation, but it may well reflect
the synchronous sense of past and present that is reflected in spiral
narratives carved into the ivory tusks on display at the Buffalo fair. The
pamphlet presents information about Africa, about his own Christian faith, a chronology of African history, information about different
regions of Africa (probably written by someone else, perhaps Pene), the
names of individual Africans who participated in the 1901 fair, accounts
of Tevi's multiple travels across the United States, including notice of
his appearances at world fairs, museums, amusement parks, and of his
participation in Buffalo Bill's Far West and Pawnee Bill's Far East shows
that travelled across the USA in the first decade of the twentieth century.
The pamphlet was assembled later, perhaps for purposes of sale at the
Wild West shows in which he participated.

Partly educational, partly reflective, partly status-enhancing, *A Tour
Around the World* offers evidence that would support the argument that
African village shows are best understood in terms of performance and
of the ability of Africans to make meaning for themselves. In addition,
there is incontrovertible evidence that Tevi and his troupes should be
regarded as among the most widely travelled Africans of their age.
There are, however, currents in the pamphlet's river of words that make
me suspicious about the completeness of this reading. For example,
we learn next to nothing about the conditions endured or enjoyed by
the Africans on their voyages to and from the United States: we learn
next to nothing about the treatment of the Africans who performed at
world fairs and Wild West shows, and nothing at all about the responses
of audiences to the African shows. Reading silences is always a tricky
business, but the silences on these matters are troubling. There are
also several passages in the pamphlet where Tevi seemingly valorizes
the superiority of whiteness and sings the praises of Christianity, thus
giving the vaguest of hints that he might well have been complicit in
advancing the 'civilizing' agendas of European and American imperialists at the expense of Africans.

So how should we understand Tevi? My take on him is as follows.
Tevi was multicultural to the core, an emigrant and an immigrant in
an era that witnessed massive population shifts from the eastern to the

western hemispheres. Furthermore, in an age that witnessed the birth of modern nationalism in Europe and the United States, Tevi leapfrogged to the postmodern future by assuming a trans-national identity, by becoming a showman who thought he could represent a proto-pan-African identity through his village exhibitions. There is no doubt that he was fully capable of negotiating contracts and multiple identities for himself across different national contexts as he criss-crossed oceans and continents. Unlike his contemporary, the African Ota Benga, who exhibited himself in multiple human zoo formats in the United States and later committed suicide, Tevi was more at home in the world. He actively constructed a stateless identity for himself, all the while encouraging at least two of his sons to study at the French colonial school in Dakar, with the result that one ultimately moved into a position of commanding influence as Togo's finance minister. To use the language of recent scholars, Tevi constructed a fluid, hybrid identity for himself that was perhaps both cause and consequence of his immersion in the world of African shows that tried to project a fictive, common identity on to all of Darkest Africa.

Was Tevi complicit in the exploitation of fellow Africans? To the extent that he aided and abetted Xavier Pene's shows, the answer, I think, has to be in the affirmative. But what about when he organized his own shows or when he subsumed these shows within Wild West entertainments? Were these dog-and-pony Africa shows put on by an African who was interested on civilizing Africa along European lines? Are they evidence that Tevi subscribed to the imperialistic messages being promoted through the Wild West shows? Or was he putting on his audiences, tantalizing them with imperial teasers to make money to support his family and advance the social position of his children? Joseph Conrad, in *Heart of Darkness*, found a great deal of complexity in the imperial encounter with Africa; we should expect no less as we explore the human zoo phenomenon. In thinking about human zoos, whether the emphasis belongs on the bars or on the spaces between them, still remains to be seen.

Notes

1 On the disease environment of one fair, see Rydell 1993.
2 Few copies of this pamphlet survive. I am grateful to Sonia Tevi and Kevin Smith for making this copy available to me and am grateful to both for their insights. I am especially grateful to Kevin Smith and the members of the planning team he assembled to work on the 'Clouded Mirror' exhibit at the Buffalo Museum of Natural Science (2001) that focused on the African Village that Pene and Tevi assembled for the 1901 Buffalo fair.

26

The 1904 St Louis Anthropological Games

FABRICE DELSAHUT

The cold gaze of science and the eyes of athletic folk will witness to-day and tomorrow one of the most unique meets the world has ever seen.

St. Louis Republic, 11 August 1904

After a nineteenth century which had been rich in human exhibitions in Europe and the United States (in particular, the Chicago World's Fair of 1893 and the Buffalo Pan-American Exposition of 1901), in 1904 the Americans organized a new World's Fair, the Louisiana Purchase Exposition[1] at St Louis (Missouri), to coincide with the Olympic Games. The founder of the modern games, Pierre de Coubertin, had been concerned about the success of the organization, impact and originality of this American Olympiad, and he was proved right. The sporting events were spaced across more than four and a half months, lost in the chaos of the fair. What was more, two weeks before the Olympic Games began, 'Anthropology Days' were held, involving special competitions for those whom the xenophobic Americans of the time considered to belong to a lower order of humans.

Here, members of the Crow, Sioux, Pawnee, Navajo and Chippewa tribes, other peoples from the United States, Ainus from Japan, Cocopas from Baja, Syrians from Beirut, Patagonians from South America, Zulus and Pygmies from Africa, and Filipinos, Moros, Negritos and Igorots were divided in to eight different cultural groups.[2] About 100 of these 'strange' competitors, drawn from 2,000 'natives' on show at the Louisiana Purchase Exhibition, would compete in the 'savage' Olympics.[3]

In 1903, William J. McGee, the First President of the American Anthropological Association, was invited to create and administer the anthropological section of the exhibition. With the use of 'life and movement' exhibits he hoped that direct contact between Americans and 'native peoples' would provide the best 'antidote to hostility and defiance between individuals and peoples'. He also wanted to show the importance of anthropological knowledge and he did all he could to ensure the development of such knowledge during these days. In Nancy Parezo's view, he had a quite different approach towards indigenous peoples: 'his goal was to visualize unilinear evolution, fight stereotypes about indigenous peoples and gather in one place Native peoples so that American and European scientists could extend their knowledge of race through systematic first-hand observations, anthropometric, and ethnographic studies' (Parezo 2005).

The idea of the Special Olympics was suggested to McGee by John E. Sullivan, secretary to the powerful and influential Amateur Athletic Union, who had been appointed head of the fair's Department of Physical Culture, and Director of the Games. He perceived the various press articles praising the physical attributes of the natives as a direct threat to the very existence of his department and a possible challenge to the supposed natural athletic superiority of white American sportsmen. Sullivan's proposal was a timely one for McGee, who was looking for new areas in which to conduct anthropometric experimentation. For Sullivan, these Special Olympics would allow the facts of the matter to be revealed and, above all, they would serve as an indirect advertisement for the *real* Olympic Games.

The anthropological athletic meeting in fact echoed the events of the Louisiana Purchase Exposition: as an arena in which the 'exotic' Other was constructed; as a space for the theorization of racial hierarchies; and as the place where such inequalities were brought out, thereby designating peoples as 'colonized' or 'colonizable'. Although the declared objective was to test the true physical capacities of the 'natives', a close examination of contemporary documents reveals an underlying intention to demonstrate to the world in no uncertain terms the superiority of the 'white race' over ethnic minorities. This fitted the expectations of a segregationist America and the Eurocentric views of race of the turn of the century. Anthropological thought thus distributed the 'ethnic races' on the evolutionist scale. It is revealing, in this case, that a place had recently been allocated to 'American Indians'. Sport, as the cultural product of the dominant nations, became, in this context, the instrument of a highly significant graded pattern of socialization.

The Special Olympics are now part of the history of sport. The different presidents of the IOC would, in the decades which followed, be eager to present the Anthropology Days as an unfortunate moment in the history of the Olympic movement. Nevertheless, at the beginning of the twentieth century, they corresponded fully to the contemporary view of the native populations, and they stand as a perfect example of the racial views which were then current in the movement.

Games within Games

Responsibility for the organization of the Anthropology Days was given to the Departments of Anthropology and Physical Culture, along with the Chicago Field Museum. The human sciences were beginning to make their presence felt, and anthropology, in particular, was still a young discipline which needed more data based on direct observation 'on the ground'. In the nineteenth century, fieldwork had been of secondary importance, and it was the theoretical work of ethnologists based on second-hand information drawn from travellers and missionaries which occupied the centre stage. The pioneering work of Carl Lumholtz, and, after him, Frank Boas, offered new horizons which were no doubt useful to the organizers of these games. Anthropology was largely based on anthropometric measurements, which would be both used and abused by the resident scientists throughout the exposition. On the basis of these biomechanical observations and measurements, fantastic theories would be constructed, at the exhibition and later on.[4] Dr McGee's scientific credentials provided essential authority to the exercise. Science would, in any case, play an important role throughout the Anthropology Days, being part of a strategy on the part of the organizers and the press to provide reassurance for the spectators. According to Parezo 'the results of these athletic events were transformed into a so-called "scientific" conclusion about the superiority or inferiority of different groups of peoples that was transmitted to the press and accepted by countless Americans, reinforcing their preconceptions' (Parezo 2005).

On the question of sport, Sullivan introduced his own ideas, which bore little or no resemblance to the European interpretation of the Olympic principle. A sporting awareness based on nationhood took shape during the Anthropology Days and, later, the Olympics. The former comforted the white race concerning its athletic abilities, while the latter event confirmed American dominance of the sporting field and, by extension, of the entire world. Lew Carlson has demonstrated the long process of 'sportification' of American society (Carlson 1989). When this young and turbulent nation first came into being, sport was not considered to be a divine blessing. According to the ascetic moral code of the theocratic leaders of New England, the only way to please and serve the Lord was to work and confront hardship. To take the easy route of games was to follow the Devil's path to laziness and idleness. The believer, guided by the Holy Spirit, should not submit to chance, which was often associated with sporting results. All forms of games were therefore banned in Connecticut and Massachusetts.

In the nineteenth century, a change in values, demographic move-ment, and technological developments affected the American way of life. There was a general relaxation of puritanical principles, and the loss of belief in the power of hard work gave entertainment a new legiti-macy, especially for the rapidly expanding urban population. While the physical benefits of exercise were emphasized from the Civil War onwards, certain figures began to attribute patriotic and democratic values to sport. In 1896, the national leader, Henry Cabot Lodge, would declare to the students of Harvard: 'The time given to athletic contests and the injuries incurred on the playing field are part of the price which the English-speaking race has paid for being world conquerors' (1989: 20). Thirty years later, General MacArthur, head of the American Olympic delegation, would announce: 'nothing has been more charac-teristic of the genius of the American people than their genius for athletics' (1989: 20).

These days in 1904 would reinforce the link between anthropology and physical culture within the strange two-headed organization which ran them. This double organization led to a number of ambiguities regarding the analysis of results. Two lines of thought ran through the series of trials. For Sullivan, the trials were intended to disprove claims concerning the physical abilities of the 'savages', which he considered to be ill-founded and to preserve the integrity of the Olympic Games. For him, the predictable failures of the indigenous sportsmen would prefigure the success of the American athletes in the main Games.[5] For McGee, it was essential to wait for the outcome. If the natives had the potential for true physical prowess, only anthropology and its various areas of research was in a position to measure and study it.

Whether in the grandiose context of the exposition or the more intimate frame of the sporting events, the organizers took constant care to confirm and even to justify a developing American imperialism by all possible means. The America of 1904 was a nation which was confi-dent in its 'manifest destiny'.[6] The Americans, with President William McKinley at their head, saw their victory in the Spanish American war as a manifestation of divine intervention.[7] The sociologist Franklin H. Giddins, from Columbia University, claimed that the victorious battle of Manila Bay was the most important historical event since the victory of Charles Martel in 732 because 'the great question of the twentieth century is whether the Anglo-Saxon or the Slav is to impress his civiliza-tion on the world' (Carlson 1989: 24).

The sciences were called on to make their own contribution to this process, not least through the new scientific field proposed by McGee:

anthropogenics. This would justify the aims of the imperial mission and would allow the new ideology of 'raciology' to locate each race in the human series. In the face of this, the tribes from the Philippines had great difficulty in expressing their gratitude to the New World. The Negritos rejected any sort of cooperation with the scientists, refusing, among other things, to compete in an archery event because such weapons were unknown to them. In the opinion of the anthropologists, all 'primitives' used bows and arrows.[8] They also refused to allow casts to be made of their heads by the New York Natural History Institute, despite the promise of a dollar for each cast. The *St. Louis Republican* saw this intransigence as the proof that the Negritos, unlike their Igorot neighbours, were 'the lowest type of inhabitants of the Archipelago' (*St. Louis Republican*, 11 August 1904).

The Anthropology Days would also allow scientists, following Professor McGee, to carry out psycho-physiological research on vision, hearing, smell, touch, pain thresholds and mental agility. Robert S. Woodworth, Professor of Psychology at the University of Columbia, would demonstrate in a report published in *Science* in 1910 that 'savages' had more acute sensory perceptions than Europeans (Hoberman 1999). Although most of these parameters clearly depended on the athletic ability of the subjects, the relationship between racial physiology and the physical aptitude of the subjects was not explored; the pitiful results of the competitions were considered by the observers of the time to speak for themselves.

In the world beyond the scientific investigations, symbolic and rhetorical flourishes were making their own, more trivial, contribution to the justification of racial hierarchies. These Olympic Games were the first at which gold, silver and bronze medals were awarded. But the organizers did not extend this honour to the 'savages' who participated in the Anthropology Days. Instead of a medal, the winners were presented with an American flag and a few dollars. Expressions such as 'barbarians', 'dog-eaters', 'primitive peoples', and 'strange races of men' were employed, while the use of 'hairy Ainus' and 'cannibals' to define subgroups of the African group[9] maintained social distance and a difference in status between the visitors and the performing peoples. According to Matti Goksyr: 'The people collected for the Anthropology Department in St. Louis were not exhibited as technicians or craftsmen, but simply as freaks' (Goksyr 1990: 300). Ota Benga, a young pygmy, was exposed accordingly as a missing link. The organizers, keen to undermine the myth of the natural athlete, were faced with the problem of the romantic perception of the 'noble savage', who lived by the laws of instinct and natural wisdom, adapting to different natural environments; contrasting with corrupt modern man, who was alienated by industrialization, which hampered the fulfilment of his desires. It was this ideal type which would, indirectly, compete against the 'white race' in the 1904 Olympics.

Proving White Superiority

'We have for years been led to believe from statements made by those who should know and from newspaper articles and books, that the average savage was fleet of foot, strong of limb, accurate with the bow and arrow and expert in throwing the stone, and that some, particularly the Patagonians, were noted for their great size and strength, and owing to the peculiar life that many have been called upon to lead they have been termed natural athletes. We have heard of the marvellous qualities of the Indian as a runner; of the stamina of the Kaffir, and the natural all round ability of the savage in athletic feats' (Sullivan 1905: 249). The clear intention of this report in the special Olympic number of *Spalding's Official Athletic Almanac* was to demonstrate that that the supposedly natural physical abilities of the different races should be tested scientifically, and to challenge the generally held belief that 'people of colour' had superior sensory and physical abilities through their participation in Anglo-American athletic events and in a few traditional sports of their own. The performances were then compared with those of white athletes.

The programme included two Anthropology Days. On the first, the participants competed among themselves, within predetermined tribal groups, in events drawn from the Olympic programme. From the outset it became clear that the results would be well below expectations. The 100-yard dash was won by George Mentz, who was presented as an 'Americanized Indian', in a rather poor time (11.4 seconds). Last in this race was Lamba, a 'Pygmy', in a time of 14.3 seconds. The author of the report commented, not entirely fairly, that the young African certainly lived an outdoor life, hunting, running, swimming, jumping and using the bow and the spear, and that this life might be described as 'naturally athletic', but that despite this, it took him more than 14 seconds to run 100 yards, a distance over which any American athlete would have beaten him with 40 yards to spare.

The second day showed the 'savages' in a better light, in that they were given the chance to show what they could achieve in some of their so-called 'ancestral practices'. The most remarkable performance was that of an Igorot from the Philippines, who climbed a 15-metre telegraph pole in 20 seconds. The audience was disappointed, though, by the javelin-throwing and the archery, which did not demonstrate the hypothetical abilities of 'savage peoples'. At the end of the day, the Cocopas from Mexico gave a demonstration of their game of Shinny, the predecessor of field hockey. But this was judged of little interest because there was no teamwork, instead showing what was seen to be a purely individual attempt on the part of the players. Last, the Pygmies resorted to their 'favourite past-time', a mud fight, which was compared with the snowball fights of American children. The demonstration was greatly enjoyed by the public and the skills of the participants in dodging, throwing and running were emphasized.

These tribal games thus served to demonstrate in no uncertain terms the shining superiority of the Caucasian race over ethnic minorities. The report in Spalding bears witness to this, despite a certain ambiguity, offering a real lesson in 'popular ethnography' (MacAloon 1981: 134). The performances in the different events, on the whole, were scoffed at when set against the expectations or, rather, the fantasies of the organizers of the tribal games.[10] The Patagonians, whose size had led the observers to hope for exceptional performances in the shot put, produced 'such a ridiculously poor performance that it astonished all who witnessed it' (Sullivan 1905: 251). The report also emphasized that the American champion, Ray Ewry, jumped further without a run-up than any 'savage' who was allowed one. The mediocre feats of the Ainus led to a comment in the report that they still had much to achieve in their physical development. The report adds: It can probably be said, without fear of contradiction, that never before in the history of sport in the world were such poor performances recorded for weight-throwing' (1905: 253). Sullivan could not find words strong enough to express his disappointment, not in the results, which he expected, but in the attitudes of the natives during the events. Nancy Parezo summarizes this as follows: 'Natives certainly did not regard the competitions with the seriousness that Sullivan imbued his "sacred" games and the cult of strenuous living' (Parezo 2005).

William McGee disputed the validity of this condemnation. He explained that these 'counter-performances' were due to the native competitors' 'lack of education' and even lack of previous practice in the different sports, but these explanations failed to satisfy either the observers or the public. At the same time, he underlined the extreme friendliness of the Ainus ('the most polite savages the author has ever encountered', he wrote), and their active participation in all the events.

By contrast, the Pygmies, whose participation was obtained in exchange for a few watermelons, did not receive the same glowing report, being presented as mischievous, taking nothing seriously other than their own traditional sports.

McGee also suggested that the natives did not participate fully in the contests for the simple reason that 'many of them did not perhaps know that they were expected to do their very best' (Sullivan 1905: 257). The report underlined, equally, that another day would have been necessary to allow the various translators time to explain the events to the participants. The heats of the 100 yards illustrate this. The start was signalled by a pistol shot and the finishing line was marked by a white tape stretched across the track at chest height, which must be broken by the winner. It took courage and patience for the officials to explain to the eight (or ten) runners that they should start off when they heard the gun and should keep running until they had passed the tape. The report even noted that Dr Martin Delaney, of the University of St Louis, had to demonstrate what to do to the competitors.

A lack of motivation, moroseness, lack of understanding of the events, insufficient or non-existent training, and compulsory participation may all have contributed to the performance of the athletes. It remains the case, though, that these factors, while they were identified by everyone, were sidelined after the event in order to support the theory of white racial superiority. The manipulated results proved 'conclusively that the savage has been a very much overrated man from an athletic point of view' (1905: 257). And Sullivan stated further: 'From a scientific standpoint, it proves conclusively that the average savage or foreigner is not equal to the white man. The savages are not even strong, to say nothing of skill' (St Louis 1904a: 50). The lesson was striking: 'Scientific men will refer to this event for many years to come. Lecturers and authors will in the future please omit all reference to the natural athletic ability of the savage unless they can substantiate their alleged feats' (Sullivan 1905: 259).

Although the conclusions drawn by Sullivan and McGee were identical, the routes by which they arrived at them were nevertheless quite different. The general context, their responsibilities and their loyalty to their own departments could only lead to different approaches to the Anthropology Days. Sullivan was incapable of thinking beyond the framework of sport, and he linked all the decontextualized physical performances of the native competitors with the sporting performances of his own beloved Olympics. In the first instance, he criticized McGee, arguing that the latter's theories had no scientific basis and only misled the spectators. As for the 'savages', he concluded that it was impossible for their performance to be better, given that they had failed to inherit either the intellectual abilities linked to understanding or the physical abilities linked to adaptation to the environment. McGee took a more moderate approach and, for a time, shared the views of Stephen Simms, the curator of the Field Museum whose task it was to announce the events each day, criticizing, in particular, the conditions under which the events took place and their integrationist character.

It can be noted, though, that the performances of the Native Americans were particularly highlighted and the use of the term 'Americanized Indian' to refer to them is revealing in this respect (see Magnaghi 1983–84). This echoed the arrangement of a stand at the exposition, where tribes were scattered around a hill in their natural habitats. At the summit of the hill there was a school filled with Native American children. The organizers could not have found a more obvious metaphor for the evolutionist and integrationist theories of the time. The native peoples of the United States were at the top of the hill, on their way to civilization, and visitors could observe 'the "civilizing" effects of Christianity, nationalism, and the Protestant work ethic amongst native children' (Troutman and Parezo 1998: 20).

The Impact of the Tribal Games

The Anthropology Days and, after them, the Olympic Games, were nationally influential in the United States, providing reassurance to an emerging world power. Nowadays, since the break-up of the Soviet Union, geopolitical experts rightly emphasize the loss of balance in world power. There is no super-power against which the United States can pit its athletes. Through the use of peace-making missions, they are now free to defend their interests anywhere in the world. This situation might appear to be entirely new, but its origins are to be found in the history of the United States. At the beginning of the last century, a strong feeling of superiority already influenced the organization of major international shows such as those in Chicago in 1893, Buffalo in 1901, and St Louis in 1904.

These events were seen as an opportunity to celebrate the power of science and technology. At their best, they reflected certain values of the young American democracy, such as the spirit of enterprise, curiosity, intelligence and success. At worst, they were part of a new ordering of the world and its peoples, defining what was superior and what was uncivilized. This strongly hierarchical vision of the world obviously justified internal segregationist policies and colonial aspirations. The Anthropology Days would make the American people aware that it was now the usual way of things to impose their own paradigm throughout the world, and that it was even a duty to do so. The American sporting success at the Olympic Games, following on from the Anthropology Days, nourished the craze for national sporting activities. It also allowed the International American Committee to extend its influence over future Olympic activities, especially in the choice of events.

We should certainly not exaggerate the influence of this interracial athletic spectacle beyond the United States, but it certainly allowed the construction of a certain perception of alterity. It brought a scientific legitimacy to racism and would long serve as a point of reference. These tribal games also fed the popular imagination and, as Allen Guttmann has underlined, legitimized colonialism (Guttmann 1984: 20). 'The amusing feature' of the 'Little Men' involved in a mud fight which was generally reported by the press (*St. Louis Republic*, 11 August 1904: 5), constituted an astonishing display which led both American and European spectators to feel morally justified in bringing modern sports (along with the rest of civilization) to the rest of the world.

The Anthropology Days were used for decades as a demonstration of white racial supremacy. A Swedish sporting encyclopaedia of 1943 referred to the results of them, concluding that 'it is not possible to make sports stars out of Africa Negroes'. The German researcher Arthur Grix had earlier taken a similar view on the lack of tactical intelligence of the Tarahumaras from Mexico (Goksyr 1990: 303). But it is the prophetic comment of Coubertin which has entered the official history of the Games: 'As for that outrageous charade, it will of course lose its appeal when black men, red men and yellow men learn to run, jump and throw, and leave the white men behind them.' In the final analysis, the Western images of distant peoples were constructed on difference, through colonial wars, evangelizing missions, the romantic concept of the 'noble savage' and other shows involving human zoos. By confirming difference, the Anthropology Days influenced popular ideas in a way which continues today, and is more widespread and insidious than we might think. The image of Eric Moussambani battling against the waters in the Homebush Bay Aquatic Centre at the Sydney Olympics in 2000 deeply divided sports enthusiasts.[11] For some he was the very picture of what is best in the Olympics: disinterested sportsmanship. But others saw him as mere entertainment. The press remarked cynically that the winner, the Dutchman Peter Van den Hoogenband, had covered twice the distance in a slightly quicker time. Here is an echo of the remark by the *St. Louis Globe-Democrat* that the Moros performance in swimming resembled 'ducks in the water'.

These Anthropology Days also served, after a fashion, to delay the access of minorities to the Olympic Games. Fine performances at the games by the 'half-civilized' were generally not mentioned, unlike those at the Anthropology Days. Following the research carried out at St Louis and the results of the Anthropology Days, the sporting ability of 'savages' remained an entirely marginal issue for many years.

Coubertin, who was at first unenthusiastic about the extension of athletic activities to the poorer classes of Western society and even more so about the 'savages' of the colonies, would later radically alter his opinion, declaring that the Olympic Games are the property of no single country or race and that all peoples should be admitted to them without debate. This view gradually spread but, as we know, this was in the context of a globalization of sport based on the quest for profits, and marked by a loss of diversity. Coubert's Olympic principles nevertheless survived beyond the games themselves. Certain so-called 'regional' sports have even survived without being subject to the control of the all-powerful International Olympic Committee. Banished from the temple, poorly represented or forbidden for political or economic reasons, the First Nations have redefined the essence of sport: sport without conscience is man's downfall.

This definition lies at the heart of indigenous sporting events in which traditional games allow cultural practices to be rediscovered or maintained. This core principle has led in recent years to the introduction of games events which are free of the taint of all media and commercial influence, for example the World Eskimo-Indian Olympics and the Amazonian Games, which offer an alternative approach derived from Coubertin's philosophy. In the face of international rejection, a new sports culture has been constructed from indigenous values. The minority games compensate for their absence from the Olympics, and the Olympic spirit reigns over the far north and the Amazon.

Notes

1 Celebrating the 1803 Louisiana Purchase, the exposition covered 486 hectares (1,200 acres) in the heart of St Louis and included more than 200 buildings. The event celebrated a glorious past, acknowledged the accomplishments of the present, and offered a glimpse into the possibilities of the future. Between 30 April and 1 December, 19,695,000 fair-goers experienced a living tribute to achievement and progress through working exhibits, inventions, and innovations.

2 The groups were Africans, Asians, Filipinos, Ainus, Tehuelche (or Patagonian) Indians, Cocopas, Pueblos and Americanized Indians.

3 As part of the festivities an exhibition on the Boer War was staged. Two members of the Tswana people, Lentauw (whose real name was Len Tau) and Yamasani (Jan Mashiani), who had joined the South African Boer War Exhibition Company in Pretoria, were invited to the exhibition and also to the Anthropology Days and the Olympic marathon.

4 On observing the lack of enthusiasm of the Native Americans who took part, a Yale geographer, Ellsworth Huntington, put forward a curious theory concerning the long Siberian migratory path. According to him, 'it is not improbable that long sojourns at way-stations on the cold, Alaskan route from central Asia may have weeded out certain types of minds. Perhaps that is why the Indian, though brave, stoical, and hard, does not possess the alert, nervous temperament which leads to invention and progress' (Huntington 1919). On the motivity of the Ainu, scientists attempted to demonstrate that their 'bodyward or centripetal movements' were strongly characteristic of a 'lowest' or 'vestigial culture'.

5 Of the 84 events which are generally agreed to have formed the Olympic programme, half included athletes only from the United States. Of the 681 athletes who attended the Olympic Games, 525 were Americans. The 156 others represented 11 different nationalities, the lowest number of competitors from nations other than the host nation in the entire history of the modern Olympic Games. The Americans managed to walk away with 79 gold medals out of the 94 available.

6 During the nineteenth century, the United States took the opportunity to extend their effective sovereignty from the Caribbean to the Pacific, considering it to be their 'manifest destiny' to control the continent from one Ocean to the other.

7 In military terms, the Spanish American war of 1898, despite its brevity, propelled the United States on to the world stage. The rapid economic growth which had followed the end of the Civil War turned the United States into a global power and many citizens thought that their country should be active beyond its borders.

8 One explanation for this is to be found in the theory of the American anthropologist Lewis Henry Morgan (1818–81), often considered to be the founder of the discipline because he was the first to conduct his work 'in the field'. This evolutionist theory distinguished a superior stage in the 'savage' state, characterized by the invention of the bow and arrow and wooden utensils, and the use of baskets woven from bark or reed. All these 'savage' characteristics were strongly represented and deployed in the course of the exhibition. The second factor which led to this assumption was the allegorical figure of the 'savage', whose characteristic accoutrements were his bow, arrows, feathers and even beads, which had been constructed by European travellers, who interpreted the new world they encountered through their own cultural reference points, among them, the writings of the Enlightenment.

9 One of the Africans was labelled 'Cannibal' by the organizers in the records of the 'Throwing baseball' event.

10 100-yard (90m) run, 16-pound (7.25kg) shot-put, 440-yard (400m) run, running broad jump, bolo throw, baseball throw, 56-pound (25kg) weight throw, 120-yard (110m) hurdles, throwing the ball for accuracy, 1-mile (1.6km) run, javelin (25 feet/7.5m), pole-climbing, running high jump, archery and tug of war.

11 At the 2000 Olympics, the swimmer from Equatorial Guinea completed his 100 metre freestyle race in 1 minute 52 seconds, alone in the pool after the elimination of his two rivals for false starts. He had not achieved the appropriate qualifying times, but obtained his place as the result of a rule which allowed competitors from developing countries to participate. Before arriving in Sydney, Eric Moussambani, who had learned to swim only eight months previously, had never even seen a 50-metre pool, having carried out his training in a 20-metre pool.

27

From the Diorama to the Dialogic: A Century of Exhibiting Africa at the Smithsonian Museum of Natural History

MARY JO ARNOLDI

Over the past two decades renewed scholarly interest in African material culture, in conjunction with critical histories of African museum displays, has generated a significant and growing body of literature. Scholars have addressed the life history of African objects in public collections, the politics of representation, the relations of power, and the historical practices which underlie the appropriation of African objects into Western collections and their subsequent recontextualization and interpretation in public displays (Arnoldi and Hardin 1996; Cannizzo 1989; Coombes 1994; Mack 1991; Schildkrout and Keim 1998; Vogel 1988). These studies of the history of anthropological representations of Africa and Africans in museum displays have analysed the concepts which frame these displays and the ways that these exhibits, as the public face of anthropology, have shaped the Western popular imagination about Africa.[1]

In analysing the relations of power and the politics of museum display, Ivan Karp noted: 'The sources of power are derived from the capacity of cultural institutions to classify and define peoples and societies. This is the power to represent, to reproduce structures of belief and experience through which cultural differences are understood' (Karp 1992: 1–2). Over the past century museums confidently and authoritatively proclaimed that their cultural exhibits were based on the most current anthropological thinking of the day. However, in most large museums, permanent exhibits remained on view over several generations. Whether because of a lack of money, of staff, or of the will to change, most major museums' anthropology exhibits have a lifespan that extends well beyond the viability and legitimacy of the anthropological theories they espouse.

The Smithsonian over this past century has suffered from this same inertia. Over the last 100 years there have been only two permanent exhibits which featured African objects at the Museum of Natural History. The first permanent exhibit was installed in the opening decades of the twentieth century. In 1922 it was modified, a portion of the original African section was removed, and a new exhibit was installed, which featured 2,700 Congo artefacts that were donated by the artist/collector Herbert Ward. The original ethnology exhibit and the 1922 Ward Congolese exhibit, which was installed in a separate gallery space adjacent to the older African displays, remained on view until the 1960s. In the 1950s the museum launched an ambitious programme to renovate its exhibits, and in the early 1960s it closed the old African exhibits and began planning the installation of a new permanent hall dedicated to African cultures. The new exhibit, 'The Cultures of Africa', was completed in 1967. It remained on view with few modifications for a quarter of a century, until it was dismantled in 1992.

The decision by the Natural History Museum to close The Cultures of Africa was the result of an increasingly vocal public criticism of this exhibit. The criticism began in the 1980s with groups of professional Africanists. In the early 1990s the critique gained public notoriety when local African and African-American communities began to register their displeasure with this exhibit through a well orchestrated letter-writing and media campaign. As public pressure mounted, the museum was shaken out of its inertia and complacency. In 1993 it moved to develop a new African exhibit (Kreamer 1997: 52–53). In his introduction to *Museums and Communities: The Politics of Public Culture*, Ivan Karp noted that 'museums are not exempt from history, and the communities that have been eliminated from museums or denigrated by them now insist that museums rectify their errors – errors that can be viewed in out-of-date-exhibit halls' (Karp 1992: 12). I had a very pragmatic and immediate interest in the history of the African exhibits at the Smithsonian National Museum of Natural History because of my curatorial involvement in the development of the new permanent exhibit, *African Voices*, which opened in December 1999.

The Department of Anthropology African Collections: 1867–1998

The first African collections came into the Smithsonian in the late 1850s and the museum continues to acquire objects into the present. Currently there are over 13,000 African objects in the anthropology collections at the Museum of Natural History. By comparison, the department's holdings in Native American objects numbers well over 100,000 objects. The largest single African collection is the Herbert

Ward collection of 2,714 Congolese objects that was donated to the institution in 1921.

Prior to the Ward donation in 1921, there were only 2,805 African objects on record comprising 173 accessions. Two-thirds of these accessions included fewer than ten objects, and there were only five accessions of more than 200 objects. Of these early accessions, 55 included objects from North Africa, Egypt and the Sudan; 29 were from West Africa (primarily Liberia); 25 were from Central Africa; 20 were objects from southern Africa, primarily South Africa, and 13 included objects from East Africa and Madagascar. The donation of the Ward collection in 1921 nearly doubled the number of African objects housed at the museum.

Objects came into the collections from a variety of sources. A number of the earliest accessions were objects from Liberia that had originally been donated to John Varden's Washington City Museum. These included African objects collected by, among others, Commodore Matthew Perry and Reverend Ralph Gurley. Between 1842 and 1845, Perry commanded a United States naval squadron that was assigned to patrol the West African Coast to seize illegal slaving vessels and return captives to Africa. Reverend Gurley was an agent for the American Colonization Society in Liberia and first visited the region in 1824. He donated a group of objects from Liberia to John Varden's Museum, which operated in Washington in the 1830s. The collections were transferred to the National Institute for the Promotion of Science in 1841 and, beginning in the late 1850s, the Institute's collections were given over to the Smithsonian.

Other early collections included those donated by members of the US Eclipse Expedition of 1889. This scientific expedition sailed to southern Africa aboard the USS *Pensacola* in October 1889 to record a total eclipse of the sun. While there observation of the eclipse was not successful, they did return with hundreds of ethnological objects from Sierra Leone, Ghana, Nigeria, the Congo, Angola and South Africa. Individual members of the expedition who donated objects to the museum included zoologist William Harvey Brown and the missionary and linguist Heli Chatelain.

Through this early period the donors to the collections included diplomats, military men, commercial agents, missionaries, biologists, ethnologists, and purveyors and collectors of ethnographic materials. Hoffman Philips, who had been the first American Consul to the court of Menelik II of Ethiopia, presented the museum with his collection of Ethiopian materials, which included, among other items, a number of painted scrolls. Emory Taunt and Richard Dorsey Mohun, two American commercial agents working in the Congo, made collections of several hundreds of Congolese objects for the museum. In the early 1890s the museum acquired the collection of Reverend E. H. Richards, which consisted of over 200 objects from Mozambique. In 1889 Talcott Williams, journalist and educator, made a collection of Moroccan musical instruments for the museum. He also donated utensils, pottery, tools and costumes.

The African collections were augmented by objects obtained from world fairs and expositions, including the 1876 Centennial Exposition in Philadelphia, the 1884 New Orleans Exposition, and the 1893 World's Columbian Exposition in Chicago. The Department of Anthropology also regularly engaged in the standard practice of exchanging objects with other museums and educational institutions. African objects were brought into the collections from American institutions including Oberlin College, the Cincinnati Museum and the Glenn Island Museum of Natural History, as well as from European museums such as the Trocadéro in Paris, the British Museum in London and the Völkerkunde Museum in Leipzig. In several of these transactions, the museum exchanged Native American objects for African objects.

Unlike fine arts museums, the collecting mandate for African ethnology was broad and included the full range of 'arts and industries of mankind'. African objects in the anthropology collections include textiles, costumes and jewellery, domestic objects such as furniture, pottery and baskets, and tools and equipment related to various local industries, such as metalworking and weaving, and items associated with animal husbandry, hunting and fishing. There are a number of weapons in the early accessions: the Ward collection, for example, consists of over 1700 spears, knives, arrows, etc. By comparison there is a relatively small number of carved masks and statues in the early collections.

Many of the early collections had little or no documentation associated with the objects. Over the last quarter-century, however, a greater emphasis has been placed on acquiring documented research collections. In the late 1950s, Dr Gordon Gibson was hired as the department's first Africanist curator. During his tenure in the department he made several field collections of Herero and Himba materials, and he sought out gifts of well-documented collections. He was involved in acquiring the Lamb collection of 1,500 West African textiles and looms. The Department of Anthropology and the Smithsonian's National Museum of African Art own the collection jointly. More recently, field collections of contemporary crafts from Niger and Kenya, industrial roller print textiles from West Africa, and recycled materials from West and East Africa have been added to the department's holdings.

Smithsonian Ethnology Exhibits: the Late Nineteenth Century to 1960

The museum's first ethnology halls included a small section devoted to Africa. During the late nineteenth century and well into the twentieth, ethnological research and exhibits in the anthropology department were in a large part shaped by the scientific philosophy of Otis T. Mason, the Museum's first curator of anthropology. Mason's early training was in the natural sciences and his subsequent approaches to ethnology were firmly rooted in its methods and theories.

Mason's system of museum classification was an elaboration of Gustav Klemm's Kulturgeschichte. Klemm's method was based on the natural sciences and it demanded first that a subject be analysed in all its developmental variety; from these particulars the larger historical picture – through the stages of savagery, barbarism and enlightenment – could be drawn (Hinsley 1981: 88). In Mason's version of the Leipzig model, his primary focus was on the notion of invention:

> Mason defined invention broadly: as changes in materials and processes; as modifications in structure and function of artifacts; as changes in the inventor of society. The concept referred, in fact, not merely to mechanical devices but to cultural processes. [...] All people invented, but primitive man saw dimly and thought imperfectly [...]. This vision produced an ambivalent judgment in which such peoples received credit as human participants, but clearly inferior ones. (Hinsley 1981: 88–89)

Although Mason's strongly developmental scheme and his biologically inspired belief in the underlying unity of all objects was already being seriously challenged by Boas in 1887 (Jacknis 1985: 77–80), on an 1889 visit to Europe he nevertheless found confirmation of his theories and methods in the Pitt Rivers Museum in Oxford, at the Musée Guimet in Paris and in Dresden (Hinsley 1981: 109). Mason's developmental scheme continued for decades to be an important influence in the ethnology exhibits at the Smithsonian.

On this same European tour, Mason was also influenced by other approaches to exhibiting that he saw in various European museums and at the Paris World Fair. Mason incorporated some of these ideas in the plan for the Smithsonian's American Indian exhibits at the 1893 Chicago World's Columbian Exposition. In collaboration with William Henry

Holmes, anthropologist and artist, and with advice from the Bureau of American Ethnology, Smithsonian anthropologists constructed a series of dioramas of American Indian groups based on 'geo-ethnic' units. These life-sized and realistically rendered mannequins represented specific groups of American Indians engaged in various activities in daily life or ritual in the appropriate environmental settings. These life group dioramas enjoyed a tremendous popular success at the Chicago World Fair, and they subsequently became one of the key features of government anthropology exhibits and were quickly embraced by other American museums (Hinsley 1981: 109; Jacknis 1985: 81–82).

   In 1902 Holmes published an article in which he laid out the organization and philosophy of the Smithsonian's ethnology exhibits. According to Holmes, the arrangement was by geo-ethnic units and the centre-piece of each section was a family life-group diorama. These family groups were purported to be representative of 'primitive' people prior to contact with civilization. Most showed 'families' or groups of people of different genders or ages engaged in some characteristic activity illustra-tive of their lives. Extending out from the central diorama on each side were cases organized in parallel rows, in which objects illustrating the arts, industries and history were arranged in descending order of their importance to the culture being featured (Holmes 1902: 356–57). These early Smithsonian life groups were intended to link the prevailing ideas by Smithsonian anthropologists about environmentalism with theories of race and evolution. The implied standard of comparison was always contemporary Western civilization and the 'primitives' were carefully defined as developmentally inferior in every category.

   The African section contained only one diorama. This diorama featured a Zulu family that had been originally created by Smithsonian anthropologists for display at the 1915 Panama-Pacific International Exposition in San Francisco. Following the exposition it was reinstalled in the Smithsonian's permanent ethnology halls. The label that accom-panied the Zulu diorama made the theoretical linkage between environ-mentalism, race and evolution quite clear. It read: 'The Zulu-Kaffir and related Bantu tribes live in the semi-arid southern extremity of the African continent. They are physically strong and energetic and not as dark as the true Negro. In respect to military and social organization they are superior and in arts and industries compare favorably with other Africans. They depend upon maize and wild fruit principally for their vegetal food supply, and on cattle, goats, chickens and wild game for their animal food. The group shows a section of the house with a doorway; a fireplace on which a woman is cooking mush; a woman dipping beer from a large pottery jar; a woman from the field with a hoe; a water carrier poising her jar on her head; a man playing the marimba or xylophone; and a boy driving a goat. The group represents these people as they existed some years ago before they were affected by contact with white men' (National Anthropological Archives n.d.).

According to the department's exhibit plan, second in importance to the central life group dioramas were the miniature dioramas of dwelling groups. These miniatures were intended to illustrate key features of the environment and to illustrate types of housing and home arts and industries. Surrounding the model dwelling were cases consisting of objects intended to illustrate these activities. The label for the model Zulu dwelling read: 'Dwelling Group of the Zulu – South Africa. The Zulu are representative of the populous and powerful Bantu family. They live in a semi-arid country and subsist on maize, wild fruits, domestic animals and game. They inhabit well-planned villages under the rule of a chief. Their villages are circular and surrounded by a fence. The houses have dome shaped frames thatched with grass. The family occupations are carried on outside the houses. Storehouses, small houses for animals and other purposes are scattered among the dwellings. The Zulu make pottery, baskets, wooden vessels, brew beer and work iron into weapons and agricultural implements' (National Anthropological Archives n.d.).

Installed in the vicinity of the life-group diorama and the model dwelling was a single figure of a Zulu man. The label accompanying this mannequin read in part: 'their strong political and military organization and prowess in war have brought them prominently before the world'. It is noteworthy that several of the Zulu labels included descriptors like 'well-organized villages under the rule of a chief', and 'strong political and military organization' and 'prowess in war'. These descriptors alluded to the 1879 Zulu defeat of the British at Isandhlwana which was widely reported in the European and American press and contributed to the characterization of the Zulu in the popular imagination as a militaristic society and surprisingly worthy adversaries. While these descriptors played into certain tropes about the nature of 'savages', they also inadvertently undermined, without necessarily overcoming, these same tropes by highlighting the political and military sophistication of Zulu society.

Because the department's African collections were relatively small, seven single figures, which were created to represent different racial types in Africa, took the place of the fully fledged dioramas in the remaining African sections. Installed geographically from north to south, these figures included a Berber man and a Berber woman who were identified in the label as the white race; a Somali man identified as belonging to Hamitic stock; a Wolof Man and a Bambara man who were classified as Sudanese Negroes; a Chagga man and a Zulu man identified as Bantu stock. Clearly implied in the orientation from north to southern Africa in this installation was a racial hierarchy.

The life group dioramas and model dwellings which served as organizing features of the ethnology exhibits, however, did not overturn Mason's original taxonomic and developmental orientation to the study of material culture. As Hinsley notes: 'Although Mason to some extent transcended the bald evolutionism of the Klemm model of "Kulturege-schichte", the life groups orientation that he and Holmes pioneered in Washington served rather than questioned the superiority of Victorian American culture' (1981: 112).

The Installation of the Ward Congo Collection: 1922

In 1922 a section of the older African ethnology hall was removed to make room for a permanent exhibit of the Herbert Ward Congo collection (2,714 objects). This new display represented a shift in the style of ethnology exhibits, but not in their interpretative intent. The Smithsonian curators consciously worked to capture some of the drama that Herbert Ward had achieved in his private installation of his collection in Paris. To this end they hung curtains over the windows to recreate a sombre atmosphere evocative of a 'jungle'. They mounted antelope and elephant heads on the walls, surrounded by African weapons and other objects arranged in decorative patterns.

In Washington, however, museum curators separated the Congolese objects and the zoological specimens from Ward's bronze sculptures. The Congolese objects were organized by type and material in cases that ran around the perimeter of the exhibition space more closely in line with the taxonomic interests of the museum. The museum placed text labels in each of the cases for the edification and education of the public. The label text reinforced the visual relationships set up as typological developmental sequences. For example, one label, *Native Fetiches and Wood Carvings*, read:

> The African native displays much skill in carving wood. He does not hesitate to boldly attempt the fashioning of the human form in his fetiches and this barbaric sculpture achieves what to him are satisfying works of art and which convey their interest to civilized man. Stools, headrests, and domestic utensils are worked with a view to pleasing forms and decoration. (NAA, Smithsonian Institution).

The 19 bronze sculptures representing Congolese figures played a major role in this exhibit (Arnoldi 1997). Rather than being integrated with the African objects, as they had been in Ward's Paris display, the bronzes were all positioned in the open space within the gallery, forming a secondary exhibition within the larger display. Without a tremendous leap of the imagination, the bronzes could be comfortably read as 'life groups'. Although the Ward sculptures are self-consciously 'European Fine Art' and clearly not ethnographic 'life-groups', they do share a formal and philosophical kinship with the Smithsonian's 'life-groups', the realism of which is equally arresting. In his book on the *Image of Blacks in Western Civilization*, Hugh Honour noted:

> Ward's statues are life-size, sometimes larger, and so disturbingly lifelike that they give the impression of truth to nature – though not the whole truth. His choice of subjects, the ways in which he posed the figures, and the facial expressions he gave them, reflect his belief that the Congolese were in a state of arrested development... They are not images of 'savages' so much as of 'savagery' as understood in his time – of scientific, techno-logical, social, artistic and religious 'backwardness'. (1989: 220–22)

Ward's bronzes shared with the Smithsonian life-group dioramas the same hyper-realism and the same implicit narrative about the 'primitives'. The 'life-group dioramas' developed by Holmes generally presented way-of-life scenes, which always depicted 'primitive people' before contact with 'civilization'. Installed as a group, the Ward sculp-tures, like *The Tribal Chief* and *The Idol Maker*, could have been read as 'life groups' supporting the museum's narrative about race and evolution. Romantic ideas about lost innocence after contact would have been further reinforced in Ward's sculptures such as *The Fugitives* and *Distress*. William Henry Holmes wrote of the Ward bronzes, 'Thus Ward's genius has presented in an attractive, even a fascinating manner, a people whose status, according to his own story, is at the very bottom of the ladder of civilization, a people living in a manner hardly above that of the beast of prey and excelling the brute in brutality, for the lowest brute does not systematically hunt and kill and feast upon the bodies of his own kind' (Holmes 1924: 125).

For Holmes and his fellow curator Walter Hough, the inclusion of the Ward bronzes along with the African objects was considered a visually powerful developmental sequence. Holmes had devoted much of his research to the study of 'primitive' art and he held strong views about the progressive evolution of art. For Holmes, art had evolved 'from geometric, nonideographic to delineative forms; from motives of religious superstition to refined sense of beauty, from imitation to

spontaneity' (Hinsley 1981: 105). The Ward sculptures must have represented to Holmes – who was no lover of modernism – examples of the
highest achievement in Western art. By placing the bronzes alongside
the decorated weapons and the African carvings, the public could see for
themselves the evolution of art. Reaffirming this point of view, Walter
Hough wrote, 'The maker of an African sword and Praxiteles were one
in the effort to express themselves in terms of art. The steps from the
aboriginal craftsman to the sculptures of Mr. Ward are plain to those
who study the development of art' (Hough 1924: 41).

What is especially ironic is that the theory of cultural evolution was
already being seriously challenged as a viable theory in American anthropology in the very decades that these early exhibits were installed at the
Smithsonian. How much more outdated and pernicious they become
when one remembers that they stood as the public face of Smithsonian
anthropology for over sixty years.

The Cultures of Africa Hall: 1967–1992

In the 1950s, the Museum of Natural History embarked upon an
ambitious two-decade plan to renovate and update its exhibits. The
impetus for change came primarily from inside the museum. Curators
and administrators recognized the outmoded style and content of all of
the museum's Anthropology Department exhibits. Planning for the new
African exhibit began in the early 1960s and the new exhibit opened to
the public in 1967. The orientation of the new hall was primarily regional,
beginning with North Africa and ending with southern Africa, echoing
the geo-ethnic organization of the earlier African displays. Nearly 60
per cent of the displays were organized by ethnic group. Other cases
were organized around topical themes, such as money and markets,
home industries, musical instruments, objects of leadership, etc. The
approach to the objects was essentially a functionalist one, where short
text labels highlighted the object's context of use. The objects were not
dated and no attempt was made to distinguish between those objects
no longer used and those in current usage. Little attempt was made to
extend the displays to include reworked and appropriated objects that
were in use everywhere in Africa in the mid-twentieth century.

The design of the Africa Hall did depart from that of the earlier
ethnology halls. Displays were installed in regional groupings within a
series of concentric circles. West and Central Africa occupied the largest
areas in the hall, a reflection of the greater numbers of objects from
these regions in the African collections. The museum chose to draw

an analytical distinction between 'traditional' and 'modern' Africa and between rural and urban sites, in line with much museum anthropological thinking of the day. While the opening paragraphs of the exhibit brochure acknowledged a complex and diverse contemporary Africa, the museum chose to ignore this reality and to focus on a 'traditional' Africa in its displays. The exhibit brochure set the orientation and tone for the hall: 'There is, however, another Africa – where the visitor will find little to remind him of home. This is rural Africa, traditional Africa, most of Africa. Here, where outside influence is only beginning to penetrate, most Africans still follow their traditional cultures, or ways of life, which are little known or understood by the rest of the world.'

The phrase 'where outside influence is only beginning to penetrate' was a romantic and indefensible notion in the 1960s, when this exhibit was conceptualized. Despite the few labels in the hall and portions of the exhibit brochure copy which acknowledged Africa's long and dynamic history and its global connections, the overwhelming message created was an Africa outside time. While diversity among 'traditional' African cultures was foregrounded in the exhibit, this diversity was primarily explained in terms of adaptations to different environments and ecological niches. This cultural ecology approach was well suited to the museum's naturalist paradigm. Diversity within any one African society, however, was essentially ignored. Individual African societies were presented as holistic and unified in their beliefs, values, and practices, echoing the normative ethnographic accounts published from the 1930s through the 1950s. Like its predecessor, the anthropological framework of this new Africa Hall was already outdated by the time it opened, and its displays did not engage newer anthropological theories current in the 1960s (Ortner 1984: 126–66). While it was certainly the museum's intention to valorize African 'traditional' cultures, the reification of an idealized 'traditional' Africa, not surprisingly, reinvented a contemporary variation of the primitivism paradigm of the earlier ethnology displays.

Life-size dioramas and smaller scale models remained a popular feature of the new hall. These dioramas, were not, however, the centrepieces of the exhibit narrative, but were interwoven through the case displays. There were three dioramas: the Lunda Initiation Dance, the Herero and Himba, and the Bushman. There were also two miniature models: Zimbabwe 400 years ago and Northern Cameroon Ironsmelting. Unlike the original life groups, which were installed in cases and could be viewed from all sides, the newer style of diorama, by this time popular in museums throughout the United States and elsewhere, presented the scene against an elaborately painted backdrop. The Lunda backdrops were based on field photographs and a great deal of attention was paid to accurately depicting environmental details, built structures and background figures. The Lunda Initiation Dance departed from the theme of Holmes's 'family groups' and featured the public dance ceremony during young men's initiation rites. The diorama was peopled by seven life-size figures, five of masked dancers and two representing initiates. Since the museum collections did not include the appropriate objects, the costumes and fibre masks were field-collected for this display. A series of brief explanatory labels, which discussed aspects of initiation and masking, were installed outside the case. Like all of the labels in the museum's halls they were written in the third person; a presentational style that underscored the museum voice and the authority of science. Neither the objects nor the scene were dated, and the diorama was framed in a timeless ethnographic present.

The choice of scenes for the Herero and Himba and the Bushman dioramas were more reminiscent of Holmes's earlier 'family groups'. While conceived of in the newer style, they both showed domestic scenes, with mixed age and genders engaged in a variety of activities. Relationships among the mannequins and painted figures were presented as self-evident. The focus in the the the Bushman diorama was on the ecological niche that they occupied. A woman is shown in front of a dwelling engaged in making ostrich-shell beads. Men are shown making and testing bows and arrows for hunting. In the background painting, adults and children are shown engaged in domestic and leisure activities.

The Herero and Himba diorama employed a slightly different dramatic technique. The mannequins were installed within a house. The visitor had actually to step slightly forward to peer into the dimly lit house, dramatically exaggerating the voyeurism of the visitor's gaze. The figures represented people of different ages, who were dressed in quite different costumes. Some of the women and girls were dressed in leather headdresses and aprons, while another woman was dressed in a tailored cotton dress in a Victorian style. This latter style of dress was introduced into the Herero and Himba areas by Christian missionaries at the turn of the century, and this style of dress was an important marker of one's Christian faith. No attempt was made in the labels to discuss the differences in the costumes and their role as markers of complex and different identities in these societies.

The two miniature models were constructed with the same attention to detail as were the life-size dioramas. The Ironworking model featured smelters in the Mandara Mountains in Cameroon. Based on photographs, the model accurately portrayed the smelting furnace and the iron extraction process. The explanatory labels were written in the present tense, never mentioning that in many parts of Africa the smelting industry had already begun to decline in the late nineteenth century as imported iron became more widely available. In fact most research on African smelting over this past half- century has required reconstructing furnaces and processes already abandoned a generation or more before the research was undertaken.

The Zimbabwe diorama was particularly interesting in that it showed Africans as the builders of the thirteenth- to fifteenth-century stone buildings and enclosures at Great Zimbabwe. The model success- fully challenged early popular theories that these sophisticated stone complexes could not have been built by Africans, but were built by Phoenician or Arab outsiders. By the 1980s, Africanists had begun to voice their criticism of the Africa Hall regularly in letters to the museum administration and to the curators. Smithsonian Africanist staff themselves and colleagues from outside the institution criticized the hall on several counts. One of the most frequently voiced criticisms of the exhibit by scholars and various other publics was that it presented African societies as having experienced little history and no change. For many anthropologists the organization of the hall was also chaotic and did not reflect clear, overarching themes. The displays also relied far too much on presenting materials as examples of types of African cultures and institutions, and did not represent the diversity of social and personal experience in Africa, where age, gender, education and personal history are all to be factored into how people experience and make sense of their worlds. Outdated and pejorative nomenclature for societies appeared in label texts and culturally loaded terms reinforced stereotypes of Africans as primitive, exotic and savage, and contributed to the misinterpretation of cultural practices.

Issues of museum representations, the politics of museum displays, and the relationship of museums to the communities were being debated among anthropologists, cultural historians and museologists (see Karp and Lavine 1991; Karp, Kreamer and Lavine 1992). At the Museum of Natural History, curators and other staff in the Department of Anthro- pology urged the museum to move expeditiously towards redoing all of the anthropology exhibits, which were deemed at best out of date, and at worst offensive to the peoples and cultures represented. While in principle the museum administration recognized the need for change, in practice it was slow to initiate any change. It was interest groups outside the Smithsonian who were instrumental in pushing for change in the Africa Hall and its closing in 1992 (Kreamer 1997: 52–53).

New Strategies: the 1922 Development of a New African Exhibit

While the museum did sequester funds to upgrade the 'Cultures of Africa' exhibit, it became clear that merely changing texts, installing new groups of objects, or repainting and relighting the displays would not adequately address the professional and public critiques levelled against the old Africa Hall. In 1993, the museum agreed with the curatorial staff that a new exhibition needed to be created, although additional funding for the project remained a critical issue throughout the life of the project. At various junctures, the lack of funds to support this project contributed to significant delays in its development process.

In 1993 an exhibit team was constituted. Its first task was to access critically the old exhibit and to develop a broad statement for the new hall, which would articulate the primary objectives and goals for a new exhibit and suggest major themes and exhibition strategies. After much debate, a working consensus was reached that the target audience would be family groups, defined as inter-generational groups of visitors. This category is the museum's largest visitor population. Because a high proportion of our museum visitors have little or no knowledge of either historical or contemporary Africa, the team agreed that baseline information about Africa would need to be provided throughout the exhibit. The team was also concerned that the exhibit should engage more knowledgeable and motivated visitors, especially African-Americans and Africans living in or visiting the United States, and structured groups such as elementary and secondary school students. These latter groups were identified as a secondary audience or a 'stakeholder audience' for the exhibit.

From the beginning of the development process, the exhibit team worked closely with a large number of Africanists and scholars of the African Diaspora locally, nationally and internationally, and with local African and African-American communities. While earlier exhibits sought collaboration with anthropologists outside the Smithsonian, Kreamer noted that, 'The controversies of the early 1990s convinced NMNH staff that they should expand the process of exhibition development to include substantive and ongoing participation by members of diverse communities and stakeholder audiences' (Kreamer 1997: 54).

Over the life of the project a core group of between 35 and 60 advisors participated in the exhibit development. They included Smithsonian staff, many of whom are members of the Smithsonian African-American Association; an engaged group of Africanist and Diasporan scholars from outside the Smithsonian Institution, who represented different disciplines and a variety of perspectives, and a committed group of African immigrants from the local region. Advisors met the exhibition staff at critical junctures. Input from the advisory groups was instrumental in reworking and revising the exhibit at every stage, from the initial statement of goals and objectives through to the final script. A final script and design was completed in September 1998 and the exhibit opened to the public in December 1999.

The collaborative process began in earnest in 1994. A community research specialist was hired to identify members of the advisory group and to work with communities in the local region. A draft statement of ideas, which included objectives, goals and a thematic outline, was presented to the advisory groups at a series of meetings held at the Smithsonian. The framing statement was critiqued on several levels. Based on the discussions at these meetings, the exhibit goals, objectives and themes were modified and sharpened. The exhibit team and the external advisors agreed broadly along the following lines: the exhibit should demonstrate both Africa's long and dynamic history and Africa's contemporary face; it should include peoples of African descent living outside Africa, both historically and in the contemporary period; it should give a balanced view of Africa and challenge existing stereotypes and assumptions about Africa and Africans in the popular imagination. Moving from these generally agreed-upon abstract objectives and goals to fashioning an exhibition script and design was the challenge for the museum team.

It was decided that the exhibit be organized thematically, rather than by geo-ethnic groupings. A thematic organization, it was hoped, would subvert the static and ahistorical representations of the older exhibits, where individual African societies were imagined as unconnected from one another through time and in space. It would also allow for the exploration of shared themes relevant to African societies across the continent and beyond, historically and in the contemporary period.

One of the primary objectives of the exhibit was to fashion exhibit stories that would focus on the constructive aspects of material culture, i.e. how people shape objects and how particular uses of objects shape people. Objects, like words, are means by which humans engage and shape their world. An approach to material culture that underscores human agency allows for an examination of objects and the material experience in terms of production, identity, and representation (Arnoldi and Hardin 1996: 11). Certain physical constraints shaped the design of the exhibit. The exhibit hall is a rectangular space with two separate entrances, one at each end of the hall. Because the visitor could enter from either end of the hall, a linear narrative was not feasible. Moreover, it was determined that each entrance would need its own orientation section. Rather than repeat the same orientation texts and displays at each entrance, we decided that one entrance would introduce the exhibit themes from the perspective of the long and dynamic history of Africa, while the other would introduce the exhibit themes from the perspective of contemporary global Africa.

A pathway that features ten history stories serves as the central spine of the exhibit. It begins with the emergence of humanity in Africa and ends with a display dedicated to contemporary health issues and challenges in Kenya. While the history pathway is linear, each moment is a discrete story and the visitor can explore the path from either direction, working backwards or forwards in time. In each of the history moments, objects, quotations from historical and living persons, labels, photographs, maps and a time line are used to tell the story. Four thematic galleries branch off the history pathway: two on either side of the pathway. These include Wealth in Africa, Working in Africa, Living Spaces and Global Africa. These thematic galleries are linked to one another by two discrete transitional spaces. Living Spaces and Global Africa are connected by a historical story of Kongo religion in Africa and its adoption in the Americas. Wealth in Africa and Working in Africa are connected by a contemporary market story, which features vendors' stories from the Makola market in Accra, Ghana.

Each of the history moments incorporates themes explored in the adjoining galleries, with the intention of setting up a resonance between historical and contemporary stories. For example, along the history pathway the theme of early urbanism in Africa is introduced through the story of Jene-Jeno in Mali (200 BCE to 1400). This history moment is in physical proximity to the Living Spaces gallery, which features contemporary urban stories. Those history moments dedicated to colonialism and independence are adjacent to the Global Africa gallery. In the Global Africa gallery, telling the story of the Atlantic slave trade posed one of the greatest challenges. Given the emotional resonance of this story for our stakeholder audience, and the historical complexity of this story, we realized that it could not be told through object displays alone, nor could it be told outside the longer history of Africa and its global reach.

We decided to use a variety of techniques that included objects, soundscapes, fibre optic maps, and films. To set the Atlantic slave trade into the larger story of Africa's global connections, we created a fibre optic map display that highlights the great diversity of African journeys beyond the continent, beginning with Hannibal leading his North African army against Rome, including the eighteenth- and nineteenth-century trans-atlantic slave trade, and ending with recent migrations of Africans world-wide. Within the exhibit we also created a small theatre, the 'Freedom Theater', and produced two twenty-minute films that run consecutively through the day. The first, *The Atlantic Slave Trade,* focuses on a story of enslaved peoples taken from Ghana to Virginia and from Nigeria to Brazil, and speaks to the ways in which these enslaved peoples created community and resisted their oppression. The second film, *The Struggle for Freedom,* focuses on the history of the Pan-Africanist movements in Africa and the Caribbean, and on Africa's struggles against European colonialism. It ends with an exploration of the more recent common-alities between the American Civil Rights Movement and the South African anti-apartheid movement.

Organizing the galleries thematically posed a series of exhib-iting challenges. Most visitors are familiar and comfortable with the geo-ethnic organization, since that continues to be the standard in most anthropology museums up to the present. Many visitors also prefer a single narrative that moves them through the exhibit space. In order to make the thematic organization of the exhibit comprehensible to the visitor, a set of hierarchical text labels and design elements were devel-oped. Each thematic gallery is introduced with a large gallery text label prominently placed at the entrance to the gallery space. This text intro-duces the theme and makes connections between the various stories the visitor will encounter in the gallery.

Each individual display or story in the gallery includes a series of hierarchical texts. A large main text relates the regional or local story to the broader gallery theme. Each display includes a map, or series of maps, to locate story in Africa or the wider world. Subtexts, panels, focus labels and object labels, in descending size, provide more detailed information about the story and the objects on display. At various stages in the development process the team tested stories, constellations of objects and photographs, and the label texts with museum visitors. This testing provided important insights about the intended and unintended messages being communicated by objects, images and words. In some cases it meant abandoning a story or text altogether, or radically refash-ioning it to make it comprehensible and engaging.

The team and the outside advisors agreed that the exhibit should include a variety of perspectives, especially those of Africans and people of African descent who are represented in this exhibit. African voices in the exhibit include cultural voices drawn from African poetry, proverbs, songs and adages; excerpts from historical and contemporary speeches and writings by Africans and peoples of African descent worldwide; and excerpts from interviews with the individuals whose stories are featured in the exhibit. African voices play the central role in the exhibit: they are prominent at every level in the text hierarchy and throughout the installation, and are heard in the exhibit in videos, films and soundscapes.

The primary focus in the thematic galleries is contemporary Africa. Some advisors, many of whom are African-American, felt strongly that urban sites should be featured exclusively in the thematic galleries in order to subvert the image of a 'primitive' Africa, which is so strongly associated with rural Africa in the American popular imagination. African advisors on the extended team took a different view. While they agreed that it was important to feature urban Africa in the thematic galleries, they disagreed that it should be the exclusive focus. They argued passionately that contemporary rural Africa should not be ignored. In their view, the exhibit should include contemporary urban and rural stories, and the dynamic historical and contemporary connections between rural and urban areas should be highlighted as an essential part of African history and the very fabric of contemporary African life.

The team struggled to develop stories and engage exhibiting strategies that could address these concerns and the different points of view. The thematic galleries, as they are constituted, include contemporary and historical stories from urban and rural settings, although contemporary urban and rural stories are emphasized. The objects selected draw upon existing collections and also include objects that were specially commissioned or collected for this exhibit. All objects in the exhibit are dated and, where possible, we have identified the individuals who have made the objects and included their biographies as part of the exhibit story. In the Wealth in Africa gallery for example, a case that explores how people use objects to register changes in social status contains a Luba chief's staff from the late nineteenth century, a Mende woman's initiation mask from the late 1960s, and a contemporary current graduation gown from the University of Ghana in Legon. In this same gallery we feature contemporary Malian artists and fashion designers who create and work with traditional mud-dyed textiles. We locate the production of these textiles in both rural and urban settings and discuss the local, national and international markets for their consumption. We also explore the international marketing of products like bed linens, towels, coffee cups, wrapping paper and shopping bags, based on this Malian textile.

In displays where historical objects are featured, labels clearly indicate whether similar objects are being produced and used today. Where an object is no longer in use, the historical object is installed next to a more contemporary object that has replaced it. For example, an iron bundle from the late nineteenth century, once exchanged as bride wealth in the Cameroon, is installed next to a stack of Cameroon CFA notes. The label addresses changes in the material repertoire and in bride wealth practices in contemporary Cameroon.

A century after 'life groups' were first introduced into the museum, dioramas remain a popular exhibit genre. Despite the representational problems inherent in this genre, the new exhibit includes several variations on dioramas. The team struggled with the ways to exploit the dramatic potential of the diorama, but reconfigure and refashion it in ways that would extend its interpretive potential. We freely borrowed a number of successful strategies from other museums that have experimented with this form. In the Makola market display, for example, we feature four women vendors currently working in this market. The market includes an installation of the four stalls and the products these women sell. The visitor is introduced to each woman through a life-size photographic cutout. In contrast to mannequin displays, there is evidence from audience studies that photographic cutouts are seen by museum visitors as more contemporary than standard mannequin displays. Rather than being of generic Africans, the photographs are of the actual women whose stories are featured in the display. The text labels adjacent to the photograph are in their voices and are excerpts taken from interviews that were conducted with them in 1997. In these texts the women speak about the market organization, the economic value of the work they do, the particular goods they sell, who buys these goods, and their hopes and aspirations for the future.

The gallery devoted to Living Spaces we opted for a different strategy. We installed a Somali nomadic house, an *aqal*, which was collected in the mid-1980s. Somali women from the Washington region worked with the team to choose the domestic objects for the contemporary display. These included locally produced objects, such as baskets, leather cases and mats, along with imported goods, such as a short-wave radio, truck keys, plastic buckets and rope, and an AK47 automatic weapon. The house and its contents allowed us to feature aspects of a contemporary nomadic lifestyle, as well as a centuries-old architectural form that remains viable in the early twenty-first century. As this story took shape, some of the American advisors and a few of the African advisors on the extended team felt that the installation of the portable house would be too easily misread by our visitors as an example of a 'primitive' dwelling. The Somalis on the extended team, however, spoke eloquently in defence of using the house. They emphasized that the *aqal* is a central symbol of Somali family life, of marriage, history and cultural identity, no matter where they are living today. The defence of the *aqal* as an object of cultural memory was compelling, and it inspired the team to shift the interpretive perspective of the display. If we could communicate the centrality of the house in the Somali imagination, would we be able to transcend the 'primitive' trope.

We soon realized that we could not accomplish our goal through the use of objects and texts alone. We chose to install the house without mannequins, and we set up a life-size video screen next to the house. Two Somalis, Abirahman Dahir and Faduma Mohammed, both of whom grew up in nomadic households in Somalia and now live in Washington, tell their stories in a series of short video sequences. Their personal stories touch on the house's adaptability to the harsh environment, its construction, and the changes it has undergone over time. Abdi identifies the *aqal*, camels and poetry as the most important symbols of Somali life. He speaks of the house's central role in marriage rituals, and he recites a poem dedicated to the *aqal*. Faduma shares her memories of growing up in a nomadic camp, of playing with friends, of learning to make her first mat, etc. It was the goal of the exhibit to move the installation from a static diorama to a dynamic dialogic display. By using objects, photographic murals and texts, along with the life-size video display of personal testimony, we hoped to communicate different stories about the house – as a technologically sophisticated dwelling, as a focal point for key cultural values and gendered practices, and as a central object of memory in the Somali imagination. Anecdotal evidence, as well as more formal visitor studies, has revealed that the life-size video does draw people to the display and that the personal testimonies of Abdi and Faduma engage them with the exhibit. The visitor studies confirmed that most people spend some time at the Somali house.

In developing this new exhibit, the team needed to address explicitly how it could be designed to respond to changing concepts, interests and themes, both within anthropology and cultural history and in terms of its representation of Africa and Africans. The exhibit was conceptualized as a work in progress, rather than a finite product, a philosophy that is foreign to the culture of exhibiting at the Natural History Museum and anathema to most museum administrators. A Focus Gallery was created within the exhibit. In this gallery, small temporary exhibits would be installed annually which would expand on one of the themes or stories in the permanent hall, or introduce new themes not covered in the exhibit. Since the opening of African Voices in 1999, the project created four temporary exhibits in this space, with the fifth exhibit to open in 2008. However, I am only cautiously optimistic that we will be able to continue the programme or to update the exhibit. Given the constraints of a limited staff, diminishing budgets, and competing exhibition priorities in the museum, it is clear to me that it will take the continued pressure and involvement of the museum staff and our stakeholder audiences to keep the administration invested in making changes to African Voices in a timely manner.

Note

1 This chapter was originally published as an article in *Cahiers d'Études africaines*, 39.3–4 (1999), 701–26. It was edited and updated by the author in 2007.

28

Human Zoos in Switzerland

PATRICK MINDER

'Freak shows' occurred frequently in Switzerland from 1880 to 1939, held for the most part in caravans, on town squares, at pubs, cafés or at refreshment stands and restaurants, and occasionally in parks or gardens near such establishments. These shows, which local newspapers announced and advertised, were professionally promoted events. For example, the 1890 visit to La Chaux-de-Fonds of Kobelkoff, the Human Torso, a Russian exhibiting himself all over the world, led to three articles being published in *La Sentinelle* (Pajot 2003: 34–36). Typically, the exhibition tent would be set up on the square in front of the railway station. These shows now and again stirred criticism, but to no effect.

From 1875 to 1939 in French-speaking Switzerland there were no fewer than thirty-nine shows and anatomical museums.[1] However, it was not considered acceptable to exhibit individuals from the same milieu as that of the spectators. This illustrates just how important it was to show the Other as different and exotic. 'Freaks' were exhibited individually or collectively. Where the person was sufficiently deformed or sensational, he or she sufficed to ensure the success of the show. To cite just one example, *l'homme poileux* [*sic*] (the hairy man), Rham-A-Sama, was exhibited in Lausanne, Geneva and Fribourg before his death in a hospital in Paris.[2] Some double acts enjoyed particularly enduring popular success, such as that of the giant Van Albert and the dwarf Seppettoni, whose shows lasted for more than 20 years in French-speaking Switzerland (Minder 2005: 172).[3] Although the Lilliputian's dances and the giant's charming conversation were appreciated, other double acts were of a more dubious nature.[4] The exhibition of two disabled people in a travelling menagerie of rare wild animals aroused some very critical reactions, yet such shows were never banned.

Science and Exhibitions

The idea of associating science and exhibition was of major importance and the impact it had should not be underestimated. Among the general public at the end of the nineteenth century, belief in positivism and determinism were common. Raciology, which had its roots in physical anthropology, used such paradigms to elaborate reasoned hierarchical systems, empirically supported by anthropometric measures. Whenever a scientist was called upon to give an expert opinion on a 'freak' exhibited in a show, the frontier between fiction and reality became so blurred that even the most sceptical minds were troubled. How could one not believe the 1931 announcement concerning 'a young girl whose body is completely covered in crocodile skin several centimetres thick', who had become a 'famous scientific phenomenon'? Why doubt her rarity and her undeniable scientific interest? Publicity would go so far as to specify that 'Doctors are particularly welcome.'[5]

Africans were introduced as showcase items into these tumultuous low-life entertainment practices of the Western world. In 1887, Galibi, 'the negro contortionist from the Congo', was presented to the public as the Snake Man.[6] Even more interesting is the case of 'two negro prisoners of the Dahomeyan war' exhibited at the Schweizerhalle in Fribourg in December 1896. In the days following the show, the two men were to be found serving as waiters in the establishment, and the publican announced their presence as 'another curiosity' for his regular customers to come and see. Might this proprietor have extended by his own initiative the Africans' employment to two additional days, thus illustrating the flimsy nature of their work contracts? A preference for exhibiting Africans in groups or tribes, accompanied by women and children, meant that there were few men on individual display.

Unlike other people or groups of people with deformities, the Africans were exhibited in circuses or 'ethnological exhibitions', as were, for example, the 'Compagnie de la Nouvelle-Guinée', and Indian fakirs. Swiss town parks, sufficiently large restaurants and zoological gardens served as a backdrop for the exhibited. Swiss French daily newspapers and illustrated weeklies from 1879 to 1939 suggest a figure of seven 'African villages'.[7] Some of the groups are listed in the detailed tables established for the zoological garden of Basel and for the city of Zürich. This cross-referencing clearly shows that the troupes travelled across Europe and all over Switzerland, with the managers seeking to obtain the best return on the shows they had organized. An estimation of the total number of exhibitions of humans in Switzerland gives a figure of well over 100 presentations.

The interruption of 1914–18 barely affected the fashion for exhibitions. Although troupes of Laplanders, Inuits and Sinhalese were also programmed, they remained a minority, which means that a further observation can be made: if groups performing in circuses are excluded from the figures, African villages occupy an even more important place in the statistics. So the question is: what exactly was the Swiss public shown and why were the African villages so fascinating? The best-documented exhibitions took place in Geneva in 1896 and in Lausanne in 1925. Unlike other exhibitions, these villages were set up and associated with festivities that ranged across the whole of Switzerland and were designed to attract the entire population, whatever their language or their religion.

It is supposed that the impresarios of the African troupes shown throughout Europe amassed large amounts of money and made their fortunes by enthusiastically indulging in this practice. The archives leave no doubt as to the real profitability of these shows. But why were African villages a feature of important national events?

The African Village of 1896 in Geneva

The Geneva village was part of an ensemble called the Parc de Plaisance, and was proposed by a member of the committee who cited as references the 1893 Chicago and 1896 Berlin exhibitions.[8] The central committee received other propositions for the construction of villages or exhibitions. All were refused, because a monopoly had been granted to the project that had economic and pedagogical dimensions.

The African village was situated on the fringes of the park, on a plot measuring approximately 3,200 square metres (3,840 square yards), rented for 35,000 francs.[9] This location was not a random choice. As the village was not totally integrated into the exhibition site, the village administrators were able to charge a supplementary fee over the official entrance ticket to it. The settlement was composed of adobe huts with a mosque that attracted everyone's attention. A small lake completed the ensemble. The visitors moved freely around the village and mixed with its inhabitants. The only restriction imposed was that they were not to enter the huts. Although clearly on display, the inhabitants of the village were not treated as animals in cages, since there were no bars separating the spectators and the indigenous people.

Three tribal chiefs led the troupe of Africans from Senegal. The arrival of the inhabitants was celebrated on 27 April 1896 by a huge procession: the municipal band opened the march and was followed by a four-horse landau carrying the organizers; and then, depending on the contemporary source, came between forty-two and fifty carriages, open and garlanded, completed by four donkeys, monkeys, parrots and everything necessary for cooking and making music. Funds were collected along the route for 'l'Hospice général, les Cuisines populaires de Plainpalais et les Cuisines scolaires'. A short film of the procession walking inside the enclosure of the Parc de Plaisance still exists.[10]

The indigenous characters were welcomed with a large bonfire. The festivities began on Friday 8 May 1896 with the celebration of the baptism of a girl born during the crossing from Dakar to Marseille. The baptism was conducted according to Muslim rites and served as a pretext to attract a large audience. It also necessitated the sacrificial offering of a sheep. This aspect of the ceremony aroused negative reactions to the celebration of a pagan rite, but did not in any way affect its success. On this occasion, the organizers sold a special entrance ticket priced at 2 francs. The event also caused alarm at the idea of a 'black invasion', with the accompanying fears of miscegenation and mixing of cultures that would threaten Swiss identity.

Other religious ceremonies attracted the public, including the Tabaski ceremony,[11] during which the throats of sheep were cut. However, after the intervention of the Animal Protection Society, this procedure was no longer carried out in public. The final celebrations were those that marked the start of the Muslim New Year, accompanied by music, dancing, singing, torchlight processions, crossbow-shooting, races, equestrian extravaganzas and wrestling, all of which aroused great curiosity.

Unfortunately, a death occurred during the exhibition. A young African man, who had managed to dodge the obligatory check-up before departure, finally received much-needed medical attention upon his arrival. This intervention was, however, too late. During his illness his countrymen visited him regularly; and on his death, they performed their traditional laying-out of the corpse. The funeral procession, which took place on 25 August 1896 at the Cimetière de Saint-Georges in Geneva, consisted of a hearse followed by five closed carriages carrying the marabouts and about twenty people. The deceased was buried in an individual tomb with a small tumulus, from which each African removed a handful of earth to take back to the dead man's sister. His uncle ordered a gravestone,[12] and a meal was offered to the children of the African village in memory of the young man.

Daily Life in the Village

The general state of health of the Africans from the moment of their embarkation was a concern for the organizers and apparently continued to be so after their arrival. The troupe received visits from doctors three times a day. Bad weather plagued the exhibition from May to October 1896. Suffering from the cold temperatures, the Africans were issued with military blankets, and on the day of their departure it even snowed. These meteorological conditions aroused the public's sympathy for them.

Wrestling matches were organized in the village, notably against three Turkish champions from the Imperial Palace of Constantinople. The keenest interest was shown in the question of whether the white champions would get the better of the 'coloured champions', who were supposed to be vested with an almost animal strength that had to be controlled. On two occasions a magic show was organized within the village enclosure. With their own stereotypical vision of Africa, the organizers apparently thought that they could impress the indigenous people on display.

It was imperative that the exhibition should be profitable. People could have their photographs taken, surrounded by members of the troupe, for the not very modest sum of 3 francs. This idea, entrusted to the talent and expertise of the official photographer, was a great success. Sources are rare regarding the activities of the troupe outside those typically reserved for the exhibitions and the African villages. A young African man refused to drink the alcohol offered by some merrymaking visitors, but he was happy to drink water with them. People in Neuchâtel tried the same thing, also unsuccessfully, with a child whom they estimated to be three or four years old. On another occasion, a mother, suspecting the presence of alcohol in a mint sweet given to her child by a female spectator, snatched it away, tasted it and spat it out contemptuously. Although considered inferior, the Africans surprised the Swiss with their moderation. Moreover, despite all that was sanctioned as exotic strangeness, morality was not something to be trifled with, and according to the press the Africans never contravened the norms. In the words of a witness: 'It is a lesson for Christians!'[13]

Although the members of the troupe could leave the enclosure, there were certain restrictions. They were to avoid creating too much contact with Europeans. It was feared that they would refuse to go back home or that they would become 'civilized' beings after all, in which case their 'authenticity' would be lost, thereby destroying the basis on which the success of the exhibition rested. For publicity reasons, the members of the troupe were occasionally allowed to leave the exhibition enclosure. The Africans became living advertising hoardings. It is known that on at least two occasions members of the Plainpalais tribe went to the theatre.

The most commonly criticized 'vice' of the Africans was their supposedly constant begging. Some press articles mention how the white people made their contribution in an original way, that is to say by throwing the small coins into the water to see the young black men dive and bring them to the surface in their mouths. Swiss-German dailies openly complained of this begging, which pushed the village management to take action, though unsuccessfully. This begging continued to be commented upon even after the festivities had ended.

At the end of the exhibition, the moment of departure led to wild speculation. Rumours were rife as to the possibility of romances having blossomed during the event. This was, of course, the ultimate taboo. A white man could not marry a black woman and the idea of a white woman seducing an African man broke all codes. According to some newspapers, black men had hurriedly proposed marriage to young women.[14] Worse still, they refused to leave Switzerland. Nothing could be further from the truth, however, as historical sources contradict these rumours.[15]

The life of the African village in Geneva was particularly disturbed on two occasions: once when the director, Alexandre, sued by the central committee, ran away; and once when the tribal chief was sent home and the troupe went on strike – an exceptional event in the history of ethnological exhibitions.[16] Though there were sometimes fights between spectators and indigenous people, or among the indigenous people themselves,[17] cases of managers abandoning the troupes or running away were, unfortunately, more frequent.[18] It is difficult to find any traces in the Geneva archives of this incident, which was conveniently forgotten without any official report being made, but contemporary newspaper reports suggest that the head of the troupe was suddenly sent home with his family, just a few days after the official opening. The organizers did not give the rest of the troupe any explanation. After a two-hour wait without any news, fearing for the life of their leader, the inhabitants of the village packed their bags, whereupon, in order to prevent them leaving, the exhibition police arrived to explain the situation.

What is surprising about this particular event is the enormous impact in the press of an affair which was of relatively minor importance. When looked at from a Western perspective, in terms of the relationship between colonizers and colonized, it becomes easier to understand. The indigenous people were reputed to be rebellious, and 'pacification' had not yet been completed. If the Africans sought to leave, it was because they were untameable, savage and dangerous, reflecting what was said about their nature and manners. The managers were shaken as the village emptied and bags were packed. Contemporaries did not understand that the attitude of the Africans though the whole incident hinged on a misunderstanding: in the eyes of the organizers, the stupidity of the inhabitants of the village indicated that they really did not understand the issue at all. It is the most revealing indicator of the nature of the relationship between the Africans and the Swiss visitors to the Geneva Exposition of 1896.

A lecture given by Emile Yung, an anthropologist in Geneva, was based on the study of the inhabitants of the African village. The approach of Yung, purportedly a scientific one, shows to what extent the Swiss scientific world of the period was fascinated by the exhibition of non-European people, to the point of losing all critical distance. At the end of the Exposition, 80 objects from the village were deposited with the Geneva Museum of Ethnography. It would be interesting today to make a detailed study of the labelling of each of these objects, whose origins remained dubious and vague, and to measure the scientific weight that would now be given to the inventory of the collection.[19]

Pompously announced in the newspapers as 'Anthropological Characteristics of the "Nigritic" Race Studied Using some of its Representatives from Western Sudan – Kinship of this Race with Other African negroes, its Geographical Distribution' [trans.], Yung's lecture attracted a full house. The professor was welcomed with 'prolonged bravos'. At the foot of the rostrum were located 'fifteen negroes, men, women and children, chosen by the speaker from the various tribes of the African village'. There followed a series of considerations of a scientific nature: first the skin – the palm of an individual was compared, 'jokingly', to that of a workman; then the head and the cranial volume – using the skull of a Genevan and the skull of a black African, Yung reminded the audience of the theories of the Frenchman Paul Broca, and told of his meeting with Quatrefages; then the foot – the 'rolling walk' of the African is caused by the weight being placed on the outside part and not the inside part of the sole of the foot; and, finally, analysis of the nose and the hair – 'frizzy, smooth or bushy'.

There is no doubting the seriousness of such a scientific inquiry. At the time, however, it met only with approval and praise from the audience. It should also be noted that the lecture ended with 'the presentation of different types, some very accommodating, others somewhat bored and intimidated – a marabout, a zebu shepherd, an old man of 82, a suckling child and various types taken from all walks of life'.[20]

A more accurate assessment can be made of what could be described as a *union sacrée* between the world of science and the system of stereotypes in effect at the time: colonial scientism, the fusion and confusion of Western scientific thought and the stereotyped perception of the Other. The general public accepted a scientific discourse for which it lacked the critical means and the tools with which to question. Moreover, we can see to what extent the message of the anthropologists and ethnologists was based on a series of clichés. The 'human zoo' satisfied the curiosity of ordinary people and also of scientists. All the strength and power of the stereotype relating to the African were expressed here.

The African Village of 1925 in Lausanne

This event owed its success to just one man, Henri Muret, a trained engineer, founder in 1919 of the Bureau industriel suisse, then Vice-President and President (1939–45) of the Office suisse d'expansion commerciale (OSEC). Muret was the first director of the Swiss Fair in 1919 and founder of the First International Fair of Colonial Products – often called the First Colonial Fair – in Lausanne. He was obsessed by the idea of how best to develop Swiss business abroad. In his opinion, Switzerland was a victim of crisis: it had chronic unemployment and its fearful attitude regarding the future was pushing it towards an inexorably fatal isolation and towards a loss of national identity through the uncontrolled exodus of its citizens. But Henri Muret remained convinced that salvation was to be found in the use of propaganda and through the contribution of Swiss expatriates, the true intermediaries of the Swiss federal state, which, in his opinion, was too weak to boost the economy on its own.

Given the circumstances linked to the organization of the fair, Muret proposed prolonging the event and avoiding a deficit by 'killing two birds with one stone', thus recouping as much as possible at the financial level and promoting the strategy of commercial development. So an African village was created with a very clear objective, as indicated in the prospectus:

> The village display will thus not only be attractive and informative, but will also serve as commercial propaganda, for it will allow our commerce and our industry to create needs among the peoples of Africa so as to incite them to be more productive. (Verschave and Guillerme 1925: 19)

Seventy Africans, Foulas from Guinea and Senegal, arrived on 25 June 1925 via Vallorbe. They were transferred from the station to the site of the fair in two buses, arousing the curiosity of bystanders. The troupe moved into the village, which was given the very symbolic Latin name of 'Tibidabo', i.e. 'I will give you'. The village measured 1,500 square metres (1,800 square yards), and precise plans still exist indicating the functions of the dwellings. These plans remain rare in the history of African villages, much documentation having systematically disappeared from the archives. The managers of the fair took care of construction, housing and maintenance. A contract was signed for a period of three months. The Africans settled in and the village opened at the same time as the exhibition halls. It remained open to the public for four days after the end of the event, which had been set for 26 July 1925. The site was positioned beside the hall of exotic products in Beaulieu, a location that was not without significance: unprocessed colonial commodities were displayed next to the inhabitants of the countries which had supplied them, the implication being that only those in the West were capable of transforming these materials because of their high level of civilization and their mastery of technology.

The organizers of the fair managed the admissions. To access the village, people had to walk alongside a thatched fence to reach a square where there was a small lake. The whole site was dominated by a mosque. Mr Fleury Tournier, a war veteran wounded in the First World War, recruited the Africans for the village. The contracts of engagement specified the smallest financial detail, including the expenses to be paid by the organizers. However, the wages of the Africans did not appear in any budget or in any account: they were included in the sum attributed to the French promoter.

Given the length of the stay, there are few details regarding what happened in the village. There were dances and the Tabaski ceremony on the tenth day of the month. A member of the Lausanne police force was responsible for law and order, and a few workmen passed through from time to time to maintain and check the security of the site. Judging from the rare photographs that have survived, the public were permitted to mingle with the inhabitants. The departure of the Africans aroused little curiosity and nothing appears to have been reported in the press – with just one exception: another romance, if the duty policeman is to be believed.

The troupe was then expected in Berne, in Basel at the zoological garden, and in Zürich. Basel was already occupied by a troupe of Sinhalese;[21] Berne and the Committee of the Agricultural Exhibition declined to host them, as did the town of Zürich because of the refusal of its police force to authorize the opening of a site. Finally, it was the Zürich commune of Alstetten that played host to the Senegalese until 25 September 1925.

Two Different Models: 1896/1925

While the African village of 1896 was presented in the early stages of what would become a phenomenon throughout the Western world, the 1925 village was held at the end of this trend. The aims of the two events also differed: whereas the first village was intended primarily to entertain, the second was intended to inform and propagandize. The event and the venue determined the size of the troupe and the duration of the exhibition. This also explains why the sources differ in abundance, diversity and quality from one village to the other.

In the eyes of contemporaries, the Exposition Nationale of 1896 differed greatly from the Colonial Fair of 1925. The context had also changed: the First World War constituted an important break in the history of human zoos in Switzerland. Soldiers from all over Africa had fought in Europe. The phases of conquest and 'pacification' had occurred before 1914. The European powers, with their territories now united into empires, were consolidating their acquisitions. Propaganda was used to establish definitively the union of the colonizer and of the colonized. Switzerland only followed events indirectly. Its resources were limited to the domain where it did not need to take political risks, i.e. the economy, the only place for the articulation of any of the colonial ambitions the country might have had. Since the Swiss state was unable to organize a colonial exhibition on the European model, the circuses and the zoological gardens were the next best thing (Razac 2002: 82–89).

Stereotypical attitudes towards the Africans persisted during the entire period with surprising consistency, mainly because of the similarities between the people organizing these events: the 1896 Exposition Nationale organizers wanted to unite the nation in one place, ensuring national salvation by projecting the greatness of the country. The managers of the 1925 Colonial Fair were, first and foremost, industrialists and businessmen. For them, what mattered most was to trigger something in the mind of the spectator, who would then become a more active consumer. Any means would serve to achieve this conversion.

The structure of the African village barely changed. Its construction was ephemeral and artificial, but supposedly as authentic as possible. It was intended that the visitor would believe he was seeing 'real Africans', not 'actors of a troupe of indigenous people'. The fusion of fact and fiction occurred because people could enter into the decor and partici- pate in the performance. Moreover, through such artifice the show was contrived to portray the everyday life of individuals from somewhere else. Africans existed; they were different, and that fact was sufficient reason for their being exhibited. The popular success of these shows in Switzerland was based purely on the existence of these exotic beings.

Was the human zoo merely an object of popular curiosity, or an instrument of colonial propaganda? A spontaneous answer would be 'both'. But in fact, this mise en scène was the result of colonial strate- gies. The construction of the Other around stereotypes, set in cardboard scenery with potted palm trees, was nothing but a show, but it was thought to resemble reality to such an extent that reality yielded to the illusion. Scientific authority carried enormous weight in the elaboration of this artifice, for scientists were those who set the standards by which it was judged.

Paradoxically, few traces remain today of these exhibitions, which had been so popular. Some posters, a few rare photographs and a small collection of artefacts deposited in the Geneva Museum of Ethnography are reminders of these episodes from the past. The African village remains a façade for economic propaganda with a colonial touch. As Swiss politicians did not show any inclination for expansion, the creation of colonies became an old-fashioned idea. The desire to colonize popula- tions was relinquished and replaced by a feeling of missed opportunity; the idea of conquest had come to an end. Switzerland emerged too late in a world that was already fully engaged in making colonial empires profitable. However, it did not refrain from maintaining the illusion of power through its human zoos.[22]

Notes

1 This figure is a minimum as it is based on a systematic consultation of *La Senti- nelle* and *La Liberté*, two regional newspapers having a relatively modest influ- ence in French-speaking Switzerland. For the period 1887 to 1904, *Le National Suisse* and the *Feuille d'Avis de Neuchâtel* were consulted by Valérie Sierro, of the Neuchâtel Museum of Ethnography, who very kindly shared her notes with me.

2 On Rham-A-Sama, see the anthropological description by Professor Eugène Pittard of Geneva and intended for the general public in *La Patrie Suisse* 142 (1899), pp. 58–59; see also *La Liberté*, 38 (17 February 1899), pp. 2–3, 58 (12 March 1899), p. 3, and announcement p. 4, and *La Liberté*, 59 (Tuesday 14 March

1899), p. 4. On his death, see the paragraph in *La Liberté*, 18 (Wednesday 24 January 1900), p. 3.

3   See *La Sentinelle*, 144 (Saturday 23 June 1917), p. 6 (Brasserie du Jura in St-Imier), and Issue 38 (Thursday 15 February 1923), pp. 3–4 (La Chaux-de-Fonds); *La Liberté*, 77 (Saturday 2 April 1932), p. 8, Issue 82 (Friday 8 April 1932), pp. 5–6 (Hôtel de la Croix-Blanche in Fribourg), and Issue 94 (Friday 24 April 1937), pp. 4, 11 (Hôtel de la Croix-Blanche in Fribourg).

4   The Mexican couple, Maximo and Bartola, were exhibited in Berlin in 1900 (see Brändle 1995: 80, 83).

5   *La Liberté*, 12 (Friday 16 January 1931), p. 5.

6   According to the *National Suisse*, 18–21 June 1887, Galibi performed at the Brasserie Hauert situated at 12, rue de la Serre, La Chaux-de-Fonds. He apparently performed again in Neuchâtel at the Place du Port at the central Grand Théâtre. See *Feuille d'Avis de Neuchâtel*, Tuesday 21 June 1887, p. 3.

7   For French-speaking Switzerland, this includes the African Village of the 1896 Swiss National Exhibition in Geneva, the Togomandingos troupe visiting Fribourg in 1903 after having been to Geneva, Lausanne, Vevey, Payerne and Zürich, a Senegalese village in Fribourg in 1909, the African Village of the Luna-Park in Geneva in 1911, the village at the Swiss Fair in Lausanne in 1925 which then went to Zürich, an African village in Geneva in 1927 and an African village in Lausanne, which then visited Fribourg, La Chaux-de-Fonds and Zürich in 1930. These troupes may well have performed in other places in Switzerland and Europe.

8   The 1893 World's Columbian Exposition, Chicago, is known for having made a big profit. This probably did not escape the notice of the central committee, as the plans and prospectuses for the Exhibition of Anvers of 1894 and the 'Prospectus of the Cotton States and International Exhibition to be held at Atlanta, September 18th to December 31st, 1895' can be found in the State of Geneva Archives, Exposition nationale, box 54, dossier 976, Rapport final VIII Le Parc de Plaisance.

9   State of Geneva Archives, Jur Civ AAa 239 dossier no. 3574, 'Location du terrain du parc de plaisance. Prix minimal.' The rental price of land generally varied from 25 to 50 francs per square metre. The land for the African Village was rented at approximately 10.95 francs per square metre. The situation at the edge of the site and the size of the surface rented explains this lower-than-average price.

10   Entitled *Ces quatre dernières vues*, and dated 7 May 1896, this very short film shows the 'Arab procession' [no. 310 to 313] 'filing past the film theatre of Lumière's cinematograph during the exhibition.' The cameraman was Alexandre Promio. The inventory indicates that this film was first shown on 12 June 1896 in Madrid at a private projection for the Queen Regent of Spain. The first public projection was in Lyon on 14 June 1896. CNC Film Archives at Bois d'Arcy, in Paris. However, there is no doubt that the footage was filmed on 27 April 1896. The film was shown in the documentary *Zoos humains* by Pascal Blanchard and Eric Deroo, 2002.

11   *Tribune de Genève*, 118 (22 May); *Le Genevois*, 119 (Monday 25 May), p. 3; and *Le Nouvelliste vaudois*, 122 (26 May 1896). On the Tabaski ceremony or Aïd-el-Kebir in Senegal, from where the inhabitants of the African Village of Geneva

came, see Armelle Chatelier http://www.senegalonline.com/francais/histoire/religions/tabaski.htm (07.09.06). On the calendar and determining the date of the ceremony, see Loïc-Michel Perrin, *Le lexique du système calendaire-chronométrique wolof*, annexe 1, pp. 654–74, www. linguistique-wolof.com (07.09.06).

12 In *La Liberté*, 276 (Thursday 26 November 1896), p. 2 it is specified that the inscription on the small monument 'is not in Arabic, but in the Wolof dialect'.

13 *Le Courrier de Genève*, 148 (Friday 26 June), p. 3. This phrase is not reprinted by *Le Nouvelliste vaudois*.

14 *Le Nouvelliste vaudois*, 210 (Saturday 5 September 1896), p. 2. The newspaper mentions three young Swiss girls, whose parents did not seem to approve of their choice of husbands, and 'One of the couples is thinking of opening a café called The Black Continent. Another is talking about a business, a farm, etc.'.

15 This is denied by the *Geschäftsblatt* of Thun, 76 (Saturday 19 September 1896), p. 2. A review of the marriage register of the commune of Petit-Saconnex and those of 45 Genevan communes for 1896 and 1897 confirms that this was untrue, State of Geneva Archives.

16 Gérard Lévy, a French expert in the history of photography, confirms the exceptional case of the revolt that he calls a 'strike'. However, he is mistaken about the date ('1915 approximately') and indicates a single cause for the event (the fact that the wages were not paid). Film *Zoos humains* Pascal Blanchard and Eric Deroo, Arte 2002, first broadcast 29 December 2002.

17 On a fight between Africans and Europeans at the Nubian Village of the Milan Exhibition, see *La Liberté*, 146 (Friday 29 June 1906), p. 2.

18 On Dahomeans abandoned in Marseille see *La Liberté*, 242 (Wednesday 18 October 1893), p. 3.

19 *Le Temps*, Friday 15 September 2006, p. 37, reprints an interview with the newly appointed curator of the Geneva Museum of Ethnography (MEG), Jacques Hainard. Since the beginning of 2007 an exhibition is devoted to Alfred Bertrand, donor of objects collected during his numerous expeditions. See also Issue 46 of the review *Totem*, edited by MEG.

20 *Le Genevois*, 136 (Saturday 13 June 1896), pp. 2–3, and *Là Tribune de Genève*, 137 (Saturday 13 June 1896), p. 2. All of the elements mentioned in this paragraph appear in these two accounts, which seem to be relatively true to reality, but with a few differences: *La Tribune de Genève* mentions 23–25 specimens instead of 15, for example. The age of the old man might also be questioned. This conference was given in a revised form by Yung on 7 October 1896 to the *Société suisse des professeurs de gymnase*, meeting at a congress in Fribourg. See *La Liberté*, 243 (Sunday 18 October 1896), p. 2.

21 The troupe of John Hagenbeck, composed of 38 Ceylonese and three elephants, performed there from 27 May to 10 June 1925. *See* Staehelin, 1993: 92–93, 158.

22 Translated by Margaret Lainsbury, Fribourg. Many thanks to Martha Ritchie for her help and advice.

29

Living Ethnological and Colonial Exhibitions in Liberal and Fascist Italy

GUIDO ABBATTISTA AND NICOLA LABANCA

This contribution aims to provide a brief overview of some of the most significant manifestations of the phenomenon of living ethnological exhibitions in the Italy of the Liberal and Fascist eras.[1] To this end, two introductory remarks of a methodological nature seem to be appropriate. The first is that the phenomena known as 'human zoos' belong to a wider category of historical forms of 'use', i.e. 'public use', of live 'specimens' of alien races – those perceived as different, admirable or terrible (in their nature, appearance, ability or pathology) – in the context of representations and rituals of political power (triumphs, regal ceremonies, parades and pageants), social power (festivals, celebrations, theatrical entertainment, processions, displays for fairs and markets), or cultural power (collections, exhibitions of curiosities and wonders, places of scientific observation). The second remark is that, in our opinion, investigation on this kind of event, with reference to the specific contexts, modes and aims of the late nineteenth and early twentieth centuries, should only use general categories – such as racism, propaganda, colonialism, commodification, reification, exploitation, or even newly coined categories such as animalization – with great caution. Such elements were certainly present in the socio-cultural events inspired by the ideas of racial hierarchy and the exaltation of Western supremacy, but historical research should not be limited to compiling lists of episodes. It should instead bring to light not only general and common traits but also specific historical characteristics in the context of history and environment, focusing on the ambiguities that render general paradigms more problematic.

Living Ethnographical Exhibitions in Liberal Italy (1884–1914)

In the history of post-unification Italy, except for a few minor examples comparable to ethnic-themed exhibitions – such as the presentation of American Indians to ecclesiastic authorities for missionary purposes, and sporadic observations regarding ethnic African individuals (Giovanni Miani's Akkas or Romolo Gessi's Akka girl called Saìda; see Puccini 1999; Abbattista 2005) – the first authentic living exhibition did not take place until 1884. The Italian General Exhibition held in Turin in that year was the new nation-state's first great national exhibition and represented an opportunity to illustrate not only the new nation's economic, social and artistic achievements but also Italy's first colonial enterprise in eastern Africa, in the area of the bay of Assab. For the first time, in addition to a rather poor exhibition of products from the Abyssinian region, living native Danakil, or 'Assabeses', were brought to Italy. This first living ethnographical exhibition, enclosed in its pretend African village and enlivened by solemn receptions, public promenades and displays, and theatrical appearances (Torino 1884a, 1884b; Abbattista 2004), reveals, when closely scrutinized, how public curiosity, aroused by these black self-proclaimed princes, did not necessarily imply acceptance of the triumphalist 'African mirages' of a fledgling colonial policy at all. The six figures from Assab, who were able histrionically to transform themselves from passive 'specimens of the human race' into unpredictably capricious actors, did not provoke racist judgements or behaviour, but rather benevolent and paternalistic forms of humour and even protests of a humanitarian tone.

A change was evident in the Palermo National Exhibition in 1891–92 (immediately after the foundation of the Eritrean colony), at which the Eritrean display exalted the civilizing enterprise that Italy had begun. The large village populated by 'sixty-five natives, five mules and several sheep of Abyssinian race' was intended to give the public an authentic view of African life, including examples of types of people, family groups, domestic arts, crafts, music, dances and forms of entertainment (Palermo 1892). The exhibition was explicitly intended to be different from the one held in Turin, which was criticized as an 'evil and grotesque [...] African swindle' with a 'bunch of ragged people'. However, as in Turin, anthropological science was absent and official ethnography still concentrated on analysing and publicly illustrating the unexpected multiplicity of Italian cultural varieties. Evidence that could be qualified as outspokenly racist, explicable by a proper racist etiology, was limited and marginal. The very idea of confining a sample of 'different' people in an enclosed space for the benefit of a public composed of white, European and 'civilized' spectators is obviously in itself a symptom of a mentality tending towards racism, but open manifestations of racism at the time remained sporadic and in the minority compared to paternalistic and philanthropic declarations.

The quarter of a century between 1890 and 1914 represented a golden period in Italy for living ethnographical exhibitions, thanks to events occasioned by national expositions and fairs, belonging to the world of theatrical and mass entertainment, or even originating from missionary initiatives. An example of the latter sort was the event that took place during the Italian–American exhibition in Genoa in 1892 (to mark the fourth centenary of the discovery of America by Columbus), and that was the work of the Salesian Fathers.

On this occasion, alongside the collections of objects of ethnographic interest from Tierra del Fuego and Patagonia, the Catholic missions' display included a reconstruction of a small village with a little church (as if it were a natural part of the village) and a group of native South Americans. Naturally intelligent and docile, these 'beautiful examples of their race' were then taken for an audience with Pope Leo XIII as a demonstration of the civilizing work of the missionaries. It was not intended as a 'spectacle for the idle curiosity of others'. 'This reification,' stated the organizers, 'would have been beneath us and you.' What they were offering was the edifying example of 'savages' 'already reconquered in the light of faith [....] initiated in the much longed for rebirth' (*Illustrazione popolare* 1892: 750).

By the end the century, entrepreneurs specializing in exhibitions, circuses and shows, and organizers of European tours of troupes of 'exotic artistes' also appeared in Italy, thus fully realizing the commercial aspect of exhibitions of alterity. The commodification of the 'actors' was certainly an important aspect, but it would be an error to ignore the element of voluntariness and inclination to bargain that characterized the relationships between entrepreneurs and actors. The 1898 National Exhibition held in Turin highlighted the evolution of this genre of ethnographical exhibition (Torino 1898). It included an Eritrean exhibit – with individuals from Eritrea and Abyssinia – and an exhibition of sacred art with a missionary section which displayed objects from South America, China and India, and where whole families gathered in prayer, studied, or were involved in making and embroidering clothing. Africans were also present, but in a somewhat less edifying show, which was already known in European capitals due to the sinister infanticidal and anthropophagous fame of its leading actors: the Corps of the Amazons, Wild Women of Dahomey. This was a troupe of over 50 people, led by the Swiss entrepreneur Albert Urbach. A real Dahomean village was set up in Turin's parco del Valentino. Although this exhibition was comparable to the genre of exotic-themed entertainment, visitors of the time were conscious of the presence of elements belonging to a real, living, ethnographical exhibition. The numerous visitors timorously attracted to the Amazon village on the banks of the River Po could observe not only demonstrations of wild dances but also rituals, ceremonies, costumes and typical scenes of the lives of an African population (Amazzoni 1898).

The Italian public was becoming accustomed to these 'ethnic shows', thanks to one of the greatest ethnic and evocative circuses, Buffalo Bill's Wild West show, which was present in Italy in 1890 and again in 1906. Towards the end of the nineteenth century, Italy – along with the rest of Europe – was crossed by many convoys, especially from Africa, the main attraction of which was the eccentricity and diversity of their leading actors, who were often described using animalistic metaphors. The 'bizarre and interesting' convoy of the Dinka of Sudan arrived in November 1895, led by the entrepreneur Delle Piane. These 42 'fun Negroes', who had already passed through much of Europe, including the zoo in Basel, arrived at the variety theatres of Milan and Turin. Their performances, as well as those of the 'dwarves of the Lilliputian troupe and their pocket-size horses and elephants', were in constant demand by a public attracted by a 'piece of Africa on stage'; a 'live picture of habits and customs' from a part of the world that 'horrible as it is, is becoming increasingly fashionable' (*Corriere della Sera* 1895). This combination of the informative and the pleasurable was highlighted by an expression that had become common: 'live ethnographic exhibition'. In almost the only case in Italy, the Dinka attracted scientists too. Cesare Lombroso (1835–1909), the famous psychiatrist and criminologist, and Mario Carrara (1866–1937), physician and anthropologist, carried out a detailed anthropometric and psychological–behavioural study. Between wild animal metaphors and analogies with criminals, the two scholars defined the 'savages' as 'slow', with intellectual capacities confined to memory, and 'primitive' in their aesthetic tastes. Their 'extraordinary apathy' was described as a question of character, rather than a consequence of their state of confinement: 'apart from the brief moments in which they were required to put on shows, they lay around all day on their bedding, just like oxen in a stable, repulsed by any movement, even if they would have earned by it, such as the study that we wanted to carry out on them' (Lombroso and Carrara 1896a; 1896b).

Another example of an ethnic show took place in 1903, when the Togolese and Mandingo companies arrived on the stages of Turin. These two troupes comprised 15 native Togolese and 11 natives of Sierra Leone, who had been through Germany, Switzerland and Russia. In October 1903 these 'dark gentlemen with their respective ladies' arrived by train in Turin, where they had 'put up tents and laid branches on the streets' (*Gazzetta del Popolo della Domenica* 1903).

The comments in the periodical press revealed that reactions were not unanimous. While some were not fooled by this type of show and highlighted the ideological and racial implications, others made overtly racist remarks. The national daily, *Corriere della Sera*, said of the Dinka that the 'savages' exhibited gave 'an impression of the race that the Europeans claim they wish to civilize, but which, if they were more truthful, they should confess to wanting to exterminate, as if they were a race of monkeys' (*Corriere della Sera* 1895). On the contrary, these black people were maliciously caricatured in the satirical weekly magazine *La Luna* as belonging to 'an inferior race' (*La Luna* 1895). Aspects of cruel brutality were suggested in comments such as those recorded in the diary of a visitor to Turin in 1898 (and no ordinary one, as he was a member of the Italian Parliament): 'We are going to the Exhibition to see the Dahomey Amazons, who, together with some warriors belonging to their race, do typical dances and games [....] Like a group of apes or dogs, these negroes go around the world led by a German entrepreneur, who was cruel enough to take them as far as Siberia. The cold and different customs took the life out of these wretched people, but when they die, the entrepreneur says with a cold smile, 'we get fresh ones sent over' (Guiccioli 1973: 235–36).

By the beginning of the twentieth century, the presence of African villages and 'natives' in exhibitions had become a well-established custom. In 1902, the International Exhibition of Modern Decorative Arts in Turin presented, among various exotic attractions, a 'Sudanese and South-Oranese' village populated by 'black creatures', thanks again to Delle Piane. This 'characteristic portrayal of customs and environment' was not, however, particularly successful. The great 'black festival', 'triumph of the black race', with cavalcades, mock battles, Moresque dances, parades among the crowds and Sudanese banquets, received a decidedly lukewarm reception. There were, in fact, signs of the 'public's stubborn scepticism' (*Gazzetta del Popolo* 1902: 4).

At the Milan Sempione exhibition in 1906, there was a colonial display and a village: a 'wonderful genuine reproduction of an African village inhabited by about 100 natives of the Eritrean colony'. This open-air spectacle included rides on elephants and in vehicles drawn by zebras, and choreographic shows with displays of exotic animals, all vouched for by the professionalism of a great entrepreneur and exhibitor of men and animals, the German Carl Hagenbeck. However, the Milan exhibition contained much more than this: African and oriental scenes steeped in magic, seduction and mysticism were reproduced in large areas, such as 'Cairo in Milan' with vehicles, stores, bars, mysterious rooms and the frenzied music of the 'Dance of the Dervishes'; or the 'Nubian Village' – 'a spectacle impressive in its cruel colourful beauty,' crowded with 'beautiful specimens of the race: strong-limbed, square-built men and women, some as black as soot, others of the most attractive tar colour.' A phantasmagoria of ethnic groups, customs, languages, crafts, mock homes and workshops, scenes and portrayals of everyday life – almost foreshadowing 'holy utopia: the ideal and real brotherhood of peoples' (Milano 1906: 179–80).

The great International Exhibition held in Turin in 1911 to mark the fiftieth anniversary of the Kingdom of Italy was no less impressive. It included two ethnic exhibitions: an Eritrean village and a Somali village. The former, part of the 'great Eritrean display', was populated by 'artists and workers', goldsmiths and weavers, with their examples of 'characteristic and rudimental industry' and their 'strange new jobs', which were able to render attractive a colony that for many was little more than a sterile expanse of stones and brambles. With its 30 natives – 'wonderful specimens of the human race' – the Somali village was intended to present a 'corner of Somalia', a region that had become an Italian colony in 1905. Again the laudatory intent was clear: diversity was evoked not to highlight distance between races, but to prompt approval of the Italian colonial enterprise. The colonial themes were, however, again accompanied by a grandiose exotic show. Ernest Pourtauborde, a professional organizer of 'intelligent' attractions, along with Lucien Jusseaume, the famous *peintre-décorateur* of the Opéra in Paris, were entrusted with setting up the great 'oriental festival', an 'ethnographic exhibition caught in the midst of action'. Reconstructions evoking countries such as Algeria, Tunisia and Egypt were to be found alongside corners of Madagascar, Senegal, Congo, Dahomey, Niger and displays inspired by Indochina, China and Japan. Observers had a round perception that this was a magnificent example of the progress that 'popular entertainment' had made: 'a voyage to the Orient for around half a lira' (Torino 1911: 246–51).

The last important example of a live ethnographic exhibition before the First World War was the Genoa International Exhibition of 1914. The Libyan War had just ended, with the Italian conquest of Cyrenaica and Tripolitania: the Genoa exhibition was therefore literally labelled 'imperialist' in its style, with 'warlike' slogans and trophies of Italy's victory over the Turks (*Illustrazione Italiana* 1914: 622; Genova 1914). The conquest of Libya was celebrated with photographic, statistic and archaeological documents, as well as with the presence of 'live soldiers', the *zaptiè*, 'faithful soldiers from down there'. These native police forces were given the task of symbolizing the civilizing project of a colonial empire 'formed over thirty years of pain, patience and oblivion'.

Presence and Absence under Fascism

After half a century as a unified country – a minor milestone for other European countries but perceived as important in Italy – the country was still a Liberal power, but saw itself as different and greater (Labanca 2002b; Del Boca 1976–1984; Del Boca 1986–1988). We have already seen how in 1914, only three years after the exhibition to mark the fiftieth anniversary of unification, Liberal Italy had shown the first signs of a certain disinterest towards the exhibition of 'native bodies'. Few natives were seen at all in Genoa, except in the uniforms of the *zaptiè* and *askari* (Bono 1992). It is hardly surprising that none were seen in the world war years, nor even in the numerous colonial-themed exhibitions that began to be organized when the flames of the conflict had been extinguished. Only in 1920, for example, were colonial exhibitions organized in Milan, Padua, Trieste and Naples – a sign of the post-war revival of expansionist circles – but to see Africans, one was more likely to have to visit *non*-colonial exhibitions. At the 1922 Fair held in Milan, for example, a traditional meeting-place for the world of business in one of the country's few truly industrial cities, Italians could admire a colonial pavilion guarded by a large squad of *askari*.

After centuries of pre-unification fascination with the exotic, and half a century of unification lived between the exotic and the launch of colonialism in the strict sense, a mere decade (between the exhibitions to mark the fiftieth anniversary of unification and the advent of Fascism) was sufficient to bring about a change of content and tone in these events. The *askari* were obviously as African as the Hottentot Venus, Saìda or the Akka, but compared to them they were (or, rather, people were led to believe they were) Westernized; although they were armed, their presence was less perturbing than that of the wild Africans of previous times, or of those who had been 'deported' to 'native villages': their presence was, in fact, organized and regimented. They were the personification of Africa under Italian command – no longer wild and free.

The eagerness for strength and power that colonial Italy both represented and produced became recognizable in the extreme nationalism of the Fascist movement, which came into power in October 1922, and in January 1925 proclaimed the end of the Liberal state, creating a 'liberticide' and reactionary regime.

It would obviously be wrong automatically to expect an immediate change of tone in the colonial exhibitions and the displays of 'native bodies'. Therefore it was still possible, in the early years of Fascism, to visit colonial exhibitions that seemed to belong to another era. It is understandable that the colonial pavilion at the Vatican Universal Missionary Exhibition of 1925 could not be extremely Fascist, and it is unsurprising that the small colonial trade exhibitions that continued to be set up in 100 Italian cities still resembled those of former Liberal Italy, also because they did not involve the presence of Africans.

However, the general climate was changing, not only in Italian Africa, but in Italy itself. An article in a colonial journal published at the end of 1925, when Italian colonial exhibitions were organized in Lausanne, Monza, Naples and Fiume, observed that when such exhibitions held in Italy were compared with those of other European powers, it was painful to admit that 'extremely useful lessons' needed to be learned from the 'expert organization of the exhibitions in France, Holland and Belgium', and that Italy should 'observe how much needs to be done to achieve the patient and perfect organization of which such States have demonstrated themselves to be undisputed masters' (*Italia Coloniale* 1925).

Nevertheless, for a regime that had placed much emphasis on imperialism and Africanism, the exhibitions were increasingly necessary for cultural and purely political reasons: it was a question of fighting 'our national defeatists' campaign of denigration [which] had been very successful in its aim of convincing [the world] that our colonial empire was no more than a big box of burning sand' (*Italia Coloniale* 1925). The colonial section of the 1928 Turin Esposizione Internazionale Industriale ed Agricola, showed that the regime was trying to talk of Africa and colonies as much as possible. Here, there was a colonial zoological display which, according to the press attracted 'continuous processions of visitors' (*Italia Coloniale* 1928b), and a total of four colonial villages, one for each colony: Eritrea, Somalia, Libya and now also Rhodes. They were organized around an exedra-like central area (a clear Roman reference), from which paths led to the inevitable *tukul*, the 'snake charmers', the 'Kassala dog' trainers and the keepers of 'small Somali lions'. As well as animating the exotic areas (the 'particular fauna' was emphasized in the Cyrenaica sector), the 'natives' were expected to demonstrate how they produced wealth for Italy: thus there were Libyan carpet workshops, doum palm basket-makers, Eritrean leather workers, goldsmiths, painters, blacksmiths, mother-of-pearl artists, etc.

In short, the 1928 exhibition aimed to 'maintain local colour as faithfully as possible' (*Italia Coloniale* 1928a). On close inspection, however, the African villages smacked of old, Liberal Italy, and of cheap exoticism. The decision of the hypothetical future king of Italy, Prince Umberto, to choose the young Somali, Nur Mohamed, from among all the Africans present and *adopt* him, as the contemporary press reported, was a gesture somewhere between beneficent and paternalistic in character, and possibly somewhat inconsistent with the imperial and military tone that Fascism had begun to try to give Italian colonies and Italians. The times, however, were not in favour of the 'local colour' dear to Liberal Italy or Prince Umberto's foreign or national adoptions: in the 1930s the winds were blowing in the direction of strengthening and stabilizing the Fascist regime.

This was revealed by a significant and, all in all, timely episode. At Littorio Airport on 8 June 1930, a 'representation of a colonial guerrilla warfare' was staged 'to extol the effective actions of the air force in the colonies' (*Italia Coloniale*, 1930c). Thus far, no Africans seemed to be involved. However, to emphasize effectively the 'modern' results obtained by the Fascist air force when bombing Libyan or Somali anti-colonial rebels and the relative civilian populations (sometimes using gas), the regime's meticulous and megalomaniac organization had 'reproduced a whole Arabian village and wanted a large group of Arab horsemen specially brought in from Tripolitania to participate'.

However, Fascism was careful not to use only the brutal aspect of war and weapons. Also in 1930, the Minister of Colonies' Research Office arranged Italy's participation in the International Missionary Exhibition at the Vatican (*Italia Coloniale* 1930b), the presence of African notables at the 'august wedding' of Prince Umberto (*Italia Coloniale* 1930c) and, most important, it organized the participation of Italian representatives in the great international colonial exhibitions. We do not know much of the Liberal Italian participation in the Inter-Allied Colonial Exhibition held in Paris in 1922, but we do know what lengths and costs the Fascist regime went to in an attempt to give its empire an image of present-ability, such as at the Anversa International Exhibition of 1930 (*Italia Coloniale* 1930a) and especially the Paris Exposition colonial internationale of 1931.

According to the research carried out to date, it seems no 'native bodies' other than 'Westernized' *askari* and the notable subjects were present, or at least they were not greatly encouraged or advertised. One category of Africans that was allowed to appear in public were the subject notables – or notables pleading to be subjected to the Fascist authorities. The presence of *askari*, who were rhetorically defined as 'faithful followers', was also encouraged – and not in small groups, as in '*Italietta*' (pre-Fascist Italy, seen as an unimportant nation), but in the immense numbers that Fascism was fond of. For the first anniversary of the Empire on 8 and 9 May 1937, enormous numbers of 'coloured' soldiers from all the Italian colonies were made to march through Rome in a colossal demonstration (*Italia Coloniale* 1937). The colonial press reported the event with a play on words '*L'impero era sulla Via dell'impero*' [The Empire was in Empire's boulevard] (*Italia Coloniale* 1937). The demonstration was no longer based on the 1911 model or that of Turin in 1928; if anything, it was more similar to the Littorio Airport event, but on a much grander scale.

The question remains, however, why progressively fewer Africans were seen in Fascist era colonial Italy, while the regime spoke increasingly of colonies. In this imperial – and at the same time native-phobic – context, the news that the Fascists were going to organize a colossal event to celebrate the conquest of the Empire – on an even more impressive scale than that in Rome in 1937 – inevitably caused quite a sensation. The event-exhibition was to be held in Naples; it was intended to rival all previous international exhibitions in grandeur and to create permanent attractions. Fascism had finally understood that it could not continue to *talk* of overseas and present itself as an empire without *showing* it. It even considered making the exhibition a regular event, with the title 'Triennial Show of Italian Territories Overseas'. The organizers of the exhibition intended to 'reconnect the Fascist Empire with Caesar's Empire' and show the world 'the masculine and virile side of Fascist and Imperial Italy' (*Italia Coloniale* 1939).

We shall not examine the planning and realization of the Triennial Exhibition in Naples (Dore 1992) in detail here. Regarding the aspect of concern to us, the event would have been animated by the presence of Africans: 'a series of villages will host the most characteristic ethnic groups', and there were even plans to create a 'faithful reproduction of a Saharan oasis'. One in particular was supposed to recreate, within the enclosure of a single village, the whole 'ethnic mosaic of Ethiopia' (*Italia Coloniale* 1940). The exhibition was planned to host hundreds of thousands, perhaps millions, of visitors: the grandeur and 'construction' – or artifice – were to be the key characteristics of the event. It was to be, the press specified, 'the Imperial city'. And not just any empire, but the empire that had been ruled by racial legislation since 1937, for a country in which anti-Semitic legislation had been in force since 1938.

The use of the conditional is not by chance: just one month after the inauguration of the exhibition, Benito Mussolini declared war on France and Great Britain. The exhibition, with all its planning, collapsed. Not only the exhibition, but the entire imperial project – the real project in Africa, for which much blood had been shed – fell into ruin, leaving the propaganda (the Naples event, in which significant resources had been invested) meaningless. This was merely a premonition of the end of the regime in July 1943, and of Mussolini himself in April 1945.

To conclude, the greatest opportunities (Labanca 1992) that Italians had to see live colonial subjects in the 1920s and 1930s were the exhibitions of 1928, 1937 and 1940 (to which we could add the less important but precursory exhibition of 1930), i.e. not many for a country with an openly imperialist policy. All of these events had very particular characteristics and not all of them were on a large scale: the 1928 exhibition was held in Turin, in the extreme north-west of the country; the 1937 exhibition was essentially a military parade; the 1940 event was a failed investment, considering the sudden declaration of war. They could be seen as a demonstration of weakness.

Yet we should not forget that, unlike the rest of Europe, on the occasion of the assault on Ethiopia Fascism had offered the Italians a *mass* opportunity – 500,000 soldiers and militarized workers – to see more 'native bodies' than any other colonial power (except Great Britain in 1899–1902 and France in 1954–62). This, on the contrary, would seem to be a demonstration of strength. In considering Italian colonialism, the question of the strength or weakness of Italy's colonial project arises again, this time in the guise of the exhibitions of natives. Was all this strength or weakness? Was it a common characteristic of colonial Europe at the time, or did it reflect an Italian or Fascist trait? Further research is required before a definite answer can be given. It should be pointed out that such studies in Italy are only very recent (Labanca 1992; Abbattista 2004). Research on the topic therefore requires development, as well as a differentiated analysis that emphasizes the diversity of the dynamics, in the various contexts, of exhibition projects that often differed from each other – inspired as they were by curiosity and admiration, study, care and education, or mere propaganda.

This would improve our understanding of the complex background to Republican/modern Italians' attitude towards 'native bodies' circulating in the streets and squares of Italy – who are now no longer colonial subjects and no longer definable as natives. In Europe in general and certainly in the specific case of Italy, it is incorrect to use direct and continuous links between the colonial image of natives and the postcolonial image of immigrants. The long history of exhibitions of 'native bodies' has obviously changed drastically over the last thirty years, in which many immigrants have passed through the country and a percentage of men and women from Africa, Asia, Latin America and (more recently) Eastern Europe have settled in Italy. This is a new experience for Italy (Labanca 2002b), and – for many Italians – may be seen as yet another (or perhaps the last) chapter in the longer history of the migration and display of natives in the country of 'good Italians', on which this chapter has focused.

Notes

1 This text is the common work of both authors. Guido Abbattista was responsible for the section on 'Living ethnographical exhibitions in Liberal Italy (1884–1914)' and Nicola Labanca for that on 'Presence and absence under Fascism'.

30

Exhibiting People in Spain: Colonialism and Mass Culture

NEUS MOYANO MIRANDA

In the local news items in the Barcelona papers on 25 July 1897, details appeared of the exhibition of a group of Ashanti, from what is now Ghana, on a piece of ground in Ronda Universidad. The Ashanti arrived amid great expectation on 21 July in a boat from Marseilles, and it was announced that they would be exhibited until 21 November: 'The Ashanti. A black people, 150 individuals. Open night and day – Ronda de la Universidad 35 – Admission 1 peseta, Thursdays fashion day, admission 2 pesetas.'

The spectacle had enormous repercussions for the life of the city, an aspect reflected in both the local and illustrated press, which similarly documented their stay in Barcelona, Madrid and Valencia.[1] But aside from the picturesque nature of the visit of a group of Africans (the first in Barcelona), this exhibition – like others that took place between 1887 and 1930 – enables us to analyse the image of colonized non-European peoples that would be disseminated in Spain during that period.

In Spain various exhibitions of human groups took place in a variety of different contexts: the Philippines Exhibition (1887), mounted by the Ministry for Overseas Territories in the Parque del Retiro in Madrid; the above-mentioned exhibition of Ashanti (1897) in Barcelona, Valencia and Madrid; and of Inuits from the Labrador Peninsula (1900) in the Jardines del Buen Retiro in Madrid and in the Nuevo Retiro in Barcelona. In the early twentieth century, an exhibition took place of around 100 Senegalese belonging to different ethnic groups in the Parque del Tibidabo (1913), and in 1925 there was another, of black inhabitants of Equatorial Guinea, in the same park. Finally, the 1929 Ibero-American Exhibition in Seville included a village from (what was then) Spanish Guinea. Three of these exhibitions were of a private nature, and the first and last were mounted by the central administration. This distinction makes for a difference as to the form and purpose of the exhibitions. (This study will not allow for consideration of other spectacles relating

353

to this theme that took place around the same time, such as Buffalo Bill's Wild West show, which visited Barcelona in 1889, and the oriental and 'Moorish' villages that could be seen in the Barcelona and Seville exhibitions of 1929.)

The Exhibitions

Human exhibitions would form part of the visual system created from the mid-nineteenth century onwards – a system reinforced by the powerful propaganda mechanisms that photography permitted. For many, exhibitions were a way of getting to know other 'exotic' peoples, but this was a denigrating form of spectacle that survived in Europe and the USA until the 1930s, too long for it not to have become a persistent feature in the Western imagination.

Associated with the exhibitions were emerging forms of visual communication: photographs that took the form of cartes de visite, tourist albums and postcards. The illustrated press rapidly incorporated photography in the 1880s (Riego 2001), and cinema would not long afterwards also be incorporated into this nineteenth-century visual system. The Lumière brothers' first films depict an end-of-century event that was undoubtedly a significant one in the city of Lyon, where the *cinématographe* was itself invented: i.e. the exhibition of Ashanti people in the 1897 exhibition, the same people who would travel to Barcelona, Madrid and Valencia shortly afterwards.

The first Spanish exhibition to include the human displays – the Philippines General Exhibition of 1887 – was, in fact, an initiative of the central government in Madrid, promoted by, among others, the politician, historian and poet Víctor Balaguer. The economic and human resources available for such events at the time cannot be compared with private initiatives. In fact, the Philippines Exhibition reproduced an indigenous village, in imitation of the 'Villages indigènes' seen in international exhibitions in Paris in 1878 and especially of the colonial exhibition in Amsterdam in 1883 (in both of which Spain had taken part). The exhibition mounted by the Ministry for Overseas Territories did not set out to present a 'savage' spectacle, but to demonstrate that, given the influence of the Spanish protectorate, some natives could be 'civilized' and reclaimed for industry. Thus, alongside the Igorot village, other equally popular structures displayed an indigenous population in European dress or with traditional clothes working in the tobacco and textile trades.

In the discussions prior to the exhibition, the possibility was considered of bringing a group of Filipinos to Spain. They would have had various duties, working as park guards, or involved in the sale of goods and in the construction of the different cane and abaca buildings. In the event, an enclosure was erected to house the Igorot Camp, as it was called, in which a group of Filipinos was displayed throughout the exhibition solely as a demonstration of the different ethnic groups that inhabited the islands.

In order to accommodate the different exhibition spaces, buildings and landscaped areas (still in existence) were laid out in the Parque del Retiro in Madrid. The Royal Pavilion of the earlier Mining Exhibition was renovated for that purpose, and formed the space reserved for presentation of collections and materials either coming from the Philippines or borrowed from private collections. The Crystal Palace was also built as a hothouse for the display of exotic plants, in the style of the glass pavilion created for the Great Exhibition of 1851 in London.

Set up alongside the Crystal Palace was a railed area for the Igorot Camp, a fenced-off space that was to house the huts of the natives representing the different 'races' from the Philippines. A brook and a reservoir were also laid out (where Filipinos were expected to display their canoeing skills), as well as a cane bridge to allow access across the reservoir to the compound. All the cane buildings were constructed by the Filipinos who had been brought from the islands, constituting a colony of 55 people in total.

The camp – or space intended for the presentation of the life-size huts and their inhabitants from the Philippines, and for the public performance of different rituals – was a space surrounded by a narrow stream. It was reached via small bridges that crossed the river, and was in the centre of the space intended for the Philippines Exhibition, next to the central building and the Crystal Palace. The camp was separate from the building designed to display the islands' most important businesses: the Philippines Tobacco Company building, where Malay women could be seen employed in the manufacture of cigars, and the fabric-weaving building, where a number of women demonstrated the manufacture of the different textiles produced in the islands. Given this contrast, the comparison was inevitable between those who could be acculturated, who dressed in a different way and represented a greater degree of civilization, and the 'savages', exhibited semi-naked and seen performing rituals and dances.

One difference from the commercial exhibitions was that there were no females in the camp, perhaps because the exhibition of practically naked women was considered indecent. The enclosure was fenced off by a railing or palisade made of cane. To reach it, the visitor went through an entrance displaying a horse's skull on two poles (Florez and Piquer 1887: 28). The complex clearly showed that visitors were entering a non-Christian area, and was clearly separated from the rest of the more civilized fellow countrymen who were used in the different productions outlined above. The compound represented the village of those resistant to civilization, where one entered the land of the 'savage'.

Attributed in the press of the time to this group were all sorts of atrocities and acts of immorality (including cannibalism), with the result that they were observed and separated from the rest of their compatriots. In an adjoining space called the Deer Park were a number of animals from the islands. Among the activities on display was the presentation of typical rituals and sacrifices, for which animals (most notably pigs and hens) were provided. Never shown, on the other hand, was the typically Filipino custom of eating dog flesh, a taboo for Western civilization that was nevertheless commercially exploited in the Philippines Exhibition held in Louisiana in 1904. The spectacle also consisted of the enactment of daily activities, in the open air and inside the huts, as was customary in other human exhibitions of the period.

By presenting a fenced compound, which it was necessary to enter in order to be transported to another time and place, the aim was clearly to make visitors feel they were in another world, one where they might begin to forget their everyday life and be immersed in another unknown or 'savage' civilization. Context was particularly important, as is revealed by the fact that in the photographs of the time the Igorots do not usually appear with Westerners and the setting is carefully prepared, as in studio portraits in which a painted backdrop is used to imitate the jungle. The photographers Laurent and Marqués de Bergés each created albums devoted to the exhibition in which this sense of separateness is clearly shown.

Ten years later, in 1897, the exhibition of Ashanti people took place in Barcelona, Madrid and Valencia. In July 1897, the Ashanti were installed on a piece of ground in Barcelona's Ensanche district. The space was not large for an exhibition on the scale of that planned, as a journalist pointed out in *La Ilustración Artística* (issue 815), but it was set up in a very central spot, almost on Plaza de Cataluña, and not far from the areas given over at the time for recreational and mass entertainment. Until 1890 the great panorama of the Battle of Waterloo was also found near there. With the extending of the Ensanche, these spaces disappeared or moved to the outskirts of the city.

One of the inconveniences the location presented was that it had no trees, no uneven ground and none of those decorative features normally found in this sort of exhibition, in which the scenery was, as has been suggested above, an important part of the staging. The organizers appear nevertheless to have managed to make the most of the location. Extending on either side of the land were two rows of huts, dormitories and workshops, and erected in the centre were four shelters plus the kitchens, where the Ashanti spectacle was staged. Unlike in the Philippines Exhibition, the group in this instance included women and, above all, children. A school was exhibited, and, as well as carrying out their daily chores, the Ashanti sold pyrogravured objects and jewellery. There was a blacksmith (who made arrowheads), a carpenter and a weaver.

The character of the exhibition was different in Madrid, where a group of some 50 individuals moved to the so-called Jardines del Buen Retiro, a wooded space where the Africans erected their shelters and huts. These gardens were run by the businessman José Jiménez Laynez, who had leased the land from the City Council. This was a recreational space offering various activities and games, small open-air theatres, cafés and other facilities. Also announced were the different performances the Ashanti put on, consisting of dances and pitched battles, as well as their mealtimes, between noon and 1pm, which also formed a spectacle in their own right in all the human exhibitions we have managed to document.

Also taking place in the Jardines del Buen Retiro between March and April 1900 was an exhibition of Inuit people, who, en route from London to Paris, were displayed there. This involved seven families from the Labrador Peninsula with their dogs, sledges and fishing canoes. The staging of everyday life – the sight of skins being tanned and harpoons handled, and the making of their characteristic ivory objects – also constituted the main attraction of these Inuits. Hired by the American businessman R. Taver, they came equipped with all the materials required for their typical way of life (Verde Casanova 1993: 88). From 3–13 May the Inuits were also in Barcelona, in a variety theatre called the Nuevo Retiro, also close to Plaza de Cataluña.

Between March and August 1913, an exhibition was staged in Tibidabo of 100 Senegalese, who were installed at the top of the mountain. (Tibidabo was a recreational space, popular among day trippers from Barcelona, with various attractions, restaurants and cafés that still exist. It was not in the centre of Barcelona, but in an elevated situation near the city.) A number of huts were built in a semicircle, and in the centre of these the different everyday activities of the Senegalese took place, including the manufacture of various products, which were put on sale. Once again, one of the principal spectacles was their mealtime, as stereoscopic photographs taken by amateur enthusiasts show.[2] The exhibition was also reported in the press, which had by now greatly evolved in its presentation of such subjects, with images by the photo-journalists Josep Maria Sagarra and Frederic Ballell. Clear in many of them is the spontaneous reaction of members of the public watching the events, which enables us to elucidate the response of Western specta-tors to these groups.

In 1925 at this same location, but in another part of the park, the Tibidabo Society, prompted by the great success of the earlier exhibi-tion, displayed a Fula tribe from Equatorial Guinea, travelling under contract with the French businessman Tavier. The final exhibition we have currently located, once again in the context of an official display, is the 1929 Ibero-American Exhibition in Seville. The colonies that Spain still occupied were represented there by groups seen as typical. In this instance, the gardens next to the Spanish Guinea pavilion housed a group of Guineans in their huts. These performed dances every night (Rodríguez Bernal 1994: 381). There is also evidence of a Moorish Quarter, clearly an imitation of the famous Rue du Caire that had been seen in the 1889 Paris Exposition. At no time did the Latin American countries represented, now independent of Spain, exhibit any of their inhabitants.

The Participation of the Scientific Community

At the end of the nineteenth century, the Museum of Natural Sciences in Madrid created its anthropology section, drawing on the knowl-edge of Manuel Antón, the museum's curator, who had studied with Quatrefages in the Natural History Museum in Paris. At that time, in the early years of the discipline, expeditions were rare and the collection of objects, data and photographs was often entrusted to travellers who were not themselves anthropologists. For that reason, Europe's anthro-pological societies drew up precise guidelines governing the taking of photographs.

The exhibiting of ethnic groups provided an undeniable opportunity for such activity. From the very first, then, the Spanish Natural History Society and the Museum of Natural Sciences participated in all the exhibitions that took place in Madrid, taking photographs and anthro-pological measurements for their archives, in the same way that they collected photographs from the Philippines or other places, even taking advantage of other exhibitions that were being organized elsewhere in Europe. In the case of the Philippines Exhibition of 1887, during which three people from the indigenous community died, a mould of the body of one of the victims, a woman from the Caroline Islands, was made. Manuel Antón had to confront the Church on this issue, as he explains in one of the articles he published in El Globo. The fact that the Caroline Islands woman was a Catholic played an important part in the Church's negative response to scientific use of her body (Thode-Arora 2002b: 3).[3]

In the museum's laboratory, identity photographs were also taken of the individuals in the 1897 Ashanti exhibition, and of the Inuits in 1900. Likewise, photographs were acquired that had been produced by other studios of the time, which were commercial photographs taken during the exhibitions. In all these instances, the photographs did not meet the standards that anthropometry was then establishing, but adhered instead to a model that had been consolidated in the nineteenth century, in particular to illustrate national types.

The comments of anthropologists in the Anales de la Sociedad para la Historia Natural also bear witness to the visits they made to the exhibitions. Manuel Antón was even present at a birth during the 1897 Ashanti exhibition, probably invited by the impresarios who were behind the event. In 1900 an extended report on Inuit customs was reproduced in the Anales. On the occasion of the exhibition, the museum also acquired a series of some 50 pieces of Inuit handicraft and clothing, as well as a number of photographs. But along with its supposedly objective purpose in the classification of human races, photography was also able to disseminate an image of the non-European Other that would remain engrained in the nineteenth-century visual system. Far from being objective, that image helped create a stereotype endorsed not only by an anthropological science in which the idea of evolution predominated but also by colonial interests committed to demonstrating the inferiority and incapacity of the colonized – an image that has arguably survived until today.

The Observed

Little is known about the individuals who formed part of the ethnographic spectacles taking place throughout Europe. In the case of the Philippines Exhibition of 1887, as has been mentioned above, some 50 people were recruited to construct the traditional buildings in the park and, as is indicated in the earliest projects (Exposición Filipinas 1887: 46–52), to work as uniformed guards there. In practice, these individuals were meant to figure in the camp as 'savages', although we know that some of them had undergone colonial education. The selection took place, in the case of the Igorots in the camp, in order to illustrate different Filipino communities. Each individual represented one of the highland ethnicities that inhabited the island.

Neither is much known about how they received their remuneration, although it is recorded that the 'savages' earned 25 pesetas a month and the 'civilized' 60 pesetas (Sánchez Gómez 2003: 63).[4] Neither was anything ever said about the state's responsibility with respect to the death of the three people that occurred in Madrid. The Igorots received food and animals for the various sacrifices that took place in the compound and for their own nourishment, as well as medical aid.

As in other similar cases in Europe, the Igorots were accompanied by an intermediary, Ismael Alzate, a mestizo who we see featured in many contemporary photographs, always dressed in European style. In the photograph Fernando Debas took of part of the group of Igorots and of Ismael Alzate himself, the latter is in a clearly differentiated and dominant posture vis-à-vis the rest of the group. This image reproduces a structure similar to that in other photographs and postcards of entrepreneurs with their ethnic groups in Europe. The comment of the anthropologist Manuel Antón on the back of this photograph (held in the archives of the Madrid Anthropology Museum) is indicative of this relationship: 'Philippines Exhibition 1887. [...] Group of Igorots from Menguet-Tinguianes with their manager Ismael Alzate, killed afterwards by these same Igorots in the Philippines.' We have not been able to authenticate the veracity of this highly significant comment.

The Filipinos were eagerly welcomed in Madrid. They were presented to the Queen at the opening of the grounds, and made the occasional outing to the theatre. There were some complaints about their food, which the organizers attempted to put right. Although we do not have the direct testimony of the Filipinos involved in the exhibition, we do have comments of their compatriots from the magazines they published in Spain. The Philippines was an extremely old Spanish colony, which found itself at a critical stage of its relationship to its colonizer. As it is, Spain lost the colony to the USA a few years after the exhibition. Enlightened figures such as José Rizal[5] or Graciano López Jaena openly criticize the use of their compatriots as 'savages' (a formula that was initially unknown to them because it had no place in the first conception of the exhibition, as is made clear above) and especially the image given of the islands in the mother country (Sánchez Gómez 2003: 224–64; López Jaena 1889: 245–46).

The case of the Ashanti village is a different one. In the first place, the indigenous actors were contracted by a private business manager, in this instance Ferdinand Gravier. Unlike the Filipinos, it appears that the contracting of the Ashanti was due, instead, to opportunity and to the perceived exoticism of this people. In fact, the British ended up appropriating the colony, after a long, hard struggle with the population, a fact that is remarked upon time and again in the press reports of the time. The arrival of the British also offered the opportunity to negotiate with a European colony regarding the arrival of the natives. Another of the characteristics of the Ashanti people, which made them a candidate on the various occasions in which they were exhibited in Europe (e.g. their exhibition in Paris in 1887 and Lyon in 1897, prior to their exhibition in Spain), was what was perceived by contemporary observers as their exotic and eye-catching nature, both in the costumes and ornaments their chiefs wore and the ceremonial of their performances in the exhibitions. In addition, the African peoples always offered spectacles of music, dance and battles, all of which attracted the attention of European audiences. This fact, along with the daily spectacle of mealtimes and the manufacture of handicrafts, constituted the principal attraction of the Ashanti.

The Ashanti were one of the first African peoples to be presented in Europe. There can be no doubt that due to their skin colour they also offered the apparent spectacle of savagery, not unlike that offered by the Filipinos. In both instances their perceived ferocity and backwardness was reported in the press of the period, along with other, more condescending commentaries[6]. Without doubt, the spectacle of the semi-naked bodies of the Ashanti was a further inducement to the public to attend their exhibition. Certain pieces of information lead us to reflect upon this issue. *La España Cristiana* (9 October 1897) devoted an article to the Ashanti exhibition taking place in Valencia's Teatro Pizarro.[7] The magazine criticizes the indecency of their nakedness and the religious transgression involved in displaying non-Christian cults in public in a denominational state such as Spain.

As regards the daily life of these indigenous people in the major cities of Spain, considerable information is available. The press not only reported the arrival of the Ashanti but also treated their stay as an ongoing event. It appears that they were not allowed to leave the compound in Ronda Universidad, the Jardines del Buen Retiro or the Teatro Pizarro in Valencia alone, but were invited to participate in various civic events, such as the anniversary party of the Red Cross, an outing to a bullfight, or the christening in Betlem Church of the Ashanti baby born in Barcelona (the group's attendance at which clearly constituted a further spectacle).

In this instance Gravier, the business manager, acted as a genuine publicist in continually drumming up local interest. The naturalists' visits to the Madrid exhibition were announced in the press, along with those of the Queen and the princesses, who were accompanied on one occasion by M. Cavanne, curator of the Bordeaux Museum of Natural History. Such reports undoubtedly contributed to the show being granted a cultural significance, as well as to attracting Madrid's high society. In Madrid the Ashanti were also invited to a function in a theatre in the city. In all these cases, the movement of the tribe was eagerly anticipated, and huge crowds were continually reported by the press.

In the early twentieth century, the exhibitions of Inuits, Senegalese or the Fula tribe of Equatorial Guinea generated no less curiosity, but the indigenous peoples involved participated less in public festivities, either because they were located far from the city centres, as was the case with the summit of Tibidabo, or, equally, because the relationship with the African, East Asian or Inuit guests had – as we will see below – changed.

The treatment the Inuit people from Labrador received in the Madrid of 1900 in the same Jardín del Buen Retiro was less festive than that accorded to the Ashanti. In this instance, according to the reports of the Madrid Society for Natural History and of the press, it may be said that more importance was granted to the customs of this people than to their physical attributes.[8] Their representation was, on the other hand, as trivializing and stereotypical as that accorded to other ethnic groups. Aspects perceived as the more 'savage' traits of the Eskimos (Inuit) – such as their consumption of raw meat, or the shared mealtimes of dogs and people – were privileged in press reports, as had already been the case with the Ashanti. The attraction of the 'savage' continued to predominate. In none of the cases mentioned do we have information about the remuneration or the conditions of the journey to Europe of these tribes.

The difficulties encountered at the Spanish frontier by the group of Senegalese exhibited on Tibidabo in 1913 meant that Dr Andreu, the well-known pharmacist and businessman behind this exhibition, would have to intervene. We know from a letter he sent to the Chief of Police in Barcelona that he contracted the group through a French businessman for 150,000 francs. (This was undoubtedly the same group that had participated in exhibitions in various cities in the neighbouring country.) The price of the visit to the tribe was incorporated in the cost of the 30-céntimo ticket for the funicular railway that went up to Tibidabo. A big crowd was doubtless anticipated in order to compensate for such a sizeable investment. As on other occasions, the presence of the Senegalese gave rise to a series of reports in local newspapers and in the illustrated press. The Senegalese demonstrated various occupations relating to their different ethnic groups. A birth also occurred, and among the group there was an albino. There was, in addition, a draughtsman who sold postcards, such as those that have been found with the indication 'Tibidabo 1913' and signed Abdulayé. These are the work of the painter Abdulayé Samb, and through them the group can be identified with the group that was also, in 1904, 1906 and 1911, in Nantes, Amiens and Le Mans respectively (Bergouniou 2001: 267).

In the cases of the Eskimos (Inuit) and the Senegalese, the sale of these postcards and of other handmade artefacts was probably crucial to the daily economy of the people exhibited. Unlike other contemporary spectacles relating to other ethnic groups, such as Buffalo Bill's Wild West shows, these people were not providing a theatrical performance – rather, their existence constituted a spectacle in its own right. Although on the odd occasion a list of times was established for visits, they could not avoid being continually observed, nor could they go off to their homes after the show.

The Observers

A symbiotic alliance between scientific opinion and colonial interest determined the mechanisms whereby the image of other cultures were to be disseminated in Spain. The treatment given in the daily and illustrated press to the visits of these groups, regular at this time in cities such as Barcelona and Madrid, together with a number of photographs that have been found (especially those clearly produced by amateur photographers), give us an idea of the racist assumptions that can gradually transform and mould the image of the Other.

Interpretation of the photographs that have been preserved is complex, since a methodology that might help us to analyse them does not exist. Even so, we shall attempt to comment on the set of images we have found of each group. In the case of the Filipino people, the official nature of the exhibition not only led to numerous comments in the press (as well as to the visit of the royal household and of members of the government) but also provided images of extraordinary quality by the French photographer Jean Laurent, who lived in Madrid and was official photographer to the Queen. Due to the early date of the event and its official character, it remains difficult to discover more spontaneous images. Amateur photographs nevertheless exist for the exhibition of the Ashanti and Senegalese in Barcelona and of the Inuits in Madrid. These give a more direct view of the events themselves, as well as of the iconography inherent in press photography, which also evolved during the years between exhibitions.

The official photographs of the Ashanti – i.e. those published in all the illustrated press, and acquired by the then Museum of Natural Sciences – were the work of the Barcelona photographer Xatart. The numerous occasions on which these are used in the press for the 1897 exhibitions that took place in Barcelona and Madrid lead us to believe that Xatart had an agreement with Gravier for publicity regarding the exhibition. One of the first cinematic documents of the Lumière brothers reproduces this group of Ashanti at the Lyon exhibition. These same films were shown in Barcelona, in the well-known Studio Napoleón on the Ramblas (head office of the Lumière company), at the same time as the exhibition was taking place in Ronda Universidad. In this way, just as the Ashanti were permanently prominent as performers during their stay in Barcelona as a result of the variety of activities in which they were involved, they were likewise present in film screenings and in one-off spectacles, such as the 'geographical session' between Vasco da Gama and an Ashanti woman that took place in the Jardín Español, a Barcelona variety theatre, on 23 August 1897. All in all, the visit of the Ashanti was posited as a spectacle that would mobilize the entire city, as was typical of spectacles with the Gravier hallmark in other European cities.

Moreover, the mechanisms of publicity had undergone major developments in the years dividing the Philippines Exhibition in 1887 from the Ashanti one in 1897. The latter would also be profusely illustrated in the press, no longer through woodcuts, but with images taken directly from photographs and accompanied by generally anecdotal or funny comments, such as those in Barcelona's L'Esquella de la Torratxa or the Madrid magazines Blanco y Negro and Nuevo Mundo.

In Spain, there is not a profusion of postcards depicting the exhibition of ethnic groups similar to that available in France from the end of the nineteenth century. The photographs which particularly catch the eye, however, are a collection of preserved stereoscopic views on paper and glass, positives and negatives, of the Ashanti and the Inuits of the Retiro in Madrid, and of the Senegalese in Tibidabo in Barcelona. These are photographs by amateur enthusiasts, people probably with cultural interests, which portray an Ashanti family in front of its hut, an Inuit family, and the Senegalese figures eating a meal in Tibidabo. Like that of the Ashanti, the Senegalese eating their meal was an event announced in the press, as was the mealtime of the Inuits and their dogs. We have already mentioned that the performance of daily activities formed one of the main attractions, along with dances, mock battles, etc. There can be no doubt that the attraction of the meal was especially degrading for its indigenous participants, not least because it was announced as if it were an event in a zoo. In this instance, the occasional visitor portrays the moment at which a group of spectators is present at the mealtime of the Senegalese. The visitors are observing the scene from close up, but at no moment do they make contact with the diners.

In the photographs already mentioned we see, for the first time, the presence of Europeans alongside the natives. These Europeans observe the scene, in which the observed – as on other occasions – do not return their gaze, as if they were acting on a stage. The circus-like qualities of these kinds of event are made clear for the first time. The same scene is encountered in another stereoscopic photograph of the Inuits in the Buen Retiro (Sánchez Gómez 2005: 31–60). Given that the card mounts and the plates lack all identification, we suspect that an amateur photographer was also involved, one of the many who visited the exhibition (Verde Casanova 1993: 96). The relationship with the Spanish public is crudely reflected here: an Inuit woman and child in traditional costume seated in front of their canoes and tents are observed by the crowd, which observes the mere fact that these people exist.[9]

The scenes stress the relationship of superiority that is established between the observers and the observed. The other two stereoscopic plates about the Ashanti show two families. In one of them, the young woman has her breasts exposed in a pose that is rarely seen in the other photographs, which would have been unusual for a European woman and can be seen as a characteristic erotic photography. Had the photographer asked the girl to reveal herself? Was such nudity seen as somehow different to a white woman's? The photographer's gaze clearly reveals a key aspect of the general attitude of the public, i.e. the sexual attraction that contemplation of these tribes awakened, which had already been made explicit in that of the Filipinos, who were almost exclusively clothed in loincloths, displaying bodies that were smooth and athletic.

The press reports coinciding with the exhibitions are also highly indicative of this relationship, whose evolution over time can be seen in the progressive withdrawal of scientific authority: in the case of the Filipino and the Ashanti exhibitions in Madrid, the viewpoint of the occasional scientist (e.g. Manuel Antón in *El Globo* and in the *Anales de la Sociedad de Historia Natural*) was incorporated, whereas in the later exhibitions the people exhibited were uniquely observed as fairground entertainment and their natural abilities were in general disparaged in the press. In every instance, the public success of the exhibitions was nevertheless extraordinary, which guaranteed their almost continuous presence in the press as long as the displays lasted. The Ashanti Exhibition in 1897 merited the occasional paternalist ceremonies and associated commentary. Due to the event's great success, the Ashanti were included in a few social gatherings, such as that of the Red Cross, in which they participated along with other groups. Their reported fierceness when taking on the British was emphasized, as was the attractiveness of their bodies. But in the case of the Senegalese in Tibidabo, the ethnographic comments about the characteristics of the various groups gradually become more frequent, with associated value judgements about their laziness or inadequacy.

Unlike other exhibitions from the previous century, such as the Philippines Exhibition, the barriers which separated the public from the village were practically eliminated so that the public could get close to and all but enter the huts of the indigenous people. However, not only from what one deduces from the photographs but also from comments in the press, it appears that the actual distance between the two remained obvious and that the lack of contact and interaction with the public was total. This all contributed to the persistent formation of stereotypes detached from any genuine interest in other peoples.

This article has not inventoried all the ethnic shows and exhibitions of this kind that took place in Spain. However, the evolution in time of those we have identified is sufficiently illustrative of the image the country projected of these 'exotic' tribes. The role of the Church may differentiate Spain from other European countries. In a few instances, it acted as a protector of individuals who were christened, by welcoming them under its umbrella and defending them from the intrusions of science. But in other cases, the Church undoubtedly performed an active function in the exhibitions themselves. If this was not as an organizer of some form (as seems to have been the case in the Philippines Exhibition), it was at least reflected in the Church's failure to denounce the existence of such exhibitions at a time when it undoubtedly had sufficient power to oppose such spectacles as not recommendable for practising Christians due to their indecency and inclusion of 'pagan' rites.

Many question are left unanswered. Study of the Ibero-American Exhibition in Seville, and of others as yet barely identified, might perhaps provide more details about the organization of events of this kind. There can be no doubt that in 1925, when the second exhibition of the Fula tribe took place in Tibidabo, other interests and sensibilities had emerged in Spanish society regarding Africa and African art, adding new variables to the relationship with non-European peoples. Many doubts also remain concerning issues such as the motivations and the situation of the people observed and the identities of the contractors. With the elements we have to hand, we can already outline the difference between the 'official' exhibitions organized by the administration and their private equivalents, the former guided by clearly political and colonialist motivations, the latter linked to recreational and cabaret-type entertainments that soon abandoned any attempt at scientific justification. The participation of anthropologists and museum curators, which briefly justified the exhibitions, disappeared extremely quickly.

Photography and the mass media, emerging by 1887 and consolidated by 1929, contributed towards fixing stereotypes, which themselves contributed to an increase in the Manichaean division between civilization and barbarism in the eyes of a society that identified itself as progressive. While it is true that the images created by culture are to be situated somewhere midway between internal psychic reality and the external world (Winnicott 1982), the medium of the mass-market human exhibition has undoubtedly contributed to fixing an image of inequality, of which modern Spaniards have done little to rid themselves.

Notes

1 In Barcelona, *La Ilustración Artística*, 815 (9 August 1897), p. 519, p. 522; *L'Esquella de la Torratxa*, 968 (30 July 1897), 969 (6 August 1897); 972 (27 August 1897); *La Vanguardia* and *El Diario de Barcelona* for the entire period of the exhibition. In Madrid, *La Ilustración Española y Americana*, 35 (22 September 1897), pp. 174, 184, and photograph; *Nuevo Mundo*, 195 (29 September 1897), n.p.; *Blanco y Negro. Revista Ilustrada*, 334 (25 September 1897); *El Heraldo, La Iberia* and *Época* (between 15 September and 30 October 1897).

2 Stereoscopic photograph, 'A group of Senegalese, Barcelona, 1913', © Centre Excursionista de Catalunya (Barcelona).

3 Hilke Thode-Arora also mentions the opposition of the Church to baptized individuals being exhibited as 'savages', as in the case of the Inuits from Labrador who travelled to Europe in the 1880s.

4 Sánchez Gómez makes the comparison with other incomes of the time. The compound's 'white' guards would get 75 pesetas a month and the overseer some 120. Sánchez Gómez's book is the most extensive and best-documented on the Philippines Exhibition.

5 Author of the novel *Noli me tangere*, among other works, in which he criticizes the Spanish colonial regime.

6 *See Blanco y Negro* (Madrid), 25 September 1897: 'Because there have been
   people who, drawing near to see them from close to, asked their companion: Do
   they bite? Nothing of the kind. You can touch them and they don't do a thing.'

7 *See La España Cristiana*, 340 (9 October 1897), p. 2799: 'The Ashanti tribe,
   which was going about Barcelona and Madrid almost stark naked, has also
   come to work in the Teatro Pizarro in Valencia, pitching their tents with public
   admission so that all might get to know their customs and religious ceremonies. This was what the daily press of the capital announced, adding that it
   will be a curious spectacle worth seeing. Journalists: can religious ceremonies
   of a dissident cult be held in public without breaking the laws of the country?
   Can Catholics attend the ceremonies of a dissident cult without offending
   against the First Commandment of God's law? It might be an extremely curious
   spectacle that is worth seeing, if it were permitted for Christians; but what you
   give to the public in announcing these indecencies is a shameful spectacle
   that reveals your ignorance in trivial matters, and is worthy of being lamented
   with abundant tears. What we must ask the Authorities is to apply Article 11 of
   the current Constitution, and not to allow black Ashanti or white Ashanti to
   celebrate their religious ceremonies in public.'

8 A publicity brochure was published on the exhibition in 1900 by R. Velasco
   Impresor: *Los habitantes del Polo Ártico en los Jardines del Buen Retiro de Madrid.
   Primera exhibición en Europa de una aldea esquimal* [The Inhabitants of the Arctic
   Pole in the Jardines del Buen Retiro in Madrid. The First Exhibition in Europe
   of an Eskimo Village].

9 Stereoscopic photograph, 'The Inuits in the Jardín del Buen Retiro, Madrid,
   1900', © Patrimonio Nacional (Madrid).

31

The Zoos of the Exposition Coloniale Internationale, Paris 1931

HERMAN LEBOVICS

Could there be a more striking example of domination than the act of consigning those peoples you consider to be inferior to a museum when they are dead, or to a zoo when they are alive? The Paris Exposition Coloniale Internationale of 1931 is a paradigmatic demonstration of the stakes of such power games. I shall therefore suggest that the 1931 Exposition (in the way of all colonial exhibitions) was one of those human zoos where the strange beasts of the colonies *and of France* were to be seen.

The Exposition Coloniale Internationale opened its doors in the Bois de Vincennes on the outskirts of Paris, in the spring of 1931. Elegantly located on 110 hectares (just over 270 acres) of land around the Daumesnil Lake in the Bois de Vincennes, it provided French and foreign tourists with a synoptic vision of productions from around the world, representing in its pavilions all the overseas colonies and territories of France, Holland, Belgium, Denmark, Portugal, Italy and the United States. A large section devoted to France itself sang the praises of advanced technologies and the luxury industries, while along the length of the imposing façade of the permanent Colonial Palace, sculpted by Alfred Janniot, the French 'civilizing mission' was portrayed.

It should be noted that the builders of the exhibition had an aquarium and a zoo constructed, which were devoted to the fauna of the southern hemisphere. This was the work of Carl Hagenbeck in the same naturalist style as the Hamburg zoo. Why were the zoo and the aquarium essential? They certainly provided a treat for the children. And, of course, they gave the French an idea of what foreign animals were like. But, above all, they were there to convince visitors that the human zoo constituted by the colonial exhibition was nothing of the kind. Indeed, if you construct a zoological garden and vast aquaria of exotic fish, it goes without saying that the peoples and pavilions on show in the exhibition could not themselves possibly be seen as a human zoo. Thus, when visitors encountered the inhabitants of the colonies in traditional dress, went for boat trips on the lake on typical native vessels, refreshed themselves in cafés and restaurants serving exotic dishes, or placated their children, bored of culture, by offering them fairground rides and other amusements, they did not suspect that all these experiences were a continuation of the zoo in a different form.

Living as we do in the postcolonial period, we tend to underestimate the sometimes Herculean efforts of the imperial propagandists to gain the support of the people for the conquest and administration of an empire and to make them accept their destiny as an imperial race. Other than perpetuating a xenophobic nationalism, the greatest efforts of the rulers of the expansionist nations were directed towards the creation of national support for the empire.

Can it be said that, thanks to several new ideas, the exhibition, that simulacrum of the tropical empire, *that copy without an original,* achieved its objective of enhancing the nation's colonial consciousness? Other universal exhibitions had already contained colonial sections. Indeed, for more than forty years the French Republic had made use of its exhibitions to show the colonial 'natives' to the French. A first 'native village' had been constructed at the 1889 Paris Exposition Universelle, in order to give the French a sense of their new colonial territory, but also to impress the native employees by presenting the French way of life to them. The Marseille exhibitions of 1906 and 1922 had been entirely devoted to the colonies. But in 1931 the strategies of presentation became more subtle, showing that a true classicism had developed in the art of the colonial exhibition.

The 1931 Paris Exposition presented pavilions carefully constructed down to the smallest detail, evoking cultures which had no connection to each other, and setting them out along vast promenades at the edge of the city. The experience of decolonization has brought us awareness of the flagrant techniques of seduction deployed to convince the public of the achievements of the empire. Nevertheless, the novelty of the 1931 Exposition, which was to promote an enlarged vision of a new imperial France and a new definition of what it was to be French, is worthy of closer analysis.

The Parisian Surrealists, who were as discerning in their knowledge of images which perpetuated the bourgeois hegemony as they were skilled at subverting them, gave their own view on the intentions and methods of the Exposition. 'Do not visit the Colonial Exhibition,' read the large letters of a tract produced by Paul Éluard, André Breton, Louis Aragon and Yves Tanguy, to name only the most famous of its authors.

These artists called for the boycott of the exposition, not only as a protest against colonial massacres and exploitation but also, and most importantly, in order to declare their rejection of 'Greater France' as a *concept-escroquerie* [a fraudulent concept] which lay at the heart of the enterprise. The tract continued: 'They are setting out to give the French a sense of ownership which they must acquire in order to be able to hear the distant sound of gunfire without being moved. They are setting out to extend the refined landscape of France, already greatly enhanced before the war by a song on bamboo cane, to include a view of minarets and pagodas.'

The Exposition provided the French public, on both an existential and a symbolic level, with the feeling that they had rights of *ownership* over all these marvels. It was constructed right in the capital city of France, at the instigation of colonial governors and heroes. The 'native performers', who were obliged to wear their traditional costumes while on the site, were the 'animals' most in the public eye. But, even more importantly, the exhibition set out the vision of a Greater France' by including the native cultures in the high culture of European France.

The Exposition Coloniale Internationale opened its doors on 6 May 1931. Before looking at the pavilions in more detail, we should distinguish the two faces of the exhibition. The guide, the contents of the pavilions and the photographs portrayed the Empire from a romantic perspective, as a fable, a marvel, a curiosity. But there were also other representations of France and its colonies which preferred to emphasize the practical benefits they brought to their citizens. I think that the persuasive power of the spectacle lay above all in this dialectic of marvellous realism, in the alternation, from one pavilion to the next, between the fantastic and the useful. Such stunning constructions confirmed, in the eyes of the visitor, the truth of the graphs and statistics, precisely because these abstract figures on the realization of the colonial project were so different from the images. Through a simple juxtaposition, the imaginary gave plausibility to the factual.

Rather than divide this discussion into issues relating to the 'aesthetic imagination' on one side, and the 'facts' on the other, I shall distinguish two aspects of the simulacrum represented by the exhibition, which I shall call the 'Fabulous' Exhibition and the 'Educational' Exhibition. After entering the exhibition through the Colonial Gate and following the route recommended by the guidebook, we follow a giant loop around the central lake. The Fabulous Exhibition begins with the Madagascan Pavilion, which is a large reproduction of the bucranium tower (decorated with ox skulls). Inside this pavilion you are greeted by a presentation of the human populations of the Grande Ile. But we do not have time to visit the whole pavilion, so we regretfully continue on our way. Further on, we reach the large pavilions devoted to the work of the Protestant and Catholic missionaries. The Protestant building preserves the simplicity which is associated with the Reformed Church in France. The Catholic building is more magnificent, with more decoration. The tiled façade is decorated with flowers, figures and symbols which celebrate the diversity and universality of the Catholic faith. Inside, the visitor gazes at an azure sky filled with gold stars. A Western-style Jesus – showing which race true Christianity is descended from – appears on a vast stained-glass window behind the altar.

The guidebook then advises us to visit the pavilions representing Guinea, French India, Somalia and the French possessions in the Pacific, Tahiti in particular. With this island, the fabulous comes to the fore. Having paid lip service to its food exports (vanilla) and natural resources (phosphates and pearls), the guidebook plunges us into the world of Pierre Loti and Gauguin (Demaison 1931: 39). We continue towards New Caledonia, the New Hebrides, Martinique, Réunion and Guadeloupe. In the New Caledonia Pavilion, André Maurois saw the walls covered in 'brown and white paintings in a primitive style which makes them modern', while the women seemed to come straight out of a Gauguin painting: 'Gauguin's women exist; I have seen them in the New Caledonia pavilion' (Maurois 1931: 13). When modern curators in France and, most of all, in the United States, speak of preserving the intellectual and artistic traditions of the West, they are unfortunately obliged to include in our heritage the voyeuristic appropriation of women from the tropics of a now-classic colonial pornography.

But let us move from the languorous evocation of island life to the *sacred* beauty of the Indochinese pavilions, occupying 6 hectares (15 acres). They are dominated by the temple of Angkor Vat, flower of the Khmer architectural style. Here, the very form of this square structure, whose sides were 70 metres (230 feet) in length, demonstrates the achievements of French colonization. The 5 towers are 45 metres (148 feet) high (the central tower is 10 metres [33 feet] higher still) and it rests on a foundation of carved and decorated stone. Are these not, reflects the guidebook, 'the image of the five countries of the Indochinese Union today, brought together and strengthened by us?' (Demaison 1931: 39)

The Senior Resident, Pierre Guesde, and the section's technical director, Henri Gourdon, hoped to convey a face of Indochina: 'To attract and retain the visitors' interest, it was essential to draw on all the seductions of the picturesque and the irresistible magic of art.' To create a beautiful ending to their visit, André Demaison advised the visitors to 'return to watch Angkor as the sun sets behind the five domes of the palace' (1931: 67).

French West Africa, a territory nine times larger than France, was represented by a magnificent red clay palace whose tower was 45 metres (148 feet) high and which, according to the guide, was constructed in the Sudanese style. Once out of the area surrounding the palace, which covered 4 hectares (nearly 10 acres), visitors could sample the variety and colours of African life. They could watch young women weaving carpets, a new skill taught to them by the White Sisters. And, not far away, they could find a 'fetish' village, where 200 'natives' would perform their daily tasks before their eyes. Indeed, native villages were invariably an obligatory element of exhibitions, serving as a zoo within the zoo. They were the evidence that the exhibition as a whole was nothing but a human zoo.

Just behind the Moroccan pavilion, in a peaceful courtyard, could be found a tiny building, open to one side, where rows of benches and a blackboard were set out. Seated on the benches, and thereby infantilized, were Senegalese riflemen, Arab traders, or others, depending on the time of day. Brought to France to be displayed in the Vincennes exhibition, they were thereby united in their struggles with the complexity of written French. In the building devoted to hunting in Africa, dioramas recreated jungle scenes, including a number of disparate objects recalling the life of the explorer Émile Bruno Bruneau de Laborie, who had been killed by a lion the previous year. One can wonder whether, in the eyes of those who had not yet been won over by the project of Greater France, this reminder of the dangers of the real animals of deepest Africa did not weaken the message of the Exposition to some extent.

Seven countries decided to accept the French invitation and to have their own pavilions in the Bois de Vincennes. These were Belgium, Brazil, Denmark, the United States, Italy, the Netherlands and Portugal. At this time, there existed what the historian Charles-Robert Ageron has called a 'colonial Holy Alliance' (1984). Just as the Tsar, following the Napoleonic Wars, had called on rulers menaced by the rise of nationalism to join his campaign to stamp out revolution, so the Minister for the Colonies, Albert Sarraut, wanted to unite all the imperialist nations in a defence against the new wave of nationalism and Bolshevism. The Bolsheviks had condemned colonialism from the outset, and the support that the Comintern provided between the wars to independence movements in the colonies was an additional cause for concern. In the year before the opening of the 1931 Exposition, the nationalist Yen Bai uprising, followed by a communist peasant's revolt (also in Vietnam), showed the strength of opposition to French rule in Indochina. The presence in Paris of pavilions from other nations therefore aroused the hope that the new nationalisms and colonial leftist movements would be contained and rejected by a new international fraternity among the imperialist countries. In addition, the latter were bound by a *universal racism*. The presence of the United States at the Exposition is an illustration of this.

The United States did not sign the Treaty of Versailles, although France had hoped for an American commitment to European security. It did, however, participate in the celebration of the European empires. The symbolism of the US pavilion is very revealing, as the Americans chose to construct a replica of Mount Vernon, George Washington's house. Perhaps in order to negate the fact that George Washington had led the first successful anti-colonial uprising in the New World, the wings of the Mount Vernon residence and the neighbouring structures contained stands from Alaska, Panama, the Philippines, Samoa, the Virgin Islands, Hawaii and Puerto Rico. But the portrayal of black slaves and their little huts was conspicuous by its absence from the 1931 Paris Exposition version of Mount Vernon. Here, American lives were dehumanized and made invisible.

Any concern that the Fabulous exhibition was an obstacle to the public's understanding of the Educational exhibition can be laid to rest by a final visit to the home country's pavilion. The traditional luxury products which made French workmanship famous were on show, alongside demonstrations of modern industrial technology: agricultural and forestry tools, aeronautics, cars and electrical equipment. To understand the political content of these displays, we should pay less attention to their contents than to their contexts and juxtapositions. By situating ancient Asian temples and 'primitive' African huts next to the finely tuned blades of electric turbines, the organizers introduced a dialectic of ancestral stability and modern dynamism into the public mind, presenting visitors with a picture of splendid but retarded cultures, who depended on France to show them the way forward to a shared future. The coexistence in the Bois de Vincennes of scenes of tropical life and of European civilization informed the public of the benefits of capitalist modernization in Greater France.

A photograph, published in *L'Illustration* (May 1931), of the machine exhibition in the French gallery is probably the most appropriate representation of the vision of Greater France. Three people are standing in the foreground, and while they may not be intimidated, they are at least dwarfed by the presence of the vast machines. The man is dressed in a dark suit, a white shirt and a hat, while the women are in dark bulky coats and traditional lace headdresses, apparently country people from a remote part of France. Born of an ancient tradition with its own patois, costumes and culture, they have come to admire the new techniques which will henceforth be part of their French culture in the widest sense. This is what Greater France planned for its tropical inhabitants: their local customs would be preserved, while capitalist technology, under Parisian control, would undertake to help them, while enfolding them, submerging them, and exposing them.

Since 1931 we have become more adept at perceiving the techniques of political domination at work in images. It can therefore seem hard for us to imagine the power of the impact on the French public produced by this collection, on the outskirts of Paris, of so many exotic temples, mosques and 'primitive' huts, of strange and oddly dressed peoples with their dances and bizarre ceremonies, of parading colonial soldiers and of marvellous technologies. The French government put all its efforts, as never before, into filling its subjects with what Robert W. Rydell has called an enduring imperial vision (1984 [1974]: 561–94). Drawing on the inaugural speech given by Paul Reynaud, Raoul Girardet describes the exhibition as an 'apotheosis': 'Never since the beginning of the Third Republic at least, never in the course of the entire history of our country even, never had so many voices cried out with so much strength and confidence to celebrate the magnificence of overseas expansion' (Girardet 1968: 1085–86).

Is it possible to measure the success of such an event? What might be understood by 'success' in such a case? It is certain that the exhibition was a triumph from a financial point of view. In less than six months in the middle of a major economic depression and despite the dull and cloudy weather of the early months, there were more visitors than to the Paris Universal Exhibition of 1889 (33.5 million, as opposed to 32.3). The exhibition made a profit of 30–35 million francs (the equivalent of 15 million euros today) generated by the entry fees, subscriptions, and the very popular zoo.

Léopold Senghor, who began at this time to develop the concept of Negritude, remembers that he and his student friends (no doubt following the example of the Surrealists, given that Senghor knew some of them and had probably seen the pamphlet calling for the boycott of the event) viewed the exhibition simply as a celebration of colonialism and did not attend it. We should probably look on the exhibition as an imperialist ceremony of self-validation and the initiation of French visitors into the new society of spectacle.

After 1931, leaving aside a few modest contributions by the colonies to exhibitions based on other themes, no other colonial exhibitions were ever organized in France, unlike Italy, Portugal and Belgium. From the 1930s onwards, the peoples of the colonies increasingly refused to present themselves like lions and monkeys in a 'naturalist-style' zoo. This type of show had come to the end of its life that autumn in the Bois de Vincennes. Exhibitions such as human zoos, which also allowed whites to believe that they were protected against the captive peoples they displayed, lost their effectiveness.

The International Colonial Exhibition of 1931 had made superb and spectacular use of electricity, as much in the form of stage lighting effects as in the illumination of ancient temples or of ritual art objects. When the beams of coloured light banished the darkness surrounding the Totem fountain, where the sacred arts of different cultures were blended and baptized together, when they shone out around Angkor Vat, visitors witnessed the transubstantiation of independent antique cultures into simple ornaments of European civilization. Torn out of the dark, lit up by electric power generated in France, non-European identities were surrounded by European identity, and we can understand more clearly what price had to be paid in order to belong to Greater France. Obviously, the organizers of the exhibition, like the authors of government policy, wished to see the reproductions of the Bois de Vincennes become a reality for the peoples of the Empire, and one which was centred on France.

Postface
Situating *Human Zoos*

CHARLES FORSDICK

The contributors to this volume, in an eclectic yet coherently focused
series of chapters, convincingly identify, define, theorize and histo-
ricize the phenomenon that the editors dub – with undoubted, yet justified provocation – the 'human zoo'. In exploring, through a comprehen-
sively wide range of examples in Asia, Europe and North America, the
practice of displaying certain human groups for the entertainment and
supposed education of others, the studies gathered in this collection
outline the historical evolution of displays of this type. The contributors
track the pre-histories of these exhibitions and identify the moments
and modes of their emergence. Finally, they explore the contexts in
which human zoos were consolidated, the processes according to which
they declined, and the forms in which they persist. As such, the volume
– and the wider project of which this book serves as a further stage
– builds on the substantial research devoted to 'freak shows' (Bogdan
1988; Garland-Thomson 1996; Adams 2001; Mitchell 2002) and to
other displays of human subjects (Altick 1978; Schneider 1982; Thode-
Arora 1989; Lindfors 1999a) that has been published in Europe and
North America since the late 1970s. *Human Zoos* federates such diverse,
focused studies, suggesting the interconnectedness of phenomena
often seen to be geographically and culturally disconnected (and accordingly discrete). It is for this reason that the volume constitutes a significant contribution to studies of exoticism and racism from postcolonial
perspectives and, more particularly, of the role of these phenomena in
the elaboration of the 'exhibitionary order' (Mitchell 1992) on which the
ideological justification of colonialism invariably depends.

This collection illustrates – especially in Rosemary Garland-Thomson's
opening chapter – the associations of the human zoo with earlier traditions of displaying Otherness. At the same time, it reveals a process
of progressive differentiation and clear periodization, as the prurient
public attraction to various forms of spectacularized human difference

was slowly replaced, as the nineteenth century unfolded, by a more particular and more specifically racialized attention to the display of non-Western peoples. As the editors make clear in their introduction, and as individual contributions underline, these processes of exhibition – without necessarily being restricted to a narrow historical moment – were consolidated and intensified in the Age of Colonial Empires. The human zoo became particularly visible in the period between the beginning of the Scramble for Africa and the onset of the First World War, when it served as a means of staging, in a popular form, theories of unilineal evolution and associated notions of Social Darwinism.

The apogee of the phenomenon cannot be understood, however, without careful attention to the prehistory of the phenomenon, as well as to its complex and ongoing afterlives. In relation to the notion of legacy, one of this volume's principal aims is to suggest the ways in which such exhibitions – popular cultural forms exemplary in their inherent ephemerality – had a lasting impact on the collective imagination of self and Other, in particular in Western cultures, but also (as Arnaud Nanta makes clear in this volume) in non-Western contexts, such as Japan. Central to these processes is an awareness of the emerging role of racialized and often racist discourses of science and anthropology, evident in the transformation of the human zoo from a purely commercial form of entertainment towards one based on a mixed economy of motivations, in which official colonial propaganda and the dissemination of associated cultural assumptions both played central roles. It is in this area that the phenomenon of the human zoo illuminates an interdependence, similar to that discussed and popularized by Edward Said in *Orientalism* (1978), between science, spectacle and colonial power. The actual forms that this interrelationship takes are often obscure. Central to criticisms of colonial discourse studies remains an awareness of the field's persistent uncertainty as to whether – to take the example offered by Said – the 'Orientalist' tendencies of Western constructions of knowledge passively reflected their lived colonial context, or whether such tendencies betokened instead a more complexly generative process in which ideology, epistemology and environment existed in a relationship of mutual self-fashioning and self-perpetuation. In the former case, that of a passive reflection of context, the identification of examples of such tendencies may be seen to encourage researchers to compile illustrative lists; but as this volume suggests, in the latter case, that of more complex interdependence, the study of material phenomena such as the human zoo permits close engagement with the interrelationships of epistemology, ideology and cultural form, encouraging the exploration

– in particular sites, at particular moments – of the specific workings of racism and colonialism, as well as of the means of their popularization and perpetuation through cultural forms.

As these preliminary observations imply, whereas the volume itself locates the phenomenon of the human zoo historically, geographically, culturally and ideologically, the aim of this postface is to reflect more abstractly on work regarding the human zoo itself. It explores the circumstances in which such a scholarly project emerged, and assesses the impact of the research it involves on a wide field of cross-disciplinary scholarship, relating in particular to colonial history and to postcolonial studies. In attempting to locate *Human Zoos* (as well as the consolidated body of research that this book has already inspired), the aim of these concluding observations is twofold. On the one hand, the postface presents the specific sets of national circumstances in which the notion of 'human zoos' emerged, exploring the field of colonial history and postcolonial memory in contemporary France; on the other hand, there is a wider discussion of the ways in which this volume transcends – and has, since its initial publication, always transcended – the circumstances of its immediate production to reflect a series of wider debates regarding the colonial past and its relationship to the postcolonial present.

The publication in 2002 of the first French edition of the current volume – *Zoos humains: de la Vénus hottentote aux reality shows* – met with a predictably mixed critical reaction. The book's success is evident in its subsequent release in a paperback edition in 2004, as well as in its almost immediate appearance in Italian translation. Whereas a number of historians welcomed the efforts of the collection's editors to excavate an often occluded element of France's colonial past, others were scandalized both by the 'postcolonial' emphases of the human zoos project and by the ways in which it was seen to privilege what its principal critic, Claude Liauzu, dubbed 'Barnum history', i.e. the perceived exaggeration and elevation to a metonymic status of a sensationalist aspect of colonial history, called to play a metonymic role in the study of empire. To understand this reaction, there is an initial need to situate the book in the wider context of reflections on and often acrimonious debates about colonial history and postcolonial memory in turn-of-the-century France (Aldrich 2005). It is significant, for instance, that *Zoos humains* appeared in the year following the seventieth anniversary of the 1931 Exposition Coloniale (Lemaire, Blanchard and Bancel 2001), a major historical event of the interwar period in France that passed largely uncommemorated that year, despite its undoubted impact on the development of French attitudes towards colonized peoples (and, to a certain extent, of the attitudes of the colonized themselves towards the French). The Exposition had featured in Pierre Nora's *Lieux de mémoire* collection (1982–93), where Charles-Robert Ageron's chapter devoted to the event constituted the editor's one concession to discussion of the role of empire in his narrative of French national history. Ageron's emphasis tended, however, towards the statistical, assessing the numbers of *French* visitors to Vincennes and exploring discrepancies between the intended and actual impact of these visits on public support of the colonial project that the exhibition was supposed to foster. The experiences of the indigenous performers brought to France in order to staff the event (while simultaneously providing hints of 'local colour') are largely absent, as are references to the Kanak recruited for the human zoo on a site adjoining that of the main exhibition (Daeninckx 1998; Dauphiné 1998).

The fact that – despite its widespread impact on national life, in terms of admissions, of the considerable traces it left in popular cultural artefacts, and of its legacy in the form of an imposing museum building at the Porte Dorée – an event such as the 1931 Exposition had slipped from French public memory in the postcolonial period might be seen as a striking instance of 'silencing the past' (Trouillot 1995), more general processes of which occurred in France in relation to the colonial dimensions of national history. It is arguable in this context that the traumatic implications for France of the Algerian War of Independence (and the effective end of empire that the conclusion of this conflict in 1962 betokened) triggered a disavowal of the colonial period (obscured not least by what Henry Rousso has called the 'Vichy syndrome'), as well as an associated resistance to any recognition of traces of that past in the present. *Human Zoos* was one part of a concerted effort on the part of the historians and scholars associated with ACHAC (Association Connaissance de l'Histoire de l'Afrique Contemporaine) to challenge such a situation. Additional publications by members of this collective have sketched out a wide-ranging research agenda, exploring, for instance, the contradictions of Republicanism and colonialism (Bancel, Blanchard and Vergès 2003), the persistently diverse nature of modern, postcolonial France (Blanchard and Bancel 2006), and the ways in which a failure to factor discussion on empire into understandings of national identity – dating back, it is argued, to the 'loss' of Saint-Domingue in 1804 – has generated a *fracture coloniale* within French society (Blanchard, Bancel and Lemaire 2005).

One of the principal contributions of ACHAC to current debates has been the group's willingness to introduce into France the assumptions and logic of postcolonial critique, thereby overturning the intellectual exceptionalism that has tended to dismiss such a body of thought as undesirably 'Anglo-Saxon' and revealing the blind spots – particularly in terms of ethnicity and colonial history – of French republicanism itself. Indeed, it is unlikely that the rapid French engagement with postcolonialism, positive as well as negative, in the wake of the 23 February 2005 law (requiring pedagogic recognition of the 'benefits' of colonialism) and the November 2005 *banlieue* riots would have been possible without the groundwork already carried out in volumes such as *Zoos humains, La République coloniale* and *La Fracture coloniale*. The at-times hostile critical reception of *Zoos humains* itself revealed not only the underlying 'colonial fractures' by which early twenty-first-century French society was, in general, structured and divided; it also more specifically highlighted the presence of such fault lines in the field of current French colonial historiography.

Much of the most original research on the French Empire is currently conducted by those from outside France – by scholars such as Robert Aldrich, Alice Conklin, Laurent Dubois, Jim House, Eric Jennings, Herman Lebovics, Gregory Mann and Todd Shepard – leading some commentators to identify a 'paxtonization' of the field, reminiscent of the shifts that reshaped the historiography of Vichy in the 1970s. There is always a risk that any such emphasis ignores the rich traditions of writing colonial history within France itself, where the scholarship of pioneering scholars such as Charles-Robert Ageron, Charles-André Julien and Pierre Vidal-Naquet has now been complemented by the more recent work of a range of historians working in a number of geographical fields, including Yves Benot, Marcel Dorigny, Laure Pitti and Emmanuelle Saada. The critical responses to *Zoos humains* – to which the editors allude in their introduction – nevertheless reveal the highly contested territory that any specifically 'French' history of France's overseas colonial expansion may be seen to represent. Within this field, the work of historians associated with ACHAC, inflected by openly postcolonial concerns without always directly adopting the specialized lexicon or set of references with which postcolonial critique is often linked, reveals a sustained attempt to create connections between historical periods, to unearth traces of the colonial past in the postcolonial present. In a French context, the underpinnings of their work depend on two key assumptions. The first is that the wishful association of the 1962 Evian Accords with a clean break from the colonial past reveals a bad faith that is no longer sustainable in the context of the increasingly apparent, increasingly troubled postcoloniality of contemporary France (see Bancel 2007). The second is that despite the best efforts of French republican historiography – epitomized, perhaps, in Nora's *Lieux de mémoire* project discussed above – to distinguish between the domestic situation and what happens *outre-mer*, there is a need to recognize that colonialism was, and to a certain extent remains, an integral, constitutive element of French republican identity rather than an aberrant phase of it, now conveniently to be consigned to history (see Bancel, Blanchard and Vergès 2003; Wilder 2005). Both of these assumptions suggest that contemporary France – like other former colonizing powers – may be characterized as 'post/colonial', i.e. revelatory of what Chris Bongie has called the 'intimate (dis)connection of the colonial and the postcolonial' (1998: 12).

This emphasis on national traditions of historiography may seem outmoded, not least at a time when – through processes of translation, electronic communication and general academic mobility – historians perhaps 'travel' more than ever before, with the result that fields of historical enquiry are themselves increasingly comparative, transnational and even globalized. Yet the initial response and continued hostility to the 'human zoos' project in France reveal the persistent need to recognize and explore the specific circumstances of the writing of history – circumstances very much reflected in the controversies surrounding the current volume. As I have suggested above, criticism of *Zoos humains* came from across a very broad spectrum, ranging from the politically engaged historiography of scholars such as Claude Liauzu, to the more recent revisionist 'takes' on colonial history, according to which the study of phenomena such as the human zoo constitutes a form of expiation for empire and reveals a desire for self-flagellating postcolonial repentance (Lefeuvre 2006) or even penitence (Bruckner 2006).

Identifying and exploring the specific circumstances of the production and reception of historical narratives reveal the ways in which historiography, as well as, by extension, the intellectual struggles by which it is constantly characterized, are to be rooted in a wider set of socio-cultural and political circumstances and related to the ideological debates in which these are reflected. It is awareness of these circumstances and debates that permits understanding of the context in which *Human Zoos* first emerged. The social upheaval throughout France in autumn 2005, centred on the frustration of young French people of immigrant origin resident in the country's major conurbations, brought to wider attention a series of questions about race, racism, contemporary French identity and the persistent social inequalities with which these are to be associated (Cole 2007) – questions whose pre-history is in part explored in this volume. After several decades of rejecting British and North American 'multiculturalism' (or 'communitarianism') as anathema to the universal applicability of French republican values, the French political elite was forced to face the explosive manifestations of what Laurent Dubois (2000) has evocatively called the *république métissée* [hybridized republic], i.e. a postcolonial, multi-ethnic society, the recognition of whose largely ignored structural inequalities will engender considerable readjustment and upheaval. The association, by leading intellectuals such as Achille Mbembe, of the social movements of November 2005 with the unresolved legacies of colonialism, is to be interpreted in relation to a series of key events that had occurred since 1999, the year in which the French parliament eventually recognized that the Algerian conflict had actually constituted a 'war'.[1]

Against the backdrop of specific events such as these, a range of interest groups, with clear and often competing stakes in the processes of representing the colonial past, began to rise in prominence: the Harkis, or Algerians who had supported the French against the FLN, demanded recognition of their historical role and subsequent lack of acknowledgement; surviving *tirailleurs sénégalais* – a generic term for colonial infantrymen – pushed for recompense for their contribution to two world wars, and were rewarded at first symbolically with memorials, and later, after the success of Rachid Bouchareb's *Indigènes* (2006), in material terms with the restoration of their pensions; the *pieds-noirs*, descendants of French settlers in Algeria forced to relocate to France in 1962, became increasingly militant, and are credited with being one of the principal lobbies behind the notorious fourth clause of the 23 February 2005 law; in the same year, a new group emerged, provocatively entitled the Indigènes de la République, claiming that France's ethnic minority populations were suffering from social inequalities that resulted from the persistence of colonialism's racist hierarchies.

Simultaneously, as has often been the case in post-1789 French culture, the museum became the site of competing performances and interrogations of national identity, at once claiming to acknowledge the implications of postcoloniality, while reverting at times to colonial practices of categorization and display of other cultures and other peoples. One of Jacques Chirac's *grands projets*, the Musée des arts premiers at the Quai Branly, was accused by its critics of exoticizing non-European cultures, of occluding many of its artefacts' colonial provenance, and of perpetuating Manichaean divisions that continue to distinguish Western (and more particularly French) art from that with a non-Western origin (see

Price 2007). Also central to these debates about the appropriate means of displaying traces of colonialism in France – with those traces understood in their widest possible sense – was the former Musée permanent des colonies at the Porte Dorée, briefly considered as a venue for what would become the Quai Branly museum, but subsequently transformed into the Cité Nationale de l'Histoire de l'Immigration. The controversies surrounding the foundation of this museum and the selection of its contents are ably explored by Mary Stevens (2008), who highlights the troubling implications of situating an institution devoted to the study of immigration in a building originally devoted to – and architecturally encoded for – the propagation of pro-colonial propaganda

It is firmly within this wider immediate context of contemporary France – and not least in relation to ongoing debates about the appropriate postcolonial means of displaying traces of the colonial past – that the original emergence of *Human Zoos* is to be situated. In the light of this wider set of circumstances, the reception of the book is no longer, or at least not only, an academic spat over historical exegesis but begins instead to reflect in miniature the controversies and conflicts characterizing late twentieth- and early twenty-first-century approaches to the questions of colonialism, ethnicity and the legacies of empire in contemporary France (and elsewhere). The volume belongs to a small body of texts that has acquired – in the minds of some of its critics – the status of Trojan horse, smuggling into France an alien body of thought suspiciously dubbed *le postcolonialisme* (see Bancel and Blanchard 2006).

Postcolonial thought is a clear example of what Edward Said dubbed 'traveling theory', i.e. it emerged as a loose body of French-language writings generated in the fields of anti-colonialism and deconstructionism that crossed the Atlantic and took root in the North American academy, where they re-emerged as the critical phenomenon commonly known as 'postcolonialism'. Debates over the reception or rejection of postcolonial thought in France often comment ironically on the tendency for misrecognition of what has now – through the work of scholars such as Jean-Marc Moura, or through translations of, for instance, Edward Said and, more recently, Homi K. Bhabha and Stuart Hall – been received back in France. The risk in such a self-congratulatory approach is that those on the outside looking in fail to acknowledge, on the one hand, the pre-existence of scholarship that fulfils the definition of a loosely defined 'postcolonial' project without the need for any obligatory association with the canonical references of postcolonialism, and, on the other, evidence of projects in which anglophone and francophone scholars, far from being divided by their distinctive intellectual practices, have been able to elaborate an internationalized research practice in which the creative synergy of their various different approaches becomes apparent. Already in its initial form, when published in French, *Human Zoos* illustrated both of these aspects. The volume constituted an attenuated reflection on exoticism and ethnicity, largely absent from much postcolonial criticism in English; its present translation into English reminds us forcefully that the translation of texts and ideas in the postcolonial field is a multi-directional process (and not just a mono-directional transfer of material in English into other languages); and finally, the genuinely international range of contributors to the volume – broadened in this new English-language edition of the collection – is a reminder of the potential advances that international collaboration across scholarly traditions may genuinely permit.

It is the relationship between studying the human zoo and wider shifts in Humanities and Social Science research to which this postface now turns, for although the understanding of the French context of the volume as outlined above is essential, the appearance of an English-language edition – containing a significant number of contributions to the 2002 collection, supplemented by a series of newly commissioned chapters, as well as by work previously published elsewhere – actively places the phenomenon of the human zoo in its necessarily international context. Moreover, since the initial publication of the collection, the term 'human zoo' has entered critical currency, taken on a rhetorical function, and is now used by activists and journalists to describe phenomena ranging from the treatment of illegal immigrants in the USA to the transformation of long-necked Padaung women into tourist attractions in Thailand. Such a shift towards an international field is wholly appropriate, for – dependent on the displacement of exhibited people, and drawn into the international circuits related to emergent consumer capitalism on which the dissemination of popular cultural forms rely – the exhibition of human beings is itself an inherently transnational phenomenon. It is manifest within a range of different cultural contexts, emerging in each with differing emphases and implications. The essays gathered in this volume provide a vocabulary and the conceptual apparatus for discussion of such a genuinely international phenomenon, the apogee of which accompanied the most intensive period of modern colonial expansion.

More importantly perhaps, *Human Zoos* provides the material for reflection on a crucial stage in the exoticization of the inhabitants of 'elsewhere'. Avoiding the risks of prescription and the disabling taxonomic anxiety that is often related to this, the editors map the complex exhibitionary field relating to the human zoo, offering a clear periodization that underlines the phenomenon's rise to prominence in the late nineteenth and early twentieth centuries. At the same time, however, they insist on genealogies and affiliated forms, exploring other forms of display that inform study of the explicitly racialized human zoo, without necessarily replicating its practices. Attention is also paid to alternative media, such as cinema, photography and the museum, which adopt, perpetuate or interrogate the human zoo's logic of display.

Prior to the publication of this collection, the term 'human zoo' had been largely understood – particularly in the context of studies in human behaviour – as shorthand for a mode of anthropology that foregrounded the similarities of animals and people. Desmond Morris used the expression, for instance, as the title of his revolutionary 1969 study in sociobiology, *The Human Zoo*. A sequel to his earlier *Naked Ape* (1967), Morris's book draws analogies between urban environments and the zoo. Applications such as this, with their implicitly democratic and universalizing reach, respond neatly to the inherent hubris of human progress. They remind us that anthropocentric understandings of the world – as well as the 'speciesism' (a term coined by Raymond Corbey in this volume) that such understandings often seem to imply – risk blinding us to residual connections between people and other animals; at the same time, however, such observational use may fall into an ahistoricity that ignores the ways in which the pseudo-scientific equation of animals and humans was once applied, not generally, but instead to very specific ethnic groups for very specific ideological purposes.

The discussion of animalization is central to certain of the modes of colonial discourse identified by Edward Said in *Orientalism*, or to certain of the practices of constructing and controlling difference that Gayatri Spivak has called 'othering'. Parodying such critical approaches, Terry Eagleton sees in them risks of an intellectual dead end:

> The bad news is that otherness is not the most fertile of intellectual furrows. Indeed, once you have observed that the other is typically portrayed as lazy, dirty, stupid, crafty, womanly, passive, rebellious, sexually rapacious, child-like, enigmatic and a number of other mutually contradictory epithets, it is hard to know what to do next apart from reaching for another textual illustration of the fact. (Eagleton 2002: 2)

While Eagleton's critique is pertinent for certain self-fulfilling strands of colonial discourse studies already discussed above, according to which scholars comb texts for the presence of pre-existing sets of stereotypes, it does not reflect the more attenuated attention to the historically grounded workings of exhibition and exoticization that the contributions to the present volume reveal. The rapid expansion and evolution of postcolonial studies in the anglophone academy resulted in a clear move from an at times reductive attention to colonial discourse in the 1980s, towards an active and nuanced engagement in the 1990s with the complexities of postcolonial literature and culture themselves. The shift of attention from the (former) colonizer to that of the (former) colonized responded to a central aspect of postcolonial criticism itself, reflected widely elsewhere in scholarly practices in the humanities and social sciences – namely, the rejection of hegemonic canonicity, or archival authority, in favour of the recovery of subaltern voices, or of (hi)stories 'from below'. The risk inherent in such a manoeuvre is that the work on representational histories and exhibitionary practices, and on the stereotypes, hierarchies and taxonomies that underpin these, was not necessarily brought to the stage of development or recognition it merited. This tendency is particularly clear in postcolonial attitudes to exoticism, customarily presented as a straightforward process of translation and domestication, in which agency is denied and essence solidified.

The entry on the concept in *Key Concepts in Post-Colonial Studies* (Ashcroft, Griffiths and Tiffin 1998), written by three of the most prominent and pioneering critics in the postcolonial field, arguably illustrates this under-theorization of questions of exoticization and display. Citing an article by Renata Wasserman (1984), the glossary appears to posit a universalized and largely ahistorical exhibitionary order by which exoticism is regulated: 'Exotics in the metropoles were a significant part of imperial displays of power and the plenitude of Empires' (1998: 95). It is clear that in recent years, and in particular since the publication of *Zoos humains*, research in this area has progressed considerably, not least in publications by contributors to this volume (e.g. Maddra 2006; Poignant 2004).[2] The epithets identified in Eagleton's quotation above might be applied to a number of the descriptions of human zoos included in this volume, not least because the phenomenon depends on a clear stage-management of Otherness in the light of popular and scientific stereotypes. The human zoo is to be associated with a willed suppression of the processes of cultural hybridization and mobility triggered by colonialism (and undoubtedly inherent in all resilient cultures, as anthropologists such as James Clifford remind us), and depends on an associated 'denial of co-evalness' (Fabian 1983) that ensures the relegation of non-Western cultures to the lower rungs of a civilizational hierarchy. Far from identifying and reconstituting a taxonomic catalogue of pre-existing, stereotypical character traits, however, the volume reveals the ways in which such categories emerge, are subsequently validated and consolidated, and are also associated with particular ethnic groups, often creating shifting hierarchies between those groups. Crucially, the contributors negotiate the distance between the general and the specific, showing how what might at first appear to be a universal set of exhibitionary practices and cultural assumptions, associated in particular with the height of colonial modernity (and often, as a result, dependent on clear cases of inter-colonial rivalry), can only be fully understood in relation to the different sets of circumstances, cultural, historical and ideological, in which those practices and assumptions emerge. The stage-management of Otherness is modulated and adapted according to its immediate context.

As such, *Human Zoos* may even be seen to contribute to a certain materialist critique of postcolonialism, elaborated by scholars as diverse as Frederick Cooper and Benita Parry, engaging with those who would endeavour to interpret colonialism only in terms of hybridity or inter-cultural contact, downplaying the actual hegemonies on which systems of colonial control depend and the very real violence invariably deployed to enforce them. In one such intervention, Parry – reiterating Edward Said's call for recognition of the 'gravity of history' – denounces a field of study in which 'an air-borne will to power was privileged over calculated compulsions, "discursive violence" took precedence over the practices of a violent system, and the intrinsically antagonistic colonial encounter was reconfigured as one of dialogue, complicity and transculturation' (2004: 4). In the examples that constitute *Human Zoos*, there are moments of 'dialogue, complicity and transculturation', not least when indigenous peoples accepted the potentially strategic essentialism provided by the human zoo in order to articulate the specific demands of the ethnic groups they represented; but much of the volume is about the practical, structural role of popular racism in the justification and perpetuation of colonialism, and of other forms of subjugation, domination and denial of human rights. Although a major contribution to the field of 'representational' studies, *Human Zoos* therefore highlights the dependence of any 'epistemic' or 'discursive' violence on actual, tangible forms of coercion and control. The collection accordingly provides further exploration of what many see as the foundational thesis of postcolonial criticism, as explored by Edward Said in *Orientalism*, according to which the genesis of popular stereotypes has its foundations not only in orders of knowledge but also in lived relations of power. In the series of careful case studies that constitute this volume, readers are warned against the pitfalls of any approach that reduces the very real trauma of colonial contact to consideration of discourses or epistemes.

The human zoo provides a key example of the stage-management of colonial contact (and, at times, of the processes of internal colonialism) in the metropole itself, revealing the imbalances of power on which this depended and the control of colonized bodies on which it relied. It is significant that contributors to the volume repeatedly remind the reader that the voices and experiences of the exhibited remain elusive, systematically excluded from archival traces and exoticized in contemporary cultural artefacts. Scholars such as Elizabeth Edwards and Roslyn Poignant have underlined the ways in which photography may provide the beginnings of a remedy to this lack, with visitors' snaps, official postcards and cartes de visite often providing troubling traces of the lives of the observed, glimpses of the return of a gaze. It is perhaps for this very reason that Didier Daeninckx's *Cannibale* (1998) has attracted such sustained critical attention, for the fictional text attempts to narrativize, from the perspective of its protagonist Gocéné (its once-exhibited and observed narrator), the experience of existing in a human zoo (in this case, the Kanak village on the fringes of the 1931 Exposition coloniale mentioned above). Duped by promoters, forced to perform a stage-managed – literally cannibalized – version of New Caledonian culture, and then doubly animalized as half of their number were exchanged for crocodiles (the property of Hagenbeck) and sent to perform in Germany, Daeninckx's characters are denied coevalness with visitors to the exhibition of which they form a part. They are observed, policed and subjected to constant control. The novella is a clear illustration of the ways in which the licence permitted the author of fiction – a licence to negotiate censorship, to explore taboo subjects, to speculate at points where the archive fails to yield silenced details of the past – allows the telling of history in a manner often impossible for conventional historiography.

The implications of Daeninckx's narrative are, therefore, both historical and contemporary. Underpinning his story is an emerging interwar anti-colonialism, evident among the colonized and some French political activists, as for both of these groups the dehumanizing mechanisms of the human zoo reflect in microcosm the wider systems of colonial power. At the same time, however, by situating the 1931 exhibition within the contemporary frame of the 1980s' independence struggle in New Caledonia/Kanaky, his work forces reflection on questions of colonial legacy and memory. The importance of Daeninckx in popularizing contemporary French debates regarding the colonial past cannot be underestimated. His *Meurtres pour mémoire* (1984), a detective novel also set in the 1980s, explored connections between the Occupation and the 1961 massacres of North Africans in France and highlighted the racialization of society on which both depended. Daeninckx's work presents, explores and problematizes the interconnectedness of the colonial past and the postcolonial present. *Cannibale* explicitly underlines the ambiguities of the 'post' in 'postcolonial', disruptively revealing the chronological reduction of that epithet as a marker of posteriority to be at best prematurely celebratory, at worst deliberately obfuscatory.

The human zoo did not disappear in 1931, when the popularity of the Kanak village at the Exposition coloniale was rapidly eclipsed by a sense of public unease over such overt displays of colonial power. On the one hand, as Eric Deroo makes clear in this volume, cinematography provided an efficient proxy, permitting the transfer of the human zoo's exhibitionary logic to the screen and no longer necessitating the recruitment of human actors (not least at a time when, in the aftermath of the First World War, French colonial subjects were playing an increasingly prominent role in French labour and intellectual life [Miller 1998]). On the other hand, after a relatively long period of absence (there was, however, a Congo village at the 1958 Brussels World Fair), the phenomenon has made an unexpected return, with – since the 1980s – numerous post-colonial human zoos attracting attention in the world media and triggering inevitable controversies. Like their colonial predecessors, these modern manifestations are similarly international, with recently recorded cases including those in Belgium (in Yvoir, 2002), France (in Nantes, 1994), Germany (at Augsburg Zoo, 2005) and the USA (at the Woodland Park Zoo, Seattle, 2007). These contemporary manifestations often offer conservationist alibis, and justify themselves in terms of an anaemic sense of 'cultural awareness', cross-cultural solidarity or associated philanthropy. The sub-Saharan African people displayed – there are no reports of members of ethnic groups from other continents in these recent phenomena – are often presented as 'cultural interpreters', elements of a growing zoological emphasis on the 'cultural resonance' of exhibits apparent since the 1980s. There is a compelling pedagogical case, not least in the light of ongoing debates regarding the intersections of postcolonialism and ecocriticism, for new displays that challenge perceptions of other landscapes as 'human-free', but surveys carried out in the 2005 African village at the Augsburg Zoo (Glick Schiller, Dea and Höhne 2005) suggest that the continued use of human subjects as exoticized zoo exhibits has, in practice, a retrogressive or even negative effect on the perception of those from other cultural and ethnic groups. Visitors to the Augsburg case regularly associated Africans with wild animals and nature, revealing the ways in which the integration of humans into a zoo environment continues to be part of a process of racialization; some protesters against the Augsburg situation even evoked as a precedent the colonial Völkerschau of interwar Germany.

In all of the recent cases listed above, human subjects were employed to stage-manage 'authentic', essentialized versions of their own cultures of origin, versions belied by the globalization of cultural identities associated with postmodern, postcolonial mobility. The frameworks adopted were firmly zoological, as opposed to anthropological, perpetuating the colonial logic epitomized by cartoons such as Hergé's *Tintin in the Congo* – discussed in this volume by Jacquemin – according to which humans living on what is customarily seen as an undifferentiated African continent are, like fauna, part of an exotic backdrop. Therefore, although venue was perceived to be the principal focus of criticism in each of these cases, there are connections between the exhibitionary practices of these events and those explored in the main body of this collection. Given the historical attention to the nineteenth- and early twentieth-century phenomenon of the human zoo represented by research in volumes such as this, the genealogies of these contemporary avatars of the human zoo become quite apparent. Although recent displays of non-Western peoples in the contexts of zoos or wildlife parks can be compared to the phenomenon of reality television, whose anthropozoomorphic dimensions have not escaped critics (Razac 2002), the comparison remains an imperfect one; nor can the contemporary human zoo be explained away by analogy with the anthropological spectacles in which volunteers from white majority populations – in events bordering on performance art – have temporarily inhabited enclosures at zoos in London (August 2005) and Adelaide (January 2007). To present non-Western people in close proximity with animals is inevitably to evoke the exhibitionary orders that this volume explores, to re-excavate the assumptions of cultural and civilizational superiority/ inferiority that many historical examples of the human zoo served to foster. I am not, of course, outlining straightforward continuities, or suggesting that a scientific and popular racism evident in the later nineteenth century, having been sublimated for over three-quarters of a century, has re-emerged, unchanged. Any such conflationary historiography of convenience, linking similar phenomena despite their very different contexts of production, would illustrate what Frederick

Cooper has characterized as the postcolonial critic's sleight of hand, the tendency to 'leapfrog legacies' (2005: 17–18). The project underpinning this volume signals instead a distinctively postcolonial scholarly practice, more rigorous and more searching than that against which Cooper warns, that nevertheless seeks to explore the interconnectedness of colonial past and postcolonial present.

Notes

1 Also notable is the increasing recognition of the historical role of human zoos in popular culture, in a film such as Régis Warnier's *Man to Man* (2005).
2 The following year, General Paul Aussaresses admitted to the systematic use of torture in Algeria; in 2001, the same year that the Loi Taubira acknowledged that the transatlantic slave trade constituted a crime against humanity, the Mayor of Paris, Bertrand Delanoë, inaugurated a memorial to the victims of the 1961 massacre of FLN demonstrators in Paris.

General Bibliography

Secondary Material

Abbattista, G. (2003), 'La rappresentazione dell'altro', in U. Levra and R. Roccia (eds), *Le esposizioni torinesi, 1805–1911. Specchio del progresso e macchina del consenso*, Torino: Archivio Storico della Città di Torino, pp. 253–68.

—— (2004), 'Torino 1884: Africani in mostra', *Contemporanea*, 7.3, pp. 369–410.

—— (2005), 'Gli interessi antropologici di Carlo Marchesetti', in G. Bandelli and Montagnari Kokelj (eds), *Carlo Marchesetti e i Castellieri 1903–2003*, *Atti del Convegno Internazionale di Studi*, Trieste: Editreg, pp. 67–85.

—— (2006), 'Africains en exposition (Italie XIXe siècle) entre racialisme, spectaculaire et humanitarisme', in G. Abbattista and R. Minuti (eds), *Le problème de l'altérité dans la culture européenne*, Naples: Bibliopolis, pp. 23–43.

—— and R. Minuti (eds) (2006), *Le problème de l'altérité dans la culture européenne*, Naples: Bibliopolis.

About, N. (2001), *Proposition de loi autorisant la restitution par la France de la dépouille mortelle de Saartjie Baartman, dite 'Vénus hottentote', à l'Afrique du Sud*, texte n° 114 (2001–02), presented to the Sénat 4 December 2001.

Ackernecht, E. H. (1956), 'P. M. A. Dumoutier et la collection phrénologique du Musée de l'homme', *Bulletins et Mémoires de la Société d'anthropologie de Paris*, 2, pp. 289–310.

Adam, M. (1984), 'Racisme et catégories du genre humain', *L'Homme*, 34.2, pp. 77–96.

Adams, B. (1997a), 'A Stupendous Mirror of Departed Empires: The Barnum Hippodromes and Circuses, 1874–1891', *American Literary History*, 26.4, pp. 34–55.

—— (1997b), *Barnum: The Greatest Showman and the Making of US Popular Culture*, Minneapolis: University of Minnesota Press.

Adams, D. W. (1995), *Education for Extinction: American Indians and the Boarding School Experience, 1875–1928*, Lawrence: University Press of Kansas.

Adams J. A. (1996), 'The American Dream Actualized: The Glistening "White City" and the Lurking Shadows of the World's Columbian Exposition', in D. J. Bertuca (ed.), *The World's Columbian Exhibition: A Centennial Bibliographic Guide*, Westport, CT: Greenwood Press, pp. xiv–xxix.

Adams, R. (2001), *Sideshow USA: Freaks and the American Cultural Imagination*, Chicago: University of Chicago Press.

Affergan, F. (1987), *Exotisme et Altérité*, Paris: PUF.

—— (1991), *Critiques anthropologiques*, Paris: Presse de la FNSP.

Agamben, G. (1998), *Homo Sacer, Sovereign Power and Bare Life*, Stanford, CA: Stanford University Press.

Agee, W. K., P. H Ault and E. Emery (1989), *Introduction aux communications de masse*, Brussels: De Boeck–Wesmael.

Ageron, C.-R. (1984), 'L'Exposition coloniale de 1931. Mythe républicain ou mythe impérial?', in P. Nora (ed.), *Les Lieux de mémoire. La République*, vol. 1, Paris: Gallimard, pp. 561–94.

Aguirre, R. (2005), *Informal Empire*, Minneapolis: University of Minnesota Press.

Aimone, L. and C. Olmo (1993), *Les Expositions universelles: 1851–1900*, Paris: Belin.

Akazawa, T. (ed.) (1995), *The 'Other' Visualized*, Tokyo: University of Tokyo Press.

Akoun, A. (1991), *Afrique noire, Amérique, Océanie: mythes et croyances du monde*, Paris: Brepols.

Aldrich, R. (2005), *Vestiges of the Colonial Empire in France: Monuments, Museums and Colonial Memories*, Basingstoke: Palgrave Macmillan.

Alexander, E. (1990), *The Venus Hottentot*, Charlottesville: University Press of Virginia.

Alloula, M. (1986), *The Colonial Harem*, trans. M. Godzich and W. Godzich, Minneapolis: University of Minnesota Press.

Allwood, J. (1977), *The Great Exhibitions*, London: Studio Vista.

Altick, R. D. (1978), *The Shows of London*, Cambridge, MA, and London: Belknap Press of Harvard University Press.

Ames, E. (2003), 'The Sound of Evolution', *Modernism/Modernity*, 10.2, pp. 297–325.

—— (2006), 'Seeing the Imaginary: On the Popular Reception of Wild West Shows in Germany, 1885–1910', in P. Kort and M. Hollein (eds), *I like America: Fictions of the Wild West*, Frankfurt: Prestel, pp. 213–29.

Amiet-Keller, M. (1974), *Die Kolonisation im Urteil schweizerischer Staatstheoretiker, Wirtschaftstheoretiker und Historiker (1815–1914)*, Bern and Frankfurt: Lang Herbert und Peter.

Amselle, J.-L. and E. M'Bokolo (eds.) (1985), *Au cœur de l'ethnie: ethnies, tribalisme et État en Afrique*, Paris: La Découverte.

Anderson, E. (1981), *Streetwise: Race, Class and Change in an Urban Community*, Chicago: University of Chicago Press.

Anthias, F. (1992), 'Connecting Race and Ethnic Phenomena', *Sociology*, 26.4, pp. 421–38.

Anthropological Pavilion (2005), 'Engeki jinruikan jôen o jitsugen sasetai kai' [Society for the realisation of the Anthropological Pavilion's performances], in *Jinruikan: fûin sareta tobira* [The Anthropological Pavilion: The Sealed Door], Tokyo: Artworks shuppan (n.p.)

Anton, J. (2000), 'L'incroyable destin controversé du vieux "Negro de Banyoles"', *Courrier International*, 16 November, pp. 48–49.

Appelbaum, S. (1980), *The Chicago World's Fair of 1893*, New York: Dover Publications.

Apter, A. (1995), 'Reading the "Africa Exhibit"', *American Anthropologist*, 97.3, September.

Arago, F. (1987), *Le Daguerréotype. Rapport fait à l'Académie des sciences de Paris en 1839*, Paris: L'Échoppe.

Archives fédérales suisses (2000), *Expos, idées, intérêts, irritations*, Berne: Archives fédérales suisses.

Arlettaz, G. and E. Barilier (1991), *Les Suisses dans le miroir. Les expositions nationales suisses. De Zürich (1883) à l'ex-future expo tessinoise de 1998, en passant par Genève 1896, Berne 1914, Zurich 1939, Lausanne 1964 et l'échec de CH-91*, Lausanne: Payot.

Armstrong, M. (1993), '"A Jumble of Foreignness": The Sublime Musayums of Nineteenth-Century Fairs and Expositions', *Cultural Critique*, 23, pp. 199–250.

Arnoldi, M. J. (1997), 'Herbert Ward's "Ethnographic Sculptures" of Africans', in A. Henderson and A. Kaeppler (eds), *Exhibiting Dilemmas: Issues of Representation at the Smithsonian*, Washington: Smithsonian Institution Press, pp. 70–91.

—— and K. Hardin (1996), 'Efficacy and Objects', in M. J. Arnoldi, C. Geary and K. Hardin (eds), *African Material Culture*, Bloomington: Indiana University Press, pp. 1–28.

——, C. M. Kreamer and M. Mason (2001), 'Reflections on "African Voices" at the Smithsonian's National Museum of Natural History', *African Arts*, 34.2, pp. 16–35.

Ashcroft, B., G. Griffiths and H. Tiffin (1998), *Key Concepts in Post-Colonial Studies*, London: Routledge.

Assayag, J. (1999), *L'Inde fabuleuse. Le Charme discret de l'exotisme français (xviie–xxe siècles)*, Paris: Editions Kimé.

Aubagnac, G. (2002), 'En 1878, les "sauvages" entrent au musée de l'Armée', in N. Bancel, P. Blanchard, G. Boëtsch, É. Deroo and S. Lemaire (eds), *Zoos humains: de la Vénus hottentote aux reality shows*, Paris: La Découverte, pp. 349–54.

Aubert, M. and J.-C. Seguin (1996), *La Production cinématographique des Frères Lumière*, Paris: Bibliothèque du film/Mémoires du cinéma.

August, T. G. (1979), 'Nineteenth-Century Exoticism in France: the Formation of French Colonial Attitudes', *Historicus*, 1, pp. 70–80.

August, T. G. (1985), *The Selling of the Empire: British and French Imperialist Propaganda, 1890–1940*, Westport, CT: Greenwood Press.

Baartman (2002), 'Loi relative à la restitution par la France de la dépuille mortelle de Saartjie Baartman à l'Afrique du Sud (n° 2002–323 du 6 mars 2002)', *Journal officiel*, 56, 7 March 2002.

Bachofen, J. J. (1967), *Myth, Religion and Mother Right. Selected Writings*, Princeton: Princeton University Press.

Bachollet, R., J.-B. Debost, A.-C. Lelieur and M.-C. Peyrière (1994), *Négripub, l'image du Noir dans la publicité*, Paris: Somogy.

Badger, R. (1993 [1979]), *The Great American Fair: The World's Columbian Exposition and American Culture*, Chicago: Nelson Hall.

Badou, G. (2000a), *L'Enigme de la Vénus hottentote*, Paris: J.-C. Lattès.

—— (2000b), 'Sur les traces de la Vénus hottentote', *Gradhiva*, 27, pp. 83–87.

Baillette, F. (1997), 'Racisme et nationalismes sportifs', *Quasimodo*, 3–4, Montpellier: Éditions Quasimodo & Fils.

Bal, M. (1996), *Double Exposures. The Subject of Cultural Analysis*, London: Routledge.

Baldassari, A. (1994), *Picasso photographe, 1901–1906*, Paris: Réunion des musées nationaux.

—— (2002), '*Corpus ethnicum*: Picasso et la photographie coloniale', in N. Bancel, P. Blanchard, G. Boëtsch, É. Deroo and S. Lemaire (eds), *Zoos humains: de la Vénus hottentote aux reality shows*, Paris: La Découverte, pp. 340–48.

Bambridge, T. (2002), 'Les premiers *Polynésiens* en Europe et l'imaginaire occidental', in N. Bancel, P. Blanchard, G. Boëtsch, É. Deroo and S. Lemaire (eds), *Zoos humains: de la Vénus hottentote aux reality shows*, Paris: La Découverte, pp. 151–58.

Bancel, N. (1996), 'De l'indigène à l'Africain', in P. Blanchard, S. Blanchoin, N. Bancel, G. Boëtsch and H. Gerbeau (eds), *L'Autre et Nous*, Paris: Achac/Syros, pp. 239–42.

—— (ed.) (2007), *Retours sur la question coloniale*, Paris: Culture Sud.

——, L. Bencharif and P. Blanchard (eds) (2007), *Lyon, Capitale des outre-mers*, Paris: La Découverte.

—— and P. Blanchard (2000), 'Les Représentations du corps des tirailleurs sénégalais', *Africultures*, January, pp. 36–43.

—— and P. Blanchard (2006), 'Mémoire coloniale: résistances à l'émergence d'un débat', in P. Blanchard and N. Bancel (eds), *Culture post-coloniale, 1961–2006: traces et mémoires coloniales en France*, Paris: Autrement, pp. 22–41.

——, P. Blanchard, G. Boëtsch, É. Deroo and S. Lemaire (eds) (2002; paperback edn 2004), *Zoos humains: de la Vénus hottentote aux reality shows*, Paris: La Découverte poche.

——, P. Blanchard and F. Delabarre (eds) (1998), *Images d'empire. Trente ans de photographies officielles sur l'Afrique française (1930–1960)*, Paris: La Documentation française et de La Martinière.

——, P. Blanchard and L. Gervereau (eds) (1993), *Images et Colonies*, Paris: ACHAC/BDIC.

——, P. Blanchard and S. Lemaire (2000), 'Ces zoos humains de la République coloniale', *Le Monde diplomatique*, August, pp. 16–17.

——, P. Blanchard and F. Vergès (2003), *La République coloniale: essai sur une utopie*, Paris; Armand Colin.

—— and J.-M. Gayman (2002), *Du guerrier à l'athlète. Éléments d'histoire des pratiques corporelles*, Paris: PUF.

—— and O. Sirost (2002), 'Le Corps de l'Autre: une nouvelle économie du regard', in N. Bancel, P. Blanchard, G. Boëtsch, É. Deroo and S. Lemaire (eds), *Zoos humains: de la Vénus hottentote aux reality shows*, Paris: La Découverte, pp. 390–98.

Banta, M. and M. Hinsley (1986), *From Site to Sight: Anthropology, Photography and the Power of Imagery*, Cambridge, MA: Peabody Museum Press.

Banton, M. (1983), *Racial and Ethnic Competition*, Cambridge: Cambridge University Press.

—— (1987), 'La Classification des races en Europe et en Amérique du Nord: 1700–1850', *Revue internationale des sciences sociales*, 39.1, pp. 49–66.

Baratay, E. (1997), 'Un instrument symbolique de la domestication, le jardin zoologique aux XIXᵉ–XXᵉ siècles', *Cahiers d'histoire*, 42.3–4, pp. 677–706.

—— (1999), 'Les représentations de La Nature, l'exemple des zoos', *Raison présente, Sciences et politiques de La Nature*, 132, pp. 39–46.

—— (2002), 'Le frisson sauvage: les zoos comme mise en scène de la curiosité', in N. Bancel, P. Blanchard, G. Boëtsch, É. Deroo and S. Lemaire (eds), *Zoos humains: de la Vénus hottentote aux reality shows*, Paris: La Découverte, pp. 31–37.

—— and E. Hardouin-Fugier (1998), *Zoos. Histoire des jardins zoologiques en Occident (XVIᵉ–XXᵉ siècle)*, Paris: La Découverte.

Barbier, M.-C. (2003), 'Le Rapatriement de la Vénus hottentotte', *Revue Alizés*, 24 [see http://www2.univ-reunion.fr/~ageof/text/74c21e88-609.html].

Baridon, L. and M. Guédron (1999), *Corps et arts. Physionomies et physiologies dans les arts visuels*, Paris: L'Harmattan.

Barkan, R. (1961), 'De Kipling à Jean Rouch, de La Croisière noire à Come back, Africa: vers un cinéma universel', *Cinéma 61*, 54, pp. 65–74.

Barlet, O. and P. Blanchard (2005), 'Les "Zoos humains" sont-ils de retour?', *Le Monde*, 28 June, p. 25.

Barletti, E. (1992), 'Fotografia e Missioni in Bolivia. L'album di Padre Giannecchini', *AFT. Archivio Fotografico toscano*, 16, pp. 59–69.

Barrows, S. (1990), *Miroirs déformants. Réflexions sur la foule à la fin du XIXe siècle*, trans. Suzanne Le Foll, Paris: Aubier.

Barthe, C. (1992), 'Les Omaha de Bonaparte', in B. Coutancier (ed.), *Peaux-Rouges. Autour de la collection du prince Roland Bonaparte*, Thonon-les-Bains: L'Albaron/ Photothèque du Musée de l'homme, pp. 62–73.

Barthe, C. and B. Coutancier (1995), 'Au Jardin d'acclimatation: représentation de l'autre (1877–1890)', in P. Blanchard, S. Blanchoin, N. Bancel, G. Boëtsch and H. Gerbeau (eds), *L'Autre et Nous*, Paris: Achac/Syros, pp. 145–50.

Barthes, R. (1983), *Selected Writings*, ed. Susan Sontag, London: Fontana.

Baschet, E. (1987), *La France au-delà des mers. Histoire d'un siècle, 1843–1944*, Paris: L'Illustration.

Bates, R. S. (1965), *Scientific Societies in the US*, Cambridge, MA.: MIT Press.

Bathia, C. (1993), 'L'Afrique Noire à Rouen: Exposition nationale et coloniale de Rouen de 1896', *Plein Sud*, 3, pp. 24–31.

Baudrillard, J. (1987), 'Au-delà du vrai et du faux ou le malin génie de l'image', *Cahiers internationaux de sociologie*, 82, pp. 139–46.

Baumgart, W. (1982), *Imperialism: the Idea and Reality of British and French Colonial Expansion*, Oxford: Oxford University Press.

Beard, P. and G. Turle (1992), *The Art of the Maasai*, New York: A. A. Knopf.

Beaugé, G. and J.-F. Clément (1995), *L'Image dans le monde arabe*, Paris: CNRS éditions/Iremam.

Beauvoir, J.-M. (1977), *Los shelk'nam. Indígenas de la Tierra del Fuego. Sus tradiciones, costumbres y lengua 1915*, Punta Arenas: Editorial Atelí.

Bell, W. S. (ed.) (1967), *A Cabinet of Curiosities*, Charlottesville: University Press of Virginia.

Belluati, M. (1991), *Immagini di immigrazione giornalistica sui rapporti interetnici*, Turin: Università degli Studi di Torino.

Benali, A. (1998), *Le Cinéma colonial au Maghreb*, Paris: Éditions du Cerf.

Benedict, B. (ed.) (1983), *The Anthropology of World's Fairs, San Francisco's Panama Pacific International Exposition of 1915*, Berkeley, CA: Scolar Press.

—— (1991), 'International Exhibitions and National Identity', *Anthropology Today*, 7.3, pp. 5–9.

—— (1994), 'Rituals of Representation: Ethnic Stereotypes and Colonized Peoples at World's Fairs', in R. Rydell and N. E. Gwinn (eds), *Fair Representations*, Amsterdam: VU University Press, pp. 28–61.

Benjamin, W. (1984), 'Paris, die Haupstadt des XIXe', in *Allegorien kulturen erfahrung, Ausgewählte scriffen 1920–1940*, Leipzig: Reclam, pp. 106–11.

Bennett, T. (1988), 'The Exhibitionary Complex', *New Formations*, 4, pp. 73–102.

—— (1996), *Early Japanese Images*, Rutland, VT: Charles E. Tuttle.

Benninghoff-Lühl, S. (1984), 'Die Ausstellung der Kolonisierten: Völkerschauen von 1874–1932', in V. Harms (ed.), *Andenken an den Kolonialismus*, Tübingen: Institut der Universität Tübingen.

Benoist, J. and J.-L. Bonniol (1994), 'Hérédités plurielles. Représentations populaires et conceptions savantes du métissage', *Ethnologie française*, 24, pp. 58–69.

Bensa, A. (1988), 'Colonialisme, racisme et ethnologie en Nouvelle-Calédonie', *Ethnologie française*, 2, pp. 188–97.

—— (2006), *La Fin de l'exotisme: essais d'anthropologie critique*, Toulouse: Anacharsis.

Berger, J. (1977 [1972]), *Ways of Seeing*, London: British Broadcasting Corporation; Harmondsworth: Penguin Books.

Bergougniou, J.-M. (1997), 'Le Village noir à l'Exposition d'Angers en 1906', *Archives d'Anjou*, 1, pp. 145–58.

—— (1999), 'Le Village noir à l'exposition de Toulouse en 1908', *Gavroche*, 107, pp. 1–6.

—— (1999), 'Le Village sénégalais à l'exposition internationale d'Amiens en 1906', *Les antiquaires de Picardie*, 652, pp. 175–208.

—— (2001), 'L'Exposition de Chicago 1893. Des Noirs dans la ville blanche', *Gavroche*, 115, pp. 64–71.

——, R. Clignet and P. David (2001), *Villages noirs et visiteurs africains et malgaches en France et en Europe*, Paris: Karthala.

Berkeley Art Center (1982), *Ethnic Notions, Black Images in the White Mind and Exhibition of Afro-American Stereotype and Caricature*, Berkeley, CA: Berkeley Art Center.

Berkhofer, R. F. Jr. (1978), *The White Man's Indian: Images of the American Indian from Columbus to the Present*, New York: Random House.

Betts, J. R. (1959), 'P. T. Barnum and the Popularization of Natural History', *Journal of the History of Ideas*, 20, pp. 353–68.

Bhabha, H. (1983), 'The Other Question: the Stereotype and Colonial Discourse', *Screen*, 24.6, pp. 18–36.

Bibliothèque Nationale (1995), *L'Africaine ou les derniers feux du grand opéra. Les Dossiers du Musée d'Orsay*, Paris: Bibliothèque Nationale.

Biddiss, M.-D. (1966), 'Gobineau and the Origins of European Racism', *Race*, 7.3, pp. 255–70.

Bigham, M. R. (2000), 'Savagery in the Shadows of Civility: Africans on the Midway', unpublished MA thesis, University of North Carolina, Wilmington.

Birke, L. (1999), 'Bodies and Biology', in J. Price and M. Shildrick (eds), *Feminist Theory and the Body*, New York: Routledge, pp. 42–49.

Birx, J. H. (1992), 'Ota Benga: The Pygmy in the Zoo', *Library Journal*, 117.13, pp. 130–42.

Blachere, J.-C. (1981), *Le Modèle nègre. Aspects littéraires du mythe primitiviste au XXe siècle*, Dakar, Abidjan and Lomé: NEA.

Blanchard, P. (2000), 'Le Zoo humain, une longue tradition française', *Hommes et Migrations*, 1228, pp. 44–51.

—— (2000), 'L'invention du corps du colonisé à l'heure de l'apogée colonial', in G. Boëtsch and D. Chevé (eds), *Le corps dans tous ses états*, Paris: CNRS éditions.

—— (2001), 'Les représentations de l'indigène dans les affiches de propagande coloniale: entre concept républicain, fiction phobique et discours racialisant', *Hermès*, CNRS Éditions, 30, pp. 149–69.

—— (2002), 'Les zoos humains aujourd'hui?', in N. Bancel, P. Blanchard, G. Boëtsch, É. Deroo and S. Lemaire (eds), *Zoos humains: de la Vénus hottentote aux reality shows*, Paris: La Découverte, pp. 417–27.

—— (ed.) (2006), *Sud-Ouest, Porte des outre-mers*, Toulouse: Milan.

—— and N. Bancel (1998a), 'L'invention de l'indigène', *Passerelles*, 16, pp. 161–77.

—— and N. Bancel (1998b), *De l'indigène à l'immigré*, Paris: Gallimard, Découverte 317.

—— and N. Bancel (2000), 'De l'indigène à l'immigré. Images, messages et réalités (1). Le retour du colonial (2)', *Hommes et Migrations*, 1228, pp. 6–30, 100–14.

——, N. Bancel and S. Lemaire (2001), 'Des zoos humains aux apothéoses coloniales', *Africultures*, 43, pp. 48–57.

——, N. Bancel and S. Lemaire (2005), *La Fracture coloniale: la société française au prisme de l'héritage colonial*, Paris: La Découverte.

——, S. Blanchoin, N. Bancel, G. Boëtsch and H. Gerbeau (1996), *L'Autre et Nous*, Paris: Achac/Syros.

——, and G. Boëtsch (1994), 'La France sous Pétain et l'Afrique, images et propagande coloniale', *Canadian Journal of African Studies*, 28, pp. 1–32.

—— and G. Boëtsch (eds) (2005), *Marseille, Porte sud*, Paris: La Découverte; Marseille: Jeanne Laffitte.

—— and A. Chatelier (1993), *Images et Colonies. Nature, discours et influence de l'iconographie coloniale liée à la propagande coloniale et à la représentation des Africains en France, de 1920 aux Indépendances*, Paris: Achac/Syros.

—— and É. Deroo (2000a), 'Sauvage ou assimilé?', *Africultures*, 25, February, pp. 44–50.

—— and É. Deroo (2000b), 'Du sauvage au bon noir. Le Sens de l'image dans six représentations du tirailleur sénégalais', *Quasimodo*, 6, pp. 167–71.

—— and É. Deroo (eds) (2004), *Le Paris-Asie*, Paris: La Découverte.

——, É. Deroo, D. El Yazami, P. Fournié and G. Manceron (2003), *Le Paris arabe*, Paris: La Découverte.

——, É. Deroo and G. Manceron (2001), *Le Paris Noir*, Paris: Hazan.

—— and S. Lemaire (eds) (2003), *Culture coloniale (1871–1931). La France conquisé par son Empire*, Paris: Autrement.

—— and S. Lemaire (eds) (2004), *Culture impériale (1931–1961). Les Colonies au cœur de la République*, Paris: Autrement.

Blanckaert, C. (1988), 'On the Origin of French Ethnology: Wiliam Edwards and the Doctrine of Race', in G. W. Stocking (ed.), *Bones, Bodies, Behavior: Essays on Biological Anthropology, History of Anthropology*, Madison: University of Wisconsin Press, pp. 18–55.

—— (1993), 'La Science de l'homme entre humanité et inhumanité', in C. Blanckaert (ed.), *Des Sciences contre l'homme*, 2 vols, Paris: Autrement, pp. 14–45.

—— (1994), 'Des Sauvages en pays civilisé. L'Anthropologie des criminels (1850–1900)', in L. Mucchielli (ed.), *Histoire de la criminologie française*, Paris: L'Harmattan, pp. 55–88.

—— (ed.) (1996), *Le Terrain des sciences humaines. Instructions et enquêtes (XVIIIᵉ–XXᵉ siècles)*, Paris: L'Harmattan.

—— (2002), 'Spectacles ethniques et culture de masse au temps des colonies', *Revue d'Histoire des Sciences humaines*, 7, pp. 223–32.

—— (2005), 'Fondements disciplinaires de l'anthropologie française au XIXᵉ siècle', *Politix*, 29, pp. 29–54.

——, A. Ducros and J.-J. Hublin (eds) (1989), 'Histoire de l'anthropologie: hommes, idées, moments', *Bulletins et mémoires de la Société d'anthropologie de Paris*, 1.3–4.

Blier, S. P. (2002), 'Les Amazones à la rencontre de l'Occident', in N. Bancel, P. Blanchard, G. Boëtsch, É. Deroo and S. Lemaire (eds.), *Zoos humains: de la Vénus hottentote aux reality shows*, Paris: La Découverte, pp. 136–41.

Bloom, P. (2002), 'La subversion des hiérarchies du savoir dans *Les Statues meurent aussi*', in N. Bancel, P. Blanchard, G. Boëtsch, É. Deroo and S. Lemaire (eds), *Zoos humains: de la Vénus hottentote aux reality shows*, Paris: La Découverte, pp. 355–64.

Blot, M. (1908), 'Les Gallas au Jardin d'Acclimatation', *La Nature*, 36.2, pp. 225–27.

Blume, E. (2006), 'Joseph Beuys' "I Like America and America likes Me"', in P. Kort and M. Hollein (eds), *I like America. Fiktionen des Wilden Westens*, Frankfurt: Prestel, pp. 358–71.

Blume, H. (1999), 'Ota Benga and Barnum Perplex', in B. Lindfors (ed.), *Africans on Stage: Studies in Ethnological Show Business*, Bloomington: Indiana University Press, pp. 188–202.

Blumin, S. M. (1989), *The Emergence of the Middle-Class, Social Experience in the City, 1760–1900*, Cambridge: Cambridge University Press.

Blunt, W. (1976), *The Ark in the Park. The Zoo in the Nineteenth Century*, London: Hamish Hamilton.

Bode, C. (1981), *Struggles and Triumphs: or Forty Years' Recollections of P. T. Barnum*, New York: Penguin.

Boëtsch, G. (2003), 'Sciences, savants et colonies', in P. Blanchard and S. Lemaire (eds), *Culture coloniale*, Paris: Autrement, pp. 55–66.

—— (2006), 'Arabes/Berbères, l'incontournable raciologie du XIXe siècle', in H. Claudot-Hawad (ed.), *Berbères ou Arabes? Le Tango des spécialistes*, Paris: Editions Non Lieu, pp. 23–38.

—— and Y. Ardagna (2002), 'Zoos humains: le "sauvage" et l'anthropologue', in N. Bancel, P. Blanchard, G. Boëtsch, É. Deroo and S. Lemaire (eds), *Zoos humains: de la Vénus hottentote aux reality shows*, Paris: La Découverte, pp. 55–62.

——, N. Chapuis-Lucciani and D. Chevé (2006) (dirs.), *Représentations du corps: Le biologique et le vécu; Normes et normalité*, Nancy: PUN.

—— and D. Chevé (eds) (2000), *Le Corps dans tous ses états*, Paris: CNRS éditions.

——, H. Claudot-Hawad and J.-N. Ferrié (2002), 'Des Touaregs "sauvages" aux Egyptiens "urbains": les gradations de l'émotion exotique', in N. Bancel, P. Blanchard, G. Boëtsch, É. Deroo and S. Lemaire (eds), *Zoos humains: de la Vénus hottentote aux reality shows*, Paris: La Découverte, pp. 142–50.

—— and J.-N. Ferrié (1989), 'Le paradigme berbère, approche de la logique classificatoire des anthropologues français du XIXe siècle', *Bulletins et mémoires de la Société d'anthropologie de Paris*, new series, 1.3–4, pp. 257–76.

—— and J.-N. Ferrié (1993), 'L'Impossible objet de la raciologie. Prologue à une anthropologie physique du nord de l'Afrique', *Cahiers d'études africaines*, 129, pp. 5–18.

—— and J.-N. Ferrié (1997), 'Le Regard anthropologique', in P. Blanchard and N. Bancel (eds), *Images d'empire*, Paris: La Martinière; La Documentation française, pp. 52–75.

—— and J.-N. Ferrié (2003), 'Du Maure à la Mauresque: les métamorphoses d'un stéréotype dans les représentations savantes et vulgaires', in G. Boëtsch, Z. Samandi and C. Villain-Gandossi (eds), *Individu, famille et société en Méditerranée entre construction d'un savoir anthropologique et stéréotypes*, Tunis: CERES (Série sociologie, 26), pp. 87–105.

—— and M. Fonton (1994), 'L'Ethnographie criminelle: Lombroso aux colonies', in L. Mucchielli (ed.), *Histoire de la criminologie française*, Paris: L'Harmattan, pp. 139–56.

——, Ch. Hervé and J. J. Rozenberg (2007), *Corps normalisé, corps stigmatisé, corps racialisé*, Paris: De Boeck.

—— and E. Savarèse (1999), 'Le Corps de l'africaine: érotisation et inversion', *Cahiers d'études africaines*, 153, 39.1, pp. 123–44.

—— and E. Savarèse (2000), 'Photographies anthropologiques et politiques des races sur les usages de la photographie à Madagascar, 1896–1905', *Journal des Anthropologues*, 80–81, pp. 247–58.

—— and C. Villain-Gandossi (2001), *Stéréotypes dans les relations Nord/Sud*, Paris: Hermès, 30.

Bogdan, R. (1986), 'Exhibition of Mentally Retarded People for Amusement and Profit, 1850–1940', *American Journal of Mental Deficiency*, 91, pp. 120–26.

—— (1988), *Freak Show: Presenting Human Oddities for Amusement and Profit*, Chicago: University of Chicago Press.

—— (1993), 'In Defense of Freak Show', *Disability, Handicap and Society*, 8.1, pp. 91–94.

—— (1996), 'The Social Construction of Freaks', in R. Garland-Thomson (ed.), *Freakery: Cultural Spectacles of the Extraordinary, 1886–1931*, New York: New York University Press, pp. 23–37.

—— (2002), 'La Mise en spectacle de l'exotique', in N. Bancel, P. Blanchard, G. Boëtsch, É. Deroo and S. Lemaire (eds), *Zoos humains: de la Vénus hottentote aux reality shows*, Paris: La Découverte, pp. 49–54.

Boime, A. (1990), *The Art of Exclusion: Representing Blacks in the Nineteenth Century*, Washington: Smithsonian Institution Press.

Bondeson, J. (1997), *A Cabinet of Medical Curiosities*, New York: Norton.

—— (2000), *The Two-headed Boy and Other Medical Marvels*, New York: Cornell University Press.

Bongie, C. (1998), *Islands and Exiles: The Creole Identities of Post/Colonial Literature*, Stanford, CA: Stanford University Press.

Bonneuil, C. (1999), 'Le Muséum national d'histoire naturelle et l'expansion coloniale de la Troisième République (1870–1914)', *Revue française d'histoire d'outre-mer*, 322–23, pp. 143–69.

Bonniol, J.-L. (1990), 'La couleur des hommes comme principe d'organisation sociale', *Ethnologie française*, 4, pp. 410–18.

—— (1992), 'La Race, inanité biologique mais réalité symbolique efficace', *Mots. Les langages du politique*, 33, pp. 187–96.

Bono, S. (1992), 'Esposizioni coloniali italiane. Ipotesi e contributo per un censimento', in N. Labanca (ed.), *L'Africa in vetrina. Storie di musei e di esposizioni coloniali in Italia*, Treviso: Pagus.

Bottari, M. (1984), *Genova 1892 e le celebrazioni colombiane*, Geneva: F. Pirella.

Boucher, P. (1992), *Cannibal Encounters: Europeans and Island Caribs, 1492–1763*, Baltimore and London: Johns Hopkins University Press.

Bourdieu, P. (1965), *La Distinction. Critique sociale du jugement*, Paris: Éditions de Minuit.

Bourguet, M.-N. (1993), 'La Collecte du monde: voyage et histoire naturelle (fin XVIIᵉ–début XIXᵉ siècle)', in C. Blanckaert et al. (eds), *Le Muséum au premier siècle de son histoire*, Paris: MNHN, pp. 163–96.

Bourlard-Collin, S. et al. (1983), *L'Orient des provençaux. Les Expositions coloniales*, Marseille: Vieille Charité.

Brace, C.-L. (1982), 'The Roots of Race Concept in American Physical Anthropology', in F. Spencer (ed.), *A History of American Physical Anthropology, 1930–1980*, New York: Academic Press, pp. 11–29.

Bradford, P. V. and H. Blume (1992), *Ota Benga: The Pygmy in the Zoo*, New York: St Martin's Press.

Brändle, R. (1992), 'Die Wilden bleiben noch ein paar Tage ausgestellt', *Die Wochen Zeitung*, 23, p. 5.

—— (1995), *Wildfremd, hautnah. Völkerschauen und Schauplätze Zürich (1889–1960)*, Zürich: Bilder und Geschichten.

—— (2002), 'La Monstration de l'Autre en Suisse: plaidoyer pour des micro-études', in N. Bancel, P. Blanchard, G. Boëtsch, É. Deroo and S. Lemaire (eds), *Zoos humains: de la Vénus hottentote aux reality shows*, Paris: La Découverte, pp. 221–26.

Brantlinger, P. (2003), *Dark Vanishings: Discourse on the Extinction of Primitive Races, 1800–1930*, Ithaca, NY: Cornell University Press.

Brauman, A. and Demanet S. (1985), *Le Parc Léopold, 1850–1950. Le Zoo, la cité scientifique et la ville*, Brussels: Archives d'architecture moderne.

Bravo, M. (1996), 'Ethnological Encounters', in N. Jardine, J. A. Secord and E. C. Spary (eds), *Cultures of Natural History*, Cambridge: Cambridge University Press, pp. 338–57.

Breckenridge, C. A. (1989), 'The Aesthetics and Politics of Colonial Collecting: India at the World Fairs', *Comparative Studies in Society and History*, 31, pp. 195–216.

Breitbart, E. (1997), *A World on Display. Photographs from the St. Louis World's Fair, 1904*, Albuquerque: University of New Mexico Press.

Bréon, E. (ed.) (1989), *Coloniales, 1920–1940*, Billancourt: MMBB.

Bridges, W. (1974), *Gathering of Animals: An Unconventional History of the New York Zoological Society*, New York: Harper and Row.

Brown, J. K. (1984), *Contesting Images: Photography and the World's Columbian Exposition*, Tucson: University of Arizona Press.

Brown, R. D. (1976), *Modernization: The Transformation of American Life, 1600–1865*, New York: Hill and Wang.

Bruckner, P. (2006), *La Tyrannie de la pénitence*, Paris: Grasset.

Bucher, B. (1977), *La Sauvage aux seins pendants*, Paris: Herman.

Bullard, A. (1997), 'Self-Representation in the Arms of Defeat: Fatal Nostalgia and the Surviving Comrades', *Cultural Anthropology*, 12.2, pp. 179–211.

—— (1998), 'The French Idea of Subjectivity and the Kanak of New Caledonia: Recuperating the Category of Affect', *History and Anthropology*, 10.4, pp. 375–405.

—— (2000), 'Paris 1871/New Caledonia 1878: Human Rights and the Managerial State', in L. Hunt, M. Young and J. Wasserstrom (eds), *Human Rights and Revolutions*, Lanham, MD, and Oxford: Rowman Littlefield, pp. 79–98.

—— and Dauphiné J. (2002), 'Les Canaques au miroir de l'Occident', in N. Bancel, P. Blanchard, G. Boëtsch, É. Deroo and S. Lemaire (eds), *Zoos humains: de la Vénus hottentote aux reality shows*, Paris: La Découverte, pp. 118–26.

Burg, D. F. (1976), *Chicago's White City of 1893*, Lexington: University Press of Kentucky.

Burke, P. (1978), *Popular Culture in Early Modern Europe*, London: Temple Smith.

Cannadine, D. (2001), *Ornamentalism. How the British Saw Their Empire*, New York: Oxford University Press.

Cannizzo, J. (1989), *Into the Heart of Africa*, Ontario: Royal Ontario Museum.

Carlson, L. (1989), 'Giant Patagonians and Hairy Ainu: Anthropology Days at the 1904 St. Louis Olympics', *Journal of American Culture*, 12.3, pp. 19–25.

Carol, A. (1995), *Histoire de l'eugénisme en France. Les Médecins et la procréation, XIXe–XXe siècle*, Paris: Seuil.

Castelli, E. (1998), *Immagini & Colonie*, Montone: Tamburo Parlante.

Çelik, Z. (1992), *Displaying the Orient*, Berkeley: University of California Press.

—— and L. Kinney (1990), 'Ethnography and Exhibitionism at the Expositions universelles', *Assemblage*, 13, pp. 33–59.

Centlivres, P. (1982), *Des Instructions aux collections: la production ethnographique de l'image de l'Orient*, Coll. 'Passions', Neuchâtel: Musée d'Ethnographie, pp. 33–61.

Cerreti, C. (1995), *Colonie africane e cultura italiana fra Ottocento e Novecento. Le esplorazioni e la geografia*, Rome: Centro d'informazione e stampa universitaria.

Chailleau, L. (1990), 'La Revue orientale et américaine (1858–1879): ethnographie, orientalisme et américanisme au XIXe siècle', *L'Ethnographie*, 36.1, pp. 91–107.

Chalaye, S. (1997), 'Du Dangereux indigène au cannibale sympathique, les images du théâtre à l'époque coloniale', *Africultures*, 3, pp. 37–43.

—— (1998), *Du Noir au nègre, l'image du Noir au théâtre de Marguerite de Navarre à Jean Genet (1550–1960)*, Paris: L'Harmattan.

—— (2001a), 'Imaginaire colonial: fantasme et nostalgie', *Africultures*, 43, pp. 21–25.

—— (2001b), *Nègres et images*, Paris: L'Harmattan.

—— (2002), 'Théâtre et cabarets: le "nègre" spectacle', in N. Bancel, P. Blanchard, G. Boëtsch, É. Deroo and S. Lemaire (eds), *Zoos humains: de la Vénus hottentote aux reality shows*, Paris: La Découverte, pp. 296–305.

Champion, C. (1990), 'Fortunio, un rêve romantique indien dans le Paris d'Haussmann', in 'Rêver l'Inde', *Corps Ecrit*, 34, pp. 57–64.

Champion, C. (1991), 'L'Inde dans la fiction populaire française', in D. Lombard (ed.), *Rêver l'Asie. Exotisme et littérature coloniale aux Indes, en Indochine et en Insulinde*, Paris: EHESS, pp. 43–68.

Chandler, A. (1990), 'Empire of the Republic: the Exposition Coloniale Internationale de Paris, 1931', *Contemporary French Civilization*, 14, pp. 89–99.

Chapman, A. (1986), *Los selk'nam. La vida de los onas*, Buenos Aires: Emecé Editores.

——, C. Barthe and P. Revol (1995), *Cap Horn, 1882–1883. Rencontre avec les indiens Yahgan*, Paris: La Martinière; MNHN; Photothèque du Musée de l'homme.

Charles, J.-C. (1980), *Le Corps noir*, Paris: Hachette.

Chase-Riboud, B. (2003), *Hottentot Venus*, New York: Doubleday.

Chiappelli, F. (ed.) (1976), *First Images of America. The Impact of the New World on the Old*, 2 vols, Berkeley: University of California Press.

Chiarelli, B., P. Chiozzi and C. Chiarelli (1996), *Etnie. La scuola antropologica fiorentina e la fotografia*, Firenze: Alinari.

Chiarelli, C. (2001), 'Cinegiornali di argomento africano nell'Archivio dell'Istituto Luce', in *AFT, L'immagine dell'Africa indipendente*, http://www.aft.it/convegni/htm/p-africa.htm, pp. 32–33.

Chikappu, M. (2001), *Ainu moshiri no kaze* [The Wind from Ainu's land], Tokyo: NHK shuppan.

Choay, F. (1965), *L'Urbanisme, utopies et réalités. Une anthologie*, Paris: Seuil.

Christout, M.-F. (1990), 'Rêver l'Inde à travers la danse. De la fascination exotique à la connaissance', in 'Rêver l'Inde', *Corps Ecrit*, 34, pp. 85–94.

Clair, C. (1968), *Human Curiosities*, New York: Abelard-Schuman.

Clark, T. B. (1940), *Omai, First Polynesian Ambassador to England*, London: Colt Press.

Claudot-Hawad, H. (1996), 'Touaregs et autres Sahariens entre plusieurs mondes. Définitions et redéfinition de soi et des autres', *Les Cahiers de l'Iremam*, 7–8.

Clement, A. J. (1967), *The Kalahari and Its Lost City*, Cape Town: Longmans.

Clifford, J. (1986), 'On Ethnographic Allegory', in J. Clifford and G. E. Marcus (eds), *Writing Culture: The Poetics and Politics of Ethnography*, Berkeley: University of California Press, pp. 98–121.

—— (1988), *The Predicament of Culture*, Cambridge, MA; London: Harvard University Press.

—— (1996), *Malaise dans la culture: l'ethnographie, la littérature et l'art au XXᵉ siècle*, trans. M.-A. Sichère, Paris: École nationale supérieure des Beaux-Arts.

Cloyd, E. L. (1972), *James Burnett, Lord Monboddo*, Oxford: Clarendon Press.

Cohen, W. B. (1974), 'Literature and Race: Nineteenth-Century French Fiction, Blacks and Africa, 1800–1880', *Race and Class*, 16.2, pp. 181–205.

—— (1980), *Français et Africains. Les Noirs dans le regard des Blancs 1530–1880*, Paris: Gallimard; Bloomington: Indiana University Press.

Cole, D. (1985), *Captured Heritage: The Scramble for Northwest Coast Artifacts*, Norman: University of Oklahoma Press.

Cole, J. (2007), 'Understanding the French Riots of 2005: What Historical Context for the "Crise des banlieues"', *Francophone Postcolonial Studies*, 5.2, pp. 69–100.

Coleman, W. (1964), *Georges Cuvier, Zoologist: A Study of the History of Evolution Theory*, Cambridge, MA: Harvard University Press.

Collectif (1994), *Barbares et Sauvages. Images et reflets dans la culture occidentale*, Caen: Presses universitaires de Caen.

—— (2006), *Le Douanier Rousseau. La jungle à Paris*, Paris: RMN.

Collier, J. and M. Collier (1986), *Visual Anthropology. Photography as a Research Method*, Albuquerque: University of New Mexico Press.

Collomb, G. (1992), *Kaliña. Des Amérindiens à Paris*, Paris: Créaphis.

—— (1995), 'Les Kaliña et le droit de regard de l'Occident', in P. Blanchard, S. Blanchoin, N. Bancel, G. Boëtsch and H. Gerbeau (eds), *L'Autre et Nous*, Paris: Achac/Syros, pp. 151–57.

—— (1997), 'La Question amérindienne en Guyane. Formation d'un espace politique', in M. Abélès and H. P. Jeudy (eds), *Anthropologie du politique*, Paris: Armand Colin, pp. 41–66.

Comas, J. (1951), *Les Mythes raciaux*, Paris: UNESCO.

Condillac, A. (1984), *Traité des sensations*, Paris: Fayard.

Congo (1996), 'Soixante-trois Neuchâtelois au service de sa majesté Léopold II, Roi-Souverain de l'Etat indépendant du Congo (1885–1908)', *Musée Neuchâtelois*, 1, pp. 11–28.

Conklin, A. (1997), *A Mission to Civilize. The Republican Idea of Empire in France and West Africa, 1895–1930*, Stanford: Stanford University Press.

Contreras, J. and I. Terrades (1984), 'L'exhibició d'aixantis a Barcelona, l'any 1897', *L'Avenç*, 72, pp. 30–36.

Cook, J. W. (1996), 'Of Men, Missing Links, and Nondescripts: The Strange Career of P. T. Barnum's "What is It?" Exhibition', in R. Garland-Thomson (ed.), *Freakery: Cultural Spectacles of the Extraordinary, 1886–1931*, New York: New York University Press, pp. 139–57.

Coombes, A. (1994), *Reinventing Africa: Material Culture and Popular Imagination in Late Victorian and Edwardian England*, New Haven, CT: Yale University Press.

Cooper, F. (2005), *Colonialism in Question: Theory, Knowledge, History*, Berkeley: University of California Press.

Copans, J. and J. Jamin (eds.) (1978), *Aux origines de l'anthropologie française. Les mémoires de la Société des Observateurs de l'Homme en l'an VIII*, Paris: Le Sycomore.

Coquery-Vidrovitch, C. (2003), 'Le Postulat de la supériorité blanche et de l'infériorité noire', in M. Ferro (ed.), *Le Livre noir du colonialisme. XVIe–XXIe siècle: de l'extermination à la repentance*, Paris: Robert Laffont, pp. 646–91.

Corbey, R. (1988), 'Alterity: the Colonial Nude', *Critique of Anthropology*, 13.3, pp. 75–92.

—— (1989), *Wildheid en beschaving. De Europese verbeelding van Afrika*, Baarn: Ambo.

—— (1990), 'Der missionar, die heiden und das Photoï', *Zeitschrift für Kulturaustausch*, 40, pp. 460–65.

—— (1993), 'Ethnographic Showcases, 1870–1930', *Cultural Anthropology*, 8.3, pp. 338–69.

—— (1997), 'Inventaire et Surveillance, l'appropriation de la nature à travers l'histoire naturelle', in C. Blanckaert (ed.), *Le Muséum au premier siècle de son histoire*, Paris: L'Harmattan, pp. 541–57.

—— (2002), 'Vitrines ethnographiques: le récit et le regard', in N. Bancel, P. Blanchard, G. Boëtsch, É. Deroo and S. Lemaire (eds), *Zoos humains: de la Vénus hottentote aux reality shows*, Paris: La Découverte, pp. 90–98.

Corrales, E. M. (2002), *La imagen del magrebi en España. Une perspectiva histórica siglos XVI–XX*, Barcelona: Edicions Bellaterra.

Coslin, P. and F. Winnykamen (1981), 'Contribution à l'étude de la genèse des stéréotypes: attribution d'actes positifs ou négatifs en fonction de l'appartenance ethnique', *Psychologie française*, 26.1, pp. 39–48.

Courcelles, D. (ed.) (1997), *Littérature et Exotisme XVIe–XVIIIe siècle*, Paris: École nationale des chartes.

Cousin, B. (1993), 'Histoire et iconographie: état des lieux', *Xoana*, 1, pp. 141–48.

Coutancier, B. (1992) '"Jaune" et ses compagnons', in B. Coutancier (ed.), *Peaux-Rouges, Autour de la collection du prince Roland Bonaparte*, Thonon-les-Bain: L'Albaron/Photothèque du Musée de l'Homme, pp. 48–61.

—— and C. Barthe (2002), '"Exhibition" et médiatisation de l'Autre: le Jardin zoologique d'acclimatation (1877–1890)', in N. Bancel, P. Blanchard, G. Boëtsch, É. Deroo and S. Lemaire (eds), *Zoos humains: de la Vénus hottentote aux reality shows*, Paris: La Découverte, pp. 306–14.

Crettaz, B. and J. Michaelis-Germanier (1983), 'Une Suisse miniature ou les grandeurs de la petitesse', *Extrait du Bulletin annuel du Musée d'ethnographie de Genève*, 25–26, pp. 62–185.

Cross, W. E. (1991), *Shades of Black. Diversity in African-American Identity*, Philadelphia: Temple University Press.

Cuisenier, J. (1983), 'Droits de la personne sur son image', *Ethnologie française*, 13.2, pp. 103–10.

Curtin, P.-D. (1964), *The Image of Africa British Idea and Action, 1780–1850*, Madison, University of Wisconsin Press.

Cuvier, G. (1978 [1800]), 'Note instructive sur les recherches à faire relativement aux différences anatomiques des diverses races d'hommes', in J. Copans and J. Jamin (eds), *Aux Origines de l'anthropologie française*, Paris: Sycomore, pp. 171–76.

Dabydeen, D. (1987), *Hogarth's Blacks. Images of Blacks in Eighteenth-Century English Art*, Athens: University of Georgia Press.

Dæninckx, D. (1984), *Meurtres pour mémoire*, Paris: Gallimard.

—— (1998), *Cannibale*, Lagrasse: Verdier.

Dardaud, G. (1985), *Une Girafe pour le roi*, Paris: Dumerchez.

Darnell, R. (1977), 'History of Anthropology in Historical Perspective', *Annual Review of Anthropology*, 4, pp. 399–417.

Daston, L. and Park K. (1998), *Wonders and the Order of Nature, 1150–1750*, New York: Zone Books.

Dauphiné, J. (1998), *Canaques de la Nouvelle-Calédonie à Paris en 1931. De la case au Zoo*, Paris: L'Harmattan.

David, P. (1998a), 'Le Village Noir à l'Exposition d'Orléans de 1905', *Bulletin de la Société archéologique et historique de l'Orléanais*, new series, 15.119, pp. 25–50.

—— (1998b), 'Les Villages Noirs aux Expositions de Brest de 1901, 1913 et 1928 en histoire et en images', *Cahier de l'Iroise*, 177–178, pp. 49–59, 59–69.

—— and J.-M. Andrault (1995), 'Le Village Noir à L'Exposition de Nantes en 1904 en histoire et en images', *Annales de Bretagne et des Pays de l'Ouest: ABPO*, 4, pp. 108–25.

Davidov, J. F. (1998), *Women's Camera Work, Self/Body/Other in American Visual Culture*, Durham, NC: Duke University Press.

Davis, J. M. (2002), *The Circus Age: Culture and Society under the American Big Top*, Chapel Hill: University of North Carolina Press.

De L'Estoile, B. (2001), 'Des Races non pas inférieures mais différentes: de l'Exposition coloniale au Musée de l'homme', in C. Blanckaert (ed.), *Politiques de l'anthropologie: pratiques et applications en France (1860–1940)*, Paris: L'Harmattan, pp. 391–473.

—— (2003), 'From the colonial exhibition to the Museum of Man. An alternative genealogy of French anthropology', *Social Anthropology*, December, pp. 59–79.

—— (2005), 'Musée des origines ou musée post-colonial: que faire de l'histoire?', *Histoire de l'art et musées*, Paris: École du Louvre, pp. 53–71.

—— (2007), *Le Goût des autres. De l'Exposition coloniale aux Arts premiers*, Paris: Flammarion.

De la Casinière, N. (1994), 'Les Ivoiriens du Safari Parc, nourris, logés mais pas payés', *Libération*, 21 April, p. 35.

Debrunner, H. W. (1979), *Presence and Prestige, Africans in Europe. A History of Africans in Europe before 1918*, Basel: Afrika Bibliographien Basel.

—— (1991), *Schweizer im kolonialen Afrika*, Basel: Basler Afrika Bibliographien.

Dehon, E. (1945), *La Nouvelle politique coloniale de la France*, Paris: Flammarion.

Del Boca, A. (1976–1984), *Gli italiani in Africa orientale*, 4 vols, Roma-Bari: Laterza.

—— (1986–1988), *Gli italiani in Libia*, Roma-Bari: Laterza.

—— (1992), *L'Africa nella coscienza degli italiani. Miti, memorie, errori, sconfitte*, Roma-Bari: Laterza.

Del Rio, G. and J.-P. Velot (1996), 'L'Exposition coloniale, Paris, 1931', *Mwà Véé*, 13, pp. 8–12.

Delanoë, N. (1982), *L'Entaille rouge: terres indiennes et démocratie américaine, 1776–1980*, Paris: François Maspero.

Delgado, L., D. Lozano and C. Chiarelli (2002), 'Les zoos humains en Espagne et en Italie: entre spectacle et entreprise missionnaire', in N. Bancel, P. Blanchard, G. Boëtsch, É. Deroo and S. Lemaire (eds), *Zoos humains: de la Vénus hottentote aux reality shows*, Paris: La Découverte, pp. 235–44.

Delon, M. (1977), 'Corps sauvages, Corps étranges', *Dix-huitième Siècle*, 9, pp. 27–38.

Deloria, V. Jr. (1981), 'The Indians', in *Buffalo Bill and the Wild West*, New York: Brooklyn Museum.

DeMallie, R. J. (1984), *The Sixth Grandfather: Black Elk's Teachings Given to John G. Neihardt*, Lincoln: University of Nebraska Press.

Demoor, F. and J.-P. Jacquemin (2000), *Notre Congo/Onze Kongo (la propagande coloniale belge: fragments pour une étude critique)*, Brussels: CEC.

Denis, D. (1997), 'La Revanche des dominés', *Quasimodo*, 3–4, pp. 47–60.

Dennett, A.-S. (1997), *Weird and Wonderful, The Dime Museum in America*, New York: New York University Press.

Deroo, É. (2002), 'Le Cinéma gardien du zoo', in N. Bancel, P. Blanchard, G. Boëtsch, É. Deroo and S. Lemaire (eds), *Zoos humains: de la Vénus hottentote aux reality shows*, Paris: La Découverte, pp. 381–89.

—— and E. Champeaux (2006), *La Force noire*, Paris: Tallandier.

——, G. Deroo and M.-C. de Taillac (1992), *Aux Colonies*, Paris: Presses de la Cité.

—— and S. Lemaire (2006), *L'Illusion coloniale*, Paris: Tallandier.

Descola, P. (1992), 'Le Sauvage, un mythe épuisé', *Sciences et Avenir*, 90, pp. 6–10.

Destutt de Tracy, A.-L.-C. (1970), *Eléments d'idéologie*, Paris: Librairie Philosophique J. Vrin

Dias, N. (1991), *Le Musée d'ethnographie du Trocadéro*, Paris: CNRS éditions

—— (1994), 'Photographier et mesurer, les portraits anthropologiques', *Romantisme*, 84, pp. 37–50.

—— (1997), 'Images et savoir anthropologique au XIXᵉ siècle', *Gradhiva*, 2, pp. 87–97.

—— (1998), 'The Visibility of Difference', in S. Macdonald (ed.), *The Politics of Display. Museums, Science, Culture*, London: Routledge, pp. 36–52.

—— (2004), *La Mesure des sens. Les anthropologues et le corps humains au XIXᵉ siècle*, Paris: Seuil.

Didi-Hubermann, G. (1986), 'La Photographie scientifique et pseudo-scientifique', in J. C. Lemagny and A. Rouillé (eds), *Histoire de la photographie*, Paris: Bordas, pp. 71–75.

Dikötter, F. (1992), *The Discourse of Race in Modern China*, Stanford: Stanford University Press.

Dixon, R. M. W. and B. J. Blake (1979; 1983), *Handbook of Australian Languages*, vol. 1 (1979), vol. 3 (1983), Amsterdam: John Benjamins.

Donald, J. and R. Ali (eds) (1992), *Race, Culture and Identity*, London: Sage.

Dore, G. (1992), 'Ideologia coloniale e senso comune etnografico nella mostra delle terre italiane d'Oltremare', in N. Labanca (ed.), *L'Africa in vetrina. Storie di musei e di esposizioni coloniali in Italia*, Treviso: Pagus.

Dornel, L. (2004), *La France hostile. Socio-histoire de la xénophobie, 1870–1914*, Paris: Hachette littératures.

Dörner, K. (1984), *Bürger und Irre. Zur Socialgeschichte Wissenschaftssoziologie des psychiatric*, Frankfurt: Europäische Verlagsanstalt.

Douglas, B. (1999), *Across the Great Divide*, New York: Harcourt.

Dozon, J.-P. (2003), *Frères et sujets. La France et l'Afrique en perspective*, Paris: Flammarion.

Dreesbach, A. (2005), *Gezähmte Wilde: Die Zurschaustellung 'exotischer' Menschen in Deutschland 1870–1940*, Frankfurt-am-Main: Campus.

Driver, F. (2001), *Geography Militant. Cultures of Exploration and Empire*, Oxford: Blackwell.

Dubois, J. (1994) (ed.), *Album Peaux-Rouges de Roland Bonaparte*, Paris: Photothèque du Musée de l'homme.

Dubois, L. (2000), 'La République métisée: citizenship, colonialism, and the borders of French history', *Cultural Studies*, 14.1, pp. 15–34.

Duchet, M. (1971), *Anthropologie et Histoire au siècle des Lumières*, Paris: Maspero.

Duclos, F. (1991), 'La Société de géographie: sa bibliothèque et ses collections photographiques', *L'Ethnographie*, 109, pp. 179–85.

Ducros A. (1992), 'La Notion de race en anthropologie physique: évolution et conservatisme', *Mots*, 33, pp. 121–42.

Dufour, P. (1999), 'Le Baroud d'honneur des Amazones du Dahomey', *Historia*, 636, pp. 30–32.

Dupertuis, C. W. and J.-M. Tanner (1950), 'The Pose of the Subject for Photogrammetric Anthropometry with Especial Reference to Somatotype', *American Journal of Physical Anthropology*, 8, pp. 27–48.

Durand, G. (1962), 'Les Catégories de l'irrationnel, prélude à l'anthropologie', *Esprit*, 1, pp. 71–85.

—— (1993), *Les Structures anthropologiques de l'imaginaire. Introduction à l'archétypologie générale*, Paris: Dunod.

Durant, A. and J. Durant (1957), *A Pictorial History of the American Circus*, New York: A. S. Barnes.

Duvernay-Bolens, J. (1995), 'L'Homme zoologique. Race et racisme chez les naturalistes de la première moitié du XIXe siècle', *L'Homme*, 133, pp. 9–32.

Eagleton, T. (2002), *Figures of Dissent: Reviewing Fish, Spivak, Zizek and Others*, London: Verso.

Edwards, E. (1988), 'Representation and Reality: Science and the Visual Image', in H. Morphy and E. Edwards (eds), *Australia in Oxford*, Oxford: University of Oxford/Pitt Rivers Museum, pp. 27–45.

—— (1990), 'Photographic Types: The Pursuit of Method', *Visual Anthropology*, 3, pp. 235–58.

—— (ed.) (1992), *Anthropology and Photography 1860–1920*, New Haven, CT, and London: Yale University Press.

—— (1995), *Picturing Paradise: Colonial Photographs of Samoa (1875–1925)*, Daytona Beach: Daytona Beach Community College.

—— (2001), *Raw Histories, Photographs, Anthropology and Museums*, Oxford: Berg.

—— (2002), 'La Photographie ou la construction de l'image de l'Autre', in N. Bancel, P. Blanchard, G. Boëtsch, É. Deroo and S. Lemaire (eds), *Zoos humains: de la Vénus hottentote aux reality shows*, Paris: La Découverte, pp. 323–30.

—— and J. Hart (eds) (2004), *Photographs Objects Histories*, London: Routledge.

Edwards, P. and J. Walvin (1983), *Black Personalities in the Era of the Slave Trade*, London: MacMillan.

Eissenberger, G. (1996), *Entführt, verspottet und gestorben. Lateinamerikanische Völkerschauen in deutschen Zoos*, Frankfurt: IKO, Verlag für Interkulturelle Kommunikation.

Elias, N. (1978), *La Dynamique de l'Occident*, Paris: Fayard.

—— and J. Scotson (1997), *Les Logiques de l'exclusion*, Paris: Fayard.

Ellingson, T. (2001), *The Myth of the Noble Savage*, Los Angeles: University of California Press, Berkeley.

Elroye, M. G. (1990), *Facing History, the Black Image in American Art, 1710–1940*, Washington, DC: Bredford Art Publishers.

El-Wakil, L. and P. Vaisse (2000), *Genève 1896. Regards sur une exposition nationale*, Geneva: Georg Editeur.

Emin, T. (2002), 'Monstres et phénomènes de foire: les numéros d'attraction de Coney Island et les eugénistes de Long Island (1910–1935)', in N. Bancel, P. Blanchard, G. Boëtsch, É. Deroo and S. Lemaire (eds), *Zoos humains: de la Vénus hottentote aux reality shows*, Paris: La Découverte, pp. 178–91.

Erikson, E. (1965), 'The Concept of Identity in Race Relations. Notes and Queries', *Dædalus*, 95.1, pp. 145–70.

Erlmann, V. (1999), '"Spectatorial Lust": The African Choir in England, 1891–1893', in B. Lindfors (ed.), *Africans on Stage: Studies in Ethnological Show Business*, Bloomington: Indiana University Press, pp. 107–34.

Ernest, R. (1998), *Les Mondes coloniaux dans les expositions universelles à Paris (1855–1900). Le cas de l'empire français*, mémoire de maîtrise, Université de Paris-X Nanterre.

Étambala, Z. A. (1989), 'Présences congolaises en Belgique, 1885–1940: exhibition, education, emancipation, paternalisme', unpublished doctoral thesis, KUL, Louvain.

Evans, R., K. Saunders and K. Cronin (1975), *Race Relations in Colonial Queensland, a history of exclusion, exploitation and extermination*, St Lucia: University of Queensland Press.

Ewald, D. and C. Peter (1992), *San Francisco Invites the World: The Panama-Pacific Exposition of 1915*, San Francisco: Chronicle Books.

Ezra, E. (1995), 'The Colonial Look: Exhibiting Empire in the 1930s', *Contemporary French Civilization*, pp. 33–49.

Ezra, E. (2000), *The Colonial Unconscious. Race and Culture in Interwar France*, Ithaca, NY, and London: Cornell University Press.

Fabian, J. (1983), *Time and the Other: How Anthropology Makes its Object*, New York: Columbia University Press.

Falguières, P. (2003), *Les Chambres des merveilles. Le Rayon des curiosités*, Paris: Bayard-Centurion.

Fanon, F. (1952), *Black Skin, White Masks*, New York: Grove Weidenfeld.

Fanoudh-Siefer, L. (1980), *Le Mythe du nègre et de l'Afrique noire dans la littérature française de 1800 à la deuxième guerre mondiale*, Dakar: NEA.

Farnum, A. L. (1992), *Pawnee Bill's Historic Wild West: A Photo Documentary of the 1900–1905 Show Tours*, West Chester: Schiffer Publishing.

Fauvelle-Aymar, F.-X. (1999), 'Les Khoisan dans la littérature anthropologique du XIXe siècle: réseaux scientifiques et constructions des savoirs au siècle de Darwin et de Barnum', *Bulletins et mémoires de la Société d'anthropologie de Paris*, 11.3–4, pp. 425–71.

—— (2002a), 'Les Khoisan: entre science et spectacle', in N. Bancel, P. Blanchard, G. Boëtsch, É. Deroo and S. Lemaire (eds), *Zoos humains: de la Vénus hottentote aux reality shows*, Paris: La Découverte, pp. 111–17.

—— (2002b), *L'Invention du Hottentot. Histoire du regard occidental sur le Khoisan, XVe–XIXe siècles*, Paris: Publications de la Sorbonne.

—— (2003), 'Les Tribulations de la Vénus hottentote?', *L'Histoire*, 273, pp. 79–84.

Favrod, C.-A. (1989), *Étranges Étrangers. Photographie et exotisme, 1850–1910*, Paris: Centre national de la photographie.

Feest, Ch. F. (1993), 'Buffalo Bill et l'image des Indiens en Europe', in H. Lomosits and P. Harbaugh (eds), *Lakol Wokiksuye, la mémoire visuelle des Lakotas*, Nimes: Les Indiennes de Nîmes/Mistral, pp. 62–84.

Feuchtwang, S. (1973), 'The Colonial Formation of British Social Anthropology', in A. Talal (ed.), *Anthropology and the Colonial Encounter*, London: Ithaca Press, pp. 71–100.

Fiedermutz-Laun, A. (2004), 'Adolphe Bastian, Robert Hartmann et Rudolf Virchow: médecins et fondateurs de l'ethnologie et de l'anthropologie allemande', in C. Trautmann-Waller (ed.), *Quand Berlin pensait les peuples. Anthropologie, ethnologie et psychologie (1850–1890)*, Paris: CNRS éditions, pp. 61–76.

Fiedler, L. (1978), *Freaks: Myths and Images of the Secret Self*, New York: Simon and Schuster.

Findling, J. E. and K. D. Pelle (1990), *Historical Dictionary of World's Fairs and Expositions 1851–1988*, Westport, CT: Greenwood Press.

Fisher, J.-L. (1983), *Races imagées et imaginaires*, Paris: Maspero.

Flint, R. W. (1977), 'The Evolution of the Circus in Nineteenth-Century America', in M. Matlaw (ed.), *American Popular Entertainment. Papers & Proceedings of Conference on the History of American Popular Entertainment*, Westport, CT: Greenwood Press, pp. 188–95.

—— (1983), 'The Circus is the World's Largest, Grandest, Best Amusement Institution', *Quarterly Journal, Library of Congress*, 40, p. 3.

Forgey, E. (1994), 'Die grosse Negertrommel der kolonilalen Werbung. Die Deutsche Afrika–Schau 1935–1943', *WerkstattGeschichte*, 9, pp. 25–33.

Foster, A. (1988), *Behold the Man. The Male Nude in Photography*, Edinburgh: Stills Gallery.

Foucault, M. (1961), *Folie et déraison. Histoire de la folie à l'âge classique*, Paris: Plon.

—— (1978), *Surveiller et punir*, Paris: Gallimard.

Fournié, P. and L. Gervereau (2000), *Regards sur le monde. Trésors photographiques du Quai d'Orsay. 1960–1914*, Paris: Somogy.

Fox, C. (1979), *Old-time Circus Cuts. A Pictorial Archive of 202 illustrations*, Mineola, NY: Dover Publications.

——, R. Porter and R. Wokler (eds.) (1995), *Inventing Human Science. Eighteenth-Century Domains*, Berkeley: University of California Press,

Fox, P. (1989), 'The Imperial Schema: Ethnography, Photography and Collecting', *Photofile*, 4, pp. 10–16.

Frazier, E.-F. (1957), *Race and Culture, Contacts in the Modern World*, New York: A. Knopf.

Fredrickson, G. (1971), *The Black Image in the White Mind. Character and Destiny, 1817–1914*, Middletown, CT: University of New England Press.

Fretz, E. (1996), 'P. T. Barnum's Theatrical Selfhood and the Nineteenth-Century Culture of Exhibition', in R. Garland-Thomson (ed.), *Freakery: Cultural Spectacles of the Extraordinary, 1886–1931*, New York: New York University Press, pp. 97–107.

Freud, S. (1930), *Psychologie collective et analyse du moi*, Paris: Payot.

Frye, Jacobson M. (1998), *Whiteness of a Different Color*, Cambridge, MA: Harvard University Press.

Gala, I. (1980), *Des Sauvages au Jardin. Les Exhibitions ethnographiques du Jardin d'acclimatation de 1877 à 1912*, Paris: Bibliothèque du musée des Arts et Traditions populaires.

Garland-Thomson, R. (ed.) (1996), *Freakery: Cultural Spectacles of the Extraordinary,*

1886–1931, New York: New York University Press.

—— (ed.) (1997), *Extraordinary Bodies: Figuring Physical Disability in American Culture and Literature*, New York: Columbia University Press.

—— (2002), 'Du Prodige à l'erreur: les monstres de l'Antiquité à nos jours', in N. Bancel, P. Blanchard, G. Boëtsch, É. Deroo and S. Lemaire (eds), *Zoos humains: de la Vénus hottentote aux reality shows*, Paris: La Découverte, pp. 38–48.

Garrigues, E. (2001), 'Les Villages Noirs en France et en Europe ou le zoo humain', *L'Ethnographie*, 2, new series, pp. 11–54.

Gates, H. L. (1987), *Figures in Black*, New York: Oxford University Press.

Geary, C.-M. (1986), 'Photographs as Materials for African History: Some Methodological Considerations', *History in Africa*, 3.13, pp. 89–116.

—— (1990), 'Impression of the African Past: Interpreting Ethnographic Photographs From Cameroon', *Visual Anthropology*, 3, pp. 285–315.

—— and V. Webb (1998), *Delivering Views. Distant Cultures in Early Postcards*, Washington, DC, and London: Smithsonian Institution Press.

Gere, F. (1980), 'Imaginaire raciste, la mesure de l'homme', *Cahiers du cinéma*, 315, pp. 36–42.

Gidley, M. (1992), *Representing Others. White Views of Indigenous Peoples*, Exeter: University of Exeter Press.

Gilbert, J. (1993), 'Fixing the Image, Photography at the World's Columbian Exposition', in N. Harris, W. De Wit, J. Gilbert and R. W. Rydell (eds), *Grand Illusions: Chicago's World's Fair of 1893*, Chicago: Chicago Historical Society, pp. 101–32.

Gilman, S. L. (1982), *On Blackness without Blacks: Essays on the Image of the Blacks in Germany*, Boston: G.K. Hall.

—— (1986), 'Black bodies, White bodies. Toward an Iconography of Female Sexuality in Late Nineteenth-Century Art, Medecine and Literature', in H. L. Gates (ed.), *"Race". Writing, and difference*, Chicago: Chicago University Press.

Gilroy, P. (1991), *'There Ain't No Black in the Union Jack': The Cultural Politics of Race and Nation*, Chicago: University of Chicago Press.

Girard, R. (1998), *La Violence et le sacré*, Paris: Hachette Poche.

Girardet, R. (1968), '"L'Apothéose de la plus grande France": l'idée coloniale devant l'opinion française (1930–1935)', *Revue française de science politique*, 18.6, pp. 1085–144

Giraud, M. (1988), 'Ethnologie et racisme: le cas des études afro-américaines', *Ethnologie française*, 3, pp. 153–57.

Glick Schiller, N., D. Dea and M. Höhne (2005), *African Culture and the Zoo in the 21st Century: The 'African Village' in the Augsburg Zoo and Its Wider Implications*, Halle: Max Planck Institute for Social Anthropology.

Gliozzi, G. (2000), *Adam et le nouveau monde. La naissance de l'anthropologie comme idéologie coloniale: des généalogies bibliques aux théories raciales (1500–1700)*, Lecques: Théétète/Le Champ social éditions.

Gloor, P.-A. (1986), 'L'Anthropologie en Suisse romande. Une Esquisse historique', *Anthropologischer Anzeiger, Société suisse d'anthropologie*, 44, pp. 305–13.

Goglia, L. (1989), *Colonialismo e fotografia. Il caso italiano*, Messina: Sicania.

Goksyr, M. (1990), '"One certainly expected a great deal more from the savages": The anthropology Days in St. Louis, 1904, and aftermath', *The International Journal of the History of Sport*, 7.2, pp. 297–306.

Goldberg, D. T. (ed.) (1990), *Anatomy of Racism*, Minneapolis: University of Minnesota Press.

Goldie, F. (1963), *Lost City of the Kalahari: The Farini Story and Reports on Other Expeditions*, Cape Town: Balkema.

Goldmann, S. (1985), 'Wilde in Europa', in T. Theye (ed.), *Wir und die Wilden. Einblicke in eine kannibalische Beziehung*, Rohwolt: Thomas Theyde, pp. 243–69.

—— (1987), 'Zur rezeption der Völkerausstellungen um 1900', in *Exotische Welten, europäische Phantasien*, Stuttgart: Institut für Auslandsbeziehungen; Ausstellungskatalog, pp. 88–95.

Goodall, J. R. (2002), *Performance and Evolution in the Age of Darwin*, London: Routledge.

Gosden, C. and C. Knowles (2001), *Collecting Colonialism, Material Culture and Colonial Change*, Oxford: Berg.

Gouda, F. (1995), *Dutch Culture Overseas. Colonial practice in the Netherlands Indies, 1900–1942*, Amsterdam: Amsterdam University Press.

Gould, S. J. (1996 [1981]), *The Mismeasure of Man*, New York: W. W. Norton.

—— (1982), 'The Hottentot Venus', *Natural History*, 91.1, pp. 20–27.

—— (1985), *The Flamingo's Smile. Reflections in Natural History*, New York/London: W. W. Norton.

Green, C. and F. Morris (2006), *Le Douanier Rousseau, jungles à Paris*, Paris: Réunion des musées nationaux.

Green, J. (1983), 'In Dahomey in London in 1903', *The Black Perspective in Music*, 11.1, pp. 22–40.

—— (1999), 'A Strange Revelation in Humankind: Six Congo Pygmies in Britain, 1905–1907', in B. Lindfors (ed.), *Africans on Stage: Studies in Ethnological Show Business*, Bloomington: Indiana University Press, pp. 156–86.

Green, R. (1988), 'The Indian in Popular American Culture', in W. E. Washburn (ed.), *History of Indian-White Relations*, Washington, DC: Smithsonian Institution, pp. 587–606.

Greene, V. (1978), 'Old Ethnic Stereotypes and the New Ethnic Studies', *Ethnicity*, 4, pp. 328–50.

Greenhalgh, P. (1985), 'Art, Politics and Society at the Franco-British Exhibition of 1908', *Art History*, 4, pp. 434–52.

Griffet, J. (1998), 'La Formation par l'image: regard sur la sensibilité d'une époque', *Sociétés. Revue des sciences humaines et sociales*, 60, pp. 23–31.

Griffiths, A. (2002), *Wondrous Difference. Cinema, Anthropology and Turn-of-the-Century Visual Culture*, New York: Columbia University Press.

Groeneveld, A. (1990), *Fotografie in Suriname, 1839–1939*, Amsterdam: Fragment Uitgeverij.

Grosz, E. (1996), 'Intolerable Ambiguity: Freaks as/at the Limit', in R. Garland-Thomson (ed.), *Freakery: Cultural Spectacles of the Extraordinary, 1886–1931*, New York: New York University Press, pp. 55–67.

Guerando, J.-M. de (1978), 'Considérations sur les diverses méthodes à suivre dans l'observation des peuples sauvages (1800)', in J. Copans and J. Jamin (eds), *Aux origines de l'anthropologie française*, Paris: Le Sycomore, pp. 127–70.

Guerci, A. (2007), *Dall'antropologia all'antropopoiesi. Breve saggio sulle rappresentazioni e costruzioni della variabilità umana*, Milan: Lucisano.

Guiccioli, A. (1973), *Diario di un conservatore*, Milan: Edizioni del Borghese.

Guillaumin, C. (1975), 'Les Ambiguïtés de la notion de race', in L. Poliakov (ed.), *Hommes et Bêtes. Entretiens sur le racisme*, Paris/La Haye: Mouton/EHESS.

Gusdorf, G. (1972), *Dieu, la nature, l'homme au siècle des Lumières, Les Sciences humaines et la pensée occidentale* 5, Paris: Payot.

Gusinde, M. (1982), 'Los indios de Tierra del Fuego, Los Selk'nam', *Centro Argentino de Etnología Americana*, 2, pp. 152–53.

Guttmann, A. (1984), *The Games Must Go On: Avery Brundage and the Olympic Movement*, New York: Columbia University Press.

Guyotat, R. (2000), 'Zoos humains', *Le Monde*, 17 January, p. 12.

Haberland, W. (1987), 'Nine Bella Coolas in Germany', in Ch. F. Feest (ed.), *Indians and Europe: An Interdisciplinary Collection of Essays*, Aachen: Herodot, Rader-Verl, pp. 76–89.

—— (1988a), 'Adrian Jacobsen on Pine Ridge Reservation, 1910', *European Review of Native American Studies*, 1.1, pp. 11–15.

—— (1988b), '"Diese Indianer sind falsch": Neun Bella Coola im Deutschen Reich 1885/1886', *Archiv für Völkerkunde*, 42, pp. 3–65.

Halberstam, J. (1998), *Female Masculinity*, Durham, NC: Duke University Press.

Hale, D.-S. (1998), 'Races on Display, French Representations of the Colonial Native, 1886–1931', unpublished PhD dissertation, Brandeis University.

—— (2002), 'L'"Indigène" mis en scène en France: entre exposition et exhibition (1880–1931)', in N. Bancel, P. Blanchard, G. Boëtsch, É. Deroo and S. Lemaire (eds), *Zoos humains: de la Vénus hottentote aux reality shows*, Paris: La Découverte, pp. 315–22.

Halen, P. and J. Riesz (eds) (1993), *Images de l'Afrique et du Congo-Zaïre dans les lettres belges de langue française et alentour*, Brussels: Textyles.

Hall, S. (1990), 'The Whites of their Eyes. Racist Ideologies and the Media', in M. Alvarado and J. O. Thompson (eds), *The Media Reader*, London: BFI Publishing, pp. 7–23.

Haller, M. (1984), *Eugenics: Hereditarian Attitudes in American Thought*, New Brunswick, NJ: Rutgers University Press.

Halttunen, K. (1982), *Confidence Men and Painted Women. A Study of Middle-Class Culture in America, 1830–1870*, New Haven, CT: Yale University Press.

Hammond, M. (1980), 'Anthropology as a weapon of social combat in late-nineteenth-century France', *Journal of the History of the Behavioral Sciences*, 16, pp. 118–32.

Haraway, D. (1989), *Primate Visions: Gender, Race, and Nature in the World of Modern Science*, New York: Routledge.

Harris, N. (1973), *Humbug: The Art of P. T. Barnum*, Boston: Little Brown.

——, W. De Wit, J. Gilbert and R. W. Rydell (eds), *Grand Illusions, Chicago's World's Fair for 1893*, Chicago: Chicago Historical Society.

Hartog, F. (2001 [1980]), *Le Miroir d'Hérodote. Essai sur la représentation de l'autre*, Paris: Gallimard.

Hartzman, M. (2005), *American Sideshow: An Encyclopedia of History's Most Wondrous and Curiously Strange Performers*, New York: Penguin.

Hatt, M. (1992), 'Making a Man of Him: Masculinity and the Black Body in Mid-Nineteenth Century American Sculpture', *The Oxford Art Journal*, 15.1, pp. 21–35.

Hemlow, J. (1958), *The History of Fanny Burney*, Oxford: Oxford University Press.

Hennissant, S. (1994), 'The Best Specimens in all our Colonial Domain: New Caledonian Melanesians in Europe, 1931–1932', *The Journal of Pacific History*, 29, pp. 172–87.

Hevey, D. (1992), *The Creatures That Time Forgot, Photography and Disability Imagery*, New York: Routledge.

Hewlett, G. (1979), *A History of Wembley*, London: Brent Library Service.

—— (1987), 'The Landscaping of Wembley Park at the Exhibition', *Wembley History Society Journal*, 6, pp. 81–89.

Hinsley, C. M. (1981), *Savages and Scientists: The Smithsonian Institution and the Development of American Anthropology*, Washington, DC: Smithsonian Institution Press.

—— (1991), 'The World as Marketplace, Commodification of the Exotic at the World's Columbian Exposition, Chicago, 1893', in I. Karp and S. D. Lavine (eds), *Exhibiting Cultures. The Poetics and Politics of Museum Display*, Washington, DC, and London: Smithsonian Institution Press, pp. 344–65.

Hirsch, F. (2003), 'Getting Know "The People of the USSR": Ethnographic Exhibits as Soviet Virtual Tourism, 1923–1934', *Slavic Review*, 112.4, pp. 683–709.

Hoage, R. and W. Deiss (eds) (1996), *New Worlds, New Animals. From Menagerie to Zoological Park in the Nineteenth Century*, London: Johns Hopkins University Press.

Hoberman, J. M. (1999), 'L'Universalisme olympique et la question de l'Apartheid', *X-Alta*, 1, *La Tentation du bonheur sportif*, pp. 25–34.

Hobson, J. (2005), *Venus in the Dark: Blackness and Beauty in Popular Culture*, New York: Routledge.

Hodeir, C. (1987), 'La France d'Outre-mer', in B. Lemoine and P. Rivoirard (eds), *Paris 1937, Cinquantenaire de l'Exposition internationale des arts et techniques de la vie moderne*, Paris: Institut français d'architecture; Paris Musées, pp. 284–91.

—— and M. Pierre (1991), *L'Exposition coloniale*, Brussels: Complexe.

Hoffenberg, H. P. (2001), *An Empire on Display: English, Indian, and Australian Exhibitions from the Crystal Palace to the Great War*, California: University of California Press.

Holmes, R. (2007), *African Queen: the Real Life of the Hottentot Venus*, London: Random House.

Holtman, J. (1968), *Freak Show Man: The Autobiography of Harry Lewiston*, Los Angeles, CA: Holloway House.

Honour, H. (1989), *L'Image du Noir dans l'art occidental. De la Révolution américaine à la Première Guerre mondiale*, Paris: Gallimard.

Höpp, G. (ed.) (1996), *Fremde Erfahrungen. Asiaten und Afrikaner in Deutschland, Österreich und in der Schweiz bis 1945*, Berlin: Das Arabische Buch.

Horkheimer, M. and T. W. Adorno (1973), *Dialectic of Enlightenment*, London: Allen Lane.

Hornberger, F. (2005), *Carny Folk. The World's Weirdest Sideshow Acts*, New York Citadel Press.

Hotta-Lister, A. (1999), *The Japan-British Exhibition of 1910: Gateway to the Island Empire of the East* (Meiji Series, 8), Richmond: Japan Library.

Hulme, P. (1990), 'The spontaneous hand of nature, savagery, colonialism and the Enlightenment', in P. Hulme and L. Jordanova (eds), *The Enlightenment and its Shadows*, London: Routledge, pp. 18–34.

Impey, O. and A. MacGregor (eds) (1985), *The Origins of Museums*, Oxford: The Clarendon Press.

Ingold, T. (1990), 'An Anthropologist Looks at Biology', *Man*, 25, pp. 208–29.

Inoue, K. (1968), *Nihon teikokushugi no keisei* [*The Formation of Japanese Imperialism*], Tokyo: Iwanami shoten.

Isaac, B. (2004), *The Invention of Racism in Classical Antiquity*, Princeton and Oxford: Princeton University Press.

Jacknis, I. (1985), 'Franz Boas and Exhibits: On the Limitations of the Museum Method of Anthropology', in G. W. Stocking (ed.), *Objects and Others. Essays on Museums and Material*, Madison, University of Wisconsin Press, pp. 75–111.

—— (1991), 'Northwest Coast Indian Culture and the World's Columbian Exposition', in D. H. Thomas (ed.), *Columbian Consequences. The Spanish Borderlands in Pan-American Perspective*, Washington, DC: Smithsonian Institution, pp. 91–118.

—— (1994), 'Franz Boas and Photography', *Studies in Visual Communication*, 10.1, pp. 1–60.

Jacob, A. (1991), 'Civilisation/sauvagerie. Le Sauvage américain et l'idée de civilisation', *Anthropologie et Sociétés*, 15.1, pp. 13–36.

Jacobson, M. F. (1998), *Whiteness of a Different Color*, Cambridge, MA: Harvard University Press.

Jacquemin, J.-P. (ed.) (1985), *Zaïre 1885–1985, Cent ans de regards belges*, Brussels: CEC; Le Noir du Blanc.

—— (1991), *Racisme, continent obscur. Clichés, stéréotypes, phantasmes à propos des Noirs dans le royaume de Belgique*, Brussels: CEC/Le Noir du Blanc.

—— (2002), 'Les Congolais dans la Belgique "impériale"', in N. Bancel, P. Blanchard, G. Boëtsch, É. Deroo and S. Lemaire (eds), *Zoos humains: de la Vénus hottentote aux reality shows*, Paris: La Découverte, pp. 253–58.

Jacquin, P. (1992), 'Buffalo Bill: de la Prairie au Champ de Mars', in V. Wiesinger (ed.), *Sur le Sentier de la Découverte: Rencontres franco-indiennes du XVIe au XXe siècle*, Paris: RMN; Musée National de la Coopération franco-américaine, pp. 97–101.

Jahoda, G. (1961), *White Man: A Study of the Attitudes of Africans to Europeans in Ghana before Independence*, New York and London: Oxford University Press.

Jauffret, G.-A. and A.-S. Leblond (1978 [1800]), 'Le Chinois Tchong-A-Sam', in J. Copans and J. Jamin (eds), *Aux origines de l'anthropologie française*, pp. 115–24.

Jay, R. (1986), *Learned Pigs and Fireproof Women*, New York: Villard Books.

Jay, R. (2005), *Extraordinary Exhibitions: The Wonderful Remains of an Enormous Head*, New York: Quantuck Lane.

Johnson, R., J. Secreto and T. Varndell (1995), *Freaks, Geeks & Strange Girls: Sideshow Banners of the Great American Midway*, Honolulu: Hardy Marks.

Jones, P. (1989), 'Ideas linking Aborigines and Fuegians, from Cook to the Kulturkreis school', *Australian Aboriginal Studies*, 2, pp. 2–13.

Jordan, P.-L. (1992), *Premier contact–Premier regard. Images en manœuvres*, Marseille: Musée de Marseille.

Jordon, W. (1968), *White Over Black*, Chapel Hill: University of North Carolina.

Kaiho, Y. (1992), *Kindai hoppô shi: Ainu minzoku to josei to* [*A Modern History of Northern Territories: About the Ainu People and the Women*], Tokyo: San'ichi shobô.

Karp, I., C. M. Kreamer and S. Lavine (eds) (1992), *Museums and Communities: The Politics of Public Culture*, Washington, DC: Smithsonian Institution Press.

—— and S. D. Lavine (eds) (1991), *Exhibiting Cultures: The Poetics and Politics of Museum Display*, Washington, DC: Smithsonian Institution Press.

Kasson, J. (1978), *Amusing the Millions: Coney Island at the Turn of the Century*, New York: Hill and Wang.

Kasson, J. S. (2000), *Buffalo Bill's Wild West: Celebrity, Memory and Popular History*, New York: Hill and Wang.

Kendall, L., B. Mathe and T. R. Miller (1997), *Drawing Shadows to Stone. The Photography of the Jesup North Pacific Expedition, 1897–1902*, Seattle: American Museum of Natural History and University of Washington Press.

Kilani, M. (1994), *L'Invention de l'autre*, Lausanne: Payot.

Kimoni, I. (s.d.), *Une Image du Noir et de sa culture, Esquisse de l'évolution de l'idée du Noir dans les Lettres françaises du début du siècle à l'entre-deux-guerres*, Neuchâtel: Messeiller.

Kinchin, P. (2001 [1988]), *Glasgow's Great Exhibitions: 1888, 1901, 1911, 1938, 1988*, Wendlebury: White Cockade Publishing.

Kiner, A. (2001), 'Les Zoos humains. La Grande Foire aux colonies', *Sciences et Avenir*, December, pp. 103–07.

Kirby, P. R. (1949), 'The Hottentot Venus', *Africana Notes and News*, 6.3, pp. 55–62.

—— (1953), 'More about the Hottentot Venus', *Africana Notes and News*, 10.4, pp. 124–34.

—— (1954), 'The Hottentot Venus of the Musée de l'Homme, Paris', *South African Journal of Science*, 50.12, July, pp. 319–22.

Ki-Zerbo, J. (1980), 'Théories relatives aux races et histoire de l'Afrique', in *Histoire générale de l'Afrique. Méthodologie et histoire africaine*, Paris: UNESCO, pp. 291–99.

Knaebel, N. (2004), *Step Right Up: Stories of Carnivals, Sideshows, and the Circus*, New York: Carroll and Graf.

Kocks, K. (2004), *Indianer im Kaiserreich: Völkerschauen und Wild West Shows zwischen 1880 und 1914*, Gerolzhofen: Oettermann.

Kopytoff, I. (1986), 'The Cultural Biography of Things, Commoditization as Process', in A. Appadurai (ed.), *The Social Life of Things, Commodities in Cultural Perspective*, Cambridge: Cambridge University Press, pp. 64–91.

Kort, P. and M. Hollein (eds) (2006), *I like America. Fiktionen des Wilden Westens*, Frankfurt: Prestel.

Kramer, P. (1999), 'Making Concessions: Race and Empire Revisited at the Philippine Exposition, St. Louis, 1901–1905', *Radical History Review*, 73, pp. 74–114.

Kreamer, C. M. (1997), 'African Voices', *Museum News*, November–December, pp. 50–55.

Kreis, K. M. (2002), 'Indians Playing, Indians Praying: Native Americans in Wild West Shows and Catholic Missions', in Colin G. Calloway, Gerd Gemünden and Susanne Zantop (eds), *Germans and Indians: Fantasies, Encounters, Projections*, Lincoln: University of Nebraska Press, pp. 195–212.

Kremer-Marietti, A. (1984), 'L'Anthropologie physique et morale en France et ses implications idéologiques', in B. Rupp-Eisenreich (ed.), *Histoires de l'anthropologie XVIe–XIXe siècles*, Paris: Klincksieck, pp. 319–51.

Kuklick, H. (1993), *The Savage Within. The Social History of Britisch Anthropology, 1885–1945*, Cambridge: Cambridge University Press.

Kunhardt, P. B. (1995), *P. T. Barnum: America's Greatest Showman*, New York: Knopf.

Labanca, N. (ed.) (1992), *L'Africa in vetrina. Storie di musei e di esposizioni coloniali in Italia*, Treviso: Pagus Edizioni.

—— (2002a), *Oltremare. Storia dell'espansione coloniale italiana*, Bologna: il Mulino.

—— (2002b), 'Le Passé colonial et le présent de l'immigration dans l'Italie contemporaine', *Migrations société*, 14.81–82, pp. 97–106.

Labrousse, P. (2000), 'Les Races de l'Archipel ou le scientisme in partibus (France XIXe siècle)', *Archipel*, 4, pp. 235–65.

—— (2002), 'L'Insulinde en images et dans les Expositions universelles: pendant ce temps les Javanaises ...', in N. Bancel, P. Blanchard, G. Boëtsch, É. Deroo and S. Lemaire (eds), *Zoos humains: de la Vénus hottentote aux reality shows*, Paris: La Découverte, pp. 169–77.

Laclau, E. and C. Mouffe (1985), *Hegemony and Socialist Strategy: Towards a Radical Democratic Politics*, New York; London: Verso Press.

Ladière, P. (1988), 'La Sociobiologie et le racisme', *Ethnologie Française*, 18.2, pp. 177–81.

Laissus, Y. and J.-J. Petter (1993), *Les Animaux du Muséum, 1793–1993*, Paris: Imprimerie nationale.

Lalvani, S. (1996), *Photography, Vision, and the Production of Modern Bodies*, New York: State University of New York Press.

Landes, D. S. (1983), *Revolution in Time, Clocks and the Making of the Modern World*, Cambridge, MA: Belknap Press of Harvard University Press.

Lane, D. (1989), *Manners and Customs of Modern Egyptians*, London and La Haye: East-West Publications.

Langaney, A. (2002), 'Collections humaines et sciences inhumaines: échantillons et reliques', in N. Bancel, P. Blanchard, G. Boëtsch, É. Deroo and S. Lemaire (eds), *Zoos humains: de la Vénus hottentote aux reality shows*, Paris: La Découverte, pp. 374–80.

——, N.-H. Van Blijenburgh and A. Sanchez-Masas (1992), *Tous parents, tous différents*, Bayonne/Paris: Chabaud/Musée de l'homme.

Laqueur, T. (1990), *Making Sex, Body and Gender from the Greeks to Freud*, Cambridge: Cambridge University Press.

Lattas, A. (1987), 'Savagery and Civilisation, towards a genealogy of racism', *Social Analysis*, 21, pp. 39–58.

Le Breton, D. (2001), *Anthropologie du corps et modernité*, Paris: PUF, coll. 'Quadriges'.

Le Normand-Romain, A., A. Roquebert, J. Durand-Revillon and D. Serena (1994), *La Sculpture ethnographique. De la Vénus hottentote à la Tehura de Gauguin*, Paris: Réunion des Musées Nationaux.

Leapman, M. (2001), *The World for a Shilling. How the Great Exhibition of 1851 Shaped a Nation*, London: Headline.

Leary, T. and E. Shones (1998), *Images of America: Buffalo's Pan-American Exposition*, Charleston: Arcadia Publishing.

Lebovics, H. (1995), *La Vraie France: Les enjeux de l'identité culturelle, 1900–1945*, Paris: Belin.

—— (2002), 'Les Zoos de l'Exposition coloniale internationale de Paris en 1931', in N. Bancel, P. Blanchard, G. Boëtsch, É. Deroo and S. Lemaire (eds), *Zoos humains: de la Vénus hottentote aux reality shows*, Paris: La Découverte, pp. 367–73.

Lederbogen, J. (1986), 'Fotografie als Völkerschau', *Fotogeschichte, Beiträge zur Geschichte und Ästhetik der Photographie*, 6.22, Berlin, pp. 47–64.

Lefeuvre, D. (2006), *Pour en finir avec la repentance coloniale*, Paris: Flammarion.

Legrand, O. (2000), 'L'École d'anthropologie de Paris 1875–1906. Histoire politique d'une institution scientifique', unpublished DEA dissertation, Paris: EHESS.

Lehmann, A. (1955), 'Zeitgenössische Bilder der erseau Völkerschauen', in *Von*

Fremden Völker und Kukturen. Beiträge zur Völkerkunde, Düsseldorf: Droste Verlag, pp. 31–38.

Lejeune, D. (1998), *Les Sociétés de géographie en France*, Paris: Albin Michel.

Lemaire, S. (2000), *L'Agence économique des colonies. Instrument de propagande ou creuset de l'idéologie coloniale en France (1870–1960)*, Florence: Institut Universitaire Européen de Florence.

—— (2002a), 'Gustave d'Eichtal, ou les ambiguïtés d'une ethnologie saint-simonienne: du racialisme ambiant à l'utopie d'un métissage universel', in P. Régnier (ed.), *Etudes saint-simoniennes*, Lyon: Presses universitaires de Lyon, pp. 153–75.

—— (2002b), 'Le "Sauvage" domestiqué par la propagande coloniale', in N. Bancel, P. Blanchard, G. Boëtsch, É. Deroo and S. Lemaire (eds), *Zoos humains: de la Vénus hottentote aux reality shows*, Paris: La Découverte, pp. 275–87.

—— and P. Blanchard (2002), 'Montrer, mesurer, distraire. Du Zoo humain aux expositions coloniales (1870–1931)', in S. Moussa (ed.), *La Construction de la notion de race dans la littérature et les sciences humaines (XVIIIe et XIXe siècles)*, Paris: L'Harmattan, pp. 343–57.

—— and P. Blanchard (2003), 'Exhibitions, expositions, médiatisations et colonies', in P. Blanchard and S. Lemaire (eds), *Culture coloniale*, Paris: Autrement, pp. 43–53.

——, P. Blanchard and N. Bancel (1999), 'L'Afrique Noire inventée: de la Première Guerre mondiale aux indépendances', *Historiens et Géographes*, special issue on 'Afrique Subsaharienne', 367, pp. 93–110.

——, P. Blanchard and N. Bancel (2001), '1931: tous à l'expo', *Le Monde diplomatique*, January, p. 10.

——, P. Blanchard, N. Bancel, G. Boëtsch and E. Deroo, (2004) (eds), *Zoo humani. Dalla Venere Ottentotta ai reality show*, trans. S. De Petris, Verona: Ombre Corte.

Léonard, Y. (1999), 'Le Portugal et ses "sentinelles de pierre": L'Exposition du monde portugais 1940', *Vingtième Siècle*, 62, pp. 27–37.

Leprohon, P. (1945), *L'Exotisme et le cinéma, les chasseurs d'images à la conquête du monde*, Paris: J. Susse.

Leprun, S. (1987), *Le Théâtre des colonies*, Paris: L'Harmattan.

—— (1990), 'Exotisme et couleur', *Ethnologie française*, 4, pp. 419–27.

Leroy-Jay, I. (1997), *La Griffe et la dent*, Paris: Réunion des musées nationaux.

Lescroart, M. (2003), 'Les Zoos humains', *Sciences et vie junior*, 161, pp. 64–69.

Lestringant, F. (1995), 'L'Entrée du Tupinamba dans la mythologie classique', *Études inter-ethniques*, 10, pp. 109–30.

—— (1997), 'L'Exotisme en France à la Renaissance. De Rabelais à Léry', in D. Courcelles (ed.), *Littérature et Exotisme XVIe–XVIIIe siècle*, Paris: École nationale des chartes, pp. 5–16.

Levine, L. W. (1988), *Highbrow/Lowbrow, The Emergence of Cultural Hierarchy in America*, Cambridge, MA: Harvard University Press.

Levi-Strauss, C. (1955), *Tristes tropiques*, Paris: Plon.

—— (1999 [1952]), *Race et Histoire*, Paris: Collection Folio-Essais, Plon.

Levra, U. and R. Roccia (2003), *Le esposizioni torinesi, 1805–1911*, Turin: Archivio Storico della Città di Torino.

Lewerentz, A. (2004), 'Les Premières années de la Société berlinoise d'anthropologie, d'ethnologie et de préhistoire et son intégration dans le paysage scientifique berlinois', in C. Trautmann-Waller (ed.), *Quand Berlin pensait les peuples. Anthropologie, ethnologie et psychologie (1850–1890)*, Paris: CNRS éditions, pp. 40–57.

Liauzu, C. (1992), *Race et Civilisation. L'Autre dans la culture occidentale*, Paris: Syros.

—— (2004), *Colonisation: droit d'inventaire*, Paris: Colin.

Lindfors B. (1983a), 'Circus Africans', *Journal of American Culture*, 6.2, pp. 9–14.

—— (1983b), 'The Hottentot Venus and other African attractions in nineteenth-century England', *Australasian Drama Studies*, 1.2, pp. 82–104.

—— (1985), 'Courting the Hottentot Venus', *Africa. Rivista trimestriale di Studi e documentazione dell'Istituto Italo-africano*, Rome, 40, pp. 133–48.

—— (1996), 'Hottentot, Bushman, Kaffir: Taxonomic Tendencies in Nineteenth-Century Racial Iconography', *Nordic Journal of African Studies*, 5.2, pp.1–28.

—— (ed.) (1999a), *Africans on Stage, Studies in Ethnological Show Business*, Bloomington: Indiana University Press.

—— (1999b), 'Charles Dickens and the Zulus', in B. Lindfors (ed.), *Africans on Stage: Studies in Ethnological Show Business*, Bloomington: Indiana University Press, pp. 62–80.

—— (2002), 'Le Docteur Kahn et les Niam-Niams', in N. Bancel, P. Blanchard, G. Boëtsch, É. Deroo and S. Lemaire (eds), *Zoos humains: de la Vénus hottentote aux reality shows*, Paris: La Découverte, pp. 203–12.

Liotard, P. (2002), 'Des Zoos humains aux stades: le spectacle des corps', in N. Bancel, P. Blanchard, G. Boëtsch, É. Deroo and S. Lemaire (eds), *Zoos humains: de la Vénus hottentote aux reality shows*, Paris: La Découverte, pp. 410–16.

Lock, M. (1993), 'The Concept of Race: an Ideological Construct', *Transcultural Psychiatric Research Review*, 30, pp. 203–28.

Locke J. (1965 [1690]), *Two Treatises of Government*, New York: Peter Laslett/American New Library.

Lombard, D. (ed.) (1991), *Rêver l'Asie. Exotisme et littérature coloniale aux Indes, en Indochine et en Insulinde*, Paris: EHESS.

Lott, E. (1992), 'Love and Theft: The Racial Unconscious of Blackface Minstrels', *Representations*, 39, pp. 23–50.

—— (1993), *Love and Theft: Blackface Minstrelsy and the American Working Class*, New York: Oxford University Press.

Lovejoy, O. (1964), *The Great Chain of Beings*, Cambridge, MA: Harvard University Press.

Luckhurst, K. W. (1951), *The Story of Exhibitions*, London and New York: Studio Publications.

Lusebrinck, H.-J. (1995), 'La Grande Nation et ses provinces. De la fonction créatrice d'identité des expositions coloniales, à l'exemple de la France', *Kolonialausstellungen. Begegnungen mit Afrika?*, Frankfurt: IKO/Verlag für Interkulturelle Kommunikation, pp. 137–58.

Lusebrinck, H.-J. (2002), 'De l'Exhibition à la prise de parole', in N. Bancel, P. Blanchard, G. Boëtsch, É. Deroo and S. Lemaire (eds), *Zoos humains: de la Vénus hottentote aux reality shows*, Paris: La Découverte, pp. 259–66.

MacAloon, J. (1981), *This Great Symbol: Pierre de Coubertin and the Origins of the Modern Olympic Games*, Chicago: University of Chicago Press.

MacCormick, E. H. (1977), *Omai Pacific Envoy*, Auckland: Auckland University Press; Oxford: Oxford University Press.

Macintyre, M. and M. MacKenzie (1992), 'Focal Length as an Analogue of Cultural Distance', in E. Edwards (ed.), *Anthropology and Photography, 1860–1920*, New Haven, CT, and London: Yale University Press, pp. 158–64.

Mack, J. (1991), *Emil Torday and the Art of the Congo 1900–1909*, Seattle: University of Washington Press.

MacKenzie, J. (1984), *Propaganda and Empire: The Manipulation of British Public Opinion, 1880–1960*, Manchester: Manchester University Press.

—— (ed.) (1986), *Imperialism and Popular Culture*, Manchester: Manchester University Press.

—— (2002), 'Les expositions impériales en Grande-Bretagne', in N. Bancel, P. Blanchard, G. Boëtsch, É. Deroo and S. Lemaire (eds), *Zoos humains: de la Vénus hottentote aux reality shows*, Paris: La Découverte, pp. 193–202.

Maddra, S. A. (2006), *Hostiles? The Lakota Ghost Dance and Buffalo Bill's Wild West*, Oklahoma: University of Oklahoma Press.

Maffesoli, M. (1985), *La Connaissance ordinaire. Précis de sociologie compréhensive*, Paris: Méridien Klincksieck.

—— (1988), *Le Temps des tribus. Déclin de l'individualisme dans les sociétés de masse*, Paris: Méridien Klincksieck.

Magnaghi, R. M. (1983–84), 'America views her Indians at the 1904 World Fair in St. Louis', *Gateway Heritage*, 4–3, pp. 20–29.

Malchow, H. L. (1993), 'Frankenstein's monster and images of race in nineteenth-century Britain', *Past and Present*, 159, pp. 89–130.

Manceron, G. (2002), 'Les "Sauvages" et les droits de l'homme: un paradoxe républicain', in N. Bancel, P. Blanchard, G. Boëtsch, É. Deroo and S. Lemaire (eds), *Zoos humains: de la Vénus hottentote aux reality shows*, Paris: La Découverte, pp. 399–405.

—— (2003), *Marianne et les colonies*, Paris: La Découverte.

Maresca, S. (1998), 'Les Apparences de la vérité ou les rêves d'objectivité du portrait photographique', *Terrain*, 30, pp. 30–39.

Mariaud, A. (1989), 'Des Canaques à Paris à l'occasion de l'Exposition coloniale', unpublished MA dissertation, University of Nice.

Marin, J. (1994), 'Dimension historique de l'ethnocentrisme européen dans le processus de la domination coloniale et post-coloniale de l'Amérique', in J. Blomart and B. Krewer (eds), *Perspectives de l'interculturel*, Paris: L'Harmattan, pp. 123–34.

Marongiu Buonaiuti, G. (1982), *Politica e religioni nel colonialismo italiano 1882–1941*, Milan: Giuffré.

Martin, P. and D. Moncond'Huy (2004), *Curiosité et cabinets de curiosités*, Neuilly: Atlande.

Martinkus-Zemp, A. (1975), *Le Blanc et le Noir. Essai d'une description de la vision du Noir par le Blanc dans la littérature française de l'entre-deux-guerres*, Paris: Nizet.

Maschietti G., M. Muti and P. Passerin d'Entreves (1988), *Serragli e menagerie in Piemonte nell'ottocento sotto la real casa Savoia*, Turin: Umberto Allemandi.

Mason, P. (1998), *Infelicities, Representations of the Exotic*, Baltimore, MD: Johns Hopkins University Press.

—— (2002a), 'En tránsito: los fueguinos, sus imágenes en Europa, y los pocos que regresaron', *Culturas de Patagonia*, Santiago de Chile: 12 miradas, Ediciones Cuerpos Pintados.

—— (2002b), 'Une troupe d'Onas exhibée au Musée du Nord: reconstruction d'un dossier perdu de la police des étrangers de Bruxelles', in N. Bancel, P. Blanchard, G. Boëtsch, É. Deroo and S. Lemaire (eds), *Zoos humains: de la Vénus hottentote aux reality shows*, Paris: La Découverte, pp. 245–52.

Massa, A. (1974), 'Black Woman in the White City', *Journal of American Studies*, 8, pp. 319–37.

Matsuda, K. (1996), 'Pabilion gakujutsu jinruikan' [The Anthropological Pavilion], *Nihon gakuhô* [Japan Bulletin], 15, pp. 47–70.

Maxwell, A. (2000), *Colonial Photography and Exhibitions. Representations of the Native and the Making of European Identities*, Leicester: Leicester University Press.

—— (2002), 'Montrer l'autre: Franz Boas et des sœurs Gerhard', in N. Bancel, P. Blanchard, G. Boëtsch, É. Deroo and S. Lemaire (eds), *Zoos humains: de la Vénus hottentote aux reality shows*, Paris: La Découverte, pp. 331–39.

May, K. H. (1993), 'German Stereotypes of Native Americans in Context of Karl May and Indianertümeleï', in N. Clerici (ed.), *Victorian Brand Indian Brand: The White Shadow on the Native Image*, Turin: Il Segnalibro, pp. 82–83.

McClintock, A (1994), *Imperial Leather. Race, Gender and Sexuality in the Colonial Contest*, London: Routledge.

McConachie, B. A. (1993), 'Museum Theater and the Problem of Respectability for Mid-Century Urban Americans', in *The American Stage, Social and Economic Issues from the Colonial Period to the Present*, New York: Cambridge University Press, pp. 65–80.

McCullough, E. (1957), *Good Old Coney Island*, New York: Charles Scribner's Sons.

—— (1976), *World's Fair Midways*, New York: Arno Press.

McLarun, A. (1981), 'Prehistory of the Social Sciences. Phrenology in France', *Comparative Studies in Society and History*, 23, pp. 3–22.

McMurtry, L. (2005), *The Colonel and Little Missie: Buffalo Bill, Annie Oakley, and the Beginnings of Superstardom in America*, New York: Simon & Schuster.

McNamara, B. (1974), 'Congress of Wonders, The Rise and Fall of the Dime Museum', *Esquire*, 20.3, pp. 216–32.

Merle, I. and E. Sibeud (2003), 'Histoire en marge ou histoire en marche? La colonisation entre repentance et particularisation', unpublished conference paper, delivered at 'La politique du passé: constructions, usages et mobilisation de l'histoire dans la France des années 70 à nos jours' [http://histoire-sociale. univ-paris1.fr/Collo/Merle.pdf].

Meunier, C. (1992), *Ring noir: Quand Apollinaire, Cendrars, Picabia découvraient les boxeurs nègres*, Paris: Plon.

Miles, R. (1980), 'Class, Race and Ethnicity: A Critique of Cox's Theory', *Racial and Ethnic Studies*, 8.3, pp. 169–87.

Miller, C. L. (1998), *Nationalists and Nomads: Essays on Francophone African Literature and Culture*, Chicago: University of Chicago Press.

Minder, P. (2002), 'La Construction du colonisé dans une métropole sans Empire: le cas de la Suisse (1880–1939)', in N. Bancel, P. Blanchard, G. Boëtsch, É. Deroo and S. Lemaire (eds), *Zoos humains: de la Vénus hottentote aux reality shows*, Paris: La Découverte, pp. 227–34.

—— (2005), 'Le Corps monstrueux à la foire. Nains d'ailleurs, nains de chez nous', in G. Boëtsch (ed.), *Le Corps de l'Alpin: perceptions, représentations, modifications*, Marseille: Editions des Hautes-Alpes, pp. 167–82.

Mitchell, M. (2002), *Monsters. Human Freaks in America's Gilded Age*, Toronto: ECW.

Mitchell, T. (1988), *Colonising Egypt*, Cambridge: Cambridge University Press.

—— (1989), 'The World as Exhibition', *Comparative Studies in Society and History*, 31.2, pp. 217–36.

—— (1992), 'Orientalism and the Exhibitionary Order', in N. B. Dirks (ed.), *Colonialism and Culture*, Ann Arbor: University of Michigan Press, pp. 289–317.

Monestier, M. (2007), *Les Monstres: histoire encyclopédique des phénomènes humains*, Paris: Le chercher midi.

Montagu, A. (1971), *The Elephant Man*, New York: Outerbridge/Dienstfrey.

Montaut, A. (1990), 'Le Rêve du philologue au XIXe siècle, flexions et origine', in 'Rêver l'Inde', *Corps écrit*, 34, pp. 45–55.

Morris, B. (1992), 'Frontier Colonialism as a Culture of Terror', *Journal of Australian Studies*, 35, pp. 72–87.

Morris, D. (1967), *The Naked Ape: A Zoologist's Study of the Human Animal*, London: Jonathan Cape.

—— (1969), *The Human Zoo*, London: Cape.

Morton, P. (2000), *Hybrid Modernities. Architecture and Representation at the 1931 Colonial Exposition, Paris*, Boston: MIT Press.

Moses, L. G. (1991), 'Indians on the Midway: Wild West Shows and the Indian Bureau at World's Fairs, 1893–1904', *South Dakota History*, 21, pp. 205–29.

—— (1996), *Wild West Shows and the Images of American Indians, 1883–1933*, Albuquerque: University of New Mexico Press.

Moura, J.-M. (1998), *La Littérature des lointains. Histoire de l'exotisme européen du XXe siècle*, Paris: Champion.

Mouralis, B. (1999), *République et colonies*, Paris; Dakar: Présence africaine.

Moussa, S. (ed.) (2002), *La Construction de la notion de race dans la littérature et les sciences humaines (XVIIIe et XIXe siècles)*, Paris: L'Harmattan.

Mulvaney, D. J. (1989), *Encounters in Place. Outsiders and Aboriginal Australians 1606–1985*, St Lucia, University of Queensland Press.

Myers, R. H. and M. R. Peattie (eds) (1984), *The Japanese Colonial Empire (1895–1945)*, Princeton, NJ: Princeton University Press.

Nanta, A. (2001), 'Ethnologie ou anthropologie physique? La Question de "l'origine des Japonais" dans la genèse de la Société d'anthropologie de Tokyo (1884–1913)', *Ebisu, études japonaises*, 28, Tokyo: Maison franco-japonaise, pp. 110–32.

—— (2003), 'Koropokgrus, Aïnous, Japonais, aux origines du peuplement de l'archipel. Débat chez les anthropologues, 1884–1913', *Ebisu, études japonaises*, 30, Tokyo: Maison franco-japonaise, pp. 123–54.

—— (2006), 'L'Altérité aïnoue dans le Japon moderne', *Annales HSS*, 61.1, pp. 247–73.

Naranjo, J. (ed.) (2006), *Fotografía, antropología y colonialismo (1845–2006)*, Barcelona: Gustavo Gili.

Navailles, J.-P. (1996), *Londres victorien. Un monde cloisonné*, Seyssel: Champ Vallon.

Nederveen Pieterse, J. J. (1992), *White on Black. Images of Africa and Blacks in Western Popular Culture*, New Haven, CT, and London: Yale University Press.

—— and B. Parekh (1995), *The Decolonization of Imagination. Culture, Knowledge and Power*, London: Zed Books.

Negroni, F. de (1992), *Afrique fantasmes*, Paris, Plon.

Nesteby, J.-R. (1982), *Black Images in American Films, 1896–1954: The Interplay Between Civil Rights and Film Culture*, Washington, DC: University Press of America.

Nickell, J. (2005), *Secrets of the Sideshows*, Lexington: University Press of Kentucky.

Niemeyer, G. H. W. (1972), *Hagenbeck. Geschichte und Geschichten*, Hamburg: [n. pub.].

Ôe, S. (ed.) (1993), *Kindai Nihon to shokuminchi [Modern Japan and its Colonies]*, 8 vols, Tokyo: Iwanami shoten.

O'Neil J. (1996), *The Authority of Experiences: Sensationist Theory in the French Enlight-enment*, University Park, PA: Pennsylvania State University Press.

Ortiz, R. D. (1992), 'Aboriginal People and Imperialism in the Western Hemisphere', *Monthly Review*, 4, pp. 1–13.

Ortner, S. (1984), 'Theory in Anthropology since the Sixties', *Comparative Studies in Society and History*, 16.1, pp. 126–66.

Ory, P. (1989), *L'Expo universelle, 1889. La mémoire des siècles*, Brussels: Complexe.

Osborne, M. A. (1994), *Nature, the Exotic, and the Science of French Colonialism*, Bloomington: Indiana University Press.

Oschinsky, L. (1959), 'A Reappraisal of Recent Serological, Genetic and Morphological Research on Taxonomy of the Races of Africa and Asia', *Anthropologica*, 1, pp. 1–25.

Paesons, N. (1999), '"Clicko", Franz Taaibosch, South African Bushman Entertainer in England, France, Cuba, and the United States, 1908–1940', in B. Lindfors (ed.), *Africans on Stage: Studies in Ethnological Show Business*, Bloomington: Indiana University Press, pp. 203–27.

Pajot, S. (2003), *De la femme à barbe à l'homme-canon. Phénomènes de cirque et de baraque foraine*, Le Château d'Olonne: Editions d'Orbestier.

Pala, S. (1981), *Exposition coloniale internationale de Paris, 1931*, Paris: Bibliothèque de la Ville de Paris.

Palma, S. (1999), *L'Italia coloniale*, Rome: Editori Riuniti.

Paré, A. (1982), *On Monsters and Marvels*, Chicago: University of Chicago Press.

Parezo, N. (2005), 'Anthropology Days, Fabricating and Testing Racial Strength and Endurance at the 1904 Louisiana Purchase Exposition', Third Annual Meeting of the Cultural Studies Association, University of Arizona, Tucson, April [http://www.csaus.pitt.edu/conf/viewabstract.php?id=161&cf=2].

Parry, B. (2004), *Postcolonial Studies: A Materialist Critique*, London, Routledge.

Parsons, Q. N. (1988), 'Frantz and Klikko. The Wild Dancing Bushman: A Case Study in Khoisan Stereotyping', *Botswana Notes and Records*, 20, pp. 71–76.

Paust, B. (1996), *Studien zur barocken Menagerie in deutschsprachigen Raum*, Worms: Wernesche Verlagsgesellchaft.

Peabody, S. and T. Stovall (eds) (2003), *The Color of Liberty. Histories of Race in France*, Durham, NC, and London: Duke University Press.

Peacock, S. (1995), *The Great Farini: The High-Wire Life of William Hunt*, Toronto: Viking.

—— (1999), 'Africa meets the Great Farini', in B. Lindfors (ed.), *Africans on Stage. Studies in Ethnological Show Business*, Bloomington: Indiana University Press, pp. 81–106.

Pegler, M. and Rimmer G. (1999), *Buffalo Bill's Wild West*, Leeds: Royal Armouries Museum.

Péharpré, S. (1992), 'Les Indiens des salons parisiens', in V. Wiesinger (ed.), *Sur le Sentier de la Découverte: Rencontres franco-indiennes du XVIe au XXe siècle*, Paris: RMN/Musée National de la Coopération franco-américaine, pp. 105–11.

Pelc, O. and M. Gretzschel (1998), *Hagenbeck. Tiere, Menschen, Illusionen*, The Professional Correspondence of Franz Boas (1878–1943), Hamburg and Wilmington [microfilm].

Penel, J.-D. (1982), *Homo Caudatus, l'homme à queue d'Afrique Centrale, un avatar de l'imaginaire occidental*, Paris: SELAF.

Penny, H. G. (2006), 'Illustriertes Amerika. Der Wilde Western in deutschen

Zeitschriften 1825–1890', in P. Kort and M. Hollein (eds), *I like America. Fiktionen des Wilden Westens*, Frankfurt: Prestel, pp. 140–57.

Pernick, M. (1996), *The Black Story, Eugenics and the Death of "Defective" Babies in American Medicine and Motion Pictures Since 1915*, New York: Oxford University Press.

Piault, M.-H. (2000), *Anthropologie et cinéma*, Paris: Nathan.

Picard, L. (2000), *Dr. Johnson's London. Life in London 1740–1770*, London: Phoenix Press.

Pickering, M. (1991), 'Mock Blacks and Racial Mockery: The "Nigger" Minstrel and British Imperialism', in J. S. Bratton (ed.), *Acts of Supremacy*, Manchester: Manchester University Press, pp. 179–236.

—— (2001), *Stereotyping: The Politics of Representation*, Basingstoke: Palgrave Macmillan.

Picque, B. (1993), 'De l'acclimatement à l'acclimatation. Étude du discours hygiéniste sur la colonisation dans la seconde moitié du XIXe siècle', unpublished MA dissertation, Université de Paris I.

Pinney, C. (1992), 'The Parallel Histories of Anthropology and Photography', in E. Edwards (ed.), *Anthropology and Photography, 1860–1920*, New Haven, CT, and London: Yale University Press, pp. 74–95.

Pirotte, J. (ed.) (1982), *Stéréotypes nationaux et préjugés raciaux aux XIXᵉ et XXᵉ siècles*, Louvain-la-Neuve: Université de Louvain.

Piton, N. (2002), 'Entre science et spectacle: des Aborigènes sur la scène des Folies Bergère', in N. Bancel, P. Blanchard, G. Boëtsch, É. Deroo and S. Lemaire (eds), *Zoos humains: de la Vénus hottentote aux reality shows*, Paris: La Découverte, pp. 289–95.

Pizzorni, Itié F. (1992), 'Roland Bonaparte (1858–1924)', in B. Coutancier (ed.), *Peaux-Rouges, Autour de la collection du prince Roland Bonaparte*, Thonon-les-Bains: L'Albaron/Photothèque du Musée de l'Homme, pp. 10–31.

Poignant, R. (1980), *Observers of Man*, London: Royal Anthropological Institute.

—— (1990), 'Surveying the Field of View', in E. Edwards (ed.), *Anthropology and Photography 1860–1920*, New Haven, CT, and London: Yale University Press/The Royal Anthropological Institute.

—— (1997), 'Looking for Tambo', *Olive Pink Society Bulletin*, 9.1–2, pp. 27–37.

—— (2002), 'Les Aborigènes: "sauvages professionnels" et vies captives', in N. Bancel, P. Blanchard, G. Boëtsch, É. Deroo and S. Lemaire (eds), *Zoos humains: de la Vénus hottentote aux reality shows*, Paris: La Découverte, pp. 103–10.

—— (2004), *Professional Savages: Captive Lives and Western Spectacle*, Sydney: University of New South Wales Press.

Poliakov, L. (1975), 'Le Fantasme des êtres hybrides et la hiérarchie des races aux XVIIIe et XIXe siècles', in L. Poliakov (ed.), *Hommes et bêtes. Entretiens sur le racisme*, Paris/La Haye: Mouton, pp. 167–82.

Pomian, K. (1987), *Collectionneurs, amateurs et curieux. Paris, Venise: XVIᵉ–XVIIIᵉ siècle*, Paris: Gallimard.

Poole, D. (1997), *Vision, Race and Modernity. A Visual Economy of the Andean Image World*, Princeton, NJ: Princeton University Press.

Pouillon, F. (1993), 'Simplification ethnique en Afrique du Nord, Maures, Arabes et Berbères (XVIIIᵉ–XXᵉ siècles)', *Cahiers d'études africaines*, 129, pp. 37–50.

Price, S. (1989), *Primitive Art in Civilized Places*, Chicago: University of Chicago Press.

—— (2007), *Paris Primitive: Jacques Chirac's Museum on the Quai Branly*, Chicago: University of Chicago Press.

Prochaska, D. (1989), 'L'Algérie imaginaire. Jalons pour une histoire de l'iconographie coloniale', *Gradhiva*, 7, pp. 29–38.

Puccini, S. (1999), *Andare Lontano. Viaggi ed etnografia nel secondo Ottocento*, Rome: Carocci.

Putnam, F. W. (1994), *Portrait Types of the Midway Plaisance: Chicago World's Columbian Exposition 1893*, St Louis: Thompson.

Pyenson, L. (1993), *Civilizing Mission. Exact Sciences and French Overseas Expansion, 1830–1940*, Baltimore, MD, and London: Johns Hopkins University Press.

Quasimodo (2000), *Fictions de l'étranger*, Montpellier: Quasimodo & Fils.

Quison, C. A. (1991), 'Ethnographic Knowledge and the Display of Philippine Igorots in the Louisiana Purchase Exposition, 1904', unpublished MA dissertation, University of New York, Stony Brook.

Qureshi, S. (2004), 'Displaying Sara Baartman, the "Hottentot Venus"', *History of Science*, 42, pp. 233–57.

Rauch, A. (1989), 'Parer, paraître, apparaître. Histoires de la présence corporelle', *Ethnologie française*, 2, pp. 145–54.

Razac, O. (2000), *Histoire politique du barbelé*, Paris: La Fabrique éditions.

—— (2002), *L'Ecran et le Zoo: spectacles et domestication des expositions coloniales à Loft Story*, Paris: Denoël.

Reddin, P. (1999), *Wild West Shows*, Urbana and Chicago: University of Chicago Press.

Reiss, B. (1999), 'P. T. Barnum, Joice Heth and Antebellum Spectacles of Race', *American Quarterly*, 51.1, pp. 78–107.

—— (2001), *The Showman and the Slave: Race, Death, and Memory in Barnum's America*, Cambridge, MA: Harvard University Press.

—— (2002), 'P. T. Barnum, Joice Heth et les débuts des spectacles raciaux', in N. Bancel, P. Blanchard, G. Boëtsch, É. Deroo and S. Lemaire (eds), *Zoos humains: de la Vénus hottentote aux reality shows*, Paris: La Découverte, pp. 23–30.

Renieu, A. (1928), *Histoire des théâtres de Bruxelles*, Paris: Ducharte & Van Buggenhoudt, pp. 877–87.

Reszler, A. (1986), *Mythes et identité de la Suisse*, Geneva: Georg Éditeur.

Revel, E. (1942), *Leconte de Lisle animalier et le goût de la zoologie au XIXᵉ siècle*, Marseille: Imprimerie du Sémaphore.

Revol, P. (1996), 'Observations sur les Fuégiens: du Jardin d'acclimatation à la Terre de Feu', in C. Blanckaert (ed.), *Le Terrain des sciences humaines, XVIIIᵉ–XXᵉ siècles*, Paris: L'Harmattan, pp. 243–96.

Reynaud-Paligot, C. (2006), *La République raciale, 1860–1930*, Paris: PUF.

—— (2007), *Races, racisme et antiracisme das les années 1930*, Paris: PUF.

Reynolds, D. (1995), *Walt Whitman's America*, New York: Knopf.

Riach, D. C. (1973), 'Blacks and Blackface on the Irish Stage, 1830–60', *Journal of American Studies*, 7.3, pp. 231–41.

Richards, T. (1990), *The Commodity Culture of Victorian England: Advertising and Spectacle, 1851–1916*, Chicago: University of Chicago.

Richmond, (1978), 'Migration, Ethnicity and Race Relations', *Ethnic and Racial Studies*, 1.1, pp. 12–18.

Riego, B. (2001), *La construcción social de la realidad a través de la fotografía y el grabado informativo en la España del siglo XIXe*, Santander: Universidad de Cantabria.

Ritvo, H. (1990), *The Animal Estate. The English and Other Creatures in the Victorian Age*, London: Penguin Books.

Rivet, D. (1988), *Lyautey et l'institution du Protectorat français au Maroc 1912–1925*, Paris; L'Harmattan.

Rodriguez Bernal, E. (1994), *Historia de la Exposición Ibero Americana de Sevilla de 1929*, Seville: Servicio de Publicaciones del Ayuntamiento de Sevilla.

Rony, F. T. (1992), 'Those Who Squat and Those Who Sit: The Iconography of Race in the 1895 Films of Félix-Louis Regnault', *Camera Obscura*, 28, pp. 263–89.

Roquebert, A. (1994), 'La Sculpture ethnographique au XIXe siècle, objet de mission ou œuvre de musée?', in A. Le Normand-Romain et al. (eds), *La Sculpture ethnographique: de la Vénus hottentote à la Tehura de Gauguin*, Paris: Réunion des Musées Nationaux, pp. 18–29.

Rosa, J. G. and R. May (1989), *Buffalo Bill and his Wild West: A Pictorial Biography*, Lawrence: University Press of Kansas.

Rosello, M. (1998), *Declining the Stereotype*, Hanover, NH: University Press of New England.

Ross, K. (1995), *Fast Cars, Clean Bodies*, Boston: MIT Press.

Rothfels, N. (1996), 'Aztecs, Aborigines, and Ape-People: Science and Freaks in Germany, 1850–1900', in R. Garland-Thomson (ed.), *Freakery: Cultural Spectacles of the Extraordinary, 1886–1931*, New York: New York University Press, pp. 158–72.

Rothman, D. (1971), *The Discovery of the Asylum, Social Order and Disorder in the New Republic*, Boston: Little Brown.

Rouillé, A. (1991), 'La Photographie entre controverse et utopie', in S. Michaud, J.-Y. Mollier and N. Savy (eds), *Usages de l'image au XIXe siècle*, Paris: Créaphis, pp. 249–56.

Rudwick, E. M. and A. Meier (1965), 'Black man in the "White City": Negroes and the Columbia Exposition, 1893', *Phylon*, 26, pp. 354–61.

Ruscio, A. (1996), *Le Credo de l'homme blanc*, Brussels: Complexe.

—— (2002), 'Du Village à l'exposition: les Français à la rencontre des *Indochinois*', in N. Bancel, P. Blanchard, G. Boëtsch, É. Deroo and S. Lemaire (eds), *Zoos humains: de la Vénus hottentote aux reality shows*, Paris: La Découverte, pp. 267–74.

Russell, D. (1970), *The Wild West: A History of the Wild West Shows*, Fort Worth, TX: Amon Carter Museum of Western Art.

—— (1973 [1960]), *The Lives and Legends of Buffalo Bill*, Norman: University of Oklahoma Press.

Rydell, R. W. (1984 [1974]), *All the World's a Fair. Visions of Empire at American International Expositions 1876–1916*, Chicago: University of Chicago Press.

—— (1993), 'A Cultural Frankenstein? The Chicago World's Columbian Exposition of 1893', in N. Harris, W. De Wit, J. Gilbert and R. W. Rydell (eds), *Grand Illusions, Chicago's World's Fair for 1893*, Chicago: Chicago Historical Society, pp. 143–70.

—— (1993), *World of Fairs: Century of Progress Expositions*, Chicago: University of Chicago Press.

—— (1999), 'Darkest Africa. African Shows at America's World's Fairs, 1893–1940', in B. Lindfors (ed.), *Africans on Stage, Studies in Ethnological Show Business*, Bloomington: Indiana University Press, pp. 135–55.

—— (2002), 'Africains en Amérique: les villages africains dans les expositions internationales américaines (1893–1901)', in N. Bancel, P. Blanchard, G. Boëtsch,

É. Deroo and S. Lemaire (eds), *Zoos humains: de la Vénus hottentote aux* reality shows, Paris: La Découverte, pp. 213–20.

—— and N. E. Gwinn (eds) (1994), *Fair Representations: World's Fairs and the Modern World*, Amsterdam: VU University Press.

Ryhiner, N. E. (1995), *Die afrikanische Nacht. Skandal im Basler Zoo*, Basel: GGS–Verlag.

Said, E. (1978), *Orientalism*, New York: Pantheon.

—— (2000), *Culture et impérialisme*, Paris: Fayard; Le Monde diplomatique.

Sakamoto, H. (1995), 'Chûgoku minzokushugi no shinwa' ['The Myth of Chinese Nationalism'], *Shisô*, 849.3, pp. 61–84.

Sakano, T. (2005), *Teikoku Nippon to jinruigakusha* [The Japanese Empire and the anthropologists], Tokyo: Keisô shobô.

Sánchez Gómez, L. (2003), *Un imperio en la vitrina. El colonialismo español en el Pacífico y la exposición de Filipinas de 1887*, Madrid: Consejo Superior de Investigaciones Científicas.

—— (2005), 'Exhibiciones etnológicas vivas en España. Espectáculo y representación fotográfica', in *Maneras de mirar. Lecturas antropológicas de la fotografía*, Madrid: CSIC, pp. 31–60.

Savitt, T. L. (1978), *Medicine and Slavery: The Diseases and Health Care of Blacks in Antebellum Virginia*, Urbana: University of Illinois Press.

Saxon, A.-H. (1980), *P. T. Barnum: The Legend and The Man*, New York: Columbia University Press.

Saxton, A. (1990), *The Rise and Fall of the White Republic: Class Politics and Mass Culture in Nineteenth-Century America*, London and New York: Verso.

Scherer, J.-C. (1990), 'Historical Photographs as Anthropological Documents: A Retrospect', *Visual Anthropology*, 3.2–3, pp. 131–85.

—— (1992), 'The Photographic Document: Photographs as Primary Data in Anthropological Inquiry', in E. Edwards (ed.), *Anthropology and Photography, 1860–1920*, New Haven, CT, and London: Yale University Press, pp. 32–41.

Schiebinger, L. (1993), *Nature's Body. Gender in the Making of Modern Science*, Boston: Beacon Press.

Schildkrout, E. and C. Keim (eds.) (1998), *The Scramble for Art in Central Africa*, Cambridge: Cambridge University Press.

Schiller, F. (1979), *Paul Broca. Founder of French Anthropology, Explorer of the Brain*, Berkley/Los Angeles/London: University of California Press.

Schmidt, N. (2000), *Abolitionnistes de l'esclavage et réformateurs des colonies, 1820–1851. Analyse et documents*, Paris: Karthala.

Schmidt-Linsenhoff, V. (1986), *Plakate, 1880–1914, inventarkatalog der Plakatsammlung des Historischen Museums Frankfurt*, Frankfurt: Frankfurt Historisches Museum.

Schneer, J. (1999), *London 1900. The Imperial Metropolis*, New Haven, CT: Yale University Press.

Schneider, G. (1982), 'Das deutsche Kolonialmuseum in Berlin und seine Bedeutung im Rahmen der preussischen Schulreform um die Jahrhudertwende', in *Die Zukunft beginnt in der Vergangenheit*, Schriften des Historischen Museums 16, Frankfurt: Historisches Museum Frankfurt am Main, pp. 155–99.

Schneider, W. H. (1977), 'Race and empire, the rise of popular ethnography in the late nineteenth century', *Journal of Popular Culture*, 11.1, pp. 98–109.

—— (1981), 'Colonies at the 1900 World's Fair', *History Today*, 31, pp. 31–36.

—— (1982), *An Empire for the Masses, the French Popular Image of Africa, 1870–1900*, Westport, CT, and London: Greenwood Press.

—— (1990), *Quality and Quantity. The Quest for Biological Regeneration in Twentieth-Century France*, Cambridge: Cambridge University Press.

—— (2002), 'Les Expositions ethnographiques du Jardin zoologique d'acclimatation', in N. Bancel, P. Blanchard, G. Boëtsch, É. Deroo and S. Lemaire (eds), *Zoos humains de la Vénus hottentote aux reality shows*, Paris: La Découverte, pp. 72–80.

Schudson, M. (1978), *Discovering the News: A Social History of American Newspapers*, New York: Basic Books.

Schwartz, V. (1998), *Spectacular Realities: Early Mass Culture in Fin-de-Siècle Paris*, Berkeley: University of California Press.

Schwarz, W. M. (2001), *Antropologische Spektakel. Zu Schaustellung "exotischer" Menschen. Wien 1870–1910*, Vienna: Turia and Kant.

Scott, D. (1980), 'The Popular Lecture and the Creation of a Public in Mid-Nineteenth Century America', *Journal of American History*, 66, pp. 791–809.

Scott, G. M. (1991), 'Village Performance: Villages at the Chicago World's Columbian Exposition, 1893', unpublished PhD dissertation, New York University.

Sears, C. (1997), *Africa in the American Mind, 1870–1955: A Study in Mythology, Ideology and the Reconstruction of Race*, Berkeley: University of California.

Sekula, A. (1986), 'The Body and the Archive', *October*, 39, pp. 3–64.

Sell, H. B. and C. Weybright (1955), *Buffalo Bill and the Wild West*, New York: Oxford University Press.

Sellers, C. (1980), *Mr Peale's Museum: Charles Wilson Peale and the First Popular Museum in Natural Science and Art*, New York: W . W. Norton.

Seltzer, M. (1992), *Bodies and Machines*, New York: Routledge.

Sennett, R. (1974), *The Fall of Public Man*, Cambridge: Cambridge University Press.

Servan-Schreiber, C. (2002), 'L'Inde et Ceylan dans les expositions coloniales et universelles (1851–1931)', in N. Bancel, P. Blanchard, G. Boëtsch, É. Deroo and S. Lemaire (eds), *Zoos humains de la Vénus hottentote aux reality shows*, Paris: La Découverte, pp. 159–68.

Sharpley-Whiting, D. T. (1999), *Black Venus: Sexualized Savages, Primal Fears, and Primitive Narratives in French*, Durham, NC: Duke University Press.

Shephard, B. (1986), 'Showbiz Imperialism: The Case of Peter Lobengula', in J. M. MacKenzie (ed.), *Imperialism and Popular Culture*, Manchester: Manchester University Press, pp. 94–112.

Shohat, E. and R. Stam (1994), *Unthinking Eurocentrism, Multiculturalism and the Media*, London and New York: Routledge.

Shyllon, F. (1977), *Black People in Britain, 1555–1833*, London: Oxford University Press.

Sibeud, E. (2002), *Une Science impériale pour l'Afrique? La construction des savoirs africanistes en France, 1878–1930*, Paris: Éditions de l'EHESS.

Singleton, M. (2004), *Critique de l'ethnocentrisme. Du missionnaire anthropophage à l'anthropologue post-développementiste*, Paris: Parangon.

Simmel, G. (1981), 'Essai sur la sociologie des sens', in *Sociologie et épistémologie*, Paris: PUF.

Sloan, M. and F. W. Glasier (2002), *Wild, Weird and Wonderful: The American Circus 1901–1927*, New York: Quantuck Lane Press.

Sontag, S. (1973), *On Photography*, New York: Dell.

Spencer, F. (1992), 'Some Notes on the Attempt to Apply Photography to Anthropometry during the Second Half of the Nineteenth Century', in E. Edwards (ed.), *Anthropology and Photography 1860–1920*, New Haven, CT, and London: Yale University Press, pp. 99–107.

Staehelin, B. (1993), *Völkerschauen im Zoologischen Garten Basel, 1879–1935*, Basel: Basler Afrika Bibliographien.

Stallybrass, P. and A. White (1986), *The Politics and Poetics of Transgression*, Ithaca, NY: Cornell University Press.

Stanton, W. (1960), *The Leopard's Spots: Scientific Attitudes Toward Race in America, 1815–59*, Chicago: University of Chicago Press.

Starr, P. (1982), *The Social Transformation of American Medicine*, New York: Basic Books.

Stearns, R. (1995), *Photography and Beyond in Japan: Space Time and Memory*, Tokyo: Hara Museum of Contemporary Art and Harry N. Abrams.

Steiger, R. and M. Taureg (1984), 'Körperphantasien auf Reisen. Anmerkungen zum ethnographischen Akt', in G. Barcher and M. Köhler (eds), *Das Aktfoto. Ansichten vom Körper im fotografischen Zeitalter. Ästhetik, Geschichte, Ideologie*, Munich: Bucher, pp. 116–36.

Steins, M. (1972), *Das Bild des Schwarzen in der Europaeischen Kolonialliteratur*, Frankfurt Am Main: Thesen Verlag.

Stencell, A. W. (2002), *Seeing is Believing. America's Sideshows*, Toronto: ECW Press.

Stepan, N. (1982), *The Idea of Race in Science: Great Britain 1800–1960*, London: Macmillan Press.

Stevens, M. (2008), 'Re-membering the Nation: the Project for the Cité nationale de l'histoire de l'immigration', unpublished PhD dissertation, University College London.

Stewart, S. (1984), *On Longing, Narratives of the Miniature, the Gigantic, the Souvenir, the Collection*, Baltimore, MD: Johns Hopkins University Press.

Stocking, G. W. (1968 [1982]), *Race, Culture and Evolution. Essays in the History of Anthropology*, Chicago: University of Chicago Press.

—— (1984), 'Qu'est-ce qui est en jeu dans un nom? La Société d'ethnographie et l'historiographie de l'"anthropologie" en France', in B. Rupp-Eisenreich (ed.), *Histoires de l'anthropologie (XVIe–XIXe siècles)*, Paris: Klincksieck, pp. 421–32.

—— (1987), *Victorian Anthropology*, New York: Free Press.

Stoler, A. L. (1995), *Race and the Education of Desire*, Durham, NC: Duke University Press.

Stone, D. A. (1984), *The Disabled State*, Philadelphia: Temple University Press.

Strother, Z. (1999), 'Display of the Body Hottentot', in B. Lindfors (ed.), *Africans on Stage: Studies in Ethnological Show Business*, Bloomington: Indiana University Press, pp. 1–60.

Sturani, E. (2001), 'Das Fremde im Bild. Überlegungen zur Lektüre kolonialer Postkarten', *Fotogeschichte*, 79, pp. 13–23.

Subiros, P. (2007), *Apartheid. The South African Mirror*, Barcelona: CCCB.

Sullivan, J. E. (1905), 'Spalding's Official Athletic Almanac for 1905', *Special Olympic Number*, New York, pp. 249–64.

Tagg, J. (1988), *The Burden of Representation*, London: Macmillan.

Taguieff, P.-A. (1988), *La Force du préjugé. Essai sur le racisme et ses doubles*, Paris: La Découverte.

—— (1991a), 'L'introduction de l'eugénisme en France: du mot à l'idée', *Mots*, 'Langages du politique', 26, pp. 23–45.

—— (1991b), 'Doctrines de la race et hantise du métissage. Fragments d'une histoire de la mixiophobie savante', *Nouvelle revue d'ethnopsychiatrie*, 17, pp. 53–100.

—— (1994), 'Eugénisme ou décadence? L'exception française', *Ethnologie française*, 24.1, pp. 81–103.

—— (2001), 'La confluence des fatalismes: emprise globalitaire, dérives identitaires', *Les Temps modernes*, 613, pp. 131–57.

—— (2002), *La Couleur et le sang. Doctrines racistes à la française*, Turin: Mille et une nuits.

Taillac, P. de (2007), *Les Paradis artificiels, l'imaginaire des drogues, de l'opium à l'ecstasy*, Paris: Hugodoc.

Takahashi, T. (2005), *Yasukuni mondai* [The Question of the Yasukuni Shrine], Tô: Chikuma shobô (french translation scheduled for 2008, Paris: Demopolis).

Takaki, R. (1979), *Iron Cages: Race and Culture in Nineteenth Century America*, New York: A. Knopf.

Taussig, M. (1992), 'Culture of Terror. Space of Death', in N. B. Dirks (ed.), *Colonialism and Culture*, Ann Arbor: University of Michigan Press, pp. 118–43.

Taylor, F. W. (n.d.), *Scrapbooks*, Los Angeles: Department of Special Collections, UCLA Press.

Taylor, J. G. (1981), 'An Eskimo abroad, 1880. His diary and death', *Canadian Geographic*, October/November, pp. 38–43.

Taylor, J. and K. Kotcher (2002), *James Taylor's Shocked and Amazed. On and Off the Midway*, Guilford, CT: Lyons Press.

Taylor, P. M. (1988), 'Anthropology and the "Racial Doctrine" in Italy Before 1940', *Antropologia Contemporanea*, 11.1–2, pp. 45–58.

Testart, A. (1981), 'Pour une typologie des chasseurs-cueilleurs', *Anthropologie et sociétés*, 5.2, pp. 177–221.

Thevet, A. (1997 [1557]), *Les Singularitez de la France antarctique, autrement nommée Amérique, et de plusieurs terres et isles découvertes de nostre tems*, Paris: Magellane.

Theye, T. (ed.) (1985), *Wir und die Wilden, Einblicke in einer kannabalische Beziehung*, Reinbek: [n. pub.].

—— (1989), *Der Geraubte Schatten, Die Photographie als Ethnographisches Dokument*, Munich: Munich Stattmuseum.

Thinius, C. H. (1975), *Damals in St. Pauli, Lust und Freude in der Vorstadt*, Hamburg: Christians.

Thode-Arora, H. (1989), *Für fünfzig Pfennig um die Welt, Die Hagenbeckschen Völkerschauen*, New York and Frankfurt: Campus Verlag.

—— (1991), 'Das Eskimo-Tagebuch von 1880. Eine Völkerschau aus der Sicht eines Teilnehmers', *Kea. Zeitschrift für Kulturwissenschaften*, 2, pp. 87–115.

—— (1992), 'Die Familie Umlauff und ihre Firmen. Ethnographica-Händler in Hamburg', *Mitteilungen aus dem Museum für Völkerkunde Hamburg*, 22, pp. 143–58.

—— (1993), 'Die Hagenbeckschen Völkerschauen. Indianer Nordamerikas in Europa', in *Indianer Nordamerikas. Kunst und Mythos*, Mainz: Ausstellungskatalog der Internationalen Tage Ingelheim, pp. 80–87.

—— (1996), 'Charakteristische Gestalten des Volkslebens, Die Hagenbeckschen Südasien-, Orient- und Afrika-Völkerschauen', in G. Höpp (ed.), *Fremde Erfahrungen. Asiaten und Afrikaner in Deutschland, Österreich und in der Schweiz bis 1945*, Berlin: Das Arabische Buch, pp. 109–34.

—— (1997), 'Herbeigeholte Ferne. Völkerschauen als Vorläufer exotisierender Abenteuerfilme', in J. Schöning (ed.), *Triviale Tropen. Exotische Reise und Abenteuerfilme aus Deutschland zwischen 1919 und 1939*, Munich: Text + Kritik, pp. 18–33.

—— (2002a), 'Abraham's Diary. A European Ethnic Show from an Inuk Participant's Viewpoint', *Journal of the Society for the Anthropology of Europe*, 2.2, pp. 2–17.

—— (2002b), 'Hagenbeck et les tournées européennes: l'élaboration du zoo humain', in N. Bancel, P. Blanchard, G. Boëtsch, É. Deroo and S. Lemaire (eds), *Zoos humains: de la Vénus hottentote aux reality shows*, Paris: La Découverte, pp. 81–89.

—— (2002c), 'Indianer und Inuit in Europa: Völkerschauen', in Eva König (ed.), *Indianer 1858–1928: Photographische Reisen von Alaska bis Feuerland*, Heidelberg: Edition Braus, pp. 69–73.

—— (2008), 'Commercial ethnographic exhibitions in nineteenth- and early twentieth-century Germany', in Prem Poddar, Rajeev S. Patke and Lars Jensen (eds), *A Historical Companion to Postcolonial Literatures: Continental Europe and its Empires*, Edinburgh: Edinburgh University Press, pp. 227–28.

Thomas, K. (1971), *Religion and the Decline of Magic*, New York: Scribner's.

—— (1983), *Man and the Natural World*, New York: Pantheon Books.

Thomas, N. (1998), *Hors du temps. Histoire et évolutionnisme dans le discours anthropologique*, Paris: Belin.

Thomson, A. (1987), *Barbary and Enlightenment: European attitudes towards the Maghreb in the 18th century*, Leiden and Cologne: E. J. Brill.

Thuillier, G. (1977), 'Un Anarchiste positivise: Georges Vacher de Lapouge', in P. Guiral and É. Temime (eds), *L'Idée de race dans la pensée politique française contemporaine*, Paris: CNRS éditions, pp. 48–65.

Todorov, T. (1982), *La Conquête de l'Amérique. La question de l'autre*, Paris: Seuil.

—— (1989), *Nous et les autres. La réflexion française sur la diversité humaine*, Paris: Seuil.

Toffin, G. (2006), *Ethnologie. La quête de l'autre*, Paris: L'Acropole.

Toole-Stot, T. R. (1971), *Circus and Allied Arts. A World Bibliography 1500–1957*, Derby: Harpus.

Tort, P. (ed.) (1996), *Dictionnaire du darwinisme et de l'évolution*, Paris: PUF.

Trautmann-Waller, C. (ed.) (2004), *Quand Berlin pensait les peuples. Anthropologie, ethnologie et psychologie (1850–1890)*, Paris: CNRS éditions.

Treichler, H. P. (1985), *La Suisse au tournant du siècle. Souvenirs du bon vieux temps*, Zürich: Sélection du Reader's Digest.

Trennert, R. A. (1987), 'Fairs, Expositions, and the Changing Image of Southwestern Indians, 1876–1904', *New Mexico Historical Review*, 62.2, pp. 127–50.

Trouillot, M.-R. (1995), *Silencing the Past: Power and the Production of History*, Boston: Beacon Press.

Troutman, J. W. and N. J. Parezo (1998), '"The Overlord of the Savage World": Anthropology and the Press at the 1904 Louisiana Purchase Exposition', *Museum Anthropology*, 22.2, pp. 17–34.

Truettner, W. H. (1986), 'Science and Sentiment: Indian Images at the Turn of the Century', in Ch. C. Eldredge, J. Schimmel and W. H. Truettner, *Art in New Mexico, 1900–1945: Paths to Taos and Santa Fe*, New York: Abbeville Press Publishers, pp. 17–41.

Truzzi, M. (1979), 'Circus and Side Shows', in M. Matlaw (ed.), *American Popular Entertainment*, Westport, CT: Greenwood Press, pp. 175–85.

Tucher, A. (1994), *Froth and Scum: Truth, Beauty, Goodness, and the Ax Murder in America's First Mass Medium*, Chapel Hill: University of North Carolina Press.

Twitchell, J. B. (1990), *Carnival Culture. The Trashing of Taste in America*, New York, Columbia University Press, pp. 57–65.

Ukigaya, S. (2005), 'Les expositions hygiénistes, les modèles anatomiques et les marionnettes réaliste', *Ebisu*, 34, pp. 3–37.

Ulmann, J. (1987), *La Nature et l'éducation. L'idée de nature dans l'éducation physique et l'éducation morale*, Paris: Klincksieck.

Valensi, L. (1977), 'Nègre/Négro: recherches dans les dictionnaires français et anglais au XIXe siècle', in P. Guiral and É. Temime (eds), *L'Idée de race dans la pensée politique française contemporaine*, Paris: CNRS éditions, pp. 157–70.

Van Den Berghe, P.-L. (1970), *Race and Ethnicity: Essays in Comparative Sociology*, New York: Basic Books.

Van Geertruyen, G. (1991), 'Démons sans merveilles, peuples sans histoire. Comment l'Occident a perçu les Africains à travers les siècles', in *Racisme, continent obscur. Clichés, stéréotypes, phantasmes à propos des Noirs dans le Royaume de Belgique*, Brussels: CEC-Texstyles, pp. 19–44.

Van Warmelo, J. (ed.) (1977), *Anthropology of Southern Africa in Periodicals to 1950*, Johannesburg: Witwatersrand University Press.

Van Woerkens, M. (1995), *Le Voyageur étranglé. L'Inde des Thugs, le colonialisme et l'imaginaire*, Paris: Albin Michel.

Van Wyk Smith, A. (1992), 'The Most Wretched of the Human Race, the Iconography of the Khoikhoin (Hottentots), 1500–1800', *History and Anthropology*, 5.3–4, pp. 285–330.

Vanstone, J. W. (1993), 'The Ainu Group at the Louisiana Purchase Exposition, 1904', *Arctic Anthropology*, 30.2, pp. 77–91.

Varigny, C. de, (1987), 'Magiciens de l'Inde', *Les Grands Dossiers de l'Illustration, L'Inde, histoire d'un siècle, 1843–1944*, Paris: Sefag; Le livre de Paris, pp. 82–83.

Vaughan, C. A. (1996), 'Ogling Igorot: The Politics and Commerce of Exhibiting Cultural Otherness, 1898–1913', in R. Garland-Thomson (ed.), *Freakery: Cultural Spectacles of the Extraordinary, 1886–1931*, New York: New York University Press, pp. 219–33.

Venturino, D. (2003), 'Race et histoire. Le paradigme nobiliaire de la distinction sociale au début du XVIIIe siècle', in S. Moussa (ed.), *L'Idée de 'race' dans les sciences humaines et la littérature (XVIIIe et XIXe siècles)*, Paris: L'Harmattan, pp. 19–38.

Vercoutter, J., J. Leclant, F. M. Snowden Jr. and J. Desanges (1976), *L'Image du noir dans l'art occidental. Des pharaons à la chute de l'empire romain*, Paris: Gallimard.

Verde Casanova, A. (1993), 'Fotografía y antropología: Inuit en Madrid, 1900', *Anales del Museo de América*, 1, pp. 85–98.

Vergès, F. (2002), 'Des îles à rêver?', in Bancel N., P. Blanchard, G. Boëtsch, É. Deroo and S. Lemaire (eds), *Zoos humains: de la Vénus hottentote aux reality shows*, Paris: La Découverte, pp. 406–09.

Vervaeck, S. (1968), *Inventaire des archives du ministère de la justice. Administration de la sûreté publique (Police des étrangers). Dossiers généraux*, 834 (Troupes d'étrangers exhibés en public. 1888–1904).

Viatte, G. (2002), *Le Palais des colonies. Histoire du musée des arts d'Afrique et d'Océanie*, Paris: Réunion des Musées Nationaux.

Vogel, S. (1988), *Art/Artifact. African Art in Anthropology Collections*, New York: Center for African Art.

Walker, I. (1997), 'Phantom Africa, Photography between Surrealism and Ethnography', *Cahiers d'études africaines*, 147, pp. 635–55.

Walthew, K. (1981), 'The British Empire Exhibition', *History Today*, 31, pp. 34–39.

Walvin, J. (1973), *Black and White. The Negro and English Society, 1555–1945*, London: Allen Lane, The Penguin Press.

Warren, L. S. (2005), *Buffalo Bill's America: William Cody and the Wild West Show*, New York: Knopf.

Wartelle, J.-C. (2004), 'La Société d'anthropologie de Paris de 1880 à 1914', in *Revue d'histoire des sciences humaines*, 10, pp. 125–70.

Wastiau, B. (2000), *Exit Congo: Essai sur la vie sociale des chefs d'œuvre du Musée de Tervuren catalogue de l'exposition*, Tervuren: Musée royal de l'Afrique Centrale.

Webb, V.-L. (1992), 'Fact and Fiction. Nineteenth-Century Photographs of the Zulu', *African Arts*, 25.1, pp. 50-59.

Weinberger-Thomas, C. (1988), *L'Inde et l'imaginaire, Purusartha*, Paris: Editions de l'Ecole des Hautes Etudes en Sciences Sociales.

White, R. (1994), 'Frederick Jackson Turner and Buffalo Bill', in J. R. Grossman (ed.), *Frontier in American Culture*, Berkeley: University of California Press, pp. 7–65.

WHS (1974), *The British Empire Exhibition*, Wembley: [n. pub.].

Wiebe, R. (1967), *The Search for Order 1877–1920*, New York: Hill and Wang.

Wiesinger, V. (1992), *Les Sauvages à Paris au XIXe siècle. Sur les sentiers de la découverte, rencontres franco-indiennes du XVe au XXe siècles*, Paris: RMN/Musée national de la Coopération franco-américaine.

Wilder, G. (2005), *The French Imperial Nation-State: Negritude and Colonial Humanism between the Two World Wars*, Chicago: University of Chicago Press.

Williams, E. A. (1994), *The Physical and the Moral. Anthropology, Physiology and Philosophical Medicine in France 1750–1850*, Cambridge: Cambridge University Press.

Wilson, D. (1993), *Signs and Portents, Monstrous Births from the Middle Ages to the Enlightenment*, London: Routledge.

Winnicott, D. W. (1982), *Realidad y juego*, Barcelona: Gedisa.

Witschi, B. (1987), *Schweizer auf imperialistischen Pfaden. Die schweizerischen Handelsbeziehungen mit der Levante 1848–1914*, Stuttgart: Steiner-Verlag.

Woerkens, see Van Woerkens

Woodham, J. (1989), 'Images of Africa and Design at the British Empire Exhibitions between the Wars', *Journal of Design History*, 2, pp. 15–33.

Woody, H. (1998), 'International Postcards. Their History, Production, and Distribution (c. 1895–1915)', in C. Geary and V. Webb (eds), *Delivering Views. Distant Cultures in Early Postcards*, Washington, DC: Smithsonian Institution Press, pp. 13–45.

Worden, G. (2002), *The Mutter Museum of the College of Physicians of Philadelphia*, Philadelphia: Blast Books.

Wright, R. (1927), *Hawkers and Walkers in Early America: Strolling Peelers, Preachers, Lawyers, Doctors, Players, and Others, from the Beginning to the Civil War*, Philadelphia: J. B. Lippincott Company.

Yee, J. (2000), *Clichés de la femme exotique: un regard sur la littérature coloniale française entre 1871 et 1914*, Paris: L'Harmattan.

Yengoyan, A. (1994), 'Culture, Ideology and World's Fairs: Colonizer and Colonized in Comparative Perspectives', in Robert W. Rydell and N. Gwinn (eds), *Fair Representations: World's Fairs and the Modern World*, Amsterdam: VU University Press, pp. 62–83.

Yoshimi, S. (1992), *Hakurankai no seijigaku* [The Politics of Expositions], Tokyo: Chûô kôron sha.

—— (2005), *Banpaku gensô: sengo seiji no jubaku* [How the Chimera of the Universal Expositions Fascinated Postwar Politics], Tokyo: Chikuma shobô.

Zantop, S. (1997), *Colonial Fantasies: Conquest, Family, and Nation in Precolonial Germany, 1770–1870*, Durham, NC: Duke University Press.

—— (2002), 'Close Encounters: Deutsche and Indianer', in Colin G. Calloway, Gerd Gemünden and Susanne Zantop (eds), *Germans and Indians: Fantasies, Encounters, Projections*, Lincoln: University of Nebraska Press, pp. 3–14.

Zerilli, F. M. (1995a), 'Il debattito sul meticciato. Biologico e sociale nell'anthropologia francese del primo novecento', *Archivio per l'Anthropologia e la Etnologia*, 85, pp. 237–73.

—— (1995b), 'Il *Questionnaire sur les métis* della Société d'anthropologie de Paris, 1908', *La Ricerca folklorica*, 32, pp. 95–104.

Zoo (1993), *Zoo. Mémoires d'éléphant. Le Zoo de Genève à Saint-Jean entre 1935 et 1940*, Geneva: Maison de quartier Saint-Jean.

Contemporary Sources (cited in the Volume)

Abel, L. (1888), 'Les Hottentots', *La Science illustrée*, February, p. 198.

Aimone, L. and C. Olmo (1990), *Le esposizioni universali*, Turin: Umberto Allemandi.

Alphand, A. (1892), *L'Exposition Universelle internationale de 1889 à Paris*, Paris: Ministère du Commerce et de l'Industrie.

Amazzoni (1898), *Corpo delle Amazzoni, donne selvagge del Dahomey*, Turin: ed. Albert Urbach/L. Wolf.

Annales (1889), 'Pita, le Canaque à l'Exposition', *Annales de l'Extrême-Orient et de l'Afrique*, 3, pp. 78–81.

Anthony, R. (1927), 'L'anthropologie, sa définition, son programme, ce que doit être son enseignement', *Bulletins et Mémoires de la Société d'anthropologie de Paris*, pp. 227–45.

Anthropologie (1889), *La Société, l'Ecole et le laboratoire d'anthropologie de Paris à l'Exposition universelle de 1889*, Paris: Imprimerie nationale.

Armand, D. (1862), 'Aperçu sur les variétés de races humaines observées de 1842 à 1862, dans les diverses campagnes de l'armée française', *Bulletins et Mémoires de la société d'anthropologie de Paris*, 3, pp. 553–68.

Atgier, E. (1909), 'Les Touaregs à Paris', in *Bulletins et Mémoires de la Société d'anthropologie de Paris*, 5th series, 10.3, pp. 222–42.

Barnum, P. T. (1855), *The Life of P. T. Barnum, Written by himself*, New York: Redfield.

—— (1872), *Struggles and Triumphs*, Buffalo: Warren/Johnson (reprinted 1930, New York: Macmillan Company).

Barry, R. (1901), *The Grandeurs of the Exposition: Pan-American Exposition, 1901*, Buffalo, NY: Robert Allen Reid.

Baston, G. A.-R. (1790), *Narration d'Omaï*, Paris: Rouen.

Beaglehole, J. C. (ed.) (1955), *The Voyage of the Endeavour, 1768–1771*, Cambridge: Cambridge University Press [for the Hakluyt Society].

Beauregard (1922), 'Ministère des colonies', *L'Exposition coloniale de Marseille*, Marseille: Commissariat général de l'exposition, pp. 70–78.

Behrendt, R. (1931), *Die Schweiz und der Imperialismus. Die Volkswirtschaft des hochka-pitalistischen Kleinstaates im Zeitalter des politischen und ökonomischen Nationa-lismus,* Zürich, Leipzig and Stuttgart: Rascher und Cie Verlag.

Bert, P. (1882), *La Première année nouvelle d'enseignement scientifique, sciences natur-elles et physique: l'homme, les animaux, les végétaux, les pierres, les trois états des corps,* Paris: Colin.

Bertillon, A. (1865), *Traité sur les races humaines,* Paris: Masson.

—— (1882), *Les Races sauvages,* Paris: Masson.

Binet, E. (1900), 'Observations sur les Dahoméens', *Bulletin de la Société d'anthropo-logie de Paris,* 5th series, 1, pp. 244–53.

Blanchard, R. (1886), 'Sur le tablier et la stéatopygie des femmes boschimans', *Bulletin de la Société d'anthropologie de Paris,* 3rd series, 3, pp. 348–59.

—— (1909), 'À propos des nègres pies', *La Nature,* 38.1, pp. 3–8.

Bloch, A. (1902), 'Quelques remarques sur l'anthropologie des Hindous exhibés au Jardin d'Acclimatation', *Bulletin de la Société d'anthropologie de Paris,* 5th series, 3, pp. 780–87.

—— (1909), 'Observations sur les nains du Jardin d'Acclimatation, nains déjà décrits et avec les pygmées', *Bulletins et Mémoires de la Société d'anthropologie de Paris,* 5th series, 10, pp. 533–74.

Blumenbach, J.-F. (1804 [1795]), *Decas collectionis suae craniorum diversarum gentium,* Gottingen: J. Dietrich.

Boas, F. (1911), *The Mind of Primitive Man,* New York: The Macmillan Company.

Bompas George, C. (1885), *Life of Frank Buckland,* London: Smith, Elder and Co.

Bonaparte, R. (1884), *Les Habitants de Suriname. Notes recueillies à l'Exposition coloniale d'Amsterdam en 1883,* Paris: Le Jardin d'Acclimatation.

—— (1890), 'Les Somalis au Jardin d'Acclimatation', *La Nature,* 18.2, pp. 247–50.

Bonnafont, D. (1863), 'Notice sur les trois chefs touaregs qui sont venus à Paris', *Bulletin de la Société d'anthropologie de Paris,* 2nd series, 4, pp. 104–17.

Bordier, A. (1877a), 'Rapport de la commission nommée par la société d'Anthropologie pour étudier les Esquimaux du Jardin d'Acclimatation et Observations à propos du procès-verbal', *Bulletin de la Société d'anthropologie de Paris,* 2nd series, 12, pp. 575–86, 606–08.

—— (1877b), 'Les Esquimaux du Jardin d'acclimatation (rapport lu dans la séance du 22 novembre 1877)', *Mémoires de la Société d'anthropologie de Paris,* 2nd series, 1, pp. 448–61.

—— (1878a), 'Les Gauchos au Jardin d'Acclimatation', *La Revue scientifique,* 2nd series, 8.1, pp. 137–38.

—— (1878b), 'Les Gauchos au Jardin d'Acclimatation', *La Nature,* 6.2, pp. 295–98.

—— (1878c), 'Les sciences anthropologiques à l'exposition universelle', *La Nature,* 6.2, pp. 129–31, 210–14, 358–62 and 408–10.

—— (1881), 'Calotte cérébrale d'un Esquimau du Labrador', *Bulletin de la Société d'anthropologie de Paris,* 3rd series, 6, pp. 16–19.

—— (1884), *La Colonisation scientifique et les colonies françaises,* Paris: Reinwald.

Boue, G. (s.d.), *Les Squares et les jardins de Paris. Le bois de Boulogne,* Paris: Le Jardin d'acclimatation.

Bouteiller, M. (1956), 'La Société des observateurs de l'homme, ancêtre de la Société d'anthropologie de Paris', *Bulletins et Mémoires de la Société d'anthropologie de Paris,* 7, pp. 448–65.

Brehm, A. E. (n.d.), *L'Homme et les animaux,* Paris: J. B. Baillière.

Broca, P. (1865), *Instructions générales sur l'anthropologie*, Paris: Masson.

—— (1879), *Instructions générales pour les recherches anthropologiques à faire sur le vivant*, Paris: Masson.

Brongniart, C. (s.d.), *Histoire naturelle populaire. L'homme et les animaux*, Paris: Marpon & Flammarion.

Buffon (1792/1749), *Histoire naturelle de l'homme*, Paris: Plassan.

Bulletin de la Société d'anthropologie de Bruxelles (1888–89), 7.

Bulletin de la Société d'anthropologie de Bruxelles (1889–90), 8.

Bulletin de la Société d'anthropologie de Bruxelles (1890–91), 9.

Burgess, G. (1910), 'The Wild Men of Paris', *The Architectural Record*, 28.5, pp. 15–20.

Burnet, J. (1973 [1773–92]), *Of the Origin and Progress of Language*, 6 vols., Menston: Scolar Press.

Camper, P. (1791), *Dissertation sur les variétés naturelles qui caractérisent la physionomie des hommes des divers climats et des differents âges*. Paris and La Haye: HJ Jansen.

Capitan, Dr (1882), 'Sur les procédés qu'emploient les Galibis pour la fabrication de la poterie', *Bulletin de la Société d'anthropologie de Paris*, 3rd series, 5, pp. 649–51.

Carrington, G. (1871), *Colonial Adventures and Experiences by a University Man*, London: Bell and Daldy.

Castelnau, F. de (1851), *Renseignements sur l'Afrique Centrale et sur une nation d'hommes à queue qui s'y trouverait, d'après le rapport des nègres du Soudan, esclaves à Bahia*, Paris: P. Bertand.

Chaigneau, Y., M. Chauzy and F. Guerziero (1931), 'Les groupes sanguins des indigènes de race noire', *Archives de l'Institut de Pasteur de Tunis*, 20.4, pp. 452–55.

Chantre, E. (1884), 'Observations anthropométriques sur cinq Zoulous de passage à Lyon', *Bulletin de la Société d'anthropologie de Lyon*, 3, pp. 72–75.

Chicago (1894), *Midway Types, A Book of Illustrated Lessons about the People of the Midway Plaisance World's Fair*, Chicago: Chicago Engraving Company.

Chudzinski (1881), 'Sur les trois encéphales des Esquimaux morts de la variole, du 13 au 16 janvier 1881, dans le service de M. Andrieux, à l'hopital Saint-Louis', *Bulletin de la Société d'anthropologie de Paris*, 3rd series, 4, pp. 312–18.

Cockburn, J. A. (1907), 'The Franco-British Exhibition', *Journal of the Society of Arts*, 56, 29, pp. 23–33.

Collignon, R. (1896a), 'Présentation d'indigènes de Madagascar et du Soudan', *Bulletin de la Société d'anthropologie de Paris*, 4th series, 7, pp. 483–87.

—— (1896b), 'Visite de l'exposition ethnographique du Sénégal et de Madagascar au Champ-de-Mars', *Bulletin de la Société d'anthropologie de Paris*, 4th series, 7, pp. 487–88.

Conducré, E. (1858), 'La photographie au Muséum d'histoire naturelle', *La Lumière*, 8.16, pp. 1–2.

Conolly, J. (1855), *The Ethnological Exhibitions of London*, London: John Churchill.

Corra (1882), 'Extrait d'une notice publiée sur les Fuégiens', *Bulletin de la Société zoologique d'acclimatation*, 3rd series, 9, pp. 5–8.

Coudereau, H. (1877), 'Sur la composition du lait chez la femme esquimau', *Bulletin de la Société d'anthropologie de Paris*, 2nd series, 12, pp. 637–39.

—— (1892), 'Les Caraïbes. À propos des individus exhibés au Jardin d'acclimatation', *La Nature*, 20.1, pp. 246–50.

Coup, W. C. (1901), *Sawdust and Spangles*, Chicago: Herbert S. Stone and Co.

Cunningham R.-A. (1887), 'Lettre du 25 novembre 1885', in *Galton Papers* (Manuscript 227/6), University College London.

Cuvier, G. (1817), 'Extrait d'observations faites sur le cadavre d'une femme connue à Paris et à Londres sous le nom de Vénus hottentote', *Mémoire du muséum*, 3, pp. 259–74.

Dally, E. (1882), 'Observations sur les Galibis', *Bulletin de la Société d'anthropologie de Paris*, 3rd series, 5, pp. 796–819.

Dampier, W. (1697), *A New Voyage Round the World*, London: Adam and Charles Black.

Darwin, C. (1839), *Journal of researches into the geology and natural history of the various countries visited by H. M. S. Beagle under the command of Captain FitzRoy, R. N., from 1832 to 1836*, London: H. Colburn.

Daudin, H. (1926), *Les Classes zoologiques et l'idée de série animale en France à l'époque de Lamarck et de Cuvier 1790–1830*, Paris: Alcan.

Davenport, C. B. (1913), 'State Laws Limiting Marriage Selection in Light of Eugenics', *Eugenics Record Office Bulletin*, 9.

—— (1940), *Medical Genetics and Eugenics*, Philadelphia: Woman's Medical College of Pennsylvania.

Debroka, M. (1929), *Les Tigres parfumés. Aventures au pays des Maharajahs*, Paris: Les Éditions de France.

Demaison, A. (1931), *Paris 1931. Exposition coloniale internationale. Guide officiel*, Paris: Mayeux.

Deniker, J. (1880), 'Quelques observations et mensurations sur les Nubiens qui ont été exposés à Genève en août 1880', *Bulletin de la Société d'anthropologie de Paris*, 1880, 2rd series, 12, pp. 594–603.

—— (1883a), 'Étude sur les Kalmouks', *Revue d'anthropologie*, 2nd series, 6, pp. 673–703.

—— (1883b), 'Sur les Araucaniens du Jardin d'acclimatation', *Bulletin de la Société d'anthropologie*, 3rd series, 3, pp. 664–75.

—— (1883c), 'Sur les Kalmouks du Jardin d'Acclimatation', *Bulletin de la Société d'anthropologie*, 3rd series, 3, pp. 754–85.

—— (1886), 'Quelques observations sur les Boshimans', *Bulletin de la Société d'anthropologie*, 3rd series, 9, pp. 570–78.

—— (1889), 'Les Hottentots au Jardin d'acclimatation', *Revue d'anthropologie*, 4, pp. 1–27.

—— (1891), 'La caravane égyptienne au Jardin d'acclimatation de Paris', *La Nature*, 19.2, pp. 195–98.

—— (1896), 'Les indigènes de Madagascar exposés au Champ-de-Mars', *Bulletin de la Société d'anthropologie de Paris*, 4th series, 7, pp. 480–83.

—— (1907), 'Les Touaregs à l'exposition coloniale', *La Nature*, 35.2, pp. 167–70.

—— and R. Collignon (1897), 'Les Indigènes de Madagascar exposés au Champ-de-Mars', *L'Anthropologie*, 7, p. 620.

—— and L. Laloy (1891), 'Les Races exotiques à l'Exposition universelle de 1889', *L'Anthropologie*, 1, pp. 257–94, 513–46.

Dickens, C. (1853), 'The Noble Savage', *Household Words*, 11 June, pp. 337–39.

Douwes Dekker [pseud. Multatuli] (ed.) (1876), *Max Havelaar*, Rotterdam: Hoeven.

Du Chaillu, P.-B. (1861), *Explorations and Adventures in Equatorial Africa*, London: Murray.

Du Couret, L. (1854), *Voyage au pays des Niam-Niams*, Paris: Martinon.

Dumesnil, A. (1906), 'Une caravane hindoue au Jardin d'Acclimatation', *La Nature*, 34.2, pp. 215–18.

Duval, M. (s.d.), *Précis d'anatomie artistique*, Paris: Quantin.

Duveyrier, H. (1864), *Les Touaregs du Nord*, Paris: Challamel.

Eden, C.-H. (1872), *My Wife and I, in Queensland*, London: Longmans; Green & Co.

Edwards, W. (1829), *Des caractères physiologiques des races humaines considérées dans leurs rapports avec l'histoire, lettre à Amédée Thierry*, Paris: Compère Jeune.

Equiano, O. (1789), *The Interesting Narrative of the Life of Olaudah Equiano, or Gustavus Vassa, the African*, London: published by the author.

The Erdermanne; or, Earthmen from the Orange River in South Africa (1853), London: John K. Chapman.

Exposición Filipinas (1887), *Catálogo de la Exposición General de las Islas Filipinas* (1887), Madrid: Establecimiento Tipográfico de Ricardo Fé.

Exposition (1867a), 'Conclusion, Exposition Universelle de 1867', in *Matériaux pour l'histoire primitive de l'homme*, vol. 3, Paris: [n.p.].

—— (1867b), *L'Exposition universelle de 1867 illustrée*, Paris: Dentu et Petit.

—— (1878), 'Rapports sur l'Exposition Universelle de 1878', *L'Angleterre et les Indes anglaises*, 18, Paris: Librairie scientifique, industrielle et agricole, Maison Eugène Lacroix, pp. 114–28.

—— (1889a), 'Paris and its Exposition', *Pall Mall Gazette*, 49, pp. 11–12.

—— (1889b), *L'Exposition Universelle Internationale de 1889 à Paris. Catalogue Général Officiel. Exposition Rétrospective du Travail et des Sciences Anthropologiques*, Section 1, Anthropologie Ethnographie, Lille: Imprimerie L. Danel.

—— (1889c), *Sommaire sur le Village Canaque*, Paris: Lanier.

—— (1930), 'Comment l'Armée et la Marine participent à l'Exposition', *Bulletin d'information*, 8, p. 4.

Farini, G. A. (1973 [1886]), *Through the Kalahari Desert: A Narrative of a Journey with Gun, Camera and Note-Book to Lake N'Gami and Back*, Cape Town: G. Struik Ltd.

Fellows, D. and A. Freeman (1936), *This Way to the Big Show*, New York: Halcyon House.

Festival of Empire, Imperial Exhibition, Pageant of London (1911), London: n.pub.

Finch-Hatton, H. (1885), *Advance Australia: An Account of Eight Years' Wandering and Amusement in Queensland, New South Wales, and Victoria*, London: Allen & Co.

Fisher, G.-A. (1885), *Das Masai-Land, Bericht über die im Auftrage der Geographischen Gesellschaft, Hamburg ausgeführte Reise von Pangani bis zum Naivasha-See*, Hambourg: Friedericksen.

FitzGerald, W. G. (1897), 'Side shows', *Strand Magazine*.

Flament, L. (1885), 'Le Congo à Anvers', *Science et nature*, 88, pp. 129–32.

Florez, A. and R. Piquer (1887), *Crónica de la Exposición de Filipinas*, Madrid: Manuel Ginés Hernández.

Foa, E. (1891), 'Dahomiens et Egbas', *La Nature*, 19.2, pp. 199–202.

Forbin, V. (1909), 'Nègre blanc', *La Nature*, 37.2, p. 384.

Frazier-Soye, (1931), *Quand l'Inde française était à Paris. Les plus beaux souvenirs de l'Inde française à l'Exposition coloniale et internationale*, Paris: Frazier-Soye.

Fulbert, Dumonteil J.-C. (1886), *Une Visite aux Cynghalais du Jardin d'acclimatation*, Paris: Imprimerie Dubuisson.

—— (1887), *Les Achantis de l'Afrique équatoriale*, Paris: Imprimerie Dubuisson.

—— (1889), 'Les Lapons du Jardin d'Acclimatation', *Le Magasin pittoresque*, 2nd series, 7, pp. 37–39.

Garnier, M. (1879), *La Nouvelle-Calédonie à l'Exposition de 1878*, Paris: Delagrave.

Gautier, T. (1852). *Caprices et Zigzags*, Paris: Victor Lecou.

Genova (1914), *Esposizione internazionale di marina, igiene marinara, mostra coloniale italiana e mostra italo-americana Genova 1914: catalogo ufficiale*, Genova: G. B. Marsano.

Géo-Fournier, G. (1934), 'Les "Femmes à plateaux"', *La Nature*, 2928, pp. 400–03.

Gibbs-Smith, C.-H. (1950), *The Great Exhibition of 1851: A Commemorative Album*, London: HMSO.

Girard de Rialle (1877a), 'Les Esquimaux du Jardin d'Acclimatation', *La Nature*, 2.2, pp. 390–95.

—— (1877b), 'Les Nubiens du Jardin d'Acclimatation', *La Nature*, 2.1, pp. 198–203.

—— (1877c), 'Les Nubiens du Jardin d'Acclimatation', *La Revue scientifique*, 7.7, pp. 154–57.

—— (1878), 'Les Lapons au Jardin d'Acclimatation', *La Nature*, 6.2, pp. 7–11.

—— (1882), 'Les Galibis du Jardin d'Acclimatation', *La Nature*, 10.2, pp. 182–87.

—— (1883a), 'Les Araucaniens au Jardin d'acclimatation de Paris', *La Nature*, 11.1, p. 154.

—— (1883b), 'Les Cinghalais au Jardin d'Acclimatation', *La Nature*, 11.2, pp. 131–34.

—— (1883c), 'Les Kalmouks au Jardin d'Acclimatation', *La Nature*, 11.2, pp. 305–08.

—— (1884), 'Les Peaux-Rouges au Jardin d'Acclimatation', *La Nature*, 12.2, pp. 3–7.

—— (1890), 'Histoire rétrospective du travail et des sciences anthropologiques', in E. Monod (ed.), *L'Exposition universelle de 1889*, Paris: Dentu, pp. 289–302.

Godron, A. (1872), *De l'espèce et des races dans les êtres organisés et spécialement de l'unité de l'espèce humaine*, Paris: Baillière.

Gratiolet, L. P. (1854), *Mémoires sur les plis cérébraux de l'homme et des primates*, Paris, Bertrand.

Hagenbeck, C. (1909), *Von Tieren und Menschen. Erlebnisse und Erfahrungen*, Berlin: [n. pub.].

Hagenbeck, C. (1951), *Cages sans barreaux, Roi des zoos*, Paris: Nouvelles Éditions de Paris.

Hagenbeck, J. G. (1932), *Mit Indiens Fahrendem Volk*, Berlin: [n. pub.].

—— (1883), 'Les Peaux-Rouges, indiens Omahas', *Science et nature*, 1, p. 1.

—— (1886), 'Note ethnographique sur les Bosjesmans', *Bulletin de la Société d'anthropologie*, 3rd series, 9, pp. 567–70.

—— (1887), *Les Études ethnographiques et archéologiques sur l'Exposition Coloniale et Indienne de Londres*, London: [n. pub.].

—— (1907), 'L'album des habitants du nouveau monde d'Antoine Jacquard, graveur poitevin du commencement du XVIIe siècle', *Journal de la Société des americanistes de Paris*, 4.2, pp. 224–37.

Hartmann, R. (1880), *Les Peuples de l'Afrique*, Paris: Baillière.

Hebert, G. (1912), *L'Éducation physique virile et morale par la méthode naturelle*, Paris: Vuibert.

Heeres, J. E (1899), *The Part Borne by the Dutch in the Discovery of Australia* [Nicolas Witsen's account of 1705], London: Luzac.

Herisson, R. (1910), 'Les Touaregs', *Sciences et voyages*, 94, pp. 5–9.

Holmes, W. H. (1902), 'Classification and Arrangement of the Exhibits of an Anthropology Museum', *Journal of the Anthropological Institute*, 32, pp. 353–72.

—— (1924), 'Herbert Ward's Achievements in the Field of Art', *Art and Archeology*, 18.3, pp. 113–25.

Hough, W. (1924), 'An Appreciation of the Scientific Value of the Herbert Ward African Collection', in *The Herbert Ward African Collection*, Washington, DC: United States National Museum, pp. 37–49.

Hovelacque, A. (1882), *Les Début de l'humanité. L'homme primitif contemporain*, Paris: Doin, Marpon et Flammarion.

Houzé E. and V. Jacques (1884), 'Communications sur les Australiens du Musée du nord, Séance du 28 Mai 1884', *Bulletin Société d'anthropologie de Bruxelles*, 3–4, pp. 21–24.

Huard, C.-L. (1889), *Le Livre d'or illustré de l'exposition universelle de 1889*, Paris: Boulanger.

Huguet, Dr J. (1902), 'Sur les Touareg', *Bulletin de la Société d'anthropologie de Paris*, 5th series, 3, pp. 614–42.

Huntington, E. (1919), *The Red Man's Continent. A Chronicle of Aboriginal America*, New Haven, CT: Yale University Press.

Illustrated Memoir of an Eventful Expedition into Central America Resulting in the Discovery of the Idolatrous City of Iximaya, in an Unexplored Region (1853), London: [n. pub.].

Italia coloniale (1925), 'Le mostre coloniali di Losanna, Monza, Napoli e Fiume', *L'Italia coloniale*, 2.10, p. 183.

—— (1928a), 'La mostra coloniale di Torino', *L'Italia coloniale*, 5.7, p. 141.

—— (1928b), 'La chiusura della mostra coloniale di Torino', *L'Italia coloniale*, 5.11, p. 215.

—— (1930a), 'I cavalieri zuarini ricevuti dal ministro delle colonie', *L'Italia coloniale*, 7.7, p. 136.

—— (1930b), 'La mostra missionaria in Vaticano', *L'Italia coloniale*, 7.11, p. 214.

—— (1930c), 'Le colonie alle nozze auguste', *L'Italia coloniale*, 7.2, pp. 23–25.

—— (1930d), 'Tripoli-Anversa', *L'Italia coloniale*, 7.2, p. 32.

—— (1937), 'L'impero sulla via cara ai cesari trionfatori', *L'Italia coloniale*, 14.5, p. 66.

—— (1939), 'L'intensa preparazione per la Mostra triennale delle terre italiane d'Oltremare', *L'Italia coloniale*, 16.4, p. 94.

—— (1940), 'Il sovrano ha inaugurato a Napoli la Mostra triennale delle terrei italiane d'oltremare, superba rassegna delle imponenti realizzazioni del Regime', *L'Italia coloniale*, 17.5, p. 41.

Ivoi, Paul d' (1900), *Le Docteur Mystère*, Paris: Combet et Cie.

Jacquinot, H. (1846), 'Zoologie. Considérations générales sur l'anthropologie suivies d'observations sur les races humaines de l'Amérique méridionale et de l'Océanie', in *Voyage au pôle Sud et dans l'Océanie sur les corvettes l'Astrolabe et la Zéli*, Paris: Gide [n. pag.].

Jalabert, L. (1931), 'L'Exposition coloniale internationale', *Étude, revue catholique générale*, Paris [n. pag.].

Janvier, L. J. (1884), *L'Egalité des races*, Paris: Rougier.

Jeunesse, A. (1868), *Le Bois de Boulogne*, Paris: Philippart.

Juillerat, P. (1881), 'Les Fuégiens du Jardin d'Acclimatation', *La Nature*, 9.2, pp. 295–98.

Kahnweiler, D.-H. (1946), *Juan Gris, sa vie, son œuvre, ses écrits*, Paris: Gallimard.

Knox, R. (1850), *The Races of Men, A Fragment*, London: Henry Renshaw.

Krehbeil, H. E. (1893), 'Folk-Music in Chicago, vol. II, Cannibal Songs of the Indians', *New York Tribune*, 6 August.

Laibe, Lt. (1911a), 'Les Touaregs', *La Nature*, 1995, pp. 177–79.

—— (1911b), 'La race targui', *La Nature*, 2012, pp. 33–34.

Laloy, L. (1900), 'L'Extrême-Orient à l'Exposition universelle', *La Nature*, 28.2, pp. 307–08.

Lawrence W. (1819), *Lectures on Physiology, Zoology and the Natural History of Man*, London: J. Callow.

Le Bon, G. (1879), 'Sur les Nubiens du Jardin d'Acclimatation', *Bulletin de la Société d'anthropologie*, 3rd series, 2, pp. 590–92.

—— (1881), 'Sur les applications de la photographie à l'anthropologie à propos de la photographie des Fuégiens du Jardin d'acclimatation', *Bulletin de la Société d'anthropologie*, 3rd series, 2, pp. 758–60.

Letourneau, C. (1880a), 'Rapport sur les Nubiens du Jardin d'Acclimatation', *Bulletin de la Société d'anthropologie de Paris*, 3rd series, 3, pp. 655–60.

—— (1880b), *La Sociologie d'après l'ethnographie*, Paris: Reinwald.

Linnaeus, C. von (1758), *Sistema Naturae*. Editio decima, Laur: Salvius.

LoBagola, B. K. (1930), *LoBagola: An African Savage's Own Story*, New York: Knopf.

Lombroso, C. and M. Carrara (1896a), 'Contributo all'antropologia dei Dinka', *Giornale della R. Accademia di Medicina di Torino*, 59.4, vol. II, Bocca, Turin, pp. 377–94.

—— (1896b) 'Contributo all'antropologia dei Dinka', *Archivio di Psichiatria, Scienze Penali ed Antropologia criminale*, 17-4, Bocca, Turin, pp. 1–15.

López Jaena, G. (1889), 'Filipinas en la Exposición Universal de Barcelona', in Ateneo Barcelonés, *Conferencias públicas relativas a la Exposición Universal de Barcelona*, Barcelona: Tipo-litografía de Busquets y Vidal, pp. 239–54.

Louis, A. (1888), 'Les Hottentots', *La Science illustrée*, 10, pp. 198.

Lumholtz, C. (1889), 'Chez les Cannibales', *Le Tour du monde*, 25, pp. 10–12.

Madieu, J. (1916), *Le Cinéma colonial*, Algiers: [n.pub.]

Manouvrier, L. (1881), 'Sur les Fuégiens du Jardin d'Acclimatation', *Bulletin de la Société d'anthropologie de Paris*, 3rd series, 4, pp. 760–90.

—— (1882), 'Sur les Galibis du Jardin d'Acclimatation', *Bulletin de la Société d'anthropologie de Paris*, 3rd series, 5, pp. 602–43.

—— (1883a), 'Rapport sur les Araucans du Jardin d'Acclimatation', *Bulletin de la Société d'anthropologie de Paris*, 3rd series, 6, p. 728.

—— (1883b), 'Rapport sur les Cinghalais du Jardin d'Acclimatation', *Bulletin de la Société d'anthropologie de Paris*, 3rd series, 6, pp. 713–26.

—— (1885), 'Sur les Peaux Rouges du Jardin d'Acclimatation', *Bulletin de la Société d'anthropologie*, 3rd series, 8, pp. 306–47.

Martial, R. (1934), *La Race française*, Paris: Mercure de France.

—— (1942), *Les Métis*, Paris: Flammarion.

Martin, H. (1878), 'Allocution sur "la science de l'homme"', *Bulletin de la Société d'anthropologie de Paris*, 3rd series, 1, pp. 5–8.

Matsumura, A. (1903a), 'Ôsaka no jinruikan' [The Anthropological pavilion at Ôsaka], *Tôkyô Jinrui gakkai zasshi* [*The Journal of the Tokyo Anthropological Society*], 205.4, pp. 289–92.

—— (1903b), 'Report about the 1903 exposition', *Tokyo Jinrui gakkai zacharie* [*The Journal of the Tôkyô Anthropological Society*], 205.4, pp. 294–96.

Maurois, A. (1931), *Sur le vif, L'exposition coloniale*, Paris, Degorce.

Meigs, J. A. (1857), *Catalogue of human crania in the collection of the academy of natural sciences of Philadelphia, based upon the third edition of Dr Morton's 'Catalogue of Skulls'*, Philadelphia: Lippincott & Co.

Mériel, P. de (1902), 'Les Hindous du Jardin d'Acclimatation', *La Nature*, 30.2, pp. 266–70.

MIHN (1860), *Instructions pour les voyageurs et les employés dans les colonies sur les manières de recueillir, de conserver et d'envoyer les objets d'histoire naturelle*, Paris: Éditions Martinet.

Milano (1906), *L'Esposizione illustrata di Milano 1906. Giornale Ufficiale del Comitato Esecutivo*, Milan: Sonzogno.

Moncelon, M. (1885), 'Présentation d'un Canaque Néo-Calédonien', *Bulletin de la Société d'anthropologie*, 3rd series, 8, p. 353.

Mortillet, G. de (1877), 'Exposition Universelle de 1878. Palais du Trocadéro', *La Nature*, 6.2: pp. 273–74.

—— (1878), 'Ouverture de l'exposition des sciences anthropologiques', *Bulletin de la Société d'anthropologie de Paris*, 3rd series, 1, pp. 220–25.

Morton, S. (1844), *Crania Aegyptiaca, or Observations on Egyptian Ethnography, derived from Anatomy, History and the Monuments*, Philadelphia: J. Pennington.

Nadaillac, M. de (1889), 'Les sciences anthropologiques à l'Exposition universelle de 1889', *La Nature*, 17.2, pp. 7–10.

—— (1891), 'Les Peaux-Rouges', *La Nature*, 19.1, pp. 278–82.

National Anthropological Archives (n.d.), *Records of the Anthropology Department*, Washington, DC: Smithsonian Institution.

Novicow, J. (1897), *L'Avenir de la race blanche. Critique du pessimisme contemporain*, Paris: Alcan.

Olivier (1931), *Exposition coloniale de Paris 1931, rapport général présenté par le gouverneur Olivier*, Paris: Imprimerie Nationale.

Olivier, E. (1882), 'L'étude scientifique de la Tunisie', *Revue des sciences pures et appliquées*, 21, pp. 45–76.

'On the Unity of the Human Race' (1854), *Southern Quarterly Review*, 10, p. 299.

Palermo (1892), *Esposizione Nazionale in Palermo 1891–92. Guida della Mostra Eritrea*, Palermo: Città di Castello.

Putman, F. W. (1893), 'World's Columbian Exposition Scrapbooks', 2, Harvard: Harvard University Archives.Quatrefages, A. de (1867), *Rapport sur les progrès de l'anthropologie*, Paris: Imprimerie nationale.

Queenslander (1880), 'Nevernever to Queenslander', *The Way We Civilise, The Queenslander*, 8 May, p. 28.

Rabot, C. (1889), 'Les Lapons au Jardin d'acclimatation', *La Nature*, 17.1, pp. 154–57.

Raspe, R. E. (1948), *Singular Travels, Campaigns and Adventures of Baron Munchausen*, London: [n. pub.].

Raymond, P. (1893), 'Les Païr-Pi-Bri au Jardin d'acclimatation', *La Nature*, 20.2, pp. 182–86.

Regnault, F. (1893), 'Les Dahoméens au Champ-de-Mars de Paris', *La Nature*, 21.1, pp. 371–74.

—— (1895), 'Exposition ethnographique de l'Afrique Occidentale au Champ-de-Mars, à Paris, Sénégal et Soudan français', *La Nature*, 24.2, pp. 183–86.

Robinson, H. (1881), *The Zulu Spy: Giving an Authentic History. Farini's Genuine Zulus, One of the Many Leading Features of the Barnum and London Circus*, New York: New York Popular Publishing Co.

Roland, B. (1884), *Les Habitants du Suriname à Amsterdam*, Paris: A. Quantin.

Rousselet, L. (1874), *L'Inde des Rajahs*, Paris: Hachette.

—— (1890), *L'Exposition universelle de 1889*, Paris: Hachette.

Rowe C. S. (1931), 'Rowe's Diary', *Cummins & Campbell's Monthly Magazine*, April–June, Townsville, [n.pag.].

Royer, C. (1873), 'Sur un homme velu né en Russie, et sur son fils, âgé de trois ans et demi', *Bulletin de la Société d'anthropologie de Paris*, 2nd series, 8, pp. 718–37.

Saint-Hilaire, G. de (1871), 'Le Jardin d'acclimatation', *La Revue scientifique*, 2nd series, 1.16, p. 361.

Saint-Hilaire, G. de and F. Cuvier (1824), *Histoire naturelle des mammifères avec des figures originales, coloriées, dessinées d'après des animaux vivants*, Paris: Belin.

Saltarino, S. (1895), *Fahrend Volk: Abnormitäten, Kuriositäten und interessante Vertreter der wandernden Künstlerwelt*, Leipzig: Weber.

Sanger, 'Lord' G. (1908), *Seventy Years a Showman*, London: C. Arthur Pearson.

SAP (1877a), 'Séance du 15 juillet', *Bulletin de la Société d'anthropologie de Paris*, 2nd series, 12, pp. 476.

—— (1877b), 'Séance du 18 octobre', *Bulletin de la Société d'anthropologie de Paris*, 2nd series, 12e, pp. 520.

—— (1895), 'Séance du 18 juillet', *Bulletin de la Société d'anthropologie de Paris*, 4th series, 6, p. 479.

Schœlcher, V. (1840), *Abolition de l'esclavage. Examen critique du préjugé contre la couleur des Africains et des sang-mêlés*, Paris: Pagnerre.

Seba, A. (2006 [1734–1765]), *Le Cabinet des curiosités naturelles* [Locuplerissimi rerum naturalium thesauri 1734–1765], Cologne; London; Los Angeles; Madrid; Paris; Tokyo: Taschen.

Sexton, G. (1855), 'Anatomical View of the Question of Men with Tails', in *Men With Tails, Remarks on the Niam-Niams of Central Africa*, London: W. J. Golbourn, pp. 12–18.

Siepi, J. (1937), *Petite histoire du Jardin zoologique de Marseille*, Marseille: Imprimerie Municipale.

South American Missionary Society Magazine (1890), 1 February, pp. 29–30.

Spiller, G. (1911), 'Le problème de l'égalité des races humaines', in *Mémoires sur le contact des races communiqués au 1er Congrès universel des races tenu à l'Université de Londres du 26 au 29 juillet 1911*, London: King & Son, pp. 33–43.

St. Louis (1904), 'A novel athletic contest', *World's Fair Bulletin*, 5.11, p. 50.

—— (1904), 'Interracial meet arranged at fair', *St. Louis Republic*, 11 August, p. 8.

—— (1904), 'Pigmies indulge in mud fight', *St. Louis Republic*, 13 August, p. 5.

Stumpf, C. (1886), 'Lieder der Bellakula-Indianer', *Vierteljahresschrift für Musikwissenschaft*, 2, pp. 405–26.

Sullivan, J. E. (ed.) (1905), *Spalding's Official Athletic Almanac for 1905*, New York: American Sports Publishing.

Taillebois, E. (1882), 'Les Caraïbes à Paris', *La Science populaire*, September, p. 129.

Terrier, A. (1907), 'Le Journal des Voyages à l'Exposition coloniale, les éléphants de l'Inde', *Journal des voyages*, 540, p. 3.

—— (1909), 'L'oasis en fête', *Journal des Voyages*, 656, p. 22.

—— (1909), 'Les distractions de l'Oasis', *Journal des Voyages*, 660, p. 135.

—— (1909), 'Les Guerriers de l'Oasis Saharienne', *Journal des Voyages*, 667, pp. 253–54.

Thorp, R. W. (1957), *Spirit Gun of the West: The Story of Doc W. F. Carver*, Glendale, CA: Arthur H. Clark.

Tissandier, G. (1889a), 'Les Cosaques du Kouban au Jardin d'Acclimatation', *La Nature*, 17.1, pp. 97–98.

—— (1889b), 'La rue du Caire à l'exposition universelle', *La Nature*, 17.1, p. 839.

Topinard, P. (1872), *Étude sur les races indigènes de l'Australie*, Paris: A. Hennuyer.

—— (1878), 'Essai de classification des races humaines actuelles', *Revue d'anthropologie*, 1rd series, 4, pp. 499–509.

—— (1881), 'Discussion sur les Fuégiens', *Bulletin de la Société d'anthropologie de Paris*, 2nd series, 3, December, pp. 774–89.

—— (1883), 'Les Cinghalais au Jardin d'acclimatation', *Revue d'anthropologie*, 2nd series, 6e, pp. 195–99.

—— (1885), 'Présentation de trois Australiens vivants', *Bulletin de la Société d'anthropologie*, 3rd series, 8, pp. 683–98.

—— (1886), 'Présentation de quatre Boshimans vivants', *Bulletin de la société d'anthropologie*, 3rd series, 9, pp. 530–67.

—— (1887), 'Les Boshimans à Paris', *La Nature*, 16.1, pp. 125–26.

—— (1888a), 'Les Hottentots au Jardin d'Acclimatation', *La Nature*, 16.2, pp. 167–70.

—— (1888b), 'Les races humaines', *La Nature*, 16.2, pp. 341–43.

—— (1889), 'La stéatopygie des Hottentots du Jardin d'acclimatation', *Revue d'anthropologie*, 3rd series, 4, pp. 194–9.

Torino (1884a), *Torino e l'Esposizione Italiana del 1884. Cronaca illustrata della Esposizione Nazionale-Industriale ed Artistica del 1884*, Turin-Milan: Roux e Favale e Fratelli Treves.

—— (1884b), *L'Esposizione Italiana del 1884 in Torino illustrata*, Milan: Sonzogno.

—— (1898), *1898. L'Esposizione Nazionale*, Turin: Roux & Frassati.

—— (1911), *L'Esposizione di Torino 1911. Giornale ufficiale illustrato*, Turin.

Trollope, A. (1873), *Australia and New Zealand*, London: Chapman and Hall.

Tsuboi, S. (1903), 'Jinruikan to jinshu chizu' ['The Anthropological Pavilion and the map of distribution of human races'], *Tôyô gakugei zasshi* [*The Journal of the Oriental Arts*], 261.4, pp. 163–66.

Tyler, J. S. (1847), *The Bosjesmans: A Lecture on the Mental, Moral, and Physical Attributes of the Bush Men*, Leeds: C. A. Wilson.

Tyson, E. (1699), *Orang Outang sive homo sylvestris, or the Anatomy of a Pygmie compared with that of a Monkey, an Ape and a Man*, London: Th. Bennet & D. Brown.

Ujfalvy, C.-E. (1883), *Les Kalmouques*, Paris: Jardin zoologique d'acclimatation.

Vallois, H. (1932), 'Rapport sur l'Exposition coloniale et les congrès', *L'Anthropologie*, 42, pp. 55–70.

—— (1944), *Les Races humaines*, Paris: PUF.

Varigny, H. de (1889), 'Le Palais des colonies à l'Exposition universelle de 1889', *La Nature*, 17.2, pp. 277–79, 347–48.

—— (1890), 'La Tunisie à l'Exposition universelle de 1889', *La Nature*, 11.1, pp. 365–66.

Verneau, R. (1890), *Les Races humaines*, Paris: Baillière.

—— (1916), 'Le Centième Anniversaire de la mort de Sarah Baartman', *L'Anthropologie*, 27, pp. 177–79.

Verniquet, D. (1802), *Exposition d'un projet sur le Muséum d'histoire naturelle et sur une ménagerie*, Paris: Huzard.

Verschave, P. and C. Guillerme (1925), *Au Village noir – Organisation de Villages exotiques – F. Tournier*, Paris: A. Tournon.

Verschuur, G. (1893), 'Voyage aux trois Guyanes', *Le Tour du monde*, 66, pp. 1–80.

Virchow, R. (1886), 'Bushmänner', *Verhandlungen der Berliner Gesellschaft für Anthropologie, Ethnologie und Urgeschichte*, annexe to *Zeitschrift für ethnologie*, 18, pp. 221–39.

Warnier, A. (1867), 'Exposition de l'Algérie', *L'Exposition universelle de 1867 illustrée*, Paris: Dentu et Petit, pp. 182–86.

Werth, L. (1931), 'Un Vieux noir dansait', *Le Monde*, 29 August, pp. 6–7.

White, C. (1799), *An Account of the Regular Gradations in Man and in Different Animals and Vegetables*, London: Charles Dilly.

Wright, T. (ed.) (1904), *The Correspondence of William Cowper*, London: Hodder and Stoughton.

Z, Dr (1886), 'Les Cynghalais au Jardin d'acclimatation de Paris', *La Nature*, 14.1, pp. 231–34.

Z, Dr (1887), 'Les Achantis au Jardin d'acclimatation', *La Nature*, 10.2, pp. 249–50.

Zaborowski, S. (1893), 'Visite aux Dahoméens du Champ-de-Mars', *Bulletin de la Société d'anthropologie de Paris*, 4th series, 4, pp. 327–38.

Zeltner, F. de (1903), 'Les Achants', *La Nature*, 31.2, pp. 71–74.

Zimmerman, W. F. A. (1864), *L'Homme. Problèmes et merveilles de la nature humaine, physique et intellectuelle*, Brussels: Muquardt; Paris: Schultz & Thuillié.

9781846311741